Phil Vasby

$9.50

D1271684

BETTER TEACHING
IN SECONDARY SCHOOLS

BETTER TEACHING
IN SECONDARY SCHOOLS

REVISED EDITION

MARVIN D. ALCORN · JAMES S. KINDER · JIM R. SCHUNERT
San Diego State College

HOLT, RINEHART AND WINSTON, INC.
NEW YORK · CHICAGO · SAN FRANCISCO · TORONTO · LONDON

Preface

The revised edition of *Better Teaching in Secondary Schools* is designed to give beginning teachers practical help in solving the complex problems of teaching in this scientific era. Each aspect of the teaching-learning situation is analyzed, from the concrete procedures used in constructing a test or developing a daily lesson plan to the more subtle processes used in motivating students or building classroom morale.

Today's schools are forcibly influenced by world-wide social, political, and economic upheavals. In this nation, teachers are confronted with such problems as racial integration, population expansion and migration, and economic dislocation accompanying automation. In the light of these problems, the authors stress the need for classroom teachers to be concerned with the common, as well as diversified, needs of *all* students, regardless of racial or cultural backgrounds or future occupational goals. Furthermore, it is pointed out that satisfaction of such needs demands a balanced curriculum which is best achieved in the comprehensive high school. The success of such a school depends upon a continuing supply of teachers better prepared than ever before.

Better Teaching in Secondary Schools not only re-emphasizes procedures that have been successful in the past, but also introduces teachers to promising current developments in methods and materials of instruction. For example, the book discusses team teaching and programmed learning; explains how to use educational television and the newer techniques of evaluation; and describes the audio-lingual method of teaching language.

In this text the approach to the problems of the teacher is realistic. Step by step, the teacher is given practical assistance with every phase of teaching, from making an initial class analysis to evaluating and reporting student progress. Although precisely what a teacher and his students do is a major emphasis, classroom procedures are not separated from tested theory nor from the subject matter taught. The authors recognize that method, theory, and content are inseparable.

This edition of *Better Teaching in Secondary Schools* is a complete and comprehensive revision of the original edition. Coverage is in depth. Recommendations are supported by the most recent findings of research and by the authors' extensive teaching experience in high school and college. Furthermore, the revision rests firmly on its predecessor's widespread use in the classroom. Pertinent suggestions for improvement have come from the many users: college professors, high school teachers, and student teachers.

The introductory chapters of the book provide an orientation to teaching. Special attention is given to the opportunities in teaching, to the roles of the teacher, and to the techniques employed in studying students, schools, and communities.

Part Two deals with the theme of instructional planning. Following an over-all analysis of the subject, the three specific areas covered in detail are unit planning, daily planning, and cooperative planning. This section concludes with a discussion of organization for more effective group (large and small) and individual planning for instruction.

Part Three, "Using Instructional Materials," explores the resources of the more conventional as well as the newer types of instructional materials and the best methods of their utilization. One chapter is devoted to the so-called "new instructional media." Some of these materials are still in the experimental stage and their general acceptance awaits further research and testing.

In Part Four, the authors analyze the complex factors related to school discipline. Many practical suggestions are given to the teacher for building group morale, for developing constructive procedures of classroom management and control, and for using appropriate remedial measures when correction of misbehavior becomes necessary.

Part Five describes the nature of the present-day curriculum, traces its background of development in this country, and analyzes the forces that appear to be shaping the school program of the immediate future. In addition, current trends and development are briefly summarized.

Part Six includes discussion of evaluation principles and appraisal techniques. The special skills involved in building tests, marking and reporting, and interpreting standardized tests are comprehensively developed in separate chapters. Concrete examples of these skills are given together with charts and figures to illustrate the more complex concepts.

The book closes with an optimistic, yet realistic, outlook on the teaching profession. Job opportunities are pointed out, salary levels shown, and the growth possibilities described.

Professional assistance in the writing of this book has come from many persons. We deeply appreciate this encouragement. We wish also to express our indebtedness to the many school systems which have so generously supplied us with pictures. Further acknowledgment of assistance is made to the various authors and publishers who have allowed us to quote or summarize their materials.

SAN DIEGO, CALIF.

FEBRUARY 1964

M. D. A.

J. S. K.

J. R. S.

Contents

BETTER TEACHING
IN SECONDARY SCHOOLS

PART ONE

Introduction to Secondary School Teaching

CHAPTER 1

Orientation to teaching as a profession

What greater or better gift can we offer the republic than to teach and instruct our youth?—*Cicero*

Cicero's words are as true today as they were 2000 years ago. Teachers still provide valuable and unique professional service to the nation. By guiding students in the acquisition of knowledge and in the development of high ideals and true appreciation of the freedoms and the responsibilities of American citizenship, and by assisting them to develop the skill of clear and critical thinking, teachers contribute significantly to the character of the adults who will determine America's future. To a considerable extent it is true that the destiny of a nation lies in the hands of those who guide its youth. Experienced teachers appreciate the critical importance of that role. But is the opportunity to give service a motive sufficiently strong to keep the nation's schools manned by competent teachers? Are there not other important opportunities in teaching?

TEACHING OFFERS MANY OPPORTUNITIES

The thousands of young men and women who each year enter college classes leading to careers in teaching seldom are fully aware of the many opportunities awaiting them. They have decided to teach for a great variety of reasons and look upon their decision with varying degrees of assurance. Some are absolutely certain they want to teach, others are a bit unsure, and a few gravely doubt the wisdom of their choice. Sometimes doubts are accentuated by the picture of teachers and teaching frequently presented on television, at the theater, and in the public press.

Is the average woman in teaching really a frustrated, unloved old maid?

Are men teachers typically undersexed, underpaid, and overworked? Do teachers usually live apart from the community? Are they frequently dominated by administrators, dictated to by parents, and bullied by students? Prospective teachers may well ask such questions even though they usually remember their own high school teachers with favor. Repeated confrontation with the type of story judged newsworthy by the mass communications media may well lead beginners to doubt the validity of their own experience. Therefore, in an effort to give needed balance to the beginner's picture of the teaching profession, the next paragraphs review infrequently published evidence and arguments which support the conclusion that teaching offers many opportunities.

Opportunity to Gain the Respect of Youth and Share Their Enthusiasm

Teachers have the opportunity to gain the respect and admiration of youth, and share in their zest for life. Many veteran teachers agree that among the greatest rewards of teaching are the feelings of appreciation expressed over the years by their students. The beginning teacher who received the following note, quoted verbatim, was well rewarded for his efforts to motivate a "reluctant scholar."

> Dear Mr. _____,
>   What I have to say isn't very much. I'm only one out of all the boy in the 5 period class. But I hope you don't hold it agin't me for the way I felt about you at the begining.
>   I didn't think very much of you. I thought you where just a man who thought he new it all. Well, I was bad to you. But you still was nice to me in more then one way. I don't know how to thank you for what you did for me. But I'll never forget. Your one of the Best men I've known. You see I don't have a father, He died but your just like him in a lot of way's.
>   Please go on with your teaching, and I hope fore the best fore you.
>   Your Pal
>   _____
>
> P.S. Thank's again. Please don't mine the writing or the spelling, Im not so good at it.

Teachers also rank high among their compensations the opportunity to work in an atmosphere charged with the hope and the enthusiasm of youth. In the book and motion picture, *Goodbye, Mr. Chips*, this idea is well illustrated by an admirer who says to the schoolmaster, "I should think you would never grow old in a world where everyone is young." Unfortunately, teachers, like all mortals, grow old in years, but while doing so they retain a remarkable opportunity to remain young in spirit.

Furthermore, it has been stated that in the minds of succeeding generations the ideas and the ideals of great teachers gain immortality.

Opportunity to Earn Community Respect

Perhaps because they expect to find in teachers attributes they wish their youth to acquire, communities usually are ready to grant teachers respect and social acceptance considerably above that granted most nonteachers of like age, education, and income. Contrary to once-popular opinion which maintained that teachers tended to be isolates, research published by the National Education Association in 1957 revealed that approximately 90 percent of a nationwide sample of teachers felt accepted in the social life of their communities. Less than 1 percent felt ignored or rejected (11:32). In the final analysis, social acceptance seldom is automatic. It must be earned by each individual. Nevertheless, teaching offers that opportunity.

Opportunity for Security and Independence

Teachers, through tenure laws, usually enjoy job security in a given school system, yet retain the sense of independence and freedom which springs from the knowledge that the demand for good teachers is nationwide. Birth-rate statistics insure that the demand will remain high for years to come.[1]

Research indicates that most teachers are happy in their work and intend to remain in the positions they hold.[2] On the other hand, teachers have comparative freedom to move should they wish to do so. For example, one study found that the typical teacher had taught for four or five years in each of three school systems (11:17). Tenure in a given job, together with the opportunity to move almost at will, forms an unbeatable combination favorable to the development of feelings of security and independence. Few, if any, occupations can equal these opportunities now available in teaching.

Opportunity to Earn a Regular Income

Teaching offers opportunity, without investment beyond education, to earn income that is regular, perhaps modest, but no longer meager in an increasing proportion of the nation's schools.

In 1960, the United States Bureau of Census reported the national

---

[1] Research Division of the National Education Association, *Teacher Supply and Demand in Public Schools, 1962*, NEA Research Report, 1962–R8, p. 5.

[2] Research Division of the National Education Association, "The Status of the American Public-School Teacher," *NEA Research Bulletin*, vol. 35, no. 1 (February 1957), p. 37.

annual salary median in elementary and secondary school teaching to be $4581 for women teachers and $6063 for men teachers. The comparable figure for men in professional-technical employment other than teaching was $7143. These data reveal that men teachers working thirty-six weeks per year were earning only 15 percent less than other professional-technical workers whose work year was usually about 30 percent longer. Women in teaching were earning at about the same rate per month of employment as women in other occupations requiring comparable education (12:15–16).

The 1962–1963 survey of the National Education Association found that as yet there is tremendous variability in teaching salaries from school district to school district across the nation. Some districts paid some teachers more than $10,000 per year; others paid no one more than $5000; and a few districts paid some teachers less than $2000. Thus it appears that a teacher's salary depends upon the policy of the school district in which the teacher works.

In an increasing number of states, however, salary minimums are set by state law. Thirty-four states had such laws in 1962. Led by California with a minimum of $4500 for teachers having a bachelor's degree, Delaware, New York, Washington, Texas, Illinois, Massachusetts, Rhode Island, and Wisconsin all set a base of at least $4000, below which no local district could venture. On the other hand, six states still had legislated minimums below $3000 and fourteen states had no minimums at all. The NEA survey noted that seven states in 1962 required school boards to pay at least $6000 to experienced teachers with a master's degree, whereas only three states had comparable regulations in 1960 (12:31–32).

The NEA survey also found that in the year 1961–1962 75 percent of elementary and secondary teachers earned $4500 or more; 40 percent earned $5500 or more; 20 percent earned $6500 or more; and 8 percent earned $7500 or more. Professional supervisory, guidance, and administrative staff members averaged $9294 annually. In addition, it was determined that the salary average for instructional staff members had increased from $3450 in 1952 to $5716 in 1962, a gain of 65.7 percent in ten years. When it is realized that the national average income for teachers in the early 1940s was $1400, it must be granted that teachers' salaries, while not yet equal on an annual basis to those of top professions, are indeed improving (12:5, 17).

Furthermore, teaching offers the opportunity to earn salary increments based upon specific schedules of service and advanced study or travel, rather than upon individual bargaining or political maneuvering. In the above study, approximately 70 percent of American teachers reported that advanced study was either required or urged by their school district.

Opportunity for Variety of Service within the Profession

Education offers many professional roles in addition to teaching. The NEA research division's biennial survey lists more than fifty different employment classifications in education, most of which require professional preparation as a teacher, teaching experience, and additional college study.[3]

Opportunities vary from administrative and supervisory positions such as principal, dean, department head, supervisor, and superintendent to special service positions such as curriculum coordinator, librarian, audiovisual director, psychometrist, counselor, guidance worker, and researcher. Depending upon the level of responsibility accepted and the size of the district served, salaries in these positions range from about 25 percent above the average for teaching to more than four or five times that amount. Many teachers find added challenge and opportunity within the profession in these administrative, supervisory, and special service roles.

Opportunity for Scholarly Life

Teachers have the opportunity to pursue, in depth, a favorite study and to interest young people in its possibilities. In fact, many teachers are first attracted to teaching because of their intense interest in a particular field of study. Teaching not only offers them the opportunity to pursue their major intellectual interest and to inspire others to share the same interest but provides lengthy vacation periods in which teachers may conveniently engage in graduate study.

Opportunity to Work in an Atmosphere of Friendship and Culture

Teachers work with professional colleagues who characteristically have stimulating minds and high ideals. They share common intellectual interests, educational background, ethics, and professionalism, all of which form the basis for a pleasant working atmosphere in the typical school. Teaching provides superior associations. It is not likely to attract to its ranks those who would place money above morality. Consequently, among all the professions, teaching is most free of the "fast buck" artist. Neither is the profession likely to attract those who, ignoring human values, would accept "cutthroat" competition as an avenue to success, since eminence in teaching is gained by working well with colleagues, not by pushing them aside nor taking their livelihood from them. Teachers place high value on scholarship, service, and moral character. They are friendly and fair working associates.

[3] Research Division of the National Education Association, *NEA Research Bulletin,* vol. 39, no. 3 (October 1961), p. 72.

Opportunity to Enjoy Academic Freedom

High school teachers typically enjoy at least a fair measure of the academic freedom so cherished by the professorial members of the profession. Unlike the close supervisory control which dominates the worker in many occupations, in teaching individuals usually enjoy exceptional freedom of decision in their daily work. The trend of supervision in schools is toward action based on concepts of cooperation, not dictation. The major purpose of this type of supervision is the cooperative improvement of instruction. Teachers thus feel that they work with supervisors and administrators, not for them. These distinctions are important contributors to the pleasant atmosphere in which teachers work.

Opportunity to Live a Full Life

Teachers have an excellent opportunity to live a life with family and friends, and particularly to enjoy frequent vacations with them. According to research, teachers participate in more community activities, belong to churches in greater numbers, and vote more regularly than the average citizen (11:32–34). Teachers are active in their communities, but they also find time to see the world. During their frequent vacation periods, teachers can be observed in all the outstanding recreational areas of the United States and in almost every land where travel is encouraged. Teachers are inveterate students and travelers.

Finally, it must be emphasized that the stereotype of a teacher as a frustrated old maid is untrue. Research in 1960 revealed that more than half of the teachers in American high schools were men,[4] over 80 percent of whom were married. Likewise, more than half of the women teachers were married. Furthermore, research also showed that marriages involving a teacher tended to be considerably more stable than the national average. Only 12 percent of teachers were divorced, separated, or widowed, whereas the comparable statistic for all workers in the United States was 23 percent (11:10–11).

Neither is it true that teachers typically are frustrated in their work. According to research, 86 percent of men teachers expect to teach until retirement and only about 15 percent say that it is either certain or probable that they would choose not to teach if they were given the opportunity to relive their lives (11:38). Therefore, with the backing of nationwide research, it can be concluded that the typical high school teacher in America is a happily married male who intends to teach until

[4] Research Division of the National Education Association, *NEA Research Bulletin,* vol. 39, no. 1 (February 1961), p. 28.

retirement and who would again choose to be a teacher if he were to reselect his lifework.

In the preceding discussion, consideration has been given to opportunities offered by the teaching profession. It must be remembered, however, that such opportunities are neither gifts nor the results of chance. They are products of continuous efforts on the part of the teacher to acquire the knowledges and skills demanded of his profession. Some of these demands are suggested in the following paragraphs.

KNOWLEDGE AND SKILLS REQUIRED IN TEACHING

The mediocre teacher tells. The good teacher explains. The superior demonstrates. The great teacher inspires.—*William Arthur Ward.*[5]

What Is Teaching?

At the outset, anyone who plans to become a teacher needs to give thoughtful consideration to the question: "What *is* teaching?" Unfortunately, a clear answer to that question is sometimes clouded by those who confuse fact and fiction.

One fiction is the notion that "if a person knows his subject, he is able to teach it." The author once supervised a student teacher whom he chided for lecturing too much to his junior high school students. In reply, the young man said, "What am I supposed to do? After spending four or five years in college accumulating information, now I am not permitted to tell what I know." He clearly demonstrated a common misconception about the nature of teaching. Telling is not teaching. It is the process of giving information.

Another fiction concerning teaching is expressed in the cliché, "Teachers are born, not made." While it is true that some candidates for teaching are more richly endowed than others, yet *all must learn how to teach.* No one would think of going to a doctor who lacked the knowledges and skills required of his profession, nor would anyone employ an engineer to build a bridge if he had never learned how to build bridges. Yet, teaching, which requires skillful ability to diagnose learning difficulties and skillful engineering to deal with human materials, is apparently considered by those who recommend little or no professional preparation as a job requiring no specialized knowledge or skills.

Closely related to both of the above-named fictions are a number of fallacies concerning *methods* of teaching. They go something like this:

[5] *Phi Delta Kappan,* vol. 43 (November 1961), p. 59.

"Educationists recommend that prospective teachers study methods *rather than* subject matter"; "Methods courses take up so much of the student's time he receives insufficient preparation in his subjects"; and finally there is the propaganda device of labeling all education courses as "methods" courses. In answer to the foregoing fictions, there is abundant evidence that education does not monopolize the program of the prospective teacher. The fact is that of total graduation requirements, education courses represent a maximum of 18 to 21 percent (1:1463). And, it may be added, educators are content to keep it that way.

In the light of these fictions, a few comments concerning the need for a teacher to know his subject are relevant. Products of higher education with a strong emphasis upon academic education themselves, educators have never discounted for one moment the need for teachers to know the subjects they teach. They do object, however, to a consideration of subject matter mastery as the ultimate end of education. They also object to a number of fictions concerning this so-called mastery.

First of all, no prospective teacher, no matter how many college units he accumulates, is adequately prepared in anything. There are at least two reasons for this. For one, new developments in all areas of knowledge are taking place at such a dizzy pace that every teacher has to study diligently and continuously lest he become a purveyor of irrelevant, if not false, information. Furthermore, the hackneyed expression, "The only way to learn a subject is to teach it," has much truth in it. As a teacher begins to teach his subject, it takes on new meaning. He develops new insights, motivations, and perspective, as well as a degree of humility. Furthermore, no subject can be taught until it is organized, and that organization must be in terms of the needs and maturity of the students.

Scholarship in teaching is important, but the meaning of the term has not always been made clear. Scholarship is certainly more than the accumulation of thirty-five, fifty, or even sixty units of credit in a particular subject. It is as much a state of mind as anything. To attain it, a person must not only be equipped with the tools of learning but must also have the desire and the intellectual curiosity to broaden his understanding of the world of people, events, and things.

Fallacious notions about teaching are due to easygoing, superficial generalizations about a complex process. Before attempting to define or explain the meaning of teaching, one must know what teachers do, what functions they perform. It soon becomes evident that teachers play not just one but many roles. As a result of considerable deliberation by various groups of educators, the following six roles of the teacher have been identified:

1. As a director of learning
2. As a counseling and guidance person
3. As a mediator of the culture
4. As a member of the school community
5. As a link between school and community
6. As a member of a profession[6]

In order to understand what knowledges and skills are required by the profession, the teacher must know what *he must do*—what functions he must perform—in order to fulfill the six roles expected of him. Some of these activities, most of which are discussed at length in other parts of this book, will be indicated in the following paragraphs.

As a Director of Learning

In developing competence as a director of learning, the teacher plans interesting and meaningful learning experiences for his students; develops satisfactory relationships with his students and effective classroom management and control; uses a variety of instructional materials and procedures effectively; provides for individual differences; and appraises, records, and reports student growth and achievement.

As a Counseling and Guidance Person

In discharging his responsibility for counseling and guidance of students, the teacher seeks to know his students and their needs; uses various sources and procedures for studying his students; learns how to interpret and use data concerning his students effectively; works closely with the guidance office, referring special problems to appropriate specialists; and uses group guidance techniques in an effective manner.

As Mediator of the Culture

"Culture is activity of thought and receptiveness to beauty and humane feeling. Scraps of information have nothing to do with it."[7] The teacher is not merely a conveyor of information nor a transmitter of the cultural heritage. Through the use of many media, not books alone, the teacher helps students gain a knowledge of and respect for our democratic institutions—their history, traditions, and processes. By means of varied experiences—reading, travel, observation, work experience, participation in

[6] C. E. Fishburn, "Teacher Role Perception in the Secondary School," *The Journal of Teacher Education*, vol. 13 (March 1962), pp. 55-59.

[7] Alfred North Whitehead, *The Aims of Education and Other Essays*. New York: The Macmillan Company, 1929, p. 1. Used by permission of Macmillan. British and Commonwealth rights have been granted by Ernest Benn, Ltd., London.

school and community groups—students learn to understand and appreciate the moral and spiritual values, the infinite variety, and the problems
of their culture. The role of the teacher as a mediator of the culture has
been well expressed in these words:

For five and twenty years . . . I have been giving sight to the blind. I have
given understanding to some thousands of boys. . . . My boys have learnt the
history of mankind so that it has become their adventure; I have had languages
taught to make the past live again in their minds and to be windows upon
the souls of alien peoples. Science has played its proper part; it has taken my
boys into the secret places of matter and out among the nebulae. . . .[8]

As a Member of the School Community

The new teacher needs to be accepted as a member of the professional
family with which he works each day, both for personal and professional
reasons. The establishment of harmonious relationships with his co-
workers contributes to his own happiness and to his effectiveness as a
teacher.

In order to gain acceptance as a member of his school community, the
beginning teacher is advised to observe a few simple rules.

1. First of all, he needs to be a good listener and a willing worker.
No matter how much he should be tempted to do it, the novice should
refrain from giving advice. He still has too much to learn to do that.

2. The well-bred, truly professional teacher is always considerate of
the feelings of others. By being temperate in speech, dressing in good
taste, and respecting the customs and traditions of the school, the newcomer soon wins acceptance by his co-workers. Criticism, whether it be of
another teacher or food in the cafeteria, is to be avoided at all costs.

3. The new teacher needs to become familiar with the correct procedures for securing the many services the school has to offer. Because the
modern school must of necessity be highly organized and staffed by
specialists, proper channels of communication have to be followed. In
securing supplies and in obtaining the assistance of nonteaching personnel—librarians, custodians, secretaries—the teacher must observe
established regulations and procedures. By being considerate and re-
fraining from making excessive demands of them, the teacher soon discovers that nonteaching staff members will go beyond the call of duty in
helping him.

No classroom is an island. Although the classroom teacher seemingly
works alone with his students day after day, he is always a part of a

---

[8] H. G. Wells, *The Undying Fire.* New York: The Macmillan Company, 1919, p. 61.
Used by permission of the executors of the H. G. Wells' estate.

professional team. The members of that team stand ready to give assistance to the beginner within their ranks. All he has to do is to learn the rules of the game and play his part as best he can. Newcomers in any situation always lack the status of the more experienced. However, by exercising tact and good judgment, by observing established customs and regulations, and by demonstrating a willingness to carry his fair share of responsibility as a faculty member, the new teacher can soon gain acceptance as a respected member of the school community.

As a Link between School and Community

Another vital role the teacher plays is to help establish a closer bond between the school and the larger community. Suggestions for improving relationships between parents and teachers have been included elsewhere (see Chapter 19). But there are other laymen, citizens and taxpayers, to be considered as well. The process of building better bridges of understanding between school and community poses a number of problems. For instance, one difficulty pertains to the concept of the community itself. A *community* is usually thought of as a geographical area in which the residents are bound together by common interests, ties, and traditions. When the author began teaching in a small rural high school, he was advised to make no disparaging remarks about anyone because the people were all related. Today, the situation is rapidly changing. As large urban centers replace the intimate neighborhoods of an earlier agrarian society, well-defined communities, as originally conceived, cease to exist. Thus the teacher may very well ask, "What is my community that I am expected to serve?" The best he can do is to work closely with the parents of his students and become an active, well-informed citizen of the larger political and geographical area of which the school is a part.

Closely related to the problem of identification of communities is the subject of public relations. Probably with some justification, teachers have often been criticized for being unaware of the importance of good relations with the public. They have been content to leave the whole matter in the hands of administrators or public relations experts. The problem is further complicated by the fact that there are many publics, not just one. Because of that fact, there is more reason than ever for teachers to play their role in improving school-public relations. It is true that good teaching with its product of happy, successful students is the best avenue to good public relations that a school can have, yet every teacher has his own circle of friends to whom he can act as an interpreter of the school and its program.

As a teacher becomes aware of the close link between the school and community, he conceives of the community as a laboratory for learning or as an extension of the classroom. The criticism that the school program is "a two-by-four curriculum" confined to the two covers of a textbook and the four walls of the classroom, as someone so succinctly said, no longer holds true. By using community resource speakers in the classroom, by taking students on field trips to study community functions and organizations, or by directing surveys of community life to study real problems, the teacher adds a new dimension to learning that takes place in the classroom.

There is a personal reason why the teacher should mingle with the people of the community. As has already been suggested, working with youth is a rewarding experience; yet, the teacher needs the additional emotional and intellectual stimulus of association with other adults. Although he associates every day with his professional colleagues, he occasionally needs to get away from shop talk and the cares of the classroom by meeting, socializing, and working with people from other occupations as well.

The teacher needs to know his community—its composition, values, impact on youth, and its resources for learning. That the out-of-school environment of boys and girls has a direct bearing on what they learn in school no one will deny. As the teacher attempts to assess these environmental influences, he may very well seek answers to such questions as the following: How do students spend their free time? Do they work? If so, what do they do? Or, do they merely loaf on the streets? What are the occupations of parents? Do both parents work outside the home? Does the community provide adequate recreational facilities for youth? What character-building agencies are available for teen-age boys and girls? What commercial amusements—motion pictures, materials on newsstands, television programs—are competing for the time and tastes of adolescents? To what social, economic, and moral pressures are students subjected? The school does not operate in a vacuum.

In the development of good citizenship, the improvement of communication skills, and the elevation of the cultural levels of students, teachers must have community support. Students themselves cannot operate successfully in two conflicting worlds, one represented by the school and the other by the neighborhood or community.

How does a teacher get to know his community? He may make a tour of it, observing its homes, churches, business and industrial firms, and parks and playgrounds. He may read the local newspapers, noting weekly entertainment guides and the activities of clubs, churches, and other agencies which serve youth. The teacher should attend social and cultural functions and visit libraries, museums, and other cultural centers. He may talk with citizens engaged in various occupations and he may offer his services as a speaker for certain occasions. By becoming an active, interested citizen of the community, the teacher increases his effectiveness in the class room and strengthens the ties between school and community.

As a Member of a Profession

In playing his role as a professional person, the first mark of the teacher is this: *He takes pride in his profession.* He never feels obliged to apologize for his choice of a vocation. Instead, he believes in the worthwhileness, the significance, of teaching as a career. He never loses faith in the improvability of human nature. Although other occupations may seem to offer more attractive rewards, the teacher who truly loves his work would not exchange jobs with anyone.

As a member of a profession, the dedicated teacher exhibits a second quality: *He is loyal to his profession.* Not for a moment does he consider teaching as a steppingstone to some other occupation. He is loyal to his professional colleagues, never stooping to petty gossip about them nor exhibiting a contemptuous attitude toward opinions which may differ from his own.

The teacher of integrity works constantly to improve himself as a person and as a member of the profession by maintaining high standards of personal and professional conduct, by continuing to grow professionally (reading, studying, and actively participating in professional organizations), by cultivating an appreciation for the best in our culture, and by continuous self-evaluation.

In conclusion, it might be pointed out that the foregoing discussion of the six roles of the teacher has stressed *the importance of interpersonal relations* as much as anything. Studies of personnel failures in business and industry indicate that most employees fail, not because of a lack of necessary knowledge and skills, but because of their inability to work with others. By logical inference, the same thing is true of teaching. Almost without exception, every function of the teacher has a more or less direct bearing on his harmonious relations with others, particularly students.

THE CHARACTERISTICS OF SECONDARY SCHOOL STUDENTS

In order to expedite the establishment of harmonious relations with students and thereby enhance the fulfillment of the teaching roles discussed in the previous paragraphs, teachers must study the characteristics of students and how those characteristics affect learning. This study includes the generalizations applicable to students as a whole in addition to detailed specifics concerning the personality of each class and of each student. The following section of this chapter will be devoted to discussion of outstanding physical, intellectual, social, and emotional characteristics of students and what those characteristics imply for teachers.

The Developmental Tasks of Youth

Students typically enter the seventh grade at 12 years of age and complete the twelfth grade at age 18. Thus, they enter secondary school as children and leave as young adults. During that six-year span, most students are in adolescence, a stage of development known for its rapid physical growth and its perplexing problems of adjustment. Adolescents are in an in-between status—too young to be accepted as adults, but too old to view themselves as children.

Teachers who understand the nature of adolescents know that typically they are self-centered, yet they seek acceptance by their peers. They wish to be independent of adults, yet they seek security in adult approval. However, when adult values and peer-group values are in conflict, adolescents adopt the values of their own age group. Consequently, each older generation occasionally feels that the younger generation certainly is headed for ruin. Adolescence, in popular parlance, is an age of rampant delinquency in which automobiles are status symbols, telephones are recreational devices, and "rock and roll" is an ever present prop. Nevertheless, even though each characterization is partially true, youth also has its serious side.

Teen-agers as a whole are good citizens, but they do have problems which to them are serious. These problems have been extensively studied by psychologists, including Havighurst, who have identified a number of "developmental tasks" including:

1. How to gain acceptance by individuals and groups of adolescent age
2. How to become psychologically and economically independent of adults, especially parents
3. How to adapt to a changing physique and a more mature role in relationships with age mates, particularly with members of the opposite sex
4. How to prepare for marriage and family living
5. How to select and prepare for a profitable and satisfying adult occupation
6. How to acquire a sense of values and a system of ethics to serve as a guiding beacon amid the morass of apparently conflicting realities in adolescent and adult life[9]

[9] Robert J. Havighurst, *Developmental Tasks and Education*. New York: David McKay Company, Inc., 1950, pp. 30–63.

Teachers must realize that concern with these problems is typical of American youth. The boy who never is quite ready to give an assigned oral report to his English class, and the girl who refuses to shower after exercise in physical education are not likely to be rebelling against either their teachers or the required activities of their classes. The boy, newly anxious to be attractive to the opposite sex, may well be overly conscious of his pimply complexion or his inability to control his changing voice, while the girl may be fearful that a shower would spoil her meticulous hairdo.

The expert teacher, recognizing the basic problems involved, would not seek solutions in use of physical force or automatic failure; but, dependent upon his knowledge of the individual students and the educational goals involved, he would try such possible actions as use of a prerecorded speech or a written report in the first case, and perhaps the use of an ample shower cap in the second. In any event, the teacher who understands the problems of youth will be better prepared to help students reach satisfactory educational goals.

Students Are Individuals

The greatest single fact to note about students is that they are tremendously different. They differ in physical ability, growth rate, health, intelligence, emotional development, social development, home background, interests, abilities, knowledges, skills, work habits, citizenship, and in endless other ways. Students, no matter how they are grouped, are essentially individuals of greatly differing characteristics.

Physical Development

No topic is more important nor more perplexing to teen-agers than their physical development. The following discussion first points out the physical stature and physical maturity characteristics of secondary school students and then elaborates on their implications for teachers.

PHYSICAL STATURE   In terms of averages, girls at ages 12 and 13 (grades seven and eight) exceed boys in physical stature. At age 12 boys average about 57 inches in height; girls are about an inch taller. The height of approximately two thirds of 12-year-olds lies within 3 inches of the average. However, the shortest boy at this age may be about 4 feet tall, while his classmate of greatest height may be more than 18 inches taller. By the time they are seniors in high school (18 years old), boys average 68 or 69 inches in height, about 5 inches in excess of the average for girls (10:90).

PHYSICAL MATURITY   Perhaps of greatest effect upon a student's self-concept during his high school years is his progress toward sexual maturity. According to statistics, about 20 percent of the girls, but practically none of the boys, have entered puberty prior to enrollment in seventh grade at about 12 years of age. At age 14 (in ninth grade), 85 percent of the girls have entered puberty and half of them have attained physical maturity.

The comparable figures for boys at age 14 are approximately 40 percent and 10 percent respectively. Two years later, when the majority are in the eleventh grade, 90 percent of the girls are physically mature, and only 60 percent of the boys. At age 18, when the average high school student is graduated, practically all have attained physical maturity (10:151).

IMPLICATIONS FOR TEACHERS   Teachers realize that physical differences readily accepted by adults are frequently the cause of great concern to adolescents. Most students desperately want to be like their peer group. Many of those who deviate from the norm more than they think desirable worry to the point that it affects their school adjustment. The fat and the thin, the short and the tall, and the late maturing as well as the early maturing—all need the special understanding of their teacher. Some overcompensate; a few withdraw; most just "grin and bear it"; but all, nonetheless, require sympathetic understanding.

Teachers, through their attitude, leadership, and counseling, can help students realize that it is normal for individuals to develop at different rates. Physical education teachers, in particular, can accomplish much through adjustment of goals and activities to the needs and abilities of individual students. Above all, teachers must remember that students at this age seek acceptance and fear ridicule and rejection.

Health and Handicaps

High school teachers instruct approximately 150 to 200 students each day. Research-based estimates indicate that in an average group of that number:

1. Five to ten will have speech defects requiring attention if therapy has not been provided in the elementary school (1:1333).
2. Three to six are afflicted with hearing loss serious enough to require medical attention (1:997).
3. Twenty to fifty require corrective lenses to achieve "normal" vision.[10]
4. Ten to fifteen suffer from known allergies such as eczema, asthma, hay fever, and hives (1:1002–1004).
5. One to ten have epilepsy, diabetes, or cardiac disability (1:1003).

[10] Howard L. Kingsley and Ralph Garry, *The Nature and Conditions of Learning.* Englewood Cliffs, N.J.: Prentice-Hall, Inc., 1957, p. 184.

IMPLICATIONS FOR TEACHERS What are the implications of these data? The answer is clear. Teachers are not expected to have the skills of doctors or nurses, but they are expected to be alert to the physical and health status of their students so that seating rearrangements can be made, educational goals and activities can be modified for individuals, and ailing students can be referred to the appropriate medical service.

In addition, teachers are expected to be ready to cope with emergencies that might have been foreseen. Likewise, by developing the ability to recognize colds and other contagious illness in early stages, teachers can contribute to reduction in the spread of such illness. It is also known that early detection and remedy of sight, speech, and hearing defects can reduce educational retardation common to many physically handicapped. Thus, it is easy to understand why teachers give high priority to careful observation of students and to study of their health records and reports.

Intelligence

Differences in intelligence among students are more subtle to determine than physical differences; nevertheless, intellectual differences are just as real and just as extensive. The most commonly used intelligence tests place approximately two thirds of a given age group between intelligence quotients (IQ's) of 84 and 116; approximately 14 percent between 116 and 132; and the same percentage, between 84 and 68. Only 2 percent have IQ's above 132, and 2 percent fall below 68. These percentages will vary somewhat, depending upon the test used and the group measured.

Since a disproportionately large number of those who drop out of school have IQ's below average, high school teachers can expect that the average IQ of their classes will exceed 100. Also, more than one sixth of their students will have IQ's above 116. However, in most schools there will be classes having an IQ average below 100, and in some schools all classes may average below that figure. It is not unusual to find an IQ difference of fifty or more points between the highest and lowest scoring member of a class. This fact poses a difficult problem for educators.

ABILITY GROUPING One attempted solution has been to assign students to classes on the basis of intelligence quotients. Ordinarily, two or at most three classifications are used. This procedure reduces the ability range in any one class but fails to achieve homogeneity with respect to ability to learn specific subject matter. Teachers of so-called homogeneous classes should keep in mind that their classes, too, are composed of individuals who differ widely.

Research has revealed that trait differences within an individual are so great that persons with like intelligence scores will have other very different attributes. It has been shown that homogeneous grouping with re-

spect to one ability has reduced the range of other abilities only approximately 20 percent.[11] For example, in typical heterogeneous ninth-
grade English classes, students range about six years in attributes such
as mental ability, grammar ability, and reading ability—from performance
that is typical for seventh graders to that which is average for high school
seniors.

If these classes are regrouped into three levels according to mental
ability, the range of mental age in each class section can be reduced to
two years, but each class section would still retain a range of approximately 4.8 years in grammar performance, in reading, and in other abilities. Similar grouping according to other factors would have similar results.
Thus it appears obvious that when a teacher desires homogeneous grouping, he must regroup for each change of activity. Such frequent change is
feasible only within the class.

IMPLICATIONS FOR TEACHERS   Other factors being equal, students of
higher IQ can be expected to understand directions and explanations more
easily, to learn more quickly, to retain their learning for a longer period of
time, and to apply what they have learned to new situations more adeptly.
With respect to academic learning they are richly blessed.

In addition, students of high IQ, when compared as a group with those
of average and low IQ, also show greater originality, greater determination, greater perseverance, and greater interest in intellectual tasks and
academic subjects. They demonstrate greater ability to reason, to generalize, to synthesize, and to deal with abstract concepts. Students of
superior intellect also tend to be more mature physically, emotionally, and
socially. They are not necessarily more talented artistically nor mechanically, but through more intensive effort they seem to develop their special
talents more effectively (1:584–585).

Of course, to these research-supported generalizations there are many
exceptions. Nevertheless, teachers must reject the old saws of "a strong
back and a weak mind," and "easy come, easy go," since they describe the
exception, not the rule. (Further discussion of the meaning and interpretation of intelligence quotients is found in Chapter 18.)

Achievement in Subject Matter and Basic Skills

Research has revealed that differences in educational achievement among
students at the extremes of any grade level are so great as to be almost
unbelievable.[12] For example, with a typical seventh-grade class of

[11] Walter W. Cook, "The Functions of Measurement in the Facilitation of Learning,"
   Educational Measurement, E. F. Lindquist, ed. Washington, D.C.: American Council on Education, 1951, p. 19.
[12] *Ibid.*, p. 11.

thirty to forty students, the lowest achievers in arithmetic, reading, science, history, and English make scores no better than those made by average fourth or fifth graders, while the highest achievers in the same seventh-grade class make scores equal to the ninth- or tenth-grade average. The typical range in achievement within one school grade is six to eight grades. This achievement variability persists throughout the secondary school and continues in college.

Further research involving eight to twelve hours of testing more than 35,000 high school and college students in a large eastern state showed that 22 percent of the high school seniors exceeded the college sophomore average, and 10 percent of the high school seniors exceeded the average for college seniors. In a similar study conducted within a single college all students were tested in English, fine arts, social studies, science, and mathematics. It was found that had the graduation list been made up of the highest quarter of the student body on the basis of the test results, the graduating class would have included 15 percent of the freshmen, 19 percent of the sophomores, 21 percent of the juniors, and only 28 percent of the seniors.[13]

IMPLICATIONS FOR TEACHERS   Lest teachers become discouraged by these facts of variability among students, they should remember that the distribution of achievement like that of intelligence is normal. The middle two thirds of a class is typically not more than one grade level ahead or behind the class average in any single trait. This knowledge is of value to teachers, but has led many to conclude erroneously that by removing the lowest sixth and the highest sixth from a typical class, the remaining group would range only three years on additional traits involved in learning. Research refutes this conclusion by showing that students who are alike in one aspect of a subject may be very different in other aspects of the same subject. This fact was illustrated in the preceding section on intelligence.

Knowing that students in the same school year differ widely in knowledge of subject matter as well as in ability to read, write, speak, spell, and compute, alert teachers include study of these factors as they prepare to teach a class. Armed with this information, teachers compare present performance of students with their past performance and with their estimated potential.

Students who are not working up to capacity can be identified and encouraged to improve, students who are low for their grade can be given remedial help, and high achievers can be commended and encouraged to work on more advanced assignments. The old practice of using identical assignments and activities for all students in a class is then replaced with

[13] *Ibid.*, pp. 10–15.

the more modern practice of modifying both the pace and the procedure to bring about maximum learning in a particular class.

Social and Emotional Development, Interest, and Adjustment

Some of the social and emotional characteristics of adolescence were mentioned in an early part of this chapter. Here it will be emphasized that awareness of a student's social and emotional status may be the real key to success in his instruction.

TYPICAL BEHAVIOR   Gesell has described typical behavior of students at various secondary school ages. He states that the seventh grader and eighth grader are noted for their enthusiasm and their intense interest in physical action.[14] Boys will snatch a classmate's possessions just for the joy of chasing and being chased. Gesell also observes that students at that stage of development find it almost impossible to stand in line without considerable jostling and horseplay. They are responsive, however, to appeals to group loyalty; they are proud to be members of a team or club; and in eighth grade they seem to concentrate better and enjoy school more than they did a year earlier.

In the ninth grade, at age 14, "he is quieter within himself, even though . . . more noisy with the group. . . . His contemplation of his own personality is becoming less uneasy, dissatisfied, and defensive, more calm and judicious."[15] It should be noted, however, that while the 14-year-old quite readily criticizes his classmates, he is not yet able to take criticism objectively. In the words of a teen-ager, "He can dish it out, but he can't take it." Teachers, when conducting group evaluations, should keep in mind that adolescents are extremely sensitive to peer opinion.

According to Gesell, the tenth grader sometimes exhibits a hostile attitude toward school and toward teachers. Dropouts are frequent in the sophomore year.[16] In the eleventh and twelfth grades, students show the results of steady growth toward social and emotional maturity. They realize that college, trade school, military service, or work are just over the horizon and they seek to make the most of their remaining school opportunities.

Teachers also can gain clues to effective motivation from research describing adolescent interests in motion pictures, music, television, radio, books, magazines, stories of adventure (boys), stories of romance (girls), famous people, hobbies of collecting, boy-girl relationships, and, above

[14] Arnold Gesell, *et al.*, *Youth: The Years from Ten to Sixteen.* New York: Harper & Row, Publishers, 1956.
[15] *Ibid.*, p. 204.
[16] *Ibid.*, pp. 241, 270.

all, from adolescents themselves (1:1105–1109). Of particular importance is the fact that adolescent interests can be broadened and directed. However, the attention span of junior and senior high school students is likely to be limited. "Adolescents are usually willing to explore new areas, but are unable to sustain concentrated attention if there is not an immediate satisfaction gained from them."[17]

Experienced teachers realize that even though the above statements are valid generalizations, individual students also differ greatly in these characteristics. A student's social and emotional development is dependent to a large degree upon his home background and upon the behavior patterns accepted by the adolescent group with which he regularly associates.

DIFFERENCES ASSOCIATED WITH SOCIOECONOMIC LEVELS   It is important for teachers, largely the product of middle-class homes, to realize that almost 60 percent of the nation's school-age youth are from homes of low socioeconomic classification. Between 35 and 40 percent are from middle-class homes, and about 3 percent are children of the upper class (2:174).

Patterns of values, beliefs, and acceptable behavior differ somewhat from home to home within the same social class but, in general, the differences between classes are drastic with respect to work habits, acceptance of responsibility, occupational outlook, the guidance of children, attitude toward money, morality, manners, uncouth language, proper grammar, physical combat, punishment, the arts, music, reading, home study, education, teachers, and schools. There is little wonder that sociologists and teachers look to the home first when seeking causes of social and emotional behaviors of children and youth.

It should also be noted that

the adolescent has not yet learned to compartmentalize his life; an emotional experience in one area is likely to affect all his other relationships. Parental denial of a request or a quarrel with a schoolmate, for example, may cause a young person's school work to suffer.[18]

No doubt, all teachers benefit from developing understanding and a degree of tolerance of the differences that exist in American social structure.

SERIOUS PROBLEMS OF ADJUSTMENT   Early identification of pupils who are potential leaders as well as those who have adjustment problems can

---

[17] Roland C. Faunce and Morrel J. Clute, *Teaching and Learning in the Junior High School*. Belmont, Calif.: Wadsworth Publishing Company, Inc., 1961, p. 41.
[18] Lester D. Crow, Harry E. Ritchie, and Alice Crow, *Education in the Secondary School*. New York: American Book Company, 1961, p. 91.

do much to keep the learning atmosphere of a class at its optimum. Alert teachers are particularly conscious of the fact that a few students have potentially serious behavior problems.

Research indicates that while the incidence of serious maladjustment may vary greatly from community to community and from school to school, it may not be unusual for a teacher to have three or four individuals with serious adjustment problems among the 150 to 200 students he teaches each day (1:139). About the same number, in some cases the same students, have been brought before the juvenile court prior to the age of 19.

In court cases, and in school misbehavior, boys outnumber girls about five to one. Boys' offenses against the law most frequently are stealing or malicious mischief; whereas girls are cited for "ungovernable behavior, running away, and sex offenses."[19] There is evidence, however, that considerably more than 2 percent of adolescents at one time or another are involved in infractions of law. In a study of 6000 illegal actions including 600 serious infractions, all of which were committed over a five-year period by 114 boys, only 1 percent of the cases resulted in court action (1:366). Exact figures are not available, but there is reason to believe that the incidence of psychological maladjustment among teen-agers is also a serious problem (1:824).

With the seriously maladjusted, the teacher's proper role is that of an important but subsidiary member of a professional team which cooperates in the diagnosis and treatment of problems. In large schools, the psychiatrist, sociologist, psychologist, visiting caseworker, and the special teacher are the professionals who direct the study and treatment of each case. In small schools the school counselor or principal may take the leadership role. In the opinion of experts, "Help to an individual delinquent can come only through individual study and diagnosis followed by treatment carefully prescribed and systematically carried out, utilizing all community resources."[20]

The classroom teacher, even though he has had "a case just like this last year," or has had experience "straightening them out in the Marines," should never take it upon himself to solve such problems singlehanded. His role in each case is to follow the prescription of the personnel professionally prepared for the job. For a community to leave such problems in the undirected hands of a well-meaning classroom teacher is like turn-

---

[19] William Kvaraceus, "Delinquency," *Encyclopedia of Educational Research*, 3d ed., Chester W. Harris, ed. New York: The Macmillan Company, 1960, p. 366. Used by permission of Macmillan.

[20] *Ibid.*, p. 368.

ing an ailing child over to a witch doctor in spite of the availability of twentieth-century medical care.

TYPICAL DISCIPLINE PROBLEMS   The school misbehaviors of seventh- and eighth-grade boys are most often: talking, fighting, throwing things, and truancy. The misbehaviors of girls in those grades are most often: talking, gum chewing, eating candy, fighting, and immorality. In the senior high school, common difficulties involve noisy conduct, rudeness to faculty and to other students, lying, petty thievery, and damage to property (1:139).

According to research conducted by the National Education Association, some misbehaviors occur in the best of schools, but the incidence of serious difficulty seems greatest in schools located in the slum areas of large urban centers. In these schools only 15 percent of the teachers report that their students are "exceptionally well behaved," whereas the corresponding figure in "good" residential areas is 47 percent. In the same study involving a nationwide sample of 4000 teachers, more than two thirds rated student behavior not nearly as bad as pictured by movies, press, and radio; seven teachers out of eight reported that fewer than 5 percent of their students were troublesome, one out of three found fewer than 1 percent of their students in that category, and one in four reported complete absence of troublemakers (1:139).

It is evident that the problem of discipline, even though overrated by mass communications media, still remains a concern of many teachers. In Chapters 11–13, the teacher's role in maintaining discipline is fully discussed. It may be well for beginning teachers to study that section carefully before taking charge of a class.

Special Talents, Experiences, and Goals

The teacher who acquaints himself with his students' special talents, educational experiences, vocational plans, and educational goals finds in that knowledge a remarkable reservoir from which he can draw to keep his classes at peak performance. In almost every class, there are students who have special interests and talents in such subjects as music, drama, speech, mechanics, and athletics. Many will have selected at least tentative vocational and educational goals. Some will have traveled broadly, others will have had interesting work experiences. All of these facts can be used by the expert teacher better to motivate learning.

The Adolescent's Workday

Teachers should be alert to the fact that competing for the attention and efforts of adolescents are many ideas and activities other than those associated with the academic life of schools. In addition to the school's activity program designed to aid in the social, emotional, physical, artistic, and cultural development of youth, there are also the important developmental programs of church, home, and other community organizations and agencies.

Some teen-agers, typically the products of middle- and upper-class homes, are notorious joiners. They frequently find themselves involved in an impossible schedule of community club activities, church responsibilities, and special lessons or tasks scheduled by the home—all in addition to the leadership roles they assume in the curricular and the cocurricular programs of the school. Other students, more typically the product of homes of less fortunate economic circumstance, have an equally heavy schedule because they are required to work to help support themselves and their sometimes numerous brothers and sisters.

In these days of the twenty-five- to forty-hour work week for adults, some parents are looking critically at the expanding demands upon adolescents. Without question, proper coordination of the various programs requires a great deal of awareness, cooperation, and a measure of compromise on the part of all, including the classroom teacher.

Knowledge of a student's complete schedule makes it possible for teachers to plan activities and assignments more realistically and effectively. Most teachers accept the principle that each school subject should have a right to its share of a student's time and effort, but none should demand uncompromising and monopolistic control.

SECURING INFORMATION ABOUT A PARTICULAR CLASS

In addition to being scholars in subject matter and experts in the various teaching techniques, teachers need to know the learning-related characteristics of each class and its individual students if the best possible job of teaching that class is to be accomplished. Teachers need to answer such questions as: What proportion of the class is fast moving, average, or slow intellectually? As a group and as individuals, are they eager to learn or are they indifferent or antagonistic to school in general or to this subject in particular? What is the level of their achievement in the subject and in the fundamental skills needed? What clues to class motivation can be gained from the interests, experiences, and special talents represented? Which students have special problems of health, growth, adjustment, or learning? What clues to better instruction can be gained from knowledge of their home and community environment? Which students can be depended upon for cooperation and leadership toward desired ends?

All the above questions and many more are important in teaching. The answers are not automatic. They are not granted with successful completion of a college course, nor do they necessarily accompany years of teaching experience, although both can be factors contributing to successful solutions.

Data basic to answers must be secured and studied for each new group of students. The needed information can be obtained in many ways and from various sources including school records and reports of all types, comments of teachers and school personnel, student essays, interviews, and questionnaires, teacher observation, and conferences with parents.

Records and Reports

The keeping of records and reports varies considerably from school to school. However, the files in the offices of the principal or counselor provide such facts as information concerning the academic progress of each student (subjects taken and grades in each), scores on group intelligence tests, reading scores, and results of standardized achievement tests. School files ordinarily include other miscellaneous items of information which are of value, such as data about the family, health records (serious illnesses, past examination results, and recommendations concerning health problems), and anecdotal reports of significant behavior recorded by observant teachers.

Unofficial Information

Fellow teachers and other school personnel often know many valuable bits of information—material which never gets into official records—about students, families, and neighborhoods. Counselors, homeroom teachers, the visiting teacher, former teachers of the students, principals and vice-principals, and other staff members may have gained some keen insights or valuable information pertaining to students.

However, some words of caution need to be given concerning the use of unofficial information about students. Never give or receive such information except for confidential, professional use. Teachers must also screen hearsay evidence carefully to distinguish probable fact from mere gossip or biased opinion. They will particularly have to guard against prejudice toward students with a bad reputation. The student who is branded summarily as a hopeless problem has no chance for redemption, whereas many, if not most of the problem cases work out of their difficulties when given proper guidance and opportunity.

Information from Students

Quite often the most significant data concerning a student are those things which he says about himself. Autobiographies, informal talks, questionnaires, interest inventories, discussion of hobbies, and open-end questions are all useful devices whereby the student gives information about himself.

The open-end question, for example, can be used to get an expression of attitude or feeling on the part of the student. The student is asked to complete a statement somewhat as follows. "I like class activities which _____" or "I like teachers who _____" or "I can study best when _____." The possibilities are unlimited for exploring student attitudes in this manner. However, best results cannot be obtained unless there is good group morale and excellent teacher-student rapport.

Interviews with students should be conducted in private and without encouraging them to reveal information they or their families would not choose to share. For example, to determine parents' occupations usually is acceptable, but to ask about incomes, political preferences, or religious beliefs is unwise. As a matter of principle, the right to privacy and the rules of good taste should be observed in all data-gathering processes. Enquiries should be restricted to matters which teachers, students, and parents clearly recognize as related to planning of instruction and motivation of learning.

Observation of Students

Much can be learned by careful observation of students in many situations—in class discussion, in committee work, during study, in the library, on the school grounds, at school functions, and wherever the student has opportunity to demonstrate behavior in which the teacher is interested. Observation can be used for several purposes: to get the feeling of a class and how it reacts, to determine the effectiveness with which a group studies or carries on school activities, to evaluate instruction, and to gain clues concerning an individual's adjustment and growth.

Specific techniques of observation including use of rating scales, check lists, and anecdotal records are discussed fully in Chapter 15. Here it will merely be pointed out that to furnish reliable evidence, observation must be carefully conducted over an extended period of time. Otherwise the behavior observed might be misleading or unimportant. Therefore teachers should be particularly careful in reaching conclusions based on observation alone. When combined with other information, however, observational evidence frequently can provide the clues which complete the picture.

Conferences with Parents

In most teaching situations the opportunity to meet parents is quite limited. Teachers should therefore seize every opportunity to make their acquaintance by meeting them at Parent-Teacher Association functions, open houses, and at class programs and demonstrations. In some instances, classroom teachers visit the homes of their students, but as a rule home visits are reserved for the experienced visiting teacher. Successful home visitation requires considerable tact and skill.

ORGANIZING AND USING INFORMATION ABOUT STUDENTS

In the process of gathering data about students, teachers need to keep several important considerations in mind. First, such material is for *use*, not for storage in a dead file. Second, the information must be kept strictly *confidential*, to be used for professional purposes only. Unless items are coded or recorded in an anonymous manner, personal data should be kept under lock and key and made available only to authorized persons. Unfortunately some teachers are afflicted with wagging tongues. They are inclined to relieve their tensions by gossiping about their students freely in the cafeteria or some other public place. Such practice is highly unprofessional. Third, teachers need to use information about students *intelligently*. This skill involves collection and organization of data, correct and judicious interpretation of the facts, and wise application to teaching situations.

Organization of Information

In the organization of student information, it is well to make a general description of the class, and also to keep an individual record for as many students as possible. Summary sheets, graphs, and charts help to give meaning to the data. Chapter 2 contains a sample class analysis of the type that is prepared by student teachers. Such analyses require investment of much time and effort, but return dividends in increased class achievement. Many experienced teachers regularly take the time to make similar analyses. They are alert to a major finding of educational and psychological research: "The learner, whether animal, child, or adult, moves most efficiently toward a prescribed objective when the process of instruction is best adapted to *him*. This would seem to demand some knowledge of *him* on the part of the teacher."[21]

Use of Information

In making intelligent use of information about his students, a teacher must consider especially the data which are significant in his particular

[21] H. Orville Nordberg, James M. Bradfield, and William C. Odell, *Secondary School Teaching*. New York: The Macmillan Company, 1962, p. 64. Used by permission of Macmillan.

class. For example, a low reading score may not be significant in a physical education class while health status and physical coordination would be very important. On the other hand, reading skill is quite necessary in a social studies class where success depends to a great extent on ability to read. Furthermore, in interpreting data, teachers must guard against making hasty generalizations or drawing dogmatic conclusions. Test score interpretation is a skill which involves understanding of the concepts of normal and nonnormal distributions, errors of measurement, and systems of standard scores. A later chapter deals fully with these problems.

Finally, teachers must always remember that each student is a person, not just another name or statistic. Each one has his hopes and fears, his strengths and weaknesses, his advantages and his handicaps, his virtues and his faults, and his own optimum route to learning. The teachers who proceed scientifically to search for those optimum routes are most likely to discover them and thereby receive the top reward in teaching: high student achievement.

Selected Readings

1. American Educational Research Association, *Encyclopedia of Educational Research*, 3d ed., Chester W. Harris, ed. New York: The Macmillan Company, 1960.
2. Burton, William H., *The Guidance of Learning Activities*, 3d ed. New York: Appleton-Century-Crofts, 1962. Chapters 7, 8.
3. Carter, William L., Carl W. Hansen, and Margaret G. McKim, *Learning to Teach in the Secondary School*. New York: The Macmillan Company, 1962. Chapter 4.
4. Chandler, B. J., *Education and the Teacher*. New York: Dodd, Mead & Company, Inc., 1961. Chapters 15, 16.
5. Crow, Lester D., Harry E. Ritchie, and Alice Crow, *Education in the Secondary School*. New York: American Book Company, 1961. Chapter 4.
6. Faunce, Roland C., and Morrel J. Clute, *Teaching and Learning in the Junior High School*. Belmont, Calif.: Wadsworth Publishing Company, Inc., 1961. Chapter 2.
7. Grambs, Jean D., William J. Iverson, and Franklin K. Patterson, *Modern Methods in Secondary Education*, revised ed. New York: Holt, Rinehart and Winston, Inc., 1958. Chapter 1.
8. Haskew, Laurence D., and Jonathon C. McLendon, *This is Teaching*, revised and expanded. Chicago: Scott, Foresman and Company, 1962. Chapters 1, 6, 10, 11.
9. Klausmeier, Herbert J., *Teaching in the Secondary School*. New York: Harper & Row, Publishers, 1958. Chapter 2.
10. Mouly, George J., *Psychology for Effective Teaching*. New York: Holt, Rinehart and Winston, Inc., 1960. Chapters 1–7, 15, 16.
11. National Education Association, Research Division, "The Status of the American Public-School Teacher," *NEA Research Bulletin*, vol. 35, no. 1. Washington, D.C.: Research Division of the National Education Association, February 1957.

12. National Education Association, Research Division, *NEA Research Bulletin*, vol. 40, no. 1. Washington, D.C.: Research Division of the National Education Association, February 1962.
13. Nordberg, H. Orville, James M. Bradfield, and William C. Odell, *Secondary School Teaching*. New York: The Macmillan Company, 1962. Chapters 1, 4.
14. Rivlin, Harry N., *Teaching Adolescents in Secondary Schools*, 2d ed. New York: Appleton-Century-Crofts, 1961. Chapters 1, 2.
15. Wellington, C. Burleigh, and Jean Wellington, *Teaching for Critical Thinking*. New York: McGraw-Hill Book Company, Inc., 1960. Chapter 15.

CHAPTER 2

Preparation for teaching

One characteristic of a profession is that it requires an extended period of specialized preparation on the part of the candidate before he is authorized to become a practitioner. This is becoming increasingly true of teaching. Preservice preparation includes a series of graduated steps for admission to teacher education and for advancement toward receipt of a license or credential, culminating in student teaching. Before undertaking this last and most important phase of preparation, the teacher candidate is advised to take careful inventory of his own assets, to reassess the requirements for teaching, and to evaluate his own fitness for the teaching profession.

BEFORE STUDENT TEACHING

By believing in a better world than the real world, and better people than real people, the happy teacher lives as few others can, in peace with herself and her community. She may be much less effective than she realizes; she may even be an incompetent. The source of her happiness, however, is not hypocrisy but that most attractive and ennobling of human failings: hope.—*Martin Mayer*[1]

An Inventory before Student Teaching

As the prospective teacher approaches the most important phase of his professional preparation, observation of and work with students in the classroom, he may very well take further stock of his motives for becoming a teacher. It is important that the teacher candidate ask himself what satisfactions he wants from life. Teachers have listed a number of reasons for choosing their career: among them, interest in teaching a particular subject (especially true of men), the desire to be of service, security and permanency of employment, and good working conditions. One study

[1] Martin Mayer, *The Schools*. New York: Harper & Row, Publishers, 1961, p. 27.

concludes that teachers have less need or desire than the general public for "prestige, income, and professional recognition."[2] In the preceding chapter, basic satisfactions of teaching, as well as the several roles of the teacher, were summarized. The prospective teacher is advised to give thoughtful consideration to these things. By all means, he should recognize that teaching is more than a bread-and-butter occupation. It is the fine art of helping boys and girls grow toward maturity.

The prospective teacher needs to give careful consideration to his *attitudes toward teaching*. Although it has already been pointed out that teacher satisfaction is relatively high in the profession, still 15 percent of all teachers in service certainly or probably would not re-enter teaching.[3] These teachers fail to achieve the satisfactions teaching has to offer and probably render a double disservice to the profession: They fail to give students the help to which they are entitled and they discourage promising high school candidates from considering teaching as a career. One perceptive high school senior made the comment about a very poor teacher: "I had thought of becoming a teacher, but, if he is representative of the profession, I think I shall decide on some other occupation."

The prospective teacher needs to become informed about *professional requirements* as early as possible and to work diligently toward their fulfillment. Such requirements usually include a program of general education, specialization in one or more teaching fields, courses in professional education, and laboratory experiences with boys and girls. Each requirement is designed to contribute to an important aspect of teacher preparation, a fact that is not always clearly recognized by the neophyte in the profession. No doubt very few teachers have completed their professional preparation without later regretting that they did not spend more time and effort on some neglected phase of the program.

Every sincere prospect for teaching desires, no doubt, to become an effective, if not a superior, teacher. That calls for another inventory—an assessment of one's *personal qualifications for teaching*. What are the qualities of the effective teacher? For over a half century attempts have been made to find the answer to that question, but there are still no criteria upon which common agreement has been reached.[4] Efforts to establish such criteria have been based on three factors: product, expressed in terms of student behavior; process, defined in such terms as

[2] Earl W. Anderson and Elfreda M. Rusher, "Staff—Characteristics," *Encyclopedia of Educational Research*, 3d ed., Chester W. Harris, ed. New York: The Macmillan Company, 1960, p. 1359. Used by permission of Macmillan.
[3] Research Division of the National Education Association, *NEA Research Bulletin*, Vol. 35 (February 1957), p. 38.
[4] Harold E. Mitzel, "Teacher Effectiveness," *Encyclopedia of Educational Research*, 3d ed., Chester W. Harris, ed. New York: The Macmillan Company, 1960, p. 1481.

the ability of the teacher to maintain effective discipline or rapport with his students; and "presage criteria," based on such factors as intelligence, adjustment, and character of the teacher. All have their limitations. For example, when the product criterion is used, it is impossible to isolate the unique contribution of the school or any one teacher from that of other agencies or to determine how the school affects ultimate behavior.[5]

A recent, comprehensive study, directed by David G. Ryans (past president of AERA), seems to throw the most light on the qualities of a good teacher. He reports the following characteristics appear to be associated with effective teaching: superior intelligence and school achievement; "good emotional adjustment"; favorable attitudes toward pupils and enjoyment of relationships with them; generosity in appraising the motives and behavior of others; strong interests in reading and cultural matters (art, literature, music); "participation in social and community affairs; early experience caring for children and teaching (such as reading to children and taking a class for a teacher)"; family support or identification with teaching; and "strong social service interests."[6, 7]

Someone has said that preparation for retirement begins in kindergarten. The same generalization could be made about teaching. The summary of characteristics associated with effective teaching, just indicated above, suggests that the prospective teacher needs to engage in many kinds of significant preprofessional experiences. Working with community-sponsored youth groups, participating in cocurricular activities with peers (especially in a capacity of leadership), and broadening cultural interests are ways in which future teachers may well lay the foundation for their career. Fortunate is the person who begins in his youth to engage in activities which stand him in good stead later as a teacher. The profession has been remiss in failing to identify promising candidates for teaching in the elementary or secondary school and encouraging them to consider teaching as a vocation. In some cases, high school students who show an interest in teaching are provided opportunities for observing and assisting pupils in the elementary school.

Directed Observation

Probably directed observation of classroom learning activities is second only to student teaching as a means of preparing the teacher candidate for the assumption of full-time responsibilities in teaching. There is an

[5] *Ibid.*, pp. 1483–1485.
[6] David G. Ryans, "Predictions of Teacher Effectiveness," *Encyclopedia of Educational Research*, 3d ed., Chester W. Harris, ed. New York: The Macmillan Company, 1960, p. 1490. Used by permission of Macmillan.
[7] *Phi Delta Kappan*, vol. 42 (January 1961), p. 147.

increasing tendency to introduce "laboratory experiences prior to student teaching."[8] Observation of and work with pupils in the classroom before actual student teaching has a number of advantages. First of all, the teacher candidate can get a better idea of whether or not his choice of teaching as a vocation has been a wise one. Sometimes vocational choices are made on a nebulous, unrealistic basis. The demonstrated insights and actual performance of the prospective teacher in observing and assisting pupils with their learning may also be used as a criterion for the prediction of future success. Finally, these laboratory experiences serve as a valuable introduction to student teaching itself.

In order to profit most from his experience in directed observation, the observer must make his observations intelligently and systematically. First of all, it is advisable to take careful notes as a basis for future study and discussion with the teacher conducting the class. What should the beginning observer watch for? The most fruitful study of any teaching situation is a study of the learners themselves—their varied social, emotional, and intellectual reactions; their differences and similarities in abilities, achievement, and home backgrounds; and their fluctuation in behavior in different situations. The observer needs to be aware of the physical environment—its comfort, attractiveness, cleanliness, and evidences of cooperative housekeeping. The observer should note the routine organization of the classroom—time schedules, student traffic, and distribution and storage of materials. By all means, the observer should carefully consider the procedures used in classroom management and control—standards maintained, responsibilities of teacher and students respectively, rapport between the teacher and the class, and general classroom atmosphere.

Usually the student teacher has a few days of observation, followed by a period of assisting and presenting parts of the lesson, before assuming full responsibility for teaching the class. By making the most of these opportunities, he should be able to make a smooth transition from an observer to a full-fledged teacher.

Observation, even the most informal type implied in the foregoing discussion, presents a number of problems. Many variables must be kept in mind: individual behaviors, different situations (classroom, playground, and so on), sampling, objectivity, and the competence of the observer. As a newcomer to the profession, the prospective teacher must be aware of his own limitations. Occasionally a beginning observer may be unduly critical of classroom procedures or situations which he does not fully comprehend because of his own immaturity and inexperience. Conse-

[8] Laurence D. Haskew, "Teacher Education—Organization and Administration," *Encyclopedia of Educational Research*, 3d ed., Chester W. Harris, ed. New York: The Macmillan Company, 1960, p. 1459. Used by permission of Macmillan.

quently, he must avoid jumping to unwarranted conclusions. It has already been suggested that observations should be recorded. This should be done with as much objectivity as possible, primarily by the omission of biased interpretations from the record. The observer should have an adequate sampling in order to give his observations more reliability. It is obviously illogical to draw any final conclusions about a student on the basis of only one or two examples of his conduct. Furthermore, a study of student behavior under varied conditions is advisable, for the student is quite often a different person in the formal classroom than he is in other settings.

STUDENT TEACHING

As the prospective teacher enters the final and most important phase of his professional preparation—student teaching—he must become fully aware of the purposes and functions of the experience. Briefly stated, student teaching marks the transition from student to teacher. And what a transition that is! One day the candidate for teaching is a student; the next day he is a teacher. After spending fifteen or sixteen years as a student, the prospective teacher may understandably have difficulty in making a sudden adjustment to the many roles of the teacher. When he takes his place *behind* the teacher's desk, he finds himself giving instructions and sometimes orders, and, much to his surprise, he finds students complying with his requests.

As the first shock of strangeness and self-consciousness wears off, the student teacher will need to get his bearings. For one thing, the amassing of units and grade points, which may have been a major concern in his academic life, should no longer seem so important to him. The student teacher must also realize that student teaching is not designed primarily for his convenience nor as a laboratory in which his students are the guinea pigs. The welfare of students, their learning, always has priority. Only by careful preparation and by conscientious performance daily in the classroom can the student teacher justify his continued presence as a guest of the school in which he teaches. The student teacher must also realize that he is not fully prepared as a teacher when he has completed his student teaching assignments. At best, student teaching is only a partial, even unrealistic, introduction to full-time teaching. Because he is frequently assigned to a limited number of classes often more or less carefully selected and to a superior cooperating teacher whose presence is felt in the classroom, the student teacher is sheltered from many problems which he will ultimately face when he is entirely on his own. Some student teachers who have had no problems develop a cocksure, "I-have-it-made" attitude, largely because of their good fortune rather than their teaching skill. Beginners can always benefit from the advice of experience.

The following major section of this chapter is addressed specifically to the beginning student teacher. The advice offered comes directly from three professors with many years of teaching in high schools and indirectly from the more than one thousand student teachers they have supervised in junior and senior high schools during the last twenty years. Careful consideration of suggestions based on their experience should help to accelerate a beginner's progress toward successful teaching.

It is thoroughly normal behavior for a student teacher to approach his first actual teaching with some degree of perturbation. No doubt you are wondering what successes lie ahead. What failures? What will your response be to the challenges of teaching? Will you be strong or weak in discipline? Will students respect you? Will they learn? Will supervisors be sympathetic and helpful? These questions and many more, according to research, trouble those who enter this most important phase of professional preparation.[9] Unfortunately there is no crystal ball which can supply immediate answers.

Nor is there any set of prescriptions which can guarantee success to all. The best advice at this stage is to avoid dwelling on advance fears. There is a job to be done, and once action begins, preliminary tensions will be replaced with the satisfactions of growth accomplished. Be assured that many co-workers are vitally interested in your problems and can do much to help you solve them. It is of utmost importance that you learn to work harmoniously with these persons, recognize their value, and come to earn their cooperation. Who are your co-workers? What can be expected of them? How can their respect and cooperation be earned?

Know Your Supervisors

A cooperating teacher at your assigned school, together with supervisors from the college, will observe and direct your teaching with one purpose in mind: they want you to succeed. They will help you plan your work, suggest a variety of activities and source materials, and constructively evaluate your teaching techniques. In periodic conferences they will strive to help you improve such factors as the quality of your voice, the appropriateness of your dress, the efficiency of your classroom organization, your rapport with students, and the overall effectiveness of your teaching methods. At the conclusion of your student teaching experience, they will write recommendations which should help you get a teaching position. They can be important contributors to your success. To help you receive

[9] John U. Michaelis, "Teacher Education—Student Teaching and Internship," *Encyclopedia of Educational Research*, 3d ed., Chester W. Harris, ed. New York: The Macmillan Company, 1960, p. 1478.

full benefit from supervisory assistance, several points must be emphasized.

THE COOPERATING TEACHER IS YOUR SPONSOR IN THE SCHOOL   He is the main source of information concerning the customs, regulations, and services of the school. He will help clarify your precise position in the school's social structure. Determine through him at the beginning of the term your duties and privileges as a junior member of the faculty. Get his approval before you request the special help of school staff such as the nurse, counselor, principal, secretary, or custodian. In like manner, do not ask faculty members, other than your supervisor, to contribute to your classes unless your cooperating teacher gives complete approval. Avoid the error of one student teacher who, within his first week, aroused the ire of an entire faculty by officiously seeking guest speakers, models of art, bulletin displays, and other products of faculty effort. Your cooperating teacher can usually provide the help you will need. If supplementary assistance is advisable, he will know where, when, and how to request it. Furthermore, your cooperating teacher is legally responsible for the progress of the class he has turned over to you. Therefore, all your teaching must be subject to his approval. Check your plans with him before you teach.

SUPERVISORS ARE YOUR FRIENDS   Discuss your problems frankly with them. Relate your successes; admit your failures. Avoid alibis or rationalizations. Making excuses may save your ego temporarily, but the cost will be loss of opportunity to improve. Certain ethical and personal considerations should govern the relationship between a student teacher and his supervisors. Eight suggestions follow.

1. Be prudent. No one admires a tale bearer. If a disturbing situation should arise between you and one of your supervisors, discuss the problem directly with him, or if that does not seem feasible, take the matter to the director of student teaching. Do not spread your problems of teaching among your friends. Your supervisors and the director of student teaching are responsible persons. They alone are professionally prepared to help solve the problems which may perplex you. It would be poor policy to risk deterioration of supervisory relationships by broadcasting the problems which are solvable professionally.

2. Be loyal. If one of your students should criticize a regular staff member of the school, do not fall into the trap of agreement, either overt or implied. For example, a student, for motives of his own, may tell you he prefers your teaching to that of the cooperating teacher. Such a statement may be music to your ears and therapy for your entire personality, but by all means you should resist rigorously any temptation to be a

receptive listener. One student who comments in this manner may be blunderingly sincere; while another may be attempting only to gain personal advantage. In either case the basic impropriety of such remarks should be recognized and dealt with promptly. At no time should you or your students get the idea that you are in any sort of competition with your cooperating teacher. The two of you form a professional team that can operate effectively only when loyalty on the part of each is automatic.

3. Accept responsibility. Take over full teaching responsibility as soon as your cooperating teacher recommends it. Be regular in attendance and be on time. If an emergency should arise to prevent your attendance at a class or a conference, inform your supervisors as soon as it is humanly possible. Messages of this nature are usually handled by the school secretary. There is almost no adequate reason to excuse your failure to inform the cooperating teacher prior to an enforced absence or tardiness.

4. Give attention to details. Have your lesson plans carefully prepared in advance so that your cooperating teacher can inspect them and discuss anticipated problems with you. Keep up to date in recording and reporting. Have attendance reports ready when they are needed in the central office. Give immediate attention to all tasks assigned by your supervisors. Neglected minutiae have a way of developing into full-fledged problems.

5. Show initiative. Avoid becoming a mental parasite, existing only on the ideas of others. Give continuous thought to your work so that you will not appear at planning sessions empty-handed and devoid of ideas. Professional periodicals and books in your college library are rich in ideas for better teaching.

6. Seek advice and follow it. Do not merely shop around until you find an opinion that agrees with your own. Supervisors take pride in observing the successful application of their suggestions, and are thus stimulated to share their rich knowledge and experience. On the other hand, they are not entirely immune to discouragement or impatience when their advice is ignored.

7. Be a good listener. All too many student teachers fall short of their potential as teachers because they have not learned to listen. Do not become a person who is so busy planning his response or searching for excuses that he is deaf to the suggestions of his supervisor. To be a good listener requires effort and practice as well as basic courtesy.

8. Be absolutely honest in self-evaluation. Be frank and honest with yourself and with your supervisors. Only then will real communication be possible. Anything less than absolute honesty in continuous self-evaluation and in periodic supervisory conferences will very seriously retard the progress that should be yours.

SUPERVISORS DIFFER   Supervisors—all successful teachers—occasionally differ among themselves concerning specific teaching practices. Student teachers should realize that differences of opinion among supervisors are the normal result of varying backgrounds of education and experience. Avoid making an issue of them. For example, most student teachers will be given teaching responsibility after a week or two of observation while a few may be plunged into full responsibility at once. Still others may be denied teaching privileges for a month or more. Some supervisors will demand extensive daily lesson plans; others may be satisfied with bare outlines or nothing. Do not be disturbed by such inconsistencies. Treat them with tact. Throughout your entire career you will encounter an abundance of conflicting opinions. The sooner you learn to live with them, the better. A guiding principle might well be to adapt supervisory advice to the specific requirements of the school in which you do your student teaching, but also keep in mind that the experience gained must be broad enough to prepare you for success in the many different schools which soon may offer you a teaching contract.

Know the School's Administrators

The administrative head of the school is the principal. He is directly responsible for providing effective leadership of the school and of its entire educational program, including the classes taught by student teachers. To student teachers he usually appears to be a rather mysterious person hidden away in a remote office. However, even though he may not see you regularly, he knows you are in the school and feels some responsibility for your success. He probably knows more about you than you suspect since he undoubtedly examined your papers when he helped select your cooperating teacher. Through conferences with supervisors most principals keep informed concerning the progress of the student teachers in their building. Some principals briefly visit classes taught by student teachers, although such visits are seldom made during the first weeks of student teaching.

The principal will expect you to adapt quickly to the requirements of your position and become a cooperative and creative member of the school community. He will expect not only that you do a good job of instruction but also that you carry your share of the extra duties of teaching. Many schools provide manuals which contain the school regulations together with specific suggestions to guide the orientation of new teachers. If such a manual exists at your school, study it carefully.

A principal is a good person to know. Not only is he a man rich in educational experience, but he also specializes in understanding human relations. Furthermore, he is chiefly responsible for the selection of his staff and through his friends can effectively recommend teachers for positions in other schools.

Quite obviously, the principal is an important person in the school community. Student teachers should not stand in awe of him. Neither should they rush to his office in an ill-concealed attempt to win attention. In some schools, the principal makes a practice of inviting each student teacher into his office for a friendly conference. In others, he can be seen only when the student teacher requests an appointment. Your cooperating teacher can advise you of the custom in your school. If you are given the opportunity of an interview with the principal, put your best foot forward. It is likely that he will direct the conversation; however, if he can be drawn out, he can undoubtedly contribute much to your knowledge of such topics as the qualities that contribute to the success of a beginning teacher, the relative supply and demand of teachers in neighboring areas, or the desirability of administration as a career in education. Answer his questions honestly, but avoid introducing any discussion of grievances or personalities. He is interested in your personality and potential as a teacher and not in your ability to analyze critically the internal relationships of his staff.

One or more vice-principals (or a dean of boys and a dean of girls) complete the administrative staff of most large schools. The duties of vice-principals usually include the accounting of student attendance and the enforcement of discipline. Customarily, it is to the vice-principal that rebellious, truant, or tardy students are sent. You and your cooperating teacher should discuss your proper role in dealing with attendance or discipline problems. Be sure you understand the policies and procedures accepted at your school before you take charge of the class.

As head of the school, the principal will do all that is possible to provide a pleasant working atmosphere. You can contribute to that goal by observing certain rules of operation:

1. Complete reports accurately and on time. The administrative staff learns to know you through your reports of attendance, marks, and so on. The impression the reports make is important.

2. Keep a strict accounting of books and supplies. The materials of instruction are costly. You are expected to use them sensibly and keep accurate records of books which are issued to students.

3. Enforce and follow the regulations of the school. If a regulation forbids smoking on the school grounds, you will be expected to follow the regulation yourself and to assist in its observance by your students. Some students will take immediate advantage of new teachers who fail to learn or to observe the school's regulations.

4. Keep the principal informed of field trips and other changes in the regular schedule of your classes. Clearance in the principal's office is usually required for all field trips and other deviations from the regular class schedule (this will usually be done through your supervisor).

5. Avoid disturbing the classes of other teachers. Their work is just as important as yours. They have every right to be free from disturbances caused by the irresponsibility of neighboring classes. For instance, do not permit your students to be noisy or to roam the halls; you are responsible for their conduct during the entire class period.

6. Follow a strict code of professional ethics in all your relationships. Many of the problems of beginning teachers arise from the fact that the teacher has been unaware of the proper procedure to follow. Study the codes adopted by your school and the leading professional organizations in education. They will be helpful.

Know the Teaching Staff

The reception you will receive from the regular teaching staff will be governed by your own attitudes and actions. If you are courteous, professional, and not overly aggressive, you will soon earn acceptance as an important junior member of their society. Be sure, however, to remember continually that you are in their midst to receive advice, not to give it. You lack prestige on two counts: you are a learner and a newcomer. Keep in mind that, like the owl, you can gain a reputation for wisdom by being silent. You will be wise to remain comparatively silent when the occasional informal gatherings develop into gripe sessions or turn toward the discussion of personalities. You might temporarily gain satisfying attention and apparent status by freely volunteering your opinions concerning topics such as the comparative uselessness of college courses, the awesome gap between educational theory and practice, the relative demerits of campus leaders, the entertaining peculiarities of your associates, or the inadequacy of instruction received by your students from their former teachers. At best, the status gained by such idle talk would be a transitory illusion. If you should be tempted to seek such attention, remember that the successful student teacher follows a professional code of ethics. He works through his cooperating teacher in all relations with the school staff, says nothing in the absence of his supervisor that he could not say without embarrassment in his presence, and acknowledges the maxim that "he who would build himself up does not attempt to tear others down."

Your cooperating teacher has to cooperate with other teachers in many ways. As you assume increasing responsibility for the class assigned to you, you will need to work closely with other teachers. For instance, the type and quality of control you set up in your class will be influenced by the control other teachers exercise in their classes. The behavior of students in your class will, in turn, be reflected in other classes. Each teacher has to learn to work within the framework of patterns to which students have been accustomed. The noise in your classroom may disturb the class next door. When you assign homework, be sure that you do not make excessive demands which conflict with the assignments of other teachers. Whenever you take your class on field trips during the school day and those trips cut across other periods, you are interfering with some other teacher's work. If you rearrange the seats in your classroom and then leave them in disorder for the next class, you are not being thoughtful. Neither is it thoughtful to monopolize bulletin board space or to leave a room with chalkboards unerased. Untidy desks and paper-strewn floors also testify to a teacher's carelessness. Thoughtless actions lead to misunderstandings, and accumulated misunderstandings can easily destroy harmonious relationships among members of a teaching staff. No student teacher can afford to be careless. Thoughtfulness pays in terms of improved staff relationships.

Know the Nonteaching Staff

The school's specialized personnel includes the nurse, the librarian, the counselors, the cafeteria manager, the secretaries and clerks, and the custodians. All these people are able and willing to help you unless you ignore them. Never become deluded with the notion that you are better than some of the staff members because you have had greater educational advantages than they. They can teach you much if you are teachable. The principal's secretary knows the inner workings of the school much better than you do and can help you avoid mistakes. She can make school resources more accessible to you, pave the way to better relationships with other staff members for you, and speak a good word for you to the principal. The custodian is also a valuable person to know. Quite often he is a respected citizen in the school community and a friend of long standing to students as well as to faculty members. Be considerate of him in keeping your room neat and clean and by respecting his work schedule. He is a busy man, but he can always find time to give a bit of friendly advice to the beginner or to lend a helping hand when it is needed. Each of the other persons in specialized services also can contribute to your success. Confer with your cooperating teacher concerning how they might best be approached.

Know Yourself as a Teacher

Now that you are entering the most important phase of your professional preparation, you should take another inventory of your qualifications for teaching. Many factors are vital to success. Student teaching is intended to provide opportunity for improvement. No one is perfect. Have you identified the specifics in which your needs are greatest?

CHECK YOUR MASTERY OF BASIC SKILLS AND SUBJECT MATTER   Do you qualify as a teacher in the mastery of skills and subject matter? Your communications skill, study habits, and ability and willingness to plan and to organize your work—these are all important. Regardless of your teaching field, students and their parents expect you to know your subject and to speak, write, and spell with the skill of a teacher.

ASSESS YOUR ABILITY TO WORK WITH PEOPLE   "Unsatisfactory response to supervision" is a recurring comment of supervisors of student teachers. While no supervisor expects you to be a "yes" man without initiative or will, he does expect to see evidence of gracious and responsive acceptance of wise counsel. How do you react to constructive criticism? Supervisors sometimes state, "Any suggestion I make to John seems to bounce back in my face," or "When I try to help Helen, she immediately goes on the defensive and begins to rationalize," or "I might help Bill if he ever came to see me." Supervisors are your friends. It is not their purpose to destroy your self-esteem, but to help you become an effective teacher. Criticisms are given in a spirit of kindly helpfulness. When you master the art of working with others, most of your problems in teaching will vanish.

DEVOTE ADEQUATE TIME TO STUDENT TEACHING   How much time are you willing to give to your teaching? Some student teachers fail to do themselves justice by attempting to do too much besides their teaching. If you can take seventeen hours of college work, hold a job for forty hours a week, become a social lion on campus, and, at the same time, do a creditable job of student teaching, you are indeed a most unusual person. When you enter a profession, you dedicate yourself to the skillful performance of the services of that profession. Student teachers with "so little time" often say, "I must work," "I must finish in June," or "I must" do this and that. Most professions would not tolerate the halfhearted performance that a few student teachers exhibit during their internship. While you are not expected to be a social recluse, your professional activities must come first. Whenever you spend too much time on other things during student teaching, certain important functions suffer—adequate planning or preparation, keeping appointments with supervisors, making necessary reports on time, and maintaining vitality, enthusiasm, and even temper in the classroom. If you are too busy to do a satisfactory job of student teaching, you are too busy. Your alternatives are to reduce your load or drop your teaching.

RE-EXAMINE YOUR PERSONALITY   How would you assess your personality and its effect on others? Do you possess integrity, sincerity, a sense of responsibility, forcefulness and conviction, sympathy and understanding, and a keen sense of values? How do you rate on warmth, tact, voice, attractiveness, sense of humor, manners, neatness, and friendliness?

Perhaps through introspection, you should re-examine your personality for teaching. Beware of becoming one of the following:

1. The "sophisticated scholar." He is overly critical of all—except himself.
2. The "born teacher." His mind is closed to suggestion. He has known since birth exactly how best to teach.
3. The "reformer." He scoffs at the abilities of his teaching colleagues. He entered teaching only to save it as a profession.
4. The "pseudo educationist." He is so convinced of the importance of method that he neglects to learn all he can about the learner and the content.
5. The "pseudo psychologist." He is so convinced of the importance of the learner that he neglects to learn all he can about method and content.
6. The "pseudo academician." He is so convinced of the importance of content that he neglects to learn all he can about method and learner.

The personality pictures listed above are not as easy to improve as is knowledge of subject matter, but insofar as they are learned characteristics, they can be changed through effort and training. Many student teachers make that effort successfully.

DEVELOP THE HABITS YOU EXPECT TO POSSESS AS A REGULAR TEACHER
What habits are you developing? The habits you display as a student are likely to be the ones you exhibit as a full-time teacher on your first job. As a teacher, you are expected to encourage habits of promptness and regularity of attendance in your students. For example, have you checked your own college class attendance habits lately? This is but one illustration.

Occasionally, a supervisor finds it necessary to remind a student teacher that he is expected to dress in a manner more appropriate to teaching and to exhibit more exemplary habits of personal cleanliness. The woman who dresses in the style of evening wear, and the man who appears ready for a picnic are both out of place in the business office of education, the classroom. Laboratory jackets, gym clothing, and other uniforms as well as dress shirts should be laundered regularly. Cleanliness of hands and fingernails, frequent haircuts and shaves, or hairdos and facials are all details that should be taken care of automatically. It should never be necessary for a grown man or woman to suffer the embarrassment of being told that his mode of dress or degree of cleanliness fails to meet professional standards. However, approximately 10 percent of student teachers have failed in one or more of these particulars. You can avoid possible embarrassment for yourself and for your supervisors by giving daily attention to grooming.

All in all, you need to see yourself always as a teacher and a leader of young Americans. You share with home and church a large measure of responsibility for the learning, the attitudes, and the actions of tomorrow's adults. Recognize the importance of your job. Dress to look like a leader in this important profession. Abandon mannerisms peculiar to the college campus and be proud of your selection of teaching as an occupation. Then you will have made a long stride toward success in the eyes of your students and those of your future professional colleagues.

Know What Teachers Do

"I thought I was hired to teach school" is sometimes the plaint of the first-year teacher. In looking ahead to the time not far away when you will be a regular, full-time teacher, you need to realize that you will be expected to do more than teach your classes. There will be supervisory duties (on the playground, in the lunchroom and the halls, at assemblies and athletic events); cocurricular activities to sponsor; parent-teacher and staff meetings to attend; and community campaigns to sponsor. The inefficient teacher who can never get his classwork done or the isolationist who frets about the extra things to do is likely to be an unhappy person. But the person who enjoys working with parents, students, and fellow teachers in various cooperative endeavors will find these experiences outside of class valuable roads to professional growth. Whether or not you derive much benefit from these activities will depend to a great degree upon your mental acceptance or rejection of them.

Know School Resources and Regulations

Learn all you can about school policies and regulations governing such items as the following: health and safety (what to do in case of a fire drill or a student injury); care of the building and other school property; conduct of students and faculty on the school premises (for example, smoking); use and conservation of supplies; attendance of students and staff members; faculty committees; school activities and organizations; school calendar; daily and assembly schedules; use of library and textbooks; detention and referral discipline; homework; marking and reporting student progress; and changing location of classes or transporting students from the school grounds. A faculty handbook is often used to supply much information concerning policies and regulations dealing with the above items. However, your cooperating teacher is always your primary source of information in clarification of school policy.

While you are learning the school's regulations, get acquainted with the school plant. Visit administrative offices, the cafeteria, shops, laboratories, gymnasium, nurse's office, library, attendance office, and guidance or counselor's office for your particular grade level. Learn what functions these centers perform or what services they render.

Find out what audio-visual equipment and materials are available, how they are procured, and what regulations govern their use. Obtain the same type of information about the library, science laboratories, or shops if they are facilities to be used by your class.

Learn to accept any physical limitations graciously. In many communities the school population has outstripped school buildings and equipment. If there are policies or regulations with which you do not agree, remember that you are professionally obligated to support them until they are changed by democratic means.

In getting to know your school, you have been urged to learn to know your co-workers, your own assets in relation to the teaching situation, and the policies and regulations of the school, as well as its resources. You will probably not learn everything suggested in the preceding paragraphs during the short time you serve as a student teacher. Yet the better informed you are, the more likely you are to succeed. It should be obvious by now that teaching involves much more than a mastery of one or two subject matter areas in college classes. A great body of knowledge is to be learned and many competencies are to be gained by direct apprenticeship on the job.

If you are not thoroughly acquainted with the community in which you are doing student teaching, you should make a community study as described earlier in this chapter. You are then ready to study your students.

Know Your Students: A Sample Class Description

The following section of this chapter contains a sample class description and analysis representative of those regularly completed by student teachers under the supervision of the authors of this text. The expression and the factual content are largely those of the reports from which the study was abstracted. The students described may seem unique, but almost all are characteristic of students regularly appearing in the classes of all teachers. It would benefit the instruction of every student teacher and most regular teachers to do similar studies.

My third-period class in ninth grade science at Central High School enrolls nineteen boys and sixteen girls. Each is identified only by number in this report. Their ages range from 13 to 16 years. From observation it appears that all are well adjusted to school and to their classmates, although school records reveal four received unsatisfactory citizenship ratings last semester, one for unexcused absences, two for repeated chatter and nonattention, and one for fighting on the school grounds and for general insubordination. One additional student is under direction of the county youth authority and has a history of law violation. On the other hand, seven students, five girls and two boys, received "outstanding" as a rating in citizenship last semester. One of this group is ninth-grade president. Several other students in this class also are active in the cocurricular program of the school. Evidently this class is quite typical in its attitude toward school and study. It contains both positive and negative leadership potential, but most members of the class are solid "satisfactory" citizens. I have conferred

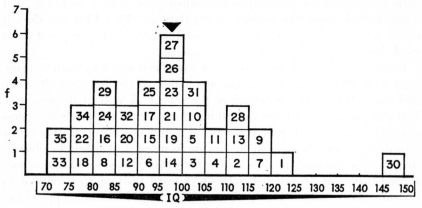

H-N test form "A" administered in ninth grade
H-N test standard deviation: 15
H-N test standard error: 5
▼ class median: 96

Fig. 2-1   *Mental ability of thirty-five students*

with my cooperating teacher on how best to work with students having problems. He has suggested a follow-up conference regarding student #30.

From observation, study of health records, and examination of the student-questionnaire results it appears that the health of this group is generally good with the exception that one girl regularly complains of headaches and one boy is subject to epileptic seizures. In addition, seven students wear glasses regularly and two others (girls) should be wearing theirs but keep them in their purses. One student has a 30 percent hearing loss and also has an apparent speech defect. Six students are concerned about acne and skin blemishes; two students are at least 20 pounds overweight; one is 6 feet 2 inches tall and concerned about it; and three others are obviously slow in their physical development.

A slow drive through the school neighborhood during which I noted the size and condition of homes and the general development of the community was very revealing. One section of homes a few blocks in length borders a park and retains a considerable portion of its earlier elegance; otherwise most of my students live in a rather old and run-down residential area which is losing its battle with the encroachment of multiple dwellings and minor business establishments. Study of parent occupations—many mothers are working at production-line tasks, and most fathers are in "blue-collar" jobs—confirms the observation that most of the students in this class are of lower to lower-middle socioeconomic background. These factors must be given careful consideration as I try to understand the motivations of each student.

Fig. 2-2   Semester grades in science of thirty-five students

Analysis of test scores in the cumulative files indicates that IQ's of this class range from 72 to 145, with the class median between 95 and 100 (see Figure 2-1). The class does not appear to be well motivated toward science study since only 20 percent earned A or B grades in the subject last semester (see Figure 2-2). Their standardized achievement scores also indicate generally low achievement. Seventy percent scored below grade level in science background last year. In a reading test also administered last year, they ranged from 4.4 to 11.8 in grade level. The class median at 7.3 was approximately one grade below average (Figure 2-3). I will have to keep these facts in mind as I prepare and select their reading materials in science.

Twelve students say they plan to go to college but most are somewhat indefinite in their choice of education and vocational goals. Eight feel that they might attend trade or business schools; five say they intend to quit school as soon as the law allows; while the remainder indicate a tentative preference for blue-collar jobs and the military.

From this survey, it appears that my third-period class is a fairly typical

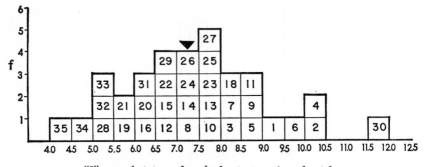

"I" test administered at the beginning of grade eight
Standard error of measurement .6 of a grade
▼ *class median: 7.3*   *No data for student #17*

Fig. 2-3   *Reading grade level of thirty-five students*

heterogeneous group; however, it is a little below average in academic interest and ability. To get them all interested in science will be a real challenge.

Analysis to facilitate better instruction of individuals

The remainder of this class analysis will be devoted to study of individuals, including those who need special attention as well as those who might make special contributions to the class.

Students who need enrichment materials and activities: Students #1 through #7 all earned A's or B's in science last semester. I plan to get them interested in special projects, including reading, term papers, special reports related to their interests, and to the best of my ability I will encourage them to keep up their good work. A few may become interested in careers in science.

Students #9, #11, and #13 seem to have potential for better work than they have been producing. Perhaps conferences with them could get them to study better. Student #30 might eventually qualify for top level assignments, but at present he is involved with problems of adjustment.

Students who need remedial materials and activities: Failing students #32 through #35 and D students #22 through #31 all can benefit from planned review, special drill based upon diagnostic tests, and use of interesting applications. They appear to need specific directions in how to study the subject of science. I am preparing a hand out of study suggestions and will guide them through the appropriate steps in supervised study at the first opportunity. Student #28 may need special remedial help in reading. In fact, as so many of this class read at an inferior level, I plan to give group instruction to them in science vocabulary and reading skills. From the mass of supplementary reading materials available, I will select those which are easiest to read and assign them specifically to this group. I also will take particular care to see that these students know (and record) exactly what is expected of them in each assignment. They will be tested frequently and given daily drill in selected areas of weakness.

Students who have interests or hobbies that could be used: Students #8 and #29 have interests in camping which I will use during the conservation unit. Student #5 has interest and some talent in art which I plan to encourage by asking her to develop bulletin boards and displays for the class. Student #4 has a hobby of raising tropical fish, student #27 collects rocks, and student #30 is a "bug" on electronics. These students will be asked to report orally to the class and perhaps exhibit their work when the class reaches the related scientific study. Students #33, #22, and #15 have relatives who work in science-related jobs. The students will be asked to inform the class about the requirements and opportunities in work of this type. The uncle of student #19 is an officer in the narcotics detail of the sheriff's department. He sometimes speaks to community groups about his work. Student #19 will be asked to invite him to speak to our class when we study the unit on alcohol and narcotics. Several other students have hobbies which I may be able to use to stimulate interest in science and which I might use as a key to discussion with them.

Students who need special consideration because of physical limitations: Students #17 and #25 seldom wear their glasses although they need them. I will assign these students to seats near the front of the room so that they can see the chalkboard. Number 26, who has a hearing difficulty, will also be given a seat near the front of the room. I must remember to look in his direction more when I speak to the class so that he can use his developing skill of lip reading. In our unit on health, I will ask a dermatologist or the school nurse to speak to our class on the health concerns of adolescents. With their assistance I also expect to develop a list of readings to help students understand these problems.

My greatest concern with the health problems of this class is to be able to do exactly the right thing should #12 have an epileptic seizure. I have conferred with the nurse and she has given me explicit instructions for this case. She also has assured me that if #12 takes his medication regularly a seizure is unlikely. The nurse will be immediately available should the unusual occur.

Students who need special consideration because of adjustment problems: Student #30 is under direction of the youth authority of this county. The caseworker in charge will confer regularly with me and with his other teachers. I will follow the caseworker's suggestions. So far #30 seems to be getting along well in this class.

Number 35 failed this course last year. He is lowest in reading ability, lowest in intelligence score, and lowest in achievement in this class. He is in a state of rebellion against all teachers and other symbols of authority. His father is unemployed and his mother has a police record as an alcoholic. A social worker is expected to be assigned to this case. Perhaps he can salvage the boy. I will cooperate but I don't feel adequately prepared to do much alone. In the meantime I will be friendly but particularly careful to keep a close check on him since I have been warned that to give him a free hand for even a few minutes may lead to classroom disaster.

Number 28 is an enigma. She is a problem not because she is poorly adjusted, but because she is too well adjusted to academic achievement below her apparent ability. She is extremely well developed and attractive for a girl of her age (and aware of it). She seems to be in a constant whirl of cocurricular and social activities. The upper-class boys as well as the more mature males in her own class all seem much more important to her—and she to them—than the "bugs and mice" of science. She can describe every detail of last night's TV spectacular but can't seem to remember a single fact of science from one moment to the next.

When I took over the class she seemed to get more interested in studying. She even volunteered to do a special report on William Harvey's description of blood flow. To this end I signed three library passes on successive days so she could research the subject. That was two weeks ago, and I am now afraid that William Harvey has lost this race to "Gunsmoke" and "Yogi Bear." In class she gives no attention to subject matter but loses no opportunity to attract the attention of her admirers. (And I'm afraid she has some designs on me!) The fact that her scholastic rating in all her classes is a straight D doesn't seem to bother her in the least. She meets all suggestions concerning study with a sweet smile, but does the absolute minimum to get by.

Mr. Jones, my cooperating teacher, remarked that last semester he too tried to direct her attention to science study, but to no avail. He added, perhaps in jest, that he no longer looked upon her with dismay, but rather with a degree of envy, since she is obviously so delightfully happy in her own little world. He concluded that it might not be psychologically defensible to upset her dreams with the disturbing facts of science, and after all she and others like her undoubtedly will create lovely, peaceful havens for their hard-driving ulcer-prone science-wise husbands a few years hence. Mr. Jones has a point there, but I'm certain he wasn't serious because we both agree that knowledge of science is important for everybody.

Students who can be depended upon to be positive leaders: Student #2 is president of the ninth grade and very popular. He is the center of a strong group which has a positive influence on this class. When the room gets noisy and I don't notice it—one of my weaknesses that must be remedied—he shushes them successfully.

Student #16 is of below-average ability according to test scores, but she works hard and sets a good example for those around her. In committee work she easily takes the leadership role and elicits productive cooperation from her group. If there were a #16 in all groups my problems in group work would be effectively reduced, if not eliminated.

Student #7 is an all-around athlete. He is active in all major sports and was a regular on the school's championship basketball team this year. He hopes to go to college and become a coach some day. He is respected by all students but is particularly effective in setting an example which helps to keep the rougher boys in line. His willing cooperation makes this an easier class to teach.

Students who need help to become effective members of the group: Observation of the class and the class sociogram both indicate that students #30, #35, and #17 are isolates in this class. I will take no action in the cases of #30 and #35 until I get the advice of experts, but student #17 appears to be a less complicated case. She transferred into this school two weeks ago from a small town in an adjoining state. She told me that she didn't like Central High because it was too big and the students were all "snooty." She customarily sits in the back of the room and talks to no one the entire period. I plan to move her seat next to #16 and ask #16 to be her sponsor. Working with #16's friendly cooperative group should soon convince her that getting acquainted requires little more than friendly reaction and acceptance by both the old and the new. I will soon give her opportunity to tell the class something about her former school and what she likes about Central High.

Refresh Your Knowledge of How Students Learn

If student teachers are to guide the learning of students most effectively, they will not only know their subject and their students, but they will keep clearly in mind the guidelines to efficient learning offered by educational psychology. A brief selected overview follows; however, serious students will recognize the need for a more complete refresher which can be provided better by restudy of a textbook in educational psychology.

LEARNING REQUIRES EFFORT Psychologists recognize learning as an active process involving attention and effort on the part of the learner. Teachers may work themselves to near exhaustion in an effort to deliver learning to students like merchants deliver products to customers, yet teachers will fail unless students themselves put forth effort. In fact, research has verified that too much teacher guidance can impede the learner.[10] Learning, therefore, is not a package that can be wrapped up and delivered. It is more like a do-it-yourself project which can benefit

[10] Howard L. Kingsley and Ralph Garry, *The Nature and Conditions of Learning.* Englewood Cliffs, N.J.: Prentice-Hall, Inc., 1957, p. 265.

from expert guidance, when needed, but which can reach completion only through the continued intent and effort of the worker. Consequently, one of the greatest concerns of teachers is the problem of developing and maintaining interest and effort on the part of their students.

SUCCESS SUSTAINS EFFORT   Research demonstrates that students will work harder, longer, and more successfully when they know the goal of their efforts, when they understand the reasons for seeking the goal, when they believe that the goal can be reached, when they want to reach the goal, and when they are promptly informed of the degree of success resulting from their efforts. Of great importance in teaching is "the desirability of insuring frequent and regular experiences of success—or reinforcement—throughout all phases of learning, but particularly in the earlier, and generally more difficult phases."[11]

Furthermore, if interest and effort are to be maintained, teachers need to organize learning into realistic tasks which can be achieved successfully by each learner.

Just as a child can sometimes be induced to eat when presented with a small portion of food, after refusing to start on a larger portion, so a student can more often be stimulated to work on a reasonable partial assignment than by assignment of the whole task all at once.[12]

On the other hand, learning experiences should not be so cut and dried as to stifle initiative and curiosity. Research in the United States and in Russia indicates that "an effective teacher . . . will be able to hold student interest by maintaining some degree of suspense as to outcomes of problems and by allowing the student to work through to discoveries for himself."[13]

EXTRINSIC INCENTIVES SHOULD BE USED WITH CAUTION   The entire problem of pupil motivation is taken up in a later chapter of this text. Only a few highlights will be pointed out for review here. It is important to note that according to the research-supported opinion of experts, "progressive loss of interest in academic learning activities . . . may be inhibited by carefully planned . . . (use) of a variety of incentives and rewards."[14] Researchers seem to agree that extrinsic incentives, such as competition, rewards, praise, and reproof can be effective supplementary instructional tools when used selectively by an expert teacher.

---

[11] Melvin H. Marx, "Motivation," *Encyclopedia of Educational Research*, 3d ed., Chester W. Harris, ed. New York: The Macmillan Company, 1960, p. 896. Used by permission of Macmillan.

[12] *Ibid.*, p. 898.

[13] *Loc. cit.*

[14] *Loc. cit.*

However, dependence upon their use must be limited.[15] At least one authority adds the specific precaution that even though organized competition and rivalry in the classroom can serve as strong incentives, they are not generally regarded as first-rate teaching procedures. Such incentives sometimes lead to undesirable social attitudes, and frequently fail to develop interest in learning which persists after removal of the incentives.[16] Specifically, it has been found that:

1. Extrinsic incentives are most useful in the earliest stages of learning when the learning itself has not yet developed to the stage of providing its own satisfaction.

2. Extrinsic incentives to be most effective should be attainable by a large proportion, if not by all, of the class. Goals which are out of reach fail to motivate.

3. Extrinsic incentives should be used cautiously and with the understanding that they are temporary substitutes for the real thing: recognition of value in the learning itself.[17]

EARLY STAGES OF LEARNING ARE CRITICAL   Psychological research has identified a number of principles associated with the acquisition of knowledge and skills.

1. Learning tasks are accomplished more effectively when drill and practice periods are spaced rather than massed. Short sessions spread over several days are to be preferred to a single long session. Longer practice and drill lessons should be interspersed with rest periods or change of pace activities to avoid the deleterious effects of fatigue and boredom.

2. Instructional emphasis should be on the correct performance, not upon the incorrect. Teacher demonstration of error may introduce desirable humor into a lesson, but as a teaching technique it rates low. A corollary of this principle is that the crucial elements of a performance should receive attention, not the noncrucial. For instance, when speed is the predominant factor of successful performance, speed should be emphasized even in the initial learning. When speed and accuracy are both important, emphasis should be on both.

3. Students should not be expected to work on several similar new learnings simultaneously. Similar but nonidentical tasks interfere one with the other in the early stages of learning.

4. Research strongly indicates that when a student has not yet identified the correct response in a learning situation, it is of paramount im-

---

[15] *Loc. cit.*
[16] Kingsley and Garry, *op. cit.*, p. 273.
[17] Marx, *op. cit.*, p. 898.

portance to reinforce that response as soon as it occurs as "even a few seconds delay . . . may mean the difference between maximal learning and no learning whatever."[18] The teaching machine industry is based upon this principle. However, in the absence of machine assistance, teachers can at least partially satisfy the learning principle by giving close supervision to practice periods, by supplying answers for out-of-class problems and encouraging immediate scoring and correction by students, and by returning all teacher-scored papers promptly. Estes summarizes this point succinctly:

In any educational context, it is important to emphasize that what becomes strengthened during practice is the behavior that actually occurs, not necessarily the behavior that is the goal of the educator. If the learner has hit upon an inferior mode of response, continued practice (without correction) will simply strengthen it. . . .[19]

RETENTION OF LEARNING CAN BE STRENGTHENED   The teacher's responsibility does not end when student learning has once reached a satisfactory level. The fact is that both older and newer learning interfere with the retention of unreinforced learning. Loss is greatest in the first few days, while over a period of a few months more than 50 percent frequently is forgotten. One researcher found that when two reinforcement periods were employed, learning loss in sixty days was less than that which occurred in one day when no reinforcement was used (10:302). Thus it is clearly the teacher's responsibility to provide a program of reinforcement. To that end research has shown that teachers should:

1. *Provide review spaced at increasing intervals.* The first review might best be placed the day following the learning, the second review, a week later, and the third, several weeks later. As a review technique, rereading is seldom as beneficial as "skimming a related source for new ideas, working through a quiz, thinking through the implications of the material, or using the knowledge as a stepping stone to more advanced learning in the field."[20] Mouly also points out that "effective review is more than just bringing the material back to the original level: it involves reorganization . . . to bring about new understandings, new insights, and new relationships that are more functional as well as more permanent than the original learning."[21]

[18] William K. Estes, "Learning," *Encyclopedia of Educational Research*, 3d ed., Chester W. Harris, ed. New York: The Macmillan Company, 1960, p. 758. Used by permission of Macmillan.

[19] *Ibid.*, p. 762.

[20] George J. Mouly, *Psychology for Effective Teaching*. New York: Holt, Rinehart and Winston, Inc., 1960, p. 303.

[21] *Ibid.*, p. 302.

2. *Encourage overlearning up to about 50 percent.* Overlearning is not a substitute for review, but serves to reduce the likelihood that learning will drop below the threshold of recall before the first review takes place. Overlearning is important, but not as important as review.

3. *Make the learning meaningful to the student.* Understanding is basic to learning and to retention. Students understand best that which is related to their own experience—past, present, and future. Experienced teachers follow this principle regularly.

4. *Encourage students to accept retention as one goal of learning.* It has been shown that goals which are clearly identified are more likely to be attained. Consciousness of the importance of remembering will improve performance in remembering. One successful technique is to point out at the time of learning the specific instances in the future when the student will be called upon to put the learning to use. Frequent tests can partially serve this purpose.

TRANSFER OF LEARNING CAN BE INCREASED   The teacher's task is only partially completed when he has facilitated the acquisition and retention of learning. He must also give consideration to maximizing the likelihood that his students will be able to use their learning wherever and whenever it might be applied. This third aspect of learning is termed *transfer*. Like the acquisition and retention of learning, transfer depends not only upon the quality of the learner, but also upon the quality of the instruction. Research amply demonstrates that "the amount of transfer induced can be increased by the method of teaching used.[22] Placing instructional emphasis upon the aspects of the subject which are expected to be transferred; encouraging generalization on the part of students; providing extensive practice in applications—all are procedures that have been found to increase the transfer of learning. It also has been shown that no particular school subject or group of subjects is outstandingly superior to any other subject or group of subjects in its contribution to a student's intellectual performance, although each subject can make contributions to improved performance in specific tasks when taught with that purpose clearly emphasized. Thus a teacher of foreign language who wishes to encourage increased understanding of English will place special emphasis upon generalization and practice in that aspect of his course. The teacher of junior high school mathematics who wishes to increase his students' future use of ratio and proportion will emphasize generalization and practice in the application of that subject to appropriate problems in

[22] J. M. Stephens, "Transfer of Learning," *Encyclopedia of Educational Research*, 3d ed., Chester W. Harris, ed. New York: The Macmillan Company, 1960, p. 1542. Used by permission of Macmillan.

geometry, physics, chemistry, art, music, homemaking, personal purchasing, and the like. In the same manner, the teacher of physical education who wishes to increase his students' application of sportsmanlike conduct and sense of fair play will place instructional emphasis upon generalization and application of those qualities not only to participation in and observation of athletic contests, but also to daily living in the school and in the community.

Teachers of all subjects should realize that the transfer of learning is a major goal of instruction, not a concomitant outcome that develops automatically. The extent to which students succeed in transfer is dependent to a large degree upon the character of the learning experiences provided. Successful teachers plan their lessons carefully to facilitate efficiency in acquisition of learning, promote greater retention of learning, and encourage wide transfer of learning.

Selected Readings

1. American Educational Research Association, *Encyclopedia of Educational Research*, 3d ed., Chester W. Harris, ed. New York: The Macmillan Company, 1960. Pages 752–767, 895–898, 1535–1542.
2. Brown, Thomas J., *Student Teaching in a Secondary School*. New York: Harper & Row, Publishers, 1960. Chapters 1, 2.
3. Carter, William L., Carl W. Hansen, and Margaret G. McKim, *Learning to Teach in the Secondary School*. New York: The Macmillan Company, 1962. Chapters 1, 3, 4.
4. Chandler, B. J., *Education and the Teacher*. New York: Dodd, Mead & Company, Inc., 1961. Chapter 8.
5. Clark, Leonard H., and Irving S. Starr, *Secondary School Teaching Methods*. New York: The Macmillan Company, 1959. Chapters 1, 2, 16.
6. Crow, Lester D., Harry E. Ritchie, and Alice Crow, *Education in the Secondary School*. New York: American Book Company, 1961. Chapters 12–14.
7. Grambs, Jean D., William J. Iverson, and Franklin K. Patterson, *Modern Methods in Secondary Education*, revised ed. New York: Holt, Rinehart and Winston, Inc., 1958. Chapter 2.
8. Klausmeier, Herbert J., *Teaching in the Secondary School*. New York: Harper & Row, Publishers, 1958. Chapter 3.
9. Massey, Harold W., and Edwin E. Vineyard, *The Profession of Teaching*. New York: The Odyssey Press, Inc., 1961. Chapters 1, 6, 10.
10. Mouly, George J., *Psychology for Effective Teaching*. New York: Holt, Rinehart and Winston, Inc., 1960. Chapters 8–11.
11. Nordberg, H. Orville, James M. Bradfield, and William C. Odell, *Secondary School Teaching*. New York: The Macmillan Company, 1962, Chapters 2, 4, 9.
12. Rivlin, Harry N., *Teaching Adolescents in Secondary Schools*, 2d ed. New York: Appleton-Century-Crofts, 1961. Chapters 3, 10, 15.

13. Schorling, Raleigh, and Howard T. Batchelder, *Student Teaching in Secondary Schools*, 3d ed. New York: McGraw-Hill Book Company, Inc., 1956. Chapter 1.

14. Schultz, Raymond E., *Student Teaching in the Secondary Schools*. New York: Harcourt, Brace & World, Inc., 1959. Chapters 1, 8.

15. Steeves, Frank L., *Fundamentals of Teaching in Secondary Schools*. New York: The Odyssey Press, Inc., 1962. Chapters 1, 2.

16. Wiggins, Sam P., *Successful High School Teaching*. Boston: Houghton Mifflin Company, 1958.

PART TWO

Planning

CHAPTER 3

Planning for instruction

Planning is a necessity in everyday life. The busy housewife sets up a schedule for the week; the businessman organizes his day at the office; parents plan ahead for the education of their children; the contractor follows a detailed blueprint in building a house; the farmer diversifies and rotates his crops. Thus planning goes on. Success or failure of each enterprise depends upon the adequacy of the planning. Some plans are for a day; others are for weeks, months, or years. Some plans are simple; others are complex. Some plans depend solely upon personal judgment; others require expert advice. Although human endeavors have always required planning, the increasing complexity of modern living demands even more preparation for effective action.

IMPORTANCE OF PLANNING FOR INSTRUCTION

Planning is as much a necessity for the teacher as for the housewife, the contractor, or the farmer. Neither ingenuity nor experience can serve as a substitute for thorough planning. Schools were created by society to provide an environment where learning can be organized effectively and economically. To discharge his responsibility well, the teacher in today's school must be better prepared and must plan more effectively than ever before. An increase in numbers and heterogeneity of the school population, rapid expansion of all fields of knowledge, newer developments in teaching methods, and an increasing volume of instructional materials of all types have compounded the complexity of instructional planning. The teacher of today must plan or perish professionally.

Before plunging blindly into the business of planning for instruction, the teacher needs to pause for reflection on changes which have occurred in educational theory and practice during the past fifty years. Tyler has concisely summarized these evolutionary trends quite well; he indicates three aspects of the curriculum which have been affected: the formulation of objectives, the selection of learning experiences, and the organization of learning experiences. First, the *nature* of objectives has changed from formal discipline to behavioral objectives. Second, the *sources* of objectives have changed from determination by subject matter specialists alone to the inclusion of four other forces: the psychology of learning, the demands of society, social and educational philosophy, and studies of the learner. And, third, the *range* of objectives has changed with the current problem of establishing priorities among a great diversity of goals becoming acute. Significant changes have also occurred in the selection of learning experiences. Notions about the *nature* of learning experiences have changed from a focus on recitation and the teacher to learning experiences of students; the *range* of learning experiences has expanded from verbal exercises to varied learning activities; and the *selection* of learning experiences has been designed to provide for individual differences or diversity in a system of mass education. Least attention has been given to the organization of learning experiences. More consideration has been given to the "ordering of content" than to changes in student behavior. Consequently, the integration of student experiences within the framework of separate subjects continues to be a persistent problem.[1]

Bearing in mind these significant changes in the teaching-learning process which have occurred during the first half of this century, the school population explosion (approximately 90 percent of the boys and girls of secondary school age are now in school as contrasted with about 10 percent in 1900), and the tremendous expansion of our cultural heritage, a teacher soon discovers that his teaching begins before he enters the classroom.

The Rewards of Planning

Specifically, what are some of the tangible rewards that the teacher may expect from carefully planning his instruction? First of all, continuous and thoughtful teacher planning gives purpose and direction to everything that takes place in the classroom. Aimless rambling, fruitless activity, and disciplinary incidents are reduced to a minimum. Wise selection and organization of varied and appropriate learning materials and activities are most likely to insure the achievement of worthwhile objectives.

Another outcome of thorough planning by the teacher is the development of an atmosphere of confidence and security in the classroom. Students gain confidence in the leadership of the teacher. The teacher, in

---

[1] Ralph W. Tyler, "The Curriculum—Then and Now," *Proceedings, 1956 Invitational Conference on Testing Problems.* Princeton, N.J.: Educational Testing Service, 1956, pp. 79–94.

turn, is freed of subject matter anxieties and nagging details of classroom management and control which stem from poor organization. Good organization is virtually synonymous with good teaching.

Still another advantage of careful planning of instruction is that it eventually becomes a timesaver. The teacher who systematically accumulates and organizes a file of supplementary references, curriculum guides, resource units, and audio-visual materials is able to enrich future learning experiences with a minimum of time and effort. Furthermore, while it is imperative for the beginning teacher to learn to build and to use complete written plans, he may well develop a pattern or habit of thinking which will later enable him to substitute mental plans for written ones. A first-year teacher summarized this last point in these words:

Even though I do not write all my plans, as I did in student teaching, I mentally go through all the steps of planning. What are my specific objectives? What materials and resources do I need? What learning activities are likely to be best in achieving my objectives? How much time should be devoted to each? And (after the lesson has been taught) how successful was the class period today? How can I determine how well my students have achieved today's goals?

At this point, the author must add that no teacher can ever completely abandon use of written plans.

From an administrative standpoint, written plans are important for two reasons: to make supervision more effective and to facilitate the work of substitute teachers. Because supervisory visits can be made only at irregular intervals, written plans provide a record of the continuity of classroom learning experience which would not otherwise be evident. This assumes, of course, that the plans are adequate and that the teacher makes incisive postanalyses of each day's work. Some principals consider written plans so important that they require new teachers to prepare both unit and daily plans as evidence of adequate preparation. Another value of written plans is to facilitate the work of substitute teachers. When the regular teacher is forced to be absent on short notice, his plans should enable a substitute teacher to carry on the work of the class as usual. As supervisory aids in student teaching, written plans are indispensable.

PRINCIPLES OF EFFECTIVE PLANNING

The right decision at the right moment is the essence of good teaching—*Goodlad*[2]

[2] John I. Goodlad, "The Teacher Selects, Plans, Organizes," *Learning and the Teacher*, 1959 Yearbook. Washington, D.C.: The Association for Supervision and Curriculum Development, 1959, p. 39.

Planning is an individual matter. The composition of a class, the nature of the subject, the goals to be achieved, and the personality and background of the teacher account for inevitable variations in planning. Yet, there are certain basic principles which are applicable to every classroom situation.

Proper planning facilitates learning. To be sure, people learn from experience, both organized and unorganized. It is, of course, also true that education takes place both inside and outside the school. However, the increasing complexity of the world, the expansion of culture, and the forces of miseducation bidding for the attention of everyone constitute a real challenge to the modern school. Never before has the school been required to teach so much to so many. There is no time for unplanned, aimless teaching. The teacher must know where he is going, how to get there, and when he has arrived. Superior planning is required to facilitate the quality of learning needed in our day.

Effective instructional planning provides opportunities for students to practice desired behavior. The statement "Learning is an active process" has been parroted so often as to become almost devoid of meaning, yet no one learns except through his own activity. But just any kind of activity is not sufficient. For example, it is not enough for the student to talk, to read, and to write about good citizenship. Learning activities must go beyond those of a purely verbal nature. The student must apply his knowledge to real life situations in order to think, to feel, and to act as a good citizen should, both in school and in later adult life.

Effective instructional planning provides for continuity in learning. This principle may be difficult to apply for the beginning teacher whose major concern is often, "What am I going to do today?" He may be justified in making short-range assignments based on a well-organized textbook as he faces for the first time five or six classes a day with two or three different preparations. Nevertheless, as he gains experience, the new teacher will need to develop plans of a higher order. As a first step toward continuity, he will relate today's lesson to those of yesterday and tomorrow. A second step, if the nature of the subject and the situation warrant it, is the development of long-range or unit plans. As the new teacher becomes more aware of the total school program and the educational problems of his students, his plans should attain a higher level of development. Helping students to bridge the gap between the logical organization of subject matter and the way they learn, to maintain continuity in their educational experiences as they go from one school level to the next, and to make a smooth transition from school to life on the outside will be reflected in the plans of the teacher who gains insight through experience. Although some of the problems related to continuity involve the school as a whole, or even more than one school level, the individual classroom teacher still has an important role to play. The teacher can help the transfer student, from the elementary or another school, feel more at home in a strange environment. He can help the student who leaves school to work or who goes to college to be more adequately prepared. The classroom teacher can help the student bridge the gap between school and life by showing the relevance of history to current affairs, by relating scientific laws to problems of everyday living, or by cultivating a taste for better art, literature, and music that will enrich the student's leisure hours forever after.

Effective instructional planning provides for correlation of knowledge and skills derived from the various subjects offered in school. Like continuity, this is another principle of good planning which the beginning teacher may not be ready to put into effect. Again expediency comes before desirability. However, as the teacher becomes more sure of himself, his subject, and his students, he can lift his eyes above his immediate concerns and catch a vision of a higher level of planning. The secondary school curriculum, traditionally organized on the basis of discrete subject matter lines, has made it difficult for the student to integrate his knowledge. Anecdotes from the classroom are replete with accounts of students who consider a teacher unfair if he requires good written compositions except in an English class or if he insists on effective speaking except in a speech class. Upon the classroom teacher, who is himself a specialist in one or two subjects, falls the task of helping each student put together the jigsaw puzzle of his fragmented school experiences. Present reactionary forces would not only perpetuate fragmentation of subject matter, extending it downward into the elementary school, but would also divorce development of the student's intellectual life from all other aspects of his personality development.

Effective instructional planning takes into consideration the readiness of the student to learn. Readiness is dependent upon such factors as maturity, previous experiences, and motivation. To function with maximum efficiency as an individual, the student must mature or develop all aspects of his personality—emotional, intellectual, moral, social, and physiological—on a unified front. In providing incentives to stimulate students to pursue school work with vigor and enthusiasm, the teacher is primarily concerned with strengthening drives which lead to sustained activity toward worthy goals (7:320). That is motivation at its best.

Effective instructional planning recognizes individual differences in student interests, needs, and abilities. Since our nation is committed to the ideal of equal educational opportunity for all youth of secondary school age, a heavy responsibility falls upon the shoulders of the classroom teacher. The public school has a twofold task: to provide mass or quantity education and, at the same time, to educate for quality. The schools also have the dual responsibility of educating for uniformity (providing students with a common heritage) and educating for diversity (capitalizing upon the unique contribution of each individual). Despite present efforts to solve the problem of diversity by grouping students subject by subject on the bases of aptitude, intelligence, and achievement, other variables which determine a student's success or failure in school are often disregarded. Just to mention a few of these significant differences, students obviously differ with respect to sex; personality (interests, emotional adjustments, relations with others); past experience; family backgrounds (socioeconomic status, national or ethnic origin, parental values and expectations for their children); and the neighborhoods from which they come. Providing for individual differences is discussed at length in Chapter 7.

Effective instructional planning enables the student to participate as much as possible in planning his own educational experiences. As already suggested, the key to learning is involvement by the student. If all he learns to do in school is to follow instructions of the teacher, then he is ill equipped to assume responsibility as a citizen in a self-governing society. However, despite the advantages often claimed for more cooperative planning in the classroom, the activities of the typical secondary school class are still largely planned and directed by the teacher alone. There will be further discussion of cooperative planning in this chapter.

PROBLEMS IN INSTRUCTIONAL PLANNING

Never before have we had so little time in which to do so much—*Franklin D. Roosevelt*

The problem of the selection and organization of instructional activities and materials has become more difficult with the expansion of available materials and teaching aids; the broadening of educational objectives, to meet the needs of all students, not just the college bound; and the increasing heterogeneity of the school population.[3]

"Educational shortages" is a common topic in educational circles. Probably the greatest shortage of the average classroom teacher is *time*. With more students of greater diversity to teach, with more to be taught, and with more duties outside the classroom and in the community, when

[3] William G. Brink, "Secondary Education—Programs," *Encyclopedia of Educational Research*, 3d ed., Chester W. Harris, ed. New York: The Macmillan Company, 1960, p. 1265.

does the teacher find time to plan his work adequately? The following verse, no doubt, expresses the feelings of many teachers in today's crowded schools:

Sounds Like Friday

By Ann Coyle

Some people say a teacher is made out of steel,
Their mind can think, but their body can't feel.
Iron and steel and hickory tea,
Frowns and gripes from nine to three.
You teach six full hours, and what do you get?
Another day older and deeper in debt.
You pay your dues in this and that,
Then for 29 more days your billfold's flat.
I was born one morning, when it was cloudy and cool,
I picked up my register and headed for school.
I wrote 84 names on the homeroom roll
And the principal said, "Well, bless my soul!
You teach six hours and what'd you get?
Cuts and bruises and dirt and sweat."
I got 84 kids and 42 seats,
Sixty-one talking while 23 sleep.
I can hardly get 'em all through the door,
And if I don't watch out they'll be sending me more.
I taught six full hours, my day is made,
But I still have 300 papers to grade.
You teach six full hours and what do you get?
Another day older and deeper in debt.
I'll go to St. Peter but I can't stay,
I gotta come back for the PTA.

(Reprinted from *San Diego Teachers Association Bulletin*, November–December 1956.)

In planning his work, the busy teacher has several alternatives. He may attempt to teach without plans or use the same plans year after year.

Neither of these alternatives satisfies the professional person. It is obvious that an effective teacher must be a highly organized person who is able to budget time wisely, think clearly, and act decisively. The experienced teacher can utilize more mental planning in lieu of the detailed written plans needed in preservice teaching. As said before, some written plans are always necessary. Equipped with curriculum guides or courses of study and textbooks, the teacher still needs to prepare an outline of suggested objectives, materials, activities, and evaluative techniques for each course. Resource units, prepared on a cooperative basis in summer workshops, constitute one of the best sources for unit or long-range planning. But in addition to making use of ready-made materials, the teacher needs to be freed periodically from the pressures of a daily teaching schedule in order to keep abreast of new developments in subject-matter areas, to become acquainted with more up-to-date materials, to explore the research and experimentation dealing with better methods, and to pause for reflection.

Another problem in instructional planning at the secondary level is the fact that the teacher may be lacking in perspective. Educated essentially as a subject-matter specialist, he can easily lose sight of the fact that such subject matter is a means to an end, not an end in itself. He would do well to keep in mind a shrewd observation attributed to the philosopher Whitehead that, as bare facts, knowledge keeps no better than fish. Unless the teacher is able to relate the subject to the student and to the way he learns, little or no learning is likely to occur. Either extreme is to be avoided: undue preoccupation with adult-centered demands or with the passing fancies of immature youth. On one hand, the teacher needs to be aware of the relationship of all subjects to the total objectives of the school; but on the other, the teacher must be sensitive to past successes and failures, present undertakings, and future aspirations of his students. The teacher who achieves proper perspective in his planning endeavors to find the best answers to the right questions. Is planning to be based upon the content and formal organization of the various subject-matter disciplines or upon personal-social goals expressed in terms of improved student behavior? Is planning to be based upon facts to be learned or upon problems of everyday living to be solved? This implies more than a narrow utilitarian view of education, for growth in appreciation and enjoyment of art, music, and literature are as important in everyday living as the development of vocational skills. Concisely stated, the chief task of the teacher is to utilize the cultural heritage, now organized in terms of separate subjects in the secondary school, to help youth achieve their present developmental tasks and, at the same time, develop an awareness of important future needs and ways to satisfy them.

Another problem in planning instruction is that of maintaining a balance between uniformity and flexibility. The need for thorough preplanning has already been stressed. But to preplan does not mean to predetermine everything that happens in the classroom. There are unpredictable variables in every teaching-learning situation. Consequently, the skillful teacher is able to change his plans, "to play it by ear," when deviations from his plans are necessary. Furthermore, if students are to be involved in planning at all, there must be flexibility enough to permit it. However, in order to avoid undesirable gaps or duplications in a student's learning experiences, it has been necessary for schools to establish guidelines in the form of courses of study or curriculum guides for teachers to follow. Once the teacher has assessed the broad limitations of the framework in which he operates, he is free to incorporate valuable student suggestions or to deviate from his own preconceived plans. A resolution to take advantage of the freedom he has is probably the most important decision the teacher makes. This freedom is often lost by over-dependence upon a single textbook, resulting in a monotonous routine and a loss of creativity, flexibility, and proper attention to individual differences by the teacher. The accumulated cultural heritage has now reached a point where textbooks may represent a hopeless number of pages to be covered. Unless a teacher exercises selectivity with respect to content, he is caught in a treadmill of assign-study-recite-test procedures with no time for the inclusion of rich and varied supplementary instructional activities and materials. How often practice teachers have been told by their supervisors in American history, for example, that they may not use pertinent films because there is no time for it.

THE KINDS OF PLANNING THAT TEACHERS DO

If a man write little, he had need have a great memory—*Francis Bacon*

Planning is an art, a "skill in performance acquired by experience, study, or observation" ("art" as defined in *Webster's New Collegiate Dictionary*). In mastering the art of planning, the teacher needs to learn how to develop long-range course and unit plans, daily plans, and cooperative plans which are all interrelated. Logically, the teacher develops them in this order: first, the course plan; second, unit plans; and third, daily plans. Cooperative planning, the highest and most difficult level, would not be used by all teachers. In practice, beginning teachers probably more often develop a term or semester calendar and go directly into preparation of daily plans.

COURSE PLANNING

Reduced to its simplest terms, course planning involves the following steps: (1) making an analysis of a particular subject to be taught; (2) listing general objectives to be achieved; (3) developing a tentative outline of content to be covered during a semester, term, or school year; and (4) setting up a tentative time allotment by days and weeks for each topic or problem in the content outline. Stated in another way, the teacher has to decide *what* is to be learned, *why* it is to be learned, the *order* in which learning experiences should take place, and the *time* to be devoted to each learning experience.

In planning course outlines, the teacher plays a major role. However, a number of factors or conditions preclude planning as a solitary, independent teacher activity. First of all, instructional planning takes place within a framework of rules and suggestions as set forth in state school codes, state and local district courses of study or curriculum guides, other school district regulations, and operational schedules. Another vital element in planning is the human factor. Classroom teachers are becoming more and more involved with their colleagues, with interested laymen, and with their students in continuous, cooperative improvement of the total school program. Furthermore, the introduction of cooperative action research ("action research" is defined as the use of research techniques by the classroom teacher to solve his own problems)[4] and the development of a team approach to teaching have further exalted the human factor in instructional planning. In fact, teaching itself is primarily an enterprise in human relations. Ability to work with others—administrators, fellow teachers, students, parents—is the first hallmark of a good teacher.

Other factors which affect course planning are instructional resources and physical facilities. Availability of text and other printed materials, audio-visual materials and services, and rich community resources is obviously a most important factor in course planning. Likewise, adequacy of physical facilities is an important element in the learning environment.

One of the first steps the teacher takes, however, in course planning is to examine the curriculum guide or course of study for his school.

The following excerpts from the Secondary School Curriculum guide of the San Diego City Schools, pages 115–116 of the 1962 revision, is used by special permission.

GENERAL SCIENCE 1–2 (8th) (two-semester course—grade 8—prerequisites: Interest, high academic ability, above average reading ability, selection by teacher and/or counselor.)

This course is offered to the most interested and able science students in the eighth grade. It includes most of the content of ninth-grade General Science 1–2 and, in addition, units in Geology and Astronomy which are normally covered in the regular eighth-grade semester course.

Areas of emphasis and time allotments:

How scientists make their discoveries	1 week
Meterology	3 weeks
Astronomy	4 weeks

[4] Marvin D. Alcorn and James M. Linley, eds., *Issues in Curriculum Development: a Book of Readings.* New York: Harcourt, Brace & World, Inc., 1959, pp. 341–342.

Geology	4 weeks
Chemistry	3 weeks
Atomic energy	2 weeks
Human body	4 weeks
Machines	3 weeks
Magnetism and electricity	4 weeks
Sound and light	4 weeks

Basic Texts:
    Davis, *et al.*, *Science, Discovery and Progress*, Book 3, 1961
    Brandwein, *et al.*, *You and Science*, 1955–1960
Supplementary Texts:
    Beauchamp, *et al.*, *Science Problems for Junior High School, Book II*, 1957
    Brandwein, *et al.*, *You and Your Inheritance*, 1956
    Brandwein, *et al.*, *You and Your World*, 1956
Guide:
    Guide for General Science 1–2, 1961 (Stock No. 31–G–8700)
Teaching Materials:
    Worksheets (stock No. 31–W–5773)

Preceding the course descriptions for science, as is the case with other subject areas, the basic purposes of the science program are given and a diagram shows course sequence for grades seven through twelve.

Procedures in Course Planning

Once the teacher has been given his course assignments and has been made aware of the curricular framework within which he is to operate, he is ready to attack the practical problem of course organization. As already suggested, he has to make decisions about objectives, scope, sequence, and time allotments.

The first decision involves objectives. The use of content, such as the textbook, for example, as a starting point is a mistake. It leads to an overemphasis upon subject matter to be learned rather than desirable behavioral changes to be achieved. In contrast to daily plans, the objectives of course outlines are more general in nature. They should, however, be socially significant, be acceptable to both teacher and students, and be achievable. The following examples of planning objectives illustrate the point:

English composition: to improve skill in oral and written composition
American history: to promote a better understanding of our national heritage
Physical education: to develop bodily vigor and coordination
Music: to encourage an appreciation of better music for enjoyment

Desirable changes in skills, understandings, appreciations, and attitudes constitute the general objectives of course outlines.

Selecting Subject Matter

In selecting course content, the teacher uses all the resources available —curriculum guides, resource units, other teachers, textbooks, audiovisual materials, and his own ideas. The selection of content or subject matter in course planning is closely related to the type of organization used. Such organization may be based on a discrete subject such as American history; a broad subject matter area, general science; or on significant problems. In terms of structure, the teacher may use a single textbook, a topical outline, or a series of units as the basis for organization. Use of the table of contents of a single textbook is likely to be least adequate. This approach tends to stifle teacher creativity and imagination; to neglect differences in interests, backgrounds, and abilities of students in today's classrooms; and to make a class too dependent on the generalizations and interpretations of a single authority.

By all means, the user of any textbook must be aware of its limitations. First of all, it represents a highly condensed, logical organization of a designated body of knowledge. And, second, it is the product of scholarly, mature minds. As such, it serves as a convenient reference and guide in the field of study, but fails to provide the bridge to student experiences or methods of learning. Improperly used, the textbook may impede learning. Student memorization of technical terms, formulas, or generalizations developed by experts may be mistaken for genuine understanding on the part of the teacher. Amusing boners which appear in examinations and the tendency on the part of students to preface remarks with "the book says" furnish evidence of the misuse of textbooks. Although modern textbooks have been greatly improved in readability, format, content, and authorship, the danger of misuse or of overdependence on them is ever present. A more complete discussion of textbooks follows in Chapter 8.

The traditional topical outline, still in common use, is especially adapted to organized subjects of a specialized type. The scope of the course, sequence of topics, inclusion of subtopics, and time allotments are relatively easy to set up and to follow. Although the topical outline represents a better approach to course planning than the use of a table of contents of a single textbook, it still has some of the inherent weaknesses of the textbook approach.

A third approach to long-range planning is the unit plan. Wherever its use is appropriate, especially in general education courses, as well as some specialized education courses, the unit plan is superior to either the single textbook or the exclusive topical outline approach to course planning.

UNIT PLANNING

To overcome the limitations of the isolated, daily assignment with its tendency to fragment learning, the unit plan of organizing instruction was developed.

The unit concept in instructional planning is an outgrowth of several movements. One of these has been changes in psychological conceptions about learning. Traditional acceptance of formal discipline—a theory that the mind is composed of separate faculties (such as memory and reason, for example), which can be strengthened like muscles through exercise— has been challenged since the turn of this century. The experiments of Thorndike and others, who found no evidence of so-called "faculties" nor superiority of any particular subjects as mind trainers, did much to discredit faculty psychology. The gestalt psychologists added another dimension to the psychological picture by concluding from their experiments that the "organism always reacts as a whole."[5] The testing movement of the 1920s made educators sharply aware of the individual differences among students. These developments have revolutionized the teaching process. No longer can a strictly academic curriculum be justified for all students on the basis of being "good training for the mind." No longer can a classroom fare of limited instructional materials and of exclusively verbal activities meet the needs of all youth now in school. The unit plan is an effective means of providing the variety and flexibility needed in today's classroom.

Another movement which lends support to the unit method of planning has been changes in educational philosophy. It has come to be recognized that the American ideal of education for all youth can never be realized in an institution restricted to the sole function of preparing students for college. Furthermore, if the unique qualities of each individual are to be cultivated, it has become obvious that a school program which meets the needs of students of varying interests, needs, and abilities must be provided. Another belief which is gaining widespread acceptance, at least in theory, is that democratic citizenship can only be achieved by the assumption of the responsibilities of such citizenship while in school.

Other factors contributing to the unitary concept of planning are changes in the nature of objectives from learning isolated facts to improv-

[5] Carter V. Good, ed., *Dictionary of Education*, 2d ed. New York: McGraw-Hill Book Company, Inc., 1959, p. 427.

ing student behavior, changes in evaluation procedures from stress on oral examination or recitation to many evidences of growth, growing dissatisfaction with the fragmentation of learning in the secondary school, and increasing recognition of the unitary nature of human development. Thus the unit method of planning instruction is an attempt to insure that integrated development of all aspects of the student's personality, not the dead storage of isolated facts, becomes the focal point of secondary schooling. A more complete discussion of the unit method follows in Chapter 4.

DAILY PLANNING

There will always be a need for daily planning of instruction. Even when the learning experiences of a class are all organized on a unit basis, it is within the daily class period that many of the unit activities—planning, working, evaluating—must necessarily occur. Unfortunately, despite the apparent advantages of the unitary approach to learning, instructional planning based almost entirely on discrete, daily assignments is still quite common, more so than theoretical treatment of the subject in methods books would lead one to believe. That teachers often use day-by-day planning rather than more unified long-range planning is probably due to a number of reasons. One is the time element. It takes much less time and thought to assign a chapter in a textbook each day than to organize a comprehensive unit, incorporating a variety of materials and activities and extending over several weeks. Another problem may be the difficulty of understanding the unit concept. The teacher who merely considers a unit as more chapters in a book or a larger block of subject matter to be learned is likely to find so-called unit planning busy work. When the teacher does not organize instruction on a unit basis, the daily plan becomes more important than ever. In some cases the nature of the class or of the subject matter itself may make the unit type of organization impractical (for example, orchestra or band, advanced courses in science or mathematics). Highly specialized courses with a definite sequence of facts or skills to be learned, without clearly defined subproblems or centers of interests, may be better structured in terms of semester outlines. Still other courses may be set up on the basis of individual project work (such as art or industrial arts) so that the class as a whole does not work on problems or projects as a group. Thus it becomes evident that daily lesson planning is here to stay, not only as a vehicle for implementation of unit plans but also as a means of insuring effective organization of learning activities where unit planning is inappropriate. Further discussion of daily planning is included in Chapter 6.

COOPERATIVE PLANNING

Cooperative or teacher-student planning has been a subject of increasing concern during recent years. However, it is a subject that is more often discussed than practiced, for most schools still use teacher-dominated methods of instruction.[6] Although proof is lacking that academic achievement is greater in classes where students participate in planning than in those where they do not, available evidence does indicate that teaching methods "which provide for adaptation to individual differences, encourage student initiative, and stimulate individual and group participation are superior to those methods which do not."[7]

Values of Cooperative Planning

So far, the claims made for cooperative planning by its advocates are unsupported by research. Nevertheless, simple logic, as well as the experience of a good many teachers, lends support to the contention that there are a number of values to be derived from teacher-student planning of learning experiences in the classroom.

In the first place, students who share in planning their own learning activities are likely to be more highly motivated. It is a normal human reaction to take pride in a venture which one has helped to plan and to feel responsible for its success. Also, whenever a student neglects his responsibility in a cooperatively planned enterprise, he may face not only the displeasure of his teacher but of his peers as well (3:63).

Another product of cooperative planning is most likely to be the establishment of stronger rapport between teacher and students, as well as among students themselves. As an authoritarian atmosphere disappears, a spirit of unity and cooperation is nourished. Unwholesome competition, even antagonism in some cases, is replaced by a "we" feeling. In analyzing the findings of social psychology, McNeil cites a number of advantages of the "nondirective school" (not to be confused with laissez-faire) over the "directive school." Tensions, aggressions, and hostilities are lessened. Students like one another. There is an increase in class cohesiveness and satisfaction. Better solutions to problems are proposed.[8]

The most important values of teacher-student planning are those which

[6] G. Max Wingo, "Methods of Teaching," *Encyclopedia of Educational Research*, 3d ed., Chester W. Harris, ed. New York: The Macmillan Company, 1960, p. 851. Used by permission of Macmillan.
[7] *Ibid.*, p. 853.
[8] John McNeil, "Toward Appreciation of Teaching Method," *Phi Delta Kappan*, vol. 39 (March 1958) pp. 295–301.

contribute to the development of more effective citizenship in our society. Development of a sense of responsibility, ability to work with others, and opportunities to make decisions—these are the priceless fruits of successful cooperative planning. When students experience twelve, fourteen, or even sixteen years of schooling in classes where they are permitted to make no important decisions, are they entirely at fault if they later exhibit apathy or indifference toward the obligations of adult citizenship? Teachers may set up and enforce regulations to insure acceptable social behavior in the classroom, but students who obey these laws are deprived of valuable experience in decision making. They have little opportunity to grow in moral stature. Students must have opportunities to make important decisions, with the possibility of making mistakes and suffering the consequences, and have some freedom in acting upon the insights they have gained. Cooperative planning offers students experience in learning to work with others. Teacher-student planning at its best makes students both willing and able to discharge their obligations as responsible persons in a world that is marked by ever-increasing interdependence.

Precautions in Cooperative Planning

To be convinced of the values of cooperative planning is not enough to insure beneficial results, for there is no one road to its achievement. In fact, such planning requires far greater skill and understanding than does a more autocratic approach to teaching. At the outset, the teacher must be aware of certain pitfalls and take precautions to avoid the dangers of chaos and frustration.

The first thing the teacher should do is to take inventory of his own assets and liabilities. He must know his students well, be well prepared in his subject, and possess leadership in organizing and directing the learning activities of youth. If he lacks experience in teacher-student planning, the teacher is advised to proceed cautiously.

A second important consideration is the composition of the class. Degree of maturity, level of ability, interests, past experiences in cooperative endeavors, and potential leadership are the assets of group members that must be assessed before the teacher plunges too deeply into cooperative planning. Quite often teachers tend to underestimate the abilities of their students. Rapport between the teacher and his students is a most important factor in determining how successful the teacher is likely to be in stimulating willingness on the part of students to assume responsibility. Obviously, it is unwise to place too much self-direction in the hands of an unstable group where control is still an acute problem.

Possible school limitations on cooperative planning must also be considered. Administrative policies, school philosophy, supervisory approval, emotional support of one's colleagues, parental understanding, class size, time limitations, and availability of resources are factors which affect the degree of cooperative planning that may be employed in the classroom.

The nature of the subject matter may also be a limiting factor. Highly specialized subjects, such as algebra or chemistry, which are organized on the basis of a definite sequence of concepts to be learned offer only limited opportunities for student decisions.

Implementation of Cooperative Planning

No doubt there are many teachers who would like to incorporate more student participation in planning classroom activities but who are not certain how to begin. At this point, it is well to remember that cooperative planning may take place either on a group or on an individual basis. For a teacher to discuss with one student how to do an individualized assignment involves no risks with respect to group control and requires no particular skill in group procedures. What the situation does require of the teacher is an awareness of individual student needs, time, and knowledge of the infinite variety of learning materials and activities that the subject for study has to offer. Cooperative planning on a group basis is another matter. The inexperienced teacher is advised to proceed gradually in the implementation of full cooperative planning by the class as a whole. Some practical steps to be taken are suggested in the discussion which follows.

Certain practices in giving students limited responsibility for classroom procedures are not new. They have been used by many teachers for a long time. A common practice is to utilize student monitors or helpers in taking care of heat, light, and ventilation for physical comfort; in distributing and collecting materials; in checking attendance; in acting as custodians of equipment; in serving as shop foremen; and in assisting as squad leaders. Giving students a choice of two or more alternatives—such as the day for a test, the time needed for the next assignment, the date when notebooks are due—is a minor step toward more student decision making.

Opportunities for group decisions frequently present themselves in the course of normal class activities. The following example illustrates the point:

Each Thursday the world history class studies current events. Class procedures had been traditional, with the teacher conducting discussion on the articles read by the students in an assigned current events paper. One Wednesday, the teacher asked the class if they would like to have a debate on an article on American foreign policy. Class members indicated considerable interest in the proposal. A student was then asked to take charge of the class and to secure volunteers to serve as chairman, debaters, and judges. Having had no responsibility for class procedures in the past, the class responded slowly at first. However, volunteers were eventually secured and the debate organized. The debate took place as scheduled. At its conclusion, many students demonstrated eagerness to discuss the issues further from the floor and there was enthusiastic consensus in favor of more debates.

Other class situations offer golden opportunities for more student assumption of responsibility. Discussion of common problems—class behavior, homework assignments, improvement of marks—is an excellent way to solve problems with greater satisfaction to all concerned. Some classes elect their own officers who call the class to order, make announcements, read the school bulletin, take care of homeroom business, and relieve the teacher of handling minor administrative details. Class officers may even be in charge of learning activities.

An eighth-grade speech teacher and her class developed a constitution and bylaws under which a class president served as chairman in charge of all class activities and a secretary kept a record of class business and acted as parliamentarian. Class officers served for one week with no one eligible for re-election until all students had had an opportunity to hold office. To insure worthwhile activities in speech and to protect the class from possible chaos, it was agreed that the teacher should introduce each new unit and should have veto power. The plan worked so well that the teacher never exercised her veto power. It was gratifying to observe how well the students took care of the usual problems which arise in speech classes, such as the monopoly of class time by a few individuals, several students talking at one time, and some students refusing to give their speeches. Not only did the students solve the usual problems as well as the teacher might have solved them, but they also absorbed two students from other classes, one from shop and one from band, who had been suspended for disciplinary reasons, and secured their participation as cooperative citizens.

A further step to the gradual development of student responsibility is the selection of committees to perform special services for the class. For example, a committee might develop a bulletin board related to the unit, assume responsibility for making the room more attractive, secure additional information for the class from a library research project, interview a prominent citizen, or visit the city council in session. In each case, the committee not only profits from a valuable experience, but also renders a service to the class. The development of an inclination to help others is both a necessary condition and an important product in cooperative planning.

In helping students to learn how to work with others, the teacher may begin on a modest scale by having students work in pairs, using student preferences as a major guide in initial pairings. These pairs may check one another's work in spelling, homework assignments in mathematics, memorization of lines in literature; review for a test; share information on a particular problem; or help each other when one has mastered some problem and the other has not.[9] Pairing is especially helpful in the orientation of new students to class.

As the teacher anticipates more and more involvement in the cooperative approach to planning, he must build upon sound foundations of both external and internal conditions which are vital to success. He should consider, first of all, the external factors which have already been mentioned, such as administrative policies, emotional support of colleagues, and parental understanding. Internal factors involve especially a spirit of class unity and a willingness on the part of students to assume more responsibility for their own learning. Even a minor factor, such as students' knowing one another's names, is important. Of course, the teacher should learn the names of his students as soon as possible. Many opportunities should be provided for students to talk, work, and play together. If a student seems isolated from the group, other members need to be encouraged to lend a helping hand. In the beginning, willingness on the part of students to become involved in planning may pose a major problem. When students have been told for years what to do, how to do it, and when to do it, they will need assurance at first that their advice is actually being sought. Some gradual steps toward more student involvement have been suggested above. What does the teacher do next?

Advanced Stages of Cooperative Planning

Full participation by a class in cooperative planning implies making important decisions in all aspects of the teaching-learning process: (1) choice of purposes or objectives, (2) selection and use of learning materials and activities, and (3) evaluation of learning experiences.

As the teacher reviews the various stages of the teaching-learning process, he must give careful consideration to the extent to which students may participate in each phase of the process and to the kinds of decisions that they may make. There is, for example, some disagreement over student participation in the choice of unit objectives. Some say it is the sole responsibility of the teacher to set up unit objectives; others maintain that students should participate fully in their selection. At any rate, by means of thorough discussion, the teacher should clarify objectives and attempt to show their relevance to student needs and concerns. Otherwise, motivation is likely to remain at a low level with an attendant loss in significant learning. It is in the selection and development of learning

[9] J. Galen Saylor and William M. Alexander, *Curriculum Planning.* New York: Holt, Rinehart and Winston, Inc., 1954, pp. 468–471.

resources and activities that the students have the most opportunity to participate in planning. The discussion approach is a good one to use. For example, in a laboratory situation such factors as safety, proper use and care of equipment, and such class procedures as getting started, working effectively, and cleaning up are always appropriate subjects for discussion. In planning a field trip or excursion, the teacher and his class need to clarify such routine procedures as permits from parents, transportation, and proper conduct; to discuss what to look for on the trip; and to plan for follow-up activities upon completion of the excursion. When the class as a whole is organized into committees to develop a project much discussion and planning are necessary. The point is well illustrated in the educational film, *Broader Concept of Method*, which is briefly summarized as follows:

> During a class discussion of damage to city parks, a student raised a question about what might be done to improve conditions in their own school lunchroom. Eventually, it was decided to make improvement of the school lunchroom a class project. As a result of a discussion led by the teacher, five subproblems were identified and made the basis for committee assignments. Each student was asked to make a first, second, and third choice of committee and assigned accordingly. The next step was to develop a "work plan" for the committees. Again under the guidance of the teacher, it was determined that each committee had to decide *what* information was needed, *how* to get the information, and *who* was to get it. During both organization and work periods, the teacher circulated among the groups, giving assistance as needed. Finally, the chairmen of the committees made reports on their findings and recommendations to the class and the principal (who came as a special guest). At the conclusion of the reports, the principal indicated that he and the lunchroom manager were ready to help carry out the recommendations of the class.[10]

Evaluation, the final phase of the teaching-learning process, is also well adapted to the discussion approach. At the beginning of a unit, the teacher and his students may discuss criteria for evaluating their work, such as the requirements for effective speaking in a speech class, the necessary steps in preparing and serving a meal in a homemaking class, or the different processes in developing a project in industrial arts. At the conclusion of a unit, the teacher and his students may use the same criteria to judge not only the finished product but also day-by-day procedures in work periods. Thus, students may participate in evaluating the effectiveness of the unit as a whole, as well as their own progress toward the achievement of unit goals. However, there is one aspect of evaluation that is the sole responsibility of the teacher. That is securing, interpreting,

[10] *Broader Concept of Method: Part II—Teacher and Pupils Planning and Working Together*, film, 19 min. New York: McGraw-Hill Book Company, Inc.

and weighing the relative importance of various types of data as a basis for translating student growth into a final mark or grade for the course.

By way of summary of the discussion on ways of implementing cooperative planning, the authors cite the following eight categories or areas which have been developed through school experimentation, reported by Miel and associates:

1. Planning the use of time for a day or for a longer period, with suggested sequences of activities for work periods, free time, or special events.
2. Planning for the care and improvement of the classroom—housekeeping, seating, or making the room more attractive.
3. Planning proper conduct in terms of people and specific situations—attending assemblies, working in laboratories, or settling misunderstandings.
4. Planning subjects and methods by suggesting topics or problems, discussing how to proceed, and locating resources.
5. Planning products and productions—developing a room mural, making Christmas cards, cultivating a school garden, planning a party, or organizing an exhibit.
6. Planning service projects—making the playground safer, beautifying the community, sending parcels overseas, making Thanksgiving donations, or acting as teachers' aides in elementary schools.
7. Planning solutions to all-school problems—taking care of lavatories, making better use of the cafeteria, or making better use of community recreational facilities.
8. Evaluating group work. The emphasis is always on "how *we* are doing."[11]

Guidelines to Cooperative Planning

By way of conclusion, it is appropriate to summarize a few important guidelines for success in teacher-student planning. Some of these may be evident in the foregoing discussion on how to implement cooperative planning; others may not.

The first consideration in cooperative planning is that it must be *honest*. Neither permitting students to do as they please nor inveigling them into accepting a teacher's preconceived plans is genuine teacher-student planning. The first is pernicious permissiveness and the second is sheer hypocrisy. Choices that students make must be honest choices. When a

11 Adapted from Alice Miel and associates, *Cooperative Procedures in Learning*. New York: Bureau of Publications, Teachers College, Columbia University, 1952, pp. 277, 302–343.

teacher decides to share more responsibility with his students, he must be emotionally prepared to accept certain conditions. For instance, the teacher must accept the fact that cooperative planning takes time. If the object of the teacher is to cover ground or the pages in a voluminous textbook, he is advised to abandon the idea of cooperative planning. In sharing decisions with a class, the teacher must be willing to surrender some of his own control of the situation at the risk of some confusion or even disorder. Above all, the teacher must have faith in his students and their ability and willingness to assume responsibility. Usually, students will justify the confidence of a teacher who has faith in them. As a further safeguard to honesty in cooperative planning, the teacher must clarify, at the outset, the boundaries within which students may exercise freedom of choice.

Another important guideline for cooperative planning is the *necessity for thorough planning by the teacher in advance.* Cooperative planning is no substitute for preplanning on the part of the teacher. Indeed cooperative planning demands more thought and preparation by the teacher than do autocratic procedures. In order to give effective guidance to students who may be immature and inexperienced in cooperative procedures, the teacher must have the ability to offer many alternative suggestions, know his materials and resources well in order to assist students in their research, possess skill in capitalizing on student questions and suggestions, and discern the infinite possibilities for the achievement of unit objectives. Thus, it can readily be observed that a teacher who is committed to cooperative planning needs thorough knowledge, organizational ability, good judgment, and imagination.

If cooperative planning is to succeed, *the respective roles of teacher and students must be clarified.* As a general guideline, Wiles suggests that it is the task of the teacher "to provide enough direction to give the pupils a sense of security, but not enough to discourage initiative."[12] Democracy is not a gift; it has to be learned and earned. Since that is the case, the democratic process of sharing responsibility with a class requires careful guidance by the teacher. Some failures are to be expected. However, if there is too much disorder, chaos, or failure in group processes, those involved develop feelings of insecurity and dissatisfaction. The teacher has to exercise discrimination in deciding when to keep hands off and when to rescue a class from its own inept operation. The respective areas of responsibility of both teacher and students must be clearly defined at the outset. When students have been assigned responsibility, the teacher not only provides the necessary freedom for students to exer-

[12] Kimball Wiles, *Teaching for Better Schools*, 2d ed. Englewood Cliffs, N.J.: Prentice-Hall, Inc., 1959, p. 109.

cise that responsibility but also provides necessary guidance as needed in defining problems, in developing leadership, in learning how to work together, and in reporting findings effectively to the class. The teacher must also remember that he has definite obligations to the school, to parents, and to the community which he cannot delegate to others. While students may participate in assisting with class routine, setting up their own rules of conduct, in planning learning activities, and in evaluating their own progress, the teacher is ultimately responsible for reporting student growth in terms of valid marks or grades, for keeping accurate records of attendance, and for maintaining an acceptable learning situation in the classroom.

Finally, it is logical to assume that cooperative planning, properly conceived and executed, should result in a number of permanent values for the student:

1. *He learns to make intelligent choices.* This involves accumulating and weighing evidence, developing value judgments, and acting upon the basis of his own decisions. He learns to do all of these things only by experience.

2. *He learns to work with others.* Developing respect for the rights and abilities of others, acquiring social skills, and knowing how to lead and how to follow are learned only through practice.[13]

3. *He learns to assume responsibility,* to stand on his own feet, and to live with decisions that he and his own peers have made. He learns all of this in the only way possible, by being responsible.

4. Finally, *he learns to evaluate his own actions,* to weigh the positive and negative results of his choices, and to develop a system of values by which to live. He becomes a responsible, moral individual by assuming responsibility for his own decisions and actions.

"Learning to plan, work, play, and live together is, like all things, an individual matter. It comes more easily to some children and teachers than others."[14] Contributing ideas, making decisions, and carrying out responsibilities help the wordy ones to make more pertinent remarks, the shy ones to become more self-confident, the aggressive ones to become more cooperative, and the lazy ones to respond to challenges.[15]

[13] Leland P. Bradford, "Developing Potentialities Through Class Groups," *Teachers College Record,* vol. 61 (May 1960), pp. 443–450.

[14] Elsa Schneider, "How Children and Teacher Work Together," *Bulletin 1952,* No. 14, Federal Security Agency, Office of Education. Washington, D.C.: Government Printing Office, 1952, p. 23.

[15] *Loc. cit.*

Selected Readings

1. Burton, William H., *The Guidance of Learning Activities*, 3d ed. New York: Appleton-Century-Crofts, 1962. Chapter 9.
2. Carter, William L., Carl W. Hansen, and Margaret K. McKim, *Learning to Teach in the Secondary School*. New York: The Macmillan Company, 1962. Chapter 6.
3. Clark, Leonard H., and Irving S. Starr, *Secondary School Teaching Methods*. New York: The Macmillan Company, 1959. Chapter 4.
4. Grambs, Jean D., William J. Iverson, and Franklin K. Patterson, *Modern Methods in Secondary Education*, revised ed. New York: Holt, Rinehart and Winston, Inc., 1958. Chapter 10.
5. Haskew, Laurence D., and Jonathon C. McLendon, *This Is Teaching*, revised and expanded. Chicago: Scott, Foresman and Company, 1962. Chapter 9.
6. McKean, Robert C., *Principles and Methods in Secondary Education*. Columbus, Ohio: Charles E. Merrill Books, Inc., 1962. Chapter 5.
7. Risk, Thomas M., *Principles and Practices of Teaching in Secondary Schools*, 3d ed. New York: American Book Company, 1958. Chapter 7.
8. Schorling, Raleigh, and Howard T. Batchelder, *Student Teaching in Secondary Schools*. New York: McGraw-Hill Book Company, Inc., 1956. Chapter 6.
9. Watkins, Ralph K., *Techniques of Secondary School Teaching*. New York: The Ronald Press Company, 1958. Chapters 1, 2, 3.

CHAPTER 4

Unit planning

It has already been suggested that a persistent problem in secondary education is that of providing greater unity and coherence in the educational experiences of boys and girls. A number of factors—the quantitative interpretation of education in terms of Carnegie units, the specialized subject matter emphasis in teacher training, and college entrance requirements—have conspired to make integration of learning difficult. Unit planning for instruction is an attempt to offset some of the disadvantages of a fragmented curriculum and to broaden the range of learning materials and activities in the classroom, even within the present framework of separate subjects. In the discussion that follows, clarification of the definition of a unit, values and limitations of unit planning, and suggestions for the development and implementation of unit plans will be considered.

THE UNIT DEFINED

The unit may be simply defined as a means of organizing instructional activities and materials into larger, related, unified patterns of learning in order to achieve significant educational objectives. According to Burton, "The important thing is to provide a combination of subject matter and processes which will have real meaning for the learner, which will aid him in continuously integrating his learning" (2:328).

One of four definitions of a unit in the *Dictionary of Education* describes the unit as "an organization of various activities, experiences, and types of learning around a central problem or purpose, developed cooperatively by a group of pupils under teacher leadership. . . ."[1] The definitions above imply that a unit includes such characteristics as the

[1] Carter V. Good, ed., *Dictionary of Education*. New York: McGraw-Hill Book Company, Inc., 1959, p. 587.

following: (1) a comprehensive coverage of a theme or problem, (2) a time allotment of more than one class period, (3) cooperative planning, (4) a variety of learning activities and materials, and (5) achievement of significant objectives. It should be noted that neither a chapter in a textbook nor a larger block of subject matter necessarily constitutes a unit. The authors contend that cooperative planning is not always a necessary element in unit planning. Teachers everywhere still prepare unit plans unassisted and teach them without consulting the class concerning what is to be done or how. The nature of the subject, the ability of the class, and the competence of the teacher are all factors which determine how much cooperative planning is practicable.

The fact that there are more than two dozen types or kinds of units can create considerable confusion in the mind of a beginning teacher who wishes to engage in unit planning.[2] Consequently, some clarification and simplification of the problem is in order at this point.

Types of Units

In textbook discussions of unit planning, it is common practice to draw nice distinctions between "experience units" and "subject matter units." In some instances, a third type, the "process unit," is introduced to add still more confusion to the concept of unit planning. The authors contend that, except for semantic reasons, an unnecessary dichotomy is set up when so-called "experience units" are contrasted with "subject matter units." Differences are a matter of degree, not kind, for the student learns neither without experience nor without subject matter or content. By the same token, violent controversies that sometimes rage in academic circles over the relative merits of methods and subject matter are pointless since both are inseparable and necessary aspects of the teaching process.

Because of their differences in function, a distinction does need to be made between a "teaching unit" and a "resource unit." In structure, they are similar, but each serves a different function. The teaching unit is prepared by the classroom teacher for use in a particular class. (For example, a teaching unit might be one on "conservation" for use in Social Studies 9 in Fremont High School during the fall semester of 1963.) The resource unit (often prepared by a group of teachers during a summer workshop) is a comprehensive compilation of suggested objectives, topics or problems related to a unifying theme, activities and materials, evaluative techniques, and references. The teaching unit, prepared by the teacher alone or in cooperation with his class, is for use by the teacher and his students. The resource unit is prepared by and for teachers. Including more suggestions than any one teacher could possibly use, the

[2] *Ibid.*, pp. 587–588.

resource unit provides the raw materials for teaching units. It is a time-saver for the busy classroom teacher. Product of a cooperative effort, the resource unit not only saves time and effort for the individual teacher but also represents the rich and varied contributions of a professional team. (Note: Sometimes a teacher working alone may develop a resource unit, but the advantages of cooperative thinking are thereby lost.) As yet, there are many areas of the curriculum for which resource units are not available.

Values of Unit Planning

It has already been suggested that less time and thought are required to develop daily plans than to construct comprehensive unit plans. But there are values in the integrated approach to planning which can never be achieved by planning on a day-by-day basis alone.

In contrast to a segmented, piecemeal approach to planning, which so often characterizes the daily assignment from a single textbook, unit planning is likely to insure more integrated, meaningful learning experiences for students. All the elements of a theme or problem are explored with a continuity that is maintained over a period of days or weeks.

Unit planning incorporates a great variety of learning activities, such as reading, writing, speaking, listening, dramatizing, experimenting, cooperative planning, researching, and reporting. Furthermore, unit planning makes use of many different kinds of learning materials, such as audio-visual, electronic devices and laboratory equipment, and community resources.

Unit planning makes possible more adequate provision for individual differences within the classroom. Because of the rich and varied materials and activities which a well-developed unit has to offer, more opportunities for student choices, greater appeal to diversified interests, and better use of a variety of talents are assured.

There is also greater likelihood that each student will achieve some measure of success when activities are not limited to those of a verbal type, as is so often the case in academic courses in the secondary school. The heterogeneity of the secondary school population today should impress upon every teacher the fact that no two classes nor any two students have the same learning experiences nor achieve identical outcomes.

Better integration of content from different subjects is possible within the framework of unit organization for instruction. This is especially true of general education subjects, those required of all students, where the block-time schedule of two or more consecutive periods under one teacher is used.

Better continuity in learning can be achieved in unit teaching. The teacher and his students are able to attack problems requiring an extended period of research and to pursue their study until possible solutions are found.

Classroom procedures are less likely to be dominated by the teacher under unit planning than under assign-study-recite procedures based upon a single textbook.

While it is true that the extent of student participation in planning is dependent upon several variables, already discussed in the preceding chapter, the unit plan provides more opportunities for the development of student initiative and responsibility than is possible under more limited and formalized types of plans. For example, where different groups or individuals are responsible for investigating different aspects of a problem, a number of desirable outcomes are possible—a better solution to the problem, more opportunities for sharing ideas, and a better use of student talent.

Unit planning is based upon sound psychological principles of learning. As already stated, the unit emphasizes learning by wholes, the continuity of learning, and the integration of student learning experiences. With more student involvement made possible by the unit approach to teaching, a higher degree of motivation is likely to occur. Research indicates that students have a stronger preference for teacher-student planning than for either a laissez-faire or an authoritative type of planning.[3] As students become more responsible for their own education, both rapidity of learning and retention are facilitated.

Limitations of Unit Planning

Not all subjects or courses are equally adaptable to unit planning. As a rule, the nonspecialized general education courses required of all students lend themselves more readily to unit organization and cooperative planning than do more highly specialized courses. The following types of classes or subjects might more appropriately use some other type of instructional plan: (1) subjects requiring mastery of a definite sequence of concepts or problems as a prerequisite for more advanced study (for example, specialized courses in mathematics or science); (2) classes in which students devote most of their time to individual projects (for example, classes in art or industrial arts); (3) classes devoted to achievement of specific skills (for example, classes in shorthand or typing); and (4) courses in which most of class time is spent in practice or rehearsal (such as band or choral groups). Even such a general education course as English often includes discrete elements which may not be related to a

[3] G. Max Wingo, "Methods of Teaching," *Encyclopedia of Educational Research*, 3d ed., Chester W. Harris, ed. New York: The Macmillan Company, 1960, p. 856.

particular unit. For instance a typical daily time budget in an English class may look something like this: ten minutes, pretest on a formal spelling word list; twenty minutes, composition papers returned and errors analyzed; and twenty minutes, reading and discussion of short poems in a literature text. Although the teacher may teach two units alternately in this case (for example, a unit on poetry and a unit on usage of pronouns), there would still probably be some discrete elements which would not be related to either unit. The point is this: not every learning activity in the classroom has to fit within the framework of a particular unit for study.

Some teachers now encounter increasing difficulty in using unit plans. Short class periods, large classes, a high degree of departmentalization, prescriptive courses of study, agitation for more specific subject titles (such as "history" or "geography" instead of the term "social studies"), mandatory use of uniform textbooks and pressure for state-wide examinations for all students—all these make unit planning more difficult.

Since unit planning implies the use of more teacher-student planning, when feasible, more varied activities, and comprehensive coverage of a theme or problem, some teachers view unit planning with misgivings. They are apprehensive of the confusion and disorder which may result from a number of individuals or small groups concurrently working on a variety of activities. The threat of discipline problems may be a real one. However, careful preparation and organization, as well as a realistic appraisal of the limitations and conditions related to cooperative planning and group work, discussed in the preceding chapter, should offer proper safeguards for an orderly, productive learning situation.

Inasmuch as unit teaching seeks to achieve greater breadth of understanding in terms of the interrelationship of all subjects, the teacher may feel insecure because of inadequate preparation in some specialized subjects. Greater breadth in preservice teacher education, continuous in-service preparation, and placement of more responsibility upon students for their own learning offer a partial solution to the problem. Teachers have to realize that they cannot be the fount of all knowledge; neither can they learn all they are expected to know during their undergraduate years in college. What teacher has not learned that the best way to learn a subject is to teach it. Furthermore, the *team* approach to teaching (with different team members specializing in different subjects) could provide another solution to the problem of subject matter mastery.

There are a number of minor difficulties that a teacher may encounter in unit teaching. Occasionally, it may be difficult to sustain interest in a single theme, topic, or problem for a relatively long period of time. This is especially true of immature or slow-learning students. The obvious solution is to plan shorter units. A related problem may be the tendency to overextend the unit, to drag out the work after objectives have been achieved. Sometimes it may seem inappropriate to include drill or remedial lessons on fundamental skills as needed and still maintain continuity in the unit. Since unit development has to take place within the frame work of daily periods of short duration, the teacher must organize each period in such a way as to maintain continuous progress toward long-range unit goals; but he can still include remedial work as needed without destroying continuity of the unit.

PRINCIPAL PARTS OF THE UNIT AND THEIR FUNCTIONS

Basically, the unit, or any other complete instructional plan, consists of four minimum essentials: objectives or expected outcomes, activities or learning experiences, materials, and evaluation. Each of these divisions of the teaching-learning process provides the answer to an important ques tion. Objectives indicate *why* any activity, lesson, or unit should be undertaken at all. They provide the answer to a petulant query that has often been voiced by students: "Why do we have to study this stuff?" Activities answer the question of *how*. They include all of the things that the teacher and students *do* to achieve the objectives. Materials provide the answer to the question of *what*. They consist of all aids or means (printed and audio-visual materials, apparatus, equipment) for implementation of the activities. Evaluation is an attempt to answer the question of *how much* or *how well*. It consists of the criteria and the procedures used by the teacher and his class to determine to what extent the objectives have been achieved.

An examination of printed units usually reveals a more elaborate structure than that suggested by the four minimum essentials listed above. In fact, if all possible items in unit structure were included, an outline of the major divisions would consist of the following titles:

    I. Setting and overview
   II. Outline of topics or problems
 III. Objectives
       A. General
       B. Specific
 IV. Activities
       A. Initiatory or introductory
       B. Developmental
       C. Culminating
   V. Materials

VI. Correlation with other subjects
VII. Evaluation
VIII. Bibliography
    A. Student
    B. Teacher

For further clarification, each of the above items in the detailed unit structure is briefly described in the following paragraphs.

Setting and Overview

The setting includes such items as unit title, subject and grade level (for example, English 9), and approximate time limit of the unit. The unit title should be concise, descriptive, and interesting. It should also suggest the unifying principle around which the unit is organized. Note the different unifying principles in the following examples.

Problem (physiology):	"How does diet affect one's health?" (or Diet in relation to health)
Project (ind. arts):	"How can an automobile owner get more service from his car?" (or Automotive maintenance)
Project (homemaking):	"How can a housewife prepare an attractive, balanced meal?" (or Preparation of balanced meals)
Topic (social studies):	"How did the people of Europe settle the New World?" (or The colonization of North America)
Activity (physical ed.):	"How does tennis contribute to better use of leisure time?" (or Tennis for recreation)
Generalization (science):	"Water is important for human survival" (Water and human survival)

As said before, the teacher may take a position from one extreme to another, from a stress on student experience to a major emphasis upon subject matter to be learned. Emphases will vary according to "the level of maturity, the experiential background, the purposes, needs, and interests of the learner" (2:329). However, the most effective planning makes student experience the focal point of teaching and uses subject matter as the means to an end, namely the improvement of the quality of student experience.

The *overview* broadly outlines the purpose and content of the unit, relating it to the preceding units and to the course as a whole. An example appears in a unit outline which is included later in this chapter.

Outline of Topics or Problems

To give structure or body to the unit in terms of a definite scope and sequence of activities and materials, some teachers find it helpful to include a content outline of topics (history), problems (science), or activities (physical education).

Objectives and Expected Outcomes

Unit objectives must have value for the student and for the society that supports the schools. The student must feel that activities to achieve unit goals have personal value for him; society must require such activities to contribute to its perpetuity. Objectives are both general and specific. They range from the general objectives of secondary education to the specific objectives of the classroom. Differences in types of objectives may be illustrated as follows:

An example from English:
Objective of secondary education: Students are expected to develop skill in the fundamental processes (also applicable to other subjects).
General objective in English: Students are expected to improve their reading skills.
Specific objective in English: Students are expected to learn how to read a book for information (using table of contents, skimming, and so on).

An example in music:
Objective of secondary education: Students are expected to learn how to use leisure time wisely.
General objective in music: Students are expected to learn to appreciate better music.
Specific objective in music: Students are expected to appreciate the close relationship that often exists between popular music and classical selections.

A further analysis of objectives appears later in this chapter under the topic of "Unit Objectives."

Activities

Initiatory or introductory activities get the unit under way. They may serve several purposes: to determine what the student already knows about the proposed unit, to relate student interests, backgrounds, and abilities to the new unit, and to motivate the class to pursue the study of the unit with enthusiasm. *Developmental* activities are the heart of the unit. These activities need to be extensive and varied, for they constitute about everything the teacher and the class do to achieve the objectives of the unit. *Culminating* activities are designed to summarize, to review, and to re-emphasize the central, unifying theme or problem of the unit. The following activities are typical: an exhibit of students' work (art), a tournament (physical education), a series of committee reports (social science), or a tea honoring mothers (homemaking).

Materials

It has already been assumed that subject matter and learning activities are inseparable. Materials (printed and audio-visual materials, apparatus, equipment) constitute the substance of the learning activities. The teacher is responsible for acquainting his students with the rich and varied sources of information and for teaching them how to locate and use accurate, relevant data in solving their problems.

Correlation with Other Subjects

Since the secondary school curriculum is so highly fragmented, the teacher must make a conscious effort at all times to integrate student knowledge in the various subjects. A short anecdote, which could be duplicated countless times, illustrates the point:

A mechanical drawing teacher was giving a test. When a student asked, "Does spelling count?" he was told that it would. The student protested on the grounds that spelling should count only in English classes.

Evaluation

The unit cycle is completed with evaluation. When all evaluation data are in, everyone concerned should know how well unit objectives have been achieved. There are several approaches to evaluation. First of all, the teacher and the class may cooperatively evaluate the successes and failures experienced in the development of the unit as a guide to future operations. As another phase of evaluation, the teacher may evaluate his own teaching of the unit. Certainly no unit evaluation is complete until the teacher has gathered all available data concerning the progress of each student and has translated it into a mark or grade to be used in progress reports to parents and as part of the cumulative record of the student. Since final marks or grades are part of the student's permanent record, each member of a class has a right to know in advance what criteria and procedures will be used by the teacher in evaluating his work for each unit.

Bibliography

A list of selected references, sometimes one for students and another for the teacher, is included at the end of the unit to supplement the materials suggested in the body of the unit. Also appendices may be added which include such items as charts and graphs, word lists, suggested class organization, and other miscellaneous items.

UNIT DESIGN

While a teacher may know that any instructional plan, reduced to its most basic elements, consists of but four parts—objectives, activities, materials, and evaluation—he may still have difficulty in organizing these into a coherent, unified sequence. The structure of a unit plan, as well as a daily plan, may be set up according to either of two formats—an outline form or a columnar or parallel form. The outline form, the one longest in use, is illustrated as follows:

UNIT: THE SHORT STORY

I. *Setting:* English 10, Mt. Miguel High School.
   Teacher—Mrs. J. M. *Dates*—October 8 through October 17.
II. *Overview:* The short story is a work of fiction characterized by a single theme treated with dramatic intensity. Any short story will have a setting, made up of scene and time, one or more characters, and a plot. As the unit progresses, we shall read several short stories written by well-known authors, attempt to analyze their characteristics and the elements that make them short stories, and try to write a short story of our own. Throughout the unit we shall be attempting to arrive at some criteria by which the value and effectiveness of any short story can be evaluated.
III. *Topics to be covered:*
   A. In *English Grammar and Composition* by Warriner, *et al.* (Chapter 14, pp. 323–340):
      1. "Finding Suitable Incidents."
      2. "Deciding the Purpose."
      3. "Deciding the Characters."
      4. "Importance of Scene and Time."
      5. "Organization of the Story."
   B. In *Adventures in Appreciation* by Cook, *et al.*:
      1. "Reward" by Jean C. Becket (pp. 152–159).
      2. "Windwagon Smith" by Wilbur Schramm (pp. 113–127).
      3. "Revolt of Mother" by May E. Wilkins Freeman (pp. 59–69).

C. Other Short Stories:
1. "The Necklace" by Maupassant.
2. "The Celebrated Sassage Factory" by Charles Dickens.

IV. *Objectives:*
A. General:
1. To develop an understanding of the short story as a literary term and type.
2. To develop an appreciation for well-written short stories.
3. To develop an understanding of the techniques necessary for writing a good short story.
B. Specific:
1. To promote an understanding of such terms as plot, character, scene, time, setting, mood, theme, and purpose in relation to the short story.
2. To develop an appreciation of the style and message of "Reward" by Becket.
3. To develop a better understanding of the narrative style of paragraph.
4. To develop an appreciation of the style and meaning of "Windwagon Smith."
5. To encourage personal desire to write narrative prose in the best style possible.
6. To foster development of intelligent self-criticism of narratives for suitability and purpose.
7. To promote understanding of "purpose" in narrative.
8. To apply criteria of purpose to "The Necklace."
9. To foster appreciation of characterization in "Revolt of Mother."
10. To develop criteria for the interpretation and evaluation of the short story.
11. To apply evaluative criteria to stories read, as well as to original work.

V. *Activities:*
A. Discuss "Reward" to cover questions on understanding of plot and character.
B. Write a paragraph on what might have happened if Joe had remained in Ware's Landing.
C. Read "Windwagon Smith."
1. Be able to apply theme to what we know of the "American ideal" of progress.
2. Explain "exaggeration" as a literary term and find examples of it in the story.
3. Be able to discuss types of characters, mood, incidents of the story.
D. Read orally "The Celebrated Sassage Factory," as an example of a subject for writing.
E. Read and discuss Chapter 14, pp. 323–327, on purpose and suitability of incident in narrative writing.

F. Write a brief narrative from personal experience.
G. Listen to a recording of "The Necklace," discuss story as to purpose and characterization and relate it to personal experiences.
H. Read aloud randomly selected samples of narrative writing and get oral criticism of purpose and effectiveness.
I. Write, in class, a vivid description of some person, read to class, and secure class criticism as to effectiveness of characterization.
J. Read and discuss "revolt of Mother" as to effectiveness of characterization and significance of theme for family life of students. Compare characterization with that of "The Necklace."
K. Read and discuss Chapter 14, pp. 335–340, on title, first draft, and revision of first draft of short story.
L. Review orally and outline on chalkboard the principles for writing a short story.
M. Write an original short story.
N. Show filmstrip-recording of "Interpretation and Evaluation of the Short Story," summarizing principles and having students apply them to stories read and to stories written by themselves.

VI. *Materials:*
A. Stories in *Adventures in Appreciation* (as listed above).
B. Chapter 14 in *English Grammar and Composition.*
C. Recording of "The Necklace" (SDSC A-V Services).
D. Filmstrip-recording of "Interpretation and Evaluation of the Short Story."
E. Story of "The Celebrated Sassage Factory" (from *Tell Me a Story* by Charles Laughton).
F. Original work of students.

VII. *Evaluation:*
A. Participation in class discussion.
B. Performance on written work.
C. Performance on tests (quizzes, unit test).

VIII. *Bibliography:*
A. Cook, Luella B., *et al., Adventures in Appreciation.* New York: Harcourt, Brace & World, Inc., 1952.
B. Laughton, Charles, *Tell Me a Story: an Anthology.* New York: McGraw-Hill Book Company, Inc., 1957.
C. Warriner, John E., and Francis Griffith, *English Grammar and Composition.* New York: Harcourt, Brace & World, Inc., 1958.

(Used by special permission of Robin Briscoe, student teacher.)

The newest and most functional design for a unit is the columnar or parallel type, illustrated in abbreviated form as follows:

UNIT: INSTALLMENT BUYING

Subject and Grade: Mathematics 9   *Approximate Time:* One Week
                                                          (October 16-20)
School: Wilson Junior High   *Teacher:* Mary Doe

Overview:

General Objectives:

Specific Objectives	Activities	Materials (or Resources)
To become acquainted with the advantages and disadvantages of installment buying.	Discuss installment buying (key questions on note cards). Show and discuss film: *Installment Buying.*	*Essentials of Business Arithmetic* by Kanzer & Schaaf; film: *Installment Buying;* pamphlet: *One Hundred Problems in Consumer Credit.*
To learn how to figure the extra costs in installment buying.	Explanation by the teacher, followed by work on problems by the class.	Problems on dittoed pages.

Evaluation: (Specific criteria and procedures for evaluating the achievement of students are to be outlined here.)

Bibliography:

It should be noted that three major divisions (sometimes four when an outline of topics or problems is included) appear in the columnar structure while the remainder of the unit is in outline form. That this type of structure is more functional than the older outline type can be seen at a glance. Parts which are inseparable in the instructional process—objectives, materials, activities—are closely related in the unit structure. Because *evaluation* appears as a separate category, it is not to be assumed that evaluation occurs only at the end of the unit. It is continuous with each evaluative activity included under the same category as other activities. However, it is necessary to have defined quite clearly both criteria and procedures, as well as relative weights assigned to each, for marking purposes.

It should be noted that the illustration of the columnar type of unit just given shows but one of a number of variations which may be used. For example, the columnar design may be reduced to two categories as follows:

Activities and Materials | *Expected Outcomes* (or *Specific Objectives*)

Or, an expansion of the columnar type of unit might include these items:

Topics or *Problems* | *Materials* or *Resources* | *Activities* | *Expected Outcomes*

Suffice it to say, the important thing is to include at least the minimum essentials of the teaching-learning process in a plan that has unity, coherence, and continuity.

UNIT PREPARATION AND IMPLEMENTATION

The first step a teacher takes in unit planning is to make a tentative list of the units he expects to teach in a given course or subject. A choice of units will need to be made within the framework of a curriculum that has been developed cooperatively by many professional people. This framework usually appears in the form of a course of study or curriculum (or teachers') guide, already illustrated in the preceding chapter.

How much freedom a teacher has in planning his work, aside from general school policies, is dependent upon the breadth and flexibility of the curriculum guide. Traditional courses of study differed considerably from modern teachers' guides. The former were highly prescriptive, stressed subject matter to be learned, were subject to revision at infrequent intervals, and were usually prepared by experts in subject fields. By way of contrast, modern curriculum guides offer many suggestions for achieving unit goals and permit considerable freedom of choice by the teacher on how to achieve those objectives. Present-day guides also stress expected outcomes in terms of desirable changes in student behavior, using subject matter as a means to that end; they are subject to continuous revision; and they incorporate the contributions of many groups (psychologists, sociologists, specialists in subject fields, and educators) in their preparation, with classroom teachers occupying a prominent role.

Although modern curriculum guides, provided at both state and local levels, allow considerable freedom for the teacher, they have been designed to establish a framework within which the teacher should operate in order to insure proper scope, sequence, and continuity for the school program as a whole. In recognition of the problem of providing for individual differences, makers of curriculum guides are further refining them to the extent that, in some cases, they are adapted to different levels of ability.

After a teacher has made a tentative choice of units for a given course, the next step is to set up a tentative time budget for each unit, subject to such revisions as may become necessary in the course of the term or semester.

Before proceeding very far in actual construction of unit plans, the teacher will need to know a number of things. Above all, he will need to know the type of students with whom he will work. Then he will need to know what instructional materials are available for implementation of the proposed units.

After the teacher has made a tentative selection of units to be developed during a term or semester, with a time allotment for each, usually his next step is to take an inventory of such available resources as physical facilities, instructional materials, and community resources. A detailed analysis of instructional materials follows in Chapters 8 through 10.

As soon as enrollments have been completed, the teacher will need *to get information about his students.* Several sources may be used—school records, the students themselves (interviews, autobiographies), parents, other professional personnel (teachers, counselors), personal observations, and the community—as discussed in Chapter 1. Armed with a knowledge of available resources and the types of students he will teach, the teacher is then ready to settle down to the business of unit construction.

UNIT OBJECTIVES

Unit construction begins with the selection of objectives. They give direction to everything the teacher and his students do. Lest unit objectives become merely window dressing, the teacher must regard them as functional, practical aspects of the total plan. The new teacher has to develop certain perceptions in order to recognize expected outcomes as the foundation of unit structure. Perspective is needed.

Objectives in Historical Perspective

Sometimes educational objectives are taken for granted. But it must be remembered that objectives expressed in terms of social and personal goals are less than fifty years old. At the turn of this century, it was assumed that the secondary school would perform such functions as preparation for college or training of the mind. It was nearly twenty years before purposes or objectives as we know them were stated. Educational psychologists began to raise serious doubts about the claims of faculty psychology. Sociologists began to stress the needs of society. Educational philosophers believed that the needs of children and youth should be given priority in teaching. At first, educational objectives were based upon analyses of the activities of adults. Later, objectives were stated in terms of meeting the needs of students in school. Educators themselves were often split into two camps: the "essentialists," who subscribed to preparation for adult life, and the "progressives," who stressed the interests and needs of children and youth. Since 1950, an attempt has been made to harmonize these two approaches to the derivation of educational objectives. Today, many factors are considered necessary in the selection of objectives. Most important are analyses of students, contemporary society, and the learning process. Other considerations include expert opinion; *local* tradition, courses, personalities, and vested interests; and accrediting agencies (1:358–359, 573).

Objectives: Theoretical or Practical?

The relationship of objectives to assigned learning activities determines the effectiveness of learning. It is at this point that the sharpest cleavage between theory and practice probably exists. Certainly no teacher in his preservice experience today has not had impressed upon him the importance of objectives. Yet, how often the relationship between stated objectives and what takes place in the classroom is purely incidental! Objectives serve for ornament, not for use. Why is this the case? There are probably several reasons.

The nonfunctional nature of educational objectives may actually be the product of preservice preparation of teachers. Repeated exposure to classical statements of objectives (the seven "Cardinal Principles of Secondary Education," the ten "imperative needs of youth of secondary-school age," and so on) can lead to familiarity or even contempt. This is especially true when the teacher in training is exposed to much theory without concurrent practical experience in the classroom. Vague, general statements of expected outcomes which sometimes appear in a teacher's plans lend further support to the useless character of objectives. Plans which include too many objectives too broadly stated serve as another deterrent to commitment to stated objectives. Despite repeated efforts to involve the total college faculty in the program of teacher education, students in training are often confused by conflicting purposes. In academic courses, stress may be placed upon mastery of subject matter; in professional courses, meeting the needs of students may be the point of emphasis. Furthermore, it is quite possible that the prospective teacher may never become aware of the fact that the purposes of the high school, as well as the type of students to be served, are by no means identical with those of the college.

Criteria for Objectives

The foregoing discussion clearly indicates the need for definite criteria for judging the value of stated objectives if they are to be functional.

First of all, expected outcomes must represent goals which are understood and accepted by the teacher and his students. It is a mistake to assume that teacher and student goals are identical. Frequently they are not. Teacher-imposed objectives are likely to be primarily concerned with remote social goals and preparation for adult life, whereas students are concerned with their own immediate problems and needs. A major difficulty in teaching is how to reconcile the goals of the teacher with those of his students and to secure genuine motivation for learning. In some way, the demands of adult society must be reconciled with the here-and-now concerns of youth. When unit goals have finally been formulated, they should represent statements which students have either helped formulate or have accepted as being worthwhile as far as they are personally concerned.

Objectives Must Be Achievable

It is futile for the teacher to set up idealistic, unattainable goals. The maturity and experience of the class, available resources and feasible learning activities, the complexity of the topic or problem under consideration, and the competence of the teacher—all of these are factors which determine whether or not a given set of objectives is achievable. It is a mistake to gear instruction below the maturity and achievement level of the students or to set the level of instruction beyond student attainment. The subject of social studies offers a good example. On the one hand, it is no longer considered advisable to limit classroom experiences of pupils in lower grades to a study of the local environment. Increasing opportunities for travel and rapid developments in communication, especially television, have expanded the horizons of even first graders to include the world, as well as outer space. On the other hand, a group of immature junior high school students may be wrestling with a problem that confounds the experts. For example, what conclusions might a teacher and his class reach with respect to a protective tariff, American foreign policy, and membership in the United Nations in relation to national interest? Aside from being controversial, the end result of such discussions may very well be a superficial grasp of a complex problem, or, what is worse, misunderstanding between the teacher and the parents of his students.

Objectives Must Provide for Diversity

Committed to the task of educating all boys and girls of secondary school age, our schools must meet the needs of students who exhibit great diversity of interests, abilities, and backgrounds. As the new teacher gains enough experience to engage in a higher level of instructional planning, his first consideration should be to provide for individual differences. The practice of grouping students according to ability and achievement into so-called homogeneous groups is becoming quite common. However, the teacher needs to keep in mind several things about grouping practices: Many classes are still grouped on a heterogeneous basis; there is never such a thing as a truly homogeneous group; and, finally, there is conflicting evidence concerning the effectiveness of so-called homogeneous grouping. Consequently, the teacher in the classroom can never escape responsibility for individualizing instruction in order to meet the needs of all of his students. Such provision for individual differences must be included in both daily and unit planning.

Objectives Must Be Both Personal and Social

Any nation that establishes and supports schools has a right to demand that education be socially useful. The schools are obligated to develop good citizens, as defined by the state. At the same time, a state such as ours demands the highest development of the unique qualities of each individual citizen. Thus, a precise balance between education for uniformity and education for diversity must be maintained. Psychologically, educational objectives must become personal goals for the student. Otherwise no real learning occurs.

Objectives Must Be Susceptible to Evaluation

As a teacher lists his unit objectives, he should consider the kind of evidence he will need to evaluate student achievement in each one. Of course, both formal means (such as tests) and informal means (such as teacher observations) may be used to gather data for evaluation. In listing objectives, the teacher may very well visualize unit development in its entirety: setting up goals, selection of appropriate materials and activities to achieve expected outcomes, and choice of procedures whereby the teacher and his students may evaluate their achievement of unit objectives. A more thorough discussion of the evaluation of objectives follows in Chapter 15.

Objectives Need to Be Properly Stated

Objectives to be achieved in the classroom must be stated in specific terms. Although the same ultimate goals may be attained, a distinction between the purposes of the students and of the teacher often must be made. Objectives should be stated so that they are grammatically consistent. Note the lack of uniformity in the following examples:

To develop understanding of _____
Helping the student develop skill in _____
An appreciation for _____

Objectives should not be confused with activities. Note the following activities which are stated as objectives:

To make a speech on the responsibilities of the citizen
To write an autobiography
To demonstrate the broad jump
To rehearse for a music festival

In the above examples, the stress is on *what* is to be done, not on *why* it should be done.

Above all, objectives need to be stated in terms of desirable changes in student behavior—changes in attitudes, appreciations, understandings, or skills. If behavioral changes are to result in continuous growth toward maturity, students must be able to satisfy basic developmental needs. Some of these are the need to develop independence in thought and action, the need to satisfy intellectual curiosity, and the need to gain social acceptance. The teacher has a responsibility not only for helping students satisfy present needs, but also for making them aware of more remote needs to be met. Once objectives have been stated in terms of desirable changes in behavior in relation to student needs, opportunities must be provided for practicing the desired behaviors, by means of appropriate learning materials and activities in the classroom.

UNIT MATERIALS AND ACTIVITIES

The heart of a unit consists of the learning activities and materials. Most of the teacher's time and effort in preplanning units needs to be devoted to the selection of the best activities and resources available since nine tenths of class time will be spent upon implementing or executing the unit.

Introducing the Unit

Heywood's familiar proverb, "Of a good beginning cometh a good end," has particular relevance to the introductory stage of unit development. First of all, it is important to get the class vitally interested. Like a good advertising manager, the teacher needs to whet the appetites of his customers. In order to do that, he must know both his customers and his product. The launching of a new unit is like the beginning of any other important enterprise. A certain amount of inertia, sometimes resistance, has to be overcome at the outset. Consequently, an appetizing sample or preview of what is to come is always in order in getting a new unit underway. Either extreme is to be avoided in the introduction of a unit: a presentation that overwhelms students in terms of difficulty or an introduction that presents no challenge to the class. A second necessary step in the introductory stage is provision for proper orientation to the unit. Clarification of objectives, definitions of problems, location of resource materials, selection and organization of appropriate activities, and the establishment of scope and sequence of events with a tentative timetable for each task—all need to be done quite early in unit development.

In arousing student interest, the teacher may use any number of approaches. *An appeal to direct experience* is one good way to stimulate class interest. Many a lagging discussion has been revived by a simple question, such as, "How many saw the television program about _____?" or "Did you hear the youth concert last Saturday night?" One new science teacher became quite adept at *personalizing problems* for a group of eighth-grade students of average ability or below. In getting students to understand the stratosphere, he began like this:

Teacher: "Bill, could you fly in the stratosphere in an open cockpit plane?"
Bill: "No."
Teacher: "Why not?"
Bill: "I would freeze to death."
Teacher: "Right. What else might happen to you?"
Bill: "I wouldn't have enough air to breathe."

A primary key to interest is student *involvement*. Sometimes students can be encouraged to share valuable experiences, hobbies, or collections which are related to the unit. Cooperative development of bulletin boards, exhibits, or centers of interest in the classroom also serves to motivate students to attack a new unit with enthusiasm. If the teacher has shown an interest in student activities, the class is more likely to respond to regular class assignments. Other approaches to a new unit which may be used are the following: excursions, resource persons, motion pictures or recordings, or well-chosen selections read to the class.

Research indicates that socioeconomic status, aptitude, and personal needs and values are important factors in the determination of student interests.[4] Different levels of maturity and varied backgrounds of experience also influence the effectiveness of any given approach to unit development as far as the members of a class are concerned.

In the final analysis, the teacher is the key factor in arousing student interest in a new unit. He needs to be imaginative, alive, and sensitive to the concerns of youth. In addition to his personal qualities, the teacher needs a cultural background of depth and breadth to share with his students.

[4] Donald E. Super, "Interests," *Encyclopedia of Educational Research*, 3d ed., Chester W. Harris, ed. New York: The Macmillan Company, 1960, pp. 729–730.

Not only is the introductory phase of the unit a time to stimulate interest and to arouse curiosity, but it is also the place where the direction, or course of action, of the entire unit is established. Some teachers provide the class with duplicated assignment guides or work plans as the last step before actual work is begun on a new unit. It is also helpful to have each student develop a brief, flexible work plan of his own. Such a plan might include proposed activities, committee assignments, readings to be done, and things to be made (4:83).

UNIT DEVELOPMENTAL MATERIALS AND ACTIVITIES

Later chapters will, of course, include more complete discussions of various materials and methods of instruction that the teacher may use. However, as the teacher considers the next stage of unit development, some guidelines for selection of materials and activities need to be indicated at this point.

Just before listing tentative learning activities and materials, the teacher may wish to include an outline of topics or problems to be covered. This provides a skeleton or framework around which learning experiences may be organized.

The first criterion of well-selected unit activities and materials is *variety*. Variety adds spice to the classroom. "A major difficulty in our educational efforts seems to be the progressive loss of interest by students in academic learning activities."[5] The pedantic teacher without imagination who relies on a single source of materials or on the same deadly routine repeated day in and day out is likely to have a dull class on his hands. Since no two students have identical experiences nor the same interests or tastes, variety insures more motivation for more students more of the time. If all students enrolled in today's schools who exhibit such great diversity of talents and abilities are to learn, variety in teaching procedures and materials becomes imperative. This point was stressed under the discussion of objectives. Slow learners need more concrete learning materials, simpler concepts, easier reading materials, and more frequent reviews. On the other hand, gifted students need more complex problems, more opportunity for individual research, and more breadth and depth of content to challenge them.

So often learning experiences in the classroom are limited almost exclusively to those of a verbal nature. The following excerpt from a unit illustrates the use of a variety of types of learning experiences:

[5] Melvin H. Marx, "Motivation," *Encyclopedia of Educational Research*, 3d ed., Chester W. Harris, ed. New York: The Macmillan Company, 1960, p. 898. Used by permission of Macmillan.

UNIT: THE ELIZABETHAN AGE

Activities: (Covering the subunit on Shakespeare's *Macbeth*)

1. In class, read and record Shakespeare's *Macbeth*, Inglis, pp. 136–199. Structure of the play and the characterization of Macbeth and Lady Macbeth should be discussed after each act.
2. Listen to the recording of *Macbeth* by the Old Vic company and compare with tape recording of students' interpretation.
3. See the following films: *English Inns* (to show how they were used as theaters); *Memories of Shakespeare* (to learn more about Shakespeare the man); and *Elizabethan Literature* (for a summary of literary types and of information about great writers of the period).
4. Outside of class, students are to read a second Shakespearean play, choosing one of the following: *Hamlet, Romeo and Juilet, Julius Caesar, Twelfth Night,* or *The Tempest*.
5. The class will divide into groups, according to the play read outside class, and conduct a panel discussion on the respective plays, following the study guide for Shakespearean plays (provided by the teacher). Selected passages are also to be read to the class.
6. Car pools are to be arranged for those who wish to see Laurence Olivier's version of *Henry V*, to be shown free on November 18 at Russ Auditorium.
7. Students will also be encouraged to see the film version of *Romeo and Juliet*, sponsored by the University of California Extension, to be shown on December 1.
8. *Macbeth* will be televised on Sunday, November 20. Students should not miss this.

(Used by special permission of Joan Knight, graduate student.)

Every student must learn in the way that is most appropriate to him— by observing, demonstrating, speaking, listening, writing, drawing, experimenting, thinking, and feeling. Consequently, provision for a variety of learning experiences in the classroom is imperative.

The raw materials of a unit may be classified according to four levels of abstraction: symbolic, pictorial, manipulative, and related to reality. These abstractions range from concrete sensory experiences to printed materials, scientific formulae, or musical scores.[6] How far a student can delve into the mysteries of abstractions depends on his academic aptitude. How far a student should pursue these abstractions is another matter. Some educators are insisting that all students should pursue an academic program of solid subjects because it has been discovered that students of lower ability can learn more than was once believed if they are skillfully taught. However, the question as to what is best for students who

[6] Fred P. Barnes, "Using the Materials of Learning," *NEA Journal*, vol. 50 (September 1961), pp. 54–56.

may be underprivileged culturally, economically, intellectually, and emotionally has not yet been satisfactorily answered.

In selecting the most effective learning activities for a unit, the teacher needs to *stress action toward desirable goals* as a second criterion. *What students do determines what they learn.* They may talk or read about good health, appreciation of better music, or how to build a boat; but, unless they practice good health, listen to good music, or actually build a boat, learning is likely to be a superficial thing. Mere verbalization about or contemplation of real experience has, no doubt, accounted for disappointing results in formal education. It is unfortunate that the word "activity" has a bad connotation for some people. Properly defined and understood, activity is relevant to learning in three ways: Learning is an active process. No one learns except by his own activity. Second, learning activity may vary from an abstract process (solving a problem in mathematics) to a simple skill (sawing a board on a straight line). Finally, no learning activity can be divorced from content or subject matter.

As a third criterion for the use of better unit activities and materials, the teacher should *build upon as much first-hand experience as possible.* Although limitation of time and space make it necessary to depend upon much vicarious experience and symbolic material in the classroom, there is no substitute for direct experience as the foundation for all abstract learning and as a means of making learning more vivid and permanent. Something vital is missing from the classroom when students read about paper making without visiting the nearby paper mill; when students discuss flowers and draw pictures of them from a book without picking and identifying the parts of the flowers growing on the school grounds; or when students talk about Indian culture without visiting the local museum housing an excellent collection of Indian artifacts. In progressing from concrete materials to effective use of symbolization, the student has to be guided through a series of gradual steps from the reality level (field trips, interviews, and so on), to the use of manipulative materials (exhibits, bulletin boards, specimens, models), to the use of pictorial materials, and finally to the abstract level or use of symbolic materials.[7]

CULMINATING ACTIVITIES OF THE UNIT

Culminating activities have already been discussed briefly. A unit may or may not include this phase of development as a separate category. When activities are included which present the highlights of the unit (by means of reports, exhibits, or assembly program), they should not rehash

7 *Ibid.,* pp. 54-58.

the entire unit, interrupt the continuity from one unit to another, include unit tests, nor be dragged in as an afterthought after the unit has already served its purpose (2:368). The teacher does well in encouraging students to share interesting discoveries or significant products of research with their classmates, but he should protect the class from the boredom occasioned by a series of uninspired oral reports. If reports are given, they should be informative, interesting, and varied in type of presentation.

UNIT EVALUATON

Since evaluation has already been mentioned briefly and is discussed thoroughly in Chapters 15 through 18, only a few principles or guidelines will be stressed here. Although "evaluation" appears as the last heading in unit structure, this does not mean that evaluation occurs only at the conclusion of a unit. Evaluation is *continuous*. This is important for two reasons: By securing evidence of student progress continuously, the teacher is more able to make readjustments in learning activities as needed and to provide for a higher degree of student motivation (1:896, 857). Evaluation should employ a variety of data-gathering instruments. This recognizes both the diversity of unit goals and the different ways in which students may make progress toward those goals. Traditionally, oral and written tests have been the chief instruments for measuring student progress while achievement in subject matter has been the major goal. In addition to using the results of written tests (oral testing has largely disappeared with the passing of the formal recitation), teachers now use data from observations, sociograms, behavioral check lists, anecdotal records, and interest inventories to secure a more comprehensive picture of student development.

The criteria and procedures for evaluation need to be stated in terms that are *definite, clear,* and *acceptable* (to the student and to the school). In some classes, where much of the activity consists of work on individual projects, it is not uncommon for the teacher to assign "A," "B," and so on to finished products in what appears to be a nebulous or capricious fashion. Before work on a unit begins, students have a right to know what criteria and procedures are to be used in evaluating their work. If the procedure is based almost exclusively on teacher judgment, then students must clearly understand what criteria the teacher will use and the approximate weight assigned to each criterion. Such specificity in evaluation is illustrated in the following excerpt from a unit plan:

Evaluation:
1. A test (50 percent objective, 50 percent essay) on the Elizabethan theater and *Macbeth* (weight—50 percent).

2. Students' panel discussion of Shakespearean play read outside class (weight —20 percent).
3. Grade on the compositions: "The Passionate Teen-ager to His Love" and "The Girl's Reply" (weight—10 percent).
4. Short papers written in class, based on one of the following series of questions:
   a. What is the theme of the second Shakespearean play you read? How does it affect you personally? Does it sharpen your insights into human motives and desires? Discuss, citing pertinent passages from the play.
   b. How does Shakespeare reveal the character of the hero or heroine in the second play you read? What are the ways a playwright can reveal character? Which of these ways or devices does Shakespeare use? Does this character seem real to you? Why or why not? (weight—20 percent).

(Used by special permission of Joan Knight, graduate student.)

In conclusion, it needs to be re-emphasized that the primary purpose of evaluation in the classroom is the improvement of learning and instruction. When both teacher and students are informed concerning progress toward accepted goals, the students are more highly motivated, and the teacher is better able to provide remedial instruction where needed, as well as correct his own limitations as a teacher.

Daily planning, the third and final aspect of instructional planning to be considered, is discussed in the following chapter.

Selected Readings

1. American Educational Research Association, *Encyclopedia of Educational Research,* 3d ed., Chester W. Harris, ed. New York: The Macmillan Company, 1960.
2. Burton, William H., *The Guidance of Learning Activities,* 3d ed. New York: Appleton-Century-Crofts, 1962. Chapters 13, 14, 15.
3. Carter, William L., Carl W. Hansen, and Margaret G. McKim, *Learning to Teach in the Secondary School.* New York: The Macmillan Company, 1962.
4. Clark, Leonard H., and Irving S. Starr, *Secondary School Teaching Methods.* New York: The Macmillan Company, 1961. Chapter 5.
5. Grambs, Jean D., William J. Iverson, and Franklin K. Patterson, *Modern Methods in Secondary Education,* revised ed. New York: Holt, Rinehart and Winston, Inc., 1958. Chapter 6.
6. McKean, Robert C., *Principles and Methods in Secondary Education.* Columbus, Ohio: Charles E. Merrill Books, Inc., 1962. Chapter 5.
7. Risk, Thomas M., *Principles and Practices of Teaching in Secondary Schools,* 3rd ed. New York: American Book Company, 1958. Chapters 8, 9, 11.
8. Rivlin, Harry N., *Teaching Adolescents in Secondary Schools,* 2d. ed. New York: Appleton-Century-Crofts, 1961. Chapter 4.
9. The Yearbook Committee, "Individualizing Instruction," *Sixty-first Yearbook of the National Society for the Study of Education, Part I.* Chicago: The University of Chicago Press, 1962.

CHAPTER 5

Daily planning

Our time is all today—*James Montgomery*

What a teacher does *before* he enters the classroom determines the success of the work for the day. Class activities may be based on an isolated assignment or on a long-range unit, but a daily plan is still a necessity. Ideally, students should be able to spend their time on comprehensive assignments, covering a relatively long period of time, without any loss of continuity. Practically, the work must be broken up into daily blocks of time, ranging from fifty minutes to two hours. There are decisions to be made, progress reports to be given, and difficulties to be overcome. All these require careful organization. While progress toward the culmination of a unit may require weeks of research by individuals and small groups, it is in the daily class period that the unit unfolds. Organization of the class, cooperative development of a work plan, reports on research findings, evaluation—these are but a few of the kinds of activities which must take place within the framework of the daily class period. Without careful daily planning, there is likely to be much wasted time, chaos, and frustration for all concerned.

Since the unit concept is not always clearly understood, and some supervisors do not practice unit teaching themselves, it is often advisable for new teachers to begin by developing well-organized daily plans before attempting to develop the more difficult unit plan.

As a prerequisite to effective daily planning, the teacher needs to know his students, as was discussed at length in Chapter 1; his subject and its potential contribution to the goals of education; his best sources of materials; the activities that are most appropriate; and the physical facilities of the school. Flexible arrangement of classroom furniture can be helpful in the development of a desirable atmosphere for learning. Because of large classes and immovable furniture in some schools, the most appropriate learning activities are sometimes difficult to achieve. Inasmuch as secondary teachers often have to share classrooms with other teachers, use of chalkboards and bulletin boards becomes a problem. In selecting learning activities and materials, the teacher needs to be governed by such criteria as contribution to objectives, economy (in terms of cost, time, and energy expended), and usability (in relation to the maturity, ability, and backgrounds of the students).

Like the unit plan, the daily plan consists of four minimum essentials: objectives, materials, activities, and evaluation. In structure, too, the daily plan may be similar, either in outline or columnar (parallel) form. Columnar structure may vary in categories as long as the minimum essentials are included. For example the columnar portion of the daily plan may look like this:

| *Approximate Time* | *Expected Outcomes* | *Activities* *(Teacher and Students)* | *Materials* |

or this:

| *Time Limits* | *Specific Objectives* | *Activities and Materials* *Teacher* *Students* | *Evaluation* |

or this:

| *Time* | *Activities (Teacher and Students)* | *Resources* |

Because they are learning how to plan for instruction and are usually teaching under close supervision, new teachers are advised to develop complete *written* plans. They may find it a timesaver to construct a format, similar to the one for the lesson plan below, duplicate it, and fill in the content for each daily plan as needed.

DEVELOPMENT OF THE LESSON PLAN

Now that the minimum essentials and structural organization of the daily lesson plan have been briefly outlined, a more thorough analysis of each step the teacher takes in developing a lesson is needed.

DAILY LESSON PLAN
(Format for Columnar Type)

Teacher: *Date:*

Subject and Grade: *Unit:*

Reminders: (Announcements, check on physical environment, administrative details—attendance, and so on, special preparation of room or equipment for lesson.)

Specific Objectives (or *Expected Outcomes*):	Evaluation: (Procedures to be used in assessing student achievement of each objective).
1.	1. (A test, for example)
2.	2. (Observation, for example)
3.	3.

(The columnar structure which follows indicates, in sequential order, everything the teacher and students *do* to achieve the specific objectives listed above.)

Approximate Time   Teacher Activities   Student Activities   Materials

Assignment: (Answers specific questions of *why, what, how, when*)

Postanalysis: (The teacher should take fifteen to twenty minutes as soon as possible after completion of the lesson to do this. It may be recorded on the back of the plan.)

Specific Objectives or Expected Outcomes

Various types of objectives, ranging from the general objectives of education to specific objectives of a daily lesson plan, have been discussed in Chapter 4. The daily plan should include only specific objectives or purposes, stated in very precise terms. For example: Students are to demonstrate ability to use correctly troublesome words which are similar in sound, spelling, or meaning (such as "principal" and "principle," "affect" and "effect," and so on). This is an appropriate objective for a daily lesson plan. Statements such as "To improve communication skills" or "To develop skills in the fundamental processes" represent broad goals of education but are not specific enough for a daily plan.

As stated before, specific objectives should be achievable, acceptable by all concerned, and subject to evaluation. Although achievement of some specific objectives may extend beyond the limits of a single class period, the teacher is advised against setting up expected outcomes that are too remote or attempting to achieve too many specific purposes in one class period. It is better to do a few things well than to gain a superficial understanding of much. In deciding on objectives for a daily plan, the teacher is cautioned against confusing either activities or subject matter with expected outcomes. Both are *means* to an end, the improvement of student behavior (thinking, feeling, and acting). Not only should expected outcomes be expressed in terms of improved behavior, but they must also be stated in terms which have meaning and value for students here and now. At the same time, specific objectives must contribute to significant goals of the society which supports the school.

The approach of a subject matter expert to a topic or problem is often quite different from that of the student. The historian may be concerned with the causes of the Civil War; the grammarian may be concerned with language structure and terminology; or the physiologist may consider any-one illiterate who cannot name the bones of the body. But the teacher must constantly ask himself, "What relevance do these facts have for the adolescent of the twentieth century?" (Or, for that matter, in achieving the goals of society.) MacLeish makes the shrewd observation that the teaching of English

always stands with a foot in the text and a foot in the world. . . . The greatest poem, removed from the ground of our being, is an irrelevance. The ground of our being without the poem is a desert.[1]

Time is too short to waste in doing meaningless exercises or in memorizing a miscellaneous hodgepodge of facts.

Introduction to the Daily Lesson

The beginning of a lesson sets the tone for the entire class period. Motivation, provision for continuity, clearly defined goals, effective organization—all must be established at the outset.

To stimulate interest, the teacher may use any number of approaches, such as: raising provocative questions, telling an interesting anecdote, giving a brief demonstration, asking students to share some of their experiences. These are but a few of the ways to introduce a lesson effectively. At the other extreme, the unimaginative teacher begins by attempting to conduct a formal recitation over "the next ten pages" assigned in the textbook. Without an "icebreaker" to precede the body of the lesson, the net result is likely to be an unresponsive class and a frustrated teacher.

Timing the Lesson

Since the typical school day is cut up into segments or class periods of less than one hour each, a teacher has to make the most of the time he has with each group of students. Lesson plan structure, illustrated before, includes a column for approximate time limits for each activity. While such limits must always remain flexible, they do help in the conservation of valuable time.

Poor timing can result in a number of problems. Some teachers fail to get the class underway promptly or leave five minutes or so at the end of the period as an unorganized, socializing activity. Such practice is a breeder of discipline problems and a waste of the students' time. Beginning teachers often experience the embarrassment of completing a lesson fifteen or twenty minutes before the end of the class period. Being panicky, talking too much and too fast, and failing to stimulate student questions or responses, the novice races through his lesson. One new

[1] Archibald MacLeish, "What Is English?" *Saturday Review*, December 9, 1961, p. 14.

teacher taught five lessons in one day and expressed the fear that he was going to finish the course during the first week. One solution to the problem of using class time profitably is for the teacher to plan more than he thinks the class will be able to do for the day. It is also advisable for the teacher to have one or two spare lessons tucked away in his desk for use when, because of poor class attendance, for example, a deviation from the scheduled lesson is better. At the other extreme of timing is the teacher who progresses at such a leisurely pace or pursues so many side lines that the final bell rings with most of the important aspects of the lesson not completed. Teachers often remark, "My students ask so many questions, I am unable to cover any ground." When students are interested enough to ask relevant questions, any teacher should be delighted, not frustrated. On the other hand, a teacher does have to guard against being side-tracked by peripheral questions, futile debate, or even delaying tactics. Then, too, the teacher is the only one who has the perspective for determining how much emphasis to give to each aspect of a course for a given term or semester. Thus, any well-organized beginning teacher needs to have a time budget for the daily lesson, to glance at it occasionally if necessary, and to decide how closely he should adhere to his schedule. Through experience, most teachers develop a time sense that makes a formal schedule unnecessary.

To conclude a lesson just as the dismissal bell rings is an art which not all teachers are able to achieve. Consequently, it is advisable to plan an "elastic ending" (7:163). A teacher may have in reserve a number of alternative activities of short duration, such as recordings, short selected readings, or critiques of class work. It is futile to assign a five-minute study period or to attempt to begin work on an activity of extended duration when little time remains. The elastic ending is, however, designed to achieve expected outcomes of the daily lesson, not to kill time.

Lesson Activities and Materials

Like the unit plan, the very heart of a lesson plan consists of learning activities and materials, the "how" and the "what" for achievement of objectives. It is best to keep lesson plan structure as simple as possible for ready reference. Usually a single sheet of 8½- by 11-inch loose-leaf notebook paper will suffice. However, most lesson plans are not complete unless they include material on additional cards or pages. By way of elaboration on this point, a *discussion* should always be based on a few key questions prepared in advance. Questions which are made up on the spur of the moment are often poorly worded and lacking in significance. Furthermore, if the teacher is not sure of his subject matter, he should jot down important facts to refresh his memory. A *demonstration* should include an outline of step-by-step procedures, to insure completeness and continuity of the presentation, and suggestions for follow-up with the class. At the outset, it is well to list the materials needed before the demonstration begins. *Audio-visual presentations* should include teacher preparation, class preparation, effective presentation, and follow-up activities. Unless all of the above suggestions are included on supplementary notes (preferably 3- by 5-inch cards) attached to the basic lesson plan, the lesson for the day is likely to be inadequate.

The Assignment

The assignment, whether for a day or on a long-range basis, is a critical phase of the teaching-learning process. A common source of teacher irritation is an inadequately prepared assignment or one which students have not done at all. How often a well-planned discussion fails miserably because the class has not studied the assignment or has read it without understanding!

A generation ago, school periods were lengthened with the hope that assignments might be prepared in class under the direct supervision of the teacher. But teachers have failed to budget class time well, often using the study period for lecture. Then, too, the school day is so short and there is so much to do, it has become necessary to have students make considerable preparation outside the class period. This brings up the subject of homework, discussed at length in another section of this chapter.

An effective assignment is one that is designed to achieve at least two objectives: to contribute to the achievement of specific objectives of the lesson plan and to motivate students to learn with a minimum of coercion (7:169). Why are these goals not always realized? The teacher would do well to make a careful analysis of his assignments. Do they provide a challenge for bright students or constitute mere busy work? To assign an able student more problems of the type that he has already mastered is a test of endurance, not learning. Are assigned tasks beyond the capabilities of slow learners? Are assignments so vague or permissive as not to be taken seriously? Is stress placed upon the memorization of unrelated facts or upon mastery of significant concepts or ideas? Too often, not enough time and thought are given to the assignment. Such an assignment as, "Take the next ten pages in the text," is a typical example. *"It would be difficult to devise an educational practice so grossly ineffective, so certainly calculated to interfere with learning, as a page assignment to a single text followed by a formal verbal quiz."*[2] Since the teacher is re-

---

[2] William H. Burton, *The Guidance of Learning Activities,* 3d ed. New York, Appleton-Century-Crofts, 1962, p. 290.

sponsible for the assignment, he is the only one who can correct its inadequacies.

What are the characteristics of a good assignment? At least four questions need to be answered for the student: What is to be done? How is it to be done? Why is it to be done? When is it due? Sometimes the question is raised: When is the best time to make an assignment? The best assignments develop naturally from ongoing class activities. Logically, an assignment should be given just prior to the time to begin work upon it. Certainly the worst time to make an assignment is at the time the bell rings ending the class period. Teachers frequently make assignments orally. It is recommended that short assignments also be written on the chalkboard and long assignments be duplicated for each member of the class.

Because it is often difficult to relate formally organized subject matter to the here-and-now concerns of youth, the alert teacher seizes every opportunity to relate the subject to current issues or problems of general interest. Whenever possible, assignments are made with reference to previous experiences, interests, and everyday concerns of boys and girls. In addition to general information about his class, both as individuals and as a group, the teacher also needs to know what information and attitudes students have with respect to the particular subject for study. Such information may be secured by means of pretests, class discussions, personal interviews, autobiographies, questionnaires, and check lists. Inasmuch as a wide range of individual differences exists within any class, even when homogeneously grouped, individualized assignments are always necessary. This has sometimes been accomplished by means of a minimum, basic assignment for the class as a whole with enrichment materials provided for average and bright students. The teacher who provides such "extra-credit" assignments, especially for gifted students, must make sure that they are not just more of the same. Enriched assignments should provide greater depth and breadth of understanding. Perhaps a better approach to differentiated assignments is provision for a variety of learning activities and materials so that students have several avenues, not just one, for achieving expected outcomes.

Even a single assignment in a heterogeneous class can be differentiated in terms of the *level* of understanding expected of students of different ability. For example, suppose a class in English, which is analyzing exercises in the correct use of verbs, comes across this sentence: "The boys had (gone, went) downtown." The very slow learner may be able to make the correct choice of "gone" only because he has been habituated to the correct usage until it sounds right to him. A more able student should be able to decide that "gone" is correct because the past participle must be

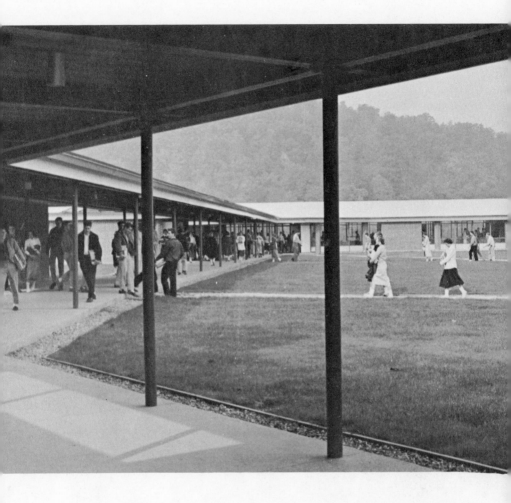

At high schools all over this nation, like the Horace Greeley High School in Chappaqua, N. Y., future statesmen, scientists, artists, craftsmen, and humanitarians are being prepared for their work. They are acquiring the basic attitudes habits, skills, appreciations, and facts that will go a long way toward setting the pattern of society for a generation. It is up to teachers to meet these young people as they are, and to provide a climate for growth and development. [*Suter, Hedrich-Blessing and Perkins & Will, Architects-Engineers.*]

When students are engaged in school activities that are important to them, very few discipline problems are likely to arise. The development of skills required in a future vocation or the personal satisfaction derived from the creation of individual projects are two worthy goals of youth that may be achieved in the school shop. A laboratory or shop, such as the one at the Butler (Pa.) Area Senior High School, provides excellent opportunities for the development of good citizenship habits and attitudes. Maintenance of a clean and orderly shop, observance of safety rules, and the students' assumption of responsibility for good working conditions all contribute to a wholesome learning environment. [*Joseph W. Molitor and Perkins & Will, Architects-Engineers, in association with Howard, Burt, and Hill, Architects.*]

A modern high school library still performs its function as a storehouse for information. In addition, it has undergone a change in appearance and adaptability. In the modern library shown here, waist-high bookshelves have replaced ceiling-high shelves, comfortable upholstered chairs can be seen in the middle room, and newspapers are racked neatly in accessible pieces of furniture. Book jackets and illustrations add interest to the room. High school students are taught to use the card files and the open shelves to find their reference materials. Good artificial lighting and acoustical ceiling and floor coverings add to the peaceful and dignified library environment. [*Bill Engdahl, Hedrich-Blessing.*]

Teachers can usually handle their own discipline problems. However, even a good teacher sometimes needs help with classroom control. At such times the teacher may turn to the school principal. Below, an apprehensive pupil awaits a conference with the principal. [*Eastman Kodak Co., from the Kodak High School Photo Awards.*]

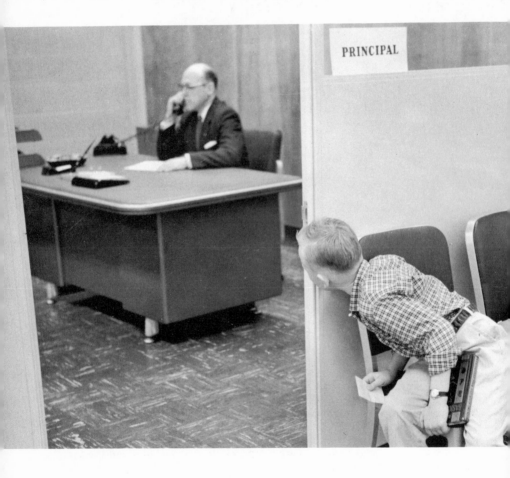

used with the helping verb "had." The college-bound student may be expected to go a step further in analyzing the sentence by indicating that the tense or time is past perfect, or action having been completed in the past.

Sometimes students do not know how to do an assignment. It is now common practice for teachers to provide study guides, to conduct lessons on how to study or read a book, to provide orientation on effective use of the library, and to use other aids to promote better study habits.

The following is an example of a study guide used in poetry:

A STUDY GUIDE FOR POETRY

1. What is the poet trying to do?
   a. To express a thought?
   b. To convey a mood?
   c. To sing a song?
   d. To rid himself of an emotion?
   e. To grasp and communicate an experience?
2. How is he going about it?
   a. What does the poem mean?
   b. What is its meter?
   c. What elements of harmony and melody appear in the poem (pauses, changes of speed, rhyme scheme, special devices—alliteration, onomatopoeia, and so on)?
   d. What is the poem's discoverable symbolism?
   e. What is the poem's prevailing tone (gay, melancholy, bitter, and so forth)?
   f. What memorable images are there (appeals to the senses)?
3. Was the poem worth doing?
   a. Is it fresh or tired?
   b. Is it too trivial or too solemn?
   c. Is it too obscure?
4. What is the psychological significance of the poem? (Or, what kind of person was the poet?)
   a. As reflected in the poem itself?
   b. As having indirectly made the poem possible?
   c. As having more directly predisposed him to write it? (For example, what moved, angered, or soured him? What does he believe in? Does his poetry reflect an obsession or persistent preoccupation?)
5. What is the personal significance of the poem, (that is, to me as a reader)?
   a. Can I be specific about the nature of my pleasure or distaste?
   b. Can I justify my pleasure or displeasure in terms of what there is in the poem, corroborated, of course, by my own emotional and intellectual experience?

c. Can I put my finger on any irrelevant reasons why I like or do not like the poem (my beliefs, temperament, and so on)?

(Used by permission of Joan Knight, student teacher.)

To insure better motivation and more effective learning, teachers today are making more use of student assistance in setting up projects, planning attacks on problems, and in organizing discussions of vital issues (for example, panels, symposiums). Research indicates that most assignments are still teacher dominated, however, with only one type of assignment typically made. Yet students dislike either laissez-faire or authoritative assignments and prefer those which are made on the basis of teacher-student planning (1:855-856). Older types of assignments stressed chapters, pages, and topics in textbooks, given authoritatively with little or no consideration for student interests, needs, and abilities. Newer types of assignments are based on units, varied activities and materials, problems, and projects with an emphasis on student motivation and involvement.

By way of summary, *a good assignment* is based on the following criteria:

1. Specific objectives are clearly stated.
2. A connection between subject matter and student needs, interests, and needs is established.
3. Outcomes which serve the purposes of our society are included.
4. Study guides and other useful aids are provided.
5. A great variety of learning activities and materials is included to provide for individual differences.
6. Guidance toward satisfactory completion of units of work, covering substantial periods of time, is assured.
7. Considerable time, thought, and energy go into the preparation of the assignment.
8. Students are involved in the development of assignments.
9. Either measurable or observable evidence of student achievement is provided each day.[3]

Homework

Assignments naturally bring up the subject of homework. Today there are increasing demands for more homework. Conant recommends a minimum of fifteen hours of homework per week for academically talented students in grades nine to twelve.[4] Illogical comparisons of American

[3] *Ibid.*, pp. 295-296. An adaptation and condensation.
[4] James B. Conant, *The American High School Today.* New York: McGraw-Hill Book Company, Inc., 1959, p. 57. Used by permission of the author and of McGraw-Hill.

education with education in other cultures, and charges that our youth are soft, sometimes delinquent, and often nonintellectual have appeared in the press, resulting in agitation for more homework. Ironically enough, despite the tendency to increase leisure time for adults, there is insistent pressure to lengthen the school day and the school year and to increase homework for youth. Some voices, like that of anthropologist Margaret Mead, have been raised in protest against pressures which would rob children of their childhood and youth.[5]

Crash programs in education have been based on unexamined and unproved assumptions. Widespread acceptance of increased homework, grouping, and mass instruction by schools, to name a few current trends, have been made on the basis of little research or without reference to known findings of research. What does research have to say about homework? First of all, opinions and practices ranging from no homework to excessive amounts differ widely. Variations occur "among schools, among classes in the same school, and among individuals in the same class."[6] It thus appears that uniformity in homework assignments is neither desirable nor practicable. A more serious question is raised concerning the effectiveness of home study assignments, for increased student achievement is the only justification for such assignments. What relationship between homework and scholastic success is indicated by experimental studies? *The results are inconclusive.*[7] Before becoming zealots of homework assignments, teachers and administrators are advised to study not only the findings of research but also to consider the problems related to home study assignments. If and when such assignments are made, certain conditions need to be set up to realize maximum values of such practice.

Homework Assignments—Problems and Recommendations

The first problem of homework is one of definition. Some teachers who keep students after school to do assigned work or assign book reports to be prepared outside of class maintain that they require no homework.[8] For a long time teachers have known that parents do their children's homework or that students copy the work of others. There is evidence that the incidence of copying increases as students progress to higher

[5] Margaret Mead, "Are We Squeezing Out Adolescence?" *National Parent–Teacher,* vol. 40 (September 1960), pp. 4–6.
[6] Ruth M. Strang, "Homework and Guided Study," *Encyclopedia of Educational Research,* 3d ed., Chester W. Harris, ed. New York: The Macmillan Company, 1960, p. 677. Used by permission of Macmillan.
[7] *Ibid.,* p. 678.
[8] Lloyd McCleary, "Homework," *Educational Leadership,* vol. 17 (January 1960), pp. 217–218.

levels with most of them experiencing no guilty feelings about the practice.[9] This brings up the problem of evaluation of homework. Obviously, the teacher who spends hours of drudgery each week in reading and scoring homework assignments is merely accumulating unreliable evidence of student progress. Whenever possible, homework assignments should be checked by students themselves. If the teacher desires evidence of completion of homework, he may quickly check written exercises, without grading them, or give a short quiz over the assignment. The best evidence of achievement for grading purposes is secured by a comprehensive test on the material, prepared and scored by the teacher.

Although not easily documented, it has often been contended that the pressure of excessive homework has been detrimental to health. Even in Russia, where everyone seems to have so much zeal for education, doctors have warned that the intense pressures of the educational system are proving detrimental to children. Certainly, home study assignments have often been a source of conflict between parents and their children. Another home problem is that of the difficulty of providing satisfactory conditions for study. Although research is inconclusive concerning the effect of distractions on learning and modern youth may be able to make reasonably adequate adaptations to distraction, students themselves express a preference for study conditions which provide "privacy, quiet, interest in the subject, freedom from worries and competing interests, absence of distracting radio and television programs, effective teaching, and well-spaced and clearly understood assignments."[10] The preceding statement not only indicates student preference but also suggests guidelines for making effective homework assignments. It is obvious that few, if any, students study under such ideal conditions as have just been indicated.

On the basis of considerable accumulated experience and limited research, it does become evident that certain conditions for home study are necessary for effective learning. First of all, administrative regulation of assignments made by various teachers is imperative. Assignments which make excessive demands of the student on certain nights, over week ends, during holidays, or in competition with other activities of youth must be avoided. One solution to the problem is provision for long-range assignments, which allows the student some flexibility in budgeting his time. Another important consideration is the type of home study assignment that is made. Individualized assignments that allow the student some freedom of choice, assignments that the student can do without the teacher's assistance, and assignments that have personal values for the student are

[9] Ruth Strang, *op. cit.*, p. 678.
[10] *Loc. cit.*

much more likely to be successful than assignments that violate these criteria. Assignments that stimulate student initiative and creativity are always in order. On the other hand, blanket assignments, with the same tasks assigned to fast and slow learners, are often done inadequately or not at all. The ideal solution to the problems related to homework would seem to be to have students complete all their preparation at school. An era of lengthened periods and supervised study attempted to eliminate home study problems. But interest in supervised study has declined and research on the effectiveness of such study is not in agreement.[11] Perhaps an increase in the number of school periods, as proposed by Conant (if it does not revive the large, ineffective study halls of the past), may make it possible for students to complete their assignments under better study conditions, under better supervision, and with more adequate facilities.

Use of the School Library

Assignments often involve use of the library. If such assignments are to be effective, the teacher must work closely with the librarian. When the teacher informs the librarian in advance of topics assigned and materials needed for research papers, the librarian is able to make such materials readily available. Assignments of materials which are not in the library, or which are in limited supply, or which are heavily used by other teachers, can be avoided. There is no better place to practice the Golden Rule than in the use of the library. The most materials made accessible to the greatest number of students is the goal. Another fact to be kept in mind by every teacher is that there are students at every grade level who do not know how to use the library. No other person is better qualified than the school librarian to assist in teaching library skills.[12] The teacher should also make use of the resources of public libraries to supplement the facilities of the school.

Evaluation in Lesson Planning

Lesson plan structure, as indicated previously, encourages the teacher to anticipate how he is going to evaluate student progress on each specific objective listed. Also, it is obvious that evaluative activities of the unit, such as tests, will appear in the activities of daily plans. Another type of evaluation which is especially helpful for student teachers or new teachers, who are usually teaching under close supervision, is the postanalysis of the daily lesson plan. It serves two purposes: It enables the teacher to analyze

[11] Ruth Strang, *op. cit.*, p. 679.
[12] Mary Peacock Douglas, "School Library—Classroom Partner," *NEA Journal*, vol. 50 (September 1961), pp. 51–53.

his successes and failures at the end of each lesson and it helps the supervisor to assess the ability of the teacher to analyze his own teaching. As soon as possible after a lesson has been taught, the teacher should take about fifteen minutes to jot down informally answers to such questions as these:

1. What did I do particularly well today? What could I have done better?
2. How well am I taking care of classroom routine and management?
3. What is the status of classroom morale? Are there any potential discipline problems? Do I need help with critical problems?
4. Are all students working to capacity?
5. Am I providing sufficient variety of activities and materials to keep the class interesting? Or do I depend too much on a single activity based on a single source?
6. Do I make provision for individual differences in student interests, needs, and abilities? Do I challenge the gifted and enable slow learners to taste success?
7. Was class tempo good or was it too fast or too slow?
8. Am I gearing instruction to the level of the class (for example, vocabulary or concepts), neither talking down to students nor going beyond their level of comprehension?
9. Am I providing opportunities for students to apply what they learn?
10. What steps can I take to remedy student failure in achievement or in self-control?
11. How do I react to supervision? How can I profit most from supervisory assistance?

SAMPLE LESSON PLANS

Now that all different aspects of the lesson plan have been thoroughly discussed, the reader may find it helpful to study the three following examples of lesson plans which were developed and used by graduate students in their preservice preparation for teaching.

LESSON PLAN ONE

Teacher: Robert Burton   *Subject:* General Science 8

School: O'Farrell Jr. High   *Date:*   May 14, 1962

Unit: The Human Body

Objectives of the Lesson:
1. Orient class to a study of the human body.
2. Provide direction for the study of the new unit.
3. Arouse interest in the unit.

Evaluation:
Evaluation will be done chiefly by observing student reaction and evident interest in the new unit.

Reminders:

Time	Teacher Activity	Student Activity	Materials
3 min.	Check roll, clear absences, and so on.		
5 min.	Ask for current events in science.	Report on current events in science.	
20 min.	Give brief overview of new unit—topics, materials, assignments, and directions for study. Compare human anatomy with that of other animals.	Raise questions and participate in discussion.	Model of human body, human skull, skull of tapir, vertebrae.
15 min.	Lead discussion on various systems of human body, indicating interesting books in school library.	Raise questions and participate in discussion.	Books and book jackets from library.
10 min.	Make assignments for the following week, outlining methods of evaluating the unit.	Raise questions about assignments, tests, and so on.	

Postanalysis: Today's lesson was apparently successful. The use of demonstration pieces, plus a little humor, stimulated interest. As a result, student participation and enthusiasm were very good. Even some of the girls responded today. It is certainly important to arouse interest in order to get the class started on a new reading assignment.

(Used by special permission of Robert Burton.)

LESSON PLAN TWO

Subject: Typing 9   *Date:* October 8, 1958
Teacher: Anne-Marie Shed
Topics: Conditioning, pace writing, skill building, dictation, review of techniques.

Expected Outcomes for the Day:
Students should:
1. Be able to type with progressively higher syllable intensity without stopping or hesitating.
2. Use correct techniques and type at a speed of 13 to 18 wpm.
3. Be more conscious of their own faulty techniques and be more eager to remedy them.
4. Understand the system and the value of self-evaluation.
Method: Review reaches for letters q, v, p, x, and z; stress techniques; and have students use self-evaluation sheets.
Materials: Textbook, pacer, keyboard chart, evaluation sheets, and numbered lists of students.

Time	Teacher Activities	Student Activities
10:25	Write instructions on board; Margin, 20 (12), tab., 5; cond. practice, p. 23, each line 3 times. Check attendance. Assign work to Fr., J. A. and D. Give help to Fr. and J. A. if desired. Set up pacer.	Type conditioning practice.
10:35	Give instructions for finger exercise and for pace writing.	Exercise fingers and do pace writing.
10:45	Assign numbers to students and place numbered sheets on board. Give skill-building instructions: 1. Insert new paper 2. Turn to p. 23, "Skill Building" 3. Type with pacer 4. Increase speed	Follow instructions and type.
11:05	Give instructions for timed writing: Do two 3-minute writings, figure wpm, figure errors and circle them, and hand in copy. Have students mark evaluation sheets.	Do timed writings. Figure and circle errors and hand in copy. Mark evaluation sheets.
11:20	Give instructions for housekeeping.	Take care of housekeeping duties.

Postanalysis: Putting Bill up front was no problem; he was good about it. Having assignments written on the board eliminated the usual buzzing and questions. During the finger exercises, I smiled encouragement at members of the class to which they responded with an eagerness to please. When I explained numbers and symbols, we ran into difficulty. Evidently I did not go into enough detail, for the class seemed confused. As a whole, the class worked well today. There were no discipline problems. In order to improve my future presentations, I must not assume anything, explain everything from the beginning, and ask questions to make sure the students understand.

LESSON PLAN THREE

Subject and grade: United States History II   *Date:* 10–3–1961

Unit: Federalists Launch the New Govern-   *Teacher:* Milton Miller
ment

Expected Outcomes:
Students will be expected to demonstrate through intelligent discussion (later a test):
1. An understanding of how the various governmental departments were set up under Washington.
2. An understanding of the political causes behind the Hamilton-Burr duel—namely, the inadequate system of electing a president and vice-president—eventually leading to the adoption of the Twelfth Amendment.

Time	Teacher Activity	Student Activity	Materials
5 min.	1. Supervise opening exercises.	1. Class president lead flag salute and read bulletin.	1. Flag and bulletin.
15 min.	2. Lead discussion of Washington's admin.: a. What exec. depts. were created by Congress under his administration? b. What courts were provided under the Constitution? c. What did the Judiciary Act of 1789 set up?	2. Participate in discussion.	2. Text: Chap. 7, Sec. 1; study sheets; chalkboard.
20 min.	3. Preview film, asking students to look for reasons behind duel and evidence of Hamilton's consciousness about his undistinguished birth.	3. Students watch for clues brought out in film preview.	3. Film: *Hamilton and Burr Duel.*

Time	Teacher Activity	Student Activity	Materials
5 min.	4. Follow-up discussion of film.	4. Ask and answer questions about film.	
5 min.	5. Put new assignment on board: Chap. 7, Sec. 2 National Bank, taxes and tariffs, and so on.	5. Write assignment in notebooks.	4. Chalkboard.

Postanalysis: Film did not come. However, discussion was successful. The diagram, showing separation of powers and checks and balances, worked very well. Putting assignment on the board gives students definite direction for their reading. I probably should spend more time in discussing the assignment.

Any one of the three plans above may not be entirely flawless, but they do represent practical, workable plans which were used with success by three new teachers.

QUESTIONS AND ANSWERS ON LESSON PLANS

Quite often beginning teachers raise specific questions about requirements for lesson plans. Some of these questions with suggested answers follow.

How long should a lesson plan be? Long enough and complete enough to be of definite help, yet not so detailed as to be confusing. Usually a single page will suffice for the basic plan. The written plan should serve as a simple, ready reference which can be easily read and which will, at the same time, preserve the continuity of the lesson without unnecessary duplication or undesirable omissions. One beginning teacher wrote three or four pages in longhand each day. As a result, he had difficulty using such a plan for ready reference. However, the one-page plan often needs to be supplemented. A discussion period should include well-worded key questions, prepared in advance. If the teacher is not sure of his material, he may also need to jot down pertinent factual information which answers the questions. Quite often it is advisable for the teacher to outline the steps of a demonstration on separate notes or cards. It is sometimes advisable for a teacher to compose a short lecture and review it a number of times so that he can give it effectively without marring his presentation with "uhs" and "wys."

What form of lesson plan is best? There is no one best form. The authors have illustrated types which can be adapted to various subjects. Usually a teacher will find a lesson plan structure he has developed himself more useful than commercially prepared plans.

How much in advance should daily plans be prepared? New teachers or student teachers, who are under close supervision, are advised to prepare plans about a week in advance, so that supervisors can give helpful suggestions before the lessons are taught. No doubt the new teacher will be allowed considerable freedom in his planning, but he should avail himself of as much supervisory assistance as possible in order to avoid costly mistakes.

Should a daily plan be rigidly followed? Never. It is neither possible nor desirable to follow plans without deviation. Unexpected changes in schedules often occur. Sometimes half of the class may be absent because of illness or conflicting activities, thus necessitating a complete shift in plans. Inflexible, teacher-made plans leave no opportunity for students to participate in planning. Studies of teacher behavior have also indicated a lack of responsiveness to student questions and answers. Sensible use of daily plans enables the teacher to make adaptations freely and, at the same time, provides him with the security and organization needed for a well-taught lesson. Beginning teachers often find it helpful to provide a time budget for each activity. This prevents unprofitable deviations, assures a better distribution of class time, provides for more variety, saves time for more important matters, and makes it more likely that planned activities will be completed on schedule.

How can a teacher avoid "busywork" in planning? Daily plans are for use, not to impress supervisors. A new teacher in physical education was asked for his daily plan. After considerable searching, he found it under a pile of other papers in the third drawer of his desk. Unnecessary duplication should be avoided. It has already been suggested that the teacher should develop his own format with appropriate headings which remain unchanged and duplicate this as a basis for all of his plans. In some cases, the same activity, such as a series of speeches in a speech class or a project in an art class, may be continued for a number of days. Obviously, a complete new plan for each day is unnecessary. The first basic plan may be used for a number of days with only minor revisions, such as reminders, special assignments, remedial activities, and daily postevaluations.

Are daily plans always part of a larger unit? Not always. As previously suggested, not all subjects lend themselves readily to effective unit planning. Also many teachers find it advisable to include remedial work on fundamental skills, to review concepts which may not even be a part of the course, or to incorporate special lessons of a timely nature which may bear no relation to the unit for study.

By way of summary, to be sure that the lesson plan includes all of the necessary items, the teacher would do well to refer to the following check list:

1. Orientation: Does the introduction clarify objectives and provide motivation for the day's activities?

2. Discussion: Are key questions listed? Are appropriate illustrations and important facts included?

3. Demonstration: Are the principal steps outlined?

4. Laboratory procedures: Are activities well organized (distribution and collection of materials, work plan, clean up)?

5. Audio-visual presentation: Are all the necessary steps for preparation, presentation, and follow up included?

6. Committee work: Are committees well organized in terms of selection, carefully defined problems, work plans, and methods of presentation of findings?

7. Activities in general: Is a variety provided to meet individual differences in needs, interests, and abilities of students?

8. Materials: Is there variety? Are the best materials provided to achieve objectives? Is each item listed specifically (for example, the text, pages, and exercises assigned; film, title, and description, and so on)?

9. Assignment: Is the assignment complete, answering the questions: why, what, how, and when? Are there modifications to fit the capabilities of fast and slow learners and to appeal to a diversity of interests and backgrounds?

10. Timing: Does the time budget provide for a complete and balanced coverage of the topic or problem for the day?

11. Application: Are opportunities provided for students to practice newly acquired skills, to utilize new knowledge, or to strengthen new insights and appreciations?

12. Evaluation: Are appropriate activities included to determine how well students are achieving expected outcomes? Is a postanalysis included which describes the impressions of the teacher concerning the achievement and behavior of his students and his own performance?

A FINAL WORD ON PLANNING

Three chapters have been devoted to three phases of instructional planning—long range, cooperative, and daily. Plans should always be tentative. The teacher should use them, but never become a slave to them. However, any plans should be done thoroughly and well in advance of their use in the classroom. While each classroom teacher is responsible for his own planning, no teacher today works alone. The classroom of yesterday may have been an academic island, unrelated to other school subjects and activities, poorly articulated with the school above or below, and isolated from community life on the outside. This is no longer the case. The modern teacher has to develop greater skill in working with many people—fellow teachers, administrators, students, parents, and resource persons of the community. Curriculum committees of the past were composed of the "experts." Today, every teacher is involved in planning the total school program. Whereas curriculum committees were at one time composed of teachers of a given subject matter area, now teachers work with teachers of other subjects and other school levels, as well as interested and informed laymen. The development of skill in planning, both on a solitary and a cooperative basis, is a prerequisite to success in teaching.

Selected Readings

1. Alexander, William M., and Paul M. Halvorsen, *Effective Teaching in Secondary Schools.* New York: Holt, Rinehart and Winston, Inc., 1956. Chapter 15.
2. American Educational Research Association, *Encyclopedia of Educational Research,* 3d ed., Chester W. Harris, ed. New York: The Macmillan Company, 1960.
3. Brown, Edwin John, and Arthur Thomas Phelps, *Managing the Classroom,* 2d ed. New York: The Ronald Press Company, 1961. Chapter 12.
4. Brown, Thomas J., *Student Teaching in a Secondary School.* New York: Harper & Row, Publishers, 1960. Chapter 6.
5. Klausmeier, Herbert J., *Teaching in the Secondary School.* New York: Harper & Row, Publishers, 1958. Chapter 6.
6. Risk, Thomas M., *Principles and Practices of Teaching in Secondary Schools,* 3d ed. New York: American Book Company, 1958. Chapter 13.
7. Rivlin, Harry N., *Teaching Adolescents in Secondary Schools,* 2d ed. New York: Appleton-Century-Crofts, 1961. Chapter 5.
8. Woodruff, Asahel D., *Basic Concepts of Teaching.* San Francisco: Chandler Publishing Company, 1961. Chapter 10.

CHAPTER 6

Class organization
for instruction

Jane has just finished her first week of teaching. Friday finds her tired and discouraged. Each of her five classes in ————— High School enrolls from sixteen to twenty-seven students. She feels the need to think over the events of the past week, to take an inventory of what has happened to her and to her students.

Jane desires to do a first-rate job of her first teaching assignment. She is aware of today's need for quality teaching. But, as she looks back over her first week she feels that things have not worked out the way they were supposed to. The students were friendly and cooperative in a social sense, but as to learning, they appear, even at this early date, not to care very much about what happens. Jane shudders to think that this might be the pattern for the year. Wasn't she "cut out to be a teacher?" She had made good grades in college in academic subjects and in education. Is she bright enough to communicate what she knows?

Jane decides to review step by step what has happened during the week. The first-period class was probably the most disheartening of all. At eight o'clock she met twenty-one girls in a general foods class. From school records and from the students themselves she knows that three are seniors, twelve are juniors, and six are sophomores. Two are repeating the course. Socioeconomically, the girls are from what are generally referred to as lower-middle homes.

During the days of orientation at the school before the students arrived, Jane had busily and happily pored over the academic records of her students, as well as the sketchy anecdotal behavior records, health reports, and other data.

Now, Jane is faced with such questions as:

1. Why are these girls taking this course?
2. What is the food problem in their several homes?
3. How can I provide instruction for this group in which interests and abilities vary nearly 180 degrees?
4. How can I tone down some of the brash and aggressive students and build up some of the shy ones?
5. Should I talk to the school nurse about the five girls who show evidence of undernourishment?
6. How can I teach Charlotte and Hetty, whose records indicate unusually high scholastic ability, without talking over the heads of the other girls?
7. From snatches of conversation, I have gathered that most of the girls are "boy crazy"; nearly all are going steady; and probably several are engaged. To what extent should matters of this sort influence planning?
8. Does Dolores really grasp what I am saying? I know that she reads poorly, her English is broken, and she is terribly self-conscious.
9. At least half of the girls show evidence of sleepiness. Are these girls out late at night?
10. How can I arouse some interest in school work for this group?
11. When I talked to the girls on the first day about what we plan to do in this class, there was not a spark of enthusiasm. How much readjustment am I justified in making in the course of study?
12. How shall I conduct the class each day?

Most teachers will not face problems of the magnitude of those faced by this beginning teacher, but they will face problems in every class and in every subject. These problems will center around motivation and interest, individual differences, student needs, aptitudes, skills, mastery of the tools of learning, health and physical problems, and others.

THE IMPORTANCE OF QUALITY TEACHING

To take a class as he finds it, to study it, to provide helpful learning experiences, and to direct the growth of the students are the tasks of the teacher. As never before, society is clamoring for quality teaching. In many quarters the schools are under attack; they are accused of doing an inferior job.

There are so many students to be taught so many things in so short a time. The teacher knows that some of the pupils are unenthusiastic, even negativistic, about school, yet these pupils must be taught something. This calls for skill in dealing with interpersonal relationships, ability to apply teaching and learning techniques which will accomplish optimum results, and patience in guiding development, which is often frustratingly slow.

Four Prime Factors in Education

Objectives, methods, materials, and evaluation are the indispensable ingredients of good education. The question of method or the best ways to structure lessons to promote acceptable learning experiences are the problems of this and the following chapter. Objectives have already been discussed. Evaluation and materials will be treated later in the book. All these phases of good teaching hinge on all the aspects of education. Classroom control, for example, cannot be discussed apart from involvement with teaching goals, with materials, and even more particularly with methods of teaching.

The Multiplicity of Method

Since the beginning of time, man has sought ways of communicating the accumulated knowledge and skills of one generation to another. Some of these methods have been spectacularly successful in certain time periods, or with certain groups of people, or for certain purposes. The teacher of today can call upon a great variety of methods to assist in guiding the learning of students.

Some of these methods are traditional and some are modern; others are still in the experimental stage. Some methods have outlived their usefulness, and have been or should be discarded. A threadbare example is the regurgitation method of memorizing isolated facts, and of repeating inane questions and answers. There are, however, occasions on which both memorization and the question-and-answer method may appropriately be used in the learning formula. But, in the main, modern learning theory calls for understandings, appreciations, positive skills, the development of judgment, independence in study, and the ability to analyze and to select a mode of action, to discriminate, and to create. Again, the connection between method and the aims of education is close.

Self-instructional techniques are much in the limelight today; also, experimentation with large and small groups is equally noticeable. It is through constant experimentation of this type that quality instruction emerges.

Someone has said that method is a teaching hypothesis. Certainly, it changes with experience and research. Change is gradual from where one is to where he wishes to go. Pupil behavior, too, changes gradually. There are hundreds of ways of handling the learning process. The teacher begins by using the one from his education and experience that seems logical to him, and with which he feels at home. But certain situations seem to call for new approaches. These should be tried little by little and with a critical, yet open mind. Wiles has put it this way:

A teacher alters his pattern of teaching a little bit at a time, undertaking the things he can do without shaking the whole structure of his method. As he tests out a new idea that he has and finds that it works, he incorporates it into his pattern. But if he tries a hunch that doesn't work, he discards it. The procedure . . . is *experimental teaching* and it is the doorway to *quality teaching*.[1]

Relating Learning to Students' Needs and Experiences

Research tends to show that the teacher-student relationship is probably more important than the teaching procedure. When the student accepts the teacher, he learns best (1:848).

It is also apparent from research and experience that students learn more rapidly and with greater permanence when the instructional techniques and the content are related to student needs and experiences. A functional educational experience promotes maximum learning. Whether the purpose be to master skills, to amass facts, or to gain understanding and meaningful knowledge, the relationship holds (1:363, 711–714).

The boy who wishes to build a sailing boat to enter in the city-wide boat building contest, or just to build a boat for personal use on a nearby bay or lake, has a need for certain skills and knowledges on which the industrial arts teacher is quick to capitalize. He knows that through this need the student will grow in the entire industrial arts curriculum. The student who is planning to enter college and has a certain career goal is eager to develop meanings and understandings as well as to amass facts. The amassing of facts alone might be the immediate goal of the student who is vying for a place on a nationally televised quiz program.

But, in relating learning to students' needs, care must be exercised not to accept a mechanical approach, because its values are limited. A rational or meaningful approach produces learning that can be generalized, that can be transferred to other situations, and that possesses greater retention value.

FACTORS AFFECTING TEACHING METHOD

The Role of the Teacher

Numerous researches have resulted in practically unanimous agreement that skill in teaching is important, but that it ranks below teacher-student

[1] Kimball Wiles, *Teaching for Better Schools*, 2d ed. © 1952, 1959 by Prentice-Hall, Inc., Englewood Cliffs, N.J., p. 302. Reprinted by permission.

relationships and group climate (3:848–849). There is no single person-ality or attitude trait, or teaching method, which guarantees teacher com-petence, but the general factor of good student-teacher relationships seems to be most closely related to competence. Students who have a high degree of person-to-person interaction with a teacher rate such a teacher high in competence.

Qualities which students admire in teachers are fairness in dealings, respect for personalities, and warm friendly relations. They respect those who have a proper command of their subject matter, and those with high ethical, social, and spiritual ideals. Good adjustment to the school and to life is another quality which rates high with students.

It has also been clearly shown that teachers who know a great deal about their students are better liked than those who take a laissez-faire attitude toward students' problems, their backgrounds, and their aspira-tions. Teachers who take the trouble to know and understand their stu-dents seem to be better adjusted personally to their work. This under-standing becomes a part of one's teaching method.

Group climate in the classroom is also important, and the teacher plays a crucial role in the creation of this climate.

Several techniques are available to help the teacher understand indi-viduals and groups. It is essential that students respect each other and develop cooperative attitudes. To explore student attitudes, teachers may use sociometry, interviews, anecdotal records, open-end questions, asso-ciation devices, and the like. Most of these procedures are reasonably objective and will assist the teacher in appraising social relationships which are likely to have a marked bearing on the learning-teaching en-vironment. These devices will be described in detail in the section on marking, reporting, and evaluating behavior and achievement.

The Relation of Method to Class Organization

Just as the teaching pattern has a close relationship to educational objec-tives, it also has a relationship to classroom organization. If the educational objective is simply the transfer of factual knowledge, the method may appropriately enough be the lecture or the recitation. The organization might be uniformly sized large groups. But, if the organization is varied or follows some of the newer plans, instructional methods will quite likely vary, too.

Class Size

For many years it has been assumed that, generally speaking, the smaller the class size, the more efficient the learning. But, since there is a close relation between class size and per pupil costs, schools have adopted a policy that enrollments should vary between thirty and forty pupils per class. No hard and fast correlations can be found between class size and pupil achievement. That large classes produce more work for teachers is not questioned, but with proper safeguards, assistance, and administrative encouragement, intellectual stimulation and growth can take place in large class groupings. It should be pointed out, however, that most researches have evaluated the knowledge of facts, whereas the attainment of other educational goals has not been carefully explored (1:224,427).

Method in Relation to Better Staff Use

Some hardheaded rational thinking has brought up the very disturbing idea that much of the contemporary school organization results in poor staff usage. These opinions are held by some of the leaders in education in Harvard University, Teachers College, Columbia University, New York University, Claremont Graduate School, Claremont College, the National Association of Secondary School Principals, and by many school superintendents and principals. One study has indicated that as much as 21 percent of a teacher's time is consumed by nonprofessional duties.[2] And, in a recent publication, the director of the Commission on the Experimental Study of the Utilization of the Staff in the Secondary School says, "About a third of a teacher's day goes to clerical and subprofessional tasks, another third to work which could just as well be done by various kinds of automated devices. A situation that provides only a third of a day for performance of work he is trained to do—and finds satisfaction in doing—contributes little to the morale of a talented, conscientious teacher" (12:8).

Some critics of contemporary education have said that the old one-room school offered more stimulation to its teachers than does the departmentalized school of today, which freezes teachers in a particular spot, a situation in which there is often no growth in responsibility or social acceptance.

It is highly questionable if the needs of an individual are met best by isolating a student with one teacher in one room with thirty-five other students for a day—the self-contained classroom—or by placing a student more or less arbitrarily with thirty-five other students for five equally spaced periods each day with a different teacher each period—the departmentalized curriculum. And, worse still, most schools are run strictly by the clock. Bells ring and students change classes every fifty or fifty-five

[2] *A Cooperative Study for the Better Utilization of Teacher Competencies.* Mt. Pleasant, Mich.: Central Michigan College, 1955, p. 11.

minutes. After a congested passage down a corridor, more bells ring, and students begin all over with a different teacher, possibly different classmates, and a different subject. Under such conditions, teachers are apt to feel that they are in a "factory" situation. European exchange teachers generally criticize this routine.

Team Teaching

At first glance this topic may seem to be strictly an administrative one, but such is not the case. "American education is in ferment. Unprecedented problems of quantity and quality call for unprecedented solutions."[3] The school problems are intensified by the population explosion, the shortage of teachers, an alarming teacher turnover, and a demand from the public for a more realistic education with evidences of substance and quality.

In an effort to effect some solutions to these problems, hundreds of experimental programs are under way. One of these programs which seems to offer promise is backed by the National Association of Secondary School Principals and numerous other professional groups as mentioned earlier. This is the "team teaching" plan.

Team teaching aims at a (1) reorganization of teachers, students, and schedules, (2) reassignment of curriculum and class schedules, (3) change in staffing patterns, and (4) more extensive use of technological aids. Is it possible to develop more fully the intellectual capacities of students through reorganizations along these lines? Can fluidity and flexibility in school organization assist educators in providing the type of education which society seems to demand? How can a better knowledge of individual differences, a better utilization of teachers, an understanding of ability groupings, a willingness to experiment with radically new ideas in class size, and the like, contribute to educational effectiveness?

The new concept of arranging teachers in teams, rather than asking teachers to go it alone, is receiving much recognition. The idea is still experimental. This is not just a new kind of cooperation among teachers; it is a way of organizing a school, a way of using a staff, and a way of using facilities to benefit the greatest majority of students. It is a way which hopefully allows every subject to be taught by a specialist, yet preserves the interrelations of content and learning. Hopefully, too, it makes optimum use of all the skills and knowledges of every staff member of a school.

The hypotheses which undergird team teaching are:

[3] Arthur D. Morse, *Schools of Tomorrow—Today*. New York: Doubleday & Company, Inc., 1960, p. 6.

The best teachers in a school are shared by more students. This statement approaches Alfred North Whitehead's remark that students need an "exposure to greatness."

Teachers are provided with a schedule which allows time for better preparation and planning. Aides are usually provided to take care of typing, mimeographing, proctoring, arranging for equipment, and the like.

Teachers get more help from the nonteaching branches of the school: test service, school office, guidance, audio-visual services, and the library.

Teachers should have, and can have, more exact knowledge of their students.

The best teachers in any system are entitled to recognition.

Teachers can grow and keep abreast of increasing knowledge.

Teachers do not plan and work in isolation. The team approach minimizes repetitious effort.

Teachers make better use of teaching techniques and technological devices.

New teachers are more quickly and easily oriented and assimilated.

Students are given new responsibility for their progress.

Students develop better study habits.

Special student needs are more easily diagnosed, and remedial assistance more easily planned.

Flexibility permits groupings and regroupings of students.

The plan provides for flexible class size.

Resource people from outside the school are more easily used.

TEAM TEACHING IN PRACTICE   By definition, team teaching implies that two or more teachers assume the responsibility for a particular phase of education for a designated group of students. The arrangement may be so complete that the entire school program follows the team plan, or it may be limited to one subject or a group of related subjects. The plan is applicable to elementary and secondary school. In one form, for example, only the English teachers for the seventh grade are involved since all teach exactly the same content, but in another school it may look something like the Ridgewood, Illinois, scheme:

the school's professional teachers have been divided into two divisions, humanities and sciences, with two teaching teams in each division. The humanities division plans courses of study for English, history, art, music and foreign languages; the sciences division, for science, mathematics, practical arts, physical education, and business education.[4]

[4] Dorsey Baynham, "A School of the Future in Operation," *Phi Delta Kappan*, vol. 42 (May 1961), p. 352.

Teaching teams vary in size and make-up according to the school situation involved. Usually, a team has a *team leader*. In this case a team of two or more teachers assume joint responsibility for instructing a group, but one member of the team is designated leader or coordinator. This person serves as chairman of the planning sessions and exercises varying degrees of leadership. Team leaders are mature, experienced teachers, and frequently they are given extra compensation. A *team teacher* is simply a fully qualified teacher who is a member of a teaching team. A *student teacher* or *intern teacher* is usually a senior college student from a teacher-education program who is assigned to a team to observe and assist under supervision from the team leader. A *teacher aide* is a noncertified person who works with the team in a part-time capacity doing clerical, library, or other routine tasks. There are numerous other arrangements for teaching teams which are variations of the above structure.

Team teaching schedules call for student time to be divided into three big blocks: large group instruction, small group instruction, and individual study with time allotments of 40 percent, 20 percent, and 40 percent respectively.

Small classes provide opportunities for students to discover subject matter, to learn its worth, and to react to it with other students and know their teachers on a rather personal basis. Small classes, also, afford teachers an opportunity to try out a variety of teaching techniques, measure individual growth and development, and provide for intergroup relationships so necessary for high school students.

Team teaching makes significant allowance for independent study, a condition that is emphasized at every turn in today's education, but one that is often difficult to manage. The facts of individual differences have been known for a long time, but it has been difficult to provide for the variety of interests and capabilities that exist. Usually the provision for individual differences relies heavily on assigned homework. There is little provision for that which is creative or truly independent. The new organization of instruction attempts to assist students to assume more responsibility for their own education. Independent learning activities make use of reading, writing, viewing, listening, doing, working with automated teaching devices, experimenting in laboratories, and engaging in many other significant activities. There will be opportunities for studying in depth. Independent study should make provision for both horizontal and vertical growth and enrichment. As teachers guide independent study, more of it can be expected of the older and more mature students. Students may spend as much as 40 percent of their time in independent study.

Individual study and large and small group instruction call for varied school facilities such as seminar rooms, large lecture rooms, and small study and work areas such as booths and cubicles. New schools are being built with provisions for such facilities. Movable partitions promote the space fluidity required by this type of organization. Already existing buildings present problems, but not insurmountable ones. Some excellent programs are now found in some of the older buildings.

TEAM TEACHING: EVALUATION But team teaching is still in the experimental stage, and in those districts where it is being given a trial, its evaluation becomes a matter of great interest. Some critics feel that students simply do not have the maturity which theoretically, at least, the plan demands. Teachers are divided in their opinions. Some accept the new arrangements enthusiastically, others disapprove. In some instances staff morale is enhanced, in others lowered. Some teachers feel that the plan downgrades all teachers except the few so-called leaders.

Does it contribute to the solution of the problem of ability grouping and individual differences? Again, arguments are pro and con. The high degree of flexibility in the program makes possible various combinations in assignments for both students and teachers. Provision is made for group work, yet there is time to study and experiment individually, to work in depth, to explore emerging interests. In some places high school seniors have earned a certain number of college credits. At the same time the noncollege student is not overlooked. He receives the same amount of assistance and encouragement, possibly more than under the conventional organization. Guidance functions are usually greater and more meaningful.

SPECIFIC ACTIVITIES BASIC TO TEACHING AND LEARNING

There are many basic activities in teaching which apply to any or all kinds of class groupings.

Communication Skills

The ability to do high school work rests chiefly on the four communication skills: reading, writing, speaking, and listening. These same skills play a significant role throughout life. They help an individual in his career and in many of the enjoyments he gets from the cultural arts. Even the fullest and wisest use of leisure time will often be based on one or more of these skills. Ideas from other people come to us through reading, a process which must be done with reasonable rapidity and with understanding. We must be able to attach meaning to words and sounds that come to us through the sense of hearing. Then, we convey our ideas through effective writing, and through clear, understandable, and often persuasive speech.

Reading

There are many subproblems in each of the communication skills. In reading, for example, students must read textbooks, novels, newspapers, science books, and poetry. They must also grasp meaning from mathematics symbols, charts, tables, graphs, maps, footnotes, and legends. Meaning must also be forthcoming from chapters, paragraphs, passages, sentences, and words.

Several false assumptions have been made about reading: that the elementary school has sole responsibility for teaching reading, that the school is at fault when all do not learn to read well, that nonreaders are incapable of learning and should be eliminated from school, and that reading is a purely mechanical skill unrelated to experience.

Even when the elementary school has done a good job of developing basic reading skills, secondary school teachers still must teach their students to understand the new words and concepts as they encounter new subject matter. Different kinds of reading ability are required in interpreting a literary selection, a mathematics problem, an issue in social studies, or a blueprint in shop. Each subject sets its own reading demands, and the teachers must help the student to cope with these demands. Books, pamphlets, periodicals, and the like have many difficulty levels. Only as students understand what they read will they be able to assimilate.

When a student is unable to read, an analysis of his problem is not as simple as finding his IQ. Causes of reading difficulty are often complex and difficult to identify. Comprehensive secondary schools rely on one or both of two methods of assisting students whose reading skills are unsatisfactory. A comparatively small number of students suffer from a reading retardation that requires special instruction; however, for those who do, there are reading clinics. For other students whose difficulties are less complicated, many schools offer a remedial reading program in the classroom. The remedial reading program tries to assist the student with a work pattern in which he slowly masters simple reading, and then moves on to more difficult types. At first his reading will be slow, but it will increase in speed as the reading-study skills are improved.

Conant singles out still another group and suggests a program:

Developmental reading is not the remedial reading program designed for slow readers. Rather, it is a voluntary instructional program intended primarily to do three things: to help students acquire skill in different sorts of reading, from close and detailed reading to scanning; to increase reading speed; and to improve comprehension of the material read.[5]

[5] James B. Conant, *The American High School Today.* New York: McGraw-Hill Book Company, Inc., 1959, pp. 67–68. Used by permission of McGraw-Hill.

Not all schools are fortunate enough to have clinics, but if they have clinics, they are staffed with persons trained to give professional assistance. Reading clinics are usually equipped with technical devices for analysis of a variety of difficulties. Follow-up programs attempt to correct handicaps and build functional corrective skills.

It has been emphasized that reading is more than a mechanical process of word recognition and correct pronunciation. Unless words provide for understanding or stimulate pictures in the mind, reading becomes a useless exercise dealing with meaningless symbols and abstractions. The foundation of understanding and comprehension must rest on concrete experience, either direct or vicarious. How this foundation is to be built raises some central problems.

MAKE A PRACTICAL BEGINNING   At the outset, it is necessary to find out the reading abilities of the students. This can be done from reading scores in the school records, from oral reading, and from simple reading tests administered in class. The teacher might also begin by thinking of himself as a reading teacher; providing varied experiences for the students; locating simple reading materials for the slow learners; securing clinical help if needed; providing the students with varied lists of reading material which will be of interest to them; and giving words meaning through association with a variety of multisensory materials. For example, how does one understand what the human heart is and does? For this understanding he reads, looks at films, handles models, looks at diagrams, and then organizes the facts.

BEYOND THE MECHANICS OF READING   Even after a student has learned to read, the responsibility of the teacher does not end. He now begins to teach discrimination in reading. In the first place the student must be taught to separate the wheat from the chaff. This involves developing a taste for better reading material and learning the skill of scanning so that the reader may judge whether or not a selection is worth careful reading. Improving taste in reading involves a slow and subtle process. The beginning is made at the student's own level of appreciation. The wise teacher never expresses surprise or scorn at what the student likes. Gradually the student raises his appreciation as he continues to read, and as he is exposed to more worthwhile material. He must be given help in his reading selections. The more poorly he reads, the less likely he will be to select reading material that is suitable. Above all, every reading experience should be an enjoyable one. Finally, improvement in reading should be a cooperative undertaking which involves parents and other teachers. Their encouragement and support are essential. An overexposure to reading material that is beyond the student's comprehension, or an overanalysis of what has been read will nullify the procedures just suggested for improving interest in reading and taste for better material.

Often students who read reasonably well develop lopsided reading tastes. They get into a habit of reading one kind of material only, and even grow to disdain anything else. A boy, for example, reads extensively, but always adventure stories; he may even narrow this adventure to westerns, pirates, war, or sea stories. Teachers have tried many techniques to secure a better balance in reading selections. Reading lists should provide variety. Visible records might be maintained, even posted, to show what is being read; the librarian is asked to exhibit books and book covers to call attention to multitype materials.

The next step in fostering discrimination is to help students distinguish between fact and falsehood. Quite often there is a naive tendency to believe that anything which appears in print is true. Normally a serious limitation of using a single textbook becomes obvious. Not only does one book fail to meet the needs of students with varying degrees of reading ability, but it encourages too much dependence on what "the book says." Through an analysis of propaganda techniques, a comparison of conflicting viewpoints, and a study of exaggerated claims often made in advertisements, students can be taught to be wary in their reading. As a part of this general point, they need to learn the value of investigating the reliability of the sources of their reading.

Improving skill, comprehension, speed, and taste in reading is not an easy matter. Communication via the printed page has much competition, some from banal reading materials, and some from motion pictures and television. Surveys of the reading habits of the adult population are disappointing in terms of taste and reading level.

Writing

No one can deny that writing is a communication skill which should be taught in school. It has a great deal of bearing on the ability to do well in school; it is an adjunct to most vocations; and it is an everyday nonjob activity. Many adults write very poorly, and for that reason find it a painful experience. Many procrastinate over the simplest of writing chores such as personal letters, requests, inquiries, newspaper notices and advertisements, invitations, and similar bit pieces.

Corporations, distributors, and purveyors recognize these facts. They never state in an advertisement that the reader should write for information, or even formulate an order. Simply fill in the attached blank. This is the only way to get the replies, even if the readers really want the goods or services advertised. Suggestions that groups contact their congressman on an issue are usually accompanied by a sample letter (of course, the specimen letter presents the point of view being advocated). Ofttimes clubs find it difficult to locate a member who will serve as secretary—the usual excuse is, "I can't write" or "I can't take notes." Instead of letter writing, the telephone and the telegraph frequently become the means of communication.

TEACHING THE WRITING SKILLS Most of what was written in the paragraphs above about reading can almost be repeated here verbatim. Change the nouns and the ideas remain much the same.

High school students should write abundantly, and in most classes. It is unfair to saddle the unadulterated burden of developing habits and skills of writing on English teachers alone. Probably students do not write enough today, but artificial pressure writing has been tried, and it has failed. In many quarters there has been an overemphasis on singling out errors, on unkind remarks about faulty unity, emphasis, or coherence.

At the same time, the rewards for good composition have been few. Some teachers appreciate writing skill and pass along a friendly note of encouragement, but most teachers merely mark the errors and hand the paper back to the student.

Here again there are vast individual differences in students. In class after class, a teacher sees students who contribute well to discussions, who volunteer to give reports, or who organize committees, but who cannot write a good test paper or a term report. And, there are those who are just the opposite.

Motivation means as much in developing writing skills as in reading or study skills. It has been truly said that teachers in assigning written work should bear in mind that students must have something to say, must have a purpose in writing it, and must have a desire to improve their writing.

Bringing reality and purpose into school composition is not easy. Letter writing should involve real letters to real people about real things. Examples are letters to the principal or the superintendent about policy or an invitation to a class affair or a request for a special permission. Rather than an oral or mimeographed invitation to parents to participate in a school function, why not a cordial written note? Opportunities arise as resource persons are invited to the school, and thanked afterwards. Field trips provide similar opportunities.

Often the school would like to convince the local paper about the soundness or weakness of certain policies on which there is disagreement. A letter to the editor, requesting that he print it, is excellent motivation. School papers or magazines should not be overlooked.

In writing, as in reading, there are mechanics that have to be mastered. Spelling, punctuation, capitalization, and sentence structure must be taught. There are also many forms of writing, for example, serious and humorous, informal letters and more formal essays. Individual tastes will incline different students to different forms.

One of the most individual aspects of the entire business is to develop in the student a habit of writing, and the ability to recognize things to write about.

Miss J. successfully uses an occasional writing round robin. A student takes a sheet of paper and writes one sentence on it. The paper is handed to another student who reads the sentence, then adds a second sentence. The paper passes to every member of the class who makes a contribution. It is a potpourri to be sure, but it accomplishes a purpose.

Mrs. N. teaches in a school which has a policy of assigning twenty minutes of each junior high school English period to formal spelling. Mrs. N. got permission to substitute a twenty-minute daily writing exercise. Students were told about the scheme and were asked to write for twenty minutes on any subject or any idea that came to mind. In the beginning some students could not get going; they were given individual help. Each day at the end of the period, Mrs. N. reminded the pupils that there would be another writing period tomorrow, and that perhaps they would like to think of something to write about. From time to time, she set up large action pictures (rodeo, a canoe shooting the rapids, a ship in a heavy gale) on the chalkrail. On such occasions the students might be asked to suggest action verbs which were written on the board. The teacher did not use the time to correct papers or fill out office reports. She moved about the room. In effect, she became a supervising writing teacher.

Among the techniques used by Mr. W. was that of occasionally playing a symphonic or orchestral record. Once it was Ferde Grofe's "Grand Canyon Suite," at another time Moussorgsky's "Pictures at an Exhibition." At still another time it was Tschaikovsky's "Overture of 1812," and at still another time a Strauss waltz. Mr. W.'s purpose was to create a mood. After each record, and the writing which followed it, he told the class the story of the selection and stressed the fact that the composer had written a great piece of descriptive literature but used a musical score instead of lines of prose. This occasional feature of Mr. W.'s composition class became quite popular.

Speaking

No activity in which students engage in school is more important to their future happiness or success than speaking. On the job, in the home, in all their relations with others, they must express themselves well in order to be understood and to be accepted by their fellows. To teach students the ability to communicate ideas effectively is a job that cannot be delegated to speech and English teachers alone. It is humiliating to meet students from other countries who can speak three or four languages fluently while the products of American schools are unable to speak one language well.

ENCOURAGING CORRECT SPEECH   Students in class should be provided as much opportunity as possible to engage in discussion, to relate good stories, to report, and to serve as chairmen of groups. The author has observed many adults, suddenly cast into roles of minor leadership, who were embarrassed by being unable to present a simple motion properly. Everyone enjoys a good story, yet how few tell one effectively. Students may well be encouraged to read good stories and to practice the art of telling them to their classmates. A simple criterion of a good book report might well be, Does it lead someone else to want to read the book? Students need to be encouraged to take pride in correct, colorful, effective speech. The importance of vocabulary building, of using the exact word to express one's meaning, and the avoidance of such stereotyped words as "fine" or "nice" to describe something can very well be stressed in every class. The use of clean speech, avoidance of slang, and the correction of lazy speech habits are taught by precept and example.

Voice is often a deterrent to effective speaking. Since no one knows exactly how his voice sounds to others, playbacks of voice recordings for each member of the class constitute the first step in the improvement of voice quality. In some instances, clinical help may be needed. Teachers themselves would do well to remember King Lear's eulogy to Cordelia: "Her voice was ever soft, gentle and low, an excellent thing in woman." Men, too, need good voices. A raspy, raucous, strident, whiny voice is not a model to be imitated.

GROUP ACTIVITIES IN SPEAKING   Although most speaking activities in life are individual matters, there are also valuable group speaking experiences which are useful in school classes as well as in situations outside of school. These activities include group discussions, dramatizations, committee reports, debates, symposiums, and panel discussions. Most of these activities are well known or have been discussed elsewhere in this book.

ORAL READING   The amount of oral reading by pupils has decreased in today's high schools. Some teachers disagree with this change, but the psychological and physiological changes taking place in teen-aged boys and girls justify it. Whenever there is oral reading, it should be voluntary. It should be done informally, that is, the reader remains at his seat or if standing to recite is customary, he stands, but he does not go to the front of the room to read.

Choral and responsive reading are widely used as oral reading activities. These are to be found more frequently in speech or drama classes than in regular English classes. When students cooperate well in group reading, an alert teacher can accomplish about everything which could be accomplished in solo reading. The tape recorder is also commonly used in connection with choral reading work. The occasional use of a recording of an expert such as Charles Laughton or Charlton Heston reading well-known literary pieces can be beneficial. Some teachers prefer to have printed copies of the readings in the hands of the students so that they can follow along with their eyes. Others prefer to have them concentrate completely on the listening.

TEACHERS' SPEECH   Although this discussion on speaking has stressed what students do, a bit of advice to teachers concerning their own speech is in order. Rough and tough language is never proper. Firm measures are required at times, to be sure, but reversion to a lower cultural level is never justified.

Another misconception that a few teachers entertain is that the use of slang is a road to popularity with adolescents. A judicious use of the right kind of slang can contribute color and force to speech. For example, a good way to express a man's depressed state is to say that he is "down and out." On the other hand, an excessive use of slang or colloquial speech cheapens language. Too much use of slang suggests intellectual bankruptcy, inability to express oneself, and a lack of refinement. Students look with suspicion on the teacher who attempts to speak their jargon; they consider such usage by an adult an invasion of the fraternity of youth.

Listening

As indicated in the introduction to the discussion of "Auditory Instructional Materials," Chapter 9, listening is a significant factor in the communications process. It has always played an important part in the educational pattern of schools, yet, in most instances, it is an act which has been little studied. It has been assumed that all students can and do listen, if told to do so. It is only within recent years that much attention has been given to the act of listening. This new emphasis seems to parallel the development of the newer mass media, and the development of extensive equipment has sharpened school sensitivity to the learning problems involved. Just as reading and written communication received a great impetus from the invention of the printing press, oral communication and listening have received a similar boost from modern electronics.

LISTENING OBJECTIVES   Many secondary school students do not read well, nor do they listen well. The ability to grasp meaning from auditory stimuli is as difficult and as important as the ability to grasp meaning from visual stimuli. The task of the teacher is to try to develop both skills in students, and to keep their use balanced and in focus.

It is now generally accepted that discriminative listening to informative speech can be taught. For a general communications course, schools have accepted such objectives as:

1. To develop a respect for listening as a learning skill
2. To eliminate bad listening habits already formed
3. To develop the basic skills, concepts, and attitudes essential to good listening habits
4. To increase markedly student experience in listening to informative speech
5. To coordinate specific listening assignments with related assignments in speaking, reading, and writing

Are goals such as these achievable?

Although all teachers can and should be concerned with developing good listening habits in students, the more active promotion of the listening objectives fall to the speech, English, music, and foreign language teachers. It is not difficult to develop a respect for listening as a medium of learning when students become aware of the fact that listening can be measured, improved, and remeasured. It is possible to chart improvement in listening habits, and research has demonstrated that grade point averages in numerous school subjects can be improved by promoting better listening. When a student becomes aware of his listening pattern, he begins self-evaluation. He may ask himself: Why am I a poor listener? How can I become a better listener? How will this help me get better grades?

Techniques for improving listening habits include:

1. Finding a central idea or ideas in the communication he is hearing, relating the contributory or embellishing ideas to the central one. Someone has said that the listener should try to "see" the central idea.
2. Trying to anticipate what the speaker will say next. This keeps the listener alert.
3. Trying to distinguish between the essential points and the details.
4. Trying to distinguish between facts and opinions.
5. Trying to separate relevant and irrelevant ideas.
6. Trying to distinguish between information and persuasion but not debating with the message.
7. Trying to relate the message to contextual clues—the announced theme, time, place, background, and other data.
8. Trying to develop a feeling of immediacy or urgency. The speaker is not going to repeat.
9. Trying to obtain a good physical vantage point for listening—not too far away, not among distractions.
10. Trying to evaluate what has been said. The evaluation may serve as a brief mental summary.

Remedial Teaching

For a variety of reasons some students will require special treatment. In some instances, the numbers are large enough so that separate classes are formed. These may be the mentally deficient or the emotionally unstable students. In other instances, remedial measures are necessitated by poor work-study skills, behavior problems, or general low achievement.

FINDING THE PUPIL WHO NEEDS HELP   Teachers need to know a great deal about their students, and only in this way can they be of most assistance. By observation, by test results, and by feedback from the student, teachers know that certain students need remedial help. To locate these students most efficiently, teachers employ a variety of evaluative devices and techniques. These range from teacher-constructed subject tests to standardized achievement tests. The construction, application, interpretation, and scope of these evaluative techniques are discussed in Chapters 15 through 18.

RETEACHING AS AN ASPECT OF REMEDIAL WORK   A chief concern is with the techniques for reteaching students who have low grades in units or in entire subjects. It is often said that reteaching is more difficult than original teaching.

Usually, both teachers and students approach remedial work with a negative attitude. It means extra time and effort. The teacher's task is to search for motivation and effective techniques of correcting the deficiencies.

Two main difficulties are discernible. At times, the trouble is basic and indicates a lack of background understanding. This calls for the development of corrective skills and fundamentals which were supposed to have been mastered previously. Corrective measures along these lines are likely to be long-term measures. Usually these measures are employed so that they parallel the normal course of study and the regular work goes right ahead.

The second difficulty is traceable to a topic or unit deficiency. For some reason the class, or certain individuals, simply failed to grasp the work, but it is apparently not due to any deep-seated background deficiency. The teacher usually reviews or reteaches in more concentrated form the topic which caused the trouble. Review here means a new view. It involves a fresh look with an attempt to produce new understanding through reinterpretation and new association. In this instance, work on the next topic of study is delayed until the group achieves a satisfactory mastery level.

Among the problems that arise in reteaching is that of what to do for those students who already understand the work. Provision must be made so that they can enrich their understanding, move ahead with new studies, or do some depth study. Possibly there is not much difference in these schemes, and the teacher may find it difficult to sell the idea to students.

Drill and Practice

Although modern educational practice tends to decry drill and repetition, they are still among the chief characteristics of practically every school. But ideas about drill have changed. Research shows that spaced, meaningful, and varied drill can be valuable instruction. Just any kind of drill or practice is no longer acceptable. In fact, a golfer, for example, may become even less proficient by practicing his errors. In the schoolroom a student may fail to learn to play a trumpet or to master factoring because he lacks motivation or understanding. Knowledge is seldom retained from one exposure and skills are not learned in a single trial. Even the professionals on the concert stage or the athletic field, for example, practice, practice, practice. But for anyone to profit from this practice certain conditions need to be met.

Drill, practice, or memory work must be meaningful. It must serve a purpose which students understand and accept. Why should they learn to spell words which they never use? Why should students be required to memorize lines of poetry which represent the teacher's choice? Why should students be required to memorize isolated facts or dates which have no significance to them? Why should laws, principles, or rules be learned? If these instances can be made meaningful, they are learned in less time and retained longer.

Drill needs to be spaced as indicated above. By and large, classroom drill tends to be spaced, but students, like golfers, may grow stale through overpractice. Boredom and fatigue cannot produce good results.

The intensity of drill has much to do with its effect on learning. Drill accompanied by vigor, mild emotional overtones, and heightened attention tends to be effective. This sort of thing is more easily accomplished in independent study than group study.

Practice must produce correct responses; they must be made satisfying in some way.

Procedures to perfect skills and factual learning should be not only interesting, but economical of time as well. Games and contests often have a legitimate use in making drill interesting. The element of time needs to be safeguarded.

Both individual and group concert exercises have their merits; the first to check accuracy of individual performance and the latter to produce a feeling of unity. Learning a foreign language, for example, calls for a great deal of drill and practice. In the past much of the drill was of the concert type. Today, the emphasis is on individual practice. Language laboratories and other new techniques make this possible.

Review

Drill and review are not the same, although the connotations are much the same. Review does not emphasize practice or repetition, but *re-view*, a *new view*, a *new look*. Review is a fresh look, or a refresher look at what has been accomplished.

Reviews are chiefly of two types: those occurring daily and those occurring at the culmination of units of work. Daily reviews involve smaller segments of knowledge or skill. The daily review is necessitated largely by the fact that conventional school organization segments learning into fifty-minute periods. Before beginning a new day's work, teachers feel that they need to "heat up" what has gone before. Such a review does put the new work into perspective. The teacher may initiate reviews by asking:

Would you like to review what we did yesterday in class?
What conclusions did we reach yesterday?
To bring ourselves up to date, what have we found out since we started studying this topic?

Review may also come at the end of the hour, or it may come at any psychological time during the period. At the end of the hour, review tends to tie together the strands which were developed and traced during the hour. Without such a review students frequently leave class feeling frustrated, asking themselves, "What is it all about?" The teacher may begin the review by remarking:

The hour is nearly over; let us see if we can arrive at any conclusions.
Will you summarize what we did today?
How did the lesson today relate to that of yesterday (or the last few days)?
Are there any questions about what we did today?
How do you think this lesson relates to the one for tomorrow?

Unit completion review stresses the long view. It may be likened to the ascent of a mountain. Once at the top, a pause is made to look back over the route traveled. This is a time to retrace some of the trials of the trip, to appraise some of the procedures, and to get the picture as a whole. This may have been done segment by segment on the way up, but now it is the over-all view that is needed. A review of this type may call for a part of a class period, a full period, or more. It may call for new outside study to fill in gaps which appear.

What would you most like to get from this review?
What is the best way for us to conduct this review?
Is the picture of ——————— clear to you?
What else would you like to know about this topic?
Would you like to record (write or tape) *some of our findings by use of an outline, summary, or check list?*
How shall I evaluate your work on this unit?

Questions and Questioning

Although the traditional teaching formula—assign, study, recite, test—has fallen into disrepute, the use of questions is another matter. It is part of the instructional method to be sure, but it is more than that. It is a useful art or tool and, in the hands of a skillful teacher, serves numerous useful learning purposes. Good questions (1) stimulate thought and encourage students to question themselves, other students, and the teacher, (2) act as a sounding board against which the correctness or acceptability of ideas may be tested, (3) promote the aims of the lesson in a concise manner, and (4) encourage discussion.

THE NATURE OF QUESTIONS   Some of the characteristics of good questions are:

They should be worded in clear, concise, and suitable terms to fit the abilities and ages of the pupils.

They should avoid vague, general queries. As far as ambiguity is concerned, the most common type of faulty question begins with, "What about . . . ?" Such a vague query as "Are there any questions?" also fails to elicit a response. Make the question specific, as in this example, "What causes the earth to rotate on its axis?"

Questions should be asked in a quiet encouraging manner. Avoid firing questions like pistol shots or conducting a third degree. Students need to be at ease and free from tension.

Key questions should be well worded and thought out in advance; however, there should be flexibility to deviate from preplanned discussion to allow for unexpected and timely questions by students.

Questions should elicit complete responses except in unison drill, not just "yes" or "no." Ask a few significant questions during a discussion period rather than innumerable, minute ones which usually capitalize on the memorization of isolated facts. This is why it was suggested in the chapter on lesson planning that a few key questions be included in daily plans.

Questions should be varied in type. Questions may be asked to elicit simple recall, comparison and contrast, choice of alternatives, classification, illustration or example, or to present a relationship. Other types may ask the students to describe, explain, outline, or organize ideas in any of several ways.

THE APPROACH TO GOOD QUESTIONING   The conditions under which questions are asked should be kept consciously in mind. Some of the positive ones are:

There should be an even distribution of questions among the members of the class. Solicit volunteers, call on others.

The conditions under which questions are asked should be varied. Use panels, debates, and other devices. At times student chairmen may conduct the discussion. A pretest may serve as a basis for a good follow-up question period.

Students should be encouraged to direct their remarks to the class. Students should answer each other insofar as possible.

Many questions should be framed so as to relate to current happenings. This is especially important in such a subject as history, for example.

Grade books should not be marked as students recite.

CUING THE STUDENT   The techniques used in the conduct of a discussion are important. There are both logical and psychological aspects to be kept in mind. Some of the recommended approaches are:

Students should have time to think about what they are going to say before answering a question. The answer may seem simple to the teacher because he has already formulated an answer, but the student has to have time to organize his thinking. A rewording of the question may be in order, yet this is often overdone.

Students should be encouraged to ask questions both of the teacher and other members of the class, but they should be discouraged from making insignificant or irrelevant queries.

Students should show each other common courtesies. Only one speaks at a time, and he should not be rudely interrupted. He should be allowed to have his say. It is also inappropriate to allow students to wave their hands in the air.

Students have a right to have their questions answered if they are germane to the discussion. Do not put questions off. If you do not know the answer, it is usually best to admit it. There may be students who have the answer; if so, bring them to your assistance.

Teachers should permit students to question their point of view. There is also a difference between factual and point of view considerations. The teacher must learn to distinguish between the honest questioner and the heckler or time waster.

It is not inappropriate to show sincere appreciation for good student responses. Commend without embarrassing. Give students as much credit as possible for honest responses, even though the responses may need to be supplemented. In cases of incorrect or ungrammatical, poorly constructed replies, use tact in making corrections. When a shy student makes his first contribution, it is better to overlook any deficiency in expression. Sometimes corrections in English for the group as a whole can be made without identifying any one person.

DIFFERENCES IN INDIVIDUALS

Every teacher knows that great differences exist in individuals in traits and behavior, yet surprisingly little in the way of adaptations is done about it. Wiles says:

Meeting individual differences is not a technique; it is a way of living. It includes accepting others, respecting their contributions, working for the kind of group operation in which each individual knows he has a part, and encouraging each pupil to give his best in each situation.[6]

Importance and Extent of Individual Differences

In Chapter 1 some of the physical and mental differences in secondary school students were presented. These carry over into practically every phase of ideation and affectivity. Some students are enthusiastic about theoretical discussions; others are not. Some students enjoy scientific knowledge; others prefer the arts. Some students are disturbed when questions and problems do not fall into neat and precise arrangements; others enjoy tackling unorganized and disarranged ideas. These individuals are challenged by the need for classification and identification. Chapter 7 will attempt to show how the content and method fit the phenomenon of individual differences.

As culture increases and society becomes more complex, these differences present many new problems. Society attempts to hold more and more of its school-age youth until graduation. There is now *more to be learned by more students.* And, the interests, aptitudes, dispositions, attitudes, aspirations, and home backgrounds vary enormously. All of these variations come to school with the students.

[6] Wiles, *op. cit.,* p. 163.

Meeting the Problem of Individual Differences

Teachers are faced with many problems in trying to care for individual differences in students. Among the broad suggestions for solving these problems are: acceleration, grouping by sections (homogeneity), flexible assignments, supervised study, laboratory study, unit planning, individual projects, and the like. Many of these suggestions will be discussed further in Chapter 7.

Acceleration has been widely tried out by high schools but with varying degrees of success. Encouraging students to finish a normal four-year program in three years has been a reasonable solution in some cases, yet in others it has led to social maladjustment and temperamental behavior. Acceleration techniques have required extra time from already overburdened teachers. New devices such as teaching machines, programmed books, and prerecorded tape lessons may make acceleration more feasible in the future.

Homogeneous or ability grouping has been and is being very widely employed as a means of caring for individual differences. The arrangement has much merit, yet it has been abused and in many instances has accomplished very little.

In recent years an attempt has been made to adapt content and method to students. An arrangement of providing parallel courses in a given subject is to be found both in junior and senior high school, for example, general mathematics or trigonometry, general science or physics, general music or orchestra.

Classroom teachers are likely to be more interested in specific suggestions which they can carry out at the classroom level, if they are teaching heterogeneous groups:

Use a *laboratory situation* in which students work as individuals or as groups on various problems and with various instructional materials while the teacher acts as consultant. Not only is it possible to insure variety in problems or projects and in the use of resources, but it is possible to make adjustments in time and in remedial work on the basic skills as needed.

Use *more than one textbook*. It is important to select reading references which vary in difficulty, as well as in appeal and in point of view.

Form *subgroups within the class*. The teacher may help one group while another group works alone. Groups should be flexible so that the composition of the group being given instruction may vary as needed.

Make assignments of different levels of difficulty. In a class which has to meet the general education needs of all students and the specialized needs of a few, differentiated assignments become a necessity. However, in any subject there should be not only basic requirements which are common to all, but also more advanced work provided for those who have the interest and ability to pursue the subject at higher levels. It should be pointed out that an assignment common to all does not necessarily mean that everyone must do the same thing in order to meet the requirements of the assignment.

Use *more group activity*. Groups should be so organized that there will be several centers of interest, requiring various skills and resources for their development.

Use *a variety of evaluation procedures*. No matter how wide a range of activities and resources is used in the class to take care of individual differences, the efforts of the teacher will be defeated if all evaluation is based on tests which measure mastery of subject matter with everyone expected to attain the same standard of achievement. In physical education, for example, evaluation that is based on skill in performance alone is inadequate in the appraisal of the total objectives of the course.

All of the procedures indicated above have been used by experienced teachers with some degree of success in providing for individual differences in the classroom. In the discussion which follows, special consideration will be given to two groups of students, the slow students and the gifted students.

Slow Learners

Some practical suggestions to help slow learners are:

1. *Try to find out why the student does not learn.* The reasons may be manifold. It is a common fallacy to conclude that all slow learners are stupid. Slow learning may or may not be due to low general aptitude.
2. *Stress concrete learning materials.* Wide use should be made of field trips, pictures, demonstrations, firsthand experience.
3. *Use shorter units*, which stress personal needs, immediate values, and practical applications.
4. Make *assignments clear and definite.* Discuss the assignment in class. Have it repeated. Talk about *how* it is to be done.
5. *Help the slow learner to succeed.* "Nothing succeeds like success.' Provide activities which he can master, and give him competition which he can challenge. This may very well be his own record.

Gifted Learners

The cause of the gifted student has become popular. Contemporary scientific, political, and cultural developments contribute to the idea that gifted students should be identified early and given some sort of special treatment. The world of today is placing more dependence on specialized personnel.

Havighurst has estimated that at least half of all gifted children never realize their full potentialities.[7] If true, this is an appalling loss. School programs have tended to neglect the gifted in contrast to the attention given the slow learner. It has been assumed that the gifted will shift for himself and will learn anyway. No one knows how much potential leadership has been lost because gifted students have been permitted to loaf day in and day out, doing assignments which never challenged them.

It has been common practice to identify gifted students on the basis of achievement and intelligence tests (labeling as "gifted" those who have an IQ above 120 or 130, for example). There seems to be little doubt about the fact that ability to do academic work or work of increasing complexity in other fields is related to scores on mental tests. However, of late years there has been definite objection to such a narrow definition of the "gifted student," especially in terms of ability to do academic work or to make a good score on a verbal mental test. While a certain degree of intelligence, as measured by tests of mental ability, is necessary to success in any field, the IQ is not always the most significant factor in successful achievement by any means. Consequently, teachers should look for various kinds of aptitudes among students. Quite often a student of average intelligence will outstrip his classmate who is rated higher in ability.

MEETING THE NEEDS OF GIFTED STUDENTS Freehill has suggested that teaching procedures for the gifted should provide:

1. *A program organized around unit topics, projects, or study themes.*

2. *Lessons organized around a problem or a purpose.* It is proper that in some of these, the severe arrangements of formal logic will give way to psychological organizations that are more truly characteristic of unsolved problems.

3. *Encouragement of side issues which develop incidental and concomitant learning.*

4. *Special emphasis on the tools of workshop learning.* These include reading skills, individual study, finding materials, observing, graphing, reporting, orderly disagreeing, and appraising opposite viewpoints.

5. *Informal classrooms with reference works more frequently used as texts.*

6. *Increasing awareness of the learning process on the part of the*

7 Robert J. Havighurst, "Conditions Favorable and Detrimental to the Development of Talent," *School Review*, vol. 65 (March 1957), pp. 20–26.

learner. Effort is expended toward insuring his participation in focusing and systematizing his work.

7. *Student involvement in planning or at least awareness of what the expected learnings are.*

8. *Participation in periodic evaluation.* Gifted students in the regular classroom should be encouraged to serve in discussions, as the person who says, "This is where we are," "This is the issue on which we disagree," or "Perhaps this will help."

9. *Student summaries which require rearrangements and conclusions as differentiated from reiterations and repetitions* (6:156–157).

Other suggestions in caring for the gifted are:

1. Encourage students to *participate widely in the learning activities* by giving demonstrations, making special reports, preparing displays, and tutoring slower students.

2. Urge gifted students to *engage in service projects* for the class, school, community (serving on committees, making surveys, conducting interviews, writing or speaking for special occasions, engaging in work experience projects). These students can make a valuable contribution and at the same time they can help counteract a tendency to use unusual ability for selfish ends alone.

3. Encourage *participation in extraclass activities.* There is no better opportunity in school for the development of leadership than that found in participation in student activities.

4. Enlist the *aid of the parents.* A gifted child is often either exploited or ignored by his parents.

The term "underachievers" has come into prominence lately. Such persons are assumed to be bright students who are not living up to their full potential academically. The extent of underachieving is not fully known, yet observation, personal experience, and measurement by standardized tests indicate it to be great. The *Encyclopedia of Educational Research* suggests that among the causes of underachievement are: (1) keeping the gifted in classes with students of lesser ability; competition with average learners is not challenging; (2) lack of enrichment programs; (3) inflexible and undifferentiated teaching methods; and (4) lack of proper encouragement. To these causes one might also add those of inadequate identification and the fact that the potential fast achiever has not developed good work-study habits early in his educational career (4:590).

SPECIAL CLASSES AND SCHOOLS FOR THE GIFTED   Metropolitan school districts have found it practical to set aside schools for high achievers. This is not possible in small districts. They can, however, identify their talented students and make provisions for special classes for all or part of their instructional programs. This is possible both at elementary and secondary school levels. Often the enrichment or acceleration for these students is in the special fields of art, music, and drama, but similar work is being done in the "solid subjects."

Some teachers enjoy working with gifted students; others feel more secure with heterogeneous groups. Teachers selected for work with gifted groups usually volunteer, and even among volunteers selections should be carefully made. These teachers are commonly referred to as master teachers. They can be expected to turn out a quality product.

Creativity

There is a relationship between giftedness and creativity. Both have been given little more than passing lip service by the schools. The public and school administration give more attention to numerous other types of pupil growth. There seems to be very little time to teach creativity, yet if schools are committed to the concept of the development of the "whole person," then why is there no obligation to develop creativity wherever possible? The answer may lie in the fact that creativity is misunderstood. It is confused with the esoteric and the narrowly individualistic.

Miel says: ". . . the quality of creativity has been shown if the individual has made something *new to himself* that is satisfying and in that sense useful to him, if he has related things that were previously unrelated in *his* experience, and if the product is 'surprising' (that is, new) to *him*." She then adds the following statement, "We wish to emphasize that the process of making something new must at some point be a deliberate one in order to be labeled creative."[8] And, Wiles says, "Creativity is a method of progress. Conformity . . . maintains the *status quo*" (13:184). Creativity holds so much promise for society, conformity is so limited. High schools need to explore and develop student creative interest. Sometimes creative talents are shown early in life; at other times they are latent and need to be uncovered. Along this line, Macomber says, "It is being recognized increasingly that creative ability is a thing of degree, not of kind, that all persons possess it to a greater or less degree in each of the many areas of human expression. . . ."[9]

CHARACTERISTICS OF CREATIVITY   Creative persons are intelligent, yet there is no one-to-one relationship between creativity and intelligence.

[8] From *Creativity in Teaching*, ed. Alice Miel. © 1961 by Wadsworth Publishing Company, Inc., Belmont, Calif., pp. 6–7. Reprinted by permission of the publisher.
[9] From *Teaching in the Modern Secondary School* by F. G. Macomber. Copyright 1952. New York: McGraw-Hill Book Company, Inc., p. 37. Used by permission.

The most intelligent persons as measured by prevailing tests are not necessarily the most creative, yet a certain amount of intelligence is required for true creativity. Many of the facets of high intelligence are marks of creative people. Creative persons understand rather easily without much formal drill and in fact are bored by drill-type assignments. They like new ideas. These traits are held in common with persons of high intelligence.

Creative persons are original. This is not just a tautology. They make responses and do things in a novel way, at least in ways that are infrequently seen. Tests have shown that those who are more facile in suggesting new ideas also tend to come up with better and more adaptive ones.

Many of the great creative figures of history have shown their originality early in life, for example, Leonardo da Vinci, Sir Francis Galton, and Wolfgang Mozart. Many school children show creative tendencies quite early. In some, it seems to fade later, reasons for which are vague. There are many pupils who start their own neighborhood papers, or who draw, explore, tinker, or venture into paths new to them.

Creative persons seem to have intuitive perception. Without teaching, they seem to possess inferential knowledge and perception. They seem to be more sensitive to deeper meanings and their implications than noncreative persons.

Esthetic interests mark creative persons. These interests are closely tied to intuitive perception, and the works of creative persons have a freshness that is often observed in dramatics, visual arts, music, writing, and speaking. Such students are said to be talented.

Creative students are prone to show more disturbances of stress and tension than other students. People do not understand them, so it is said. Since creative persons are keyed as they are, they chafe and rebel easily; they are impatient. They feel the need for independence, and conformity creates tension and turmoil.

Recently, J. P. Guilford and his students in educational psychology attempted to isolate the complex of abilities that make up creativity, and to devise a test of these abilities by asking some functional questions about everyday matters. Seven different but related abilities were identified in these studies.

1. *Sensitivity to problems* indicates awareness of defects, needs, and deficiencies in the environment. A test of this ability is a set of questions asking for the defects which might be improved in common appliances, such as a refrigerator, or social institutions, such as the school.

2a. *Associative fluency* denotes the ability to think rapidly of words that meet certain requirements, such as being synonymous, or being opposites.

2b. *Ideational fluency* refers to the rate at which a person can think of ideas. For example, a person may be asked to think of as many uses as possible for a common brick.

3a. *Spontaneous flexibility* implies the ability to strike out in a number of different directions in one's thinking. For instance, in the question about "uses of a brick," those who have much spontaneous flexibility will think of a variety of uses, taking account of the various qualities of a brick, such as weight, solidity, abrasive qualities, and size.

3b. *Adaptive flexibility* is the ability to change the direction of one's thinking in order to keep up with a changing problem situation. Thus, if one is thinking of uses of a brick, the test may require one to change from uses of a single brick to uses of several bricks at a time, to uses which require the brick to have a certain color, to uses which depend on the density of the brick.

4. *Originality* is a quality which can be demonstrated in several ways, one being the uncommonness of ideas a person has, another the ability to produce clever, "original" titles for stories, and another being the ability to see unusual consequences of outlandish hypotheses, such as, "What would happen if people had only three fingers?"

5. *Redefinition* or *improvisation* refers to the ability to operate successfully in situations requiring novel use of familiar objects, such as using a shoe to drive a nail in the wall (5:176–177).

HOW TO IDENTIFY AND ENCOURAGE CREATIVITY   Before teachers can assist creative students, three points need to be posited: teachers must know what to look for, they must want to find it, and they must know what to do about it.

Immediately one thinks of "brainstorming" as a possible way to develop a number and variety of ideas in a short time. This technique has proved fruitful in many instances with children and with adults. Ideas, all kinds, wild or conventional, are brought forth. No attempt is made to evaluate them at the time. Such a technique stimulates imagination and creativity. It can be applied to almost any problem or subject.

But, do teachers wish to locate their creative students? They have a grave responsibility, and with heavy schedules anyway, do they really want to know these students? Teachers, however, are the most altruistic people in the world. Regardless of the effort involved, they *do want to know.* And the opportunity to work with some of the creative individuals is among the most rewarding in the profession.

What can teachers do when the creative students have been identified?

They can provide stimulating experiences and an atmosphere in which these students can express their talents. Encouragement and guidance represent the assistance they need most. With the exception of an art teacher here, a drama teacher there, or a composition teacher, imagination has had few sponsors.

A provocative point of view has been expressed by Henry to the effect that since "We must conserve culture while changing it, we must always be *more* sure of surviving than adapting . . . *Homo sapiens* has wanted acquiescence, not originality, from his offspring . . . Creative intellect is mysterious, devious, and irritating."[10] Consequently the school merely gives lip service to creativity.

MOTIVATION

It might be said that motivation is the first step in the learning process. By heredity and environment students have within them drives or motives to do certain things and to resist others. Basic drives and pleasures are closely related.

They like teachers who are interested in them—in their problems and their aspirations. They appreciate teachers who give them responsibility and who provide learning experiences that are new, but that are built upon their interests. As pointed out several times in this text, teachers should know their students in as many ways as possible—backgrounds, aptitudes, interests, and skills.

SOME TECHNIQUES FOR MOTIVATING STUDENTS How can you arouse genuine interest in the work of a class? Quickly reread the case of the teacher given at the beginning of this chapter. What might Jane do to interest her students? Normally, a student is interested when he considers an activity important by his standards, and if he truly believes an activity to be important he does not need artificial stimulation. Here are some suggestions which may assist in class motivation:

1. Set up a definite *purpose* for each class period. Students must feel that the work is worth doing. Use group goals to supplement individual goals. Follow through on all assignments. If they are not important, do not make them.

2. Use a *variety* of learning activities, methods, and materials. Think about ways of introducing purposeful variety into class work. Talk to many other teachers. Read the professional journals. Introduce concrete learning materials (films, resource speakers, field trips, projects). Consider surprise, suspense, and curiosity in connection with method.

[10] Jules Henry, "American Schoolrooms: Learning the Nightmare," *Columbia University Forum.* vol. 6 (Spring 1963), pp. 24–30.

3. Encourage wider student *participation.* Get all students involved. Involvement may be only a matter of degree, but all the students belong to the class. The principle of individual differences operates here, too.

4. Place more *responsibility* on students for their own learning. Well-placed responsibility inflates the ego. Find ways of quietly promoting the idea with the better students that they have some responsibility for group progress.

5. Keep students *informed of their progress.* Hand back papers promptly. No one likes to work in the dark. Encourage students to learn to evaluate their own work.

6. *Relate school work to the world* in which we live. Tie principles and theories to contemporary developments if appropriate.

7. Set up learning situations where every student may experience some degree of *success.* Success is a prime motivator. "Nothing fails like failure." Commend if possible.

8. Establish *an environment* that is attractive and comfortable. This has been stressed at several places in this book.

9. Show *enthusiasm* for the subject you teach. "Sell" the idea of the importance of your subject. Students may have entered the class with a prejudice against it. Subtly correct it, not by preachment, but by positive action.

This chapter has tried to show that the modern secondary school is concerned about quality teaching. The achievement of this goal involves many people, agencies, and philosophies. The teacher plays an important role in teaching, but the matter of organization is also important and it must be integrated into over-all considerations of school effectiveness. Class organization, regardless of its type, must provide the foundation so that teachers can be maximally effective in relating learning to students' needs.

Selected Readings

1. American Educational Research Association, *Encyclopedia of Educational Research,* 3d ed., Chester W. Harris, ed. New York: The Macmillan Company, 1960.
2. Brickell, Henry, *Organizing New York State for Educational Change.* Albany: Commission of Education, 1961.
3. Brownell, John A., and Harris A. Taylor, "Theoretical Perspectives for Teaching Teams," *Phi Delta Kappan,* vol. 43 (January 1962), pp. 150–157.
4. DeCecco, John P., *Human Learning in the School.* New York: Holt, Rinehart and Winston, Inc., 1963.
5. DeHaan, Robert F., and Robert J. Havighurst, *Educating Gifted Children,* revised ed. Chicago: University of Chicago Press, 1961.

6. Freehill, Maurice F., *Gifted Children*. New York: The Macmillan Company, 1961.
7. Miel, Alice, ed., *Creativity in Teaching*. Belmont, Calif.: Wadsworth Publishing Company, Inc., 1961.
8. Rivlin, Harry N., *Teaching Adolescents in Secondary School*, 2d ed. New York: Appleton-Century-Crofts, 1961.
9. Risk, Thomas M., *Principles and Practices of Teaching in Secondary Schools*, 3d ed. New York: American Book Company, 1958.
10. *Team Teaching: A Research Guide for Administrators*. Pleasant Hills, Calif.: Contra Costa County Superintendent of Schools, December 1960.
11. Trump, Lloyd, "Flexible Scheduling," *Phi Delta Kappan*, vol. 44 (May 1963), pp. 367–371.
12. ———, and Dorsey Baynham, *Guide to Better Schools: Focus on Change*. Chicago: Rand McNally & Company, 1961.
13. Wiles, Kimball, *Teaching for Better Schools*, 2d ed. Englewood Cliffs, N.J.: Prentice-Hall, Inc., 1959.
14. Wrightstone, J. Wayne, "What Research Says to the Teacher," *Class Organization for Instruction*, Bulletin No. 13. Washington, D.C.: National Education Association, 1961.

Selected Audio-Visual Materials

A. *And No Bells Ring*, 56 min., b & w, sound: National Association of Secondary School Principals. This film explains the Trump plan with emphasis on the work of students in large and small groups and in individual study.
B. *Focus on Change*, 25 min., color, filmstrip and 33-⅓ rpm record: National Education Association. Focus is on team teaching and need for change.
C. *Homework: Studying on Your Own*, 10 min.: Coronet. Home study problems and budgeting time are stressed. Three high school students use a film to illustrate their problem situations and then offer some solutions.
D. *Individual Differences*, 24 min., b & w: McGraw-Hill Book Company, Inc. A teacher's praise leads a boy to discover that to be different is not to be wrong. The film stresses need for schools to shape education to the needs of individuals.
E. *Learning Democracy Through School-Community Projects*, 21 min., color, sound: University of Michigan. Experiences in democratic learning in some Michigan schools are depicted including student councils, student elections, Junior Red Cross, youth centers, a community council meeting, vocational guidance conference, school safety patrol, rural field day, and audio-visual service club.
F. *Providing for Individual Differences*, 23 min., b & w, sound: Iowa State University. This film indicates the ways in which a classroom teacher can adjust the learning environment to meet individual differences. It depicts a college class discussing the methods of handling these differences as they observed them on visits to elementary and secondary schools.
G. *Time for Talent*, 23 min., sound: Education Service, Inc. Film employing actual classroom scenes describes how a community can provide for academically talented students.
H. *Time Out for Study*. 3 filmstrips, 45 frames each: One shows planning work and organizing study schedules; the second, principles of organized study and working habits; and the third outlines notebook organization.

CHAPTER 7

Teaching methods: provisions for groups and individuals

Secondary school method has a long history. It has developed over many years, and during this time a host of methods of instruction have been used. Most of these methods have had some merit, at least for some people at some time. New methods have developed to meet new goals, but old methods pass into oblivion slowly. Secondary teachers of today are following a variety of teaching methods. Many are discussed in this chapter and, to give some organization to this discussion, these methods are grouped under headings which are involved chiefly with large group instruction, small group instruction, and individual instruction.

VARIED PROCEDURES OF LARGE GROUP INSTRUCTION

It has been said that "teachers teach as they were taught." There is some truth in this statement. The statement implies that beginning secondary school teachers tend to overdo lecturing because so much of their preparation in college was of the lecture type. The lecture method in high school has been generally attacked as a method unsuited to secondary school instruction.

The Lecture Method in the Secondary School

In spite of the fact that secondary teachers are constantly admonished not to lecture to their students, the technique is widely used. This method of teaching has been grossly abused by many teachers and their students have suffered; but, correctly used, it is functional.

At the outset it should be pointed out that there is a difference between formal lecturing and informal lecturing or "teacher talks." The short informal lecture can be used to good advantage in introducing a unit, summarizing a problem for study, providing information difficult for students to find, supplying motivation, or in sharing one's own cultural experiences with the class.

The lecture method in high school can be used to explain a problem in which students are interested, to illustrate a process by a lecture demonstration, to illustrate a point by creating a word picture, or to tell a good story. Telling the story of William Tell, relating Galileo's experience with his telescope, reviewing Irving Stone's *The Agony and the Ecstasy*, explaining the forces of aerodynamics in space conquest, or describing the emerging needs for broader world markets are merely some of the forms of the lecture. To be effective, teachers need to understand the varied forms and uses of the lecture.

HOW TO MAKE THE LECTURE EFFECTIVE The teacher talk or informal lecture can be made more effective by giving attention to the following suggestions:

1. Lectures for secondary school students should usually be short. One of fifteen or twenty minutes is possibly the maximum, and in most cases five or ten minutes may be better. Teachers must recognize that attention spans are relatively short. Although instruction by television depends chiefly on lecture, it is also highly spiced with demonstration and visual cuing. Time intervals tend to be longer, but variety is the key. Straight lecturing must still be for short periods.

2. The approach to the lecture should be informal. The language should be clear and simple, not stilted. The purpose is to inform, to enrich, to motivate.

3. Lectures should be tailored to people, and in the high school the teachers must not forget that the audience is one of adolescent boys and girls. Lecturing teachers are inclined to use words beyond the students' working vocabularies.

4. Lectures should be related to students' backgrounds, knowledges, skills, and interests. If they are not, the students are soon "lost." This results in a real problem in motivation.

5. Lectures should not rehash textbooks or other readings which the students have done, or should do for themselves. The lecture should present new and fresh ideas not readily available to the students.

6. Lecturers should avoid reminiscences or discourses on trivial personal incidents.

7. Lectures should be planned and organized so that they do not digress. In the main, the teacher should announce his purpose at the beginning of the lecture. Then, its development should stick to the theme. The exact purpose of the talk must not be forgotten as it develops. Some

lectures are like the classic report on Columbus and his discovery of America, "He didn't know where he was going when he started, he didn't know where he was when he got there, and when he returned he didn't know where he had been."

8. Talks should be replete with verbal illustrations. Illustrations can accent abstract ideas.

9. Frequently, lectures are improved if supplemented by simple visual aids such as specimens, flat pictures, or chalkboard sketches.

10. Many students, especially in the advanced classes, will be going to college. They should be told that lecturing is customary at the college level, and that some practice in learning from this technique while still in high school is in order.

11. The relatively long lecture should include a summarization at its close.

12. The teacher should give the class instruction in taking simple notes and in organizing verbal material. Students should learn to review these notes and to make them part of their cultural growth.

Lecturing is a difficult, but useful method of teaching. It involves more than verbal fluency. It is a method in itself, but it also supplements practically all other teaching devices such as demonstration, role playing, the introduction of film lessons, and group discussion. It is not merely a case of all or none; it is pervasive. Teachers will sense when their talks are effective and when they are not.

College teachers, ministers, and public lecturers often supplement their lectures with mimeographed copies of the material they have covered. This may not be a practical suggestion for the high school teacher, but modifications of the idea are worth consideration. These modifications would include mimeographed outlines, summaries, follow-up questions, or projects.

Research bearing on the lecture as a secondary school teaching method is inconsistent. Some researchers have found it notably effective, especially with older students, but other investigators have found other methods of greater value. Method must relate to the educational objectives sought by the school; thus, if the objective is to transfer knowledge or information about a topic, then the lecture method is satisfactory, but if the objective is problem solving or the building of attitudes of inquiry, other methods are preferable (3:280, 851).

Illustrations: Verbal and Visual

It has already been pointed out that illustrations can accent or underscore abstract lecture ideas. Audiences of all ages become more interested when the speaker clarifies and enlivens his talk with anecdotes, verbal illustrations, witticisms, apt stories, examples, and even pertinent reminiscences. However, injudicious illustrations cheapen the talk or render it valueless. Slang is very much a case in point.

Visual illustration, like verbal, is used to clarify, to render ideas concrete and meaningful. Good teachers try to make their talks more effective by introducing various forms of visualization. An old Chinese proverb says, "One picture is worth a thousand words." This far-reaching generalization carries a point: a few well-placed visual illustrations will often save a great deal of telling, add variety, and stimulate interest.

Audio-Visual Materials as a Part of Method

Film, radio, television, and magnetic tape recordings loom large in any discussion of large group instruction. Although these techniques and materials may be successfully used with small groups, and even with individuals, they play their most useful role in communication with large groups. Today's schools make extensive use of these materials, whether the school organization is conventional in character or whether it follows some form of team teaching. It was noted earlier that Dr. Trump's plan makes provision for 40 percent of a student's time to be spent in large group instruction. Specific techniques for the use of many instructional materials are presented in Chapters 8 through 10.

VARIED PROCEDURES OF SMALL GROUP INSTRUCTION

The differentiation between a large group and a small group is indefinite. Certainly, a group of 100 is a large group and one of nine is small. But where is the dividing line? Also, it should be noted that under certain circumstances, a group of twenty-five, for example, may be classified as large in remedial reading, but small in general music.

The Oral Recitation

One still finds much secondary school teaching making use of the traditional method, which is commonly dependent upon the "assign-study-recite-test" procedure. This is not a stimulating mode of instruction. Essentially, this method values information simply for the sake of information and rests squarely upon memorization as a technique. It emphasizes specifics—definition, classification, chronology—rather than meaningful wholes. Rote recall rather than understanding or true knowledge is fostered. This type of instruction does not produce the changes in student behavior that the schools are trying to bring about. Then too this kind of instruction fails to foster permanency in learning.

Almost every teacher can relate examples of students who recognized information only if a single memorized clue was given. John Dewey's story illustrates the point:

"What would you find if you dug a hole in the earth?" Getting no response, he repeated the question; again he obtained nothing but silence. The teacher chided Mr. Dewey, "You're asking the wrong question." Turning to the class, she asked, "What is the state of the center of the earth?" The class replied in unison, "Igneous fusion."[1]

Under the traditional recitation plan, the teacher is largely a drill master. The drill method rests on the assignment of a certain number of pages of a text to be read, problems to be solved, or exercises to be completed. The work is usually completed at home or in a study hall. A question-and-answer period the following day covers the material assigned.

Although many students apparently accept this method of school work, it is doubtful if any really enjoy it. The method is inflexible; pupil interest is usually disregarded. The method is unacceptable to teachers educated in the rationale of modern education, except in those cases where the primary purpose is overlearning by means of drill.

The use of the question in group discussion is quite a different thing from questioning in recitation.

Other Techniques

Five discussion techniques for dealing with small groups are group discussion, buzz session, panel and symposium, debate, and the working committee. All are suitable to group work, usually small groupings, although the discussion technique in the hands of a master teacher can be a potent instrument with large classes. It is reported by the former students of the late William H. Kilpatrick of Teachers College, Columbia University, that he regularly taught classes of 200 and 300 using a discussion technique supplemented by lecture. The students were, of course, adults who had elected Dr. Kilpatrick's classes in the philosophy of education. The situation in high school teaching is not exactly comparable.

Group Discussion

To discuss, says Webster, is to consider, examine, or investigate the various sides of a question, topic, or problem. A great deal of contemporary secondary school teaching is of this type, especially in literature, social studies, health, speech, and certain aspects of science. The discussion

---

[1] Quoted by Benjamin S. Bloom, ed., *Taxonomy of Educational Objectives, Handbook I: Cognitive Domain.* New York: David McKay Company, Inc., 1956, p. 29.

method ranges all the way from a narrow question and answer technique to a nondirective approach with the teacher playing a laissez-faire role. Ruja defines the method as:

interchange of questions and answers (*sic*) among students primarily with the instructor playing a role . . . of moderator. The instructor roughly defines the area of discussion and supplies information when directly asked for it or when it illustrates a point already made or . . . poses a question relevant to the topic under consideration. . . . Mostly the activity of the instructor consists in reflecting the content and feelings of students' comments, relating these to one another and to the central topic, and promoting orderly sequences of discussion.[2]

The problem for the beginning teacher is how best to sharpen the discussion technique in order to make it effective in motivating high school students. The discussion technique is an essential part of the democratic process. It assumes that the class is less teacher centered, whereas the older recitation assumed the opposite. Discussion connotes a give and take between teacher and students, and among students themselves. It assumes a willingness to share points of view, to hold an open mind, to weigh evidence. Textbooks, visual media, and all forms of instructional materials are used and weighed as the teacher guides the class through the content of his field.

Although discussion is used here in the sense of the primary technique, it will nearly always be supplemented with other techniques. Which ones used will depend upon the maturity of the students and on the subject matter. There are some courses, for example, computational mathematics, in which discussion is unsuited for the primary method. Some of the so-called "new mathematics" is suited to limited discussion.

A good discussion includes the following characteristics:

1. It has *purpose*.
2. It is based on *important information*. Although the primary purpose of the discussion may be to share ideas and opinions, it must issue from factual sources rather than "pooled ignorance."
3. It utilizes *participation by every student*.
4. It is founded on *mutual respect* for different opinions and *consideration* for one another's rights.
5. It deals with a topic, problem, or subject that has *significance* for students and for society.
6. It should lead to some *conclusions*.

INTRODUCING THE DISCUSSION   Discussions may be initiated in a number of ways. The most common procedure is, of course, by means of questioning on the part of the teacher. Other methods which provoke a good response are a panel, symposium, buzz session, debate, sociodrama, report, or demonstration.

In laying the foundation for a successful discussion, the teacher needs to take a number of precautions. First of all, *he must be prepared* and make sure that *the class is prepared*. Are the students ready? Have they prepared for the discussion? A warm-up period is often a good idea to get the attention of all the students and to create an interest in the topic. Is everyone comfortable? Is the seating arrangement conducive to discussion? A circle, semicircle, or some other face-to-face arrangement is preferable to a face-to-back arrangement.

CONDUCTING THE DISCUSSION   Actually, conducting an effective lesson through discussion follows the general pattern for lessons of all types. The essential elements are teacher preparation, student preparation and involvement, and possible follow-up such as research or experimentation.

First of all, the teacher must be prepared. This assumes thorough understanding of the content to be covered, and careful planning of the specific topic to be covered. Thoroughgoing unit and daily lesson plans pave the way for effective group discussion. In addition, Rivlin says:

Because the discussion on a topic may ramify in many directions, it is difficult for the teacher to prepare adequately on a day-by-day basis. The kind of rich background which the teacher needs cannot be secured by the teacher who reads each night only as much as he thinks he needs for the next day. More than ever, the teacher must himself be an educated person, with a scholarship that is ever fresh because it is constantly being renewed. If the teacher's background is not adequate to qualify him to lead a discussion on the topic, it may be better for him to rely on other methods of presentation and to use the discussion techniques for only those phases of the topic for which his background is adequate.[3]

Student preparation is as important as teacher preparation. Unless students have sufficient background related to the discussion topic or problem, little can be accomplished. Also, there is need for specific information about the problem being discussed. A discussion of the United Arab Republic, the Suez Canal, or Israel, if it is to do more than air superficial opinion, must rest on a political, geographical, and economic understanding as well as knowledge of contemporaneous happenings.

Insofar as the actual discussion itself goes, responsibility is shared by

[3] Harry N. Rivlin, *Teaching Adolescents in Secondary Schools*, 2d ed. New York: Appleton-Century-Crofts, 1961, p. 182. Used by permission of Appleton-Century-Crofts, © 1948, 1961.

teacher and students, although not on an equal basis. Much of the responsibility may be delegated to students. Although the teacher is seated as a member of the class while a student chairman assumes leadership, in the final analysis the teacher is in charge. The responsibility for worthwhile work belongs to the teacher and cannot be delegated. He is paid for this leadership.

There are various suggestions to help attain maximal results. Rivlin outlines eight useful techniques to help vitalize group discussions (9:185–194). These suggestions are abbreviated and restated here:

The teacher plays a prominent role in the discussion and cannot abrogate the responsibility. His maturity, scholarship, and leadership must keep the discussion relevant.

The teacher guides the discussion. Usually, the teacher poses the problem or formulates the topic for discussion. Then, he must achieve a balance between complete direction and little or no direction. He must keep the discussion moving and with significant accomplishments, yet, he must not dictate.

The teacher keeps the discussion from rambling. A clear statement of the problem is imperative. This may call for the exploration of possible interpretations, definitions, and delimitations. A statement of the problem written on the chalkboard helps to prevent rambling. At times the group may wish to develop and place on the chalkboard an outline of the topic. Significant points as they develop may be listed by the teacher or class recorder. For this purpose, an overhead projector is often more useful than a chalkboard since the recorder may make entries without leaving the discussion circle. Furthermore, such reports may be saved from day to day for further reference.

The teacher evaluates tangential remarks, and decides on their relevancy. He decides to what extent the original statement of the problem should be revised; how much new evidence, so to speak, will be admitted.

The teacher is responsible for summaries and conclusions. As discussions draw to a close, students should know that the group raised various issues, accepted certain evidence, and rejected other evidence. At times teachers will ask students to write individual summaries for their notebooks; at other times the class recorder may ditto a brief summary to be passed out to the class.

The teacher is responsible for stimulating thinking. It is necessary to keep the students actively thinking about the problem under discussion. The ability to challenge, to stimulate, and to present new horizons marks a good discussion leader. There is a close tie between this stimulation and the initial planning and preparation of the teacher.

The teacher fosters broad student participation. Some students will be inclined to sit back and let others do the work, and still other students will tend to monopolize the discussion. In both cases the firm hand of the teacher must lead. Shy students should be brought into the discussion possibly by such commonplace remarks as, "Bill, what does this point mean to you?" "Dorothy, would you like to speak to this point?" "Oscar, have you some personal information on this problem which is of interest to the class?" At the same time the fluent, extroverted, enthusiastic student must learn to listen, to share the time with others, to adapt to the situation.

The teacher must recognize individual differences among the participants. Some have unusual ability and verbal fluency, others are limited.

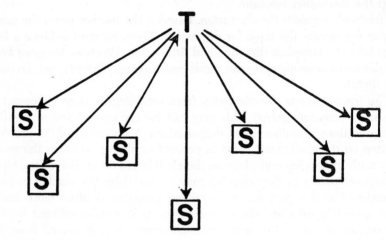

Fig. 7-1

Some come from homes where discussion is the rule; others have little or no home participation, nor are cultural topics ever subjects of conversation.

Discussion lessons, like most other lessons, *lead naturally into follow-up activities.* It is unfortunate that bells have to terminate most lessons. Students will usually be reluctant to abandon lively, stimulating discussions. The teacher may wish to suggest that an individual student, or the group, check out some of the leads developed in the class. These activities may well take the students to the library, the audio-visual department, the community, or other sources. Reporting back to the class is a natural activity.

Greater involvement may also come out of the class discussions, involvements for the group as a whole as well as for individuals. Forms of the involvement may be a field trip, a program to be given in the school assembly, or an invitation to certain other classes to join in a cooperative effort of a designated type. Individuals also may come upon ideas so appealing that they develop into a science fair project, a story or a poem that is entered in a national students' competition, or even an enduring career motive.

EVALUATING THE DISCUSSION   Clark and Starr (2:135–136) and Grambs, Iverson, and Patterson (4:240) suggest that the teacher might draw up a flow chart to assist in the appraisal of student participation. Such a chart

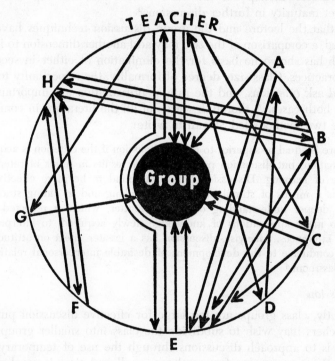

Fig. 7-2

not only shows student involvement, but also shows the instructor certain guidelines for future group teaching techniques. Figure 7-1 illustrates a dialogue or a one-way discussion.

Figure 7-2 shows the interchange of ideas among the students with the teacher primarily playing the role of moderator. Note how the teacher brings all members of the class into participation.

Analyze Figures 7-1 and 7-2. What does each tell you? Which chart more nearly illustrates Ruja's interpretation of the group discussion technique? In connection with the second chart, comment on the participation of each student. What are the chances that this class may "get out of hand?"

Several other types of appraisal include student evaluation (oral or written), group listening to a tape recording of the discussion, and a teacher postdiscussion evaluation against a set of criteria such as: 1. Did the group accomplish what it set out to do? 2. Did the group stick to the topic? 3. Were the members of the class objective? 4. Was there a shortage of facts and valid evidence? 5. Did everyone participate? 6. Did any "eager beavers" monopolize the class? 7. Will this class experience lead to greater maturity in further discussions?

Now that the lecture and the group discussion techniques have been presented, a comparison of the two may add another dimension to insight. Research has shown no basis for the elimination of either in secondary school practices. Class size, degree of formality, the opportunity to interrupt and ask questions, and the rate of presentation are important variables in both cases. A thorough search of all the literature in connection with the two methods led Stovall to write:

the lecture is equal or superior to group discussion if the criterion is acquisition of information, but discussion produces better results in terms of retention of this type of learning. Discussion has been found to be more effective than lecture as a means of stimulating critical thinking and in aiding students to attain a deeper understanding of subject matter, which is reflected in the ability to make applications of knowledge newly acquired, to interpret, and to draw inferences. Likewise, discussion has a greater effect on attitudes and is more conducive to the development of desirable interpersonal relationships in the classroom.[4]

Buzz Session

Frequently, class groups are too large for effective discussion purposes, and teachers may wish to subdivide the class into smaller groups. One method is to approach discussions through the use of temporary small groups. Buzz groups are frequently so small and time is so short that they have been referred to as *Discussion 66* (9:196), meaning six persons in a group meeting for six minutes, yet a buzz session may last for a half hour. The purpose of these groups is exploratory. They are "boosters." Hopefully, they set the groundwork to get a discussion started.

A teacher who is planning to make use of buzz sessions should plan with care. In starting a buzz group, the teacher lights a fuse that can blow up in his face if improperly handled, or he may open doors that would otherwise remain tightly closed. Preplanning and a sense of timing are

[4] Thomas F. Stovall, "Lecture vs. Discussion," *Phi Delta Kappan*, vol. 39 (March 1958), p. 256.

important ingredients in success with the technique. Specific factors in-clude the following:

1. Both students and teacher should have a clear idea of the purpose of the work they are to do and how they are to accomplish it. They do no research, hence they merely arrive at a consensus.

2. Buzz sessions must be timely. They may be announced at the be-ginning, middle, or near the close of a class period. There is a strategic time in nearly every instance. The purpose is to allow more people to express an opinion on an issue that many members of the group wish to speak about, for example, problems of school policy, grading, class events, and serious controversial subjects.

3. Buzz groups must be small so that all members will have a chance to be heard, yet not so small that there is a dearth of ideas and resources. The size may range from three to six.

4. Choosing the members of a buzz group must be simple. The groups are temporary, and their findings are accepted only as a consensus. Groups may be formed alphabetically, by seating proximity, by passing out numbered cards, or by use of similar arrangements.

5. Buzz sessions are usually short. Students are told that they will have so many minutes to buzz. Experience will help the teacher to judge what is a reasonable limit; if the time is too short, students will be frustrated; if unduly long, they dawdle and become noisy and disinter-ested. If the teacher sets a five-minute limit for buzzing, but finds that at the end of the time all are working earnestly, he can announce a time extension.

6. Very little organization is needed by the groups, probably only a chairman and a recorder. It is risky to allow the groups to make their own selections. Usually, it is better for the teacher to do it. There are several sides to this matter of selection.

7. Groups are asked to report back to the entire assembled class on the action of the group. This is usually done by the recorder, but it could be done by any member of the group. Group reports may be written on the chalkboard or delivered orally. Sometimes, the group reporters are in-structed to get together later and summarize their findings.

Panel and Symposium

Panels and symposiums may be used in either large or small classes, or in groups smaller than those considered to be of class size. The purpose is to provide an opportunity for a few well-prepared students to discuss pertinent topics. In the panel discussion, four to eight students are selected for the discussion. There is usually a free exchange of ideas among the members of the panel. The presentations are considered impromptu, but the participants are well informed, and should be students with divergent points of view.

A good panel technique places large responsibility on a chairman who may be selected by the teacher, the class, or the panel members. He acts much as a good chairman of any discussion meeting. He states the topic for consideration, introduces the panel members, and makes a statement or two concerning the topic. It is his responsibility to bring all the members of the panel into action, yet to control the discussion so that the time is not monopolized by a few. Another duty of the chairman is to recognize contributions from the floor. Finally, he summarizes the talks, closes the discussion, and dismisses the panel.

A symposium is slightly different. It requires members to prepare and present a set speech (statement) of facts or opinions regarding the topic. This is followed by discussion from the floor. The chairman has the same duties as the panel chairman.

Panels and symposiums accomplish approximately the same results. They increase discussion opportunities, and they are appropriate techniques for introduction of new materials, for enrichment as a unit progresses, for culmination of a unit of work, and for motivation.

Debate

The debate is a traditional way of promoting discussion in classes. Unfortunately, the debate is usually formal and is limited in participation to two or four of the better students in the class. Attempts have been made to modify the debate by introducing the British style or House of Commons procedure. Two students take affirmative and negative positions and present short arguments of five to eight minutes. A shorter talk is then given by a second member on each side. This debate is followed by open debate from the floor, but these talks must be in affirmative-negative sequence. The object is to balance the arguments and to objectify partisanship. The main speakers on each side more or less marshal their adherents and set the trend for the speaking sequence.

Committee

In order to divide classes into smaller groups, teachers often arrange for working committees. These committees may be brought into existence for short term assignments of a day or two, or they may be given a working schedule of two or three weeks, as, for example, in unit teaching. The use of committees was discussed in Chapter 3 in relation to cooperative planning. The discussion is brought up again here briefly to fix it in mind as one of several techniques for effective instruction of small groups.

Committees may be selected by the teachers, more or less arbitrarily, but they must recognize student tastes and abilities. There may also be voluntary participation. The purposes for which the committees exist will usually determine the method. It is well for the teacher to keep in mind natural student groupings and leaders when committee membership is considered. Certain students may work together cooperatively; others may not. A class sociogram can be of assistance to the teacher in this connection (the sociogram is discussed in Chapter 15). Committees should be small, usually five to seven members, so that they can convene easily and divide the work equitably. The teacher must remember that committees by their nature are groups working together. Working time and meeting places must not be overlooked.

COMMITTEE PROCEDURES

Assignment of specific tasks or problems
Selection of a chairman for each committee
Selection of recorders
Development of work schedules
Preparation of reports

The senior sociology class in _____ High School was discussing the economics of the family and the young married couple. It was decided to divide the class of thirty-five into committees to gather information and report. The following committees and duties were decided upon:

Committee	*Responsibility*
A. Sources of income	To consider one or both members working. Types of work. Possible pay. Other sources of income.
B. Food and shelter	Own vs. rent. Apartment vs. house. Space needed. Eat at home and eat out. Lunch at work.
C. Transportation, taxes, savings	Public transportation. Private car. Income, taxes, fees, licenses. Are savings possible?
D. Health and recreation	Insurance. Hospital and medical bills. Types of entertainment. Entertainment at home. Public entertainment.
E. Dependence on vs. independence of family	His parents. Her parents.
F. Furnishing a house or an apartment	Installment buying. Amount and quality of furnishings. "Second-hand and hand-me-downs."

Dramatization

Various forms of dramatization are employed by teachers at all school levels from kindergarten to college. Naturally, some forms are better suited to certain maturity levels than others, and some content is more appropriate. Youth enjoy the dramatic form, and, although some individuals are shy, most of them enjoy both being participants and being members of an audience. Dramatization adds realism, zest, and interest to class work on many occasions. It tends to promote cooperation and group unity. If kept within reasonable bounds, this technique or methodology can be signally effective.

The chief forms of dramatization used by secondary school teachers are extemporaneous dramatization, role playing, pantomime, and puppetry.

ROLE PLAYING Extemporaneous dramatization and role playing are much the same. There is an informal, impromptu characterization or creation of a role. This action depends upon knowledges and interpretations rather than memorized lines and actions. Historical incidents and social organization lend themselves to role playing. Teachers of English and speech accept dramatization as a natural concomitant, but the activity must fit into the course objectives or it becomes artificial and time wasting. Dramatization or role playing can be just as effectively employed in foreign language classes, or in courses stressing job application, consumer buying, and family living.

Role playing, although simple, must follow certain rules to be effective: (1) situations must be set up with care; (2) roles must be assigned thoughtfully; (3) members of the class who become the audience should understand what the actors will be trying to accomplish and should show proper behavior; (4) actors should be allowed a few minutes for consultation and strategy; (5) the presentation should then be made; and (6) an evaluation of the action by the entire group should follow immediately. The discussion should be frank but not punitive; it should evaluate the portrayal of the incident, not the dramatic merits of the performance. Often, scenes can be repeated with profit by changing the actors in the several roles.

PUPPETRY Puppetry is a specialized form of dramatization which has many values, yet it is often time consuming and difficult to dissociate from entertainment. The use of puppets and marionettes is a highly creative activity which calls for skill and understanding.

High school teachers have found puppetry useful in such subjects as home economics, social studies, foreign languages, health, and English.

Many educational television programs make extensive use of puppets in serious presentations for children and adults.

There are many other forms of dramatics that can be successfully used at times. Among these forms are pantomimes, mimicry, mock conventions, skits, and sociodramas. The authors do not make a noticeable distinction between the sociodrama and role playing. "The sociodrama is merely a form of role playing designed to give a better understanding of human relations."[5]

Demonstration

A simple way to define demonstration is to point out that it is the learning of a skill through guided performance. But, the demonstration is more than a simple act of showing a process or a skill. Although it employs concrete materials and a performance, it also presents facts and principles.

The demonstration is useful for teachers and students alike. It may be used in almost any field, and it serves well in the introduction, development, and culmination of units. Teachers tend to use the technique more in the first two stages of a unit, but students probably use it more at the culmination of a unit. For example, students demonstrate skill with typewriters, with science equipment, with sewing machines, or with the horizontal bars in the gymnasium. There are some demonstrations that students can do better than teachers.

EFFECTIVE DEMONSTRATIONS MUST BE PLANNED   The principles of a good demonstration are essentially the same as the principles of any good lesson presentation—preparation, presentation, and follow-up. Risk says, prepare the learner, guide the learner, and evaluate the learner (8:253).

Tips for a good demonstration:

Prepare well in advance by practicing the act, by readying all equipment and supplies, by being sure the demonstration will work, and by building self-assurance.

Prepare the learner in advance in what to look for. Give needed background and purpose.

Be sure everyone can see clearly.

Keep the directions simple; vary the tempo to suit the class.

Check frequently during the performance to know that each step is being followed. Explain and perform simultaneously.

Summarize the entire demonstration. Repeat, if necessary, but ask questions.

Follow up with individual or group tryouts immediately if possible.

[5] Carter V. Good, ed., *Dictionary of Education.* New York: McGraw-Hill Book Company, Inc., 1959, p. 510. Used by permission.

Students appreciate good demonstrations, and successful performance builds confidence in the teacher. A junior high school science teacher demonstrated how a volcano erupts. A plaster of Paris mound with hollow crater was made in advance on a plywood board. Then in class with the room semidarkened, the chemicals in the cone were ignited. The eruption occurred on schedule: slow action, rapid action, decreased action. Ash fell at the base of the volcano for a radius of 15 inches. The discussion after the demonstration was spirited, to say the least. Both student motivation and teacher confidence were enhanced by the experience.

Science demonstrations may involve elaborate equipment with many materials. Physical education classes, too, may involve sports or gymnasium equipment. Demonstrations in other subject areas have almost unlimited possibilities, some involving no equipment, or only a few inexpensive, easily collected materials. Mathematics demonstrations may call for templates, measuring forms, cardboard, pieces of wire, crayon, string, and other simple supplies. A student demonstration once used a yardstick, a chalkboard eraser, a clothespin, and a piece of string to show the effects of friction and centrifugal force in driving a car.

Demonstrations vary somewhat in their concreteness, yet even the more abstract ones are basically concrete. In demonstrating how pi (π) is derived and computed, the teacher might use a bicycle wheel, a cutout on a feltboard, or a drawing on the chalkboard. In the follow-up, problems are solved or applications are made. How do foreign language students achieve correct pronunciation? They listen to oral demonstrations with full explanation; then, they practice.

VARIED PROCEDURES OF INDIVIDUAL INSTRUCTION

The foregoing discussion has been related to activities involved in instruction of large and small groups. These groups are made up of individuals, and it is with and about these individuals that we are concerned. A democratic society accepts the adage that the chain is no stronger than its individual links.

The Importance of Individual Instruction

To the schools come all the pupils. This is a broad statement, because it includes the gifted, the slow, and the average insofar as scholastic abilities are involved; it also includes the shy and the aggressive; the balanced and the maladjusted; those who have a high degree of self-concern and those with concern for others; those who enjoy ideas and those who enjoy people and things; those who have natural artistic talents and those who do not. Teachers always have been concerned with individuals, whether their instruction was organized around large classes, small classes, or a single student. The question is how can teachers best give optimum service.

People must react individually in order to learn. They can profit from the shared experience of others, but in order really to learn, persons must in some way make these experiences their own. To learn, they repeat or interpret the experience. Learning is unique in many ways; it cannot be forced upon a person, except in a minor sort of way. Each person's learning pattern is his own.

In recent years there has been a resurgence of individualized work in the secondary school. The climate today favors extending capable students more than was done a few years ago; also, slower students are provided with greater personal assistance with their scholastic problems. Various plans are being tried; their applications and values vary widely. Teachers will do well to evaluate these plans and select those which seem appropriate.

Means Involved in Individual Instruction

In order to accomplish individual study and learning, teachers provide varied activities. All of the means involved in individual instruction have some merit, but some have more than others. We shall discuss the ones most commonly used.

The Unit Approach as a Method

In Chapter 3 the unit in lesson planning was discussed. By implication, at least, its use as a method of teaching was described. *The Encyclopedia of Educational Research* refers to the unit plan as one of the older "named" plans, names such as Morrison and Dalton. Most of these plans provided for students to work alone on assignments except for assistance from the teacher. The students were, however, organized as classes, some large and some small (3:222).

The unit idea applies to class groups as well as individuals. Many teachers have found committee organization useful. Rivlin devotes an entire chapter to this approach (9:107–147).

Among the values of the unit method is its provision for individual differences. Each student works at his own rate, but within a time framework. In most instances, the organization calls for each student to cover certain fundamentals, but there is provision for enrichment and extended work for those students with more ability. Slower students are given assignments of a simpler nature and with more direction from the teacher.

Learning is organized in relatively large blocks of knowledge or around comprehensive topics or big problems. Care must be exercised to see that gaps do not occur in the subject coverage. Each unit, as explained in an earlier chapter, is a rather lengthy assignment and may cover one week or several weeks.

Teachers who follow the unit plan of teaching find extensive pre-planning imperative. Each unit must be seen in its entirety before the students begin work on it. This involves objectives, procedures, materials, and planned evaluation. Some teachers involve the group in much problem solving or in cooperative efforts as topic analysis and study. To this extent the plan is one for group instruction instead of individualized instruction.

Rivlin has cogently stated the case for the unit plan in this manner:

Habits of reading widely rather than accepting the textbook uncritically, of using the library as a source of information, of helping others and of responding to suggestions from others, of working independently and of being able to serve on committees, of using information as a basis for problem solving, of regarding the school as a place where real questions are thrashed out, of respecting those who can work with things and with people as they respect those who can work with words—these are more likely to be developed under the unit plan than under other teaching procedures that do not concern themselves so directly with the development of such traits and abilities.[6]

Individual Projects and Problems

Project work allows much leeway for students to pursue interests in depth if they have the initiative, ability, skills, and persistence. All students have these traits but in different degrees. Consequently, the teacher recognizes that student projects will vary in comprehensiveness and creativity.

SELECTING A PROJECT   Teachers guide and direct students in the selection of projects, but they are careful not to dictate. Student selections are made after listening to teacher talks on significant topics, reading, observing demonstrations, solving community problems, discussing national problems, talking with peers, viewing films and television programs, and the like. For some students, the teachers may have to prepare a list of projects from which selections are to be made. The hope is that this will be rare.

Project approaches in learning are appropriate both for group and individual instruction. The chief ingredient in project teaching is motivation. Students need sufficient interest in a given activity to initiate, plan, execute, and evaluate it. Many students have enough drive and inquisitiveness to have one or more projects or problems which they would like to tackle in a concerted manner. For those who have not, the teacher's job

6 Rivlin, *op. cit.*, p. 112.

is to arouse them and to guide them into an activity which they will find interesting and worthwhile.

The main questions in deciding on projects are: (1) Is the activity of value to the student? (2) Is it appropriate for the student in terms of time and talent? (3) Are there sufficient resources—facilities, equipment, personnel—to enable a solution to be achieved? (4) Is the project pertinent to the course?

COMPLETION AND EVALUATION   Although students will require assistance from the teacher, in the main each student works out the project himself. There will be need to read, to explore, to investigate, and to create as the project progresses. Such activities cause the student to gain the knowledge, insight, skill, and appreciation that are parts of his education.

At the outset the student should know that his project will require effort on his part. He will not be able to ride along on the ideas and efforts of others. He should work out his plan and submit it to the teacher for approval. This plan will entail (1) objectives, (2) procedures or plan of attack, (3) materials needed, and (4) limitations, difficulties, or possible obstacles that can be foreseen.

Many people have the idea that the project is a useful technique only with superior students. This is not the case. Slower students profit in enormous degree from project work, but they require more assistance from the teacher, more encouragement, longer time in which to accomplish their objectives, and simpler problems. A successful individual study project may stimulate the student as no other activity can. Success is a precious coin, and all students need a certain amount of it. The student who all through school has been the last to be chosen by his peers in games or class activities, and the first to be eliminated in competition, needs the feel of success. The project may bring this feeling. Experience has shown that successfully completed projects develop confidence.

Usually, projects are judged by the teacher, but it is also important to have the student, and possibly other students, judge what has been accomplished. In an art or shop class the project is visible and is naturally seen by everyone. In social studies, science, foreign language, or in literature this may not be so. Therefore, in most instances, the work should be brought to the attention of the class. Even in making a presentation of his project, the pupil learns.

Supervised Study

Study is almost always an individual matter, although there are occasions when two or more students study together to effect problem solutions, pronunciation skills, creation of tangible devices, or planning activities.

Usually supervised study is considered a part of regularly organized class periods in which students work individually at their tasks. Teachers, as a result of their own initiative, or in accordance with school policy, use a part of each class period—quarter, half, or more—for directed or supervised study. The remainder of the period, and it may be at the beginning or at the end of the hour, is used for such conventional class work as discussion, review, teacher talks, or film study. Such occasions have real advantages because the student can call upon the teacher for assistance when it is most needed. The teacher, on the other hand, has an opportunity to see the student react as he works alone on his problems. The teacher is observer, helper, and guide. Such study or work periods may take place in the classroom, in the library, in the laboratory, in the community, or in whatever setting may be appropriate. During a study period the teacher has to be alert, judicious, and resourceful. On the spur of the moment he must often decide how much help to give a student or where to send him for additional assistance. The teacher must be sensitive to the welfare of all the students and see that the rights of all are protected. He must decide how much interchange of ideas is best for the pupils, whether there shall be quietness, or how much movement about the classroom should be permitted.

The supervised study period is not a time for the teacher to catch up on some personal reading or letter writing, or student paper correction. He must be on call by all students. Usually, he moves among the class ready to give assistance. Less closely supervised work is carried over to free periods or for work at home. Supervision in the laboratory depends upon student maturity and the nature of the work. The laboratory will be discussed in a separate topic later.

Work-Study Skills

Secondary school teachers know very well that they cannot assume that their students have learned how to work and study. Many of the procedures and habits of study must be learned in high school, because for want of these skills many students fail. The junior high school in particular is concerned with improving the work-study skills of the pupils.

Study skills are more than just the ability to read with comprehension. Also involved is the ability to take notes, to write a paper, to do reference work, to make written and oral reports, to skim and to read carefully, to get ideas from the spoken word, and to plan and outline. But study skills involve recall and association of knowledge as well as acquisition. Weakness along any of these lines often spells inefficient and unsuccessful work.

EVERY TEACHER IS INVOLVED   The promotion of good work-study habits and skills is the business of every teacher. Some schools have tried initiating general how-to-study courses, but these have met with indifferent success. Such courses are popular with neither teachers nor students. There is a specificity about how to study, a uniqueness about studying each course. Although the ability to read with reasonable speed and understanding is general, there are also specific reading skills in every subject. For example, reading and analyzing a mathematical problem involves different skills than those in reading and interpreting a poem.

Much of the effectiveness in teaching students how to study can be accomplished in making assignments. Teachers know that it is pointless to make remarks such as study well, do this carefully, and the like. Better results are achieved, first, by making sure every student knows what the assignment is, its length, purpose, and whether it involves just reading, written work, or problem solutions. To accompany and direct reading assignments, teachers furnish students with mimeographed study guides, lists of questions, outlines, exercises to be followed, or problems to be solved. Sometimes the work is written on the chalkboard, but this is a wasteful activity for the teacher, and for the students, too, if it is to be copied, and if the directions are more than simple page notations.

PUPIL EFFORT   Again, it is the pupil who must finally do the job. No teacher can do it for him, if he expects to learn. He must be so motivated that he desires to read, to learn new vocabulary, to know more about a topic, or to experiment further. Concentration is particularly an individual matter. Good study skills are basic and important, as are the habits and attitudes of work.

Teachers have been prone to assume that every child has a desire to learn, to do good schoolwork. Instructors have expected that the home would nurture this desire to learn. Today's teachers go beyond this assumption. They try to show students why they should work, why effort is important to them. This they do, not by mere admonition, but by precept, by specific acts, and by creating a learning environment.

HOMEWORK   Homework is essentially individual work, and the teacher assumes that the student possesses proper work-study skills to do it by himself.

Homework has become an issue in some communities with teachers and parents taking sides—sometimes one way and sometimes another. Many relevant questions soon arise when homework is considered. How much work is reasonable? Should it be the same for all students? How should it be evaluated? Should students with out-of-school jobs and chores be excused?

Teachers should become familiar with the policy of the school, as well as the abilities and maturities of the students. Regardless of the policy of the school, the teacher should be aware of the problems related to homework assignments.

In the first place, when a teacher assigns homework without knowing what other teachers expect of a student, as is usually the case, demands upon the student's time can easily become excessive. Furthermore, it is well to realize that a student may engage in activities other than classwork in school which he considers important, for example, private music lessons. (Homework was also discussed in Chapter 5. A review of this section will be helpful.)

WORK-STUDY SKILLS NEED MOTIVATION   The idea that good work-study skills are geared to motivation has been implied in the foregoing paragraphs. Unless the interest and the will to study are present, the teacher faces a losing battle in teaching efficient work-study skills and in building effective habits.

Wiles (11:208–209) has said, "A motivated student is one with a purpose" and "Motivation is closely associated with the values that a pupil holds." Purpose is many headed, and is developed in various ways and under various conditions. Motivation in association with attitudes and skills is learned, and there is much which teachers can do to bring it about. This is what the psychologists call the "law of effect." Teachers do have difficulty in providing "continuing reinforcement." Motivation and all other behavior patterns must bring satisfaction to the student. The subject of motivation was discussed in the preceding chapter. At this time our objective is merely to point out that the relationship between work-study skills and incentive exists and is very vital.

Investigation and Report

In independent work much emphasis is placed on locating and collecting data, on organizing material, and on reporting it.

LIBRARY   Chief among the resources for gathering information is the library. Although not all high school libraries measure up to American Library Association standards, most are sufficiently well stocked so that teachers can find the supplementary materials that the work of their students requires. In terms of general reference materials, libraries are likely to be more complete than in the matter of comprehensiveness in providing for a wide scope of interests and reading enjoyment. Use of the library is discussed in Chapter 8, but a few thoughts are relevant here.

Teachers and librarians need to work together closely. The librarian is the most strategic person in the school in assisting students in collecting data. And if the library book accumulation falls short of what teachers need, then the teachers should make recommendations for future acquisitions.

The emphasis on individual study places a new value on the library as a research center. Mahar has pointed out that more and more class library units are being developed, and that libraries are being used less and less as mass study halls.[7] As gifted students are given more encouragement, as more project assignments are made, and as the science interest continues, the library becomes increasingly important.

New types of instructional materials such as prerecorded tapes, discs, and programmed devices should be housed in the book library or the audio-visual center. In some instances, a school has a valuable collection of foreign language tapes. These may quite appropriately be catalogued and housed in a library or audio-visual center, or even in the expanded facilities of the language laboratory. Teaching machines and programmed materials must be housed somewhere—in the library, A-V center, or in a separate laboratory. Also, there must be space for their use, probably for group instructional use, but more likely for individual study.

FIELD INVESTIGATION Without question today's students do more re- search and investigation than did students of a decade or two ago. Reading and research go beyond textbook, even beyond the library, as students search for primary data in order to document their answers to dynamic questions and problems. Singly or in committee groups, students probe the community for the raw data it holds.

REPORTING Sharing the results of study and investigation has a new emphasis in the high school of today. Lackadaisical oral reports before a class are passé. Even book reports go far beyond telling the story. They resemble researched literary criticisms. Reports are made in writing and orally. Oral reports may be made individually or they may be a part of a panel or a seminar. It is not unusual to tape reports so that they can be used by other classes or individuals. Taped reports may also be kept for use in later years.

The Laboratory in Individual Study

The laboratory is becoming less of a facility where large classes of stu- dents work on common assignments performing experiments by recipes. Much of this sort of activity is performed by the teacher as demonstration. But laboratories are places for depth study, investigation, analysis, and research by bright students, and students with real, identified problems and projects. There is much about science that can be read, but there is also that which must be tested, measured, manipulated, and perceived.

Group work will also be found in the science laboratory, the industrial arts shop, and the music and art studios. A much more permissive climate prevails in these situations than in most discussion classrooms. The teacher

[7] Mary Helen Mahar, "Promising Practices in Secondary School Libraries," *National Association of Secondary School Principals Bulletin,* vol. 43 (November 1959), pp. 13–19.

allows as much freedom as the situation will permit. But when one or more students interfere with the work of others, waste time in aimless wandering, endanger the safety of fellow students, or create chaos, their freedom will have to be restricted for the good of the group. The laboratory instructor will likely circulate about the room to give help wherever needed.

Workshop and laboratory sessions for nonscience and nonshop classes are becoming increasingly popular with high schools. It is realized that learning is more than reading and talking. It is seeing, doing, manipulating—in fact it is all the ideas gathered into the "Learning Complex" listed in Chapter 8. Today, there are English laboratories, mathematics laboratories, economics laboratories, and so on. Any classroom can be arranged for laboratory-type activities. The laboratory feature calls for "space freedom," along with movable chairs, tables, counters, racks, closets, electrical connections, darkening facilities, library units, exhibit cases, tackboards, filing cases, and similar features.

Procedures or methods are more important than the physical features, because learning focuses on individuals, committees, small groups, or average size classes. All students may be on a common task, or they may be working on numerous projects or assignments. In the workshop or laboratory organization, a clear understanding by students of their goals is important.

IMPROVISING   Few schools are fortunate enough to have the variety of facilities and fixtures which modern-day organization and teaching method favor. The situation at its best was outlined above. But, if teachers do not have such ideal conditions, they can, if they wish, improvise. Students are extremely cooperative, and together with the teacher can work wonders. With the teacher's desk, a worktable, and a few side chairs, many new groupings are possible. By making shelves from plain boards and construction blocks, files from orange crates or apple boxes, tack space from a wall covered with monk's cloth or burlap, the teacher can create a working area with a new atmosphere.

Programmed Instructional Materials, Workbooks, and Other Materials Designed for Individual Instruction

In the last analysis most instructional materials are designed for individual use. Books, although used individually, are mass media. They are bought in great numbers and passed from one class or one individual to another. Workbooks, small outline maps, pamphlets, and many similar items are classified as consumable media. Programmed lesson materials (see Chapter 10) are sometimes bound as books, while in other instances, they are provided as sheets, rolls, or strips for use in a teaching machine.

Some of the programmed materials are consumed, others are not. Non-textbooks on the shelves of the library act as programmed nonconsumed learning materials. They are used by one student at a time to help solve an individual problem.

It is quite likely that the profession will see a great deal more of teaching machines and programmed learning in the years ahead. These programs base one of their chief claims on the fact that they are geared for individual instruction. The need may be for remedial assistance, for drill (reinforcement), or for advanced work in a subject or area. In the first two instances, the teacher's time is saved, and in the last, gifted high school students may be forging ahead with work ordinarily done in the first year or two of college. This is notably true in the sciences, mathematics, and foreign languages. Thousands and thousands of copies of the programmed book *English 2600* have been sold to college students over the country, not because it is a required text, but because it permits a sharpening of language skills by the individual on his own time.

Workbooks, boon or bane? Without passing on the merits of these instructional materials, it is pointed out here that they fit the program of individualized instruction. They are simple programmed materials provided for drill purposes for busy teachers. They are usually expendable, and for this reason are not as generally used as the textbook.

INDIVIDUALIZED INSTRUCTION: RECAPITULATION   Dr. Lloyd Trump has emphatically stated that the "magic number of twenty-five students to one teacher" does not represent the most productive means of utilizing a teacher's time. He suggests that the schools of the future should form three distinct groupings of students—large classes, small classes, and independent (individual) study arrangements. Under this scheme a student's time might be divided 40 percent, 20 percent, and 40 percent respectively for the three groupings.[8]

In connection with independent study, the National Association of Secondary School Principals emphasizes the desirability of differentiated assignments, rooms of various shapes and sizes, and a flexible time schedule that practically eliminates class-period bells. There would be space for students to study independently, with study cubicles in the ratio of one to four students. There would also be a new laboratory space arrangement to fit the concept of independent study accommodating science, mathematics, English, social studies, and foreign language laboratories. Similar spaces, called "areas" or "centers," would be arranged for the practical arts, fine arts, and health, physical education, recreation. The

[8] Dr. Trump is Director of the NASSP Commission on the Experimental Study of the Utilization of the Staff in the Secondary Schools. Dr. Trump's latest book was written with Dorsey Baynham as collaborator (10).

scheme also places a new emphasis on the library and the audio-visual center. Rooms and spaces would be arranged around two centers: "instructional materials center for teachers" and "learning resources center for students."

The organization of Chapters 6 and 7 on methods of teaching interlock with the three questions which Dr. Trump has posed. He assumed the acceptance of present goals and content and asked: "What can students learn largely by themselves?" "What can students learn from explanations by others?" "What requires personal interaction among students and teachers?" (10:104).

When one attempts to divide instructional method into categories and to say that this method is reserved for large classes, that for small classes, and another for independent study, one soon realizes the illogicalness of these arbitrary separations. Yet, in order to emphasize that teaching is basically related to the three questions above, the separation is made. As presently constituted, no school relies solely on one or another. In the past, some schools have tried complete organization around such plans as unit methods, project methods, and platoon systems.

The authors of this text are aware that the unit plan or the laboratory-workshop method, although emphasizing independent study, is being utilized successfully with large and small groups. In fact, the ingenuity to modify and adapt plans to local conditions is one of the notable achievements of secondary educators.

QUALITY TEACHING: A SYNTHESIS OF METHOD

At the beginning of Chapter 6, it was made clear that good teaching may result from any one or more of a great number of methods. Teachers need to keep before them constantly the thought that learning needs to be related to students' needs and experiences. It is well to point out that the needs of society also must be kept in mind, but the schools must beware of jumping in with untested curricula and methods at each wave of the development of knowledge.

Everywhere teachers with even a spark of professional spirit wish to do the best possible job of teaching. They see in it a challenge. They are willing to experiment and to try new approaches in their teaching. They expect the psychologists and research workers to help them with hypotheses and evaluations. The teacher who seeks quality in his work is constantly experimenting with new methods, tools, and evaluations. Every experience adds something. Teaching the same way, day in and day out, leads to deterioration rather than growth. A remark by Wiles sums up the idea of quality as a synthesis of method:

Quality teaching is the result of continued search for greater insight and constant effort to improve skills and procedures. It is achieved, if ever, by study, by evaluation, by experimentation, and by revision of goals, theory, and techniques in the light of new data.[9]

Selected Readings

1. Brown, Thomas J., *Student Teaching in a Secondary School.* New York: Harper & Row, Publishers, 1960. Chapters 6–8.
2. Clark, Leonard H., and Irving S. Starr, *Secondary School Teaching Methods.* New York: The Macmillan Company, 1959. Chapters 6, 7.
3. *Encyclopedia of Educational Research,* 3d ed. New York: McGraw-Hill Book Company, Inc., 1960, pp. 848–861.
4. Grambs, Jean D., William J. Iverson, and Franklin K. Patterson, *Modern Methods in Secondary Education,* revised ed. New York: Holt, Rinehart and Winston, Inc., 1958. Chapters 9–11.
5. Klausmeier, Herbert J., *Teaching in the Secondary School.* New York: Harper & Row, Publishers, 1958. Chapters 10, 12.
6. Morse, Arthur D., *Schools of Tomorrow Today.* New York: Doubleday & Company, Inc., 1960. Chapter 1.
7. Pulliam, Lloyd, "The Lecture—Are We Reviving Discredited Teaching Methods?" *Phi Delta Kappan,* vol. 44 (May 1963), pp. 382–385.
8. Risk, Thomas M., *Principles and Practices of Teaching in Secondary Schools,* 3d ed. New York: American Book Company, 1958.
9. Rivlin, Harry N., *Teaching Adolescents in Secondary Schools,* 2d ed. New York: Appleton-Century-Crofts, 1961. Chapters 6–9.
10. Trump, J. Lloyd, and Dorsey Baynham, *Guide to Better Schools: Focus on Change.* Chicago: Rand, McNally & Company, 1961.
11. Wiles, Kimball, *Teaching for Better Schools,* 2d ed. Englewood Cliffs, N.J.: Prentice-Hall, Inc., 1959.

[9] Kimball Wiles, *Teaching for Better Schools,* 2d ed. Englewood Cliffs, N.J.: Prentice-Hall, Inc., 1959, p. 282.

PART THREE

Using Instructional Materials

CHAPTER 8

Instructional materials including printed materials

A visit to most modern secondary or elementary schools will demonstrate clearly that teachers use a multitude of instructional materials. A casual visitor to a science classroom might see a variety of materials including models, specimens, charts, diagrams, chalkboard illustrations, as well as projection equipment for slides and films and opaque materials. In the social studies classroom, similar evidence of the use of a variety of instructional materials is apparent. A mathematics classroom might have a large number of so-called teaching machines, wooden-paper-string models, and templates. Trips to such other classrooms as industrial arts, fine arts, health education, English, and home economics would reveal much the same picture. Details would differ because certain curricular areas employ specialized techniques and materials. The foreign languages, for example, by their very nature lean heavily on such audio devices as record players, magnetic tape recorders, and microphones; perhaps all of these materials are provided in an integrated pattern such as a language laboratory. This is not to say that teachers of the language arts do not make use of visual-graphic-dimensional materials. Furthermore, there are numerous instructional materials and techniques which will not be evident to the casual visitor unless he happens to be present exactly at the time of use. These aids are represented by demonstrations, dramatizations, use of resource persons, field trips, surveys, off-campus interviews, and many similar devices or techniques.

There is a constantly growing array of instructional materials. At one time teachers had to rely almost solely on a single textbook, a chalkboard, and possibly an out-of-date political map. How fortunate is the modern teacher! How fortunate is the modern student! The authors of one textbook portray the old and the new in this way:

Contrast the picture of the physical environment of the Latin grammar school of colonial times with that of the modern secondary school. That the latter houses thousands of dollars' worth of instructional materials is a phenomenon which has occurred neither by accident nor the imprudent use of money. Appropriate equipment and materials are necessary aids to efficient learning. At the present time dramatic events are taking place in schools across the nation through the extended use of varied instructional materials, particularly television and teaching machines. The curricula and methodology of tomorrow's schools promise to be shaped considerably by the extent to which these innovations prove successful; it behooves the teacher to know what will be expected of him in using both new and established instructional materials.[1]

The employment of modern tools is not unique with schools. In some respects education lags behind such professional and occupational areas as medicine, communications, advertising, industry, armed services, agriculture, and others. Americans are proud to point to their accomplishments in these areas. Much of this progress is due to the fact that there is a heavy dependence on modern technology. Are we as rightly proud of our schools as we are of our medicine and our industrial output?

PROBLEMS IN SCHOOL EFFECTIVENESS

It is generally accepted that the audio-graphic communications media are effective with people of all ages. Experience tends to show that people generally remember

10 percent of what they READ
20 percent of what they HEAR
30 percent of what they SEE
50 percent of what they HEAR and SEE
70 percent of what they SAY
90 percent of what they SAY as they DO a thing

In the light of this evidence Americans can no longer afford a reading-listening school. If education is to keep pace with the ever-increasing world of knowledge, with new technology, with new ideas, and with new skills, an educational pattern must be pursued which provides effectiveness both in depth and breadth.

Formal school experience by its very nature tends to be removed from life, to be patterned and structured. To the extent that the school can capture more and more life experiences and substitute reality for artificiality, the school is a more effective agent of society. Yet, the school must

[1] H. O. Nordberg, *et al.*, *Secondary School Teaching.* New York: The Macmillan Company, 1962, p. 108. Used by permission of Macmillan.

not depend upon narrow direct experience solely. To do so builds on the *status quo* and fails to capitalize upon our racial and cultural heritage, not to mention the challenge to probe into uncharted horizons.

Burton has emphasized that the modern curriculum demands both direct and vicarious experience, but that there are "dangers of too great reliance upon vicarious experience far removed from appropriate direct experience" (1:418).

The field trip is generally regarded as being an effective means of promoting acquisition and retention of facts, conditioning attitudes, stimulating attention and interest, and illustrating and clarifying details and processes about things and places. The students who can experience more of our contemporary culture firsthand are very fortunate. Students study the Nile, the Congo, the Orient, the Louvre, the opera, the culture of Scandinavia, the booming of suburbia but it must be done vicariously for the most part. Events from history—the first Continental Congress, the birth of the French republic, World Wars I and II, westward expansion in the United States—must be studied in the same manner. Teachers are constantly striving for techniques and materials which will enable them to present their courses more realistically and meaningfully. To do this they employ the whole audio-visual repertoire.

The great novelist Thomas Wolfe expressed the viewpoint of modern educators quite well when he wrote: "the world is full of people who think they know what they really do not know." And he went on to discuss knowledge thus: "It is finding out something for oneself with pain, with joy, with exultancy, with labor, and with all the little ticking, breathing movements of our lives, until it is ours as that only is ours which is rooted in the structure of our lives."[2] The underlying thought here harks back to the expressed criticisms of such noted educators as Comenius, Rousseau, Pestalozzi, Froebel, Herbart, and Dewey. As a matter of fact, this underlying, nagging thought of the school's inefficiency has been a common bond for many renowned schoolmen. Library study will verify this statement.

Verbalism

All too frequently poorly understood word symbolization passes for mastery. This is the root of the nasty word *verbalism*. The term is applied when pupils have only vague or even wildly incorrect knowledge of the words they use, or when the words are known in a limited use instead of in their complete meaning. One child referred to caviar as surgeon eggs. Why such a boner?

[2] Thomas Wolfe, *The Web and the Rock*. New York: Harper & Row, Publishers, 1930, p. 380.

Verbal counterfeiting occurs most frequently in conceptualization and generalization. Pupils read or listen to concepts formulated into words. Soon they are able to use these same words apparently without error, yet they by no means understand the concept. For them it has been borrowed instead of derived. Teachers, quite generally, exaggerate the pupil's ability to acquire and understand concepts.

Teaching in generalities is common. Some teachers simply do not know how to illustrate to clarify meaning, and some appear to believe that to do so is juvenile and unacademic. Apt and meaningful illustrations and examples, verbal and pictorial, should be generously used. The material presented in most textbooks needs such supplementation. Correct thinking, to reiterate, must be built upon definite knowledge, clear concepts. Many instances have been reported of how badly pupils garble the Pledge of Allegiance or the Lord's Prayer when requested to write it and to discuss its real meaning. There is an inclination to think that such instances are "cute." Or, we treat indulgently the high school student who defined a complex sentence as "a thought with one independent clause and one despondent one."

In response to Polonius' question, "What do you read my lord?" Hamlet answered: "Words, words, words."[3] Then, there is the case of Humpty Dumpty who confused Alice by saying, "When I use a word, it means just what I choose it to mean, neither more nor less." Poor Alice thought that words should have definite meanings.

In high school we expect the students to read and to understand material such as: "A city is a covenant. It is the place where men contract to live together with dignity and grace, in law and order; where society publicly agrees and subscribes to unity within the civilized state of mankind. . . ."[4]

How does one grow from hazy word understanding to true knowledge? Terminology is often a hindrance to understanding for many pupils. The commonest of teaching platitudes, "study this carefully" or "you have not studied your lesson," are of no avail. The problem is not one of more time to be spent, more reading to be done, or more homework to be assigned, but one of concept formation. Someone has said that "the verbal cram is worse than worthless, it is injurious."

The abstract study of parallel lines in geometry must in some way be tied up with the parallelism of the planks of the floor, railroad tracks and ties, corn rows, streets, bookshelves, and all incidents of parallelism, concrete or abstract, wherever found. Laboratory work ordinarily clears up

---

3 William Shakespeare, *Hamlet*, Act II.
4 Olga Maynard, "A Theater in the City," *San Diego Union*, Leisure and the Arts Supplement, May 15, 1962.

many misinterpretations and misconceptions. Home economics students, for example, are not baffled by their problems. Perceptual foundations and experiences are a definite part of the laboratory procedure.

Verbalism is insidious. Fluent speech is acceptable coin for understanding in most classrooms. It is easy enough for pupils to say that to divide a fraction by a fraction, one must invert and multiply. They can easily be taught this rule, but they should also know why this rule is a rule. Students quickly learn that the circumference of a circle is πd, but have they also learned that there is a ratio involved here, and that π is a constant? Teachers know that experiments in the psychological laboratory have shown conclusively that meaningful material is more easily learned than nonsense material, and that retention is greater.

THE VALUES OF INSTRUCTIONAL MATERIALS

Modern instructional materials are not fads and frills. Some critics are quick to apply this opprobrious statement, but it is patently unjustified. Audio-visual materials are frequently misused. Teachers show movies instead of using instructional films, often in an auditorium or cafeteria instead of the regularly assigned classroom, laboratory, or shop. Many illustrative pictures and models have been employed merely because they are interesting. At times a plethora of aids is used. Pictures have been passed around the class willy-nilly. *Realia* and exhibit materials have been used promiscuously under the impression that they will make the lesson objectives concrete. Often materials have been used which have no relation to the objectives to be accomplished. A trip just for the sake of a trip or to pacify students' longing to get away from the classroom is no justification at all. Materials have been used without proper preparation by teacher and students. At other times, there has been no follow-up of the use of materials.

It is well to keep in mind these simple criteria when discussing the potential effectiveness of instructional materials: they must be properly prepared; they must be wisely selected; and they must be intelligently used. The first two of these criteria are essentially administrative in character, whereas the third, as well as the second to some extent, is teacher oriented. Any learning material, be it a textbook, pamphlet, map, or film, cannot help but add significantly to the learning situation if it meets these criteria.

Specific Values of Concrete Instructional Materials

It is difficult to enumerate all the benefits to be had from a wise use of varied instructional materials without seeming to present a panacea for all the problems of learning. But, some of these benefits are enumerated here because they have not been fully understood and accepted by all educators. Audio-visual materials as used in this instance do not include textbooks, readings, and lectures, or what one might term conventional learning materials. This should in no way be interpreted to mean that the authors repudiate conventional learning materials and methods. The values of concrete instructional materials are as follows:

1. They illustrate and clarify non-verbal symbols and images, quantitative relationships, complex relationships, abstract concepts, spatial relations, and specific details.
2. They facilitate attitude and behavior changes.
3. They show inaccessible processes, materials, events, things, and changes in time, speed, and space.
4. They promote greater acquisition and longer retention of factual knowledge.
5. They provide increased interest in learning.
6. They provide objectivity for the study of a delicate or controversial subject.
7. They stimulate interest in voluntary reading.
8. They allow all members of a group the opportunity to share a joint experience.
9. They get and hold attention.
10. They reinforce verbal messages.
11. They bring experts and multiresources to the classroom.
12. They provide for a direct interaction of students with the realities of their social and physical environment.
13. They provide integrated experiences which vary from concrete to abstract.
14. They are valuable for all age and ability groups.

All lesson planning employs four major categories: objectives, learning activities, learning materials, and evaluation. In other words, *what activities* will students pursue involving *what materials* to achieve *what objectives* and with *what evidence* of attainment of goals. The chart of the Materials-Activities-Complex is organized around three of these categories.

The objectives or goals are listed in the center of the chart, but the order here is of little value. No brief is held for it; however, the topmost listed goal is undoubtedly the capstone of educational endeavor. *Behavioral integration* refers to the personality pattern of the individual: how he thinks, acts, reacts, applies meanings and experiences, and evaluates life and society. The other objectives, although important, are in a

The Materials-Activities-Complex

LEARNING MATERIALS AND EXPERIENCES	OUTCOMES	ACTIVITIES
Symbolization Recondite signs Technical symbols Terminology Coefficients Figurative expression— reading, speaking Literal expression— reading, speaking *Vicarious Experiencing* (Second Level) Graphic presentations as found in graphs, cartoons, diagrams, blueprints, maps Still pictures Recordings, radio Motion pictures, television Models, mockups, dioramas Globes *Vicarious Experiencing* (First Level) Objects, specimens, artifacts Field trips Dramatizations Demonstrations Resource persons *Direct Experiencing* Community studies Surveys Work experiences Service projects Away-from-school interviews	1. Behavioral integration 2. Understanding 3. Attitude 4. Appreciation 5. Knowledge (facts) 6. Skill	1. Doing, building, writing, reciting, expressing, drawing, painting, planning, organizing, constructing, initiating, collecting, producing, practicing 2. Reciting, repeating, memorizing, drilling 3. Directing, ordering, controlling, curtailing, forcing 4. Experiencing, participating, investigating, aiding, adventuring, experimenting, exploring, searching, inquiring, contemplating, examining, proving, studying, finding out 5. Appreciating, enjoying, creating 6. Thinking, problem solving, understanding, generalizing, contriving, devising, organizing, planning 7. Visualizing, rendering concrete, seeing, clarifying, imagining, listening 8. Accepting, obeying, following, carrying out 9. Sharing, pooling, cooperating, helping, contributing, suggesting, discussing 10. Evaluating, judging, summarizing, formulating, considering, deciding, acting upon, concluding, reacting, questioning

way contributory to the capstone. What kind of behavioral pattern are we seeking in American secondary education? That is essentially the theme of Chapter 14, "The Curriculum of the Secondary School."

Earlier, Burton was quoted as saying that "the process of learning is doing, reacting, undergoing, experiencing." For generations educators have been using varied activities as listed in column three. Each generation rearranges and re-evaluates the list to suit its philosophy. For example, reciting was given major consideration at one period in our educational history. Although not abandoned today, it has been assigned a smaller role. Teachers should remember Margaret Mead's remark, "No one will live all his life in the world into which he was born, and no one will die in the world in which he worked in his maturity."[5] Someone has also pointed out that of today's population about 5 percent goes back to the horse and buggy days, 20 percent to World War I, 30 percent to the depression era, and 40 percent to World War II. The problem of objectives and activities is indeed a complicated one.

What learning materials are used with these activities? Perceptive teachers use every invented or developed material now known, and man's inventive genius will constantly add new ones. Supervisors of student teachers constantly look for originality and regularly discuss new techniques and methods with their student teachers and with other teacher-supervisors. Teachers are not dismayed when an occasional critic speaks of these materials and techniques as gimmicks or as hardware. They could be, but they need not be.

The first column in the above list bears a distinct resemblance to Dale's "Cone of Experience" (2:43) and to Olsen's "Pyramid of Learning Resources" (8:46).

Audio-Visual Materials: Terms and Criteria

The term *audio-visual materials* is used in most books in the field of instructional materials and the term has become standardized in education, industry, and the military; moreover, the public understands it. Although the authors use the term in this text from time to time, in the main they speak of learning or instructional or curriculum materials. Such terminology is broader and permits the inclusion of all aids.

Learning is a complex business. No one method nor instructional material will achieve modern educational objectives. Direct experience goes hand in hand with vicarious and abstract experience. Looking at pictures alone is far from adequate. Explanation and analysis are as much needed today as ever before. Not only must Johnny read but he must read more and be able to evaluate what he reads.

But what are *good* instructional materials? Intelligent well-prepared

[5] Bureau of Educational Research and Service, Ohio State University, Newsletter, (December 1960), p. 2.

teachers know what they are; however, the following criteria may be of some value since they apply equally well to all materials—printed pages, lectures, motion pictures, prerecorded magnetic tapes, machine programmed lessons, physical maps, mock-ups, or puppets:

Appropriateness—related to curriculum, units of study, daily lessons; suitable for particular age or grade level
Freedom from bias, prejudice, distortion, antisocial attitudes, untruthfulness
Recency—up to date, reflecting current thought, original or revised
Availability—obtainable when needed
Appeal—esthetic, attention holding
Technical quality—simplicity, workability
Cost—within school budget limitations

Teachers who wish more specific assistance with problems of utilization should take advantage of the many special courses in methods and materials offered in all teacher-education institutions. In addition to formal courses, there are often workshops and conferences. Specialized books and magazines are also helpful. Nevertheless, the discussion of instructional materials would fall short of a reasonable target if it did not point up some ways to use them. Accordingly, the remainder of this chapter and the two following chapters will describe instructional materials and their use.

PRINTED MATERIALS

Textbooks

Although modern secondary teachers use a wide variety of teaching materials, the textbook is still the primary tool for a vast majority of them. Over the years it has been practically revered by students, teachers, and the public.

This dependence on textbooks (usually a single text) started in early times when books were scarce and costly. Teachers were poorly prepared for their tasks and the textbook saved them from failure. However, the profession became aware of the slavish use of printed materials about the turn of the twentieth century, and since then much effort has been expended to improve the selection of textbooks. Studies and researches by individuals, committees, and commissions have followed. In 1931 the National Society for the Study of Education devoted Part II of the thirtieth yearbook to a code of ethics on textbook selection and adoption. Some assistance in the solution of the problem was given by the development of textbook rating scales during the thirties and forties.[6] These scales have helped to objectify textbook selection, but they are mechanical and have not accomplished a great deal. Much more has been achieved by curriculum groups in local areas using specific criteria developed by the group and its consultants for the selection of books in a given curricular field (5).

A significant study of the use of textbooks was made by a group of scholars at the University of Illinois. They not only surveyed the dependence placed on texts by teachers, but they went on to offer helpful suggestions for the improvement of texts and ways to vitalize their use in the classroom. The opening statement of the report highlights the problem:

At the center of the present-day educational scene in America is the textbook. It takes a dominant place in the typical school from the first grade to the college. Only the teacher—and perhaps a blackboard and writing materials—are found as universally as the textbook in our classrooms (5:3).

Some light is shed on the reasons for this dependence on textbooks when one notes the heavy schedules of teachers. Assigned classes, counseling, administrative and clerical routine, and committee work leave little time for planning and preparation. A comprehensive time study of a large group of teachers revealed that on the average only one quarter of an hour per day was devoted to daily preparation. This was coupled with some out-of-school preparation, but the total was less than forty minutes.[7] This time factor alone undoubtedly accounts for the fact that teachers fall back heavily on textbooks as "assistant teachers."

Conditions in the modern efficient high school are actually somewhat improved. Teachers are busy and time is limited, true enough, but there are ameliorating circumstances. Reading materials continue to be important and significant learning materials, but they are not slavishly followed; neither are they accepted unquestioned. The preparation of today's teachers qualifies them for a more professional and intelligent understanding of books and their use. In the first place, the range and variety of books have been multiplied. In many schools, several texts are used in a course instead of one. Paperbacks take their place along with the hard-covered books. Adequate libraries help take the pressure from single assigned texts. Thus, the teacher can draw heavily on supplementary

[6] For example, see Samuel E. Burr, Jr., *Journal of Education*, vol. 132 (May 1949); for a thorough coverage of the subject consult the index of the *Encyclopedia of Educational Research*.

[7] *A Cooperative Study for the Better Use of Teacher Competencies*, 2d report. Mt. Pleasant, Mich.: Central Michigan College, 1955, pp. 29, 33–34.

references, encyclopedias, almanacs, dictionaries, source books, work-books, magazines, pamphlets, brochures, and even comic book materials.

Values of Textbooks

There can be no question that textbooks are being improved constantly. Critical feedback from schools and teachers is a potent factor. Authors and publishers spend more time and effort to provide better quality books. Competition is strong. Within recent years textbooks have become more scientific in conception and construction. Studies are being constantly made of quality, quantity, and kind of content. These studies are being translated into textbooks at all levels and in all curricular areas. It is also noteworthy that a majority of the textbooks for today's elementary and secondary schools are either written by practicing elementary and secondary teachers, or they combine their talents with college and university specialists (5).

Furthermore, present-day textbooks actually blend with or at least integrate with many of the newer instructional media such as films, film-strips, records, and prerecorded tapes. These materials tend to reinforce each other, and frequently allow teachers to make varied approaches to their curricular problems. Take for example, almost any standard textbook in science, home economics, social studies, or foreign language. The book itself is artistic in design with generous margins, adequate spacing, large and clear type, and lucid and meaningful illustrations. A majority of the texts provide some of these illustrations in color. Pictures of color spectra, mineral-bearing rocks, national costumes, fauna and flora, festivals, ceremonies, art, landscapes, and legions of other illustrations are frequently in full color. Color adds a realism that is much needed. Chapter "closings" employ many teacher aids and suggestions, such as library references, film and filmstrip references, project activities, questions for discussion, songs, dramatizations, construction activities, study helps, and review devices. These related learning materials and aids are varied and ingenious.

A number of the standard publishing companies now produce and distribute numerous audio-visual materials which are author integrated with their textbooks. One publisher produces integrated books and sound motion pictures, another produces books and audio materials, another, books and filmstrips, and so the procession goes. And, just as publishers desire to reinforce their books with audio-visual materials, at least one audio-visual producer supplements his motion pictures with printed readers, and another is augmenting his films with preprogrammed lessons for use in teaching machines.

Books are interesting objects just to pick up. They are bound in colorful artistic covers, and frequently bold intriguing jackets overlay the covers. Such books are not limited to dramatics, social studies, or science. Just as interesting books are found in industrial arts, mathematics, music, health education, and foreign languages.

What is the point to all this? It certainly is not just a matter of beautification. It is a fact that learning can be better if the materials are varied and of better quality. Even a casual comparison of modern texts with those available years ago will add substance to this statement.

Books are written so that learning is facilitated. Content is organized, systematized, and sequaciously arranged so that greater economy may prevail. Books should be intelligently read and often reread because everyone forgets a great deal. They are a convenient ready reference for review and restudy, but most students are not aggressively enthusiastic about textbooks. Some prefer other competing mass communication media such as television, theater, motion picture; and others may prefer the more challenging and meaty books of the nontext type. Claims have been made that textbooks actually dampen and shrivel reading desires and habits.

The needs of students will determine what and how many learning materials are to be used. The chances are that the teacher will have a textbook for each class taught. He may have the option of using several texts. At any rate, the teacher must determine the needs of his students because these needs vary from community to community and from class to class. Textbooks must not be allowed to become planned courses even though they may be well organized and well written. Some textbooks provide too much material, at least on some topics, others too little. The teacher must make intelligent adaptations. He supplements with radio, television, films, tapes, paperbacks, source books, and other materials as needs dictate.

How to Use Textbooks

Teachers can and should encourage students to:

1. Read assignments rapidly for a once-over pattern. This overview will show the "flavor" of the assignment. In this survey, note should be made of topics treated; graphs, maps, and other devices included; illustrations shown; and, above all, the reasons for the assignment. This becomes essentially a skimming process.

2. Follow the skimming of the assignment by a closer reading for the meaning of words, sentences, paragraphs, graphs, and tables. This is the dictionary meaning of the verb *study*. At this time the text may raise numerous questions in the student's mind. It may stimulate thinking. It may present new data, and lead the student to go beyond the text to find

answers to questions and problems which seem to be insufficiently answered.

3. Take notes on what has been read. Not all teachers agree that this is a useful activity, but some note taking may be valuable. If it is done, students should be encouraged to do it perceptively, not mechanically. The best plan is to use an outline consisting of questions. Notes should be carefully taken and never allowed to become a jumble of disorganized, disconnected words, phrases, or sentences. At this point, the teacher should do an educational job concerning the care of books—personal, school texts, or library materials. Underscoring, writing in margins, and otherwise marking or cuing is not allowable unless the book is personally owned, and even then, there is a question of value.

4. Try mentally to recall the main ideas in the assignment after it has been read. This includes not only the topics but some of the salient facts.

5. Review notes at the completion of a unit of work, or before an examination. This review should attempt to coordinate notes, text, class discussions, laboratory experiments, and other learning activities.

6. Reread text, when needed, for clarification of vague or uncertain concepts, facts, or other knowledges. This is also a good time to evaluate what has been read. Did the author stick to facts or did he present personal opinions? Is there any evidence of bias? Did he attempt to generalize from isolated cases?

7. Understand and know how to use table of contents, index, glossaries, reference lists, and illustrations. Teachers frequently skip the preface to a text. Such an omission is unfortunate because students should know that often the preface provides useful keys in understanding various parts of the book, their relationships, why the book was written, and author motivations.

On a broader plane teachers and supervisory personnel have a responsibility to:

1. Provide a wide variety of reading materials including multiple texts, auxiliary reading materials, reference books, and library materials.
2. Encourage students to probe all reading materials for facts, answers and solutions for their problems, leads, and intellectual stimulation.
3. Encourage students to evaluate and discriminate as they read. Critical thinking will help sift fact from fiction.
4. Plan instructional units of study, projects, and problems instead of assigned pages, chapters, word or question lists in single texts.
5. Remember that words are symbols for real and concrete experiences. Help students build worthwhile experiential backgrounds.
6. Correlate text with nontext learning materials.

Some years ago, Herrick[8] tried to categorize teacher responsibility in classroom planning. His analysis has much bearing on the matter of textbook utilization. Herrick charted responsibilities and factors as shown in the accompanying table.

Levels of Teacher Responsibility in Three Types
of Instructional Planning (Modified)

AREAS OF PLANNING	DETERMINING FORCES AT EACH LEVEL		
	LEVEL III	LEVEL II	LEVEL I
Concept to be taught	Text or workbook	Text and course of study	Design of curriculum in subject field
Experiences, facts, activities, materials	Text, workbook, and teacher	Text, teacher, group of children	Teacher, group of children and resources of community
Timing and time schedules	Text, workbook, teacher, and school program	Teacher and school program	Teacher, group of children, school program

Levels I and III show the two extremes and highlight the thinking of two groups of curriculum planners. Level III places little responsibility upon the teacher, and is likely to be geared to the old formula of read-recite-test. The text here is the curriculum and inert subject matter is of utmost importance. In Level I, texts are less important and teachers have more freedom to plan and to take their instructional materials from a variety of sources. Community resources and so-called "current materials" may be very important at this level.

Beginning teachers will, in all likelihood, have little or no opportunity to voice opinions on the matter of texts. They should, however, know how to use text materials as well as know procedures for textbook selection. All teachers should thoroughly acquaint themselves with the texts which are available in their respective fields even though they may not have an opportunity to select them. The R. R. Bowker Company annually publishes a book which lists under the heading of school subjects all the textbooks of some 150 publishing houses. The books are indexed by author, title, and subject. They are also classified as to elementary, junior

[8] V. E. Herrick, "The Concept of Curriculum Design," in V. E. Herrick and R. W. Tyler, eds., *Toward Improved Curriculum Theory,* Supplementary Educational Monographs, no. 71. Chicago: University of Chicago Press, 1950, pp. 37–50; see also Lee J. Cronbach, *op. cit.*, pp. 188–216.

high, and senior high school adaptability, but the books are not rated or annotated.[9]

Workbooks

There exists a wide variety of workbooks, drill pads, exercise books, manuals, and other practice devices related to English language, foreign language, science, mathematics, and commercial subjects. Whether or not to use workbooks is debatable. As the name implies, the work or practice book provides work for the student to do—drill and practice with skills, problems to be solved, questions to be answered, tests to be taken, remedial work to be followed, words to be mastered, or experiments to be performed.

The workbook idea and its proliferation of materials grew out of the limitations of textbooks, the paucity of practice materials, and the complete absorption of the teacher's time with a multiplicity of tasks.

Research provides no clear-cut answer to the question of educational value of workbooks. At least the degree of value is undetermined. Some teachers in some subject areas get good results with them; in other instances the materials are so used as to degenerate into busy work, petty exercises, and filling in blanks. The purpose here is merely to call attention to these instructional materials so that beginning teachers will have an awareness of their values and limitations.

Some of the workbooks now available have been well planned and carefully written. Often they integrate with or accompany basic texts so well that busy teachers feel them to be educationally valuable for students. They enable students to practice skills at a rate consistent with individual abilities. For some students these workbooks achieve acknowledged motivation and practice in self-direction and independent study. The recently developed "scrambled" books are in reality workbooks prepared for individualized study. This type book is closely related to the programmed learning materials prepared for use in the so-called teaching machines.[10] Large group instruction (lecture-discussion type) needs some sort of semi-individualized bolstering. Supplementation, review, and opportunity to reconstruct are imperative. This assistance the workbook can give.

On the other side of the coin, one finds instances of slavish adherence to the workbook—students merely following mechanical directions in the laboratory or classroom. Most workbooks call for no originality of thought.

[9] *Textbooks in Print.* New York: R. R. Bowker Company, published annually in April; another worthwhile source is American Textbook Publisher's Institute, New York.
[10] For a good example of a "scrambled book" see Joseph C. Blumenthal, *English 3200.* New York: Harcourt, Brace & World, Inc., 1962.

Often there is an overemphasis on nonessential outcomes. Some workbooks, manuals, and practice pads have no apparent correlation with textbooks or courses of study, and often the materials are not well graded.

Teachers' Guides

Teacher guides bear about the same relation to teachers that student workbooks bear to students. They are guides or syllabi written by authors to accompany their books. Following the text closely, they offer assistance to busy teachers, yet in all honesty they are essentially crutches, or modernized "ponies." But, if teachers get any professional assistance from them, they undoubtedly serve a useful purpose. On the other hand, it must be said that teachers are capable and that they should prepare their own guides, syllabi, and teaching plans. Some teachers welcome these aids, others disdain their use.

About three fourths of all instructional motion pictures have accompanying teachers' guides, sometimes called study guides. These guides serve two purposes: they act as a standardized lesson plan and they substitute for a preview of the film before utilization. It is pretty generally understood that the second purpose is a makeshift one; the actual preview is preferable. Headings in these guides are usually organized as "Suggestions for Effective Use of the Film," "Suggested Discussion Questions," "Follow-up Projects," "Technical or Foreign Words or Phrases," and "Suggested Reading References." In some cases the teachers' guide will provide a complete scripting of the film. Many of these guides are quite simple, being no more than two folded pages punched for easy filing.

Teachers' guides as discussed here should not be confused with courses of study, units of study, or other curricular guides.

Reference and Supplementary Printed Materials

LIBRARY   The modern secondary school is replete with reference and supplementary books. These books are housed in different classrooms and in the library. Professionally trained school librarians are usually found on high school staffs. They work with teachers in guiding pupils in the use of the library. Together, they should assure that pupils learn proper skills in the use of the library and well-fixed habits of use, including that of reading for sheer enjoyment.

Modern libraries try to maintain proper balance in subject areas. They also balance historical and contemporary materials and events, fiction and nonfiction, reference and collateral materials, hard-cover books and paper bound pamphlets, and magazines and newspapers.

Library skills are taught in a variety of ways, depending upon school organization, philosophy, physical plant, staff, and community background. These techniques follow one of the plans below, or a combination of plans:

School librarian teaches a unit course.
Use is integrated into numerous high school courses.
Use is incorporated into a general orientation course usually required of all freshmen.
Use is unorganized and is taught informally to pupils individually when they come to the library for assistance.

It has been said that the formal classroom work of today kills enjoyment in reading and that a majority of students never read after completing high school except for desultory reading of magazines and newspapers. If such be the case, it is hardly the fault of most librarians, because they work assiduously for the opposite effect. Library rooms or suites are attractive and comfortable. Many devices are used to motivate students to come to the library, to check out books, and to read. A list of such devices is long, but it will include:

Open book shelves
Newspaper and magazine racks
Nonglare lighting
Displays and bulletin boards of new books, colorful jackets, advertisements, reviews, clippings
Special holiday book features
Easy check out of books, and in some cases magazines, phonograph records, study prints, and related items
Friendly and helpful staff assistance

Some schools have sufficient library materials so that specific matter may, on request of the teacher, be sent directly to the classroom for long-term use. As units of work follow each other, new collections of related books and pamphlets are deposited in the rooms. Teachers can best fulfill their responsibilities for directing study habits under such circumstances.

ENCYCLOPEDIAS The central core of any library is its sets of encyclopedias, and one writer goes so far as to say, "We are now in an '*encyclopedia age.*' "[11] There are more than thirty encyclopedias currently available. Although they overlap in content, they vary considerably in approach. Some are aimed at mature interests and reading levels; others are directed at youth. These sets are relatively expensive, costing from one to three

[11] W. V. Miller, "Textbooks Call For Reference Books," *Phi Delta Kappan*, vol. 33 (January 1952), p. 285.

hundred dollars. Numerous publishers bring out accompanying yearbooks which materially assist in keeping the sets up to date.

Since encyclopedias are expensive, schools should select with care. Chief criteria to be kept in mind are kinds of information needed by the particular school, organization of content in the books, accuracy and reliability, book architecture, and currency. Beginning teachers should be informed about these materials, their use, sources, and manner in which they are selected locally.

DICTIONARIES   Unlike encyclopedias, dictionaries are comparatively inexpensive. It is a common practice to provide each classroom with at least one unabridged edition or a smaller hand volume.

In addition to English dictionaries, schools often provide others, such as those in the foreign languages, biographies, familiar quotations, synonyms and antonyms, and thesauri.

ATLASES AND WORLD ALMANACS   Both of these reference sources will be found in the larger high schools. Usually both will be housed in the central library instead of the classrooms. The world almanac, usually paper bound, is essentially an annual publication and is a handy reference for thousands of facts on diverse topics.

COLLATERAL BOOKS   The *Dictionary of Education* defines collateral reading as, "(1) Reading material related to the main topic or theme being studied as distinguished from the textual or basic material of the assignment, (2) reading related to a subject that supports and enriches or broadens the experience of the reader" (6:443).

Textbooks are of necessity much condensed and often encyclopedic in nature. It is, therefore, desirable in most instances to supplement the text with other reading opportunities. At times, the general reference type of materials described in the foregoing pages will be adequate, but in many instances, extended reading will need to be of a different type.

Teachers and librarians put heavy reliance on the reading of collateral books of the nontext or trade book type. These books cover more thoroughly and in more unified fashion subjects such as specific sciences, travel, adventure, biography, history, and fiction.

Assigned or suggested collateral reading serves several positive purposes. In any high school class there is a wide difference in aptitudes, interests, and backgrounds among the students. Collateral reading allows students to explore some of their individual interests. Textual content is extended and new viewpoints are introduced. Supplementary reading often brings freshness to assignments, as well as a wider range and greater depth. Students working on projects or developing individual reports profit from this type of reading.

Recreational reading is a concern of all teachers. Selecting suitable

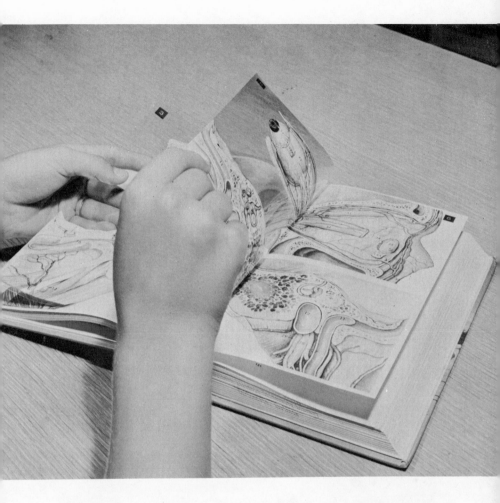

This science textbook represents an innovation of binding in colored transparent overlays. There is also an increasing use of photographs, line drawings, charts, and graphs in modern textbooks. The presence of these teaching aids lightens the task of the teacher and makes the books more attractive to the students. However, textbooks usually do not provide for individual differences. They must be supplemented so that reading material about the same subject is available on various levels. [*Courtesy Paul R. Wendt and Southern Illinois University.*]

A problem in applied mathematics may have more meaning when worked out in this manner. A king-size slide rule will interest students and its operation will be quickly learned. Society needs men and women who can think logically and critically. In groups such as this may be found the future scientists, engineers, and mathematicians who tomorrow will be designing the rockets and planes to conquer outer space. [*Courtesy Harold R. Snodgrass, Tacoma (Wash.) Public Schools.*]

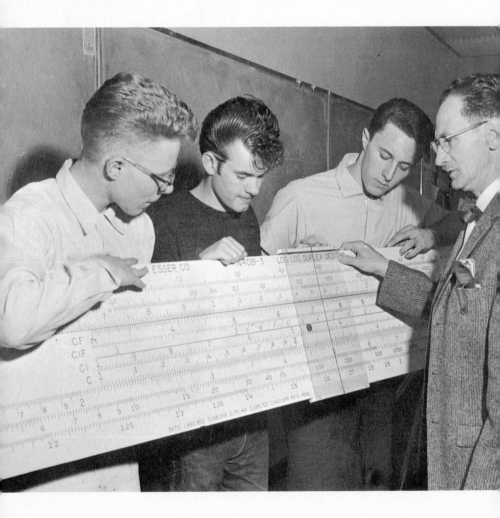

This student is using an overhead projector to explain a geometry proposition to her classmates. The projector is operated in a fully lighted room. It is portable and throws a strong image so that a light-colored wall may be used instead of a special screen. The demonstrator faces the class at all times. A pencil acts as a pointer, and the student may add or erase from the prepared material as desired. The written part of this demonstration could be prepared in advance or it could be developed step by step as the class watches. [*Minnesota Mining and Manufacturing Company.*]

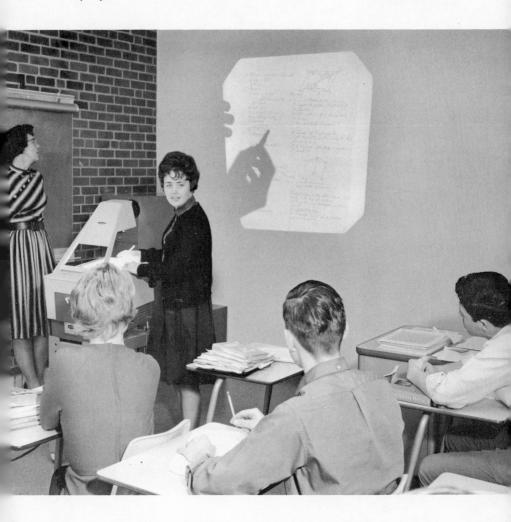

Far back in history educators employed field trips, and they are being used increasingly today. The conventional field trip is one taken to a local area, but longer trips are also coming into use. In all cases, field trips should have clearly defined objectives. They should be carefully planned and then followed up with close evaluation. Shown here is the beginning of an all-day field trip taken by twenty-two Humbolt High School senior physics students. The students flew from St. Paul to Rochester, Minnesota, for a planned day's visitation at Mayo Clinic. [*Courtesy St. Paul (Minn.) Public Schools.*]

reading materials to fit individual needs is a never-ending activity. Teachers and librarians are constantly on the alert to locate fresh subjects with varied reading difficulty levels. Only as students find content of suitable interest and difficulty do they get fun from reading. Then, and only then, can the printed page really compete with television and the motion picture in the leisure field.

Current Materials

More than a decade ago two small Stanford University publications described a state-wide California public school experiment in the use of so-called current materials. These materials were designated as follows:

They include whatever will lead to the understanding of current problems. Thus, for the Council members, "current materials" include—beyond newspapers, periodicals, and such "fugitive" source matter as pamphlets and advertising brochures—such things as excursions and field trips, community activities, expert personnel brought into class, radio broadcasts, and television among numerous others.[12]

It was the contention of the California Council on Improvement of Teaching that citizens must be able to form intelligent opinions on current issues of all types, and that the greater events of recorded history have meaning only as they relate to the present scene. After several years of study and experimentation, members of the council concluded that the use of current materials assisted in better understanding, that students became more resourceful and investigative, that there was lessened emphasis on purely verbal learning, and that class work could be given more variety and flexibility. This belief in the value of contemporary materials is still held by California educators. In its most recent publication the State Central Committee on Social Studies wrote:

A planned program in the teaching of contemporary affairs will require approximately one-fifth of the total time devoted to social studies instruction, particularly during the junior and senior high school years.

Use of approximately one-fifth of the total social studies time for instruction in current affairs should not result in arbitrary decisions to devote one day per week to such instruction. Instruction in contemporary affairs should be incorporated into the ongoing social studies program at times and points where it will be most effective.[13]

[12] Lucien Kinney and Reginald Bell, *Better Teaching Through the Use of Current Materials.* Stanford, Calif.: Stanford University Press, 1947; and, Lucien Kinney and Katherine Dresden, *Better Learning Through Current Materials,* same publisher, 1949, revised, 1952. Used by permission of Stanford University Press.

[13] *Report of the State Central Committee on Social Studies to the California State Curriculum Commission.* Sacramento: California State Department of Education, 1961, pp. 10–11.

In *Ecclesiastes* we learn "Of the making of many books there is no end. . . ." If this is true of hard-cover books, what can we say of pamphlets, brochures, newspapers, magazines, tracts, comics, and the miscellany of other printed materials?

PAMPHLETS AND BROCHURES   Materials in this classification have three main sources of origin—free or sponsored materials, materials created by the schools themselves, and materials produced by professional sources.

Free, sponsored, or low-cost pamphlets are legion in number. Literally hundreds of American (and some foreign) manufacturers and commercial groups publish thousands of pamphlets each year. Some are designed for general consumption, others are prepared specifically for the schools. And the reports from these firms indicate that pupils and teachers are requesting free materials in a mighty stream. Some may be thrown away, but many have educational value and find a place in the current materials curriculum files.

Selection of these materials by teachers and librarians becomes a task of great proportions. Obviously, the business establishments are not so much interested in the education of the youth as they are in placing their name and their product in a favorable light. Advertising is at times overt, at others, hidden. Propaganda designed to change ideas is even more dangerous than just the sale of products. Teachers considering free materials will do well to study them with great care. Since the use of free and free-loan materials has become a matter of grave concern, schools considering their use should adopt a policy statement to guide both teachers and administrative officials. Several organizations have drawn up criteria to help in the more intelligent selection and use of such materials. For example, the American Association of School Administrators has offered these criteria:

1. Define clearly the relation that such materials must bear to the basic purposes and objectives of the schools.
2. Provide specific guidelines upon which rules for selection and use can be based.
3. Give assurances to teachers concerning the limits within which they have official backing in the selection and use of materials.
4. Delegate responsibility to appropriate administrative officials or other school personnel for selection and handling of materials.
5. Provide some means of maintaining community confidence in the schools and of safeguarding against unwarranted pressures.
6. Make available necessary funds so that teachers are not forced to use free materials as substitutes for superior materials that could be purchased.

And the same association suggests that materials be checked for such biases as the following:

1. Convictions presented as facts
2. One point of view stressed in an obviously two-sided issue
3. Emphasis on what is wrong, rather than what is right
4. "Theme of presentation deals with matters of basic concern to others than the producer of the item—usually others in competition or in conflict with the producing agency"[14]

Pamphlets produced by professional or semiprofessional organizations, agencies, and groups are also widely used. It can reasonably be assumed that bias and propaganda are absent from these materials, or at least they are at such a minimum as not to be objectionable. Materials considered here are usually purchased by the school district. Pamphlets supplement standard texts, and have the advantage of timeliness. They can be revised easily and frequently at little expense. In this manner the latest events and trends can be made available. Also, it is possible to tailor content to fit specific class and individual needs. Booklet materials fit short units of study, introductory lessons, review or summarizing lessons, or nearly any lesson type. Students tend to take a favorable attitude toward pamphlets and booklets.

In some states, statutes prohibit the expenditure of public funds for unbound books. This is a problem that time is correcting. An increasing percentage of the schoolbook fund is going into the purchase of pamphlet materials.

MAGAZINES AND NEWSPAPERS If books and pamphlets are abundant, give some thought to these facts. Approximately 1900 daily and 9000 weekly newspapers are printed in the United States with a circulation of nearly 65 million. Some 7000 magazines are published with an output of 400 million copies, and of this output five of the leading magazines account for nearly 32 million copies (8:1;12:3).

Although newspapers are one of the greatest sources of information, they are poorly read by both adults and youth. Studies show that neither have habits of discrimination. Sports and comics are widely read, but editorials are read by less than one fifth of the readers.

[14] *Choosing Free Materials for Use in the Schools,* American Association of School Administrators, Washington, D.C.: National Education Association, 1955; see also criteria developed by the Instructional Materials Committee of the California School Supervisors Association, Allen Risdon, chairman, published in Sacramento by the California State Teachers Association, 1954; and *Using Free Materials in the Classroom,* Association for Supervision and Curriculum Development. Washington, D.C.: National Education Association, 1953.

Teachers should find a way to encourage discriminative reading, regular study habits, and the use of the newspaper as a source of ideas about current topics. It has been suggested that newspapers be made an integral part of classroom instruction, and that they be readily available to students in all schools. Although the newspaper may be most appropriate for use in the social studies, it carries items of value to practically every teacher in the school. Foreign language teachers know the value of foreign newspapers. Most of the larger magazines print foreign language editions of all issues. Because these have great value in the schools, they are often given to language classes along with the English editions.

Magazines range all the way from the trashy to the scholarly and sophisticated. Students are more at home with magazines than newspapers. This is due both to content and to structure. Magazine pictures and illustrations are more striking than those of the newspapers. They communicate more effectively.

The above discussion of magazines and newspapers has been slanted to publications intended for the general public. There are several magazines and newspapers aimed solely at classroom use. Normally, these are less colorful, less expensive, and less appealing. Nevertheless, they fill a useful place and justify their existence. This kind of publication is found more often in classrooms than general publications. A few of these publications for the secondary school are:

American Education Publications, 1250 Fairwood Ave., Columbus 16, Ohio: *Current Events, Every Week, Our Times, Current Science, Read Magazine*

Civic Education Service, 1733 K St. N.W., Washington 6, D.C.: *Junior Review, Weekly News Review, American Observer*

Scholastic Magazines, 33 W. 42 St., New York 36, N.Y.: *Junior Scholastic, Senior Scholastic, World Week, Practical English, Literary Cavalcade, Co-ed.*

COMIC BOOKS Probably no learning material is so controversial as the comic book or comic strip (the cartoon falls into another category). Even to mention the comic book as a learning material is debatable. Yet, more than a million of these books are printed annually, are read avidly, traded, hoarded. In reality, the negative attitude toward comics has somewhat abated by the time the child has reached junior high school, and neither teachers nor parents are so militant. There are, however, antisocial and antimoral aspects even here which should not be overlooked.

On the positive side, the picture story holds a great educational potential. Students like this medium of communication, and it may become the threshold to richer reading habits. There is reason to believe that the quality of the comics is building upward, and teachers are finding more and more ways to exploit and capitalize on the medium.

Some years ago *Scholastic Magazine* conducted an essay contest for teachers entitled "How I Teach During the First Week of School." One of the winning essays told how one teacher exploited the comics.[15] Other teachers use them regularly in bulletin board displays, either alone or in conjunction with other materials. Still other teachers have used comics as a springboard for written and spoken exercises and for motivation of creative activity in art. Coupled with the cartoon, the comic picture or series has been used in teaching grammatical structure, foreign language, safety, driver education, science, guidance principles, consumer education, salesmanship, and other topics.

Creating Reading Materials

It is an erroneous idea to think that the creation of reading materials is an activity for the elementary school only. Junior and senior high school teachers have found this a useful learning project in certain situations. Four of the many reasons for such an activity are mentioned here.

1. Students who have written something of a worthwhile nature should share it with others, as is done when a good short story or poem is published in a newspaper or magazine. But it may be more valuable to have multiple copies made and used in a more standard curricular manner. The material becomes more important, is more likely to be permanent, and is more adaptable to learning purposes.

2. Students need the experience of serious writing. Writing is more real when it is likely to serve more than a mere "exercise need." Material for reproduction and circulation must be carefully and near-professionally produced. This means factual accuracy, careful analysis, originality in presentation, and clarity of expression.

3. Often there is a paucity of material on a subject which is being studied. If students, singly or as a group, produce something of value, it should be retained as valuable source material for other students who will study the same topic. Such a situation is easily conceivable in the study of a community—industries, ethnic groups, cultural agencies, finances, or other phases.

4. The motivational value inherent in a project that will probably be

[15] Audrey Hodgins, "My Drugstore Cowboys," *Scholastic Teacher*, September 22, 1955, p. 13–T.

used by other students, either contemporaneously or in after years, is significant.

Who creates these materials at the local level? The above introduction has been entirely from the standpoint of the student. And this is probably the most important production source, but they may be produced by teachers, or by committees of teachers and supervisors, as a curriculum unit for example. There are some study guides of such outstanding worth that they could well be reproduced and made available to other teachers. This, too, has unusual motivational value at the teacher level. As a matter of fact, a high school might well assume an annual project: the publication of a yearbook, anthology, or collection of faculty writings of the year. This would in fact be "our best" for the year—poems, stories, dramas, outlines, study guides, histories, surveys, bibliographies, interviews, reports on foreign trips and study, and other writings.

How will locally produced reading materials be reproduced for use by others? There are many ways of doing it. Which one is employed will probably depend upon funds available, facilities, and the permanency sought for the publication. In some cases, extra copies may be unnecessary. A bound typewritten copy is placed on the classroom library shelf or housed in the main library. One college for years has followed a plan of binding in Manila folders all its research papers of quality and storing them in the library. They are available for graduate students year after year in much the same way that dissertations are available. Some critics fear the presence of these papers will encourage "cribbing." Of course, this is possible, but probably no more so than the presence of any other printed documents.

Important stories, poems, correspondence with foreign students, or other compositions may be printed in the school paper. This is commonplace, but it needs some build up; otherwise students may wish to fill the pages of the paper with trivia.

REPRODUCING MATERIALS   To provide multiple copies of materials, schools usually use the liquid duplicator, stencil duplicator, offset press, or letterpress techniques. Each has advantages and limitations. Teachers should know these advantages and limitations and the local production facilities. It is assumed here that all teachers know how to make "ditto" and "mimeo" copy.

Liquid duplicators, often called hectographs, are of two types. The spirit or liquid type, a direct process, is probably the most commonly used throughout the country. It is inexpensive and easy of operation by student or teacher. As high as 300 good copies can be made from one master. Copies will fade and are often messy to prepare, but they are cheap. The gelatin process is similar to the so-called spirit process, but is not in as common use.[16]

The stencil or mimeograph process is also a very common one, and the machine is easy to operate. Copy lasts almost indefinitely, and a master will reproduce 500 copies with short-run stencils or as many as 10,000 with special stencils.[17]

Offset printing as represented by the multilith or multigraph is an even more satisfactory reproduction form. Offset printing produces more professional appearing copy and thousands of copies can be made from a master. Also, photographs can be incorporated into the copy. One disadvantage is that the equipment is expensive and the preparation of masters and plates is more technical than in the preceding processes. The offset press is more likely to be found in the district school office than in building offices.

Letterpress is expensive and must be done commercially or in the school print shop. School printing is limited. Only a very unusual local publication is likely to be reproduced by letterpress. However, there may be ambitious projects, usually those produced at the supervisory or administrative level, susceptible of wide distribution, which will be set in letterpress type.

A Materials File

A majority of the contents of a materials file will be "print" or "graphic" in type. It is a cliché that a good craftsman must know how to use the tools of his trade. It might also be added that he must have the tools. This applies with equal force to teachers. In the case of teachers, many of the tools are provided by the school districts simply as a matter of course, including textbooks, reference books, maps, globes, projectors, recorders, radios, and many other materials. The provision of these teaching tools is in varying degree. Some schools supply them in abundance, others have skimpy supplies. Some districts provide what they call "basic" materials and "basic" becomes a matter of definition.

Regardless of district, teachers always feel the need for more and more specific learning materials. These needs go far beyond what is provided. Therefore, teachers make collections of their own, invent devices, reshape what they have, and give their ingenuity full rein.

[16] Anyone unfamiliar with the operation of this equipment might like to review the motion picture, *Duplicating by the Spirit Method*, 15 min., color, produced by Bailey Films, Inc. This film shows step-by-step processes.

[17] *Mimeographing Techniques*, film, 17 min., color, produced by Bailey Films, Inc., explains the process.

It is in the area of "fugitive" materials that student teachers and beginning teachers feel at a disadvantage. They simply have not been "in the business" long enough to have collected materials to supplement what is provided. Prospective teachers will be well advised to begin a materials file just as soon as they are admitted to a teacher-education program.

Intelligent long-range planning in this field will pay good dividends. By the time a prospective teacher reaches the stage of student teaching, he should have a sizeable materials file. This file, collection, or accumulation could include flat pictures, clippings, poems, bibliographies, lists of field trips, booklets or sources of free and inexpensive materials, charts, graphs, diagrams, sketches, drawings, maps, bulletin board designs and ideas, facsimiles, and other two-dimensional materials. The materials file might just as well include such three-dimensional materials as models, specimens, artifacts, or small hand tools. The industrial arts teacher, for example, will quite naturally have both types.

When materials have been collected, or as they are collected, they must be organized or catalogued in some meaningful manner. Unorganized materials are little better than no materials. There are hosts of possible classifications. The commonest one is by subject matter, topic, or area. The prospective teacher might wish to give some thought to classification by instructional concepts or values with subject-matter classifications in subdivisions. Instead of "social studies" with subdivisions of United Nations, UNESCO, U.S. Senate, Supreme Court, these subdivisions might well follow "value" or "goal" headings such as room environment, contemporary problems, individual study, committee study, oral reports, or motivation.

Storage often becomes a problem. It is the last step in the ongoing clip-collect-file-store formula. Each individual must solve this problem in his own way. School rooms are being built with facilities which include built-in drawers and cabinet space for flat and three-dimensional materials. Letter and legal-sized filing cabinets help with the storage of mounted pictures, clippings, and lists. But, before one has a classroom, one can utilize pressed board filing drawers, collapsible file boxes and folders, vertical file boxes, orange crates, or other available storage items.

Selected Readings

1. Burton, William H., *The Guidance of Learning*, 3d ed. New York: Appleton-Century-Crofts, 1962.
2. Dale, Edgar, *Audio-Visual Methods in Teaching*, revised ed. New York: Holt, Rinehart and Winston, Inc., 1954.
3. De Bernardis, Amo, *The Use of Instructional Materials*. New York: Appleton-Century-Crofts, 1960.

4. Clark, Leonard H., and Irving S. Starr, *Secondary School Teaching Methods.* New York: The Macmillan Company, 1959.
5. Cronbach, Lee J., ed., *Text Materials in Modern Education.* Urbana: University of Illinois Press, 1955.
6. *Dictionary of Education*, 2d ed. New York: McGraw-Hill Book Company, Inc., 1959.
7. Grambs, Jean D., William J. Iverson, and Franklin K. Patterson, *Modern Methods in Secondary Education*, revised ed. New York: Holt, Rinehart and Winston, Inc., 1958.
8. Kinder, James S., *Audio-Visual Materials and Techniques*, 2d ed. New York: American Book Company, 1959. Chapters 1–2.
9. Kinney, Lucien, and Katherine Dresden, *Better Learning Through Current Materials.* Stanford, Calif.: Stanford University Press, 1949.
10. *New Teaching Aids for the American Classroom.* Stanford, Calif.: The Institute for Communication Research, Part I–"The Classroom of Tomorrow"; research papers by Ralph W. Tyler, "Social Trends and Problems for Tomorrow's Schools"; Ray M. Hall, "The Nature of Tomorrow's Classroom"; and William E. Spaulding, "Old and New Teaching Aids," 1960, pp. 3–15.
11. Nordberg, H. Orville, James M. Bradford, and William C. Odell, *Secondary School Teaching.* New York: The Macmillan Company, 1962.
12. Wittich, Walter A., and Charles F. Schuller, *Audiovisual Materials: Their Nature and Use*, 3d ed. New York: Harper & Row, Publishers, 1962. Chapter 1.

Selected Audio-Visual Materials

A. *The Carpet Under Every Classroom*, 20 min., sound: Precision Films. Film shows how a good library program helps to realize the objectives of the school, with the library presented as a resource center.
B. *Duplicating by the Spirit Method*, 15 min., color, sound: Bailey Films, Inc. Detailed instruction outlines how to use the equipment and prepare stencils.
C. *Mimeographing Techniques*, 17 min., color, sound: Bailey Films, Inc. Mimeographing techniques and care of the equipment are given.
D. *Case of the Curious Citizen*, 33-⅓ rpm record, thirty-six 2- by 2-inch color slides: Audio-Visual Commission on Public Information. Two parents are taken on a tour of a typical school instructional materials center.

CHAPTER 9

Instructional materials:
conventional audio-visual type

In addition to the printed learning materials discussed in the preceding chapter, there are almost endless numbers of other learning materials, many of which will be treated in the present and following chapter. For convenience, these materials are separated into those that are rather commonplace, and those that are usually considered to be newer in chronology. Widely varying use, innovations, research, and new modifications and extensions of older devices constantly provide new dimensions. A relatively old device may lie dormant for years only to spring into dynamic prominence as research and technology push ahead.

Teachers need to remind themselves that materials which have become commonplace or which are inexpensive or near at hand are not necessarily obsolete. Often the newer media have more glamour and publicity but they do not necessarily replace other tried devices. Usually, the newer devices provide teachers with a greater range of tools with which to do the instructional job demanded by modern developments. Programmed learning materials, for example, do not replace films or field trips; they simply add depth to the teachers' instructional repertoire.

FLAT PICTURES

Pictures do not in and of themselves possess any mystical powers to teach, yet they have one of the greatest potentials of all types of learning materials. Young and old, dull and bright, have an innate liking for pictures. The appeal of pictures is universal. Children become acquainted with them long before they start to school, and adults continue to "look at" or "read" pictures long after they have completed formal schooling, in fact, as long as they live. Pictures are among the cheapest and the most readily available of all learning materials. Many of them are free. Teachers and students gather pictures from magazines, newspapers, advertisements, pamphlets, posters, circulars, and an endless number of places. But, like all other learning materials, their values vary and selection and use should be given careful consideration.

Pictures serve many purposes in the learning process. They motivate and vitalize learning and they clarify vague ideas. Abstractions nearly always need clarification, and concrete imagery should be brought to bear wherever possible. Even knowledge of concrete things, skills, and processes is often vague or limited. Pictures can assist in providing more complete and meaningful ideation.

Types of Pictures

Flat pictures consist of study prints, photographs, textbook illustrations, and unprojected pictures of all kinds. They are all much the same, although study prints usually are pictures that are more carefully selected, mounted, and curriculum oriented.

Photographs are made from either original negatives or copied from existing pictures. Usually photographic copies are more interesting than the clippings or paper pictures they are taken from because they have more warmth, definition, and detail. If needed in quantity, photographic pictures are usually mounted and sometimes laminated and are expected to serve teachers and students over a long period of time. Many school districts have photographers and equipment and provide this service for teachers; yet on the whole only a small percentage of the teachers of a district ever get much photographic assistance.

A junior high school social studies teacher felt that he needed pictures of world architecture as found in his city. None of the study prints in the local audio-visual collection told the story. He needed tailor-made materials. In cooperation with the school photographer, a set of twenty-six illustrations of local architecture representing types from the classic Greek and Roman to the severely functional modern was photographed, enlarged to 11- by 14-inch size, and mounted. These photographs along with the other more standard types of learning materials provided the content for the unit on "The Emergence of Modern Architecture."

Instead of preparing the study print set above as 11- by 14-inch mounted pictures, it would have been just as easy, probably easier, to have made the same content available as a set of 2- by 2-inch color slides. And, if properly planned, both types of pictures could have been prepared from the same negatives. More will be said about slide production later in this chapter.

Preparation and Use

Some of the purposes which flat pictures serve have already been pointed out. How can they be most effectively used? A rather common use lies in the introduction of new units of study. They orient the thinking, they set the stage for new subject matter, and they involve nearly every subject or experience unit in the curriculum.

Flat pictures could do much to motivate a class in American Literature preparing to study the short stories of Bret Harte. Pictures of the author, frontier buildings and settlements, signs or posted billboards, dance halls, derringers, costumes, snow drifts, leafless trees, cowboys and miners, and a lonely editor setting hand type by the dim light of a kerosene lamp establish the mood. Additional motivation could be provided by artists' sketches of some of the characters from "The Outcasts of Poker Flat" and "The Luck of Roaring Camp," such as Mr. Oakhurst, Kentuck, the Duchess, and Yerba Bill, or of a grave at the foot of a tree with this epitaph:

BENEATH THIS TREE

LIES THE BODY

OF

JOHN OAKHURST

WHO STRUCK A STREAK OF BAD LUCK

ON THE 23D OF NOVEMBER 1850

AND

HANDED IN HIS CHECKS

ON THE 7th DECEMBER 1850

Pictures used to introduce units need to be seen and discussed by all members of the class. They may later be exhibited on bulletin boards for study and reference.

One can hardly study pictures without enriching his experience. The nature and extent of this enrichment depend upon the amount of knowledge already possessed, the type of pictures, the manner in which the pictures are employed, and the objectives sought. Pictures do add new dimensions to learning.

Often a single picture will suffice for the objective in mind. One picture of an early cave painting found in southern France may be sufficient to arouse imagination, and it may actually be better than a dozen pictures. If, on the other hand, the unit to be studied is Iran, one picture obviously would not suffice. In introducing the symphonic orchestra, one picture would tell a great deal about the instruments involved, placement (location) of instruments, position of conductor and musicians, and possibly other facts. Additional pictures could very well detail the various instruments, types of music stands, and even meanings of the conductor's gestures.

On occasions, teachers use pictures as a test, or part of a test, of students' understanding of content. These pictures may be drawings which are mimeographed, they may be prints in quantity so that each student has a copy on his desk, or they may be in the form of a slide or a transparency. In the latter use the medium must be such that the student has a sufficient light level at his desk for reading and writing.

Techniques for using pictures are manifold, but time, place, and purpose will determine which adds most to the learning process. In some instances, the teacher may prefer to arrange a display on a bulletin board and in some way incorporate the display into the lesson structure.

Although unprojected pictures are being considered, attention must be called to the use of illustrations in the opaque and overhead projectors. In the former, pictures are projected without processing or preparation, while in the latter, they must be transferred to a transparent medium. A projected picture may be copied on the chalkboard or on butcher paper for later use so that repeated projection is unnecessary.

PROJECTED PICTURES

In the above discussion, attention was given to flat pictures. At this point attention is directed to projected pictures which are of two general types, still and motion.

Types of Projected Pictures

Practically every high school in the nation is equipped, more or less adequately, to use most types of projected materials. The motion picture, slide, filmstrip, opaque projector, overhead projector, stereoprojector, microprojector, and tachistoscope will be considered here. Only the first mentioned is a motion device, although attempts are being made to put motion or animation in slides, filmstrips, and transparencies. These attempts depend upon polarization and are still in their infancy. As yet, they are too expensive to buy and too difficult to produce locally to occasion more than an experimental use in the high school. For industry, that is another matter.

Psychological and Educational Advantages

The projected picture has several advantages over the unprojected picture as a learning material. Its use with large classes is obvious at a glance, because it removes the "front row" feature of the unprojected picture. Projected pictures have a certain amount of novelty, which arouses and maintains positive student attention. To a large extent, extraneous factors which dilute and dissipate attention are eliminated, and all members of a group become engaged in one unifying activity. Minds will wander, but "wool-gathering" is reduced. Novelty, of course, is not the only advantage of projected pictures, and if it were, their use would be largely one of fostering interest.

Contrary to opinions held by some teachers, projection materials are relatively inexpensive because they may be reused many times. Thus the cost per student may become a fraction of a cent. The cost of many other learning materials, verbal and nonverbal, may be appreciably higher. Actually, good projected materials are within the budget range of every school.

In the main, the thought and understanding which go into the preparation of most filmstrips and motion pictures are worthy of mention. They are not made overnight. Producers know that they are working for a professional market and that the general acceptance of their product depends upon its quality. These materials are actually planned in curriculum terms. Of course, this is not to say that there are no poor quality filmstrips and motion pictures, but the number is decreasing. More and more, teachers and administrators have adopted this rule concerning instructional materials: "properly prepared, wisely selected, and intelligently used."

The major psychological and professional advantage of projected pictures lies in the type of material they are *ipso facto.* These materials visualize their topics—idea, fact, skill, process, attitude—and make them concrete and comprehensible for students. Projected materials must enable the teacher to be more proficient than he would be otherwise. School districts buy materials, not to be modern, not to be spectacular, but solely to enable their teachers to do a better job of instruction.

Slides and Filmstrips

Slides and filmstrips are much alike. One is a series of related pictures arranged in fixed sequence; the sequence of the other falls to the discretion of the teacher. There are advantages for each. It might be pointed out that the use of the filmstrip is increasing much faster than that of the slide. Whether this is occasioned by convenience or by merit cannot be determined at this time.

Slides are available in several sizes but only the 3¼- by 4-inch and the 2- by 2-inch slides will be mentioned here. The former is older, but still has pronounced usefulness in connection with handmade teaching materials. It may be (1) made with India ink, pencils, crayons, (2) typed, (3) photographed on sensitive glass (positive transparency), or (4) reproduced by a diazo or related process. The 2- by 2-inch photographic slide is available commercially, usually in sets, for a great variety of subjects. It may also be easily photographed by teacher or students to document or illustrate curriculum work. Projection is simple and inexpensive. There is a tendency to use one or only a few slides of the 3¼- by 4-inch type in a class session, but more of the 2- by 2-inch size are ordinarily used. This is probably accounted for by the fact that most of the smaller slides are bought as sets and used simply because they are there.

As filmstrip and slide materials are available in great quantity and for almost all school subjects, wise selection becomes imperative. Some materials are of most use in introducing study units, while others fit developmental, drill, appreciation, and review lessons. In general, slides and filmstrips are most used with large groups, but they can be adapted to small group or individual work. Many schools which are now making provision for more individual work have fitted out screening carrels or sectioned off areas with a low light level where students can study slides, filmstrips, or even motion pictures much as they study books. With motion pictures or with record players, earphones are employed so that the sound does not bother nearby students. Filmstrips are as easily checked out from the library as a book, and projectors can be operated after a short period of instruction and practice.

Motion Pictures

The motion picture possesses practically all the advantages given above for projected materials plus the big factor of motion. Motion pictures are seldom produced on subjects which are static, although animation techniques make it possible to show static subjects with great concreteness. A law in physics, for example, needs demonstration to clarify its application, and the motion picture can do this, yet the law itself is a purely verbal description of a phenomenon. Interaction and dynamic relationships among people allow the motion picture to do a superb job. What is shyness? How do totalitarian regimes operate in daily life? How does courtesy affect friends and acquaintances? How do mores shape the lives of primitive peoples? What were the events leading up to the bombardment of Fort Sumter? How did the "blue laws" of colonial New England shape the character of the citizens? Historical films can recreate and document understandings of time relationships, causes, and effects of man's aspirations, crises, and progress. They bridge the gap of time and space.

There are a great many teachers and students, too, who have the opinion that the motion picture is on a much higher plane than the filmstrip or slide as a learning material. Such an opinion has no factual basis. They are two separate types of materials and one does not supplant the other. It is true that the filmstrip is a simpler and more compact device, but its values are significant. With the motion picture, as with the filmstrip, proper preparation, wise selection, and intelligent use are the teachers' guidelines.

Opaque Projections

Opaque projections are treated here along with filmstrips and motion pictures, yet they are quite different in type. The opaque projector is a machine which enlarges and projects images from a given medium by reflected light. In all the materials discussed above, the projection light goes through a translucent material, but in this instance, projection is from an opaque medium. One understands from a glance why opaque projection requires a dark room; indeed, the darker the better. But the big advantage of opaque projection is also apparent; materials need no processing in order to be projected. Flat pictures of any kind, colored or monochrome, charts, graphs, sketches, post cards, cartoons, book illustrations are all ready to be projected as they are. Size is the only consideration. Aside from the projector itself (a capital equipment item) there is no cost. Even small three-dimensional objects may be projected—a farthing may be enlarged so that every member of a class can see it at the same time. Even the details of milling, date, color, wear, and texture can be noted, and if another known coin is placed alongside it, comparisons are easily made.

Overhead Projections

The overhead projector is somewhat newer than the other instructional tools being discussed, but its use is increasing rapidly. Many teachers consider it indispensable in such subjects as mathematics, science, social studies, foreign language, English, business education, and health education. Chief among its many advantages are: (1) it gives a bright picture in a fully lighted room, (2) it is operated from the front of the class by the instructor who faces the class at all times, (3) the teacher can use a pencil to point out features appearing in a picture without leaving his position at the machine, and (4) materials to be projected may be prepared in advance by a variety of techniques, or they may be placed on the projector impromptu. Thus, the points made in a lesson may be summarized in concrete form for all the members of the class to see. In this instance, the overhead becomes a "whiteboard" replacing the blackboard, and it is actually easier and cleaner to use.

Other Types of Projections

Stereoprojectors, microprojectors, and tachistoscopes, although standard types of projection apparatus, are specialized and have limited use. Modern stereo materials and projectors are expensive and are chiefly limited to clinics, laboratories, graduate seminars, and analytical study. Microprojectors are especially useful in the biological sciences. Either wet or dry microscopic slides can be shown to an entire class at one time, obviating the need for microscopes for each member of the class. Also, in group projection the teacher knows that each member of the class sees the significant aspects of each slide. The tachistoscope is a still projector equipped with a shutterlike mechanism for flash recognition exposures. It can be used to increase attention span, rate of perception, and accuracy and speed of recognition. This apparatus, too, is specialized and will be operated chiefly by reading or other remedial clinicians. The preservice teacher will rarely, if ever, be called upon to use any of these specialized machines, but it is well to know of their existence and capabilities.

Utilization of Projected Pictures

Already a great deal has been said about the use of projection apparatus and learning materials. Some more specific principles of use and examples will be of value to the beginning teacher.

A teacher of American history in the eleventh grade had just completed a unit on the War of 1812. He felt that a good review was in order, but that the review would be meaningless if it were a rehash of previous lessons. Accordingly, he selected a filmstrip entitled *The War of 1812* to provide understandings, relationships, and sequence. The filmstrip was shown in the regular classroom equipped with Venetian blinds which provided a semidarkened room. The projector was operated by a student as the instructor stood in the side aisle by the chalkboard and display area. A brief introduction set the stage, and as each frame was projected a few words were said, or, in some cases, students were brought into the discussion. Twice the screen pictures were tied to special reports which had earlier been made in class by students. And, twice the instructor went briefly to a large wall map to note spatial relationships introduced in the picture. The teacher set the tempo and the time was balanced so that each facet of the topic got its just portion of time.

Instead of *The War of 1812* the teacher above could have selected any one or more filmstrips from a dozen titles available to him. For an introductory lesson or for a developmental lesson, undoubtedly the selection would have been different.

During a short period of unstructured discussion about the flag and loyalty which followed the usual Pledge of Allegiance, a junior high school teacher on the first day of the fall term decided that a series of short discussions or programs about the flag would be in order. Accordingly, he prepared a series of lantern slides. On the next day two typed slides were used: 1. P L E D G E: from Old French, *plege, pleige,* and Medieval Latin, *plebium, plevium.* Today's meaning: a promise or agreement by which one binds oneself to do something; a promise.

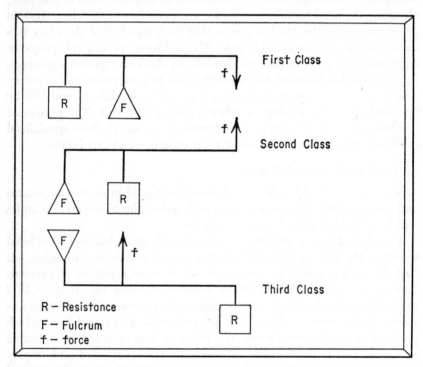

Fig. 9-1   This handmade slide was done with India ink on clear glass. The edge was bound with regular slide binding tape.

2. A L L E G I A N C E: from Middle English, *allegeaunce* and Old French, *lige, liege.* Today's meaning: devotion or loyalty to that which is entitled to obedience or service and respect.

On succeeding days one hand-drawn and lettered slide was used to illustrate the evolution of the American flag from that of June 14, 1777, with thirteen stars to the present fifty-star flag with thirteen stripes.

A general science teacher began a unit on levers with the slide illustrated in Figure 9-1.

The art class of Miss B_____ used five sets of commercially prepared 2- by 2-inch slides in the study of Japanese art. These sets were arranged to follow time developments of periods of artistic development. Each set contained from twenty to thirty-seven slides.

Some years ago the head of the English department of an eastern high school developed the idea of using 2- by 2-inch slides in his English literature courses. He photographed in color costumes worn by different characters as various Elizabethan plays were given at the high school, a nearby university, and at the town playhouse. Over a period of several years, he gathered slides of a significant number of Shakespeare's plays. The shooting was accomplished during rehearsals. Then, with a copy lens, the teacher copied frontispieces of each play to be taught. Shakespeare's plays became quite real with an emphasis on dramatic quality first and foremost. The production of the slides was accomplished with a camera which cost less than fifty dollars.

A physical education teacher in a large midwestern high school was required to teach several classes of first aid. Students sat through these classes with varying degrees of indifference as the teacher presented the advice of Red Cross handbooks and manuals, gave demonstrations, discussed lifesaving and economic losses, and provided an occasional Red Cross guest speaker. Using a 35 mm. camera the instructor photographed seventy-two slides covering lifesaving and first aid techniques. Cases were simulated but with plausible reality. For example, three slides showed convincingly the differences between first, second, and third degree burns. Skeptics of this application of the slide technique might try explaining the differences between the three types of burns without color pictures.

Use of the motion picture is quite common and in the main most effective. The principles of use given later for all projected materials should make specific examples for uses of the motion picture needless.

Overhead projectors rely to a large extent upon impromptu use or upon teacher preproduced materials on a transparency medium. Any good manual gives the details of preparation. Difficult and expensive photographic techniques are no longer a necessity. Standard equipment is now available to make copies of any printed, photographed, hand-drawn, or written material. These transparencies may be made in a matter of seconds with dry nonchemical materials and in a fully lighted room. As a matter of fact, they may be made in front of the class as needed, and projected at once.

Principles of use of projected pictures are much the same as those for other learning materials—textbooks, maps, models, or records. The particular medium involved naturally calls for adaptations and modifications.

THE TEACHER MUST PREPARE IN ADVANCE Considering the daily lesson he is teaching, the teacher decides in advance the types of learning materials which will best help accomplish his established objectives. Next comes the selection of appropriate pictures and verbal materials. This process of selection is highly important because there are so many from which to choose. These materials are precise learning media and must fit the objectives of the unit of study. They must be integrated into lesson plans, and at this point consideration should be given to correlation with laboratory, library, creative work, discussion, and composition. Method and material are inseparable. Selection of picture materials goes hand in hand with preview.

THE CLASS MUST BE PREPARED A class which is properly prepared for a learning experience profits maximally from the experience. Proper preparation of students for the use of visual materials alerts them as to why they are doing what they are doing, tells them what to look for, and shows them how to relate visual content to prior class work, thus building a readiness for the experience to follow. Students usually learn more from films, for example, if they are told in advance that they will be tested on the contents of the film. Tests are not always germane, so students should be told of other uses to which the material will be put. Unusual words, phrases, references, or locations found in the film should also be pointed out in advance.

THE EQUIPMENT MUST BE MADE READY IN ADVANCE OF PRESENTATION Whenever equipment is used, whether in laboratory, demonstration, or in film presentation, the teacher must be sure that everything is in working order. Mechanical failure or delay causes time to be wasted, confidence to be destroyed, and little learning to be accomplished. If student operators are used, they must be scheduled ahead of time.

THE PRESENTATION IS THE CULMINATION OF THE PREPARATION The presentation is made under the best circumstances possible and should proceed according to plan. With filmstrips and slides, there will likely be discussion, reading of captions, or reference to maps. Films are much more likely to be projected without interruption, yet they, too, may at times be used profitably with interruption. If so, the machine is stopped, and the lights may or may not be switched on depending upon the extent of the interruption.

EFFECTIVE FOLLOW-UP IS ESSENTIAL Seldom does good usage stop with merely showing the material. Something must follow to clarify facts, to provide concept generalization, to tie material to established objectives, to clinch benefits. Follow-up activities vary with maturity of students, subjects, teachers' objectives, and other factors. Among follow-up activities are discussions, reports, tests, creative work, and construction projects.

At times these activities may be voluntary; at other times, assigned. Involvement of students is a must.

One of the chief points of this discussion of principles of use is that these materials must be taught. They teach a few things by themselves, but not enough. Hanging a chart in front of a classroom is not going to accomplish much. It must become an integral part of planned instruction—*it must be taught.*

Keep these axioms in mind in using projected pictures:

Materials should be built into the warp and woof of lessons.
Teacher preparation is absolutely essential.
Pupil readiness is equally essential.
Follow-up activities are always appropriate.
Schedules of the right material at the right time in the right place are
     necessary.
Involvement of students should take place at every step.
Materials should be reshown or replayed as needed.
Discussion after looking and listening tends to set values in students'
     minds.
Supplementation with all sorts of related learning materials and activities
     helps give maximum results.

What Research Has to Say

The volume of research on the use of projected pictures is second only to that in the use of television. By and large it is overwhelmingly favorable. The director of secondary education in Mount Vernon, New York, says:

Learning is more efficient when subject matter can be presented in several forms than when only one is possible. For example, hearing and seeing reinforce reading to increase learning. Studying a globe adds to the meaning of a text book, and viewing a film adds even more (6:238).

An NEA research bulletin states:

In an experiment in ninth-grade science, for example, the classes that used regular teaching methods with a textbook and films learned 20 percent more facts than the control classes which used the same teaching methods and textbook but no films. This immediate improvement, of course, is valuable. But, the really significant fact is that after six weeks the film groups retained 38 percent more information than the control groups (9:10–11).

In the matter of use, research shows that the effectiveness of a film may be nearly doubled when properly handled. Note the accompanying graph (7:18):

Effect of Three Methods of Film Use on Learning (Wittich and Fowlkes)

	20%	30%	40%	50%	60%
Film only					
Introduction plus film					
Introduction, film, review, reshowing					

Other researches show that many films and filmstrips can be repeated for a class with profit. At times the repetition may follow during the same class period, at other times at a later period. McTavish has reported a research in teaching science to the effect that the second, third, and fourth showings of films produced percentage gains of 35.0, 7.4, and 1.1 respectively. Only factual knowledge was tested. Other investigators report similar results. It would seem that a second showing can be quite important, but that additional showings tend to lead to diminishing returns (7:18).

Instructional materials should be used in the regular classroom. Classes should not be shifted to an auditorium or special room. Students learn best in their regularly accustomed learning environment. This conclusion is undoubtedly the opinion of many experienced teachers, and is also the emphatic findings of controlled researches by Krasker, Knowlton, Tilton, and Stoddard (7:18).

A word of caution is also found in the research on the concentration or density of concepts in films. This relates closely to the research on values to be obtained from repeated showings.

A research study was carried out on how much a film should attempt to teach within a specified time. The variable here, the number of facts, was called the concept density. It was found that most teaching films have too high a concept density, and reduction in the teaching load of a film improves its effectiveness. On the other hand, there is a limit to how little a film should attempt to teach. Oversimplification is a possibility also. The experiment confirms, however, the well-known fact that most audio-visual materials attempt to cover too much ground. In any case, the concept density should be adjusted to the level of the class using the film. Part of this adjustment would, of course, have to be made individually for members of any class by the teacher who knows the class.[1]

[1] Paul R. Wendt, "Audio-Visual Instruction," *What Research Says to the Teacher,* Bulletin No. 14. Washington, D.C.: Department of Classroom Teachers, American Educational Research Association, 1957, reprinted 1961, pp. 22–23.

The above paragraphs are intended only to direct attention to the fact that the use of these materials has been carefully studied in laboratory and classroom. The professional literature abounds in researches which illustrate the benefits of audio-visual techniques. The references at the close of the chapter are recommended for further study.

A summary of six studies in audio-visual research dealing with science teaching was reviewed by Dean Kenneth E. Anderson at the University of Kansas Conference on Programmed Learning in the summer of 1961. Dean Anderson's final word was:

The results, discounting any "Hawthorne Effect," would seem to indicate that when the instruction via films is purposeful and planned in terms of objectives to be reached, positive increments in learning occur. . . . Teaching with or without films, television, or machines, will be effective only as we employ teachers who know their subject matter and have the know-how to put the material across. A good teacher may greatly augment his effectiveness by the proper use of mechanical aids. This means selection of good films, good television programs, and good teaching-machine programs, which fit into a planned and purposeful program of instruction.[2]

Also, it may be noted that the researches sampled here deal almost exclusively with factual learning. Research on interest, vocabulary, opinions and attitudes, problem solving, and skill formation has not been neglected. There are materials that are largely inspirational in type. These may be based on legend or they may be re-enactment of historical or literary events. Different techniques must obviously be employed in their use.

Abuses and Obstacles

Each year sees improvement in the use of audio-visual materials by teachers. Beginning teachers joining the teaching corps bring with them new techniques and insights. The contribution of projected pictures to education is an accepted fact and few, if any, communication media have the versatility of the motion picture, which happily combines motion, words, music, animation, and color. Opportunities for in-service teachers to learn more about the use of audio-visual materials and techniques also increase constantly. Workshops, institutes, summer and extension courses, yearbooks, magazine articles, and the counsel of supervisors provide new ideas and encouragement. A few states make it mandatory for teachers to learn how to use audio-visual equipment and materials properly.

Yet, with all the above, there is reason to believe that abuses and poor

2 Kenneth E. Anderson, "Audio-Visual Research," *Kansas Studies in Education*, vol. 11 (June 1961), pp. 3–14.

use still exist in some places. Some of the abuses are traceable to administrative levels while others must be laid at the doorstep of the classroom teacher. Among these abuses are:

Poor selection of materials
No relation to subject or unit of work
Lack of preparation before utilization
Inadequate or no follow-up
Reliance on a single type of material
Use of too many materials
Using materials merely to fill up time

Most of these abuses are rooted in a poor understanding of the use of instructional materials regardless of type. All of these abuses should be easy to correct.

There are also numerous obstacles to more effective use. Most of these obstacles have administrative origins. Yet in many instances teachers can, if they are willing, offset or minimize the difficulties. In the case of projected materials, an often encountered difficulty is that many classrooms cannot be properly darkened, and the acoustics are horrible. Inadequate room conditions plague effective teaching in many ways. Along with this physical obstacle is the lack of a suitable place for previewing and study of the materials before they are used in the classroom.

Many school buildings are inadequately stocked with equipment. Scheduling becomes a problem, and in some cases only the aggressive teachers get the equipment. Others tend to give up after a few "turndowns." The same difficulty obtains in getting films, maps, and other materials when needed from the central materials center. In some schools, there is a tendency to schedule "movie days." Some misconceptions are involved in such instances. First, there is no point in showing "movies"; only educational films should be shown. Next, films should not be scheduled for a stereotyped or mechanical showing because of a calendar. Films should be shown whenever they contribute to the educational goals sought by the teacher; they may, therefore, fit more appropriately on Tuesday instead of Thursday or Monday instead of Friday. Much of this improper use stems from an inadequate amount of equipment in the building. Even the local catalogues are so vague that teachers have difficulty finding materials. Delivery is at times not dependable. Often there is no stand-by equipment in case of breakdown. All this adds up to discouragement and disillusion.

But, better audio-visual usage is steadily gaining. School budgets make increasing provision for materials and equipment. Special assistance from the federal government has brought millions of dollars worth of equipment to the schools since the passage of the National Defense Education Act (NDEA) of 1958. Now school buildings are being planned with an eye to a new emphasis on the "new media" in teaching. New instructional organization, such as team teaching, tends to promote better usage. There is a noticeable upsurge in the use of audio-visual materials which steadily minimizes and eliminates many of the obstacles and abuses referred to above.

AUDITORY INSTRUCTIONAL MATERIALS

The audio experience is one of the most thrilling which man encounters. Some say that it exceeds the visual experience in depth of aesthetic emotion. An impairment of either visual or auditory senses is a severe handicap to any individual.

Audio communication involves two reciprocal acts, speaking and listening. Although the ability to utter sounds is general to the animal kingdom, intelligible language is limited to man. Listening or hearing, too, is a general ability, but when coupled with attention or the ability to concentrate it has narrow limitations. Training and developing speaking competence has been a part of the school curriculum for years, but listening had received short shrift until about the mid-twentieth century. Even now, listening—hearing, understanding, and remembering—is taught incidentally in most schools, whereas reading, writing, and speaking are given large time blocks. It is commonly understood that adult communication skills consist of about 45 percent listening, 30 percent speaking, 16 percent reading, and 9 percent writing. A Greek philosopher once remarked, "We have two ears and one mouth that we may listen the more and talk the less."

Types of Auditory Instructional Materials

The production of sound, recording of sound, and the reception of auditory stimuli have achieved wide proportions. The equipment used by schools consists of microphones, public address systems, radios, tape recorders, phonographs, earphones, and listening posts. The materials consist of disc records and magnetic tapes. Through the use of these materials and equipment, sound can be conveyed, amplified, and recorded. There are other sound instruments and materials which serve visual as well as auditory purposes, for example, sound motion pictures, sound filmstrips, videotape, and television. By putting together several pieces of equipment, the school may develop a sound laboratory or a sound system.

Uses and Purposes

Practically all high school teachers find that audio devices and techniques have values in teaching. The uses to which these devices and related teaching methods are put are manifold. The following are some of those of most value to high school teachers.

ENRICHMENT   Recorded sound adds a new dimension to culture. Nothing can replace the advantage of hearing great composers play or sing their own compositions, or world renowned orchestras brilliantly perform the orchestrations of the best composers. Through recordings the world becomes a stage for everyone to hear operatic stars, actors, poets, scientists, statesmen, and leaders from all fields.

PRESERVATION   Contemporary sounds need never be lost. They can be preserved for all time. Who has not wished that he could hear the voice of George Washington, Alexander Hamilton, Benjamin Franklin, Daniel Webster, Abraham Lincoln, or, going farther back, that of Cicero or Demosthenes. Future generations will be able to hear today's world leaders. Although Edison invented the phonograph in 1877, it has only been since 1900 that the sound of history has been recorded "live." Invention of the magnetic wire recorder and later the magnetic tape recorder did much to simplify sound recording.

RECORDING OF CONTEMPORARY EVENTS   All manner of current events can be recorded for later use. Some of these recorded events may have transient value only, as for example, the early morning recording of news items from the news fronts of the world to be used later in the day in history and social studies classes. Other recordings such as the President's message to Congress, a session of the United Nations, a court trial, or a conference may have long-range values. Many school libraries have audio copies of the abdication speech of Edward VIII, President Roosevelt's speech to Congress requesting a Declaration of War against Japan, General MacArthur's speech before Congress, and the McCarthy hearings.

PATTERN FOR REMEDIAL PRACTICE   Teachers of speech, music, and foreign language make signal uses of audio devices. It is almost imperative that these teachers have available to them sound instruments if they are to be expected to accomplish maximum results.

In remedial work repetition of a sample or pattern is almost axiomatic, but the repetition needs to be matched against the pattern. This is the basis of correct pronunciation whether in English or a foreign language. The requirement is the same for voice development in speech or singing. With the handicapped, techniques may require that the student watch his vocal cords in a mirror, sense the muscle contractions kinesthetically, or employ one or more of a dozen techniques.

Coupled with remedial work is "spot" recording of an analytical nature. A member of the football coaching staff may sit in the stands, and with tape recorder and microphone, analyze an entire game. This can be a penetrating account of the plays seen by a specialist removed from the emotions and immediate characteristic of actions on the bench. A later playback for staff or players will provoke lively discussion.

The oral-lingual approach is much in favor in foreign language instruction. It requires repetition and continuous practice. The tape recorder is indispensable.

CAPTURE OF NATURAL SOUNDS   Sounds of birds, animals, the sea, the hurricane, the jungle, eruption of a volcano or a geyser, or any other nature sounds can be brought into the classroom anywhere at any time.

CAPTURE OF SOUNDS OF INDUSTRY AND URBAN LIFE   The rhythmic sound of electronic computers and the hum of industry are equally important, and just as easily brought to the classroom. The thud of paced traffic on a freeway, the sound of screeching brakes, or the thumping of a railroad car are a part of modern life.

REPORTING AND RECORDING   Tape recorders enable teachers and students to broaden their means of reporting and recording researches, committee findings, interviews, projects, inquiries, and similar activities. Students in a junior high school social studies class developed individual projects in connection with a unit on Western Europe. Among the projects were political maps, product maps, papier-mâché relief maps, models of castles, scrapbooks of pictures, sketches, and an assortment of papers and pamphlets. Each student made a brief explanation of his project to the class. A table microphone and a tape recorder recorded the oral presentation and the questions raised by members of the class.

To what extent can teachers use this equipment for reporting and recording? How can most effective use be made of the techniques?

"VOICESPONDENTS" AND "TAPE PALS"   The magnetic tape can be to voice communication what letters are to written communication. Pen pals with students in foreign countries are common enough. Somewhat less common are "voicespondents," or an exchange of tapes between, for instance, a junior high school English class in San Francisco with a similar class in the rural midwest. High school seniors might wish to exchange tapes with their counterparts in Germany, Japan, or any other foreign country. Topics of world concern might well evoke lively interest.

Practically any device or method which creates interest, quickens anticipation, arouses curiosity, or provides similar valuable stimulation finds a place in the instructional repertory. Auditory instructional materials and equipment can often do just that. The topic of listening, important to the use of audio materials, was discussed in Chapter 6 in connection with *communication skills.*

GRAPHIC INSTRUCTIONAL MATERIALS

Graphics is a word of Greek origin used to refer to the art of expressing ideas by lines, pictures, charts, or diagrams. As used here the term is general enough to include charts, diagrams, graphs, sketches, cartoons, maps, engravings, and related media. By means of graphics man has added another dimension to communication. Graphics enable us to present ideas and facts in condensed and summarized form in a vivid and concise manner. Usually, graphic presentation means concrete presentation, but this is not always true, because some graphics become noticeably abstract.

It is difficult to conceive of modern communications without graphics. They are widely employed in education, business, industry, government, and advertising. If there is need to catch attention, present facts succinctly and quickly, or to sell an idea, graphics may be advantageously used.

Someone once defined graphics as "visual shorthand," and undoubtedly they are considered the spark plugs of reporting and selling by business, industry, and the government. Research and new innovations have reached a point where it is almost possible to refer to the science of graphics. It might be said that graphics are an essential part of the science of communication, because communication has been very simply defined as "anything that conveys meaning, that carries a message from one person to another."

The five factors which give graphics such importance in the schools have already been implied, but specifically they are communication, concreteness, creativity, motivation, and economy. Little need be said about these facts other than to remark that graphics in and of themselves may not be concrete. To be concrete, ideas and data put in graphic form must be consciously simplified, otherwise the communication may be complex and baffling. Students should be taught how to read graphics. Kinder has remarked, "The teacher who cannot read graphics suffers from a form of illiteracy; the teacher who cannot produce graphics lacks one kind of ability to communicate" (7:379). Of course, commercially produced graphics may be purchased, but those produced by teachers and students predominate.

Common Types

Practically every teacher in the secondary schools has used these materials at one time or another. In some curriculum areas they are so important that they are used constantly. Diagrammatic drawings in industrial arts are used to show flow of electricity, engine structure, stresses and strains, magnetism, and the workings of many kinds of machinery. Schematic drawings are likewise useful in botany, physics, chemistry, astronomy, and general science. Social studies teachers use them to show relationships between social agencies, institutions, and individuals. Attempts to illustrate the theory of probability in mathematics, for example, will in all likelihood call for some sort of diagrammatic device. Uses in many other subject areas are equally evident.

CHARTS Charts are effective teaching tools, and, when produced locally, usually follow the characteristics of types, design, media, and materials shown in the following listing:

Charts

TYPE	DESIGN	MEDIA	MATERIALS
1. Experience	Flip	Drawings	Paper
Story	Strip	Graphs	Poster board
News	Poster	Diagrams	Chalkboard
2. Organization		Cartoons	Magnetic board
Flow		Pictures	Flannel board
Stream		Words	
Tree		Symbols	
Tabular		Numbers	
Process		Objects	
3. Time (lines)			
4. Miscellaneous			
Issues			
Map			
Pictorial			

According to type, charts are described as follows:

Experience charts are used by primary teachers to record visually stories, news, or experiences (included here for purpose of completeness of chart types rather than appropriateness to secondary teaching).

Flow charts are used to show sequence and relationships, for example, United Nations structure, U. S. judicial districts and system, student government organization.

Stream charts are used to show how several events or items come together to form a larger event, for example, English language and its components, contributions to a campaign.

Tree charts are the reverse of stream charts. They can be used to show derivatives from a main channel, for example, genealogy, by-products from a given substance as petroleum.

Tabular charts can depict tabular data, for instance, profit and loss, balance sheets, export and import, timetables, television program schedule.

Process charts illustrate steps in making something, succession of events one depending upon another, for example, making a silk-screen print, developing a photographic picture, causes of war.

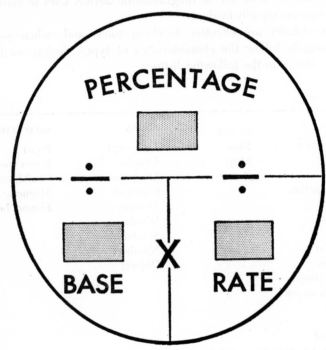

Fig. 9-2

Time charts, sometimes called time lines, show relations of historical events, chronology, growth changes, for instance, inventions of transportation, American fictional writers in time sequence.

Issue charts present side by side comparisons, contrasts, or points of view, for example, political party platforms, advantages and disadvantages of the Common Market, gold and silver money standard.

Map charts include maps, dots, and other symbols to show comparisons and relationships, for example, television coverage of national networks, population by areas, grain production, national parks.

Pictorial charts include conventional or symbolized pictures, for instance, bags of grain, ships, size of armed forces, natural resources, industrial output, basic foods in a diet, wood finishes.

In design, charts are usually flip (turn over), strip (hidden), or poster (conventional panels). Which design to choose depends upon purpose to be served and conditions under which it will be used.

Figure 9-2 is a chart produced by a junior high school teacher who found his students struggling with the percentage formula. It has three windows, one for each member of the formula: base multiplied by rate equals percentage. By stapling a revolving disc behind the face of the chart, it is possible to show in the windows any two knowns of the formula, and the chart then indicates how the unknown is found. After the formula is understood, a second disc with problems may be substituted for the formula disc so that drill can be provided. The reader might try to classify this chart as to type.

GRAPHS   A graph is a device which employs dots, lines, or pictures to show interrelated statistical information. Graphs, unlike charts, are constructed on mathematical principles, and quickly and clearly show relationships with exactness. Since they are exact, they make it possible to present quantitative data for analysis, interpretation, and comparison. For many people this visual image provides a more vivid understanding and a more lasting impression. Graphs play an important role in formal school instruction as well as in government bulletins, journalism, and all types of reporting. The more complicated the data, the greater the need for some scheme of graphic clarification.

Graphs, except for type, are much the same as charts in design, media, and materials. The five most common types are:

Circle graphs are segmented circles or pie graphs which show how a whole is divided into parts, usually on a percentage basis, for example, tax dollar, costs, budgets, school attendance. Segmented parts are often shaded, crosshatched, or colored. Sometimes pictograms are inserted. Percentages should be shown on each segment.

Bar graphs are used for picturization of comparative size by bars or columns. They are easy to construct and read, and are widely used. Instead of a single bar, the bar may be subdivided into parts of the whole— somewhat more complicated but also more adaptable. Bars may also run in two directions to show change in two different dimensions as gain and loss, for example.

Line graphs also refer to frequency polygon or profile graphs; they are designed to show changes over a span of time. Mathematically exact, they connect established points provided by ordinate and abscissa. The lines may be straight from point to point or smoothed. The latter procedure usually reduces exactness unless key points are clearly indicated.

Area graphs, by means of area, show proportions or differences in amounts. Area graphs usually employ cubes, squares, circles, or other forms which are sometimes superimposed one upon another. These graphs are easily misinterpreted.

Pictorial graphs, instead of bars, lines, or shaded areas, substitute conventional or stylized drawings of the data. The purpose of pictorial graphs is to make the data clearer and to make the graphs more appealing. Children especially prefer them, but their use with adults is outstanding as well. Pictorial statistics have become a sort of basic English of graphic presentation. Symbols have international meaning because the simple silhouettes, free from shading and detail, are readily recognizable.

Among the graphic materials available for purchase commercially is a study skills kit suitable for junior high school.[3] This kit is designed for use in independent or group study and can be integrated with the regular program in science, language arts, social studies, or mathematics. It contains separate units on tables, pictorial graphs, circle graphs, bar graphs, line graphs, charts and diagrams, and photographs. The kit serves such basic learning objectives as:

Recognizing the type of graphic form used and relating the accompanying verbal data to it
Identifying and understanding symbolic and visual images
Reading the graphic form for specific facts or details
Reading the graphic form to make comparisons of facts so as to detect relationships
Reading the graphic form to draw logical conclusions, make inferences, and form generalizations
Applying graphic skills in new situations

DIAGRAMS AND SKETCHES Other highly useful graphic materials are sketches and diagrams. They tend to be more informal and impromptu in use. There are, however, many long and carefully prepared diagrams as, for example, in electrical diagrams and circuitry.

POSTERS Posters are used to produce room environment; to promote an event, issue, or campaign; to assist in teaching an idea or a process; and to remind students of something that they may forget. Posters must tell their message quickly because they are read at a glance, and seldom if ever studied intently. Therefore, they must be simple, carry a single idea, be concise, and use wording set in banner type with bold titles that tend toward "sloganizing."

Most students enjoy making posters, although older students may try to excuse themselves on the grounds of lack of artistic ability. Posters may be purchased but this is done infrequently because the poster is

[3] *Graph and Picture Study Skills*, Kit GHII. Chicago: Science Research Associates, 1961.

designed for so specific a purpose that it must ordinarily be made to order. However, in the realm of free and inexpensive or sponsored materials there are posters galore. They may promote some of the school objectives such as proper diet and nutrition, as do the posters from the dairy council and the meat institute. Other posters may promote safety, continuous savings, or the benefits of exercise. Nevertheless, one must beware of free posters because many of them are designed to promote vested interests. On the use of sponsored materials, schools must maintain a policy which protects students from propaganda, but at the same time does not overlook materials which enhance socially approved educational objectives.

Art ability is unquestionably an asset in the preparation of charts, graphs, and posters, yet teachers with little developed art skill can make effective graphics. Measured and ruler-followed lines and geometric forms can be effective although they are likely to be formal. Freehand drawing seems best, but even without this skill, stick figure drawing is so simple that anyone can master it with little practice. Stick figures are rudimentary unadorned drawings of objects and figures. A few conventionalized lines will easily show human figures in such actions as standing, sitting, running, marching, listening, and many others.

CARTOONS Cartoons are another form of graphics. These interpretive pictures employ bold satire, exaggeration, and caricature to catch and hold attention in order to convey a message. Cartoons tend to be abstract and adult in their communication, and may therefore have to be interpreted; yet they are commonly employed by textbook authors, journalists, reporters, and others with a verbal-visual message. A cartoon can carry associated ideas better than dozens of words.

In an earlier discussion (see Chapter 8) it was pointed out that a certain English teacher found the comic and the cartoon an excellent means of starting students in a new term in a composition class. With a few thought-provoking cartoons, a few questions about them, a class can be highly stimulated. Students like to post them on bulletin boards, and if the cartoons are appropriate and germane to the subject, they can be valuable. Students also like to use them in poster construction, particularly in such matters as advertising a school dance or a picnic, in promoting a courtesy or cleanup campaign, or in discussions of school policy in the student newspaper.

No one should belittle or underestimate the value of cartoons. The beginning teacher should learn to work with them, and whenever possible exploit their uniqueness to make instruction more effective.

MAPS AND GLOBES Some teachers will directly teach maps and their uses, but many other teachers will at some time use them as auxiliary teaching materials. Maps can assist in teaching the world of today and the many interrelationships of man. Maps can also help us teach the world of the past.[4]

Maps and globes are included here with graphics, because they are graphic in character, but the map might also have been treated with flat pictures. By lines, words, symbols, and colors a map shows what the world, or part of it, looks like. Globes are scale models to show the terrestrial world and the celestial universe. Maps are in one or two dimensions and globes are in three dimensions.

Most children receive an early introduction to maps by way of the ubiquitous road map. At school, they begin more formal understanding of the map and the globe. At junior and senior high school levels, advanced understanding of the type indicated below is expected:

Use of Maps and Globes

PROGRAM	PRINCIPAL OBJECTIVES	TEACHING TOOLS
Junior Program Grades 7–8	Learning various map projections Determining latitude and longitude Locating and measuring great circle routes Demonstrating difference in time Using the International Date Line, ecliptic, and analemma Learning how to interpret information from maps Using an atlas in research	Centennial 16-inch globe, satellite mounting Relief maps Physical-political maps American history maps Desk project maps World atlases Steps in map reading
Senior Program Grades 9–12	Using many types of maps as sources of information Using different map projections Learning how to interpret political maps Using maps for the study of history Using maps to understand today's political problems	12-inch political globe, satellite mounting Political maps American history maps World history maps Chalkboard outline wall maps Desk project globes

SOURCE: *Rand McNally Handbook of Map and Globe Usage*. Skokie, Ill.: Rand McNally & Company, pp. 2–4.

[4] Those who teach map and globe orientation, including actual and relative location, scale, and symbolic representation of physical, cultural, and political features, may wish to consult *Map and Globe Skills Kit*. Chicago: Science Research Associates, 1962.

The last column in the above table lists six different teaching tools briefly explained below:

Globes like maps have numerous forms and characteristics. The more common ones are political, physical, outline, and relief. They may be made of solid substance or transparent plastics.

Relief maps are three-dimensional maps which are used to help show physical features of the earth. To a certain extent these maps replace the color and contour symbolization of the flat map. Moldings of plastics have made this type of map much more useful than the older, heavier, relief maps.

Physical-political maps are the commonest of all map forms, either as separate physical and political maps or in combination. These maps show political boundaries, physical features, and relationships of land and water.

History maps are among the numerous types of specialized maps, and are used in teaching exploration, areas at specific times, routes, and other historical events or periods. What did the known world at the time of Columbus look like? What areas in the new world were discovered and explored by various European powers? Where did the military campaigns of the Civil War take place? What were the areas of the territorial expansion of the United States?

Outline maps are available as large wall maps or as small individual paper maps. The former are suitable for discussion and chalkboard work. If these maps have slated surfaces, they may be erased and reused. They have great flexibility and promote student discussion. The individual outline maps may be purchased in bulk or produced on a duplicating machine.

Atlases are books of maps with encyclopedic information on names of places, rivers, mountains, statistics, historical incidents, and similar data.

Projected maps are those which, through technological developments, may be straightway projected from a book, travel folder, or periodical. This may be done by the use of an opaque projector, and if desired, copied on chalkboard or butcher paper for extended study. Maps may also be reproduced on transparencies for use on the overhead projector. Also, among the newer instructional materials are map slides and filmstrips for use with the 2- by 2-inch projector.

FREE AND INEXPENSIVE MATERIALS

The extensive use of so-called free and inexpensive or sponsored materials was mentioned in Chapter 8. The widespread use of these materials seems to have had its inception during the depression. Schools are no longer on relief, and they can be and are being financed in a businesslike manner. Curriculum materials, as well as all other types of materials, sup-plies, and equipment, should be handled by solid budget support. To rely to any extent upon sponsored instructional materials is an admission that teaching materials are of little importance in the learning process. Just as the "laborer is worthy of his hire," so, too, are instructional materials worthy of their price. If schools use sponsored materials, it cannot be too strongly urged that they adopt a policy statement to guide both teachers and administrative officials as to what materials may be used, under what conditions, and to what extent.

The American Association of School Administrators in cooperation with principals, classroom teachers, and supervisors has suggested that guide-lines governing acceptability of free materials be developed.[5] Factors such as size of the school system, educational philosophy, and financial status will necessitate consideration, but such criteria as the following will show the way:

A policy should be formulated, put into writing, officially adopted, and circulated among school personnel. This statement might also be given to suppliers of free materials.

Responsibility for acceptance of materials may be placed in the hands of a committee or an administrative arm such as the audio-visual or cur-riculum department, or some other department which by training and experience can make perceptive judgments.

Regulations for review of materials should not be cumbersome or elaborate.

Those in charge of accepting materials should scrutinize carefully ma-terials which "overdo the job." Some sponsors not only plan and organize the materials, but also tell teachers how to use them. This sort of thing is often found in "package deals," units, or teachers' guides.

Free or sponsored materials should be considered *supplementary, not basic* teaching materials.

The presence of bias, blatant or hidden, should be watched. Advertising in free materials is a matter of degree. Levels involving the mention of the name of the sponsor may be entirely acceptable, whereas the level of active promotion in sales or acceptance of an idea would not.

Materials should be up to date. Much of their value lies in their cur-rency.

Those responsible for accepting free materials may request as well as

[5] Choosing Free Materials for Use in the School. Washington, D.C.: American Asso-ciation of School Administrators, Department of the National Educational Associa-tion, March, 1955.

wait for sponsors to offer them. Materials sought in this manner would be expected to meet the same criteria.

Teachers who do turn to the free or inexpensive materials sources may expect to find a vast quantity of mainly unevaluated learning resources. It is not an exaggeration to say that a moderate amount of correspondence would procure a truck load of pamphlets, brochures, outlines, charts, graphs, calendars, pictures, slides, filmstrips, samples, specimens, models, kits, and numerous other items. Some of this material may have real value depending, of course, on the manner in which it is handled by the teacher. Entire learning units, in general science or health, for example, might be built on these materials.

It has been pointed out by educators that some teachers have been guilty of encouraging students to become beggars through request letters for materials. Cases exist of pupils actually asking corporations to write term papers for them, or asking them to send packets of materials, otherwise the writers might be in danger of semester failure. Such are the lengths to which the "something for nothing" idea has spread.

COMMUNITY RESOURCES AS LEARNING MATERIALS

I would have the world to be the book my young gentlemen should study with most attention. Many strange humors, many sects, many judgments, opinions, laws, and customs teach us to judge rightly of our own actions, to correct our faults, and to inform our understanding, which is no trivial lesson.— *Montaigne*

"Have you a compass?" the teacher asked the clerk in the variety store. "Well," answered the clerk, "we have compasses for drawing circles, but none for going places."—*Edward G. Olsen*

Field Trip

The term *field trip* applies to true-to-life activity engaged in by a school group which leaves the classroom and goes out to the actual source of information for learning purposes. The objectives of most field trips are to gather information firsthand about objects, places, people, or processes, and to enrich, extend, validate, or vitalize information from printed or other sources, or to try to uncover entirely new data. Whether this activity is called field trip, journey, excursion, or study trip is of no consequence. It is, however, not to be confused with nonstudy trips such as athletic events, forensic or musical contests, school hikes, picnics, sight-seeing excursions, and the like.

Field trips may not be "real-life experiencing," but their dimensions are *near real life.* Learning is concrete, sensory, and basic. Students see and observe things, places, people, and processes in life settings; they see objects in true size and in all their natural complexity; they hear natural sounds; and as the poet says, "Life is real, life is earnest. . . ."

CRITERIA FOR FIELD TRIPS Before planning any field trip, the teacher should ask himself such questions as the following:

Will the learning value from this trip justify the expense, time, and general inconvenience which it may occasion?

Does the trip coordinate closely with the study going on in the classroom?

Is this trip practical from such standpoints as time involved, transportation, costs, safety, and similar factors?

Could the same learning values be accomplished by use of films, models, resource persons, or other means?

Will this trip tend to promote good school-community relationships?

Will this trip be essentially an observational one or will students possibly be permitted limited participation in the processes or events studied?

Does the trip have generalized learning values?

Are there any unusual legal liabilities involved?

PLANNING A FIELD TRIP There are five important steps in planning and executing an effective field trip.

1. *Teacher preparation.* The teacher should:
   Contact the authorities of the area to be visited.
   Visit the area; go over details.
   Arrange for transportation.
   Check on safety, rest facilities, and so on.
   Obtain approval from school authorities.
   Notify parents; obtain consent; issue invitations for selected parents to accompany class on trip, if this is in order.
   Schedule the trip on the school calendar.
   Make arrangements with other teachers regarding absences.
2. *Class preparation for the trip.* Teachers and students should:
   Discuss the reason for the trip.
   Write out questions to be answered; list things to be checked.
   Work out ways to document the trip such as taking notes, taking pictures, recording sounds, sketching, interviewing, writing.
   Plan pretrip reading, study, film previewing.
   Discuss behavior standards for the group.
   Discuss appropriate dress.
   Plan for and appoint committees as needed.
3. *"On the Spot."* Students should:

Arrive on time at scheduled meeting place.

Stay with assigned groups or guides.

Show an active interest.

Procure samples, specimens, booklets, and so on, to take back to the school with permission of hosts.

Be courteous at all times.

See that lunch scraps and papers are neatly disposed of in case lunches are carried.

Check to see that no belongings are left behind.

4. *The follow-up.* The members of the group should:

Review the objectives of the trip.

Discuss individual and committee findings.

Discuss unexpected problems. Why did they arise?

Draft a thank-you letter to the hosts.

Display any specimens brought back along with any pictures taken or sketches made on the trip.

Discuss the benefits of such a trip for future classes.

Test the sentiment for other field trips.

Share the fruits of the trip with other classes through student reports, newspaper accounts, and so on.

5. *Evaluation.* Teacher should:

Prepare a written evaluation of the trip to be filed with the school principal, and/or the instructional materials center. (This report may be written by teacher or students, preferably by both.)

Answer for himself the questions, Was the trip worthwhile? Was it worth what it cost in time, money, and extra effort?

LIMITATIONS OF THE FIELD TRIP There are a number of problems or limitations which must be kept in mind whenever a field trip is considered. There are administrative problems, particularly to longer trips which involve student absence from several classes. The work of other classes which students miss while on trips must be made up. Costs may be heavy and some pupils may not be able to meet them without embarrassment. Transportation may be a problem. This is particularly true if nonschool transportation is involved. School and personal liability may be involved.

Extended Field Trips

The discussion above has been based on a relatively short trip—one of a class period, a half day, or at most a full day. There are, of course, many longer trips which are extremely valuable. These trips require even greater care in planning, are usually more expensive, and are hedged with more limitations, but the values may be proportionately higher. Such trips take students from their local environment to other cities, counties, states, or even to other countries. These trips may see city students visiting the country, and rural students visiting the city. Here are a few samples of extended field trips:

A Spanish class spends a week in Mazatlan, Mexico.

A French class spends a week in Quebec, Canada.

A social studies class goes to the coal fields of southwestern Pennsylvania.

A social studies class spends a week with sharecroppers and tenant farmers.

A class goes to New York City to gather firsthand data regarding urban life and problems, the United Nations, transportation, the stock market.

A science class studies firsthand archaeology and Indian culture in New Mexico or Arizona.

A science class researches field geography in the Death Valley area.

A foreign language class enrolls in a week's seminar in Monterrey, Mexico.

A culturally minded group tours the countries of Europe or other foreign countries.

The most valuable extended field trips are those which focus on a specific topic or a single community. Thus, the study of the coal mines is localized to a particular county or a particular town. Students on trips of this sort should not try to cover extensive ground, but should cover more intensively a few problems or questions. These long trips should be built on contacts with people; their objective is definitely not sight-seeing, nor are they recommended for the idly curious. The type of trips discussed here are for serious students who have well-defined interests, and who have already accumulated some understanding of the subject involved.

In the case of trips to other countries, the problems, understandings, and results are multiplied. Often there has been no prior foreign travel or study by some of the members of the group, hence more generalized culture tours may be in order, but even so, the field trip must be more penetrating than a family sight-seeing tour. Sometimes the problems of foreign study tours are staggering. They involve finances, passports and visas, border crossings, insurance, health risks, clothing, baggage, codes of behavior, and many others. Students and teachers must keep in mind that as visitors and learners, they are welcome; as critics or "well doers," they may not be.

Resource Persons

By definition these are persons not professionally connected with the school, but who come to the school, usually without pay, to share knowledge or skill with students. It goes without saying that such persons should be unbiased, and should be able to show, present, or discuss their specialty with reasonable lucidity.

Many teachers have the mistaken impression that resource persons are valuable for and limited to the elementary school. This is far from the case. Consider the many specialists available in most communities in practically every cultural, professional, vocational, industrial, and governmental field. Often the so-called average people have much to offer for a specific problem or occasion; for example, a resident who was born and reared in another country, missionary, soldier, gourmet, or a senior citizen.

Resource people can often contribute new and vital ideas which enrich and motivate learning. Students develop more respect for out-of-school people; at the same time they may develop a keener appreciation of the community. In reverse, the resource person carries a new understanding of the school program back to his job and the community.

Resource persons may be invited to the school by the teacher, by individual students, or by a committee of the class. The teacher should, however, clear all invitations with the central office.

It is well to plan carefully. Select a person who knows his subject and presents it well in language that high school students understand. Give him guidance in his presentation by providing a list of questions to answer or an outline of topics that you should like to have covered. When a speaker has been secured some time in advance, verify the date a day or two before he is to appear. Needless to say, a visiting speaker should be accorded a courteous hearing. The class should be well enough prepared so that intelligent questions may be expected. A follow-up thank-you letter is in order and may most appropriately be written by the members of the class.

Resources of an Activity or Material Nature

This term applies to those activities of people, organizations, institutions, industries, and the things and places of a local environment that the school can conceivably draw upon for furthering its educational program. Increasingly, schools are viewing their communities as learning laboratories. Students are going beyond classroom walls for study and research that are real and concrete. Teachers have found this study practically self-motivating.

Students who use their community as a study laboratory tend to become more sensitive to local needs and to local problems. By its very nature, this study causes students to use scientific study techniques in collection of data, classification, analysis, and presentation. As students study their communities, they stand to become more sensitive to value patterns and to learn to work together more cooperatively.

The literature concerning the interaction of school and community is extensive. In addition to the large number of magazine articles, several societies and associations have made community study the theme for year-books; also, there have been numerous studies for degrees at the masters and doctoral levels.

The tendency of these studies is to group community activities into three levels: (1) observational, (2) participatory, and (3) contributory.

Doubtless, most of the activities are observational in type, and remain pretty much the field trip sort. There are, however, increasing numbers of more serious studies and surveys which move into the contributory level. At this level there are both general and narrowly intensive surveys. These surveys need to be properly planned and supervised, and they depend upon experience and maturity both of teachers and students. To study intensively the problem of racial discrimination in a community, for example, calls for rare insights and judgment. Perhaps more appropriate for beginning teachers would be studies of a less demanding nature and studies which would be less likely to become involved in controversy. Examples of such are: (1) housing, (2) city trash and garbage removal, (3) sanitation, such as eradication of mosquito breeding places, (4) spare time employment possibilities for high school boys and girls. A useful project for a rural area might be a complete register of all purebred or registered livestock, poultry, and pets in the school district.

To be of real value, studies of this nature must arise from the curriculum. They cannot be imposed just for the sake of a study or problem. After completion, community studies should be properly organized for presentation to the entire class and to those who cooperated with the study, and to any interested adult groups. Throughout studies of this type, the processes of democratic group planning should be evident.

SOME SPECIFIC SCHOOL-COMMUNITY PROJECTS   Many communities sponsor what is called Business-Education Day under the guidance of the chamber of commerce. The object of B-E Day is to acquaint teachers firsthand with the materials and resources of the community. On this day business and industry hold open house for the teachers of the community. The day chosen is usually one that is a legal holiday for the schools but not for business, such as Veterans Day or Lincoln's Birthday.

Career Days are somewhat like B-E Days in reverse. In this instance representatives from business and industry visit schools for the purpose of meeting with teachers and selected students in order to inform them about working conditions and requirements in their fields. The emphasis is upon vocational selection, or upon choice of college or professional school for post-high school education.

A participatory effort is represented by the "earn-to-learn" curricular project. This type of project takes many forms in different communities and is suitable for high school and college levels. It is a sort of on-the-job training and is frequently associated with the commercial or industrial departments. This form of experience and study has serious limitations, yet through it some students are enabled to find a niche in the work world, or to gain a valuable overview before beginning their careers.

Another type of project is exemplified by one currently being developed in San Diego County in Southern California.[6] In this project there is a pooling of suitable resource material from industry so that these materials may be reproduced and distributed to the schools of the county. The project is sponsored by business and an NDEA grant. The materials involve graphic and photographic pictures from business, industry, and agriculture. The pictures are carefully selected, graded for maturity level, reproduced in uniform sizes, and distributed as study prints. Some of the study print sets have accompanying filmstrips. Similar developments include the production and distribution of three-dimensional models, kits, motion pictures, and specimens. In addition to providing products, the project is engaged in providing programs and furthering research.

This sharing of materials by business is akin to the free or sponsored materials programs described earlier. There is, however, a big difference. In this instance, many businesses cooperate in a pooled project, and the materials distributed to the schools are worked over by educators so that they are educationally sound, and they have been lifted from the realm of propaganda or company salesmanship.

Camping

In various sections of the country, schools provide limited camping experiences for students. These experiences may be at the elementary or secondary level; they may be weekly winter trips woven into the school curriculum, or they may be summer activities. In any event youngsters learn to live together, to share, and to accept responsibility. A large part of the experience is focused on the urgent business of living—cooking, making beds, cleaning up, keeping warm, and making friends.

Camping as considered here is not an activity just for the underprivileged; it is an enterprise for all students, and is considered an integral part of the total educational development. It features a blending of talents of teachers, camp counselors, and camp staff. Educationally, students have organized time for such activities as reading, discussion, listen-

[6] San Diego Community Educational Resources Project.

ing to resource persons, and engaging in serious nature study. Other activities involve athletics, hikes, crafts, dramatics, art, motion pictures, and the like.

The value of this activity in the school program is indicated by the remark that "Camping is a straight line to reality."

MISCELLANEOUS INSTRUCTIONAL MATERIALS

Many of the cheaper, less formal and older, but less spectacular instructional materials are often quite as significant as those discussed above. As a matter of fact, most teachers, good teachers, would feel heavily handicapped if they were denied some of the older, simpler instructional materials. To a certain extent, these older materials are taken for granted, but they would be sorely missed if unavailable. Teachers and students use them over and over, probably daily, without much thought as to their importance in the learning program.

The miscellany of materials to follow is grouped in two categories: special boards characterized by the key word *display* and three-dimensional materials characterized by the term *manipulation.*

Special Boards

Chalkboards

The origin of the chalkboard is obscured by time. Modern teachers take the chalkboard for granted, but would feel lost without it. Place the average teacher in a classroom without a chalkboard, and he will request one before the end of the first day. Yet, many principals are of the opinion that the chalkboard is one of the most ineptly used instructional materials. Most of the uses are not only impromptu, but they are often sloven and clumsy. An educator once remarked that for a quick, informal evaluation of a teacher, the appearance of the chalkboard is about as good as any single criterion.

VALUES AND LIMITATIONS   The chalkboard offers so many values for different subjects, different teachers, and different methods that it is difficult to do more than sample them. Some of the more outstanding ones are:

It is both a group and an individual device.
It fits the tempo of any presentation.
No special talent is required for its use.
Teachers of practically all subject content as well as all grade levels use chalkboards.

Pupil errors can be quickly and easily corrected for all to see.
It is possibly the cheapest of all instructional materials.
It is eminently convenient.
The chalkboard encourages note taking.
Chalkboard impact is heightened through the use of heavy and light crayon strokes, colored crayons, "black light," and spotlights.
Neatness, orderliness, and graphic skills add new values.
Where certain forms or designs are used repeatedly as in music, stenography, bookkeeping, logarithms, and the like, permanent rulings save time.

There are limitations, too:

Much time can be wasted at chalkboards both by teachers and students.
Most chalkboards detract from the attractiveness of classrooms.
The desirability of using the chalkboard for assigned work, except for short lists of questions, words, exercises, or problems may be questioned.
Other forms of duplication are usually better for study guides, tests, and longer exercises.
Hygienic questions may be raised at times.
Students may not be able to see chalkboard materials well without changing seat locations.
Misspelled words, poor handwriting, and slovenly use lower the effectiveness of the device.
Modern facilities and equipment such as the slide projector, opaque projector, overhead projector, and the mimeograph often serve instructional needs better than the chalkboard.

DOS AND DON'TS The following are some suggestions for improving the use of the chalkboard: Do not erase with fingers. Do not talk to the class with face to the board; take at least a 45-degree turn. Use a pointer for reference. If the classroom is shared with other teachers, leave the chalkboard neatly erased. Erase materials from the board when classes change. Old materials on the chalkboard have a certain amount of distraction for students.

Five simple methods which can add to effective chalkboard use are:
Stick figure drawings. A little practice will enable any teacher to make such drawings. (See Figure 9-3.)
Proportional squares. By this method (often called grid), a picture to be copied is ruled off into squares and then the chalkboard is marked off into similar but larger squares. Lastly, square by square the picture is drawn on the board freehand.
Template. Plywood or cardboard templates or patterns are made of

Fig. 9-3

symbols or forms used repeatedly. Forms are traced on the chalkboard whenever needed. A template has rather limited use, but is helpful in geography, science, or wherever a simple form such as a parallelogram is used over and over.

Pattern or pounce. Holes are punched in a sheet of paper or fabric to follow the outline of a design or picture, a dusty chalk eraser is patted over perforated pattern held against the board, and chalk dots are connected freehand. Patterns may be stored and reused indefinitely.

Opaque projection. Maps or drawings may be transferred from books or loose sheets to chalkboards easily by using the opaque projector and enlargement may be made to any size. This technique may be used for holiday decoration as well as more formal instructional purposes.

Feltboards

Feltboards are inexpensive if bought or they can easily be made by the "do-it-yourself" teacher. These boards are constructed of any lightweight flat-surfaced material such as plywood or heavy cardboard. The board is covered with any sort of felt, flannel, or duvetyn. Cutouts of similar material adhere to the surface so that effective displays can be created.

Feltboards have many uses for imaginative teachers who have found them helpful in language arts, science, industrial arts, health, home economics, physical education, music, social studies, driver education, foreign language, English, and other subjects. They are used in secondary schools chiefly in drill work, poster or bulletin board display, in accenting charts and graphs, and adding variety to many common learning devices. Almost any teacher of any subject may find that a flannel board can be used as a communications device.

If one stops to recall the many uses made of flannel boards on television, the teacher may be reminded of the versatility of this simple device.

A substitute material for feltboards called "hook and loop" is capable of supporting three-dimensional objects of noticeable weight such as pliers, screwdrivers, hammers, scissors, rock specimens, and similar objects. Ordinary felt or flannel will sustain only light weights such as cutouts of paper, fabric, or light cardboard.

Magnetic Boards

High school teachers often find magnetic boards of value in their teaching. Magnets adhere to any steel-base surface. A plate of painted thin sheet metal can make an attractive display board. Instructional materials equipped with magnetic holders adhere easily to the boards and can be moved about at will. Small magnets can be glued to a variety of forms, such as cardboards or small three-dimensional objects to use on the boards. In principle, the magnetic board is similar to the feltboard except that magnetism holds in the one case and friction in the other.

Physical education teachers frequently make use of magnetic boards to mark the boundaries of playing field models, and to indicate the position of players in devising plays. In like manner, home economics teachers might use magnetic boards in the discussion of furniture placement, step-saving remodeling, and table and place settings. Paper cutout parts of a whole, as for example, bone parts of the skull, might be put together in jigsaw fashion to emphasize name, location, and relative size. Business education teachers could use similar techniques in studying display styles and designs. A teacher of journalism may make effective use of a magnetic board of newspaper size to discuss layout, placement of headlines, lead articles, and advertising blocks.

Magnetic boards may also serve as chalkboards, thus adding a dual purpose to the display area of a classroom. Such a board can also serve as a bulletin board because student papers, notices, and other graphic materials may be held in place by small magnets without defacing the board or marring the papers.

Electric Boards

The electric board is in effect a programmed learning device by which students learn to associate certain facts, principles, skills, or combinations. These boards make a strong appeal to students who like to test their wits against the machine. The principle of the electric board, simple or complex, is to match up programmed information so that an electrical contact will ring a buzzer or light a small bulb.

Electric boards are used to generate interest at the beginning of a new unit of study, to drill, to review, and to test. Electric boards can be outlined as maps with many sorts of subdivisions and data which may be matched with the visual clues. The programmed data may be changed from time to time to circumvent position memorization. Students, as well as the teacher, may do the programming. Even the wiring of the device may be changed periodically to forestall memorization.

The following are some uses of electric boards:

Mathematics—nomenclature, arithmetic terms, geometrical figures, combinations
Chemistry—symbols, atomic weights, valences
Foreign language—vocabulary, grammar, easy translations
Geography—place and economic geography
History—dates, locations, leaders, epochs, movements
Commercial subjects—shorthand symbols

Health—rules, diet, proper foods
Industrial arts—tools, equipment, formulas

The more elaborate the wiring, the more flexibility the board will have. The usual board is constructed to care for pairs of matched items only, yet boards may be constructed in any high school shop which will match three, four, five, or more sets of items before a circuit is completed.

Three-Dimensional Materials

The key word for miscellaneous instructional materials dealing with those of a three-dimensional character is *manipulation*. The materials to be considered are models, mock-ups, objects, specimens, samples, artifacts, exhibits, dioramas, kits, and loan boxes. Some of these materials may be as simple as a pebble, while others may be as complicated as a turbine or a plastic model of the human body.

Learning from actual things is as old as the human race. The uneducated depend in great measure upon such everyday experiences. They rely on size, color, shape, texture, odor, and similar characteristics. In the learning process, man wishes to get his hands on the object, or to experience it directly through the sense organs.

The poem, "The Blind Men and the Elephant," by John Godfrey Saxe, illustrates how six blind men each sensed by touch six parts of an elephant and how each man thought he understood the elephant—to one it was like a wall, and to others a spear, rope, snake, tree, or fan. Each man was partly right, yet all were wrong too, because their sensory experiencing was too limited. In the classroom, great care must be exercised to prevent generalization from partially observed or experienced stimuli.

Objects, Specimens, and Models

Realia and artifacts of many types collected from a variety of sources should be mounted if necessary, labeled with the source and date of acquisition noted, evaluated, and suitably stored. They provide learning experiences as genuine as other learning materials. A flower which can be examined by every member of the class is not only an excellent way to show pistil, stamen, and calyx, but will also add meaning to the illustration found in the text. A rock specimen, a piece of coal, a shell, soil samples, a seed, dried leaves, insects preserved in formaldehyde or embedded in plastic—all these specimens taken from their natural setting can be found in most classrooms. They can be examined and studied as the need arises.

Do you remember the model of the steam engine displayed in your high school physics class, or the model of the man with removable internal organs in your health education class? Such realistic reproductions make lasting impressions. Models (miniature reproductions) or representations of things on larger scales, as a plaster of Paris paramecium, are widely used in teaching. Their construction is being constantly improved by the use of plastics, glass, and synthetic materials. Many models include all the features of the real object, often contain moving parts which operate, and they sometimes have cutaway sections to show inner workings which are not observable in the original. Models may be classified into three main types: (1) solid models which are used chiefly for recognition of external features, (2) cross-section or cutaway models which are valuable to show internal structure, and (3) working models which actually demonstrate the operation of the original. Good working models often use contrasting colors for parts so that students can follow actions or processes as they develop. This is quite common in models employing gear boxes, cables, and electric circuits.

In many instances, models are of more value to students than real objects. They can be handled, used and reused as needed, and they are likely to be more available to students. Although the more complex models will have to be purchased from school funds, teachers and students may build many of the models that they use. Cones, pyramids, and the like are easily constructed from cardboard for use in mathematics classes. A model of a city, made of cardboard or papier-mâché, can be used to demonstrate anything from safety education to housing conditions for a social studies class. Thin plywood or balsa offers opportunities in the construction of stage sets for use in drama classes.

Mock-ups

A mock-up is defined as a "contrived or simulated three-dimensional device which imitates certain aspects of the real thing." Mock-ups may be as simple as a clock dial made from a paper plate or as complicated as a turbine or a synthetic city water supply with settling beds, aeration devices, and reservoirs. Driver training laboratories may contain car mock-ups which look like stubby automobiles.

Mock-ups are frequently purchased from commercial sources, but more of them are constructed by students as parts of projects or units of work. Students taking part in local science fairs construct ingenious mock-ups or models.

With models or mock-ups, students must be aware of the fact that the model may be the same size as the original, larger, or smaller; however, most models are smaller. It must also be kept in mind that the model may have been removed from context. There may even be a noticeable simplification, a very important point in connection with models of the human body or body organs. A model of the Grand Canyon can show contour, coloring, and proportional dimensions, but it may not show such conditions as sky, sun, and climate. Photographs and motion pictures used in conjunction with models and mock-ups help to relate the simulation to reality.

Exhibits

Exhibits prepared by students are a great factor in creating pride in workmanship and accomplishment. Exhibits are frequently arranged for special occasions such as Education Week, but they have a value if prepared only for class or building display. Commercial displays and exhibits are usually more complex and involve materials which are not readily available to students such as mineral displays, working parts of machine objects, or the exhibits from museums.

Dioramas

The *Dictionary of Education* defines a diorama as "a three-dimensional representation composed of various symbolic and real materials such as pictures and specimens; it frequently utilizes both transmitted and reflected light to produce a natural scenic effect."

Both professional and pupil-made dioramas have a place as instructional materials, particularly at the junior high level. Professionally made dioramas are expensive and the range of subject matter is extremely limited. Many school systems have, however, over the years accumulated a fair collection of these objects. Some audio-visual centers employ a staff artist who occasionally finds time to construct something very special, for example, a midwestern farm scene or an Argentine rancho.

Loan Boxes and Kits

These are inexpensive materials which should be more popular than they are. Kinder defines the loan box as "a collection of related items appropriately boxed for loan to a school," and the kit as "a collection of pertinent materials gathered into a unit" (7:478).

Both loan boxes and kits are usually circulated from an instructional materials center. Health kits, first-aid kits, and tool kits are familiar. Why not similar integrated collections in science, art, home economics, and other areas? The value lies chiefly in the fact that varied materials are brought together in one place. Such a collection is a real timesaver, and sometimes the items might be difficult for a teacher to bring together without great effort, for example, marine-life kits for schools removed from the coast.

Some industries and commercial concerns offer schools loan boxes and kits of their products. These can be effective teaching devices. Among the kits of this type available to schools are those from the Bituminous Coal Institute, the telephone company, petroleum industry, and companies which manufacture small tools and shop equipment. The boxes and kits discussed here are much the same as the exhibit materials treated above.

Chapter 9 has attempted to summarize in brief form approximately an entire course in instructional materials. All the conventional materials and techniques taught in such a course are described, including their values and uses. Space consideration has limited the inclusion of examples from classroom practice. Each teacher will be able to think of many additional uses for the materials. The teacher need only ask himself, "How can I employ motion pictures, maps, recordings, or charts to make my teaching more meaningful to my students?"

Chapter 10 will continue the discussion of materials and techniques, their values and uses, with the newer media such as television, teaching machines, and language laboratories.

Selected Readings

1. Anderson, Kenneth E., "Audio-Visual Research," *Kansas Studies in Education,* vol. 11 (June 1961), pp. 3–14.
2. Cross, A. J. Foy, and Irene F. Cypher, *Audio-Visual Education.* New York: Thomas Y. Crowell Company, 1961. Chapter 12.
3. De Bernardis, Amo, *The Use of Instructional Materials.* New York: Appleton-Century-Crofts, 1960.
4. Freedman, Florence B., and Esther L. Berg, *Classroom Teacher's Guide to Audio-Visual Material.* Philadelphia: Chilton Company—Book Division, 1961.
5. Fusco, Gene C., "Technology in the Classroom Challenges to the School Administrator," reprinted from *School Life* (March–May 1961).
6. Harris, Raymond P., *American Education: Facts, Fancies, and Folklore.* New York: Random House, 1961.
7. Kinder, James S., *Audio-Visual Materials and Techniques,* 2d ed. New York: American Book Company, 1959.
8. Trump, J. Lloyd, *New Directions to Quality Education—The Secondary School Tomorrow,* bulletin. Washington, D.C.: National Association of Secondary School Principals.
9. Wendt, Paul R., "Audio-Visual Instruction," *What Research Says to the Teacher,* Bulletin No. 14. Washington, D.C.: Department of Classroom Teachers, American Education Research Association, 1957, reprinted, 1961. (Professor Wendt has collated and summarized scores of researches relating to audio-visual education.)

Selected Audio-Visual Materials

A. *Film Research and Learning,* 16 min., b & w: International Film Bureau, 1956. Film describes research studies and shows how the use of films in instruction can improve student achievement in such fields as reading, science, and social studies.

B. *Globes: Their Function in the Classroom*, 20 min., color: Bailey Films, Inc., 1960. Different types of globes and their specific use in the classroom are discussed.

C. *School Journey*, 48-frame filmstrip, color: Basic Skill Films, 1958. Classroom experience and research on the use of the school journey are summarized. The values of school journeys and procedures to follow before, during, and after the trip are also discussed.

D. *The Tape Recorder*, 6 min., b & w: Iowa State University, 1960. Outlined are a variety of uses for the tape recorder and procedures for setting up and adjusting magnetic tape recorders for use.

E. *Tips on Tape*, 25-frame filmstrip, b & w: Kent State University, 1957. The nature of tape recording, its advantages, and its use in the classroom are discussed.

F. *Using Charts and Graphs in Teaching*, 54-frame filmstrip, color: Basic Skill Films, 1959. This filmstrip explains the types of graphic materials usually employed by teachers, and their values.

Newer instructional materials

Although the National Defense Education Act of 1958 mentioned such audio-visual materials as motion pictures, television, radio, and foreign language laboratories by name, it also referred to all of these devices as the "newer instructional media." The term has caught on and is widely used today; chiefly, however, to refer to television, language laboratories, teaching machines, and programmed learning.

COMMERCIAL TELEVISION

The Social Significance of Television

In less than two decades, fifty million homes have been equipped with one or more television receivers. The growth of the use of television has been phenomenal. The expansion of the use of radio, motion pictures, automobiles, or electrical appliances for the home cannot match its growth.

The impact of this new medium of mass communication is a matter of both scorn and approbation. In some quarters it is intellectually fashionable to deride television, to accuse it of mediocrity, to blame it for a large share of the growth of social violence and juvenile delinquency, and to charge that the medium has sold out to advertisers. Some truth may be attached to these charges, but it is not possible to document any of them completely. Although television is censured for mediocrity, the same accusation is hurled against the theater, films, books, and politics; even against the educational system itself.

Some critics who find fault with television should bear in mind that individuals have many and varied specialized tastes and interests. No single program will satisfy all viewers, as no single book, play, concert, or automobile satisfies everyone.

The total American public is made up of many publics. And, each day millions of viewers exercise their prerogatives and make thousands of program selections reflecting the discrimination which comes to a viewer because of his education, family, friends, vocation, and personal temperament.

Probably no one should be too concerned about public tastes. There is reason to believe that tastes are on the upswing if viewed perspectively. Since the impact of television was first felt, the population has increased 20 percent, but at the same time the publication of books has shot up 100 percent, and that of juvenile books 200 percent; library circulation has increased 50 percent; the number of museums, 80 percent and production of classical records, 50 percent; the number of symphony orchestras has doubled. During this same period of time, college enrollments expanded 46 percent. Television cannot be given the credit for any of these statistics, but neither can it be shown to have been a millstone about the neck of cultural growth.

Unquestionably, the public has been exposed to ideas and materials which it would never have experienced so directly without television. A few examples may be of interest: (1) tours of foreign cities and countries—Hong Kong, Copenhagen, Vienna, Japan, and Venezuela; (2) political activities—UN debates, Congressional committee investigations, and debates by presidential candidates; (3) contemporary news affairs—the coronation of sovereigns, inaugurations of presidents, and the visits of foreign dignitaries; (4) revolution and strife around the world—African disturbances and the anti-American demonstrations in Japan and Cuba; (5) national and international sports—hockey, golf, and the Olympic games; (6) art and music—the Boston or New York symphonies, Britain's Royal Ballet, or Russia's Moiseyev Dancers; and (7) science and discovery—hospital care, development of new drugs, and the globe-girdling trips of the American astronauts.

EDUCATIONAL TELEVISION

Almost any television program could be educational, at least for some people somewhere. But, commercial television, in spite of the "public interest" clause in Federal Communications Commission regulations, is essentially an entertainment and mass-information vehicle. Schools can and do use commercial television, but for instructional purposes the medium is served best through *educational television*.

Television can be open- or closed-circuit. Both types are employed for educational purposes. The former is familiar as the type seen in our homes; the signal is put on the air by a broadcasting station and is picked up by any receiver in the broadcast area which can be tuned to the channel used. Closed-circuit television is not broadcast on the air. The signal goes only to receivers that are connected to the transmitter by wire or cable. For this reason, no FCC licensing is necessary. Closed-circuit television is widely used in colleges, universities, and public schools where the area to be reached is compact, or where there is need to broadcast several programs simultaneously. This, for example, is the case in the Washington County schools of Maryland where as many as six programs may be broadcast at one time.

Educational television, like commercial broadcasting, uses either "live" or "recorded" programs. Live programs are seen and heard at the instant that they are picked up by the television camera, whereas the recorded or delayed program is prerecorded on film (kinescope) or tape (videotape). Recorded programs necessitate additional equipment, some of which is rather expensive, but prerecording allows the program director a great deal of latitude and flexibility.

Growth and Status of Educational Television

An editorial in *The Saturday Review*, January 13, 1962, asked the question, "Can Educational Television Turn the Corner?" On April 14, 1952, the FCC announced the reservation of 242 television channels for educational allocation and later extended the number to 258 and then to 273. Some of these channels were VHF (very high frequency) but most of them were UHF (ultra high frequency) bands. The latter bands have been difficult to use, but technological advancements are rapidly overcoming this limitation. In 1953, KUHT, University of Houston, made its appearance as the first truly educational TV station. An educational station is defined as one that is licensed as a nonprofit organization and is organized primarily to serve the educational needs of a community.

Educational station broadcasting was 10 years old in 1961, and in its first decade the number of stations grew to 63, of which 44 were VHF and 19 UHF. Today, there are approximately 100 VHF and 45 UHF stations. A score or more stations are in the construction or advanced planning stage. At the end of 1961 there were 589 commercial stations (495 VHF and 94 UHF). Commercial stations are established for profit and are supported chiefly from advertising. Educational stations are supported by taxation, public subscription, and grants from various foundations and industry. About one third of the educational stations are owned by colleges and universities, one third by city or county school systems, and one third by civic-minded community groups. Educational and commercial stations exist side by side. There is no conflict owing to the fact that support is different and that different types of programs are broadcast. Current federal legislation will add millions of dollars to local efforts. With these funds available station building will be accelerated.

Educational television is expanding rapidly. Alabama, Florida, and Oregon are examples of a few states which have established state networks. Michigan, Ohio, California, Kentucky, and others are considering networks. Twenty-five states have ETV commissions formed by legislative action. Interstate networks will soon be a reality. There is already local interstate cooperation.

Will ETV turn the corner? The answer is that it already has. Yet, ETV like commercial TV has its own "wastelands." Program quality in the ETV stations is often substandard. Many educators confuse program quality with lowered educational standards. They seem to forget that great teachers use showmanship everywhere; they seldom bore.

Closed-Circuit Television

The above discussion has been aimed rather pointedly at open-circuit broadcasting, yet many of the implications apply to closed-circuit use. Probably no one knows how many CCTV systems there are in the United States. The number is doubtless about 400 if the count includes colleges, universities, city and county schools, hospitals and medical schools, and those used in scientific research. These facilities vary from a single camera with one or more receivers to elaborate studios which connect a great many elementary and secondary schools by cable. An example is found in Washington County, Maryland. In this instance, the system reaches out from Hagerstown to each of the fifty schools in the county. Six programs can be carried simultaneously and TV instruction is given daily for all grade levels and in many subjects. No student receives more than one hour of television instruction a day, except for a few high school students who get one and a half hours.

City school systems using CCTV are too numerous to mention and their number is steadily growing. They are to be found in small school districts such as Lennox, California (five schools) as well as populous centers such as Louisville, Kentucky. Arrangements are often made with the telephone company to place school cables from building to building on telephone poles. In other instances a wire service is leased. On college campuses, television cables usually are laid underground from building to building.

Closed-circuit television can serve quite specific purposes. It may be used for outright instructional purposes or it may be confined to enrichment or special demonstration. All age groups from kindergarten to postgraduate have been taught by television. Although some subjects lend themselves more naturally to the medium, there is possibly not a single subject which has not at some time been presented on television.

Preservice and in-service education programs have found ETV, especially CCTV, helpful in observations, demonstrations, and interviews. The observation of classroom procedures may be available to a large number of viewers without disturbing the class being observed. The effectiveness of teacher supervision can be increased significantly. A case in point here is the recently released results of an NDEA experiment at Fontana, California.[1]

Television Teaching: All or None?

Some critics of ETV seem to have the idea that students get either all or none of their instruction via television when a program is inaugurated. The practice followed by Hagerstown, Maryland, noted above, is typical. Even where television is widely used, students do not get all their course work, nor all of their work in any one course, by this medium. The following discussion will show how four types of ETV fit into this scheme in terms of use.

TOTAL TELEVISION TEACHING   There are some instances in which the total instruction is carried by the television medium. These instances are usually out-of-school adult programs and are for short duration. They are commonly listed as noncredit courses, for example, a course in Spanish offered over an educational or a commercial station. In this instance, the only help the student gets in addition to the telecast is from a textbook, a recommended set of recordings for listening drill, and possibly a syllabus.

The well-known "Continental Classroom" series in mathematics and science is essentially this type of program, yet many colleges and universities which offer credit for the series supplement it with discussions, tests, and related learning activities. Nebraska is experimenting with TV to help small high schools offer more effective mathematics and science courses for advanced students. Correspondence tutelage is the additional factor here.

MAJOR RESOURCE TEACHING   Probably most television teaching today is of resource value. Regular teachers and television teachers share the teaching responsibilities. Television makes possible the assistance of experts and of outstanding facilities which are so often denied the individual school. After major telecasts, classroom teachers follow up with laboratory experiments, discussions, library work, creative projects, or remedial exercises.

SUPPLEMENTARY TELEVISION TEACHING   Television can supplement what

[1] *Use of Closed Circuit Television to Improve Teacher Effectiveness*, a research report conducted by the Fontana School District and supported by a grant from the United States Office of Education, Department of Health, Education and Welfare. Proposal 269, Grant No. 704062.00, 77 pp.

normally takes place in the classroom. A recent report from the National Education Association says:

Here television follows a course of study in a broad way but adds to it the kinds of fruitful experiences which individual teachers find difficult if not impossible to provide. A series may present visits on film to local industries or institutions. It may feature interviews and demonstrations by outstanding authorities or local officials. Performances by musical, ballet, or dramatic groups may be used to enhance appreciation or to motivate student interest. This type of instructional television is in widespread use from the Bay Region of California to New York City.[2]

INSTRUCTIONAL OBSERVATION   This is a limited and specialized form of television in which a TV camera and a small closed-circuit system are used to enable a class to view close-up demonstrations, dissections, setting gems, or other minute operations. A microscope slide or a science demonstration can be enlarged so that every person in a large lecture hall gets an intimate view.

Television Teaching—Shared Teaching

The teacher who uses television must realize that he is a part of a team, that he shares his instructional efforts with one or more colleagues. No longer does he have complete autonomy in his classroom. To some extent the teacher who uses television in his teaching has less responsibility for purveying content and more for managing learning situations with more time for individual and group learning activities. His counseling role in the learning situation is increased. If he knows his students as he should, he now arranges appropriate learning situations for them—by individual or group—to investigate, practice, read, discuss, or to work with teaching machines, tape recorders, motion pictures, and other devices. He may incorporate field trips, the building of models, or other activities as he diagnoses the needs of his students.

On the other hand, the teacher who actually appears before the television camera must prepare each presentation with great care. He must know his subject content and he must make an effective presentation of it. He must effectively use various visuals, and he is given assistance so that he can do this. One obstacle to more effective conventional teaching lies in the fact that teachers have neither the time nor the facilities to accomplish maximum results.

Each teacher has a role to play, and the roles are complementary. Each gives up something of the age-old role, but this is replaced by a new-

2 *And TV, Too!* Washington, D.C.: Department of Audiovisual Instruction and Department of Classroom Teachers, National Education Association, 1961.

found satisfaction in outright effectiveness in a world in which ideas increase geometrically.

The Fund for the Advancement of Education outlines the separate roles of the teaching team in this manner:

Team teaching in television classes

The studio teacher, classroom teachers, and curriculum specialists cooperatively plan the course in advance and prepare teacher guides.

The studio teacher presents, explains, and demonstrates the major points of the lesson, raises questions, and stimulates student interest.

The classroom teacher prepares students for the telecast part of the lesson, answers questions, clarifies points, leads discussion, makes assignments, gives individual help, and supervises testing.

The studio teacher and classroom teacher confer regularly to evaluate the lessons and make improvements.[3]

Strengths and Weaknesses

Arguments pro and con are easy to find. Without elaboration some of the more obvious arguments regarding the strengths and weaknesses of television teaching are set forth at this time.

STRENGTHS	WEAKNESSES
1. Tests show that students taught by TV do as well or better than those taught by conventional methods.	1. Face-to-face contact of teacher and student is lacking
2. Horizons are enlarged.	2. Costs are high.
3. Unusual resources which are often unavailable otherwise are brought to the classroom.	3. Education tends to become impersonal, mechanized.
4. This method of teaching stimulates teachers as well as students.	4. Modern trends toward uniformity seem to be accentuated; to produce the "mass man."
5. Time is saved for the regular classroom teacher so that more remedial work can be accomplished.	5. Individual differences cannot be checked or attenuated.
6. Specialized learning or special problems of students can be met.	6. Many parents react unfavorably toward television instruction.
7. Many students can be taught at one time.	7. Many teachers, too, react unfavorably toward television instruction.
8. Curriculum breadth can be provided for small schools.	8. Students, if given a preference, will choose live teaching.

[3] *Teaching by Television*, 2d ed. New York: The Ford Foundation and The Fund for the Advancement of Education, 1961.

9. Every student is able to see and hear everything that takes place in the teaching process.
10. Redeployment of teacher time can be an asset.
11. Television-taught students tend to accept more responsibility for their own learning.
12. Television-taught students make greater use of the library.
13. Existing space in school buildings may be better utilized.

9. Learners tend toward passivity.
10. Scheduling of classes presents problems.
11. Television teaching gradually builds up a caste among the teachers.
12. Students tend to look upon television instruction as play.

Steps in Classroom Use

In the immediate years ahead, many beginning teachers will be located in school systems which employ television in some form; many others will not. As a part of his professional education, every teacher should realize the strengths and weaknesses of the medium and should know some of the basic principles of use.

The steps in television use are not unlike those in the use of films, recordings, resource persons, or other good instructional materials. These consist of teacher preparation, student preparation, reception, and follow-up.

It goes without saying that teachers must be prepared for television lessons as well as any other type of lesson. This preparation includes content understanding, specific objectives of lessons, emotional *rapprochement*, and best reception conditions. Study guides are as useful in TV teaching as elsewhere. Usually they suggest how to prepare for a telecast and give much pertinent information. Teachers should never turn on telecasts simply because they are tired or have nothing planned for the hour. Schools which regularly use TV usually furnish their teachers with numerous invaluable teaching aids. In many school systems these materials are prepared by a curriculum-coordinating committee.

Pupil preparation is as important as teacher preparation. Students must first be conditioned to the fact that the viewing is a learning experience and not just a pastime. The teacher is a key person in this conditioning process—he provides the difference between a negative, laissez-faire, or positive attitude toward this type of learning. Students must know the purpose of the particular lesson, what to look for, generalizations to be sought, assignments to be copied, or workbooks or texts to be followed as the viewing is in progress.

Meaningful telecast viewing can take place if teacher and students are properly prepared for the experience. Students should also be given instruction in *how to look*. They will then probably be thinking ahead about what activities will follow. Needless to say, work—books or papers—which might act as a distraction should be cleared away. For this period, the particular subject has the floor and should have undivided attention.

The reception of the telecast should take place under the best physical conditions possible. Every school which proposes to use TV should recognize this and make arrangements so that each room has the requisite number of receivers for the students involved. The sets should be placed at the proper height and in the proper location. Provision should also be made for light and acoustic control; desks and chairs should be arranged; distracting fragments on the chalkboard should be erased; and the teacher should have a place in the room which does not detract from the reception.

In nearly all instances, there are follow-up activities which result rather naturally from telecast lessons. These activities run the gamut of learning activities. If the preparation for the telecast has been well done, follow-up activities are logical and will be expected by the students. They will feel responsible for doing more than just viewing the lesson.

The culmination of the ideally taught television lesson brings together the studio teacher and the classroom teacher to evaluate the effectiveness of their work. As they evaluate and plan improvements, the preparation for the next phase of the work gets under way.

Research into Television Values

No area of modern education has been more fully researched than television. Resources from industry, foundations, and educational systems have been placed in the hands of the researchers. Literally millions of dollars have been spent.

Teachers should have some awareness of the results of this research which has covered all grade levels from primary to the graduate school. Although the research has covered many types of learning, most of it has dealt with the acquisition of knowledge and the development of skills. In 1960, Allen (8:7–8) summarized all the researches up to that time. For the high school, for example, he found sixty-seven studies from sixteen school systems. Fourteen of the studies showed results significantly favored television; five favored conventional teaching; and forty-eight showed no observable pattern favoring one or the other method for particular subject matter areas. English and literature have received the greatest research attention; next were science, social studies, and mathematics (8:12–13).

The results for the junior high school were much the same. Twenty-four studies from eight different school systems were reported. In these, two studies favored conventional instruction; three, television; and the remaining nineteen showed no significant differences. These studies were chiefly with science and social studies classes in predominantly large-class situations (8:12).

There can be no question about the fact that television will become an increasingly potent factor in instruction. It has already reached a high degree of perfection, and future developments will quite likely show even better results. Students who receive some of their instruction through this mass communication medium are not doomed for retardation, stupidity, or delinquency.

It must also be kept in mind that educational television does not replace the need for classroom teachers; neither does it represent cash savings except in unusual circumstances. Experience does show that the curriculum can be broadened, enriched, and the learning fundamentals effectively taught.

Midwest Airborne Television Instruction

As television signals tend to travel in a straight line, the curvature of the earth limits the reception of a broadcast. To overcome this to greatest extent, it is common practice to place television transmitters on hill tops and high buildings. This factor does increase the effective range of the telecast.

The Midwest Program of Airborne Television Instruction project (MPATI) was conceived so that an airplane 5 miles above the earth can serve as a broadcasting transmitter. Coverage is enormously increased. Actually, signals cover a radius of about 200 miles. Project headquarters are in northern Indiana, and the broadcast area extends over all or parts of Indiana, Ohio, Kentucky, Illinois, Michigan, and Wisconsin. (See Figure 10-1.)

MPATI was organized to broaden the range of educational offerings—science, mathematics, and foreign language, for example—to schools and to try to increase the quality of education by bringing together some of the nation's best teachers while providing these teachers with the best in the audio-visual arts.

Here is briefly how it works. Two four-engine airplanes—one is always in reserve—are equipped as flying transmitters. Over UHF channels 72 and 76, telecasts of video-taped lessons are sent from the "flying classrooms" above the Purdue University headquarters. It is possible to expand the two channels to six; in other words six courses could be broadcast simultaneously instead of the present two. It is estimated that 17,000 school districts and colleges enrolling some seven million school-age children are within the telecast area. Needless to say, not all the districts in the

Fig. 10-1 Geographical area covered by MPATI

area are participating, but for those which do, costs are nominal. Each district buys the number of receivers it needs, and study guides, lesson plans, and other printed material as suggested. The capital expenses are borne by outside agencies.

MPATI telecasting got under way in the fall of 1961, but only after some two years of careful planning. Responsibility for the experiment rests with a council of fifteen representatives of schools and colleges in the area served.

Studio teachers, sixteen in all, were gathered after a nationwide talent search. These teachers were selected because of their demonstrated teaching ability, their ability to make effective use of television in teaching, and their competence in a subject-matter field. The teachers spend an average of twenty hours preparing and taping each televised lesson which lasts twenty minutes for the elementary school and thirty minutes for the high school. They prepare from two to three lessons a week. (In most city districts using TV, the studio teacher prepares at least one lesson a day.)

Twenty-one courses were offered in the spring term of 1961–1962: of these four were college courses; six, secondary school; and eleven, elementary school.

This mammoth project has captured the imagination of many educators, but whether it will be continued into the future as a reasonable-cost educational project is still not known. There have been many difficulties but they seem to have been taken care of satisfactorily. Teachers appear enthusiastic, but whether resistance will develop is problematical.

One final word needs to be said. What does it cost? How can the money be found? MPATI has a budget of $8,500,000. The Ford Foundation contributed $7,000,000, and the remainder came from other foundations and from industry. If continued into the future on the present scale, a budget of more than $3,000,000 would be needed. But if this sum is divided by 17,000 districts, or by the potential seven million students in the area, the cost per student would be modest. Questions facing the citizens in the MPATI area are: (1) Does this program broaden the educational offerings significantly? (2) Does it improve the quality of learning? (3) Is it workable administratively? (4) Can the funds be found to pay for it?

Looking Ahead

Research has shown that students can learn as well as and frequently better by television than by conventional methods, and possibly much better with new studies and techniques in the years ahead (8; 15). The potential of television integrates the teaching arts, the graphic arts, and the electronic communication process. Television seems to demand more and in turn produces more. A national committee of teachers has summarized it succinctly in this way:

As stated before, television has no magic in itself; but well-planned lessons, in the hands of the skilled teacher, can bring rich, valuable experiences to the classroom. The television teacher, in utilizing television, should look upon it as a helping hand, an assistant who throws open the walls of his classroom, making it as broad as the world itself (1:37).

Will ETV cost some teachers their jobs? Logic says not. A paragraph from a bulletin of the North Central Association of Colleges and Secondary Schools seems to cover this question:

Educational television is not likely to cause technological unemployment. It may, however, result in some modification of the traditional role of the teacher, and especially of the teacher in a self-contained classroom who has not been accustomed to cooperating with a librarian and an audio-visual aids department in providing opportunities for learning for her pupils.[4]

THE LANGUAGE LABORATORY

The boom today in foreign language teaching is almost revolutionary. It is uncertain as to when this boom actually began but the factors involved attest to its recency. The Modern Foreign Language Association has estimated that 42.7 percent of the Foreign Service Corps of the United States lacks "adequate knowledge of any foreign language." This is the partial theme of *The Ugly American,* a recent popular novel. As the world tends to become one neighborhood, the United States seems singularly unready. Dr. James B. Conant has bluntly accused American secondary schools of doing a poor job of foreign language teaching. He has stated that those students who take foreign languages in most of our schools have a "brief exposure with very little residue," and that "to study a language for two years, or two languages for two years each, is a waste of time."[5]

Yet, when students begin a foreign language there is no question of their enthusiasm. Enrollment figures, although in themselves meaningless according to Conant, indicate wide interest. In 1958, Congress passed the National Defense Education Act authorizing financial assistance to schools for the acquisition of laboratory or other special equipment needed in the teaching of foreign languages. The funds have provided schools with installations ranging from a simple listening corner with a single playback machine to fully equipped electronic laboratories.

To many, more and better foreign language teaching has become a national imperative. The emphasis on audio equipment including language laboratories may even exceed the interest in instructional television. Researches, studies, conferences, and pamphlets appear in mounting num-

[4] *The Uses of Television in Education,* a report prepared by the subcommittee on television of the Commission on Research and Service of the North Central Association of Colleges and Secondary Schools in cooperation with the United States Office of Education. Washington, D.C.: Department of Health, Education, and Welfare, Office of Education, March 1961, p. 21.

[5] James B. Conant, *The American High School Today.* New York: McGraw-Hill Book Company, Inc., 1959, pp. 69–73. Used by permission.

bers. California has passed legislation (1961 regular legislative session) which requires the teaching of a foreign language by 1965 to all pupils in grades six, seven, and eight of the elementary school. The elementary school teaching credential may soon add a language requirement.

What Is a Language Laboratory?

A language laboratory is essentially a place where a student may practice a language just as a music student practices piano or other instruments. Gene C. Fusco, specialist in school and community relations in the United States Office of Education, says:

In its complete form the language lab is an electronic installation consisting of a booth, headset, microphone, recording facilities for each student, and a monitoring set-up for the teacher. Visual facilities may include a projection screen, a motion picture machine, and slide-, filmstrip-, and overhead-projectors.[6]

What Does a Language Laboratory Do?

In the aural-lingual method of teaching a language, the chief elements of the learning process are varied and intensive repetition. Meaningful drill and immediate correction of errors are provided. It is of prime importance not only to be able to hear oneself unhampered by other voices, but also to be able to receive criticism of one's pronunciation from the teacher, and to progress at one's own rate of learning. Language learning was once dull, wasteful, even boring. Students sat through a recitation period with the opportunity to speak only once or twice or only by concert recitation. Much time was spent listening to recitations which were stumbling, halting, and erroneous.

Elliott H. Kone, director of the Yale University audio-visual center, has summarized the advantages of the language laboratory as follows:

1. The sound of the teacher's voice reaches each student more clearly and without interference. If a teacher desires, recorded sounds of skilled native speakers may be added. As a student responds to a lesson, his voice is fed to his own ears electronically. Thus he comes closer to the quality of pronunciation that he should use.

2. In isolating a pupil's ears and presence from his class neighbors he again becomes an individual working with the teacher, now depending on his own wits and resources and his ability to respond alone.

3. It is often true that only when a student hears his own recorded voice alternately with that of the teacher that he first learns about the difference of his response from the correct pronunciation.

[6] Gene C. Fusco, *Technology in the Classroom Challenges to the School Administrator*. Reprint, *School Life* (March–May 1960), p. 4. Washington, D.C.: United States Department of Health, Education, and Welfare, Office of Education.

4. A teacher can now have the equivalent assistance of personal tutors for every student, a "library study" plan whereby each student can work with his own master tape.

5. Audio-visual materials can be used easily. The sound can be fed directly to the students' ears from a film track or any type of prerecorded material accompanying filmstrips.

6. The time necessary to master a language is relatively shortened. Many dependable observations in universities indicate that there is a 30 percent to 80 percent increase in the speed of mastering a language when the laboratory method is used.

7. The language lab democratically permits pupils to advance in their studies at their own pace according to their varied talents—but all are given an equal opportunity to master the subject.[7]

Is a Language Laboratory Entirely Verbal?

Fusco's definition of the language laboratory includes visual facilities as well as audio facilities. At Purdue University, language is considered multisensory, and nearly every conceivable "visual" is integrated into the "audio" experience. One professor has said, "Oral language becomes real when we can see what we are talking about, in the laboratory as in life situations."[8]

Ruth R. Cornfield, consultant and curriculum materials adviser to the French Cultural Services of the French Embassy in the United States, says:

To translate the words *le petit dejeuner* by showing orange juice, oatmeal with sweet cream, a bottle of pasteurized milk, toast and coffee is as false a concept of the French breakfast as one can imagine. The meaning of the word is not contained in the sound of it; it is contained in the concept. In this sense we cannot hope to teach foreign languages successfully by aural-oral methods only . . . the foreign language teacher must exert every effort to get authentic visuals with which to teach.[9]

Practically all visual materials can be useful in teaching language, but many teachers prefer the simpler materials such as filmstrip, flannel board, chalkboard, flash card, object, specimen, and model. Dramatization and pantomime are also useful, as are motion picture films and tele-

---

[7] Elliott H. Kone, "Why Have a Language Laboratory?" *Modern Techniques in Teaching Foreign Languages*, Annual Bulletin 19. Hartford: Connecticut Audio-Visual Education Association, 1960, p. 13.

[8] Elton Hocking, "The Language Laboratory," *Modern Techniques in Teaching Foreign Languages*, Annual Bulletin, 19. Hartford: Connecticut Audio-Visual Education Association, 1960, p. 64.

[9] Ruth R. Cornfield, "Not by Sound Alone," *Audiovisual Instruction*, vol. 6 (December 1960), p. 339.

casts. It should also be mentioned that extensive use is being made of integrated instructional materials such as textbooks, films or filmstrips, prerecorded tapes, and manuals.

As to equipment, the teacher should have the exclusive use of a tape recorder. The trend in the classroom is to reduce the amount of equipment in front of the student. Too much equipment tends to confuse and detract. Some teachers prefer the flexible magnetic disc to the magnetic tape. It has the simplicity of a phonograph, but can be reused for many recordings, perhaps up to five thousand times. Tape fidelity is superior, but that of the disc is sufficiently high for most practical purposes.

It seems quite likely that the beginning foreign language teacher will now, or in the very near future, be working with some sort of language laboratory. It may be as simple as a portable "audio-cart" or it may be the completely electronic classroom which is now in the emergent stage. Trump, as director of the National Association of Secondary School Principals in the Experimental Study of the Utilization of Staff, has emphasized that more vigorous efforts should be made to bring the means of communicating ideas abreast of the latest scientific advances (17:1–14).

Joseph C. Hutchinson, specialist in foreign languages for the United States Office of Education, said in an address at Indiana University:

It is clear that the language laboratory is definitely established as a basic ingredient in a successful foreign language program. The language laboratory is not only included in most predictions of what the future school will be like, but also holds promises of even transforming itself into the new concept of the teaching machine.[10]

TEACHING MACHINES AND PROGRAMMED LEARNING

The whole area of programmed learning or self-instruction is popularly associated with the "teaching machine." This term is somewhat of a misnomer, but it has caught on and will probably stay with us. Some professional educators say that "teaching machine" is more than a misnomer, that it is actually misleading. A person does not truly learn from a machine; he learns from instructional material which is in the machine. Most educators prefer such terms as "self-instructional devices," "autoinstructional devices," and "programmed instruction." Terms such as these can serve as an umbrella for teaching machines: scrambled books, tutor texts, paper sheets, rolls, cards, and folds. Finn and Perrin (3:35–49) have categorized all devices under three headings: printed media, projected media, and classroom communications systems.

[10] Joseph C. Hutchinson, an address delivered at the 1960 foreign language conference, Indiana University.

The notion that Johnny might in some mysterious way learn from a machine has captured the fancy of many people. Books, pamphlets, and articles dealing with some aspect of programmed learning are appearing in great profusion. A bibliography of more than 300 such listings is needed to cover the years of 1960 and 1961 alone. Nor should it be imagined that all these publications are readily found just in educational journals. The general public is interested. Articles frequently appear in the metropolitan newspapers, *The New York Times* and *The New York Herald Tribune;* national weekly magazines, *Newsweek, Time, Saturday Review, Saturday Evening Post;* financial publications, *Wall Street Journal* and *Barron's;* library magazines, *Library Journal* and *ALA Bulletin;* limited-reader publications, *Columbia University Graduate Facilities Newsletter* and the *Carnegie Corporation of New York Quarterly;* and in the publications aimed specifically for military personnel, engineers, research scientists, personnel managers, training directors, and others. At least three periodicals devote their entire contents to the field.

Many colleges and universities are pursuing extensive automatic tutor research. Actual use with large or small numbers can be found in many elementary schools, secondary schools, industrial training programs, and military centers around the country.

A recent NDEA publication (3:20–32) shows that in 1960 and 1961, 630 school and college subject programs were placed on the market. Some hundred firms are producing programmed instructional devices or have designs on the drafting boards. Eleven publishing houses have their own program writers. An emerging trend is for publishers to align themselves with counterpart machine manufacturers.

The Background of Programmed Learning

How did it all start? Like most modern developments the basic idea of programmed learning is very old. Some say it started with Socrates, who at the conclusion of a demonstration said to a friend:

So a man who does not know has in himself true opinions on a subject without having knowledge. At the present these opinions, being newly aroused, have a dream-like quality. But if the same questions are put to him on many occasions and in different ways, you can see that in the end he will have a knowledge on the subject as accurate as anybody's. This knowledge will not come from teaching but from questioning.[11]

A half century ago, Edward L. Thorndike foresaw what contemporary psychologists devise for the scientifically designed programmed book. He

[11] Printed in "Not from Teaching but from Questioning," *Carnegie Corporation Quarterly,* vol. 9 (October 1961), pp. 1–8.

maintained that texts often stated the habits to be formed by students but gave the students no exercises in forming them. This he felt held for books in grammar, sociology, economics, and philosophy as well as arithmetic and foreign language. He contended that students should be helped just enough at each stage of growth to lead them to help themselves and that proper ingenuity on the part of authors and publishers should overcome conventional textbook faults.

If by a miracle of mechanical ingenuity, a book could be so arranged that only to him who had done what was directed on page one would page two become visible, and so on, much that now requires personal instruction could be managed by print. Books to be given out in loose sheets, a page or so at a time, and books arranged so that the student only suffers if he misuses them, should be worked out in many subjects. . . . a textbook can do much more than be on the one hand a mere statement of the results of reasoning such as ordinary geography or German grammar is, or on the other hand a mere statement of problems, such as the ordinary arithmetic or German reader is.

On the whole, the improvement of printed directions, statement of facts, exercise books and the like is as important as the improvement of the powers of teachers themselves to diagnose the condition of pupils and to guide their activities by personal means. Great economies are possible by printed aids, and personal comment and questions should be saved to do what only it can do. A human being should not be wasted in doing what forty sheets of paper or two phonographs can do. Just because personal teaching is precious and can do what books and apparatus can not, it should be saved for its peculiar work.[12]

The actual construction of contraptions or so-called teaching machines has been traced back to 1866 when a spelling machine was produced. In 1873, a logic machine was supposed "to generate solutions to logical problems represented symbolically."[13] In the 1920s, Sydney L. Pressey of Ohio State University attempted to mechanize testing and to some extent teaching with devices that were supplementary to regular classroom teaching.

Some Causes of the Present Popularization

The popularization of teaching machines has come, however, in the late 1950s through the researches in learning and the design of a practical machine by B. F. Skinner of Harvard. Holland, an associate of Skinner, says machines could have been built hundreds of years ago, but their function

12 Edward L. Thorndike, *Education*. New York: The Macmillan Company, 1912. Used by permission of Macmillan.
13 Lawrence M. Stolurow, *Teaching by Machine*, Cooperative Research Monograph, No. 6. Washington, D.C.: Department of Health, Education, and Welfare, Office of Education, 1961, p. 17.

today rests upon "the development of a new technology—a behavioral engineering of teaching procedures."[14]

A considerable segment of American society views present teaching methods as inefficient and wasteful. It is generally agreed that the world is experiencing a population explosion of unprecedented proportions. Many people maintain that there exists an acknowledged struggle in the world merely to maintain present literacy levels, or as Alice remarked, we must run as fast as we can to stay where we are. Concurrent with this population explosion there exists a deficit in the number of qualified teachers and a dearth of classrooms. Costs are rising and there is some concern over society's ability to meet the education bill even if teachers and classrooms are found.

Everyone knows that knowledge is being generated at a fantastic rate. *Fortune* magazine (January 1959) has noted that scientific breakthroughs are coming even faster than the scientists predicted. Today's achievement may be rendered obsolete by tomorrow's development. In television, videotape succeeded kinescope, and tomorrow a thermoplastic tape may outdate videotape. Change is likewise true in every field of knowledge, especially so in mathematics and science. Occupational change upsets economics. More and better solutions are needed for the problems of education. Edgar Dale, in reviewing *Teaching Machines and Programmed Learning: A Source Book*, edited by Lumsdaine and Glaser, says: "If we merely want to teach more, teach it faster, and use better what we have learned, there is little doubt that programmed teaching will help offer us significant help" (16:58).

Characteristics of Programmed Materials

Programmed instruction takes many forms but the forms are characteristically much the same.

The word "program" is important. It denotes a planned learning pattern. The material to be learned is, then, presented to the learner sequentially. This presentation takes place bit by bit in such a way that the learner must respond to each stimulus before he goes further. Actually, the learner progresses in small lucid steps so arranged by the programmer that the learner arrives at the desired outcome with a minimum of errors. Each step is repeated and practiced so that the learner thoroughly understands it before he goes to the next step. The student always knows whether he is right or wrong. There is a low level of difficulty at each step or "frame." Only the material which is pertinent and for which the student is logically and psychologically ready is presented. The student moves slowly from simple ideas to more complex ones and to generaliza-

---

[14] *Invitational Conference on Testing Problems, Proceedings 1959.* Princeton, N.J.: Educational Testing Service, 1960.

tions. Ideas are repeated several times in new form or with different context so that the desired responses are buttressed.

Rewards come to the students in the knowledge that they understand what they are doing, and they immediately see every response that they make as right or wrong. There are no delays of hours or even days. This immediate feedback overcomes one of the greatest difficulties in conventional group instruction.

Each student proceeds at his own rate of progress. Contrary to what some skeptics have thought, students do not dawdle their time away. As a matter of fact, they accomplish much more with self-instructional learning than they do under conventional procedures. To paraphrase Dale here, research shows that students cover more content and understand it better. One junior high school teacher who attempted to program his mathematics classes with scrambled book exercises gave up after two months. His comment, "I can't keep up. They (the students) chew it up faster than I can put it together." He had never had this happen before with conventional teaching methods.

Automatic tutoring functions much like a private human tutor. The machine or book as the case may be holds the student at a given task until he is able to make a correct response repeatedly. If the student has trouble with an item, the automatic device, like the tutor, coaches him by suggesting, hinting, and cuing until the correct response is made. There is always immediate feedback; the student knows whether he is right or wrong.

Programming

The art of planning material for use in a book or a machine is called *programming*, and the planned material is *programmed instructional* material.

There are two schools of thought as to the best way to plan instructional materials; undoubtedly others will arise. One group advocates a method variously called *linear, fixed-sequence, straight-line,* or *extrinsic* programming. The plan is shown in Figure 10-2.

Fig. 10-2

In this diagram each circle represents a frame, and the arrow represents the response. The frames or steps represent small units of content. These are presented to the student in sequence, but only after he has made a correct response to the previous stimulus. The student responds on the basis of what he already knows or with the help of various cues or suggestions which he may or may not need. Each step must be completed, and the student cannot skip around. In the main, the student *constructs* his answers and fills in blanks, writes or types his answers, or manipulates dials on a machine to record his answers. Individual differences are cared for as the student works at his individual rate of speed. Examples of linear programming are the learning materials of the *TEMAC* programs produced by Encyclopedia Britannica Films, Inc., *English 2600* by Harcourt, Brace & World, Inc., and the programs of TMI-Grolier.

The second school of thought concerning programs uses a scheme

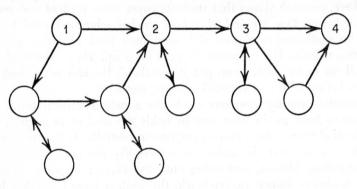

Fig. 10-3

Reproduced from *Explaining "Teaching Machines" and Programming* by David Cram, copyright Fearon Publishers, Inc., San Francisco, 1961, p. 36.

called *nonlinear, branching,* or *intrinsic.* Material is presented in small sequential steps or in larger units as desired. The learner usually has a choice of possible answers. After selecting one, he turns to the designated page and checks his response. If correct, he goes to a new exercise; if incorrect, he is told why he is wrong, and is asked to return to the original step, to reread it, and try again. This scrambling with multiple-choice responses permits more flexibility and allows more leeway for meeting individual differences. The branching program is shown in Figure 10-3.

Numerous formats have been devised for printed programmed devices: the programmed textbook, the scrambled textbook, the cut-back page booklet, and the tab-type page. Only the first two will be described here.

The programmed textbook has two types of pages, the information-question page and the answer page which follows it immediately. As a result, each page is arranged in a series of bands or panels. The learner moves through the pages in succession to the end of the book or section and then returns to page one for the second band or panel. The following example follows this format.

Example

Blumenthal, Joseph C., *English 2600: A Scientific Program in Grammar and Usage.* New York: Harcourt, Brace & World, Inc., 1960. Paper. Length: 2632 frames, 448 pp.

Each page of the book is divided into six panels (or frames), printed in alternate bands of white and light gray. On page 361, panel 1061 looks like this:

	A *fragment* means a "broken piece"—like a fragment of glass or wood. A *sentence fragment* is a piece of a sentence that is written as though it were a complete _____. 1061

The student fills in the blank and turns to page 363. Panel 1062 looks like this:

sentence
 	
1061
	To be a sentence, a group of words must pass two tests:
	  1. Does it have a subject and a verb?
	  2. Does it make sense by itself?
	
	    The large book with the brown cover.
	
	The above word group is a (*fragment, sentence*).
	1062

The accompanying frame on page 365 looks like this:

fragment 1062	*The large* BOOK *with the brown cover.* This word group is a fragment because it names something (*book*) but makes no statement about it. In other words this word group is not a sentence because it lacks a (*subject, verb*). 1063

Page 367 shows this:

verb 1063	a. *The large book with the brown cover.* b. *The large* BOOK *with the brown cover* IS *an atlas.* Which word group is a sentence because it has both a subject and a verb—*a* or *b*? _____ 1064

The above is the fifth frame on four consecutive odd-numbered pages. These frames continue in increasing difficulty to the end of the section on "Understanding the Sentence Unit."[15]

In the typical scrambled textbook, the learner begins on page one with given content and question, but he may go immediately to any one of three or four pages depending upon his selection of a response. The pages in the book are numbered in sequence but not the learning materials. The example below from *Molecular Solutions* by Darby and Mager follows this form. There has, of necessity, been a great deal of abbreviation in order to show this example.

Example

Darby, C. L., and Mager, R. F., *Molecular Solutions*. Athens, Ohio: Ohio University. Length 35 pages. Available only to qualified researchers.

Scrambled Book Page 14

This is an automatic tutoring or "scrambled" book applied to the concept of *molar* solutions. It is different from any other book you have read in that the pages are not read consecutively. On each page, you will be asked a question. The answer you choose will direct you to the page to which you should turn next. The appendix (page 35) contains all the information you should need to work through the material presented in this book. To begin, turn to page 10.

Scrambled Book Page 10

Let's begin by reviewing the definitions of solutions, solvents, and solutes. You will recall that a *solution* is a homogeneous molecular mixture of substances. The liquid in which a solid or gas has been dispersed to form a solution is called a *solvent*, and the substance dissolved, the *solute*. In the case of two liquids or two solids, each may be said to be dissolved in the other, though the one present in larger quantity is usually termed the solvent.

Now let's see how well you remember these definitions.

If you were to mix 500 milliliter (ml) of sulfuric acid with one liter of water, the water would be termed the _____.

p. 3 Solvent
p. 6 Solute
p. 13 Solution

15 From *English 2600* by Joseph C. Blumenthal © 1960 by Harcourt, Brace & World, Inc., and reprinted with their permission.

Scrambled Book Page 3

Your answer was: *solvent*

CORRECT. The substance present in a solution in the largest quantity is usually termed the solvent.

There are a variety of ways in which we could describe the quantities of solutes, their weight, volume, etc. One convention is to talk about gram-molecular weight of substances. This is simply the molecular weight of the substance expressed in grams. For example, the gram-molecular weight of water would be:

p. 15 18.02
p. 8 16.00

Scrambled Book Page 6

Your answer was: *solute*

No, the solute is that substance which is dissolved in another substance.

This latter substance is called the solvent and is usually the substance present in the largest quantity. Since a liter is equal to 1000 milliliters (ml), we have twice as much water as sulfuric acid.

If we were to dissolve common table salt in water, the water could be called the _____.

p. 3 Solvent
p. 4 Solute

Scrambled Book Page 13

Your answer was: *solution*

The term "solution" refers to the molecular mixture of the water and whatever other substance has been dissolved in it. Thus, a solution is the resulting combination of two or more substances. Now turn to page 10 and try again.[16]

Programming is unquestionably the key to efficacious learning of the automatic type. The programmed materials are prepared either for text-books or for use in mechanical devices. The cost of producing these programs is understandably high but, once produced, books may sell for five or ten dollars and machine programs from ten dollars and more.

[16] This example of a scrambled book is from an article by Joseph W. Rigney, and Edward B. Fry, "Current Teaching-Machine Programs and Programming Techniques," *AV Communication Review*, vol. 9, no. 3, Supplement No. 3, May–June 1961. By permission of the Department of Audiovisual Instruction.

Machine Devices

Many educators and most of the general public refer to instruction through the use of programmed materials as education by machine teaching. Quite obviously the machine does not teach; it is merely a conveyer of teaching or programmed materials. It puts the learner in contact with the author of the instructional materials. It might even be said to be a laborsaving device which by its novelty helps to motivate the student. It does not need to be monitored, it is patient, and it is practically impossible to cheat on it.

Since the idea of teaching machines struck the educational world in 1958 or 1959, there has been a proliferation of devices put on the market. More than one hundred companies have made teaching machine models costing anywhere from a few dollars to several thousand, the latter representing sophisticated computer-operated devices or elaborate electronic classroom systems.

Simulated Machine Devices

There are a great many devices on the market which can scarcely be called machines nor are they books. These devices are frequently of the pencil-paper variety. Then, there are some devices which are halfway between.

Among these latter devices, often costing only a few cents, are punchboards, pull-tabs, pluck cards, sliding masks, paper scanners, and chemical cards.

Educational Testing Service is preparing a variety of self-correcting exercises in the form of tests. Some of these exercises are produced to serve as homework assignments. They are very cleverly programmed materials arranged as blocks of information, as for example, a set of challenging questions to follow a poem. Item writing is the big factor here. The exercise may be one which is actually designed to teach a method of dealing with poems, not merely an examination of understanding. The technique would be used with many difficult poems. As a homework assignment, the program would follow a class discussion of the poem. Students would test themselves on the poem, but they would at the same time acquire some skill in figuring out the meaning of the next poem to be studied in class.

The programmed questions are printed sheets. A cardboard or sheet of paper covers the correct answer until the student has made his response. The sample exercise on "Spring and Fall" shows how it works. (This is an abbreviated illustration and omits the answer key to the test to be given the following day by the classroom teacher.)

Example

Spring and Fall

By Gerard Manley Hopkins

Margaret are you grieving
2 Over Goldengrove unleaving?
Leaves, like the things of man, you
4 With your fresh thoughts care for, can you?
Ah! as the heart grows older
6 It will come to such sights colder
By and by, nor spare a sigh
8 Though worlds of wanwood leafmeal lie;
And yet you *will* weep *and* know why.

10 Now no matter, child, the name:
Sorrow's springs are the same.
12 Nor mouth had, no nor mind, expressed
What heart heard of, ghost guessed:
14 It is the blight man was born for,
It is Margaret you mourn for.[17]

DIRECTIONS: With a sheet of paper, cover everything below the item on which you are working. Read the item, look back at the poem, and write the number of the best answer in the ( ) at the end of the item. Then move the sheet of paper below the next item. The number in parenthesis is the intended answer for the preceding item. If your answer was not the same, put a circle around this parenthesis. If you agree and want to discuss the item, add a question mark or exclamation point.

   1. About how old is the person addressed? 1—Six 2—Eighteen 3—Thirty 4—Fifty ( )

(1)   2. What is Goldengrove? 1—Some English flower, like goldenrod 2—A particular plant to which she has given this name 3—A patch of woods in autumn 4—A person named Goldengrove ( )

(3)   3. In line 2 "unleaving" means: 1—not leaving (i.e., staying) 2—failing to produce leaves 3—unfolding leaves from buds 4—shedding leaves ( )

(4)   4. The *opposite* of "the things of man" in line 3 is: 1—the things of woman 2—the things of children 3—the things of nature 4—the ideas of man ( )

(3)   5. In line 3 "leaves" are: 1—addressed by the question, "Can

---

[17] Gerard Manley Hopkins, "Spring and Fall." Used by permission of Oxford University Press.

you?" 2—the subject of "care for" 3—the subject of "can you" 4—the object of "care for" (   )

(4) 6. In line 7 "nor spare a sigh" means: 1—not be sparing of sighs (i.e., give many of them) 2—not give as much as a sigh 3—not express sorrow openly 4—not permit anyone to sigh (   )

(2) 7. In line 8 "worlds" means 1—large quantities 2—imaginary worlds 3—planets like our world 4—little worlds (round balls) formed by wanwood (   )

(1) 8. Which of the following is most like "leafmeal" in line 8? 1—Oatmeal 2—Bone meal 3—Piecemeal 4—Lastmeal (   )

(3) Now re-study the items you answered correctly.

Test on "Spring and Fall"

DIRECTIONS: Encircle "Yes" if the sentence is a reasonable interpretation of any part of the poem. Encircle "No" if it is not.

Yes No 1. Margaret, are you sad because your lover has deserted you?

Yes No 2. Can't you think of anything but men?

Yes No 3. As you grow older, you will be less moved by sights like this.

Yes No 4. You will not grieve, no matter how many leaves fall.

Yes No 5. But now you keep on weeping and want to know why you weep.

Yes No 6. You have to rake up the leaves that fall on your lawn.

Yes No 7. If you do not know my name, it makes no difference.

Yes No 14. The falling leaves told your heart that you, too, must die.

Yes No 15. In the title, "Fall" stands for "immortality."[18]

Why don't students cheat? Some may, but it is soon evident that it does not pay. No credit is allowed for the score on the homework. Only the test taken in class the following day is scored, and no point covered in the homework exercise ever reappears on the test except in new form. Cheating on the homework is pointless and memorization of right answers is impossible. The program is still in the experimental stage.

Writing Programs

Who should write the programs? There is no absolute answer, but it seems pretty certain that the time factor alone will rule out any more than token preparations by classroom teachers. Earlier in this discussion,

[18] Paul B. Diederich, "Self-Correcting Homework in English," *Proceedings 1959-Invitational Conference on Teaching Problems.* Princeton, N.J.: Educational Test-ing Service, 1960, pp. 80–82, *passim.* Used by permission.

a junior high school teacher pretty well summed up the case: "I can't keep up. They (students) chew it up faster than I can put it together."

It seems therefore that most of the programmed materials will have to be written by specialists at program writing, or at least by teaching teams who can pool time and resources for the job. This sort of writing demands special talents and insights. Stolurow says, "Currently program writing is more art than science" (14:101). He goes on to say that this writing will tend to be more scientific as the task is more thoroughly understood in terms of critical psychological elements and relationships. Teacher workshops and courses in programming for teachers are tackling the problem.

The broad general requirements for writing a program are: (1) thorough knowledge of subject, (2) a large amount of time, (3) patience, (4) students on whom to try out the preliminary drafts, and (5) an above-average understanding of the learning process.

Selecting Equipment and Programs

The whole domain of the teaching machine has expanded so rapidly that there is concern in many professional quarters about likely abuses. Wild claims have been made and high-pressure salesmanship is likely to enmesh unsophisticated school boards and uninformed parents.

Such national organizations as the American Educational Research Association, American Psychological Association, and the Department of Audiovisual Instruction of the National Education Association are preparing criteria to guide prospective buyers. No purchases should be made until a thorough examination has been made of the equipment and the program materials to be used in it. Is the equipment mechanically dependable? Are there available program materials? Have these materials been evaluated? Was the evaluation made under classroom conditions? Can educational programs of various companies be used in several types of machines?

Implications for Education

Research shows rather explicitly that students can learn effectively through the use of these individualized techniques. However, Stolurow says, "The research reported thus far is more provocative than definitive" (14:144). Much of the research has been done in the psychological laboratories over the country, yet there is also a volume of research reported with normal students, with exceptional students, and with non-school-connected adults, such as those persons in industry and the military.

In schools, it would seem that teaching machines and programmed materials can perform a valuable service in remedial work, drill and practice, enrichment, testing, and even in total teaching. Teachers can be freed from repetitive drill routine to provide time for more creative work. Hilgard has said, "By relieving the teacher of much of the routine, the teaching machine and program permit other opportunities greater play. If much of the *science* of teaching is taken over by the machine, the *art* of teaching will again come into its own. . . . (4:21).

Pressey believes that:

Enthusiastic programmers will soon give up trying to replace most textbooks and other core materials with thousands of "frames" viewed seriatim. Drill and rote learning may be so handled. But the larger usefulness of auto-instruction will be found in co-ordination with, not replacement of, other materials and methods. However, the programmers' efforts may bring improvement in these other materials. . . . Devices can be more simple and inexpensive than those now on the market—perhaps simply a 3″ x 5″ chemo-card on which a pupil's mark in the correct space instantly changes color . . . evaluations will show that auto-instruction can be made far more convenient and practical, and more useful, than is now generally recognized.

In a footnote Pressey goes on to say:

The efficiency may be embarrassing! A student may deserve five hours of credit though taught in a class meeting only two hours; he may finish a semester course in the first six weeks, and as an outcome finish a four-year college course in three years, or twelve years of public-school work in ten (16:37)!

At Temple University in Philadelphia, John B. Hough used teaching machines in connection with a course in "Contemporary Secondary School." Dr. Hough's research was so carefully done that he received a Phi Delta Kappa award. Of his findings, he says:

Content covered in three hours of lecture might well be covered in two hours of machine instruction. This would imply reorganization and re-allocation of instructional time where teaching machines are used. In addition, the use of teaching machines would apparently free teachers from many information-giving tasks typically performed by the lecture method, thus allowing time for those aspects of teaching which only human teachers can perform but which heretofore have been impossible because of "content priority."[19]

No serious person believes that teaching machines will replace teachers. Rather, they can take much of the drudgery out of teaching. The teacher is still essential in any school. The machine may very well multiply his effectiveness. The teacher can become a "teaching engineer" concerned with the teaching process and with students. With less routine work, more time for guidance functions is likewise available.

[19] John Hough, "Research Vindication for Teaching Machines," *Phi Delta Kappan,* vol. 43 (March 1962), pp. 240–242.

Organization in schools using teaching machines will be different from conventional organization. Teachers will tend to work more as teams using classrooms of varying sizes. Students may, at certain periods, work in regular classrooms at machines; they may work alone with a machine in a conference room or even in a cubicle. A teacher may or may not be present, and students may be working on the same content or on different content. Work with motion pictures and television will be integrated as needed.

Conventional textbooks will not be eliminated. They will simply take on a changed function. Textbooks will serve for what they are, storehouses of information. The programmed device will assume more of the teaching function.

To Use or Not To Use

Many teachers, both new and experienced, across the country will be using autoinstructional devices in one way or another; many others will not. But every teacher should be aware of their potentialities. The literature is replete with articles hailing these devices with gusto, suggesting that they are as revolutionary educationally as were the printing press, the motion picture, or television. In fact *Time* magazine has said ". . . (programmed learning) promises the first real innovation in teaching since the invention of movable type in the fifteenth century."[20] There will be other articles which view the devices with Oswellian gloom, saying that they are contraptions, a passing fad.

There are still many unresolved problems about teaching machines. Can they really produce more effective learning? Are they challenging for normal students, for gifted students? How can they be fitted into contemporary school organization? Are they valuable in the same degree for all types of learning and all types of content? Will machines used over a period of time become boring to students? Do they really care for individual differences? Are they economical in terms of adaptability and usability? Are they truly educational parameters? What is known of retention from machine learning? Can students make generalizations or transfer from machine learning as well as conventional learning?

These are some of the questions that teachers, administrators, school board members, and parents must face. The foregoing pages have opened the door. The utility of programmed learning will, in the last analysis, be demonstrated chiefly by experimentation. The forward-looking teacher will wish to see for himself what these materials can do for his students. He will experiment with the standard programs now on the market, and he will try his hand at the preparation of programmed lessons, as time

[20] *Time*, March 21, 1961, p. 36.

will allow. Professor Desmond L. Clark says: "Teaching machines are a challenge to education, for they reflect the trend in our society toward greater automation in our daily living" (16:19).

CROSS MEDIA APPROACH TO INSTRUCTION

Teaching is a multiphase business. Each teacher teaches many pupils who have different and varied needs.

Learning materials play an important part in meeting these needs, but they must be selected with a sagacity that includes an understanding of the learner, the materials and what they can do, and the needs of the social order. Printed materials can accomplish certain objectives. The film, filmstrip, record, map, and similar media accomplish still other objectives. The teacher must decide which instructional media best meet the needs of his students. Possibly, it is not a question of an instructional material or a method; it may very well be that several materials and methods should be used in a combination so that they reinforce each other. Each material or method has its own unique characteristics, but if coordinated with other instructional materials, it may assume larger significance.

A social studies teacher may be trying to show the relationship of federal spending to local economy. A field trip to a number of federal projects is taken. A film on the old Civilian Conservation Corps or the more modern Peace Corps is shown. Resource persons are interviewed. The textbook and supplementary pamphlets are read. Maps are consulted. Any one of these media is useful in extending the concept being developed but in combination, each material takes on new significance.

It has been repeatedly remarked that the various instructional materials are not to be used willy-nilly; they must be used with a purpose and they must be wisely selected. The reservoir of instructional materials is large. There has been a great deal of research bearing on each instructional material but much more is needed to show clearly what each can do: the techniques of use, the limitations. Even some of the oldest techniques can still stand researching. Is the verbal statement better made orally or in printed form? What do we know about permanence of learning through the various forms?

Television, to a certain extent, utilizes a number of media. It is a combination of many media, and theoretically, at least, might provide built-in reinforcement of the various learning materials. But, it must be kept in mind, "Audiovisual materials are the means of enriching learning opportunities. It is the teacher who supplies the skill, imagination, and guidance which means the difference between successful and mediocre use of audiovisual materials" (18:460).

ARRANGED ROOM ENVIRONMENT

Each of the three words above is important to effective learning. The first, "arranged," suggests adjustments, a proper order, or a manner best suited to a purpose. "Room," of course, refers to space. "Environment," according to Webster, refers to the surroundings, specifically, "the aggregate of all the external conditions and influences affecting the life and development of an organism," and we might add the behavior of the organism. Winston Churchill in a speech in 1944 made the statement that "We shape our dwellings and afterwards our dwellings shape us." The implication for an educative environment is clear.

In Chapter 11 it is pointed out that there is a distinct relationship between environment and discipline. There is an equally distinct relationship between environment and learning. It is difficult to show that pupil X will learn Y amount in a dismal environment, but Z amount in a cheerful environment. But testimony based on observation and experience validates it. Edgar Dale says school environment can be "educative, miseducative, or mal-educative."[21] The child who starts to school at age 6 has a functional vocabulary of some 2500 words. Where did he get this vocabulary? Was it not from his environment? This vocabulary may be larger or smaller depending upon many things, but surely on the quality of the environment.

In industry, it has been found that job output can be increased by creating a proper environment. Safety can likewise be increased. Restaurant owners are confident that environment in the way of decor, cheerfulness, and esthetics brings customers back, and may even lead to larger orders, with increased cheerfulness in paying the bills.

It is not difficult to accept the thesis that drab, unsightly, or uncomfortable surroundings may underlie tensions and negative behavior. Poor lighting, poor ventilation, and high noise level exact a toll on morale.

The school environmental influence is often more psychological than physical, yet for some unaccountable reason unacceptable physical conditions are more likely to be corrected than unacceptable psychological conditions.

Creating an Environment

An environment favorable to learning can be created in almost any school by an industrious and imaginative teacher. Surroundings conducive to a desire to learn, to cooperate, and to diminish interpersonal problems can be established. An air of mutuality can replace an air of distrust.

21 Edgar Dale, *Newsletter*, May 1961.

Students are captive audiences. They must live in the same room an hour or more each day for every school day of the year. It is not too much to expect that an unusual effort be made to make the classroom an attractive place in which to live. An environment which is stimulating and exciting can bring out the best in the students. It is no wonder that modern school architecture and modern education theory are suffused with the thought of an interesting and challenging atmosphere.

Time dimensions are important. The schools of a past era were often most uninspiring. Compulsive factors dominated education, but times change. Many beginning teachers will be assigned to modern buildings which are attractive in design, flexible in arrangement, and varied and complete in terms of equipment. These buildings are designed so that teaching methods are not frozen by space and physical factors. But other beginning teachers will be located in older school buildings, because buildings are built for a lifetime of thirty, fifty, or more years. Ingenuity becomes imperative for these teachers. They must try to make bare, colorless, and dull surroundings come alive. Chalkboards can be kept neat and uncluttered. If bulletin boards or tack areas are available, they can become the nuclei of display areas which add color and interest. Travel posters will add a modern touch. A book shelf with new and interesting books or a corner may be set aside for some specific use as space exploration, tomorrow's transportation, or understanding of our neighbors in other lands. Book jackets and a judiciously placed map, air age or political, will help update a room. Corrugated colored paperboard may cover unsightly walls or cluttered surfaces. Hangings and displays may be placed almost anywhere.

Good art is not the sole prerogative of the art department. Art is appropriate in any classroom. The mathematics teacher may borrow drawings and designs which correlate highly with his subject. Good reprints of the works of some of the art masters are always in order. But let us not hang two or three tired lithoprints of Galahad or Lafayette on the walls for students to "stare through" from September to June.

Does the community have a museum? Does it have an established and well-supplied audio-visual center? If so, it is the source of many objects, specimens, artifacts, pictures, prints, and facsimiles. Could you use a band of flags representing the nations of Asia, Africa, Latin America, or the United Nations? In addition to the museum, other sources to consider are newspapers, water districts, chambers of commerce, industrial plants, ship companies, and a list that grows too long to enumerate further.

Not all of these efforts are made just for the sake of appearances. Arranging and rearranging the environment of the classroom serves to help initiate new units of study in an interesting manner. Reality can be created, or at least simulated, and a common background experience provided for the students. Environment can help to unify and integrate ideas. Other purposes may also be served depending upon time, place, and conditions. Much of this assumes, and rightly so, that the environment of the classroom will change periodically. Subject emphases change, seasons change, and the environment might appropriately match these or other changes.

Teachers Have Assistance

The teacher need not feel that all of these changes fall solely upon his shoulders, yet he does carry the responsibility. Certainly, students in every class should assist in the rearrangements decided upon. These changes provide unique opportunities for various types of learning, and students have a built-in readiness for making innovations. Junior high school students in particular enjoy this type of activity.

The custodial and entire school staff, too, can be of great assistance. Courtesy pays great dividends in these areas. Custodians can be extremely helpful in making illustrative materials, in finding supplies, and in rearranging furniture, in making displays, in doing minor paint jobs, or in distributing equipment. The ability to win friends and influence people is as important in this connection as in any other area of interpersonal relationships. Finally, keep in mind that the parents and parent-teacher organizations are also interested in the learning environment.

THE QUALITY OF TEACHING MATERIALS

The older schools tended to rely heavily, but certainly not exclusively, on printed, text-type instructional materials Mark Hopkins used more than a log to make education meaningful. He purchased a new device, a model of a man, which cost him $600, and this he used in speeches and in teaching throughout western Massachusetts. Drama and art forms played a significant part in Greek and Roman education. Cicero, Seneca, and Quintilian advocated visual forms and the latter developed the now commonplace alphabet block. Marionettes, frescoes, and stained glass windows contributed their part to the education of the Middle Ages. Field trips and object teaching were stressed by almost every reform-teacher of the realism period. Maps were engraved for inclusion in books as early as 1478. Charts and pictures are often credited to Comenius, and such educators as Rousseau, Pestalozzi, and Froebel gave substantial substance to what might be called the modern audio-visual method.

Compromise between the Ideal and the Possible

Teaching materials, whether books or nontext types, are not perfect, but the quality is rising. Textbooks have evolved from the rustic hornbook to the sophisticated and attractive volumes of today. Educational motion pictures have grown from the dull, silent, slow-moving inflammable celluloids of the twenties to the noninflammable, sound-color films of today. Other materials have improved in like manner. And as technology strides forward, the equipment used to present these materials improves.

Textbooks are usually selected by a committee of classroom teachers, curriculum specialists, and possibly administrators. Textbook committees examine and evaluate many books before adoptions are made of basic texts, supplementary texts, and workbooks. Films and other nonprinted instructional materials are usually selected in similar manner.

Often the selection is acknowledgedly not the ideal, but it is the best available at the time. It is hoped that a producer, a publisher, or an author will improve on what is currently available, but students cannot wait. They must have learning materials, so a compromise is made, provided, of course, there is nothing harmful or misleading in the material.

Librarians and audio-visual directors should be broadly trained people in matters of curriculum and instructional methodology, as well as in their areas of specialization. They should, therefore, assist in the selection of all instructional materials.

Continued research of instructional materials and their use is needed. Materials used in today's schools are good, but they can be better. There are still books as well as films which are dull, repetitive, inartistic, generalizing, and incomplete. Possibly no single instrument is adequate in itself. The cross-media approach helps correct this shortcoming. A symphony of instructional materials produces more acceptable results than a single instrument.

This chapter has completed the discussion of devices including values and uses. These newer media are not found in all schools, but beginning teachers cannot afford to be uninformed about them for the chances are that sooner or later every teacher will be using these media in some form.

Selected Readings

1. *And TV, Too!* Washington, D.C.: Department of Audiovisual Instruction and Department of Classroom Teachers, National Education Association, 1961.
2. Cram, David, *Explaining Teaching Machines and Programming.* San Francisco: Fearon Publishers, 1961.
3. Finn, James D., and Donald G. Perrin, *Teaching Machines and Programmed Learning, 1962: A Survey of the Industry,* Occasional Paper No. 3, A Report

Prepared for the Technological Development Project of the National Education Association. Washington, D.C.: National Education Association.

4. Hilgard, Ernest L., "What Support from the Psychology of Learning?" *NEA Journal*, vol. 50 (November 1961), pp. 20–21.

5. Johnson, Marjorie C., and Catherine C. Seerley, *Foreign Language Laboratories in Schools and Colleges*, Bulletin 1959, No. 3. Washington, D.C.: U.S. Department of Health, Education, and Welfare, Office of Education, 1959.

6. Klaus, David J., "The Art of Auto-Instructional Programming." *AV Communication Review*, vol. 9 (March–April 1961), pp. 130–142.

7. Landers, Bertha, *A Foreign Language Audio-Visual Guide*. Los Angeles: Landers Associates, 1961.

8. Legislative Research Commission, *Educational Television for Kentucky*, Research Report No. 3, 1961. Frankfort, Ky.: Commonwealth of Kentucky, 1961.

9. Lumsdaine, A. A., and Robert Glaser, eds., *Teaching Machines and Programmed Learning: A Source Book*. Washington, D.C.: Department of Audio-Visual Instruction, National Education Association, 1960.

10. *New Teaching Media for the American Classroom*. Stanford, Calif.: The Institute for Communication Research, 1960.

11. *Programs, '62: A Guide to Programed Instructional Materials Available to Educators by September 1962*, The Center for Programed Instruction. Washington, D.C.: Government Printing Office, 1962.

12. Rigney, Joseph W., and Edward B. Fry, "Current Teaching-Machine Programs and Programmed Techniques," *AV Communication Review*, Supplement No. 3, vol. 9 (May–June 1961), pp. 1–122.

13. Siepman, Charles A., *TV and Our Social Crisis*. New York: Dodd, Mead & Company, 1958.

14. Stolurow, Lawrence M., *Teaching by Machine*, Cooperative Research Monograph, No. 6. Washington, D.C.: Department of Health, Education, and Welfare, Office of Education, 1961.

15. *Teaching by Television*, 2d ed., New York: The Ford Foundation and The Fund for the Advancement of Education, 1961.

16. "Teaching Machines and Language Laboratories," *Theory Into Practice*, vol. 1. (February 1962), Ohio State University, pp. 1–60.

17. Trump, J. Lloyd, *New Horizons to Quality Education: The Secondary School of Tomorrow*, Bulletin. Washington, D.C.: National Association of Secondary School Principals. Also, J. Lloyd Trump and Dorsey Baynham, *Guide to Better Schools*. Chicago: Rand McNally & Company, 1961.

18. Wittich, Walter A., and Chorles F. Schuller, *Audiovisual Materials: Their Nature and Use*, 3d ed. New York: Harper & Row, Publishers, 1962.

Selected Audio-Visual Materials

A. *An Example of a Teaching Machine Program*, 62-frame filmstrip, color: Basic: 1960. An example is given of an actual self-instructional teaching machine program.

B. *The Second Classroom*, 30 min., b & w: National Education Association, 1961. The advantages and contributions of educational television to teaching and learning are shown.

C. *Teaching by Television*, 51-frame filmstrip, color: Basic, 1957. Research is summarized on what is known about teaching by TV in relation to what TV teaching can do, how to use TV in the classroom, and how to teach over TV.

D. *Teaching Machines,* 62-frame filmstrip, color: Basic, 1960. The basic facts for understanding teaching machines and their use in instruction are presented in simplified form.

E. *Teaching Machines and Programmed Learning,* 30 min., b & w: National Education Association, 1961. This film initiates the educator into the field of mechanized learning and offers a first lesson in teaching machines and programmed learning.

PART FOUR

Providing
Classroom Control

CHAPTER 11

Building group morale

There, in his noisy mansion, skilled to rule,
The village master taught his little school.—*Oliver Goldsmith*

THE IMPORTANCE OF GOOD DISCIPLINE

"No single problem is such a challenge and causes so much teacher heartache, frustration, and failure as the problem of discipline" (8:1). Beginning teachers especially view the problem of discipline with apprehension because they realize that their success or failure at the outset will depend largely on their ability to maintain an effective learning environment in the classroom. Administrators are concerned about the ability of new teachers to control their classes because they realize that unless an orderly classroom atmosphere is achieved, very little learning is likely to occur and school problems will be multiplied. Students themselves lose respect for teachers who are unable to maintain good discipline.

It has often been said that good discipline is synonymous with good teaching. Certainly the teacher who is able to keep his students vitally interested and personally involved in constructive learning activities is likely to have few, if any, disciplinary problems.

Wherever large numbers of boys and girls are brought together to be educated, some form of grouping becomes necessary. Each group constitutes a society of its own. As in any other social group, some degree of law and order has to be maintained or the group disintegrates. The teacher, as instructional leader in the classroom, has a twofold responsibility: to help each student develop his abilities to the maximum and to promote cooperative group living.

DISCIPLINE: A COMPLEX PROBLEM

The subject of *discipline* may be a source of confusion to both teacher and parent. The term itself is objectionable to some people because it carries with it an unpleasant connotation. However, since it is a word in common usage and one which seems to have no adequate synonym, the term *discipline* must continue to be used.

At the outset, there is confusion over definition, for Oliva discovered at least twenty-five different meanings of the word "discipline" (8:5–6). For instance, discipline may be defined as self-control, external control, obedience to authority, the degree of order established in a class, a rigorous course of study, a device used to maintain order, or as a synonym for punishment. Common dictionary definitions of "discipline" include such meanings as instruction to insure proper conduct, orderly conduct, subjection to rules of conduct, a system of rules regulating conduct, and punishment. *The Dictionary of Education* incorporates such additional concepts as the subordination of immediate impulses for ultimate ideals or purposes and persistent self-direction in the face of difficulty.[1] Sheviakov and Redl believe that teachers ordinarily think of discipline in three different ways: the degree of order established in a group, the means by which order is achieved, and punishment (10:2–3).

As far as the school is concerned, the present tendency is to think of discipline problems largely in terms of "the thoughtless and irresponsible acts of young people who are not maladjusted but are just uneducated and unsocialized."[2] This point of view will serve as a basis for much of the later discussion of techniques for good classroom management and control. However, some consideration must be given to boys and girls with serious behavior problems, for a few are found in the classroom and must be given assistance with their problems.

Another problem in dealing with the concept of discipline is the lack of research on the subject. This is apparently true for two reasons: difficulties in delimiting the concept and managing so many variables (2:381). There is, nevertheless, a great deal of good advice to be found in the literature on the subject. Years of accumulated, practical experience of teachers and administrators provide a rich source of helpful suggestions to the beginning teacher. Some see little hope for helping new teachers develop skill in classroom management and control, maintaining that no two situations are identical. Although there is a certain element of truth in this contention, many types of discipline problems have been recurring with monotonous regularity ever since boys and girls began going to school. Furthermore, it has been found that certain practices usually work

---

[1] Carter V. Good, *Dictionary of Education.* New York: McGraw-Hill Book Company, Inc., 1959, p. 176.

[2] Asahel, D. Woodruff, "Discipline," *Encyclopedia of Educational Research*, 3d ed., Chester W. Harris, ed. New York: The Macmillan Company, 1960, p. 382. Used by permission of Macmillan.

while others frequently do not. The teacher who has listened to the teaching of others before entering the classroom has some knowledge of workable procedures in dealing with many situations which he is almost sure to encounter. A teacher who is not so equipped is much more susceptible to the commitment of stupid, sometimes fatal, mistakes in discipline.

Historically, the concept of school discipline has undergone a revolution in our society. In colonial times, discipline was severe with an emphasis on unquestioned obedience to authority and vindictive punishment. New knowledge of the forces of nature and the dynamics of personality, plus acceptance of a more humanitarian philosophy, have brought about a remarkable transition in disciplinary theory and practice. Unreasonable punishment eventually gave way to attempts to reform the offender, later to the prevention of misbehavior, and finally to stress on self-control. The modern concept of discipline has focused on recognition of individual differences in behavior, as well as fluctuations in behavior of each individual. Literature on the problem frequently reflects the view that individuals often need help in coping with the problems of the world around them.[3] Teachers have always realized the importance of helping students with their school subjects. What they have not always clearly recognized is the fact that students also need help with their personal and social development. The development of a superb intellect in a weak and sickly physical body, governed by the values of a moral moron, can only result in personal failure for the individual concerned and in waste to society. As the pendulum has swung from one extreme to another, from authoritarian control to self-control, there is a counter trend today which reflects the belief that both home and school have gone too far in the direction of permissiveness.

The present-day note in discipline is reflected from a number of sources. An editorial in the December 1959 issue of the *Phi Delta Kappan* cites a case of a 12-year-old boy who killed his brother and maintained, "It wasn't my fault." The editor then makes the observation that the boy is right "if we accept the orthodox sociological thesis that practically everyone and everything are responsible for the actions of the delinquent except the delinquent himself." The editor further states that

There are haunting and crippling paradoxes in both the humanitarian admonition—"to understand all is to forgive all"—and the Freudian theory—"man is largely the creature of his subconscious drives."[4]

An even more extreme reflection of this anomalous position is found in

---

[3] *Ibid.*, p. 383.
[4] Stanley Elam, "Editorial on Responsibilities, Revolutions, and Reservations," *Phi Delta Kappan*, vol. 41 (December 1959), p. 89.

the words of a senior judge in New York who said, "The philosophy of responsibility has been replaced by the philosophy of excuse."

In somewhat the same vein, Harold Taylor attacks the problem from the standpoint of the home. He points out that parents have made such a genuine effort to *understand* their children, to stake "everything on a warm and affectionate relationship" with their children, that youth have become independent and self-sufficient in a quasi-adult society of their own. As a result, the strongest force parents are able to exert is to produce feelings of guilt in their children. Consequently, "there is no longer a clear-cut authority-freedom issue for the adolescent, but instead there are ambivalent feelings of obligation, responsibility, and guilt."[5]

As the discipline pendulum swings to and fro, it will be most unfortunate if our society resorts to either extreme of authoritarian control or laissez-faire practices.

That the elders of a given society have always been inclined to feel that children and youth were degenerating is well known. While it is true that juvenile delinquency has apparently been increasing since World War II, it is still difficult to determine whether or not youth are worse than they used to be. Today, more publicity, more complete records, and more efficient apprehension of delinquents may very well distort a true picture of the situation. As far as the classroom is concerned, delinquents constitute less than 1 percent of the population.[6]

The authors take the position that an *understanding* of the nature of boys and girls—their needs, problems, aspirations, abilities, and backgrounds—is the most important factor in effective classroom management and control. In achievement of the twofold goals of American education, maximum development of the individual and the preservation of group welfare, the teacher is responsible for providing the leadership necessary to achieve both.

DILEMMAS OF DISCIPLINE

Probably nothing is more confusing about discipline to the new teacher than the conflicting points of view and discrepancies between theory and practice that he so often encounters. The classroom teacher must understand these paradoxes in discipline, learn to live with them, and formulate his own philosophy of discipline.

One of the common areas of conflict is found between the so-called

[5] Harold Taylor, "The Understood Child," *Saturday Review*, vol. 44 (May 20, 1961), pp. 47–49, 66.

[6] National Education Association, "Ten Criticisms of Public Education," *Research Bulletin*, vol. 35 (December 1957), p. 155.

This picture shows a so-called "scrambled book," which is highly unconventional. The reader does not read page by page; he reads successive bands or "frames." Note the three gray and three white bands on each page. These bands are followed in succession throughout the book. The top gray bands run the length of the book and are completed before the reader turns to the top white bands. Each band asks a question or makes a statement. The student decides on the correct answer, writes it, and then turns to the next frame to check his answer. The correct answer is printed at the left of the succeeding frame. Each frame is limited and the student can usually make a correct response. If so, he goes on to the next statement; if not, he returns to the preceding frame and tries to figure out why he was wrong. Incorrect answers are corrected immediately. Correct responses "reinforce" other responses to such an extent that learning is said to be faster, easier, and surer. [*Courtesy Royal Crooks, Seattle (Wash.) Public Schools.*]

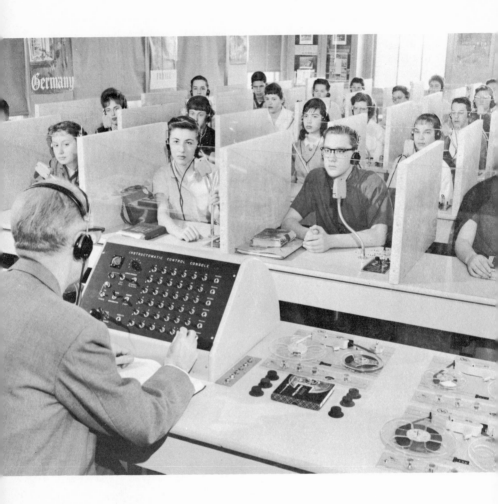

A language laboratory may be a simple arrangement of a tape recorder and headsets, or it may be a room with specially designed booths fitted out with electronic equipment, as shown here. Each student has his individual microphone for response to the lesson. The teacher sits at a console where he has complete control of the group. He speaks or plays prerecorded tapes, or he listens to the responses of the students. At his side are two recorders. He may communicate with one student, several students, or the entire class. Thus, mass instruction has been individualized. [*Courtesy Philip Lewis and the Chicago (Ill.) Public Schools.*]

In this period of scarcity of well-prepared, competent teachers, especially teachers of science, one effective, challenging teacher who uses television with all its rich complement of instructional materials and devices can reach large classes of students. Shown here is a ninth-grade class in physical science receiving instruction over television. There is evidence of note taking and of reasonable interest in the presentation on the part of most students. However, teaching by television raises many problems, and its results must be evaluated carefully. [*Courtesy Rex E. Benson and Sedgefield Junior High School, Charlotte (N. C.).*]

Across the United States, many high schools are experimenting with various types of class organization and methods of instruction. This experimental classroom in the Evanston Township (Ill.) High School offers many challenges. Numerous curricular experiences can be carried on in large classes. But the teacher must meet the interests of individual students in such a large group. In order to handle such classes successfully, teachers need experience and professional maturity. [*Perkins & Will, Architects-Engineers.*]

"guidance" point of view and the "teaching" point of view. It has been known for some time that mental hygienists and guidance specialists consider withdrawal type of behavior most serious whereas classroom teachers are most concerned with aggressive types of behavior. Guidance workers have devoted more of their attention to underlying causes of misbehavior and to individual adjustment problems. On the other hand, the classroom teacher has had to take large assortments of individuals with varied interests, backgrounds, and abilities and attempt to weld them into cohesive groups in pursuit of common goals. No doubt, differences in viewpoints between full-time counselors and classroom teachers are largely due to *differences in situations.* Teachers have been forced through necessity to do that which is expedient and to treat surface behavior rather than search for underlying causes. The counselor who works with students on an individual, face-to-face relationship basis has quite a different situation from that of the classroom teacher who is always working with groups.

Another problem which has created confusion about discipline is one of a semantic nature. As one writer has stated, "We should stop equating permissiveness (absence of discipline) with democratic discipline, and realistic adult control and guidance with authoritarianism." In the same article, the author of the above statement points out a number of "distortions of democratic discipline," such as the notion that democratic discipline implies freedom from external restraints or that teachers may abdicate responsibility for making final decisions.[7]

Another dilemma of discipline arises from a conflict of *needs.* Which shall have priority, the needs of the individual or the needs of the group? Certainly the individual must have freedom to develop self-control, to achieve maturity as a unique person who is able to think for himself. On the other hand, unless each one learns to respect the rights of others and to conform to certain rules of group living or social control, no stable society, either adolescent or adult, can ever be achieved.

Another paradox in discipline stems from disagreement over *techniques.* Should the teacher stress directive or nondirective control? Is direct modification of behavior through external control better than permitting students much freedom to experiment or learn by trial and error? Is it better for the teacher to correct surface behavior, to demand immediate conformity in the interest of group welfare, or to delay action while he seeks more evidence of causes and permits the offender to suffer the natural consequences of his own acts? Somewhere between the extremes of imposed discipline and permissive control is a sensible middle ground which is not always easy to determine. Since classroom teaching is essen-

[7] David P. Ausubel, "A New Look at Classroom Discipline," *Phi Delta Kappan,* vol. 43 (October 1961), pp. 25–30.

tially a group operation, the authors of this text believe that group welfare should receive first consideration.

Conflicting *philosophies* constitute a major source of confusion in discipline. The cultural conflict between the philosophy of excuse and of responsibility has already been discussed. Likewise, the irreconcilable positions of authoritarianism and extreme permissiveness have been suggested. Social philosophy also has a bearing on school discipline. The widening rift between liberals and conservatives in this country and the worldwide cold war between democracy and communism are conducive to a climate of fear, suspicion, and insecurity. The school is inevitably affected. Censorship of books, the harsher discipline, more and more legislative prescription of school programs, and the increasing peril of dealing with controversial issues reflect the tenor of the early 1960s. With respect to students in school, they face a very practical problem of making adjustments to the conflicting philosophies and practices encountered from class to class within the same school. As far as the teaching profession itself is concerned, not only is there widespread disagreement over theory and practice in discipline, but there are also sharp discrepancies between stated beliefs and actual classroom procedures. Perhaps some teachers are inclined to talk a better line than they are willing to follow.

The problem of conflicting *values* has already been mentioned. To complicate matters, there is always the problem of reconciling the middle-class values of teachers with the values of students who come from lower-class homes. Furthermore, the widening gap between adult values and those of an adolescent subculture is apparently becoming more pronounced.

The last area of confusion in discipline to be discussed is that relating to the *stage of development* of the student. Not only must teacher expectations be geared to the level of maturity of the learner, but also appropriate procedures must be used in each case. New teachers, especially, need to avoid several false assumptions: that high school students are as mature as college students, that all students at a given grade level have achieved the same level of maturity, or that all students without exception are capable of achieving complete self-direction. Once these realities are recognized, then the teacher has to ascertain ways to adapt control procedures to all of the variations in maturity level with which he must cope.

SOURCES OF DISCIPLINE PROBLEMS

The number and kinds of behavior problems with which the teacher of adolescents has to contend are legion. Even though the classroom teacher often has to deal with problems on the basis of expediency rather than on the basis of case studies or analysis of underlying causes, there is still an advantage in knowing why boys and girls behave as they do. No one would deny that it is far better to remove causes of misbehavior than merely to treat symptoms. Yet detection of basic causes of behavior problems is no easy matter, for it is now recognized that causes of any particular type of misbehavior may stem from many and varied sources. As each student seeks to develop self-direction, he is always influenced by three kinds of environment: physical, cultural, and interpersonal relationships.[8] Oliva has indentified the following sources of behavior problems: the student himself, the student's peer group, the teacher and the school, the home and community, and the larger social order (8:19–37). In the discussion that follows, further analysis will be made of the factors which influence behavior. In addition, preventive measures will be indicated.

Physical Environment

The physical environment of the school is an important factor in influencing the behavior of boys and girls. Dingy, crowded, unattractive school buildings are conducive to confusion and disorder. On the other hand, a physical environment that is comfortable, attractive, and orderly is likely to bring out the best in student behavior. Maintenance of proper temperature, ventilation, and lighting in the classroom is important not only from the standpoint of good discipline but also in protecting the physical health of students. Some older classrooms which are poorly arranged and drably decorated pose the problem of attractiveness. However, a teacher can, with the help of his students, brighten the dullest room with flower arrangements, attractive bulletin boards, and centers of interests (science corner, exhibits, and a book nook). In addition to maintaining a comfortable, attractive, tidy classroom, the teacher must by all means provide an orderly working atmosphere in which learning can take place effectively. More will be said about this later under the subject of class organization and management.

Cultural Sources of Discipline Problems

Of all the factors influencing student behavior, the cultural influence is probably the most pervasive and, at the same time, the most difficult to evaluate.

The shift from agrarian to industrial society has brought about changes in cultural patterns with which our social institutions have been unable to cope. The most significant change resulting from the industrial age has been the dislocation of *family life*. The self-sufficient family of the past has been replaced by a modern version which has lost more and more of its former functions to other social agencies. Modern industry has

[8] Woodruff, *op. cit.*, p. 382.

replaced the family as the center of economic life. Commercial entertainment has taken recreation out of the home. Schools have absorbed many educational functions which formerly belonged to the family. The authoritarian role of the father has all but disappeared. With both parents frequently away from home, children are left to their own devices (sometimes referred to as "door-key kids"[9]) or in the care of friends and relatives.

Needless to say, all of these changes in the role of the family have created problems in the education of youth. Lacking the guidance and support of their parents and being unable to identify themselves with the economic life of an industrial society, adolescents are often confused and even resentful. Adult reaction to these bewildered youth is often one of disapproval, or even fear.[10, 11] The problem of juvenile delinquency is not confined to American culture, however, for England has her "Teddy boys"; the Soviet Union, the *stylyagi*; and Australia, the "bodgies" and "widgies."[12]

Adolescents have developed a number of defenses against the insecurities engendered by a society they feel has neglected them. First of all, adolescents seek refuge within their own peer group, which has become more and more the source of their values.[13] The problem for adults, especially parents and teachers, is obvious. The values of adult society and of teen-age peer culture are frequently in conflict, and youth tend to show less respect for teachers and the learning they represent. Another defense against insecurity used by adolescents is resentment. Such resentment may be against school, law, or military conscription, for example, or it may be against no specific target but "resentment that is going nowhere."[14] Furthermore, parents and teachers find the resentment difficult to tolerate because it is expressed fearlessly, without a sense of guilt. A final defense against insecurity is in the realm of "impulse expression." "Young people increasingly are gratifying impulses in an unconditional manner, and this acts to threaten adult values more than the market will bear."[15]

[9] Harold J. McNally, "What Shall We Teach—and How?" *The National Elementary Principal,* May 1957, pp. 6–11.
[10] Donald McNassor, "The Changing Character of Adolescents," *California Journal of Secondary Education,* vol. 31 (March 1956), pp. 128–133.
[11] George Z. F. Bereday, Brian Holmes, and Joseph A. Lauwerys, "Editors' Introduction," *The Secondary School Curriculum: the Yearbook of Education, 1958.* London: Evans Brothers, Limited, 1958.
[12] *Ibid.,* p. 6.
[13] Robert Hess, "The Adolescent: His Society," *Review of Educational Research,* vol. 24 (February 1960), p. 10.
[14] McNassor, *op. cit.,* pp. 129–131.
[15] *Ibid.,* p. 131.

Adaptation to the expectations of adult society is made especially different for some youth in our culture. The roots of a *migrant* population are shallow and engulfed by the impersonal life of big cities. Sorokin has referred to our civilization as "a cut-flower civilization." Cut off from close circles of relatives and friends, both parents and their children lose the supporting and stabilizing influence of such intimate relationships. These migrants of the twentieth century never feel that they quite belong to any community or its institutions. There is no loneliness greater than that experienced by a stranger on a crowded city street or in the halls of a big school. What is the role of the school in dealing with these newcomers, some of whom enter the school almost every week of the year? Every teacher has a responsibility to make a special effort to help them get acquainted, feel at home, and become a part of the group. Making use of the special contributions which new students may be able to bring to the class, arranging for a student to orient each one to the work of the class, and showing personal friendliness and interest in their welfare are some of the things teachers can do to help the strangers in their classrooms.

Conflicting values between home and school have already been suggested as a source of discipline problems. The teacher, who usually subscribes to the values of the middle class, may find it difficult to understand, or even tolerate, the behavior of other social groups. Dealing with pampered, overprotected, upper-class children on the one hand and uncouth, neglected, lower-class children on the other is a real challenge for the teacher. He has to become as adaptive as the chameleon. Such actions as fighting, swearing, and smoking may be considered normal behavior in lower-class families but cannot be tolerated by teachers. Thus an inevitable conflict arises between the home and the school with the adolescent caught in the middle. Only by a slow, patient process can youth be educated to accept values of a society that may be quite different from their own.

The problem of improving the behavior of youth becomes more complex due to the fact that their world appears to be in a perpetual state of crisis. International tensions and the prospect of atomic warfare, probable interruption of normal life by military service, and inadequate economic opportunities are but a few of the social problems which create anxiety on the part of youth today.

There is evidence that the common core of accepted values in American culture has been shrinking. When adults are often confused about what is acceptable or unacceptable behavior, there is little wonder that young people are likewise confused. As boys and girls read about political scandals, game fixing by athletic heroes, sharp business practices, and corruption in high places, they no doubt find it difficult to reconcile such actions with the high ideals promulgated by the school.

In his relationship with teachers and other adults, the fact that he is treated with fairness and understanding is most important to the adolescent. Despite commitment to the principle of equality of educational opportunity, there is abundant evidence that society has fallen short of attaining its ideal. The extent of discrimination against minority groups is too well known to require elaboration here. That the school may discriminate against children of lower-class families is probably not always so clearly recognized.[16] However, every decade marks definite steps forward in meeting the needs of the underprivileged and those who have been subject to discrimination.

Dealing with Culturally Induced Problems

What can the teacher do about the anxieties and resentments created by the ills of our society? Obviously, the problem is not one for which the school alone is responsible. The home and the total community have a most significant role to play. Despite the magnitude of the problem, however, every teacher can do something to help young people satisfy their needs and make adjustments to the demands of contemporary society.

While no teacher can remove the undesirable cultural conditions surrounding some children and youth, he can provide a happy school environment, an island of security in a sea of trouble.

As far as the school as a whole is concerned, a number of things can be done to reconcile the needs and aspirations of youth with the demands of adult society. Orientation to military service, to the vocations, to school and community life, and to the critical problems of our day are necessities in the education of boys and girls. Students should be able to examine controversial issues and their own prejudices in the light of available facts and differing points of view. They must, at the same time, develop the social attributes of good manners and cooperative relationships.

Student Needs in Relation to Discipline Problems

Failure to achieve satisfaction of basic needs is a frequent source of rebellion and misbehavior on the part of adolescents. Teachers have to be constantly aware of these needs in order to help students satisfy them in acceptable ways. A primary need of everyone, child and adult, is for *affection*. The warped personality resulting from rejection by the home is almost sure to become a problem in school. Another basic human need is for *security*. Failure, lack of acceptance, and subjection to controls that are too permissive or arbitrarily repressive undermine the security of

[16] August Hollingshead, *Elmtown's Youth*. New York: John Wiley & Sons, Inc., 1949.

adolescents in their efforts to achieve maturity. *Success* is another basic need. Students who fail in school are fit subjects for discipline cases. Nothing fails like failure. Schoolwork must be within the capacity of slow learners, yet difficult enough to challenge gifted students. Classroom procedures must also be adapted to the ability and maturity levels of students.

Acceptance and recognition are necessary ingredients in the achievement of maturity. Probably nothing is more important to the adolescent than acceptance by his peers. To be one of the crowd sometimes becomes almost an obsession. Equally important, although not always so obvious, is the need for acceptance by adults, especially parents and teachers. Other qualities which are strongly noticeable in boys and girls in their teens are *curiosity, hero worship,* and a *venturesome spirit.* The wise teacher can use all of the needs of youth to an advantage. Boys and girls, especially of junior high school age, need *freedom of movement.* When they are imprisoned in their seats too long, pent up energy eventually dissipates itself in disorder (8:21–24). The foregoing list of adolescent needs is by no means complete, but it does suggest some very basic ones which cannot be ignored.

DISCIPLINE PROBLEMS ORIGINATING IN SCHOOL

Poor home and community environment, the ills of our society, and interpersonal relationships of youth are sources of discipline problems which teachers may be able to do little or nothing about. But school personnel can do something about correcting school-induced problems of misbehavior. What are some of the causes of misbehavior which originate within the school itself?

Whenever a teacher has a class that is unresponsive and bored, seeking its satisfactions in rowdy behavior or listless daydreaming, he has a right to be concerned. In seeking the source of the trouble, he may find it originates with the curriculum. Unfortunately, as the formal school program is now organized, it fails to meet the needs of many boys and girls who represent such great diversity in interests, abilities, and backgrounds. Traditionally, the secondary school curriculum has been academic and bookish. Learning has been based on the accumulated heritage of mankind as recorded in books with a singular neglect of the experiences and problems of everyday living.

A half century ago, when only a selected segment of the population (largely academic in character) of secondary school age attended school, the problem of student adjustment to the curriculum was not so acute as it is today. Now, with virtually all boys and girls between the ages of 14 and 17 in school, a strictly academic program falls far short of meeting the personal and social needs of many students, to say nothing of failure in meeting the needs of a society experiencing the most rapid socioeconomic changes in history.

There is no simple solution to the problem. In some cases, a complete overhauling of the content of certain subjects is long overdue. Perhaps in some cases, specific subjects need to be eliminated entirely. Tradition is apparently a potent factor in the retention of outmoded, nonfunctional items in the school program. Where changes have been made in existing courses, sometimes the most important goal of education has been neglected: that is, improved behavior of boys and girls. Where there is no immediate relief from the dissatisfaction of students with the curriculum, the teacher will need to exercise the utmost imagination and ingenuity to interest some students in the work to be done. Not only the curriculum, but also the methods used by the teacher are important. Monotonous routines and inappropriate instructional procedures soon lead to behavior problems.

Administration plays a critical role in the achievement of satisfactory school discipline. Administrators expect teachers to take care of their own control problems within the classroom. This is a reasonable expectation, but when a teacher encounters a problem with which he is unable to cope, he is entitled to the full backing and support of the administration. Whenever a principal fails to give teachers the help they deserve, control problems multiply and school morale deteriorates rapidly.

School Policies and Regulations

Another possible source of discipline problems arising within the school is the policies and regulations which govern achievement and behavior of its students. The conflict that often arises between home and school because of different values has already been indicated. Regulations, as well as their means of enforcement, which are either too severe or too lax may also lead to control problems. Administrators who frequently resort to physical punishment, especially for older children, soon reap a harvest of rebellion and aggressive behavior. When rules that are just and reasonable have been made, they must be enforced fairly and consistently. Enforcement of school regulations—such as regular attendance, proper conduct in halls and on the playground, and respect for public property—is the responsibility of all school personnel, not just administrators. Promotional policies which encourage just "getting by" on the one hand or result in a high incidence of failure on the other are another potential source of discipline problems. Excessive stress on examinations or competition for school marks creates not only a climate which is conducive to behavior problems but also may be a threat to the mental health of many students as well.

Personnel Relationships

How well teachers are able to work in harmony with fellow teachers, administrators, parents, and students is a vital factor in the promotion of desirable student behavior. When faculties are split into hostile, competing camps, students are forced to develop divided loyalties. They become confused and insecure. If teachers and administrators lack confidence in and respect for one another, students lose confidence in the leadership of the adults who are supposedly helping them achieve maturity. On the other hand, when the personnel of a school work together in harmony, student respect for faculty leadership, strong school spirit, and a high level of achievement in both citizenship and scholarship are encouraged.

Another type of relationship which needs to be strengthened, especially at the secondary school level, is that between teachers and parents. The improvement of student behavior is most likely to occur when parents and teachers are working together as a team. Very often students who are out of step with school policies and practices will strengthen their position by taking advantage of a cleavage between parents and teachers. The student who has to choose between loyalty to his teachers and his parents is in an unenviable position. Of course, the most important interpersonal relationships for teachers are those which exist between them and their students. Further discussion of this point will be taken up later in this chapter.

Physical Factors Related to Discipline

It has already been indicated that a clean, attractive, and comfortable physical environment is conducive to good discipline. Dingy, crowded, and unattractive buildings and classrooms breed vandalism, rowdiness, and discourteous behavior. Certainly the physical atmosphere of a school is within the power of teachers, administrators, and school board members to improve.

HOW TEACHERS AFFECT STUDENT BEHAVIOR

Of all the influences in a school which provoke misbehavior or stimulate good behavior on the part of students, the most pervasive influence is that of the teachers. Personality, character, attitudes, and observable actions are all factors that determine the effectiveness of teacher relationships, both with students and with colleagues. Some persons attract; others

repel. Since successful teaching depends so much on satisfactory interpersonal relationships, it behooves all teachers to cultivate those personal traits which attract others. It is now generally agreed that personality can be changed.

Personality of the Teacher

Is there such a thing as a teaching personality? Some teachers exhibit
vivacity; they sparkle. Others present a demeanor of gravity and stability;
they inspire confidence. Still others may demonstrate qualities of kindness, sympathy, and understanding; they radiate warmth. All of these
may be good teachers. In developing his personality, the teacher must
first of all capitalize on his own assets and not attempt to become a poor
facsimile of someone else.

First impressions are not always lasting ones, but they are important.
Physical attractiveness, cleanliness, and good manners are important
factors in the creation of a good first impression. However, in order to
wear well, the teacher must be able to demonstrate consistently exemplary
professional attitudes and evidence of strength of character. More will
be said about this later in the chapter.

Voice quality is an important consideration in teaching. Unfortunately,
most teachers do not know how their own voices sound to others. It is
surprising how often supervisors of teachers rate voice as "unsatisfactory."
As a first step to improvement, a person may listen to a tape recording of
his own voice. The experience may prove to be disconcerting, but helpful.

A well-integrated personality is mandatory for successful teaching. Not
only is a well-adjusted personality important in the maintenance of
harmonious relationships with others, but it is a necessary condition for
safeguarding one's own mental health. Teaching is basically a problem of
human engineering. It is especially important for the teacher to accept
himself (in his role as a teacher) and others. In no other profession is
the commandment, "Love thy neighbor as thyself," more relevant.
Furthermore, the well-adjusted person is able to face reality, to accept
constructive criticism without resentment, to admit failure without ra-
tionalizing, and to recognize the need for continuous self-improvement
(3:342–346).

A professor of psychiatry made an observation that is especially relevant
for teachers:

It has been the assumption of education that learning would make men wise,
mature, and creative. It is my unhappy conviction that learning alone achieves
none of these goals, but more frequently is a mask for immaturity, neurosis,
and a lack of wisdom.[17]

[17] Lawrence S. Kubie, "Are We Educating for Maturity?" *NEA Journal*, vol. 48
(January 1959), pp. 58–63.

In helping adolescents achieve the difficult task of growing up, the teacher must first of all be a mature person himself.

Teacher Attitudes

The prevailing attitudes a teacher has toward his job, his colleagues, and his students have a direct bearing on student behavior. As a member of an honored profession, the teacher should exhibit pride in that fact and continuously strive to be a credit to his profession. Many stories have been related about teachers who try to hide their occupational identity away from home or who apologetically identify themselves by saying, "I am just a teacher." If that is the way teachers feel about their profession, they cannot expect to command much respect for it, either from adults or youth. The importance of cooperative attitudes and harmonious relationships within the profession has already been indicated earlier in this chapter.

Although the attitudes a teacher has toward his profession and his colleagues may not have the most significant bearing on classroom control, his attitudes toward his students will ultimately determine his success or failure in improving student behavior. The following classroom situations illustrate the point.

One new teacher whose relationships with his students were deteriorating rapidly finally admitted that he disliked his students. Another teacher made this remark to a student teacher who asked permission to observe his class, "I don't know why you came to visit me. I hate kids." However, upon being invited to remain, the student teacher did observe the class. A report on the observation later revealed the fact that much of the class hour was spent in a series of unpleasant incidents in which the teacher was pitted against the students. Still another teacher demonstrated a mistaken attitude toward his relationships with students when he remarked, "It's the best class I have because the kids are afraid of me."

Students usually try to live up to a teacher's expectations. If a teacher expects the worst of his students, they seldom disappoint him. On the other hand, if he believes in them and shows confidence in their ability to become good citizens, students usually justify their teacher's faith in them.

It is unfortunate that a few persons enter teaching who only bring reproach on the profession. To illustrate the point, caricatures of some of these types follow (with no intention of discrediting the many good teachers who teach the subjects that are used in the illustration). Mr. Biceps of the physical education department is loud, rough, and tough. In order to impress his charges with his red-blooded manliness, he bellows at his boys, punctuating his remarks with an occasional bit of profanity. In social studies, Miss Frustration enters her classroom grimly, expecting trouble from the brats. The artists in teacher-baiting soon get into action and another unhappy hour takes place. In science, Mr. Monotony drones on wearily while his bored students doze or watch the clock. In seventh grade music, Mr. O. F. Key smiles weakly and murmurs repeatedly, "We are waiting for C_____ to help us with 'The Blackbird Song.'" Mrs. Drudge, who has taught English for twenty-nine years, seldom notices her students when she meets them on the street because of her preoccupation with the litter of ungraded themes on her desk. The teacher who catches a glimpse of his own image in these caricatures is advised to change either his attitudes or his occupation. An unhappy, maladjusted teacher creates a miserable existence for himself and his students. Needless to say, the vice-principal's office is filled with the disciplinary referrals from such unhappy classroom situations.

The Character of the Teacher

In lauding the work of a new teacher, a supervisor climaxed his remarks with "He has character." An attractive physique and a neat appearance are certainly not to be discounted in the art of influencing people but, in the long run, *what a person is* determines whether or not he will continue to draw others to him. Fairness, integrity, and consideration are not a veneer which a teacher can apply at will as he enters the classroom. The "chisler," whether he cheats in driving a car or in taking a test; the "little Caesar," who takes out his aggressions on a captive audience of students; or the parasite, who takes refuge in tenure laws, will sooner or later reveal his true self. Teachers talk much, but their actions are always more impressive than their words.

PRINCIPLES OF EFFECTIVE CLASS LEADERSHIP

Before launching a discussion of specific techniques for effective classroom management and control, the authors would like to suggest some important principles or guidelines which a teacher should keep in mind. Eventually every teacher develops his own philosophy of control. Out of this philosophy are derived certain principles that govern specific acts in the guidance of student behavior. If the principles are sound, the choice of control procedures is likely to be wise.

As a first principle, it should be remembered that the ultimate goal of all teacher control is to enable students to achieve *self-control*. Failure at this point means that students never mature nor develop the necessary skills of citizenship in a self-governing society like our own. But it must also be remembered that self-direction is not inherited. It must be learned. Furthermore, there is no formula for the achievement of self-discipline overnight. It takes time. Until students have learned to respect the rights and needs of others, the teacher has a legal and moral responsibility to provide whatever external controls are necessary to protect group welfare. The teacher always ensures that there is sufficient control to produce desirable changes in behavior. Adequate teacher support is necessary for individual security and for a happy, orderly group climate.

A second principle of good discipline, which has been implied above, concerns *group welfare*. Teachers often face the dilemma of deciding what is best for the individual or for the group. A simple solution is to do what is best for both. But there are times when the answer is not that simple. In such cases, the principle of "the greatest good to the greatest number" operates. Group welfare must come first. There will always be maladjusted students, fortunately few in number, who will not cooperate with the teacher and the class. In dealing with such students, the teacher cannot tolerate interference with the rights of the majority to learn.

School disciplinary practices need to be based on *sound principles of learning*. Just as students need help in learning history or science, they also need help in learning desirable personal and social behavior. Just as there are low achievers and high achievers in school subjects, there are also fast learners and slow learners in the achievement of self-control.

Good teaching procedures, based on sound learning theory, are recommended as the most effective means of developing good classroom control. By stressing motivation and student participation, rather than coercion and punishment, the teacher is able to get class cooperation. The principle of *readiness*, which is applicable to academic learning, is equally relevant to the development of self-control. In referring to an unfortunate experience of losing control of a class, a teacher said,

> If I were beginning again with this class, I would proceed differently. I assumed that the students had a maturity they did not yet have. After they were given more freedom than they could use wisely, I found it difficult to impose the restrictions that became necessary.

Adaptation of control procedures to different school levels, to different school neighborhoods, to different cultural backgrounds, or to different levels of maturity within a given grade or age group taxes the ingenuity of the teacher in making provisions for individual differences. There is always the danger of overestimating or underestimating a student's readiness for self-direction.

Another important principle of discipline is related to the *student's understanding of the purposes and functions of discipline*. The student must first understand the need for the school to establish and maintain certain conditions for the achievement of important objectives. He must develop favorable attitudes toward these necessary conditions for effective work and cooperation with others. He must also learn to respect the authority which may need to be exercised to protect both the rights of the individual and the welfare of the group (9:488). The student also needs to understand what is expected of him in terms of the behavioral goals and limits established by the school and society. He must be made to realize the consequences of his behavior and learn to accept responsibility for his actions. Most students wish to do the right thing, but they do not always know what is expected of them nor how to achieve these expectations.

Another principle of good classroom control is related to the fact that *no one prescription is applicable to all disciplinary problems.* Methods of classroom control vary with the student, the teacher, the place (home, school, community), the weather, or even the day of the week. Oliva draws a close analogy between the courts and the schools. The law of the land is not immutable but is subject to interpretation by the courts. Punishment for a crime, such as stealing for example, will vary according to intent, to willingness to make amends, to mitigating circumstances, or to maturity of the offender (8:86–87). When punishment is necessary, it must fit the offense, the individual or the group, and the purpose to be achieved (a change in surface behavior or a permanent change in attitude).

In helping students achieve maturity, the teacher must continuously evaluate his own behavior—his speech, courtesy, and consideration. The teacher who resorts to vulgar speech, such as profanity, or to undignified actions, such as manhandling students, soon loses the respect of his students. In order to attract students to him, the teacher must first gain their respect.

In dealing with discipline problems, a teacher has to remember constantly that *all misbehavior stems from causes.* Because of the complexity of causes and the teacher's own limitations of time, skill, and resources, the reasons for many incidents of misbehavior will remain undiscovered. As previously stated, sometimes expediency rather than delayed action for investigation of cause-and-effect relationships must govern what the teacher does to correct misbehavior. Otherwise, the welfare of either the individual or of the group may be jeopardized. However, even when a teacher is unable to remove causes of undesirable behavior, he can at least develop more sympathy and understanding for boys and girls who have adjustment problems for which they are not entirely responsible. In developing a more realistic and objective attitude toward behavior problems, the teacher can avoid sentimentality on the one hand and assumption of a dogmatic punitive position on the other.

By way of summary, then, the teacher who would exercise wise class-room control must recognize certain basic principles as the following: (1) Discipline is a complex concept. (2) The ultimate aim of teacher control is to help students achieve self-discipline. (3) There is no one solution that is applicable to all discipline problems. (4) Group welfare must be given primary consideration. (5) Like other teaching procedures, control techniques must be based on sound principles of learning. (6) Students need to understand the purposes and functions of discipline. (7) Whenever possible, the teacher should seek to discover underlying causes of misbehavior. (8) It is important for the teacher to analyze his own behavior constantly. (9) Without effective discipline, much of the valuable learning experience provided by the school will be unrealized. (10) A positive approach to classroom control is more effective than negative, repressive measures (8:85–89).

Selected Readings

1. Addicott, Irwin O., *Constructive Classroom Discipline.* San Francisco: Chandler Publishing Company, 1958.
2. American Educational Research Association, *Encyclopedia of Educational Research*, 3d ed., Chester W. Harris, ed. New York: The Macmillan Company, 1960, pp. 137–143, 381–383.
3. Brown, Edwin John, and Arthur Thomas Phelps, *Managing the Classroom*, 2d ed. New York: The Ronald Press Company, 1961. Chapters 5, 6, 7, 8.
4. Cutts, Norma E., and Nicholas Moseley, *Teaching the Disorderly Pupil in Elementary and Secondary School.* New York: David McKay Company, Inc., 1957.
5. Hand, Harold C., *Principles of Public Secondary Education.* New York: Harcourt, Brace & World, Inc., 1958. Chapter 7.
6. Herrick, Mary, *Discipline: What For and How?* Chicago: American Federation of Teachers, 1957.
7. Massey, Harold W., and Edwin E. Vineyard, *The Profession of Teaching.* New York: The Odyssey Press, Inc., 1961. Chapters 8, 9, 10.
8. Oliva, Peter F., "High School Discipline in American Society: A Primer on Democratic Discipline in Social Context," *Bulletin of the National Association of Secondary School Principals*, vol. 40 (January 1956), pp. 1–103.
9. Risk, Thomas M., *Principles and Practices of Teaching in Secondary Schools*, 3d ed. New York: American Book Company, 1958. Chapter 21.
10. Sheviakov, George V., and Fritz Redl, *Discipline for Today's Children and Youth.* New revision by Sybil K. Richardson. Washington, D.C.: Association for Supervision and Curriculum Development, 1956.

CHAPTER 12

Constructive classroom management and control

Teachers, especially those who have just completed their preservice education, are often apprehensive of their ability to control their students. Consequently, they hope for a formula for solving all of their discipline problems. It has already been pointed out that there are so many variables in specific situations involving behavior problems that it is difficult to determine in advance what action should be taken. For that reason, skeptics contend that no one can teach someone else how to solve his behavior problems. Actually the truth lies somewhere between these two extremes. The previous chapter suggested basic principles the teacher might follow in laying the foundation for effective classroom management and control. In the discussion that follows, specific actions to be taken for the *prevention* of behavior problems are outlined in some detail. The chapter concludes with the guidance role of the teacher, specifically in relation to discipline.

EFFECTIVE ORGANIZATION TO IMPROVE STUDENT BEHAVIOR

Effective organization is the first prerequisite to good discipline. A well-organized classroom provides a businesslike environment, one in which the students can get their work done with a minimum of confusion, tension, and frustration. Good class organization eliminates waste and conserves class time for significant learning activities. By handling routine matters efficiently, enlisting student help with management, and providing for a comfortable, attractive physical environment, the teacher demonstrates his organizational ability.

How much organization is necessary? That depends upon several factors. Large classes of immature students require a high degree of organization whereas smaller classes of more mature students may be conducted on a more informal, self-governing basis. Specialized class-rooms, such as shops or laboratories, must be sufficiently organized to protect students from accidents and the school from loss of equipment. Beginnings and endings of class periods, as well as transitions in activities during class sessions, frequently require special attention. Many class activities need to be organized on a fairly routine basis so that valuable class time will not be used each day in giving instructions on how to carry them out. More specific suggestions are given in the discussion that im-mediately follows.

Providing for Good Beginnings

The first day, sometimes the first week, marks a critical period in the his-tory of a class. To avoid chaos, the teacher may have to become the equivalent of a ringmaster of a three-ring circus. He must keep his stu-dents occupied as he signs program cards, organizes a class roll and seat-ing chart, and takes care of many other details. One teacher has solved this problem by recording his orientation lecture and playing it while he takes care of administrative details. Quite soon, the teacher will wish to provide a compass for the year's work by outlining requirements and future activities. He may also wish to give a pretest and administer an interest questionnaire as a basis for future assignments. Certainly, im-mediate assignments must be made with special attention given to stu-dent motivation.

Every teacher hopes to make a favorable first impression on his class. As said before, dress, grooming, and demeanor are especially important. Attention getters—beards, flashy clothes, and the like—are to be avoided. At the very first class meeting, the teacher needs to set an example of punctuality. In general, the teacher needs to be friendly but business-like; enthusiastic but reserved; confident but not overbearing; and in good humor but not frivolous.

Making Provisions for Physical Comfort

Proper regulation of temperature, light, and ventilation is necessary for good health and effective learning. This also has a direct bearing on disci-pline. Students who are uncomfortable become inattentive and unpro-ductive. This in turn may lead to minor disorders or unruly behavior. Unsightly and uncomfortable classrooms of yesterday are being replaced today by modern facilities which are more functional, attractive, and comfortable. Despite contemporary improvement, however, the teacher must still make day-by-day adjustments as needed: adjust window blinds to prevent glare, turn on lights on cloudy days, and regulate temperature and ventilation when the room becomes stuffy or drafty. Not only must the teacher be constantly aware of the necessity for such adjustments, but he should also develop student responsibility for regulating conditions which create discomfort or endanger health. Thus the teacher conserves his time for more important activities and, at the same time, provides a valuable learning experience for his students.

Providing for a Tidy and Attractive Room

The classroom should not only be comfortable, but it should also be as neat and attractive as possible. An orderly, comfortable, and attractive environment is conducive to good work habits and attitudes. The maintenance of clean floors and desks, including that of the teacher, and provision for orderly bookcases, storage cabinets, and displays are the *joint* responsibility of a teacher and his students. Even such a relatively unimportant function as the storage of supplies or equipment has more implications for discipline than may be readily apparent. Storage centers need to be decentralized to avoid traffic jams. In shops, tools should be checked systematically to avoid lost time in attempts to trace them or to assess fines against students to cover losses. Awkward situations or unpleasant incidents are thereby reduced or eliminated.

In a well-organized classroom, it is the teacher who, first of all, sets an example of good housekeeping. Then he is in a good position to insist that students do their part in keeping the classroom neat and orderly. Clean-up periods, in such classes as art, homemaking, and industrial arts, require special attention to organization. Because secondary school teachers so frequently have to share classrooms with others, they need to show special consideration by keeping chalkboards clean and by leaving the room clean and orderly. In the clean-up period for art or shop classes, there is no better opportunity for teaching students to be good housekeepers than to have them pick up after themselves and return school materials to their proper storage spaces.

No matter how modern a classroom may be in terms of design and color scheme, the teacher and his class can always make their own contribution to its beautification. Attractive bulletin boards, pictures on the wall, exhibits on window sills and interesting chalkboard designs are a few additional touches that make the classroom an enjoyable place in which to work.

When student assumption of responsibility for clean and attractive classrooms is extended to include the campus as a whole, no one could ask for better insurance against vandalism. As students take pride in the creation and maintenance of a clean, attractive, and orderly school environment, their improved behavior is reflected in every aspect of school life.

Insuring Orderly Student Traffic

The movement of students is always a potential source of minor disturbances, some of which may lead to major discipline problems. The teacher is advised to note students' movements at such times as the following: passing to and from the classroom; going to and from chalkboards, pencil sharpeners, and so on; securing and returning books and other supplies; and passing through the halls. By all means, students should have *planned* freedom of movement. Well-regulated traffic, with an emphasis on common courtesy, is conducive to improved behavior and more satisfaction for everyone.

Assigning Seats or Stations to Students

Some organized procedure for the assignment of students to definite seats or stations is necessary to expedite attendance check, to facilitate the learning of students' names, to take care of special needs (for example, students with defective vision or hearing), and to insure a more orderly working atmosphere for the class as a whole. Students may be allowed to choose their own seating positions initially; however, the teacher should not hesitate to make reassignments when the needs of an individual or the class are better served. A number of procedures may be used for checking attendance: use of a seating chart, reports by squad leaders, or response of students by numbers. A physical education teacher made the common mistake of calling the names of students as they moved around an extended area. Such procedure obviously encouraged straggling to class, horseplay, and the temptation for students to respond to one another's names. Whatever system is used, roll check should be accurate and speedy in order to discourage absenteeism or tardiness and to conserve time for learning activities.

Expediting the Distribution and Collection of Materials

A systematic method of handling instructional materials or student papers has a number of values. First of all, it conserves class time. Some teachers use the wasteful procedure of returning student papers one at a time in random fashion rather than in sequence by rows. A second value is an elimination of confusion. When permanent school property, such as textbooks or tools, is involved, proper handling and storage of such materials constitute good insurance against damage or loss. In order to provide more opportunities for student movement, the teacher should use student monitors, especially in junior high school, for the distribution and collection of materials. Being a monitor should be considered a privilege, which may be denied when a student persists in discharging his duties in a careless, noisy, or disorderly manner.

Keeping Records and Making Reports

The teacher is responsible for making accurate attendance reports, keeping complete records of student progress in scholarship and citizenship, and for providing other data needed for school records. Carelessness or tardiness with respect to such records and reports is a constant source of irritation to the school principal and, in some cases, an open invitation to delinquent student behavior (for example, inaccurate or time-consuming roll checks, sketchy citizenship records, failure to warn parents of a decline in student scholarship or citizenship). A teacher must have sufficient evidence for giving marks or grades. In reporting scholarship, he should avoid either extreme of having his record book cluttered with daily grades or marks or having it almost devoid of any grades. In reporting citizenship, the teacher is advised to keep anecdotal records of significant student behavior rather than depend upon vague remembrances or impressions derived from a recent, perhaps atypical, example of student behavior as the basis for his report. The following illustration demonstrates the point.

Mr. C. kept a complete record of each student's citizenship in his class. One boy, whose mother was PTA president, received a D grade in citizenship. When the mother came to the school very much disturbed, the teacher reviewed anecdotal records for her. On one date, when Mr. C. had told the boy he might have to call his mother, the boy had said, "If you do, she will hit you over the head with a mop." That was all the mother needed to know. She indicated she would have a heart-to-heart talk with her son.

Adequate records insure a square deal for students, more likelihood of improved student habits and attitudes, and improved public relations.

Keeping Everyone Busy

Idleness breeds disorder. The best antidote is keeping everyone busy at worthwhile tasks. When the teacher is lecturing or demonstrating or when one or more students are making a presentation to the class, attention of the group is required. During a study or work period, the teacher may have to exert gentle, insistent pressure on would-be disturbers of the peace. He can do this by circulating around the room, passing by or standing momentarily near those who are talking or idling, sometimes asking to see completed work, or catching the eye of those exhibiting poor work habits and frowning his disapproval. It is quite important that the students soon learn that they are expected to begin work immediately when the class period begins and to continue working until dismissal time.

Sometimes there is a time lag while the teacher is taking care of administrative duties. This can be corrected in a number of ways. Student monitors may take care of routine jobs while the teacher gets the class under way. Some classes have their own officers who call the group to order and get activities for the day started, even when the teacher is out of the room. A typing teacher had his class so well organized that he seldom spoke to the class for the first five or ten minutes. The students came quietly into the room, seated themselves in an orderly manner, and began working on the warm-up assignment listed on the board. Proper organization forestalls idleness and disorder.

Making Provisions for Emergencies.

There are times when regularly planned activities are unexpectedly interrupted or have to be deferred. If a physical education class that is dependent upon outside facilities is driven inside by rain, the teacher must be able to substitute other activities on the spur of the moment by showing an appropriate film, giving a chalk talk on rules and strategy of play, or joining another class in coeducational dancing. When an English teacher unexpectedly finds half of his class absent, he may read and have the class discuss a selected poem or short story, held in reserve for such an occasion. The mathematics teacher may have the class work on some interesting puzzle problems or spend the day quite profitably on remedial or make-up work. In a social studies class, for example, it is advisable to have alternate activities planned in case individual or group reports are not ready on the day assigned. The teacher should not be unduly upset by a fire drill, even in the middle of a test. By anticipating emergencies and making some preparation beforehand, the teacher can soon put his class to work with a minimum of confusion and disorder as if he had planned it that way.

Insisting on Common Courtesy

It may seem strange to include courtesy under the subject of classroom management. Manners are minor virtues which are learned through practice. Proper organization provides the necessary setting for the exercise of good manners. Once students develop a habitual pattern of mannerly behavior, details of management become less important. In order to achieve the ideal of courtesy and consideration in the classroom, the teacher will need to help his students improve their behavior in specific situations. When students are inadvertently discourteous in speech or actions, they can be taught the value of "I beg your pardon" or "I am sorry." Unfortunately, some teachers tolerate boorish behavior without making any attempt to correct it. Unless the teacher constantly encourages thoughtful, considerate relationships in the classroom, he is failing in his obligation to teach good citizenship.

At this point, it should be remembered that courtesy is largely taught by example. The teacher may insist on observance of rules of courtesy, but students are more likely to follow his example than his preachments. Sarcastic remarks, lack of consideration for the personal feelings of students, and failure to give recognition for contributions to the class provoke student wisecracks and lower class morale. On the other hand, some teachers make it a point to thank students who make a special contribution to the class—such as a report, demonstration, or operation of a motion picture projector. *The behavior that a teacher expects of himself is the kind of behavior that he may expect of his students.*

Achieving Effective Leadership

All of the foregoing items suggest many details of classroom management which are important in the maintenance of a positive learning environment. However, the teacher should not only be skillful in handling details of organization but he must also be an organized person himself. This means that he possesses the qualities of poise, assurance, and self-control which inspire confidence in his leadership. Thus the teacher needs first to become a master of himself before he can achieve the status of a master teacher, "a teacher recognized as possessing exceptional ability in the art of teaching."[1] Such mastery, of course, is not attained in a day; neither is it achieved without continuous effort on the part of the teacher to improve his own personality and character.

As a review of the items of classroom management, the reader may wish to take a self-test on the "Classroom Organization Check List" in order to ascertain how well he fulfills the managerial roles of the teacher.

Classroom Organization Check List

	NEEDS IMPROVEMENT	SATISFACTORY
1. Maintenance of desirable physical conditions		
a. Controlling light (natural and artificial)	_____	_____
b. Regulating temperature	_____	_____
c. Regulating ventilation	_____	_____

[1] Carter V. Good, ed., *Dictionary of Education.* New York: McGraw-Hill Book Company, Inc., 1959, p. 332. Used by permission.

	NEEDS IMPROVEMENT	SATISFACTORY

d. Maintaining comfortable working conditions in general

2. Improvement of appearance of room
   a. Keeping desks and floors neat and clean
   b. Keeping chalkboard clean
   c. Keeping bulletin boards attractive and up to date
   d. Using attractive, appropriate room decorations

3. Provision for orderly movements of students
   a. Insuring orderly movement to and from classroom
   b. Regulating traffic within the classroom
   c. Supervising traffic in the halls

4. Arrangement for seating students
   a. Assigning students to definite seats or stations
   b. Rearranging assignments as needed
   c. Making provisions for special needs

5. Provision for effective use of materials and equipment
   a. Preparing materials in advance
   b. Distributing and collecting materials systematically
   c. Conserving materials by proper handling, accounting, and storing
   d. Using expendable materials economically

6. Preparation of records and reports
   a. Making accurate attendance reports promptly
   b. Keeping a complete record of student scholarship and citizenship
   c. Collecting and reporting other data promptly

7. Provisions for courtesy in the classroom
   a. Insisting on mutual respect and consideration
   b. Showing special consideration for new students

	NEEDS IMPROVEMENT	SATISFACTORY
c. Making visitors feel welcome	————————	————————
8. Organization of other procedures		
a. Learning students' names quickly	————————	————————
b. Beginning class promptly and ending it on time	————————	————————
c. Keeping everyone busy	————————	————————
d. Making assignments definite	————————	————————
e. Making individual adjustments as needed	————————	————————
f. Keeping a continuous check on student progress	————————	————————
9. Achievement of instructional leadership		
a. Developing poise, assurance, and self-control	————————	————————
b. Planning ahead for effective leadership	————————	————————

SOURCE: Adapted from Schorling and Batchelder and used by special permission of McGraw-Hill Publishing Company, Inc. (10:113–114).

EFFECTIVE ACTION FOR CONSTRUCTIVE DISCIPLINE

The fundamental reason why children do not act right is because they do not have the conditions for right action—Francis W. Parker[2]

Nowhere else is the adage "An ounce of prevention is worth a pound of cure" more relevant than in discipline. Under ideal conditions the teacher is able to establish and maintain a classroom atmosphere in which discipline problems are virtually nonexistent. In reality, such a happy state of affairs is rarely achievable. Nevertheless, the teacher who consistently uses constructive control measures is likely to have few, if any, major behavior problems or crises. Just what are some of the guidelines to be observed in this constructive approach to classroom management and control? The following paragraphs include a number of pertinent suggestions.

The importance of adequate planning (discussed in Chapter 3) and of good classroom organization have already been stressed as prerequisites for effective learning and improved student behavior.

There are a number of measures a teacher may take to establish and

[2] Francis W. Parker, *Talks on Pedagogics.* New York: E. L. Kellogg and Company, 1894, p. 372.

maintain a wholesome learning environment in the classroom. He may observe such rules of action as the following:

1. *Keep constantly aware of classroom climate.* In establishing and maintaining a constructive classroom atmosphere, the teacher must always be sensitive to the personality of the group. He needs to be alert to early danger signals which may indicate a disturbance in group climate or individual behavior. The teacher who knows what each student is doing, or not doing, can quickly take care of individual problems before the class as a whole is affected.

An alert teacher never becomes so absorbed in helping individual students that he is oblivious to the problems or needs of the rest of the class. It is true that a teacher should approach any class with a positive attitude, believing in his students and accepting them as good citizens, until they prove otherwise. Yet, he must not be so naive as to think that all students have achieved sufficient maturity for complete self-direction. As a general rule, however, students do try to live up to the expectations of a respected teacher.

The teacher should see his class as individual personalities. Direct eye contact with individual students, an encouraging smile, or a nod of approval by the teacher all contribute to a wholesome classroom climate.

2. *Encourage student participation in classroom control.* Not only should students assist the teacher with routine class management, but they should also be encouraged to cooperate in setting up necessary rules for class government. The teacher is advised, however, to recognize certain limitations which may exist. For instance, if a class has had little or no experience with such cooperative procedures, the teacher will probably need to proceed with caution. In some cases, a class may be so immature or lacking in group spirit that the teacher will have to assume almost complete responsibility for control.

The teacher should always bear in mind that standards of behavior which he considers acceptable must also be acceptable to the class as a whole. The students must consider restrictions as just and reasonable. It can usually be assumed that most students wish to do what is right. If this were not so, school rules and regulations would be unenforceable.

3. *Re-evaluate teaching procedures constantly.* Good discipline is a by-product of good teaching. The teacher who uses a variety of learning activities and materials effectively will probably have few discipline problems. With proper attention to motivation and adequate provision for individual differences, the teacher establishes "conditions for right action." Bright students are challenged and slow learners taste success. When

class activities are well planned, interesting, and varied, students are encouraged to be on their best behavior.

4. *Make allowances for unusual conditions.* When students are overstimulated by a change in weather, the tide of excitement before a big game, or some other unusual factor, the teacher can well afford to be more tolerant, more liberal in his expectations of the class. He may find it wise to defer or change his assignment for the day.

5. *Communicate with students at their level.* The teacher needs to avoid either extreme: talking down to students by treating them like children or addressing them formally as adults by calling them "Mr. _____" or "Miss _____" instead of "Jim" or "Mary." If a teacher transfers from junior high school to senior high school or vice versa, he will find it necessary to make adjustments in vocabulary, teaching procedures, and expectations with respect to behavior. It might also be well to point out that some boys and girls from a particular neighborhood may be more sophisticated than those from some other community, even though they are the same age. Sometimes a new teacher who has spent four or five years as a college student may have difficulty in adjusting to his role as a teacher of adolescents.

6. *Stress "do" rather than "don't."* The wise teacher uses a positive approach to the improvement of behavior. "Do" is more effective than "don't," especially with adolescents who are going through a stage of rebellion in an effort to become independent when they resist adult restrictions imposed by teacher or parent. A further refinement of this point is the fact that *requests* are usually more effective than *commands*. Requests are less likely to arouse resentment or to place either student or teacher in a position of having to save face.

7. *Encourage more student activity.* In a positive approach to classroom management and control, the teacher strives constantly to secure more involvement, more participation, and the assumption of more responsibility on the part of every student. The net results are better motivation, more effective learning, and improved behavior.

8. *Show an interest in students' concerns.* The teacher who demonstrates an interest in the affairs of students—in their cocurricular activities, for example—often finds that student behavior improves in direct proportion to that interest. Unfortunately, some teachers regard an assignment to sponsor a cocurricular activity only as an onerous task, little realizing the potential reward in terms of better teacher-student relations.

9. *Use the voice effectively.* A low, well modulated voice has a calming effect on an unstable, restless group. If the noise level of a class begins to rise to a point where it interferes with learning, the teacher should first

gain the complete attention of his students and then address them in a quiet, positive manner.

10. *Set a good example and take appropriate action when necessary.* Nothing can supersede the personal example of the teacher. Yet he must be more than an exemplary person; he must also be a doer. Professional judgment has to be translated into action. As he deals with problems, the teacher has to be sympathetic without being sentimental, to be friendly and approachable without being intimate, and to satisfy student needs without being indulgent.

11. *Cultivate mutual respect and consideration.* The structure of constructive discipline rests on a foundation of mutual respect and consideration. This foundation is built on many little acts of kindness, tact, and thoughtfulness. The following vignettes from the classroom illustrate the point: The teacher encouraged student questions and salvaged everything he could from the answers of students to his questions. Even if an answer was entirely wrong, he made the correction with the utmost tact. . . . As a new student entered the class, he was assigned a student to help him with his orientation to the school. . . . When an observer entered the classroom, the class president gave him a textbook and plan for the day and explained what the class was doing. . . . The teacher attempted to learn the names of his students as quickly as possible. He would check his class roster and make a special effort to learn more about the students whose names and faces he could not associate. . . . A visitor sat in the rear of the classroom. Student traffic was heavy in front of him, yet every student would ask to be excused. . . . A teacher unjustly reprimanded a student in the presence of the class, discovered his mistake, and apologized to the class the next day. . . . A student questioned the teacher's solution to a problem. The teacher noted his error and thanked the student sincerely for the correction. The foregoing illustrations indicate the kinds of actions, both of teacher and students, which contribute to a wholesome classroom environment, an environment marked by mutual trust and consideration.

By way of summary, a psychologist has outlined the conditions for, what he calls, "a therapeutic environment." Briefly, they are as follows:

The first, and probably the most important, essential in a therapeutic environment is a positive attitude on the part of the teacher toward children. . . .

Another necessary condition for having a therapeutic classroom environment is that the teacher feel secure in his role as a teacher. It would perhaps be more correct to say in his "roles" as teacher, because the teacher's roles are many. . . .

A third aspect of a therapeutic environment in the school is that the work is made stimulating and interesting. . . .

In a therapeutic classroom environment, each child attains success in some important (to him) area of his school work. . . .

A fifth factor contributing to a therapeutic environment in the classroom is establishing limits. One function of the teacher is to set the boundaries for behavior in the classroom. . . .

A sixth characteristic of a therapeutic environment is that there is a group feeling among the individual members of the class. . . .

Finally, no environment can promote social and emotional growth if the physical surroundings are not conducive to such growth. . . .[3]

BEHAVIOR TO FIT THE OCCASION

Teacher expectations have a direct bearing on constructive discipline. Whether the kind of behavior a teacher expects of his students is reasonable and realistic depends upon the situation: the class setting, the nature of the activities, and the purposes to be served. In the discussion that immediately follows, suggestions are made concerning appropriate behavior for specific class situations.

Discussion

Courtesy is the key word. In the give-and-take of free discussion, the rights of everyone are to be respected. Each one has a right to express his point of view; each one is entitled to a respectful hearing. To reiterate, the teacher demonstrates the kind of behavior he expects of his students. By permitting students to make their contributions without interrupting or repeating their remarks, by giving considerate recognition to student responses, commending correct responses and correcting errors tactfully, and by being tolerant of opinions that differ from his own, the teacher establishes a proper classroom atmosphere for effective discussion.

Supervised Study

Study is often an individual matter. Consequently, under such circumstances, there should be little or no need for talking or visiting among students. If or when it is desirable for two or more students to work together, they should *work* quietly without disturbing other members of the class. The teacher who permits widespread visiting with only the caution to be quiet is neglecting his responsibility for proper supervision of study. Likewise, the teacher who sits at his desk grading papers is neglectful, for he is neither providing the help that students are likely to need nor checking on potential behavior problem cases. By circulating

[3] O. G. Johnson, "A Climate to Grow In," *NEA Journal*, vol. 46 (April 1957), pp. 233–236.

around the room, the teacher provides the guidance for study to which his class is entitled. An administrator once remarked that he usually found the teacher who did not circulate to be one who was lazy and ineffective.

Laboratory Periods

When a class is working on experiments in science, projects in industrial arts, or problems in art, a much more informal atmosphere is more appropriate than in some other types of class activities. As much freedom and informality as are consistent with safety and effective learning should be encouraged. But when one or more students interfere with the work of others, waste time in aimless wandering or fruitless chatter, endanger the safety of fellow students, or create an atmosphere of general disorder, the teacher must restrict their freedom. Even the noise level of the class is a factor to be considered. Although he should encourage freedom of movement and communication, the teacher need not tolerate either horseplay or loud, ribald speech. The sound in a working atmosphere is quite different from that in a noisy, disorganized laboratory situation.

Group Work

Regardless of the size of the group—a three-member committee, a five-man team, or the entire class—certain conditions need to be maintained. First of all, there should be a cooperative relationship with every member participating. When subgroups are formed, they are ultimately responsible for making a contribution to the class as a whole. The teacher is always accountable for effective operation of all groups in helping them to organize, to develop a work plan, to conduct their research, and to make a worthwhile contribution to the class as a whole. Large, informal groups (such as bands, teams, or choruses) require strong teacher leadership, effective organization, and acceptance of common goals to function effectively.

Field Trips or Excursions

Since trips or tours take students away from the school campus, a high degree of advance preparation and organization is necessary. Planning should be on a cooperative basis, with the teacher and his class working together, so that everyone clearly understands the purposes and problems of the particular excursion. The primary purpose of the trip, of course, is to provide a learning experience that is not available in the normal classroom setting. Problems involve protection against accidents, the maintenance of good public relations, and the prevention of discipline problems in a more or less informal, uncontrolled environment. Of course, proper administrative clearance, parental permissions, and the reduction of disruption of other classes to a minimum must be taken care of before the trip.

Student Activities

Because of the informality, freedom and opportunities for self-direction provided by extraclass activities, teachers who are sponsors of such activities have to exercise reasonable judgment in knowing when and how to temper student initiative with faculty direction to insure proper observance of school regulations and the maintenance of good public relations. Without unnecessarily restricting opportunities for student leadership and self-government, the teacher-sponsor needs to impress upon his charges the importance of such ideals as good sportsmanship, good citizenship, and responsible leadership.

Other Group Situations

There are other situations, such as those involving groups in study halls or assemblies in the school auditorium, which pose special problems in seating and supervision. Mutual responsibility for management is often shared by teachers and administrators. The degree of teacher control required is determined by such factors as the size of the group, the maturity of the students, and the nature of the activity. Again the criterion for effectiveness of control is based on the extent to which the purposes of the groups are achieved.

DEVELOPMENT OF GROUP MORALE

As an instructional leader, the teacher has a twofold responsibility: to help each individual student achieve maturity and to weld aggregations of individuals into cohesive groups for effective learning.

Any classroom observer can usually detect quite soon the climate or atmosphere of a particular class. He may sense an atmosphere of cooperation or rebellion, enthusiasm or boredom, or security or tension. Such a climate is merely a reflection of the morale of the group. Thus an aggregation of thirty-five students, for example, may become a tight little group that either accepts or rejects the educational purposes of the teacher and the school. What are some of the factors or forces which promote development of a group climate conducive to desirable behavior? There are several.

Bases of Group Morale

First of all, *a group is united by common purposes*. Just any purposes, however, will not suffice. A group may be either good or bad, depending upon the worthiness of the purposes which unite them. Obviously, a group devoted to resistance to study and learning, united on the basis of hostility toward the teacher, or prone to engage in horseplay at the slightest provocation serves no constructive educational purpose. On the other hand, whenever the teacher is able to build a strong effective group, devoted to worthwhile purposes, class morale and productivity, as well as individual learning and satisfaction, reach a high level.[4] Whenever a cohesive group discovers that specific actions are out of harmony with its objectives, the members are willing to impose certain restrictions on themselves, to limit their own freedom if necessary, in order to preserve the integrity of the group. No group can long exist without some form of control or discipline. But such control must be either self-imposed or be accepted by the group when imposed by some external authority, such as the teacher. If neither of these conditions prevails, desirable surface behavior may be achieved, but the class most likely will continue to operate as an aggregate of individuals, not as a group with common goals.

A second factor in the achievement of wholesome group morale is that opportunities must be provided for the members *to work together, to engage in cooperative action.* As suggested above, such work must be directed toward the achievement of worthy goals. Furthermore, an effective group sets for itself high standards of excellence. The precision of a drill team, the smart appearance of a band, the harmony of a chorus, the the teamwork of an athletic group, the unity of effort involved in the presentation of an exhibit or an assembly program, or the mutual feeling of achievement in the development of a science project are indicative of a high degree of group morale. The teacher may well encourage group pride—the spirit of "all for one and one for all"—and devotion to excellence in achievement. Unfortunately, in the average classroom, major emphasis is placed on individual, competitive activities, leading to a spirit of divisiveness rather than unity.

In order to improve the quality of group living, as well as the values held by individuals, a teacher needs to do less lecturing and more guiding toward desirable behavior. As a director of learning, the teacher provides the key to group spirit. He may encourage group enterprises or stress only individual performance. He may stress cooperation or competition. Ashley Montagu, the anthropologist, has pointed out that contrary to popular opinion cooperation, not competition, is the first law of survival.[5] What the student learns in the classroom or on the playing field can have lifelong consequences. Learning to work harmoniously with others may

[4] Leland P. Bradford, "The Pupil and the Group," *NEA Journal,* vol. 46 (February 1957), pp. 103–105.

[5] Ashley Montagu, *On Being Human.* New York: Abelard-Schuman Ltd., 1950.

mean the difference between success and failure for the student in his future relationships with his boss, his family, and his neighbors.

Closely associated with the necessity of cooperative action for the development of group morale is the need for *personal loyalty*. In the final analysis, group unity is based on loyalty to persons rather than on acceptance of some abstract principle. Studies of morale in units of American armed forces in World War II revealed that loyalty to one's friends and pride in one's outfit—not such abstract principles as "freedom" or "democracy," even though the importance of these concepts must be recognized— were the chief integrating factors.[6]

Problems in the Development of Group Morale

In attempting to build group morale, the teacher is admittedly faced with a number of difficulties. For one thing, each student is already a member of other groups—family, friends, team—before he comes to school. These groups compete with the school class for the student's time and, in some cases, sanction values which are in conflict with those of the school. Another problem the teacher has in developing group morale is related to school organization itself. A school day that is segmented into inflexible, fifty-minute periods provides only limited time for a class to become a cohesive group. Finally, many learning activites, especially those related to evaluation, stress individual performance with each student in sharp competition with his fellows.

Group Life versus Individual Development

In the light of certain social forces which place a premium on conformity and stifle individual thought and action, some persons feel quite strongly that group life has been emphasized at the expense of individual development. It should be pointed out that group life is not an end in itself. It is designed to improve the quality of living for the individual. *"Most human needs are satisfied through interaction with other people."*[7] When a student feels at home with his group, he is able to disagree with his peers without fear of ridicule or ostracism. When a student feels accepted by his group, he has a personal concern for the welfare of his fellows. In a class united on the basis of commonly accepted, worthwhile goals, the classroom becomes

a laboratory for learning the fundamentals of democratic behavior, for developing individual maturity, for gaining skills of leadership and membership, and for developing skills of independency and interdependency.[8]

[6] Stuart Chase, *Roads to Agreement*. New York: Harper & Row, Publishers, 1951, pp. 63–65.

[7] *Ibid.*, p. 78.

[8] Bradford, *op. cit.*, p. 104.

THE ROLE OF GUIDANCE IN CONSTRUCTIVE DISCIPLINE

For some people, the term "guidance" may suggest a specialized function which is performed only by certain certified personnel. For others, the term is loosely defined in the cliché "all education is guidance." Either conception is misleading. While the primary function of the classroom teacher is teaching, he also performs many guidance functions, one of the most important of which is counseling students.

Counseling for Constructive Discipline

As school guidance services are now organized, counseling is done by full-time counselors who are specifically certified, by teacher-counselors, and by classroom teachers. Counseling is designed to assist students in making decisions concerning further schooling, future careers, employment, and personal and social problems. Teachers operate in all of these areas. Obviously, the teachers who help students resolve their personal or social problems make a direct contribution to constructive discipline. Indirectly, teachers who direct students into courses that fit their needs and abilities, enable students to make wise choices of further education, or help them find a suitable vocational future make a definite contribution to improved classroom morale. Satisfied, successful students are seldom discipline problems.

A personnel officer once remarked, "I am looking for teachers with a guidance point of view." In order to be a successful counselor, the teacher must have a "guidance point of view." He must be more concerned about finding and removing causes of misbehavior than in treating superficial symptoms of discipline problems. He must be more interested in improving the behavior of students than in merely punishing them.

The need for each teacher of a school to become an effective counselor is critical in a system of mass education. Every student needs a confidant, an adult friend to whom he may go with his problems. Obviously, full-time counselors cannot meet that need for everyone. They are too few in number. Then, too, adolescents do not confide in just anyone. Consequently, all school personnel—athletic coach, librarian, classroom teacher, nurse—need to make themselves available as counselors and adult friends to at least a few students. If all school personnel fulfill their obligations as counselors, the dividends in terms of improved student behavior will more than repay them for the extra time and effort involved.

Reciprocal Relationships between Teacher and Counselor

Both teacher and counselor need to recognize their dependence upon each other. How does the classroom teacher assist the full-time counselor? First of all, he serves as the eyes and ears of the counselor's office. Counselors see most students only on specific occasions, if at all, whereas teachers have daily contact with them. Thus a classroom teacher occupies a strategic position in the detection of failure, maladjustment, or illness. By all means, he needs to detect quite early critical problems which he cannot solve and refer them to the appropriate counselor. Another important guidance function performed by the teacher is helping students who have received counsel for misbehavior to adjust to group living within the classroom. Students may *discuss* their problems within the privacy of the counselor's office, but they must *solve* most of their problems within the social framework of the classroom. Probably the greatest contribution a teacher makes to the guidance services of a school is doing a good job of teaching. Poor teaching fills the counselor's office with candidates for failure and punishment. On the other hand, the teacher who maintains a class in which his students are happy and successful definitely eases the load of the counselor.

How do counselors aid teachers? Not only do counselors provide teachers expert help with problem cases, but they also serve as the one best source of information about students. The authors stress repeatedly the necessity for teachers to know their students. Data may be secured in many ways and from many sources (as discussed at length in Chapter 1). But there is no substitute for discussion of a problem student with an understanding counselor and a study of the records in the counselor's files.

Counseling with Parents

Most problems of boys and girls could be solved with dispatch if parents and teacher worked more closely together than they sometimes do. Unfortunately, parents are sometimes not consulted until a problem is far advanced. They want to know how their children are getting along in school and hope the school will keep them informed, but they may hesitate to ask (12:17–18).

Secondary school teachers, who teach 180 or more students in a five- or six-period day, may well be envious of the elementary teacher in the self-contained classroom. The common practice of having each elementary teacher confer periodically with every parent is obviously not feasible in the highly departmentalized secondary school. A number of ways have been tried in the secondary school to bring parent and teacher closer together—parent-teacher association meetings, open houses, invitations to special exhibits, teas honoring mothers, and an occasional home visit. None of these measures, however, has reached all parents, or perhaps even a majority of them. Then, too, group situations, as indicated above, provide no opportunity for private, personal conferences between parent and teacher.

In informing parents of the progress of their children, in citizenship as well as scholarship, secondary school teachers have limited their communication largely to report cards. Whenever scholarship or citizenship is unsatisfactory, the report card may be supplemented by a warning notice. Such a cold, impersonal approach to the reporting of unsatisfactory progress certainly contributes little to a better understanding between parent and teacher or provides little real help to the student.

Although teacher conferences with all parents are apparently not feasible at the secondary school level, there are occasions when a teacher needs to arrange for special conferences with parents of some of his students. Whenever there is evidence that the misbehavior of a student may reach major proportions, the teacher should enlist the cooperation of parents as soon as possible. Otherwise, a problem that might have been quickly resolved could reach a crisis resulting in the suspension or dismissal of the student. In conferring with parents, the teacher is advised to keep a few important guidelines in mind, such as the following:

1. If a parent is disturbed, the teacher needs to be *a good listener.* It is good therapy for an upset individual to relieve his tensions by verbalizing his grievances. Then, too, a rational discussion of any problem cannot take place until both parties are in a state of emotional equilibrium. When a teacher is tempted to defend his own position or argue a point, he should remember that it is better to win a parent than an argument. If the teacher has made a mistake, his best defense is an honest admission of error.

2. In every parent-teacher conference where the problems of a son or daughter are the subject of discussion, the *welfare of the student* should receive primary consideration. Good points, rather than shortcomings, need to be emphasized. At the same time, however, the teacher must be honest with parents. When a student is in error, it is the responsibility of mature adults, both teacher and parents, to help him correct his mistakes and make amends for them if necessary. It is quite natural for parents to defend their children, even to be overly protective of them at times. Tagore expressed this admirable parental failing in these words: "I do not love him because he is good, but because he is my child." Nevertheless, as tactfully as possible, the teacher sometimes has to help parents become more realistic in assessing both the strengths and weaknesses of their children.

3. The skillful teacher encourages parents *to ask questions and to make*

suggestions in the course of the interview. He should avoid repeating "*I* think" but should *ask* the parent, "what can we do?" Parents like to feel their assistance is needed and wanted.

4. The teacher should *speak in simple terms.* There is a professional terminology which teachers should understand and use among themselves, but they must avoid the use of technical terms which might confuse parents or lead to further misunderstanding. The story is told of a lecturer who spoke to a group of parents and teachers about "the whole child." At the conclusion of the talk, one parent timidly asked, "What other kind of child is there?"

5. The teacher must play *a strong, positive role* in solving the problem. Once he has established a cooperative relationship with the parents of a child with a problem, he is obligated to share the objective evidence the school has bearing on the problem. When the conference is over, the teacher should summarize and record it, and follow it up with positive action when necessary.

By conducting conferences with dignity, tact, and consideration, the teacher facilitates better student behavior and improved relations with parents.

Selected Readings

1. Addicott, Irwin O., *Constructive Classroom Discipline.* San Francisco: Chandler Publishing Company, 1958.
2. Brown, Edwin John, and Arthur Thomas Phelps, *Managing the Classroom,* 2d ed. New York: The Ronald Press Company, 1961. Chapters 4, 5, 6, 7.
3. Burton, William H., *The Guidance of Learning Activities,* 3d ed. New York: Appleton-Century-Crofts, 1962. Chapter 23.
4. Carter, William L., Carl W. Hansen, and Margaret G. McKim, *Learning to Teach in the Secondary School.* New York: The Macmillan Company, 1962. Chapter 5.
5. Clark, Leonard H., and Irving S. Starr, *Secondary School Teaching Methods.* New York: The Macmillan Company, 1959, Chapter 14.
6. Gordon, Ted, *Tips to Teachers.* Los Angeles: California Education Press, Chapters 1, 2, 6.
7. Grambs, Jean D., William J. Iverson, and Franklin K. Patterson, *Modern Methods in Secondary Education,* rev. ed. New York: Holt, Rinehart and Winston, Inc., 1958. Chapters 12, 19, 20.
8. McKean, Robert C., *Principles and Methods in Secondary Education.* Columbus, Ohio: Charles E. Merrill Books, Inc., 1962. Chapters 9, 11.
9. Rivlin, Harry N., *Teaching Adolescents in Secondary Schools,* 2d ed. New York: Appleton-Century-Crofts, 1961. Chapters 13, 14.
10. Schorling, Raleigh, and Howard T. Batchelder, *Student Teaching in Secondary Schools,* 3d ed. New York: McGraw-Hill Book Company, Inc., 1956. Chapters 3, 4, 5.

11. Sheviakov, George V., and Fritz Redl, *Discipline for Today's Children and Youth,* new revision by Sybil K. Richardson. Washington, D.C.: National Education Association, 1956.

12. Stout, Irving W., and Grace Langdon, "Parent-Teacher Relationships," *What Research Says to the Teacher, No. 16.* Washington, D.C.: National Education Association (September 1958).

CHAPTER 13

Remedial classroom control

The preceding chapter emphasized a constructive approach to classroom control and management. Under ideal conditions, problems of misbehavior are virtually nonexistent, or, if aberrant behavior does occur, it never assumes major proportions. Realistically, however, sooner or later some students will commit offenses for which they must be corrected. Because of the imperfections in human nature, as well as the environmental problems influencing human development, personal maladjustments and conflicts with social regulations are inevitable.

Before specific suggestions are made for dealing with student misbehavior, brief consideration needs to be given to the nature and extent of discipline problems in school.

"A BLACKBOARD JUNGLE?"

Widespread publicity of the delinquent behavior of youth, both in fact and fiction, might soon convince one that this is a spoiled and soft and even a sometimes to be feared generation. That classroom management and control are a major concern of teachers, not to be taken lightly, has already been indicated. However, since this chapter deals with the correction or punishment of misbehavior, the point needs to be stressed at the outset that modern school rooms are *not* "blackboard jungles," populated by hoodlums. Just what are the facts about the extent and seriousness of student misbehavior in today's schools?

According to a study conducted by the San Diego city schools, teachers agreed that "poor behavior was limited to less than one out of every twenty pupils" and that fewer than "three of every 100 junior high pupils" or "two of every 100 senior high students could not be controlled satisfactorily in the classroom by the teacher."[1]

[1] San Diego City Schools, *As You See It,* "What San Diego Parents and Teachers Think of Their Schools." San Diego: Board of Education (January 1957), p. 11. A survey based on the responses of 2653 teachers and 5342 parents.

In a letter to the author, dated February 25, 1963, Dr. William H. Stegeman, assistant superintendent, in charge of the curriculum, San Diego city schools, pointed out that the findings of the study just cited were published seven years ago and concluded with this statement: "Although the picture concerning discipline and the deportment of students presented by the findings summarized in *As You See It* was not especially dark, we still are firmly convinced that the situation is much improved now." He further added that "it is our feeling that the proportion is smaller now" of pupils who cannot be controlled satisfactorily by the classroom teacher.

In another study, two thirds of the teachers reported that "real trouble makers account for fewer than 1 in every 100 pupils."[2]

The findings of these two studies are parallel in many respects. Both strongly support the conclusion that the major cause of behavior problems is unsatisfactory home conditions or family life. Both conclude "that, in general, pupil behavior is no worse than it was five or ten years ago."[3]

In the letter from Stegeman, he also reaffirmed his conviction that pupil behavior has been improving by stating that "in 1963 many of us feel pupil behavior is considerably better than it was thirteen or eighteen years ago." The kinds of misbehavior judged to occur more frequently than ten years ago are "impertinence and discourtesy to teachers, failure to do homework and other assignments, and drinking intoxicants."[4]

It is interesting to note that parents who were most disturbed about rowdy behavior in the schools apparently based their conclusions on what they had read or on hearsay. For example, parents of elementary children were concerned about conditions they had heard about in secondary school. On the other hand, parents who had direct experience with secondary schools through their children were not so much concerned.[5]

As far as discipline in the average classroom is concerned, a junior high school teacher summarized the situation reasonably well. Surveying a large class of students at work, the teacher remarked, "I wish I could meet the parents of all these boys and girls. They are to be commended for doing such an excellent job of rearing their children."

In conclusion, it should be noted that, with other things being equal,

teachers are likely to have fewer problems among pupils if (a) they feel they have sufficient authority to maintain effective control . . . , (b) they have an important voice in the determination of policies . . . , (c) most of the pupils in

2 National Educational Association, Research Division, "Teacher Opinion on Pupil Behavior, 1955–56," *Research Bulletin*, vol. 34 (April 1956), p. 104. A survey based on the responses of 4270 teachers.

3 San Diego City Schools, *op. cit.*, p. 17.

4 National Educational Association, *op. cit.*, p. 106.

5 San Diego City Schools, *op. cit.*, pp. 16–17.

school are above average intelligence . . . and (d) no pupils in their classes need psychiatric help.[6]

Of all the factors contributing to good behavior, one of the most important is the willingness of parents to help solve their children's problems.

CORRECTION OR PUNISHMENT

An earlier discussion of the definitions of discipline indicated that many people consider "discipline" synonymous with "punishment." This is unfortunate, of course, for it has already been pointed out that discipline has a much broader meaning. Nevertheless, punishment or correction is an important aspect of discipline not to be ignored. Melitta Schmideberg, a psychiatrist, stresses the importance of "negative incentives in life" by saying that

As a rule, a mixture of both positive and negative incentives is most effective, and this is also a better preparation for life . . . the effect of positive incentives is necessarily limited. We cannot get pleasure from an activity until we have learned it, and studying and working are not always fun. Everyone encounters hardship, injustice, and heartbreak in the course of life.[7]

The Role of Punishment in Discipline

Since punishment is one of the unpleasant, but educative, facts of life, the chief concern of the teacher is how to administer it so as to improve student behavior. In contrast to the past, today "correction of irrational forms of behavior has shifted from imposition of the will of a stronger person to imposition of the natural results of the act."[8] In order to make natural law more operative, the teacher needs to keep a number of principles in mind.

The purpose of punishment is to correct undesirable behavior. Before assuming his role as a dispenser of punishment, the teacher must develop proper perspective with respect to what *is* undesirable or objectionable behavior. Sheviakov and Redl make the point that "different goals are pursued differently." By way of illustration, a Boy Scout troop may practice marching, which requires precision and unity. If, however, the group is climbing a mountain, symmetry is no longer necessary and individuals may walk loosely, chase butterflies, and examine rocks as long as no one gets lost or interferes with group goals. Another example contrasts the

[6] National Education Association, *op. cit.*, p. 105.

[7] Melitta Schmideberg, "Training for Responsibility," *Phi Delta Kappan*, vol. 41 (December 1959), p. 93.

[8] Asahel D. Woodruff, "Discipline," *Encyclopedia of Educational Research*, 3d ed. New York: The Macmillan Company, 1960, p. 383. Used by permission of Macmillan.

significance of the behavior of a student who runs through the halls of the school on a Saturday afternoon in order to get to a meeting on time compared to that of his running through the same halls at recess time on a school day, interfering with the rights of others to get to class safely and efficiently (9:4–5).

Any student in need of correction must learn to make a better adjustment to the realities of life, both as an individual and as a member of society. Consequently, the type of punishment which undermines self-esteem or the development of effective interpersonal relationships is to be avoided. Thus the use of sarcasm, public reprimands, or forced apologies would be a highly questionable procedure.

The spirit in which punishment is administered is important. Punishment should not be administered in anger or in a retaliatory or vindictive mood. The teacher must remember that most aggressive acts of misbehavior are not directed at him personally. By considering such acts as attempts on the part of the offender to relieve personal frustrations, the teacher is in a better position to deal with such misdeeds in an objective manner. Corrections are always to be made in the best interests of the class and the individual concerned. Consequently, there is no place in the classroom for the teacher who inflicts punishment to relieve personal irritations or aggressions or to satisfy a desire to assert his authority or control over others. In correcting minor infractions of school rules, the teacher who can demonstrate a sense of humor is at an advantage. Not only is he better able to maintain his own self-control, but he also keeps tension from building up in the classroom.

Punishment should fit the offense. Since punishment is designed to be corrective, an offender should be encouraged to make amends for mistakes he has made and to refrain from repetition of such behavior. For example, if a student carelessly damages public property, he should either restore or replace it, or, at least demonstrate a willingness to do so. If a student willfully litters the classroom, he should be required to clean it up.

Individual differences need to be considered in punishment. "Two students may commit the same offense, but for reasons that are so different that a uniform system of punishments may be unjust and ineffective for both of them" (7:423). Not only must different reasons for misbehavior be considered, but also the sensitivity, maturity, and background of the student involved. For instance, one student may respond to a mild reproof while another may require more severe treatment for correction of the same kind of misbehavior. As knowledge of the nature and causes of maladjustment has increased,

the concept of discipline has shifted steadily from uniform demands on everyone to toleration of variations in behavior by individuals, and even to toleration of variations for a single individual when he is faced with fluctuating situations.[9]

This statement may seem to violate the principle of *consistency*, stressed elsewhere in this book. That is not the case. Problems of misbehavior should be consistently recognized and corrected. But the element of justice and fair treatment cannot be ignored. Punishment must vary according to the situation, the offense, and the offender, if it is to be truly corrective.

Beginning teachers especially need to be wary in taking the advice of an experienced teacher who may have handled a particular problem in a certain way with apparent success and then recommends the same procedure for almost every occasion. It is obvious that such an approach fails to consider differences in situations, in students (their maturity, backgrounds, and so on), in goals, and in other variables. There is also the scoffer who rejects every proposed solution to a problem by saying, "We tried that in our school and it did not work."

Individual correction works better than group correction. Disruption of class morale usually begins with disturbances created by one or two individuals. Group discourtesy begins with the first student who demonstrates discourteous behavior without being corrected. The physical education instructor who ignores the first profane remark or bit of disruptive horseplay may eventually find himself with an unruly mob on his hands. Even such minor distractions as application of make-up or combing hair should be discouraged, for they are not conducive to the best learning atmosphere. It is comparatively easy to correct the first evidences of disruptive behavior on an individual basis; but, once disorder or undesirable behavior has infected a group, it sometimes takes heroic measures to restore order.

Corrective measures should be varied. Even when corrective measures take into account the variables indicated above and seem to be fair and workable, they still need to be varied. It has been said that a housewife should not attempt to do all her laundry with the same cake of soap. Likewise, the teacher should avoid using a particular procedure with monotonous repetition just because it seems to work. Sometimes the element of novelty or surprise adds to the effectiveness of punishment.

Punishment should be used judiciously. Neither severity nor frequency of punishment is an effective deterrent of misbehavior. Stern measures should be reserved for treatment of major offenses, not minor disorders. One new teacher began sending students out of his room to sit in the counselor's office for failure to do their homework, forgetting to bring their books to class, and so on. As a result, he merely compounded his problems,

[9] *Loc. cit.*

created an atmosphere of hostility in the classroom, and left himself no control measures to be used for major offenses.

When punishment becomes necessary, "it should be swift, sure, and impressive."[10] This statement does not mean that the teacher punishes a student on impulse or when he is angry. Sometimes further investigation is needed, a cooling-off period may be advisable, the student may profit from meditating on his own misbehavior, or more thought may need to be given to the most appropriate punishment. Neither does this mean that the teacher punishes a student to impress his classmates. What it does imply is that a student who misbehaves is sure he will have to suffer the consequences of his acts. Furthermore, if the punishment is appropriate, he will be impressed with the undesirability of continuing such behavior.

A teacher who is effective in classroom management and control does not make idle threats nor forget to follow through on corrective measures. By way of illustration, a teacher may request a student to stop after class or to return after school and then promptly forget about it. Or he may warn a persistent talker that he is going to change his seat the next time it occurs, but do nothing about it. The teacher is most effective *when he follows through.*

It should always be clear to an offender why he is being punished. Usually, objectionable behavior is the kind that interferes with the rights, the safety, or the welfare of others. If this is pointed out to the misbehaving student, perhaps he can be made to realize that from the standpoint of intelligent self-interest, namely, acceptance by his peers, such behavior does not pay.

When the student has paid his penalty, the case should be closed. The teacher should make the erstwhile offender feel that he is fully accepted as a member of the class. It is the offense, not the offender as a person, that merits the disapproval of the teacher. The continually misbehaving student who is the object of resentment by a school faculty has little or no chance of rehabilitation.

Punishment should be just. Students have the highest respect for teachers who maintain strict discipline as long as they feel treatment has been fair and equitable. Such practice as punishing the group for the misbehavior of an individual or making an example of an offender to impress the class is no way to win friends nor to influence students. On the other hand, the teacher who is honest, fair, and impartial in all his dealings with his students is almost sure to have the cooperation of the majority, striving to please and gain his recognition.

[10] Leonard H. Clark and Irving S. Starr, *Secondary School Teaching Methods.* New York: The Macmillan Company, 1959, p. 265. Used by permission of Macmillan.

AN ANALYSIS OF DISCIPLINARY PRACTICES

Disciplinary practices range all the way from those that are generally approved to those that are considered questionable or objectionable by most teachers. Of course, there is still disagreement over the relative merits of a number of common practices.

Approved Disciplinary Practices

Although there is unlikely to be complete agreement on all of the items, the following disciplinary procedures have been endorsed as desirable corrective measures by sources indicated below: (1) individual conferences with students; (2) conferences with parents; (3) simple control measures (catching the eye of an offender, and so on); (4) a change in seating; (5) use of social pressure; (6) loss of special privilege; (7) student participation in school discipline; (8) rectification, restitution, and reparation; (9) "use of rewards"; (10) "temporary isolation under supervision"; (11) detention for a specific, clearly stated purpose, and (12) "referral to a school officer . . . after the teacher has exhausted all his own possibilities" (6:76–84, 1:383–384).

INDIVIDUAL CONFERENCES An individual conference with a student is the most desirable of all corrective measures the teacher might use. It enables the teacher to perform his guidance function, to obtain additional information, and to secure the reactions of the student. In some cases, it is advisable to have the student suggest his own punishment. Such a conference may be limited in its effectiveness, however, by a lack of knowledge, time, interest, or understanding of adolescents on the part of the teacher. Furthermore, some teachers may be inclined to harbor resentments toward offenders or be unable to establish rapport with them (6:76).

When an individual conference is held, it should be in private. There should be freedom from outside distractions or eavesdropping by other students or faculty members. It is never advisable to confer with two misbehaving students at the same time, unless they are mutually involved, for they are likely to reinforce each other in resisting the counsel of the teacher.

CONFERENCES WITH PARENTS Conferences with parents have a number of potential values: to strengthen relationships between home and school; to enable parents and teachers to share information and to attack the problem on a united front; and to provide the teacher with a better understanding of the student's home environment. The disadvantages of such conferences may stem from the teacher's lack of skill in interviewing and making home visits and in diagnosing and interpreting student misbehavior. Then, too, it is often difficult to arrange such conferences, either at home or at school (6:77).

Unfortunately, conferences between teachers and parents of misbehaving students often take place under unfavorable conditions. The parents may not be summoned to school until misbehavior has already reached serious proportions, perhaps to the point of expulsion. It is understandable that such parents would be on the defensive and probably in a belligerent mood. Earlier notification might forestall such a difficult situation. It should also be noted that neither a note nor a telephone call is a satisfactory substitute for the personal interview. On handling such an interview, even when parents are upset, the reader is referred to suggestions given in Chapter 12 (3:86–87).

SIMPLE CONTROL MEASURES The use of simple control measures—quiet disapproval techniques, such as eye contact, moving near trouble spots— is not likely to disturb the class as a whole, to result in "unpleasant scenes," or to have harmful effects on personality. With difficult classes, however, such control measures are ineffective. Furthermore, the teacher "attacks surface behavior only, neglecting underlying causes" (6:76). At times no action is best. The beginning teacher is often advised to avoid nagging or making issues of trivial incidents. Admittedly this poses a problem. Lacking experience, the new teacher may not have the perspective to judge what is significant or trivial in terms of the students' actions. A simple criterion may be applied: If persistence of a particular kind of behavior results in a gradual deterioration of the learning situation, then such behavior cannot be considered trivial.

The teacher must be able to distinguish between normal, exuberant actions of youth and danger signs of real aberrant behavior. Sometimes as teachers grow older, they should be reminded that they may create their own discipline problems by becoming fussier, more impatient, and less tolerant of the high-spirited behavior of normal adolescents.

CHANGE OF SEATING A change of seating may correct minor disturbances such as excessive talking. The teacher should avoid measures which create feelings of shame or resentment, perhaps making the offender even worse. For example, seating a girl among a group of boys, placing a talker conspicuously in the front of the room or apart from the group, or placing an offender at the back of the room where it is difficult to keep him under observation are changes in seating which may do more harm than good. Some teachers have found it useful to talk with the student, to suggest a change in seating to improve his behavior, and to ask him where he would like to sit.

LOSS OF PRIVILEGE When a student is punished by loss of privilege, he is made aware of the relationship between duty and privilege. For example, if one condition for participation in cocurricular activities is contingent on maintenance of satisfactory citizenship, the student soon learns that unsatisfactory behavior does not pay. Depriving a student of a privilege he has abused or temporarily confiscating a possession that is causing the trouble are punishments that fit the offense. The chief danger in this type of control if applied too long is that the student may be denied valuable learning experiences.

STUDENT SELF-GOVERNMENT   It has already been suggested that there are definite advantages to having students participate in setting up rules to govern their class. However, when a group begins to exhibit patterns of idleness or disorder, what action should the teacher take under those conditions? With a group of sufficient maturity, the teacher may profitably arrange for a candid discussion of the problem. Such a session permits students to air their dissatisfactions and provides a means whereby a teacher and his class may reach a mutual agreement on what is needed to promote a more effective learning situation.

Again the teacher needs to be warned of the danger of attempting to establish self-government in a group that is not yet ready for it. Sheviakov and Redl cite the case of a Miss Jones who undertook to use democratic procedures in a class with a bad reputation, including some of "the worst hoodlums in school." Several unfortunate results followed: bullies took over, showing favoritism toward their friends; rules were made and broken; and no fundamental improvements in school attendance, work habits, or over-all behavior occurred (9:33).

RECTIFICATION, RESTITUTION, AND REPARATION   These are forms of punishment which can be justly and impartially associated with the offense. For example, if a student charges out of the room when the dismissal bell rings, endangering the safety of himself and others, he should be made to return to the room and walk from it in an orderly manner. Or he may be required to remain in his seat each day while all other class members leave until he is willing to leave the room in an acceptable way.

Students need to develop a sense of social responsibility for making amends when they willfully destroy or take property belonging to others. A problem arises in the application of this corrective measure, however, whenever the student is financially unable to pay for damages or parents too readily supply the money themselves, thereby "destroying the educative value of the punishment" (6:78). The common practice of shop teachers of collecting money from all students when a tool is lost may be questionable on legal grounds.

REWARDS OR PRIZES   The use of rewards or prizes does constitute a positive approach to the promotion of desirable behavior. However, there are a number of dangers in this procedure: rewards may become ends in themselves; they may not be available "to all students on an equal basis;" and prizes may encourage personal selfishness and greed. If rewards are used, they should "appeal to higher motives such as group welfare, citizenship, and service" (6:78).

"TEMPORARY ISOLATION UNDER SUPERVISION"[11] This measure is sometimes a necessity when the behavior of an individual becomes completely objectionable in terms of group welfare. The offender may be set apart from the group within a classroom or referred to the office of a counselor or principal. It is not advisable to have a student stand or sit outside the classroom or to leave for some unspecified destination. When such punishment is exercised too frequently or for too long a period, it may rob the student of valuable educational experiences and increase his difficulty in making adjustment to the group.

USE OF SOCIAL PRESSURE Social or peer pressure may be an effective measure for the correction of misbehavior when used judiciously. The following example illustrates the point:

Jerry was a perpetually disturbing element in the eighth-grade social studies class. Whistling, mumbling, making sound effects, heckling his neighbors, and wandering aimlessly made up his assortment of distractions. One day the class played a baseball game for a unit review. Anyone who was on the same team as the student at bat (answering a review question) who coached his teammate received a strike against his team. Jerry's team had three men on base, two outs, and two strikes on the "batter" who had decided to try for a "home run." The teacher asked him a difficult review question. As the batter painfully concentrated on the answer, with his classmates waiting excitedly, Jerry blurted out the answer and the side was retired. The displeasure of his team, soon made evident to Jerry, served as an effective deterrent of his uninhibited behavior.

The behavior of Jerry was most likely indicative of a desire for attention. But he needed to learn how to secure recognition in more socially accepted ways, a lesson which sometimes a boy can learn most effectively from his peers. The use of social pressure is harmful if it alienates a student permanently from his group. By all means, the teacher should not himself encourage a group to reject an offender, but should arrange the situation so that the student suffers the social consequences of his own acts.

DETENTION AFTER SCHOOL Detention is one of the most widely used, and presumably most widely acceptable, forms of punishment. It is easily administered and may serve as a deterrent to further misbehavior when the student is prevented from doing something which he would very much like to do. It may also be an appropriate corrective measure for the

[11] Woodruff, *op. cit.*, p. 384.

student who is persistently tardy or wastes times during school hours.

The disadvantages of this form of punishment, however, seem to outweigh its advantages. First of all, basic causes of misbehavior are not considered. Furthermore, it is often used as a blanket form of punishment for all types of misbehavior so that correction may fit neither the offense nor the offender. In having to supervise the offender after school hours, the teacher is also punished, a fact that may be relished by the offender himself. Detention may seriously conflict with such after-school activities of the student as work, medical appointments, cocurricular activities, and school bus transportation, although some schools provide before-school detention. Finally, it is a real problem to decide what to have the student do during detention. If he just sits, nothing of value is accomplished. If he is assigned homework, he may learn to strengthen his dislike for school. If he is assigned other tasks, then the punishment is probably no longer associated with the act of misbehavior.

Detention after school cannot be justified unless it enables the teacher to give extra help or counsel to the student or it enables the student to make up work. Detention during recess or noon periods is condemned and even illegal in some states (6:79–80).

REFERRAL TO SOME OTHER SCHOOL AUTHORITY   Exclusion from the classroom is necessary when a student becomes incorrigible in the classroom, engages in serious forms of misbehavior (committing immoral acts or assaulting others, for example), or gives evidence of being emotionally disturbed or socially maladjusted. Teachers may err in either of two extremes, by sending students to the principal for even the most minor offenses or by putting up with intolerable disruptive behavior in the classroom without seeking help.

Before resorting to referrals, a teacher needs to exhaust his own resources, by trying any or all of the following measures:

Making class work more interesting
Seeking to discover underlying causes of misbehavior
Securing more information about his students
Conferring privately with an offender
Providing opportunity for special recognition
Conferring with homeroom teacher, counselor, or vice-principal
Conferring with parents
Ignoring minor annoyances which are unlikely to disturb group climate
Changing seating
Isolating an offender temporarily within the classroom
Taking away special privileges
Detaining an offender after school for reasons related to the offense

The preceding discussion has been concerned with corrective measures in classroom management and control which are generally approved in school practice. However, of the last three forms of punishment—isolation, detention, and referral—there are those who would classify them as questionable rather than acceptable procedures. Obviously, all of the corrective measures listed above are not equally acceptable. Some probably can be justified only on the basis of immediate necessity. In the following discussion, an analysis will be made of control procedures that are considered questionable or objectionable.

Questionable or Objectionable Disciplinary Procedures

There are a great number of corrective measures used in classroom management and control about which there is considerable difference of opinion. Some of these are: (1) use of corporal punishment, (2) use of group punishment, (3) forcing apologies, (4) lowering marks, (5) use of sarcasm or ridicule, (6) use of threats and repeated vocal correction, (7) assignment of extra tasks unrelated to the offense, (8) making an example of a misbehaving student, (9) arguing with students in the presence of the total group, (10) use of suspension, and (11) expulsion (6:84).

CORPORAL PUNISHMENT   The use of corporal punishment is the subject of much controversy. Opinion polls have shown that parents and particularly administrators favor it. There is also evidence that the use of corporal punishment is gaining in favor again. If used at all, such a corrective measure would obviously be more appropriate at the elementary level than in high school. When corporal punishment is authorized, there are usually definite requirements outlined for its administration, such as having witnesses, using moderation, and the like.

Except in extreme cases, when the safety of a student or the teacher himself is at stake, the teacher is advised to avoid the use of physical force in dealing with a recalcitrant student. It is better to summon assistance if needed. Physical contact with a student, such as slapping or restraining him, may result in a number of complications: he may strike the teacher; the teacher may feel it necessary to defend himself; or the parents may resort to court action (3:34–35).

GROUP PUNISHMENT   While it is true that in some instances an entire class may seem to be deserving of punishment, the teacher has to exercise discretion in its application and a finesse which may even be appreciated by the recipients. By way of illustration, an entire student body cut school on April Fool's Day. Upon their return, the principal called a general assembly and, without making any reference to the affair, announced in a suave manner, "Students, it seems that we are getting a little behind in our work. So the board and I have decided that it is advisable for us to lengthen the school day forty-five minutes from now until the end of the term." Sometimes a teacher punishes a class for the offense of an individual in the belief that group disapproval will be directed against the offender. More often than not, resentment is directed toward the teacher and he loses the support of the students who previously favored him. Group punishment is also likely to be unjust, for the innocent must suffer with the guilty.

FORCED APOLOGIES   A forced apology is objectionable in the first place because such an apology is no apology at all; it is an act of hypocrisy. A true apology is a voluntary expression of sincere regret for thoughtless behavior. By all means, the teacher should encourage a student to feel responsible for his misbehavior, to regret it, and to wish to make amends to those whom he may have wronged. For instance, the teacher may say, "Don't you feel that you owe the class an apology for what you have done?" but not, "You *must* apologize to the class before you return to it." In encouraging students to apologize for their misdeeds, the teacher must be willing to set a good example. When he has erred, he should admit it and ask the forgiveness of those he may have misjudged or treated unjustly.

LOWERING SCHOLARSHIP MARKS   The use of such a measure for the correction of misbehavior is a misuse of the school's marking system. It is perfectly logical to lower citizenship grades for misbehavior but to lower scholarship marks as punishment is unjustifiable. Such marks represent scholastic achievement and nothing else. A closely related practice, assigning demerits for various offenses, is objectionable for a number of reasons: causes of behavior are ignored, bookkeeping becomes onerous, and good behavior is not rewarded. As is often the case in the use of questionable practices, teachers may defend them by asserting the effectiveness of a particular system. Actually the results of many procedures are difficult to evaluate. They may bring about surface changes only or the desired conformity, with no fundamental changes in attitudes or future behavior of the student taking place.

SARCASM OR RIDICULE   The use of sarcasm or ridicule is another corrective measure that is often justified on the assumption that it works. The practice is objectionable, first of all, because the offender is subjected to embarrassment and loss of self-esteem. Like group punishment, it can be a dangerous weapon. The student is forced into a face-saving situation in which his status with his peers is threatened. Sooner or later, a student will respond in kind to the teacher's sarcastic remark. With the class acting as judge and jury, it is the teacher who will be laughed out of court. Whenever a teacher is tempted to resort to sarcasm, he should remember that a basic professional principle is at stake: *A teacher can expect the same respect and consideration that he shows for his students.* Furthermore, "young people learn to respect one another when they themselves have been treated with respect by understanding adults" (9:11).

THREATS AND VOCAL CORRECTION Threats and repeated vocal correction have one thing in common: they are often used as ineffective substitutes for needed action. Nothing is more futile than repetitious vocal correction. A threat may serve to notify a student that his behavior is objectionable, but it may be inconvenient, if not impossible, to carry out. Sometimes a warning may be in order, especially if the offender is told why his behavior is objectionable and will need to be corrected if continued (3:29). Where two students are involved, for example, in excessive talking, the teacher may suggest that if they wish to continue to sit near each other they must mend their ways or some changes will be made in seating. The use of threats has an additional disadvantage, especially with adolescents who are passing through a stage of rebellion against adult authority; it may constitute a challenge to be tested.

Under the subject of vocal correction needs to be mentioned the teacher who persistently scolds or nags his students. Instead of encouraging improved behavior, such practice lowers group morale and widens the breach between the teacher and the class.

The teacher also should avoid making comments to individuals or vocal corrections across the room when the class is at work. Sometimes a noisy teacher is the most disturbing element in the classroom.

ASSIGNMENT OF EXTRA TASKS The assignment of extra tasks has little or nothing to commend it as a corrective measure. Punishment is unrelated to the act of misbehavior; dislike for school work is likely to be increased; and motivation to learn is stifled.

MAKING EXAMPLES OF STUDENTS Making an example of a misbehaving student is objectionable on several counts. First of all, the self-esteem of the student is undermined. Secondly, when a student is threatened with loss of face in the presence of his peers, he may defy the authority of the teacher. Furthermore, such punishment is unjust when some student is selected as a scapegoat to serve as an object lesson for the group. Finally, the procedure is ineffective: the group is usually not impressed, and, in fact, the offender may become a martyr in the eyes of his classmates and the group itself may be encouraged to imitate his behavior.

PUBLIC ARGUMENTS WITH STUDENTS Arguing with a student in the presence of the class is decidely unwise. This is another face-saving situation in which the teacher is pitted against the student. The teacher must absolutely refuse to become involved in such arguments. Any differences between the teacher and a student which involve problems of behavior must be settled privately. Two examples illustrate the right way and the wrong way to handle the problem.

The following incident illustrates how a new teacher of physical education took care of a potentially explosive situation in a wise manner:

> The teacher and his class were returning to the gymnasium after a period of touch football. As was the usual procedure, the teacher began collecting all of the balls. When he asked one student to toss a ball to him, the boy deliberately threw the ball as far as he could in another direction. Instead of ordering the boy to get the ball, the teacher said quietly but firmly, "I'll see you in the locker room."

In the above illustration, the teacher forced neither the boy nor himself into an uncompromising face-saving situation. Neither did he provide the boy an open opportunity to further defy his authority in the presence of the class.

A second illustration demonstrates how a new teacher reached a crisis in discipline by unwise handling of a minor incident.

> J. J. announced to an eighth-grade speech class that they were to copy material she would dictate. When everyone seemed to be ready, Chuck announced that he had no pencil. Evidently this was a delaying tactic, a subtle sabotage of class procedures, for which Chuck was noted. Irritated with his behavior, the teacher sharply demanded of Chuck his reason for having no pencil. An argument ensued in which Chuck responded with wisecracks, the class burst into gales of laughter, and the teacher became increasingly confused and angry. Finally, the class became completely disorganized and J. J. made her exit in tears.

This could have been avoided in several ways: by lending Chuck a pencil; by ignoring him and letting him get his information as best he could; or by having him come in after school and copy the material on his own time for habitual failure to bring necessary materials to class.

SUSPENSION OR EXPULSION Drastic measures like suspension or expulsion, ordinarily administered by the principal or superintendent, are to be used as a last resort. When all other measures have failed and the welfare of the class is threatened, suspension or expulsion becomes a necessity. No student has a right to interfere with the rights of the majority to learn. Suspension may give the student an opportunity to reflect on his own behavior and impress parents with the seriousness of the problem. Neither suspension nor expulsion, however, removes the causes of misbehavior. Expulsion enables the school "to get rid of extreme cases," but it does not solve the problem for society (6:83–84).

CORRECTION VERSUS PREVENTION OF DISCIPLINE PROBLEMS

The foundation of good discipline is good morale, marked by an emotional climate in the classroom of "warm friendliness, pride in a good reputation, and group solidarity" (3:6). The teacher who is able to supply the guidance teen-agers need possesses qualities of "friendliness, fairness, enthusiasm, vitality, a sense of humor, a liking for (his) work, and a liking for young people" (3:138).

Teacher Sensitivity to Students' Feelings

Of all the aspects of human development, a conscious consideration of feeling or emotional activity has probably been most neglected by schools. The first book on the subject was written during this generation. Yet, of all the drives to action, sources of personal enjoyment, and keys to human values, emotions probably rank first. Pestalozzi contended that education must be of the hand, the head, and the heart.[12] Formal education has scorned the first, enshrined the second, and neglected the third. Man takes pride in being a rational animal, a claim that may be open to serious question. Acquaintance with great literature, art, and music; participation in dramatic situations of emotional significance; human relationships that stir love, sympathy, and understanding are the factors that give life meaning.

Sometimes teachers have exhibited a shameful indifference to their students' feelings. While adolescents often try to mask their true feelings, they still stand in need of a wholesome development of their affective natures. Not only must an emotional sensitivity be developed, but students also must learn to control their emotions. Discussion groups, competitive games, and recreational activities are but a few of the situations in which boys and girls may learn to develop self-control. They have to learn to take defeat without bitterness and to experience victory without arrogance.

School administrators are sometimes tempted to abolish competitive student activities because of the school rivalries and personal animosities engendered by them. However, the unlovely emotional results of such contests are not always primarily the fault of the activities nor of the contestants. Parents, coaches, and fans have often been more concerned with winning loving cups than with developing the emotional quality of good sportsmanship.

Every teacher, whether he be coach or English teacher, needs to develop emotional self-control. That is critical in insuring his own mental

12 J. H. Pestalozzi, *The Swan Song.* Edited by J. A. Green in *Pestalozzi's Educational Writings*, London: Edward Arnold & Co., 1916, pp. 268–269.

health as well as important in guiding his students toward emotional maturity. The teacher who sulks a whole semester because of some slight to his dignity, either real or imaginary, is in no condition to act as a counselor for youth. In the realm of the emotions, the teacher sets the pattern for student behavior.

The Teacher's Mental Health

In order to aid students in making better adjustments to the demands of daily living, the teacher must maintain his own mental health. Some of the simple rules of good mental hygiene follow:

Enjoy your work. Someone has said not everyone can do what he likes, but he can like what he does.

Schedule free time for interesting hobbies, wholesome recreation, and relaxation.

Protect your physical health by providing for sufficient exercise, sleep, rest, and regular physical checkups.

Cultivate friendships, both within and outside the profession.

Enjoy the beauty of the world around you.

Assist others who need your help, especially when you are disturbed or feeling sorry for yourself.

Develop self-reliance and assume your responsibilities.

Solve your problems in a realistic and courageous manner.[13]

TEN COMMANDMENTS OF DISCIPLINE

Ten rules for the development of good class morale are:

1. *Begin right.* Good grooming, enthusiasm, and warmth are important in making a good first impression. Students should be made to feel that the class is going to be a stimulating, enjoyable, and profitable experience.

2. *Be businesslike.* Class should begin on time and close on time. Plans should be ready and all routine well organized. You should be calm, composed, and dignified in manner. Good tempo, variety, and protection of the group from unnecessary annoyances should help keep the class interesting.

3. *Be alert.* Stopping the little disturbances—idling, scuffling, loud talking—often prevents more serious disorder. You need to be immediately aware of individual aberrations in behavior or disturbances in group climate.

4. *Be tactful.* Requests rather than commands, cooperative decisions

[13] Norma E. Cutts and Nicholas Moseley, *Teaching the Disorderly Pupil in Elementary and Secondary School.* New York: David McKay Company, Inc., 1957, pp. 162–163.

rather than those made solely by the teacher, courtesy rather than curtness, and respect for the rights and opinions of others instead of intolerance constitute the essence of tact and consideration.

5. *Be cheerful.* Radiate good humor, an even disposition, and peace of mind in your face, your voice, and your actions. At all costs, the authoritative manner, the peevish voice, or perpetual scowl should be avoided.

6. *Be just.* Avoid hasty judgments, partiality, or prejudicial treatment in working with students. If you make a mistake, rectify it.

7. *Be persistent.* Expect good behavior and insist on it. If you set out to settle a problem, see it through. If words are ineffective, act.

8. *Be consistent.* Consistency of behavior is indicative of maturity and self-control. Fortunate are the students who have a mature teacher who provides them with the security they need.

9. *Be decisive.* As a teacher, you are morally and legally responsible for maintaining classroom atmosphere that is conducive to effective learning. If you fail in your leadership, students become insecure and classroom conditions become chaotic.

10. *Be judicious.* Avoid scenes or crises in the classroom. Avoid uncompromising situations—public argument, sarcasm, encouragement of open defiance—in which either teacher or student is in danger of loss of face. Commend publicly; reprimand privately.

Selected Readings

1. American Educational Research Association, *Encyclopedia of Educational Research,* 3d ed. Chester W. Harris, ed. New York: The Macmillan Company, 1960.
2. Brown, Edwin John, and Arthur Thomas Phelps, *Managing the Classroom.* New York: The Ronald Press Company, 1961. Chapter 6.
3. Cutts, Norma E., and Nicholas Moseley, *Teaching the Disorderly Pupil in Elementary and Secondary School.* New York: David McKay Company, Inc., 1957.
4. Gordon, Ted, *Tips to Teachers.* Los Angeles: California Education Press. Chapters 2, 4.
5. Massey, Harold W., and Edwin E. Vineyard, *The Profession of Teaching.* New York: The Odyssey Press, Inc., 1961. Chapters 8, 9.
6. Oliva, Peter F., "High School Discipline in American Society," *Bulletin of the National Association of Secondary-School Principals,* vol. 40 (January 1956), pp. 1–103.
7. Rivlin, Harry N., *Teaching Adolescents in Secondary Schools,* 2d ed. New York: Appleton-Century-Crofts, 1961. Chapter 14.
8. Schorling, Raleigh, and Howard T. Batchelder, *Student Teaching in Secondary Schools,* 3d ed. New York: McGraw-Hill Book Company, Inc., 1956. Chapter 4.
9. Sheviakov, George V., and Fritz Redl, *Discipline for Today's Children and Youth,* new revision by Sybil K. Richardson. Washington, D.C.: National Education Association, 1956.
10. Wellington, C. Burleigh, and Jean Wellington, *Teaching for Critical Thinking.* New York: McGraw-Hill Book Company, Inc., 1960. Chapter 13.

PART FIVE

Considering
the Total
School Program

CHAPTER 14

The secondary school curriculum

"Today . . . the mechanics of curriculum survival and its adaptation in our time are the most fascinating aspects of the whole educational problem."[1]

At no time in history has the curriculum maker been confronted with a greater challenge. He is faced with the paradox of attempting to maintain cultural stability and unity in a period of revolutionary change and at the same time attempting to develop a dynamic educational program to keep pace with the needs of a changing world.

"Tradition encourages us to cling to a curriculum which seems oddly impervious to the impact of contemporary epochal discoveries, to world-shaking events, and to inexorable and profound changes in our society."[2]

"At present, all over the world the schools are faced with the necessity of adjusting their programme to the drastic change around them. Yet all over the world, nations not only cling to outmoded educational programmes but also rationalize eagerly the justification for so doing."[3]

The foregoing statements suggest some of the challenges and problems involved in curriculum development in the years just ahead. It is imperative for every teacher to become aware of the issues and problems at stake and to become an intelligent and active participant in curriculum improvement. By the very nature of his work the classroom teacher is in danger of developing a microscopic view of the total school program and its impact on contemporary life. Following daily routines, working with the same group of students day after day, and teaching the same subjects year after year may very well limit the vision of the teacher.

[1] George Z. F. Bereday, Brian Holmes, and Joseph A. Lauwerys, "Editors' Introduction," *The Secondary School Curriculum: 1958 Yearbook of Education.* London: Evans Brothers Limited, 1958, p. 25.

[2] Harold J. McNally, "What Shall We Teach—and How?" *The National Elementary Principal* (May 1957), p. 6.

[3] Bereday, *op. cit.*, p. 25.

ORGANIZATION AND OFFERINGS OF THE SECONDARY SCHOOL

Secondary school organization in this country has developed along two unique lines. First, the secondary school became part of a unitary or "ladder" system, extending from the lowest grade of the elementary school through the university. By way of contrast, the traditional type of organization of European educational systems has been in terms of a dual track, with one track for an academic (or socioeconomic) elite and another for the masses. A second unique feature of the American second-ary school is that it became a *comprehensive* school, one in which all boys and girls are educated together, regardless of differences in ability, sex, religion, race (an ideal yet to be fully achieved), socioeconomic status, or occupational goals.

Prior to 1890, the secondary school was typically a four-year school which followed eight years of elementary schooling. Since 1900, various patterns of reorganization have been developing. A common pattern that has evolved has been the six-year elementary school, followed by a six-year high school (in smaller communities) or a three-year junior high school and a three-year senior high school. Today, at least in a number of states, this twelve-year program has been capped by a two-year junior or community college (grades thirteen and fourteen).

Curricular offerings consist of subjects studied in the classroom and the student activity or cocurricular program. The curriculum varies from school to school with larger schools providing broader and more varied offerings.

The *classroom program* has been, and continues to be, organized primarily on the basis of separate, discrete subjects. The number of specific titles is extensive. However, subjects are usually classified under such categories as the following:

Language arts (English, speech, foreign languages)
Social studies (basically history and geography)
Mathematics
Science
Fine arts (art and music)
Practical arts (agriculture, industrial arts, homemaking, business edu-
    cation)
Health and physical education

Graduation requirements have been traditionally defined in terms of Carnegie units (one unit being equivalent to one period per day of a five-day week for a school year, or 120 class hours in a subject). In a four-year high school, sixteen units have constituted normal requirements for graduation.

The *student activity or cocurricular program* consists of a number of athletic events, innumerable clubs, musical and dramatic activities, school publications, and student government. Values and problems associated with these programs are discussed later in this chapter.

The Curriculum Defined

Traditionally, the *curriculum* has meant a course of study or the subjects that a student takes in school, with corresponding neglect of the objectives of education, defined in terms of changes in student behavior. Today, "the curriculum is defined as all the experiences that a learner has under the guidance of the school."[4] Philosophically, the broader definition has been widely accepted by professional educators in an attempt to unify the total program of the school. This is especially true with respect to an effort to coordinate more closely the organized class program with the student activity or extracurricular program. However, the union has been more theoretical than real, for in practice, as well as in common descriptions of the curriculum, a distinction is frequently made between organized class activities and the student activity program (3:360).

When the word "curriculum" is defined in such broad terms, further clarification of definition becomes necessary. To some persons, the organized classroom phase of the curriculum means merely a body of content. But curriculum involves not only *what* is taught but *how* it is taught as well, for the two are inseparable. However, both the *what* and the *how* are only means to an end, the improved behavior of the learner.

Aspects of the Curriculum

Not only is the curriculum divided into two different phases, the organized class program and student activities, but the organized class program is further subdivided into two categories, *general education* and *special education*. The first is designed to educate for unity; the second, to educate for diversity. General education provides the learning experiences needed by all students to become effective citizens. Special education is designed to provide for the unique interests, needs, and abilities of each student individually.

In terms of subjects or courses listed in the course of study or curriculum guide of a school, general education consists of the required subjects while special education includes the electives.

[4] Nolan C. Kearney and Walter W. Cook, "Curriculum," *Encyclopedia of Educational Research*, 3d ed. New York: The Macmillan Company, 1960, p. 358. Used by permission of Macmillan.

At this point, it should be re-emphasized that general education or special education is more than a subject or series of subjects. It should also be noted that a sharp line of demarcation cannot always be drawn between general education and special education. For example, sometimes the best vocational education (a function of special education) is that which aids students in learning how to cooperate with others (a function of general education).

BACKGROUNDS OF AMERICAN SECONDARY EDUCATION

The story of American education is the story of a "search for freedom." In the process of development of a unique system of education, the schools have been faced with certain persistent problems. Attempts to solve those problems in an evolving democracy have made the schools what they are today. A few of these problems follow: Shall education be provided for all or for an elite only? Is a democratic school system served best by local control or by a centralized, state authority? Shall control and support of education be public or private? Shall boys and girls be educated in a school common to all or shall they be segregated on the basis of sex, race, religion, social class, or intellect? Shall colleges and secondary schools offer academic or intellectual studies only or shall practical subjects be included as well in the curriculum?[5]

A superficial analysis of the above questions might lead one to believe that they have already been satisfactorily answered. However, a further study of current issues and trends, to be discussed later in this chapter, results in a more sound conclusion: namely, that some educational battles have to be fought and won by each succeeding generation.

The Latin Grammar School

The first type of secondary school established in America was the Latin Grammar School, founded in Boston, presumably in 1635. The curriculum was classical and traditional, patterned after the curricula of European schools. Admission was selective, limited to boys of high intellectual ability. The primary purpose was to provide leadership needed by the church and state. In 1647, a Massachusetts law required every "town" (a geographical area of about 20 to 40 square miles) of 100 or more householders to establish a grammar school. Failure to do so resulted in the assessment of a fine, and many towns paid the fine rather than maintain the schools.[6]

[5] R. Freeman Butts, "Search for Freedom—the Story of American Education," *NEA Journal,* vol. 49 (March 1960), pp. 33–48.
[6] Newton Edwards and Herman G. Richey, *The School in the American Social Order.* Boston: Houghton Mifflin Company, 1947, pp. 104–105.

The chief contribution of the Latin Grammar School was to establish the college-preparatory function of the secondary school.

The Academy

With the rise of a strong middle class, primarily engaged in business and industry, the need for a new type of school to meet the needs of the people became evident. An examination of the advertisements in the newspapers of Boston during the first half of the eighteenth century indicated that the practical educational needs of boys, as well as girls, of this class were being met by private teachers.[7] Consequently, when the first academy was established in Philadelphia in 1751 by Benjamin Franklin, the foundations for a practical curriculum had already been laid.

Product of an emerging industrial society, flexible in its policies and practices, and offering a great variety of subjects, the academy soon became a popular school. Its legacy for secondary education was to introduce practical courses into the curriculum, to admit girls to secondary education, and to free the schools from sectarian control. It had one serious limitation, however; it was not free. Because the academy had to depend upon tuition for partial support, many youths could not afford to attend it.

The High School

In 1821, the first high school was established in Boston. Since the curriculum was similar to that of the academy, it was probably an attempt to provide for more *public* support and control of education to meet the needs of boys who intended "to become merchants and mechanics." Later, high schools were established for girls, or "female departments" were added to existing schools. At that time, it was recognized that both the academy and the high school had a dual function: to prepare for life and to prepare for college.

Since 1890

Many educational historians classify the period since 1890 as *a period of reorganization*. The Committee of Ten of 1893 recommended "English, ancient and modern foreign languages, mathematics, natural science, history, and geography" as appropriate subjects for study by all students, ignoring differences in interests, abilities, and vocational goals. A short time later, other committees succeeded in defining a high school education in quantitative terms of units of credit. Through the activities of such committees, the high school curriculum became more or less standardized until about 1930.[8]

[7] *Ibid.,* pp. 122–125.
[8] *Ibid.,* pp. 739–741.

Prior to 1918, the primary function of the high school was regarded as preparation for college. For those students who did not plan to go to college, training of the mind provided sufficient justification for pursuit of an academic curriculum. "Objectives (for adult living, self-preservation, and so on) were neglected or regarded as secondary during the time when faculty psychology and mental discipline held sway."[9]

In 1918, the Commission on the Reorganization of Secondary Education defined the aims of the high school in terms of seven personal-social goals:

1. Good health
2. Command of fundamental processes
3. Worthy home membership
4. Vocational efficiency
5. Civic efficiency
6. Worthy use of leisure
7. Ethical character (2:93)

Since 1918, educational objectives have been stated by various commissions, most of them representing refinements or elaborations of the "seven cardinal principles" above.[10]

According to Ralph Tyler, there is a

shift in school objectives toward a more discriminating selection, toward the kinds of learning which involve intellectual skills, which require sequential experiences to reach the necessary level of competence, which involve concepts and principles that are not apparent on the surface and for this reason are not likely to be learned through the guidance of laymen.[11]

Besides Tyler, Paul Woodring and others have recognized the need to establish "an order of priority" for educational objectives, so that the schools will undertake their most important tasks first (2:84). That priority is now being strongly defined in terms of intellectual attainment, as indicated by the purposes of the Council for Basic Education and the report of the San Francisco Curriculum Survey Committee, to be discussed later in this chapter.

FACTORS AND FORCES IN CURRICULUM DEVELOPMENT

What are some of the factors and forces which have affected, and continue to affect, the curriculum of the secondary school?

[9] Kearney and Cook, *op. cit.*, p. 358.

[10] For a review of changes which have taken place in objectives and learning activities during the first half of this century, see the condensation of Ralph Tyler's article in Chapter 3.

[11] Ralph W. Tyler, "The Curriculum—Then and Now," *Proceedings, 1956 Invitational Conference on Testing Problems*, Princeton, N.J.: Educational Testing Service, 1956, pp. 79–94.

Historical Traditions

The college-preparatory function of the secondary school, a direct legacy of the Boston Latin Grammar School, still exerts a strong influence on the curriculum of the high school. Undue preoccupation with an academic tradition can seriously hamper the efforts of the school to meet the needs of all boys and girls and to deal with the persistent problems of a dynamic society.

Research

Various studies—such as studies of needs, of individual differences, of group processes, of adolescent growth and development, and of "the social structure of our society"—have had an important bearing on curriculum development.[12]

Social and Educational Philosophy

Philosophical beliefs have a pervasive influence on curriculum change. For example, many of the recurring "battles" in education have been fought over a single principle: *equality of educational opportunity*. No other country in the world has attempted to provide so much education for so many for so long a period of years. To provide education on such a massive scale has created a number of complexities: to provide mass education and still maintain quality, to educate for national unity and encourage diversity, to meet the needs of all when so many differ in so many ways. Some of these issues will be considered later in this chapter.

Special Interest Groups

There are many agencies and special-interest groups which exert pressure on the schools. State and local boards of education, state departments of education, legislatures, and accrediting agencies are official groups which set up minimum standards for school programs. A great many special-interest groups—such as patriotic groups, business, labor, political, and religious organizations—influence curricula through organized programs, publicity campaigns, and lobbying.

State Legislatures

State legislatures may actively engage in making changes in the curriculum, either directly or indirectly. Illustrations of such activity are given later in this chapter.

The Teaching Profession

The profession itself, through its leaders (such as Horace Mann and John

[12] Kearney and Cook, *op. cit.*, pp. 361–362.

Dewey), and its professional organizations, such as the National Education Association, have continuously worked for curriculum improvement.

Textbook Authors and Test Makers

Publishers of instructional materials have more influence on curriculum development than is sometimes realized. The textbook has even been referred to as the child's "other teacher." If a trend toward the adoption of state-wide testing programs becomes widespread, test makers will become even more significant as curriculum makers of the future.

Community Influences

Because the American school system is decentralized, with considerable control residing with local boards of education, the community is one of the most important factors in shaping the school program of a given locality. The character of the people—their occupations, educational level, and economic status—has a direct bearing on the type and quality of schools provided in the area.

The Teacher

In the final analysis, the classroom teacher is the most important factor in curriculum improvement. In fact, the sum total of the educational experiences boys and girls have under their teachers *is* the curriculum. Because tradition is such a strong agent in curriculum development, lasting changes are likely to occur only on a piecemeal basis. "Among the factors responsible for such piecemeal but relentless change the teachers may be singled out as the most obvious agents."[13]

IMPROVEMENT OF THE CURRICULUM

The approach to curriculum development today is different from what it was a generation ago. Formerly the entire staff of a school system, under the leadership of administrators and curriculum consultants, was organized into committees to develop goals, study problems, organize courses of study, and, after a year or two of intensive work and study, produce the school program to be used for the next few years. Now, curriculum revision is a continuous, evolutionary process. Through staff meetings, summer workshops, experimentation and research, permanent curriculum committees (with rotating membership), interschool visits, supervisory activities, and other in-service programs, the total faculty is involved in continuous curriculum revision (2:303–304).

School administrators have learned that no change takes place in the curriculum unless there is a change in teachers. Teachers must persuade

[13] Bereday, *op. cit.*, p. 26.

themselves of the need for a change and then take active part in bringing it about.

Because teacher involvement is so important, curriculum improvement depends upon the individual school approach to experimentation. If, for example, a school system decides to explore the possibilities of team teaching, a building principal and his staff are likely to conduct the experiment, not the system as a whole. Closely related to this approach is the tendency to encourage teachers to do *action research*. Simply stated, this means that a teacher uses the methods of research to study his own problems (2:341–347).

In identifying the problems of research in mathematics, Kenneth Brown of the United States Office of Education indicated equally well the needs in all other fields of study. He identified the following needs: *"First, the identification of the crucial problems. . . . Second, greater coordinating of effort in attacking the problems. . . . (and) Third, publication and widespread distribution of research"* (2:211).

THE 1950s—A DECADE OF CONCERN

During the 1950s, countless proposals and counterproposals were made for improvement of the school program. Even the most superficial examination of the history of education reveals that the schools have always had their critics. However, probably in no other period of American history has criticism of public education reached such volume and intensity as it did during the 1950s. Some of the more significant criticisms will be analyzed in this chapter.

When the National Citizens Council for Better Schools celebrated its tenth anniversary in a special issue of *Better Schools*, a caption at the top of the front page referred to the period of 1949 to 1959 as a "Decade of Concern." The first wave of criticism came just after World War II, and a second wave began about 1953, became more violent in the middle of the decade and culminated in the organization of such groups as the Council for Basic Education. As to why the defense of public education in newspapers and periodicals seldom has equal space with that of the criticisms, the editor of *Better Schools* expressed the belief that "any sharp attack upon a public institution is news" whereas "a reply that 'things aren't really as bad as the critics say' is not news."[14]

Losing Sight of the Major Purpose

That the schools fail to develop the intellect has been, and continues to be, one of the most persistent criticisms of public education. In fact, many other criticisms are related directly to this one.

[14] National Citizens Council for Better Schools, *Better Schools* (May 1959), pp. 7–8.

Among the foremost defenders of intellectualism in education are the members of the Council for Basic Education, cited in the discussion above. The Council was incorporated on July 3, 1956, with Arthur Bestor as its first president of the board of directors. Some of its avowed purposes were "to ensure

1. That all students without exception receive adequate instruction in the basic intellectual disciplines . . .
4. That teachers are thoroughly educated in the subjects they teach . . .
5. That vocational training is offered in due subordination to the school's fundamental purpose of intellectual discipline . . .
6. That school administrators are encouraged and supported" to resist diversion of school time to educational activities of minor importance, "social adjustment at the expense of intellectual discipline," and the assumption of responsibilities belonging to other agencies.[15]

The critics who contend that the public schools neglect intellectual discipline often cite foreign languages, mathematics, and science as examples, charging that the schools no longer teach these subjects or, when they are taught, the students do not take them.

Arthur Bestor, one of the best known spokesmen for intellectual emphasis in education, expressed concern over the declining emphasis on basic subjects in the schools in an interview with the staff of a national news magazine:

Q. Are the schools paying less attention to the teaching of science, mathematics, history, and foreign languages than they used to?
A. Yes, they are. In fact, lots of American high schools don't offer courses in the basic sciences and advanced mathematics, that is geometry and algebra. And an increasing percentage of American students aren't taking the courses when they are offered.
Q. How bad is that situation?
A. Well, more than half of the high schools in the United States offer no physics; roughly a quarter offer neither physics nor chemistry. And even geometry is missing in 23 percent of our high schools.
Q. Is the situation getting better or worse?
A. Worse. A responsible estimate is that last year some 1500 high schools reduced the number of their courses in science and mathematics, or dropped them entirely.
Q. Is there a relationship, do you think, between the shortage of scientists you hear so much about today and what we have been doing with education in the last thirty to fifty years?
A. A very obvious relationship. The figures of the U. S. Office of Education show that in 1900 nearly 84 percent of all American high school students

[15] Council for Basic Education, Washington, D.C.

were taking some science courses. That has dropped to only 54 percent today. In mathematics the drop has been from 86 to 55 percent.[16]

A number of replies to Bestor, two of which are cited here, indicate why some of his assumptions are misleading. First of all, Bestor bases his conclusions on only one year, failing to take into account the total four-year program of a student. Furthermore, he ignores the fact that many small schools offer advanced courses in alternate years. It should also be noted that small schools which have limited offerings enroll only a small percentage of the total high school population. The greatest fallacy, however, in Bestor's argument is suggested by the generalization, "We Are Less Educated Than Fifty Years Ago," based on declining enrollments in foreign language, mathematics, and science. That enrollments have been declining is correct, but the crux of the matter is this. In 1900, only 8 percent of the youth of high school age (14 to 17 years, inclusive) *were in school*; in 1950, 64 percent were in school. When actual numbers are compared or even the percentage of 14- to 17-year-old youths who took these "hard" subjects in 1900 is compared with the percentage of those who took them in 1950, only one conclusion can be drawn: *Substantially more boys and girls of high school age were taking foreign language, mathematics, and science in 1950 than in 1900.*[17]

To bring the figures more up to date, it should be noted that in 1959, 90.2 percent of the youths 14 to 17 years of age were in school.[18] There is also evidence that enrollments in the subjects indicated above are increasing. For example, enrollments in foreign language in California during the years 1955 to 1959 increased 60 percent in the secondary schools.[19]

The supporters of intellectualism have charged "The schools teach nothing but life adjustment education." The statement is absurd on two counts. First, it is obvious that no school confines itself exclusively to the teaching of any one thing. Second, the term "life adjustment education" is deliberately misused. It is neither method nor content. "Life adjustment education" was a movement to meet the needs of boys and girls who were not being prepared "for either a skilled occupation or higher

---

[16] From a copyrighted article entitled "We Are Less Educated Than Fifty Years Ago," appearing in *U.S. News & World Report*, November 30, 1956.

[17] Material in refutation of Bestor's argument is taken from a letter which originally appeared in the *St. Louis Post-Dispatch* from Harold C. Hand, professor of education, University of Illinois. The letter was later published in the *Phi Delta Kappan* (March 1957), pp. 254, 256.

[18] Research Division, National Education Association, *Research Bulletin*, vol. 39 (February 1961), p. 26.

[19] Ruth Parle Craig and Wilson Craig, "Modern Foreign Languages in California: New Problems and Their Solutions," *Journal of Secondary Education*, vol. 37 (April 1962), p. 225.

education." During the years 1950 to 1953, the movement spread to twenty-nine states. Special emphasis was placed on three areas: family life, vocational preparation, and citizenship (2:238–239).

The Superiority of European Education

The criticism that American education is inferior to that of Europe is closely related to the charge that American schools are anti-intellectual in character.

When asked to compare the product of the English secondary school with his American high school counterpart, Sir Geoffrey Crowther, chairman of the Central Advisory Council for Education in England, said, "He has been taught different things, by different methods, with a different purpose in view, in a different sort of school. There is no fair basis for comparison."[20]

"Each nation, out of its own historical, social, and cultural background, attempts to find answers which will solve its problems in its own way. The development of a national system of education, like that of all other institutions, is limited and determined by such background factors in the life of the nation."[21]

After contrasting American schools with those of France, Andre Maurois concludes, "It would be madness to ask either nation to act or teach according to the traditions of the other."[22]

These statements illustrate that one cannot compare the incomparable. Admirers of European education today, like the comparative educators of the early nineteenth century, seem unaware of the fact "that the educational system of one country cannot be transplanted into the soil of another" (3:319).

There are differences between the goals and practices of American and European education which cannot be easily reconciled. Leading Swedish educators, Husén and Svensson, point out that "The pattern of schools that prevails in western Europe must be characterized as selective and dual. . . . The emotional and social consequences of this selection will not be discussed here. Suffice it to say that the arrangement causes much anxiety and frustration."[23]

[20] Sir Geoffrey Crowther, "English and American Education," *The Atlantic Monthly*, vol. 205 (April 1960), p. 42.

[21] John Francis Cramer and George Stephenson Browne, *Contemporary Education*. New York: Harcourt, Brace & World, Inc., 1956, p. 3.

[22] André Maurois, "A Frenchman Appraises U. S. Schools," Education Supplement of *Saturday Review*, vol. 44 (April 1961), p. 74.

[23] Thorsten Husén and Nils-Eric Svensson, "Pedagogic Milieu and Development of Intellectual Skills," *School Review*, vol. 68 (Spring 1960), p. 37. Copyright 1960 by the University of Chicago Press.

European secondary schools provide an academic, classical curriculum for an intellectual elite; American high schools provide both an academic and practical curriculum for all youth. European schools are often segregated on such bases as sex, religion, intellect, or social class; the typical American high school is a *comprehensive* school, enrolling all boys and girls on a nonsegregated basis. European schools stress early occupational choice (about ages 10 to 12 years); American schools defer specialization and choice of an occupation.

At this point, it should be pointed out that those who compare American schools unfavorably with those of Europe are confronted with an interesting paradox.

It is one of the ironies of our times that in the decade of the Fifties, while domestic critics were castigating American schools for "anti-intellectualism" and comparing them unfavorably with those of Europe, the liberal democracies were abandoning their rigid caste system, with its emphasis on advanced education for the elite only, and beginning to adopt the kind of free, universal, public, unitary comprehensive school we take so much for granted.[24]

In conclusion, it should be said that a genuine study of comparative education is valuable for both American and European educators who may learn from one another without disparaging their respective school systems in the process.

Neglect of the Fundamentals, Particularly Reading

The authors of this text believe that all teachers must be teachers of reading. The debate of the 1950s concerning the relative merits of the phonics and the word-recognition methods of teaching reading has been revived by two books: *Tomorrow's Illiterates* by Charles C. Walcutt and *What Ivan Knows That Johnny Doesn't* by Arthur S. Trace, Jr.

In a scholarly article, appearing in the February 1962 issue of the *Phi Delta Kappan*, Arthur Gates used the findings of research to counter the most recent attacks on the teaching of reading in the public schools.[25] Using comparative test scores, dating from 1921 to 1957, Gates demonstrated that children have been showing substantial and steady improvement in reading, despite the fact that modern children are "appreciably younger" at each grade level than those a generation ago and that now more children of less ability remain in school.[26] Gates also exploded a number of myths, including the one that the phonics method never created any reading problems.

[24] Stanley Elam, "Editorial," *Phi Delta Kappan*, vol. 43 (November 1961), p. 49.
[25] Arthur I. Gates, "The Teaching of Reading—Objective Evidence Versus Opinion," *Phi Delta Kappan*, vol. 42 (February 1962), pp. 197–205.
[26] *Ibid.*, p. 198.

By comparing Russian basal readers with those of American schools, Trace concluded that American children do not learn to read nearly as many words as Russian children do nor as many as American children learned twenty-five years ago. In response to this, Gates pointed out that American children *begin* with basal readers and then expand their vocabularies by reading widely. To prove his point, he cited results of vocabulary tests (based on the 20,000 Thorndike word list and the Dale-Eichholz list) which indicated that a high percentage of fourth-grade children know 4302 words ("or four times as many as Mr. Trace gives them credit for knowing"). "Sixth-grade children . . . know well at least 10,430. This is more than the total of 8000 words found in all of Milton's writings and close to the 15,000 in the works of Shakespeare."[27]

Control of the Schools by Educators

Some critics base the blame for all shortcomings of American education, either real or imaginary, upon the charge that educators (or "educationists") have taken control of the schools from the people. Since the American school system is controlled by state legislatures and by state and local boards of education, elected by the people, this charge becomes almost an absurdity. Add to this the fact that, unlike other professions, "the agencies controlling admission to teaching consist almost exclusively of members outside the profession."[28] In addition to the official agencies above, there have been many other lay groups that have influenced policies in public education. For example, citizens advisory committees numbered "over 12,000 groups in 1957."[29]

Two other criticisms—that *the schools lack discipline* and that *teachers are not prepared in their subjects because they have to take too many education courses*—are discussed elsewhere in this text.

THE 1960s—A CONSERVATIVE REVOLUTION

The criticisms of the 1950s have apparently ebbed in volume and intensity. Now a new tide of conservatism seems to be rising. In 1956, in analyzing the sources of educational aims, Tyler noted that "primary attention is currently given to the opinions of subject specialists" (a reversion to the period between 1900 and 1918).[30] In the recommendation of Conant, that "students should be grouped according to ability, subject

---

[27] *Ibid.*, p. 203.
[28] Research Division, National Education Association, "Ten Criticisms of Public Education," *Research Bulletin*, vol. 35 (December 1957), p. 135.
[29] *Ibid.*, p. 137.
[30] *Tyler, op. cit.*, p. 83.

by subject," mastery of the subject as a major goal of education is implied.[31] A number of limitations of Conant's reports have been indicated, including his failure to give "the nature of the learner and the learning process . . . the consideration they probably deserve."[32] Contributors to the June 1960 *Review of Educational Research* furnish further evidences of an approaching "conservative revolution" in such generalizations as:

"The college subject-matter specialist increasingly is becoming a self-styled expert in curriculum planning at lower levels of education," and after the launching of Sputnik, "alleged shortcomings and strengths of education in the United States were projected against the background of European educational practices . . . A reorientation of the curriculum along traditional European lines was advocated by many. . . ."[33]

Conservative Curriculum Proposals

Conservative proposals for changes in the American public schools have come from various sources. Some proposals follow:

That a state-wide system of examinations be adopted

That preparation for teaching include more academic subjects and fewer courses in education and nonacademic subjects

That all students follow the same academic course of study

That the schools assign more homework, be stricter, and lengthen the school day, week, and year

That the departmentalized organization of the high school be extended into the elementary school

That academic subjects be taught at earlier levels, by teaching algebra in the eighth grade and requiring foreign language in the sixth or seventh grade, for instance

That the junior high school be abolished and the "eight–four" type of organization be reinstated

That a national curriculum commission be established

That organization of subjects into broad fields (such as social science or general science) be abandoned in favor of such discrete subjects as English, history, or chemistry

That modern methods be abandoned in favor of older methods which purportedly produced better results: by using the phonics approach to reading and eliminating the "readiness" concept in reading and arithmetic

[31] James B. Conant, *The American High School Today.* New York: The McGraw-Hill Book Company, Inc., 1959, p. 49. Used by permission.

[32] American Educational Research Association, "Curriculum Planning and Development," *Review of Educational Research,* vol. 30 (June 1960), p. 234.

[33] *Ibid.,* p. 193.

That education for social development or "life adjustment education" be
eliminated from the school program

Each proposal represents one or more of three positions on curriculum
development: a return to the past, an emphasis on intellectualism, and an
adoption of European patterns of education.

During an era when criticisms of education may be particularly rife, a
new teacher may be overwhelmed by what he reads and hears. In order
to achieve proper perspective, the beginning teacher needs to remember
several things. First of all, criticisms are not new; people have always
complained about their schools. Second, while a few critics appear to be
dishonest, most are probably sincere. Some are merely expressing genuine
differences of opinion, a right they have in a democracy. Others, especially
parents, may register dissatisfaction because of misinformation about what
the schools are doing. Finally, a school in which the people have a genuine
interest and concern is more fortunate than one toward which the public
has an attitude of apathy.

The Conservative Revolution in California

That conservative proposals of the late 1950s are beginning to bear fruit
is quite evident in California. Abundant evidence is furnished by the
December 1960 issue of the *Phi Delta Kappan*, a considerable portion of
which is devoted to the theme, "The Conservative Revolution in California."[34] The activities of the state legislature and the recommendations
of lay advisory committees, appointed by local boards of education, give
further evidence of the "conservative revolution."

SAN FRANCISCO CURRICULUM SURVEY COMMITTEE   A practice that seems
to be gaining favor with local boards of education in California is the
appointment of advisory committees to evaluate their school program.

The San Francisco Board of Education appointed a committee of eight
academic professors from Stanford University and the University of California to evaluate the curriculum of the San Francisco unified school
district.[35] Some of their recommendations are as follows:

That "reading be taught by a systematically phonetic method *from* the
beginning. . . ."[36] Also letters and their sounds be learned at age 6.
That "when 'social studies' begin, we prefer that they be called by their
proper names: geography, history, civics."[37]

[34] Don Robinson, "The Conservative Revolution in California Education," *Phi Delta
Kappan*, vol. 42 (December 1960), pp. 90–102.
[35] Report of the San Francisco Curriculum Survey Committee, prepared for the Board
of Education, San Francisco unified school district, April 1, 1960.
[36] *Ibid.*, p. 11.
[37] *Ibid.*, p. 11.

That "a sequence of history courses, proceeding from ancient to modern, should replace the history content in present vague social studies courses."[38]

That "essay-type examinations should be used . . . in English . . . history, geography, and civics instead of true-false and multiple-choice examinations."[39]

That "such diffuse descriptive jargon as *language arts* and *communication skills*" be abolished.[40]

That "there should be rigorous work in sentence diagramming."[41]

That the "emphasis placed on 'resource units' as a means of ordering course materials be drastically reduced."[42]

That "algebra should be started in the eighth grade, and a full year of algebra given in the ninth grade. All students should be required to take this course."[43]

That "beginning at once and proceeding as quickly as possible, a revision of the textbook program from the eighth grade on, substituting books written by specialists in the subjects concerned for books written by professors of education."[44]

1961 LEGISLATION IN CALIFORNIA The curriculum has been affected directly by new teacher certification requirements, institution of a state-wide examination program for elementary and secondary students, and direct curricular requirements.

A bill was introduced in the 1961 legislature which would have required all teachers, both elementary and secondary, receiving the standard teaching credential, to have majors and minors *in academic subject matter areas.* The bill passed, with a number of modifications, and the final effect on teacher preparation is not yet known.

The 1961 legislature also passed legislation which required all school districts to conduct a testing program, including both intelligence and achievement tests, and to provide the state department of education with results of any tests upon request of the superintendent of public instruction.[45] The legislation further provided that the state department of education shall use "the reports of test scores" for analysis, for development of state norms, or for other purposes "permitted or required by law."[46]

38 *Ibid.,* p. 12.
39 *Ibid.,* p. 14.
40 *Ibid.,* p. 23.
41 *Ibid.,* p. 26.
42 *Ibid.,* pp. 27–28.
43 *Ibid.,* p. 39.
44 *Ibid.,* p. 56.
45 Education Code, Sections 12820, 12823.
46 *Ibid.,* Title 5, 62.2, Section 85.6.

At the elementary level, two proposals reflect the conservative trend.

(b) Beginning not later than grade four and continuing through grade six or eight, as the case may be, (note: the elementary school may terminate with grade six or eight) instruction shall be given in all of the following:

(1) English as a separate subject with emphasis on thoroughness, and as a discipline separate from the subject of social studies . . .

(c) Beginning not later than grade six, and continuing through grade six or eight, as the case may be, instruction shall be given in all of the following:

(2) a foreign language or languages.[47]

At the junior high school level, "five years of history commencing with grade seven," as well as certain kinds of history, are required.[48]

Conclusions Concerning the Conservative Revolution

Although a number of the conservative developments outlined in the foregoing discussion may be disturbing to professional educators, they are not the chief cause of concern. The major issue is *the way in which curriculum change is taking place.* Dangerous precedents are being set.

In some cases lay advisory groups, some self-appointed and others appointed by boards of education and state legislatures, are making policy recommendations related to the curriculum without sufficient consultation with professionally qualified people. Even more disturbing is the fact that some such groups represent minority pressure groups and not the majority of the people.

It is recognized that society through its elected representatives has a right by majority decision based on investigation of *all* the relevant facts to make decisions about the kind of schools that are desired and needed. It should also be recognized that teachers and other educators have the right and responsibility to provide authoritative information and opinions concerning policies which they must eventually put into effect. However, participation in policy making does not give professional people alone the right to dictate educational policy. That would also be a form of anarchy.

The viewpoint of the authors is very well summarized in the minority opinions of four of the twenty-seven members of a citizens advisory commission, chosen by a joint committee of the California legislature to study the public education system. Their statement, which disagreed with the final report, reads as follows:

The undersigned disagree with the recommendations for mandatory state testing and enactment of curricular requirements by the legislature. Mandatory

---

[47] *Ibid.,* Section 7604.
[48] *Ibid.,* Section 7700.

state testing encourages uniformity and an emphasis on educational purposes that can be measured by objective tests, and it does not provide for the wide range of differences between and within local school systems. Mandatory state testing can inhibit creativity and individual incentive and be a hindrance to the development of an educational program of high quality. A school curriculum shaped by legislative action is likely to be too rigid to utilize effectively advances in knowledge and to lack comprehensiveness and balance. Decisions as to what is taught in the schools are of vital importance. They should be made only after the most careful consideration and the utilization of the best talents available, particularly those of classroom teachers. The school curriculum should be flexible enough to meet local and individual needs and encourage continual efforts for improvement.[49]

ISSUES IN CURRICULUM DEVELOPMENT

From the foregoing discussion of criticisms of the schools and conservative currents in education, a few critical issues in curriculum development become obvious.

Education for All versus Education of an Elite

If there is one educational principle to which the citizens of this country are committed, it is this: All youth of secondary school age are entitled to *equal educational opportunity.* As this nation has developed, the people have rejected aristocracy in any form, whether it be of birth, religion, government, or intellect. Yet, there are strong, insistent voices today which would create an intellectual aristocracy in the public school system. That a large number of youths in secondary school today would fail to profit from a strictly academic program is no longer debatable.

The imposition of an academic program on all boys and girls in high school would leave the school but one of two unacceptable alternatives: to fail a large number of students or to dilute the program until it would lose its value. The general public would reject the first alternative; the academic scholars, the second. Some who reluctantly admit that a large segment of the student population is lacking in both motivation and aptitude to succeed in a program that is exclusively academic suggest a third alternative: enroll such students in nonacademic courses but clearly label such courses as being inferior to academic subjects. As long as any subject can be justifiably retained in the curriculum and as long as any student is required to remain in school, *no subject should be labeled as a second-rate subject and no student should be classified as a second-class citizen.*

[49] Report of the Joint Interim Committee on the Public Education System published by the senate of the State of California, 1961, p. 63.

Related to this issue of an educational program to meet the needs of all students is the concern for *quality* in education. As a subtitle to his book, *Excellence,* John Gardner, president of the Carnegie Foundation, raises the question: "Can We Be Equal and Excellent Too?" His main thesis is that excellence is required in every line of human endeavor. Gardner condemns American confusion of values, which defines "success in terms of high personal attainment," with college attendance "virtually a prerequisite of high attainment." He then climaxes his indictment with this conclusion: *"Human dignity and worth should be assessed only in terms of those qualities of mind and spirit that are within the reach of every human being"* (5:81).

Balance in the Curriculum

As the pace of the cold war has accelerated, with its emphasis on scientific development for military survival, there has been growing concern about the maintenance of balance in the curriculum. C. P. Snow, British scientist and novelist, is convinced that "western society is increasingly being split into two polar groups—literary intellectuals and scientists."[50]

The National Defense Education Act (NDEA) has aggravated the problem of imbalance in the curriculum. Passed with the best of intentions—national defense—its stress on science and mathematics, to the neglect of the arts and humanities, has been viewed with concern from many quarters. The question of values in an unbalanced curriculum has also been raised: Will an overemphasis on mathematics and science lead to a neglect of the humanities, the primary source of our values?

Achievement of balance in the curriculum becomes even more difficult in a period of national crisis. By appeals to fear and insecurity, alarmists can exert effective pressure for the hasty adoption of ill-advised programs, changes that are adopted without sufficient study and experimentation.

Another problem is that of maintaining balance between academic subjects and practical courses. As has already been suggested, this has been a persistent problem in the history of education and is especially acute at this time.

Other problems of balance in the curriculum are:

Maintaining balance between the needs of the learner and the needs of society

Maintaining balance between education for unity and for diversity

Maintaining balance between education for cultural stability and education for social change

[50] C. P. Snow, *The Two Cultures and the Scientific Revolution.* New York: Cambridge University Press, 1961, p. 4.

Maintaining balance in participation in curriculum change, so that all who
   have a contribution to make are included
Maintaining balance in achievement of the different purposes of education (4)

Who Shall Build the Curriculum?

A major issue in the 1960s is whether or not curriculum change will be
effected by all who have a contribution to make or by vested interests or
pressure groups.

As has already been indicated, there is evidence of an increasing tendency on the part of lay boards of education and state legislatures to accept
the advice of laymen, sometimes representing vested interests, in such
professional matters as qualifications of teachers, curriculum content and
organization, and methods of teaching. When experts are called in, quite
often only those qualified in subject matter are consulted. As a result,
the needs of society and the needs of the learner may be ignored.

Strangely enough, classroom teachers, who are most responsible for
implementation of the curriculum, seem to be the last group to be consulted. As teachers have become better qualified professionally, prescriptive courses of study have been gradually superseded by curriculum
guides which have allowed teachers much more freedom of action.

There is a movement in some parts of the country toward the treatment
of teachers as hirelings rather than professionally educated people. Sometimes they are singled out as a special group to take loyalty oaths. Self-
appointed censors are telling them what textbooks they may or may not
use. Legislative restrictions are going so far as to indicate the *what, when,
how,* and *why* of teaching. State-wide testing programs may constitute a
further threat to teacher initiative and creativity in curriculum development. An enlightened use of testing can, of course, result in the maintenance of high standards of achievement. On the other hand, an un-
intelligent and unprofessional use of tests, such as making invidious
comparisons between individual school districts or teachers, can result in
curriculum stagnation. If high test scores alone become the status symbols
for a good school or a good teacher, then the test makers may well become
the curriculum makers of the future.

Public versus Private Support and Control of Education

Indirectly but ultimately related to curriculum development is the pattern
of educational control and support that a nation develops.

The right of parents to send their children to a school of their choice,
either public or private, has already been definitely established. An issue
that has not been resolved is to what extent public tax money may be

used to support private or independent schools. Since more than 90 percent of the children enrolled in independent schools are attending parochial schools, the issue involves the principle of separation of church and state or state support for religion.[51]

A basic argument for tax support of parochial schools is based on the thesis that "the denial of educational benefits to nonconforming students (those who do not conform to the religious orientation of state-controlled schools) compels their parents to pay a second time for benefits to which they have an equal right under law."[52] In assuming its proper educational responsibility, the government does not subsidize a particular educational system or institution but each individual child. A precedent has already been set by many welfare programs which make direct grants to individual citizens and allow them complete freedom of choice in the way they use their aid.[53]

Opponents of tax support for parochial schools maintain that such a policy challenges the right of the state to maintain schools, undermines a system of free, public education, creates national disunity by fostering religious rivalries, and results in a union of church and state which would be undesirable for both.

Parochial schools are receiving various kinds of aid from the government now for so-called "secular" activities (such as bus transportation) and "secular" subjects (such as mathematics and science). Yet, an analysis of the content of some of the textbooks in these "secular" subjects reveals that such books do contain sectarian material.[54]

Some of the major issues in curricular development have been discussed briefly in the foregoing paragraphs. Each teacher has a responsibility to identify issues related to curriculum change, to weigh and consider all of the arguments supporting both sides of each particular issue, and to participate actively in the solution of persistent problems facing the schools.

NEW DEVELOPMENTS IN THE CURRICULUM

Although the public schools have been subjected to a barrage of criticisms during the last fifteen years or more and many proposals for change have been extremely conservative if not reactionary, the schools have continued to make progress toward curriculum improvement.

[51] Butts, *op. cit.*, p. 41.

[52] Virgil C. Blum, S.J., "Academic Freedom and Tax Support for the Independent School," *Phi Delta Kappan*, vol. 40 (June 1959), p. 351.

[53] *Ibid.*, p. 353.

[54] George R. La Noue, "The National Defense Education Act and 'Secular' Subjects," *Phi Delta Kappan*, vol. 43 (June 1962), pp. 380–387.

Effects of Criticism on the Curriculum

Criticism may have a good or bad effect on curriculum development. Criticism that is severe and persistent, resulting in withdrawal of public support, can stifle new developments and impede progress. On the other hand, continuous, critical evaluation of the school program destroys complacency and encourages school administrators and their staffs to evaluate their curricula continuously and to make needed improvements.

Some evidences of the over-all effects of criticism on educational institutions may be deduced from the experience of the junior high school. For over a decade, the junior high school has been subject to severe criticism. Despite proposals to abolish it and to return to the "eight–four" type of organization, "the junior high school is found in 53 percent of the urban school systems." Also during the period from 1948–1949 to 1958–1959, "junior high schools were established for the first time by 15.1 percent of the school districts, and were eliminated by 1.9 percent."[55]

Developments in Teaching Methods

During the last decade or so, improvements in teaching methods seem to be progressing toward more *effective mass instruction* and toward more provision for *self-instruction*. The first has been aided by developments in educational television (ETV); the second, by the use of programmed learning materials (via teaching machines and scrambled textbooks). Both mass and self-instruction are featured in *team teaching*. Since all of these developments are discussed elsewhere, they will receive no further consideration here.

Developments in Curriculum Content

International tensions, a vast store of knowledge that is constantly increasing and changing, and recent technological advances have accelerated developments in the content of certain subjects.

The National Defense Education Act (NDEA) of 1958 gave impetus to study and experimentation in the fields of foreign languages, science, and mathematics. Federal funds were authorized on a matching basis to state and local school systems for such purposes as the following: (1) to provide instructional equipment, (2) to improve guidance and supervisory services, (3) to provide loans to students, with special consideration given to teacher trainees, (4) to promote research in audio-visual material, and (5) to organize institutes for the advanced preparation of teachers of foreign languages.

[55] Research Division, National Education Association, *Research Bulletin,* vol. 39 (May 1961), pp. 47–50.

Widespread efforts to improve content of science and mathematics courses have been especially noteworthy. A brief discussion of the major projects follows:

BIOLOGY   The Biological Science Curriculum Study (BSCS) was begun in 1958 by the American Institute of Biological Science (AIBS). The purpose of the study was to develop and evaluate new materials for three different "versions" of the biological science course, for every grade level from kindergarten through graduate school. Laboratory experimentation was organized in terms of "blocks" with each block covering a six-week period. By 1961–1962, some 400 schools were participating in the project. The first textbook materials seemed too difficult for slow learners, but the laboratory programs were accepted with enthusiasm by both teachers and students. Another AIBS project has been the development of a complete general biology course on films.

CHEMISTRY   Beginning in 1957, the Chemical Bond Approach Project (CBAP) was organized by a team of teachers from high school and college to develop a new course based on the concept of "chemical bonds." Instructional materials have been developed, tried out in the classroom, evaluated, and revised a number of times.

Participants in the Chemical Education Materials Study (CHEM) have developed a textbook, laboratory manual, and a number of films for a high school course in chemistry that uses a different approach from the one proposed by CBAP. Stress is placed on laboratory work or an experimental approach to the study of chemistry. Tryouts of the new material were first conducted in 1960–1961, followed by revision of the textbook and laboratory manual and the development of a teachers' guide.

PHYSICS   The Physical Science Study Committee (PSSC) was formed in 1956 at the Massachusetts Institute of Technology. The group has developed a new high school physics course, complete with syllabus, textbook, manuals, films, and teachers' guides. It was the purpose of the committee to prepare a course that would tell "a unified story" that extended from "the atom to the distant galaxies," to meet the needs of students who would pursue careers in science, as well as those who would not.

MATHEMATICS   Since 1952, the University of Illinois Committee on School Mathematics (UICSM), under the leadership of Max Beberman, has been redesigning mathematics courses for grades seven through twelve. They have been developing new materials and educating teachers in their use.

The School Mathematics Study Group (SMSG) began work in 1958 at Yale University to develop an improved program in mathematics for grades seven through twelve. The group has been working on a number of projects: the development of units and textbooks to be used on a trial basis, preparation of a series of monographs to arouse more interest in mathematics among able students, and provision for assistance to teachers.

GENERAL CHARACTERISTICS OF SCIENCE AND MATHEMATICS PROJECTS Most of the projects to develop "new" mathematics and science courses have a few features that are more or less common to all of them.

They are large-scale projects, involving nationwide study and experimentation.

They use a *team* approach, involving research specialists, college professors, and elementary and secondary-school teachers.

They stress learning experiences which depend upon active inquiry or experimentation by students.

They stress more active student participation.

They stress concepts which will advance understanding. In mathematics, less emphasis is placed on computation and more on mathematical structure and concepts. In science, there is an effort to break away from laboratory exercises, passive observation of demonstrations, and memorization of classifications.

They are developing tests to evaluate understanding of concepts and principles and their application in solving problems rather than the student's ability to memorize facts and parrot them back to the teacher.

They stress problem solving and application of concepts outside the classroom.

They are introducing concepts earlier in school.

They are engaging in continuous course revision.

They are attempting to provide more continuity in courses.

They are stressing the importance of mathematics and science for all students.

They are proposing *different* approaches to problems.

They are experimenting with grouping, using three to five groups.

They are providing assistance to teachers by means of handbooks, guides, pamphlets, films, tests, and summer institutes or workshops.

They are receiving generous financial aid from the National Science Foundation and other foundations.[56]

---

[56] Material has been adapted from *The School Review*, vol. 70 (Spring 1962), pp. 1–147; "Quality Science for Secondary Schools," *Bulletin* of the National Association of Secondary School Principals (NASSP), vol. 44 (December 1960), pp. 3–210; "New Developments in Secondary School Mathematics," *Bulletin* of the NASSP, vol. 43 (May 1959), pp. 1–189; and American Educational Research Association, "Curriculum Planning and Development," *Review of Educational Research*, vol. 30 (June 1960), pp. 226–228, 235–237.

OTHER DEVELOPMENTS IN CONTENT   In the area of social studies, the National Council for the Social Studies published in 1959 a report outlining a complete K-14 program.[57] The National Task Force on Economic Education has been stressing the importance of economic education for everyone.

Recent developments in English include:

More emphasis on linguistics, the science or structure of language, rather than formal grammar

Integration of the language arts—speaking, listening, reading, and writing

Improvement of writing through more emphasis on oral communication

Emphasis on *creative* writing (creativity is also being stressed in other subjects)

Introduction of developmental reading in the junior high school

Increased interest in world literature[58, 59]

The trend toward increasing enrollments in foreign languages has already been indicated. Since World War II, there has been a change in methodology as well, away from the grammar-translation method toward the audio-lingual approach. A student first learns to converse in the language before attempting to read and write it. As a part of the national defense effort, there has been increasing stress on health and physical fitness.

Because increasing numbers of young people who fail to finish high school are swelling the ranks of the unemployed, considerable attention is being given to the need for more adequate vocational preparation and retraining.

Interesting trends in the *placement of concepts and subject content* are now evident. Concepts are being introduced earlier in the educational experiences of children and are then presented in greater depth at each successive grade level. This is especially noticeable in arithmetic and science (2:145, 215). Subject content also appears at earlier levels. For example, algebra, formerly a ninth-grade subject, is now often taught in the eighth grade. The same trend is also evident in science and foreign language courses.

Education of Academically Talented Students

Recent years have witnessed increasing emphasis on the education of academically talented youth. Some of the provisions being made for these students include:

[57] American Educational Research Association, *op. cit.*, pp. 228–229.

[58] *Ibid.*, p. 235.

[59] Association for Supervision and Curriculum Development, "Language Arts in the School," *Educational Leadership*, vol. 19 (February 1962), pp. 282–311.

Acceleration—enabling students to complete their education earlier by taking more subjects each semester or by attending summer school, for example.

Segregation—placing academically gifted students in separate schools or in separate sections of courses in the same school. Homogeneous grouping, on the basis of achievement in specific subjects, is probably the most common procedure for providing for students of varying abilities.

Enrichment—providing individualized programs of greater depth and breadth for gifted students in regular classes. If several students in one class are academically talented, the teacher may use subgrouping within the classroom.

Advanced Placement—permitting students to take advanced courses in high school and, on the basis of examinations over such courses, to receive credit or advanced placement in a college or university.

Others—encouraging participation in student activities and community service projects; making arrangements for independent study; and excusing students from certain requirements on the basis of special examinations.

STUDENT ACTIVITIES

Many terms have been used to define the learning activities of the school which take place *outside* the classroom, such as *extracurricular, cocurricular, extraclass,* and *student activities.* At present, the term that seems to be gaining most widespread acceptance is *student activities.*[60]

Development of Student Activities

Student activities have a long history, dating back at least as far as the schools of ancient Greece. The idea of self-government has been an especially strong feature of the movement throughout its history. In this country, the student activity movement apparently passed "through three successive states": (1) a period of "hostility and opposition" by the faculty, (2) a second stage of "passive acceptance," and (3) finally acceptance and encouragement by school authorities.[61] Indeed, a number of these activities have now been incorporated in the class program with credit given for them.

The student activity offerings today have assumed major proportions in terms of the number of activities included in the typical high school

[60] Roland C. Faunce, "Extracurricular Activities," *Encyclopedia of Educational Research,* 3d ed. New York: The Macmillan Company, 1960, pp. 506–507. Used by permission of Macmillan.

[61] *Ibid.,* pp. 507–508.

program. Almost every activity that might appeal to youth is included in such categories as: athletics, publication, student government, speech and dramatics, musical activities, and clubs of every type and description.

The phenomenal growth of the student activity program has been due to various factors. The movement probably began in the form of student protests against a dull classroom program. Recognition of the needs and interests of students on the part of school faculties no doubt gave impetus to the movement. Recognition of the importance of having students assume more responsibility for their own education was probably another stimulus. Efforts to build better bridges of cooperation and understanding between school and community further strengthened the role of student activities in the curriculum until finally, the program was given more status by scheduling many activities within the school day and giving credit for them.

Values of Student Activities

A number of values of student activities have been implied—development of leadership, assumption of responsibility for self-government, greater student interest in school, and improved public relations. Such activities also build school morale or develop school pride and spirit to an extent that probably would not be possible with a classroom program alone. They have been an important factor in encouraging students to remain in school. That participation in student activities is important in personal development is supported by the fact that permanent records now include reports of student participation. Interviewers for employment or further schooling of students often attach some significance to past participation in student activities as one criterion for success.

Problems of Student Activities

There are a number of problems related to the student activity program. There is frequently overparticipation by the few and underparticipation by the many. The first problem can be easily solved by proper restrictions, but the second is more difficult. A high proportion of those who do not participate come from low-income families. They do not participate for at least two reasons. First of all, they do not have the money, for student activities are not always free. Hidden costs—uniforms, dues, pins, letters, trips—make participation prohibitive for some students. A second factor is related to the class structure of the school. School activities are usually dominated by students of privileged groups; consequently, students from less privileged socioeconomic groups are effectively barred from participation on social grounds.[62]

[62] *Ibid.*, pp. 509–510.

Another problem pertains to *sponsorship*. There are two aspects to this problem: securing faculty support and safeguarding faculty members from exploitation. Faculty attitudes toward student activities range all the way from hostility or indifference to excessive enthusiasm for a particular activity. The problem of sponsorship would be largely solved if all faculty members recognized the values of student activities and were willing to do their part in sponsoring them. As to exploitation of sponsors, it is now becoming clearly recognized that it is unreasonable to expect teachers to sponsor student activities as an overload. Some are being given extra pay for extra work; others are being given credit for sponsorship in their teaching schedule. The latter solution to the problem is considered preferable.[63]

Some other problems of student activities are organization of secret societies, excessive community demands on performing groups, excessive athleticism, and interruption of class activities.

Criteria for Successful Student Activities

If the student activity program is to play its proper role in the total curriculum, it must meet certain criteria.

Student activities must contribute to the *purposes* of the school.
Student activities must be well integrated with the total curriculum.
Student activities must be carefully planned and well sponsored.
Student activities must encourage participation by *all* students (alleviating scheduling difficulties, cost barriers, and social discrimination).
Student activities must be evaluated continuously.

This chapter includes a condensed summary of the nature of the secondary school curriculum and its historical development, problems and issues affecting curriculum revision, and current trends in curricular reorganization. Since the classroom teacher is the one who ultimately determines the nature and quality of educational experiences, he is the key person in curriculum improvement. In order to be an effective, intelligent participant in this vital role, he has the difficult task of keeping up with new developments, problems, and issues which affect, not only his own special fields of interest, but also the entire school program.

Selected Readings

1. Alberty, Harold B., and Elsie J. Alberty, *Reorganizing the High School Curriculum*, 3d ed. New York: The Macmillan Company, 1962.
2. Alcorn, Marvin D., and James M. Linley, eds., *Issues in Curriculum Development: A Book of Readings*. New York: Harcourt, Brace & World, Inc., 1959.

[63] *Loc. cit.*

3. American Educational Research Association, *Encyclopedia of Educational Research*, 3d ed., Chester W. Harris, ed. New York: The Macmillan Company, 1960, pp. 358–365, 506–511.
4. Association for Supervision and Curriculum Development, *Balance in the Curriculum*, 1961 Yearbook. Washington, D.C.: The National Education Association, 1961.
5. Gardner, John W., *Excellence.* New York: Harper & Row, Publishers, 1961.
6. Gwynn, J. Minor, *Curriculum Principles and Social Trends*, 3d ed. New York: The Macmillan Company, 1960.
7. Krug, Edward A., *The Secondary School Curriculum.* New York: Harper & Row, Publishers, 1960.
8. Leese, Joseph, Kenneth Frasure, and Mauritz Johnson, Jr., *The Teacher in Curriculum Making.* New York: Harper & Row, Publishers, 1961.
9. Parker, J. Cecil, T. Bentley Edwards, and William H. Stegeman, *Curriculum in America.* New York: Thomas Y. Crowell Company, 1962.
10. *Yearbook of Education: The Secondary Curriculum*, prepared under the joint auspices of the University of London Institute of Education and Teachers College, Columbia University. New York: Harcourt, Brace & World, Inc., 1958, pp. 1–33.

PART SIX

Evaluation

CHAPTER 15

Evaluation principles
and appraisal techniques

Each day teachers find it necessary to make many judgments of value. They seek the best possible answers to such questions as: What level of instruction would be most appropriate for this class? What instructional pace should be followed? Which students would benefit from remedial instruction? Which ones are ready for enrichment work? What student groupings might facilitate learning? How effective are the materials and methods of instruction now being employed? How far has each student progressed toward the goals of instruction? What mark has been earned by each student? Much of the success of a teacher today depends upon the quality of judgments he makes in answer to these complex questions. Teaching was not always as complex, however.

Evaluation in Early Schools

In the typical schools at the turn of the century, teachers were little concerned with the problems listed above. They taught small classes from a single text at a pace designed to cover the material in the comparatively short school year.

(In 1900) the schooling process consisted of following a rigid schedule of assignments and recitations based upon single textbooks. The goal was to cover the prescribed number of pages in the designated number of days. In the classroom, potential mule skinners, day laborers, and janitors sat beside embryo research physicists, surgeons, and business executives. They studied the same textbooks, heard the same recitations, pursued the same educational goals, and were marked on the same standards.[1]

In the schools of 1900, measurement of student ability and achievement

[1] American Educational Research Association, "Improving Educational Research," *1948 Official Report*, p. 75.

was crude or nonexistent. Evaluative judgment was practically limited to a term-ending decision of "pass" or "fail."

Evaluation Today: How Best to Facilitate Learning?

The task of the teacher today is exceedingly more complex. He customarily faces larger classes of students who are much more divergent in abilities and interests. The "potential muleskinners" are in schools in greater numbers and remain for a longer period of years. They prepare for a life in which there will be an absence of mules and an abundance of mechanical industrialization. American society itself is more complex. Students must be educated not only to direct effectively the forces of this industrialization but also to participate effectively in the democratic process of government, to understand it, and to appreciate it fully.

Potential research scientists are in the schools of today also in greater numbers. In many high schools such students are mastering content formerly taught only in college. Parents no longer can assist with assignments in science and mathematics because content in those fields has changed since they were in school. Science as well as technology is in a period of accelerated change. Teachers feel the sense of urgency in the nation and are receptive to the call for excellence.

Fortunately the technology of teaching also is moving forward. In addition to standardized tests of achievement, tools are being developed scientifically to measure intelligence, special aptitudes, basic skills, attitudes, and interests. Even though these instruments still are far from perfect, they are extremely useful to teachers in their study of learners. Additional innovations since 1900 include audio-visual materials, teaching machines, programmed learning, multilevel texts, teacher's guides, and supplementary curriculum materials. Many changes in teaching technique and material have taken place and under the stimulus of research, the tempo of change is increasing. Teaching is becoming an increasingly complex process in which measurement and evaluation are playing a greater role.

The modern teacher is constantly challenged by the problem of selecting from the multitude of available instructional techniques and materials, those best adapted to the learning peculiarities of his students, and best suited to the instructional outcomes he seeks—outcomes which must be adjusted so as to command the best efforts of all his students. This is the stimulating challenge of present-day teaching.

To meet this challenge, the teacher must study his class and his techniques, as well as his subject matter. If he is to use the available tools and techniques most effectively to improve student achievement, he must determine the learning characteristics of his students and keep constantly informed of the quality of learning resulting from daily instruction. In his study of student achievement, he is concerned with the attainment of a broad array of goals including knowledge, skills, attitudes, and appreciations. This very necessary part of successful teaching is broadly termed *evaluation.*

Purposes of Measurement and Evaluation

More technically, the gathering of data through use of tests and scales is termed *measurement*, whereas the whole process of decision making involving the setting of goals and the assessment of their attainment through consideration of all obtainable evidence is termed *evaluation*. The data-gathering aspect of the evaluation process commonly includes conferences with students, parents, and colleagues; the study of records; observation of performance; and measurement through testing.

The primary purpose of both measurement and evaluation is to motivate, to direct, and to improve teaching and learning. Increasingly important specialized functions include diagnosis of learning difficulties and prediction of future performance. It should be noted that determination of achievement marks remains an important though now a secondary purpose.

Evaluation: a Continuous Part of Teaching.

Problems to be solved through use of the procedures of evaluation are present at all stages of instruction. As a preliminary to planning, teachers study the achievements, abilities, interests, and attitudes of their students. With this knowledge the teacher is better able to set realistic group and individual goals. Appropriate teaching materials and learning experiences can be provided to achieve these goals. Instructional groups based on interests and abilities can be organized, either by class groupings or grouping within the class. Laggards in learning can be identified and assigned to experiences selected to remedy their deficiencies. Likewise, students of high potential for achievement can be recognized and challenged by enrichment and acceleration to work at a level better adapted to their abilities. Thus the possibility of disappointment and failure for one and boredom and mediocrity for the other can be reduced, if not eliminated.

During the progress of instruction, teachers continue to study records, to confer, to observe, to measure, and to evaluate. They are anxious to determine how well their students are progressing toward their individual and group goals. Teachers seek to determine early what adjustments in planning may be necessary. They realize that when the planned methods, materials, and activities are not producing the desired results, early discovery and revision are imperative. Such discoveries must be made while there is still time for remedial action. To wait for final products and final examinations is too late. Continuous evaluation is a necessary part of good teaching.

At the conclusion of a unit of instruction, final measurement and evaluation serve to answer three related questions: (1) How well have the unit objectives been achieved? (2) What marks have been earned by the student? (3) To what extent has the instruction been effective? All three questions are important even though the third has most direct bearing upon the major purpose of evaluation.

Accurate appraisal of student achievement is an important contributor toward maintenance of good teacher-student rapport, as well as toward maintenance of good public relations. Furthermore, accurate marks facilitate effective educational and vocational guidance. Nevertheless, critical self-evaluation on the part of the teacher bears the greatest promise for the continued improvement of instruction.

Thus it is apparent that problems of evaluation begin in the early steps of planning and continue to the final steps of reporting. Constant alertness to the principles and purposes of evaluation, combined with steady development of evaluative skills, therefore, must be recognized as essential elements in successful teaching.

EVALUATION PRINCIPLES

In the hands of the inexpert teacher, evaluation could be reduced to barren measurement and recording, while in the employ of a more proficient teacher, the process has boundless potential for the improvement of learning and instruction. Beginning teachers will find it profitable to devote considerable time to development of the knowledges and skills involved. The following section of this chapter is devoted to suggestions for those who desire to make full use of measurement and evaluation.

Broad and Realistic Goals

The achievement of all important objectives of instruction should be evaluated. For example, in physical education the attainment of the objectives of good health habits, correct safety habits, good sportsmanship, and active interest in healthful recreation should be evaluated in addition to the development of game skills and knowledge of rules. When the instructor learns all he can about the interests, needs, and abilities of his students, he can set more realistic goals for the class and for individuals. The modification of objectives so that they may serve as a challenge, and at the same time be within the reach of a student, is a practice supported by research. *The Encyclopedia of Educational Research* points out the implications for teachers as follows:

the teacher needs to insure that the learner is not given tasks where he is expected to perform beyond his present capabilities . . . the student should be offered reasonable subgoals. . . .[2]

Teachers are rapidly recognizing the principle that goals which are unrealistic fail to motivate learning and are thereby inadequate as bases for evaluation.

An Integral and Continuous Part of Teaching

The major purposes of evaluation can be achieved best when the planning of evaluation becomes a regular part of instructional planning. One should not fall into the error of limiting evaluation activities to times of stress or to a few days prior to the date that final marks are due. Provisions for evaluation should be made in all daily lesson plans as well as in the plans for each unit. Since evaluation is an integral part of teaching, haphazard evaluation practices denote haphazard teaching. The importance of continuous evaluation cannot be overstressed, particularly for beginning teachers.

Appropriate Use of Data-Gathering Techniques

Teachers should recognize that all techniques have their strengths and their weaknesses. In order to take advantage of the strengths and avoid the weaknesses, it is necessary to select techniques carefully. The following suggestions should be of value:

1. Direct observation usually provides better evidence of the attainment of skills that is provided by the indirect method of written tests. Skills in art, music, and physical education frequently can be evaluated most effectively by direct observation of both the process and the product. To appraise critically the end product alone, in many cases, would be inadequate. The boy who bats cross-handed is in need of instruction even though he occasionally hits a home run. Teachers should keep in mind that the reliability of observational data can be increased through use of rating sheets and check lists (2:932).

2. In the evaluation of knowledge, evidence of understanding based upon ability to make applications and to interpret meanings is preferable to evidence of ability merely to recall statements or facts. Newer testing techniques discussed in Chapter 16 make it possible to use objective as well as essay questions to gather evidence in this category.

[2] Melvin H. Marx, "Motivation," *Encyclopedia of Educational Research*, 3d ed. New York: The Macmillan Company, 1960, p. 896. Used by permission of Macmillan.

3. Observation and interview provide better evidence of real attitudes than can be obtained from most written tests now available. Tests tend to indicate knowledge of preferred attitudes, but frequently fail to give valid evidence of actual attitudes. Anecdotal records based on observation of the behavior of a student should provide more accurate information in this area. Sociometric devices are helpful also.

4. Teacher-made tests should be used frequently so that both student and teacher can keep fully informed of learning status and progress. Pretests and diagnostic tests as well as tests for marks can serve their purposes best when they are built for a specific class. Skill in test building and use is a necessary part of good teaching.

5. Published tests and scales usually provide norms which enable a teacher to compare scores of his class with those of regional and national groups. Furthermore, the technical excellence of many published tests can serve to stimulate better test building on the part of the teacher. Wise use of published tests in diagnosis and prognosis as well as in ordinary achievement testing can be a benefit to both student and teacher. Precautions to be observed are discussed in Chapter 18.

6. Tests that can be scored objectively usually provide more reliable evidence of achievement than is provided by essay tests. On the other hand, there is some evidence to indicate that essay tests encourage better study habits and greater retention. Some authorities maintain that the essay test could be eliminated without loss. However, the present tendency seems to be to use essay tests to measure abilities to organize and interpret information, particularly in the subjects of English and social studies, and to use objective tests for other testing situations. Teachers should avoid the overuse of any single technique.[3]

7. Any single test, observation, or other measurement reveals only a sample of the behavior of a student and should be interpreted with the knowledge that behaviors are subject to frequent change. Consequently, it should be recognized that any measurement may contain error attributable to variability in the behavior of the student as well as that error which is inherent in the measurement technique employed. Teachers should avoid placing great weight upon single measurements, particularly when the results indicate large deviations from the student's general pattern of performance.[4] Fortunately, the practice of passing or failing a student on the basis of a single test is no longer a common occurrence. Important decisions are now based upon extensive accumulations of carefully collected evidence.

[3] American Educational Research Association, *Review of Educational Research,* vol. 29 (February 1959), p. 43.
[4] *Ibid.,* p. 48.

Achievement of balance is a persistent problem in the curriculum. Traditionally, teachers have been preoccupied with transmitting information rather than effecting behavioral changes in students. Nothing short of total mobilization of all the resources—intellectual, emotional, physical—of all the people will suffice in a period of crisis. These two students are in pursuit of learning experiences that require creativity, sensitivity, perception, and emotional involvement. Excessive emphasis on scientific invention and academic achievement leads to neglect of the aesthetic, moral, and spiritual values of life. The school must continue to provide a program that develops emotional maturity and broadens the vision of those to be educated. [*Courtesy R. E. Nielsen and St. Paul (Minn.) Public Schools.*]

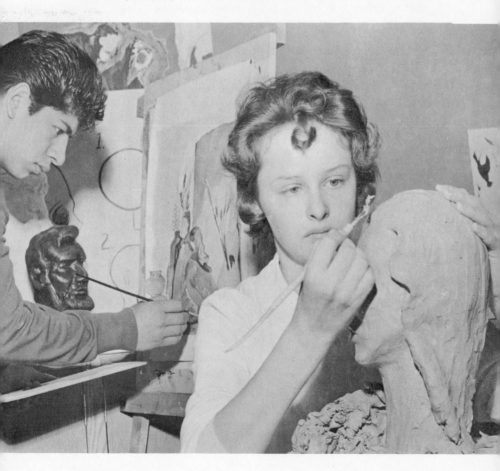

In this class at the Kellogg (Idaho) High School, some students working in small groups are experimenting while a larger group is listening to the teacher explain a principle at the chalkboard. The technique of breaking up large class groupings into subgroups is highly recommended. Student needs vary materially, and subgroupings provide an opportunity to care for such needs. However, groups should be formed for specific purposes that will change as content and learning conditions change. New groupings provide for interpersonal growth and development as the course progresses. [*Suter, Hedrich-Blessing; Culler, Gale, Martell, & Norrie; and Perkins & Will, Architects-Engineers.*]

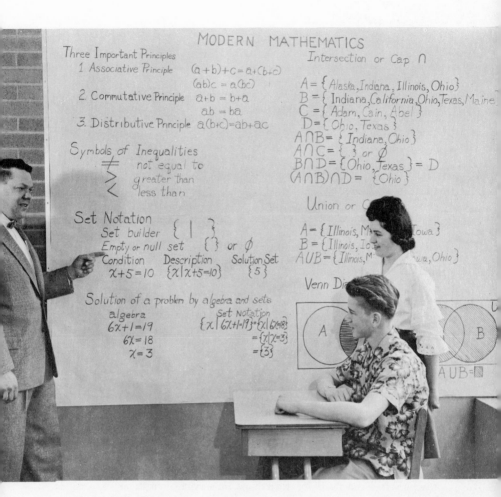

The National Commission on Mathematics has come up with a "new look" in high school mathematics. The theory of sets explained here to two ninth-grade students requires a different notation. The emphasis is on the logic of the number system. Students not only learn *how* to become skilled in computation, they learn *why* they do things with numbers and symbols. [*Courtesy Tacoma (Wash.) Public Schools.*]

To keep abreast of the new developments in the school curriculum, teachers feel the need for workshops, in-service courses at universities and colleges, and specialized reading. Workshops, such as the one shown here, take many forms, and they are characterized by informality, small working groups, total group sessions, and the use of resource persons. Workshops provide growth opportunities both for experienced and inexperienced teachers. [*Courtesy Dade County (Fla.) Board of Public Instruction.*]

Diagnostic Aspects of Evaluation

It is the responsibility of the teacher not only to determine the level of achievement of his students as they enter a course of instruction and to formulate his plans and procedures to meet their needs, but also to find and remedy the weaknesses of those students who, as the instruction progresses, are not achieving up to their capacity. In the latter responsibility, diagnostic measures are invaluable.

Published diagnostic instruments are concentrated chiefly in the subjects of arithmetic and reading. When appropriate published instruments are not available, usable substitutes can be constructed by the classroom teacher. Such tests differ from ordinary achievement tests in these respects: (1) they cover a relatively small group of objectives (for example, the use of the comma, fielding of ground balls, or the use of gestures in public speaking); (2) several items or chances should be provided to cover each specific to be tested as repetition is required to reduce the effects of chance success or error; (3) the items or situations employed should be of types that reduce chance success to a minimum; (4) the important scores are based on single items or small groups of items designed to measure the same objective; and (5) the results of the test are used for the purpose of guidance and not as a basis for marks.

Some information of diagnostic value, particularly with reference to the class as a whole, can be gleaned from regular instructional tests of achievement. Many teachers study the results of instructional tests to determine which items have been most difficult for the class. If the items are not faulty in themselves, this procedure will provide excellent clues to help direct succeeding lessons toward objectives which need furthei study. Item analysis techniques are discussed in Chapter 16.

A common teaching practice is that of discussing test results with students as the papers are returned or in conferences soon afterward. This practice is to be recommended for use provided that the teacher makes constructive comments and follows up with more detailed analysis and instruction. He should always keep in mind that mere admonitions to work hard coupled with threats of failure are inadequate substitutes for modern techniques emphasizing specific remedial instruction based upon accurate knowledge of student weaknesses.

Evaluative techniques other than testing are just as important in diagnosis as they are in the other aspects of a complete evaluation program. In fact, case studies (involving aptitude, personality, and interest measures, interviews, conferences, school records, and observations) frequently are necessary to diagnose adequately the more difficult problems.

Since learning difficulties are at times only one aspect of a complex of adjustment problems, the classroom teacher should not hesitate to ask the help of the school counselor or principal when learning difficulties persist. A complete program of educational diagnosis would seek not only to identify and remedy deficiencies but would aim to locate and remove their causes as well. Diagnostic and remedial procedures are time-consuming tasks, but they frequently yield results which make teaching a real pleasure.

Motivational Aspects of Evaluation

One of the concomitant outcomes of an effective program of evaluation is its motivating influence upon both students and teachers. Few would deny that tests encourage intensive planning and study. Some would condemn intensive study as cramming while others encourage it. Looking to research, teachers are able to substantiate both points of view. Evaluation techniques, particularly testing, have potential for both good and bad influence upon the student and the teacher. It is extremely important that this factor be taken into account by teachers and administrators.

Some teachers remember the days when their jobs depended upon the success with which their students took tests imposed by city, county, or state administrative boards. Under those conditions teachers were motivated to cast aside all other objectives and drill incessantly upon questions that were most likely to be included in the final test. Students failed or passed on the single basis of their final test score. All their prior work, successful or unsuccessful, was ignored.

It is little wonder that some teachers still retain a dislike, if not a fear, of tests traceable to their experience as students or teachers in that type of test program. Fortunately such practices are now practically nonexistent. However, teachers today can build up the same feelings of fear and tension in their own classrooms through overemphasis upon single tests or general misuse of measurement techniques.

The writer recalls observing two inexperienced teachers who misused the motivational possibilities of tests. One, disappointed in the level of understanding revealed in recitation, told the class, "Unless you know your lesson better tomorrow, we will have a test." The second teacher, unable to stop the talking that was going on during a test, stated, "If you do not quiet down at once, I will add items to this test." These teachers failed to understand the real purposes of evaluation.

Tests should not be used as threats, not even to enforce standards of study or discipline. The motivational use of tests should be based upon the research-founded principle of the "desirability of continuous use of knowledge of results,"[5] not upon the highly questionable principle of fear as a motivator.

It is generally recognized that the deliberate use of fear as a motivator, or the use of punishment or threat of punishment with fear as an almost unavoidable consequence, may have highly undesirable effects.[6]

Tests, as well as other measurement instruments, should furnish the teacher and student with evidence of their successes and needs. This information should be shared with the student and serve as a guide to his further study. The preponderance of evidence indicates that measurement techniques employed in this manner help to motivate better teaching and better learning by clarifying goals, designating means, and stimulating action.

Beginning teachers frequently ask whether tests should be announced or administered without announcement. Which practice results in more study and learning? The answer appears to be announced tests. If tests motivate prior study at all, a test that is a certainty should motivate more study than one that is only a possibility. Then any given number of announced tests should motivate more study than the same number of tests given without announcement. Furthermore, a well-known principle is that "successful motivation must not only energize action, but direct it." Therefore, if a teacher wishes to stimulate the most study prior to a test he will see that his students understand the purpose of the test, the objectives to be measured, and the kinds of items to be used. Then students will be better able to plan their study.

Of course, when tests are used to their optimum in motivation, the test results will be analyzed and used by both teacher and student to energize and direct study. The study which follows a test is as important as that which precedes it.

Beginning teachers commonly ask if individual test scores or other comparable data should be posted. Does such publicity motivate students to study better? This question must be answered with a qualified no. Posting the full results of competition in which some are invariably inferior in spite of their efforts reduces the motivational potential of tests. Regular postings should be confined to the names of those who have shown the greatest improvement and might possibly be expanded at times to include short listings of rankings within groups which have approximately equal opportunity for success. Competition serves as a motivator for those who have a fair chance to succeed. Repeated publicity of failure, particularly when such failure occurs despite honest effort, can

[5] Marx, *op. cit.*, p. 896.
[6] *Ibid.*, p. 897.

lead only to disappointment and reduction of effort. Perhaps the most effective recording of test scores might well be the record of his own ratings which each student is encouraged to keep. Competition in self-improvement is healthy motivation.

When returning tests to students, teachers should be particularly alert to the motivation to be gained from written or quiet oral commendation to those who have improved, and also from personal encouragement and specific instructional help to those who have done less well than might be expected. Seldom should tests be returned without evaluative and motivational comment.

Morale-Building Aspects of Evaluation

Well-conducted evaluation can contribute to good classroom morale by keeping each student informed of his progress and by revealing the teacher as a sympathetic guide interested in helping him move toward the goals of instruction. Poorly conducted evaluation, on the contrary, can have a disrupting effect upon morale. Announcement of failure before the group can destroy almost any student's feeling of belonging. Consequently, teachers should make special efforts to insure that their evaluation techniques will have positive effects upon morale.

Teachers can improve the morale-building potential of their evaluation by giving attention to the following suggestions:

1. Have students take part in the planning of evaluation. For example, students can help select the kinds of measurement to be used and help schedule important tests so that they do not unknowingly conflict with school activities or with tests in other classes. Students can also benefit from discussing the objectives to be measured and from constructing sample test items. Thus they can gain better understanding of the purposes and processes of evaluation.

2. Study the results of measurement with each student so as to help him recognize his needs and successes. Students welcome tests used as guides. They are eager to get accurate information about their progress. Individual attention is appreciated.

3. Avoid evaluation practices which students consider unfair. For example, students generally resent and fear surprise tests which deny them the opportunity to review. They dislike poorly timed tests which require such speed that students fail to do their best. Furthermore, use of complex, "trick" questions and open posting of achievement marks also earn low ratings from students.

4. Provide practice in new measurement techniques before using them to get evidence of achievement. Students frequently lack confidence and

become confused when confronted with unfamiliar techniques of measurement. This difficulty can be overcome through systematic use of practice and instructional measures.

5. Encourage students to evaluate themselves. Through the process of self-evaluation, students can gain a better understanding of their purposes in school. For many, the values of education then become more real, and their attitudes toward learning improve.

The Public Relations Aspect of Evaluation

The maintenance of good public relations is an important problem in any large public enterprise including the public schools. Much of the criticism of schools arises from lack of information (or from misinformation) concerning the purposes and processes of present-day American education. Teachers can contribute much toward improved understanding through a well-planned program of evaluation. Such a program would provide parents with more adequate written reports and supplement them with personal contacts as much as possible. Reporting practices should be flexible so as to include timely special reports and conferences. Parents have every right to be kept informed of their child's progress, particularly when problems appear to be developing. To confine reports to the regular card may be entirely inadequate. One may well imagine the reaction against teacher and school, as well as the personal embarrassment of the family that arrived at school with their friends on commencement night only to find that their son was not among those granted a diploma. The regular report was still being processed in the office. Meanwhile, the teacher wrongly had assumed that the boy would inform his parents of his failure to complete graduation requirements. Even in less dramatic circumstances it is equally important that the teacher and school take the responsibility for direct communication with parents.

Teachers should invite parents to share their knowledge of their child's background, interests, and needs. Conferences of this type help teachers to understand individual students and help parents to understand the school. It is becoming more important that teachers develop skill in teacher-parent conferences. However, it must be realized that even though conferences and visitation between home and school are increasing, many parents seldom, if ever, participate in these activities. Most parents still rely upon the regular report card to keep them informed. It is important that reports to parents be improved. In the secondary school there is little likelihood that report cards ever will be replaced by conferences.

As parents are being asked to give greater financial support to education, they in turn are asking for more objective information concerning instruction and learning in their public schools. Many schools are meeting this demand, in part, through use of a continuing program of standardized testing. With this information pupil gains can be determined in addition to pupil status. It means more to a parent to learn that in the ninth grade his daughter improved from sixth-grade to eighth-grade standing in reading than for him merely to learn that her final rating was one year below average. Intelligent use of standardized test results can be effective in public relations.

Teachers should be fully aware that public relations is a complex field. Practices differ from school to school. For instance, in some schools, test information is freely shared with pupils and parents; in other schools it is given out only after approval through official channels, while in still other schools such information is shared only with professional personnel. It is of particular importance, then, that teachers in training recognize the role of evaluation in public relations. They should always check their plans with their supervisors and carefully follow the policies and practices of their school. Further discussion of reporting practices is to be found in Chapter 17.

Self-evaluation

Self-evaluation by the individual students, by the class, and by the instructor are all important aspects of a complete evaluation program.

Self-evaluation on the part of students can be facilitated by: (1) teaching them the necessary graphing skills and providing the basic materials and data so that they can keep an accurate record of their progress; (2) returning graded work promptly and requesting that samples for comparison be retained by the student in his evaluation folder; (3) providing class time for instruction and practice in self-evaluation techniques; (4) providing basic information concerning the progress of the class as a whole so that students can compare their own standing with the average or quartile points of the class; (5) encouraging students to compete with their own record rather than with individual classmates; and (6) including students in the planning as well as in other phases of evaluation. Students who participate in the selection of clearly defined goals are more likely to be interested in keeping track of their progress toward those goals.

Self-evaluation on the part of a class as a whole can be facilitated by scheduling class discussions for that purpose. In these evaluation sessions, care must be taken to avoid individual comparisons. Neither commendation nor censure of individual students should be permitted. Rather, emphasis should be placed upon development of group feeling. Use such questions as: How well have we progressed as a class? What have we done best? In what have we been least successful? How can we do better? What are reasonable new goals for the class? In some circumstances class evaluations can be further stimulated by centering discussions around graphical comparisons of class averages on standardized measures with local, state, or national norms for similar classes. In comparisons of this type it is important to see that the results of discussion are constructive. In essence, evaluation of group progress by the group itself should be a natural part of teacher-student planning.

Continuous self-evaluation on the part of the instructor is an essential element in successful teaching. Each day as he prepares to revise plans for the next day's teaching, he should carefully review the effectiveness of the lessons just completed. What seemed to be particularly successful? What could be improved? Could more effective methods and materials be employed? What changes might be appropriate the next time that particular content is covered? How should the next day's instruction be adapted to meet the special needs revealed? Answers to these questions should be written into daily plans. Memory alone cannot be trusted.

Periodically each teacher should also searchingly appraise himself as a professional person. He should ask such questions as: Am I improving in professional knowledge and skill? What is the quality of my rapport with students? How well do I cooperate with my colleagues? Is my response to supervision adequate? In short, how am I doing and how can I improve as a member of the teaching profession?

The Keeping of Records

Carefully maintained records are a necessary part of an evaluation program. No one can expect to commit to memory all the collected information pertinent to the evaluation of his students. If adequate information is to be available when needed, rather extensive records must be kept. As a minimum, each teacher should maintain (1) a class record book of test scores and other ratings of achievement which indicate the status of each student at designated points throughout the school year; (2) a supplementary folder on selected students containing records of their abilities, interests, background, special goals, health, and adjustment, as well as anecdotal records, samples of work, and progress charts; and (3) a folder containing similar information about the class as a whole, in addition to the teacher's self-evaluations pertaining to his instruction of that class.

In addition to these records, teachers should encourage and assist each student to maintain an evaluation folder of his own in which he can keep his returned assignments and tests, records of his tests scores, statements of his personal goals, and copies of his periodic self-evaluations.

Evaluation and Action

Evaluation is of little benefit unless it leads to action. Determination of final marks is only a minor function of the entire process. To be effective in attaining its major purpose, the improvement of instruction and learning, evaluation must be followed by specific changes in the work of the student and the teacher. Tests should be analyzed to determine strengths and weaknesses of individual students and of the class as a whole. The remedial and enrichment work following should then be based on the knowledge gained. Evaluation conferences and interviews should also culminate in plans and action toward improvement. Only then will the full benefit of evaluation be realized.

TECHNIQUES OF APPRAISAL

It must be acknowledged that teachers in service differ greatly in their ability to apply the principles of evaluation. Many keep in step with the advancements of their profession, while some merely teach as they were taught. Consequently, beginning teachers, observing widely different practices, sometimes find it difficult to decide what measurement and evaluation skills should be developed as part of their own professional equipment. What is a teacher expected to know about these matters? The answer should be clear. To perform at the highest levels of proficiency, today's teacher finds it essential to develop skill in:

1. The use of appraisal techniques
2. Building, administering, and scoring written tests
3. Determining marks and making reports to parents
4. Interpreting scores from standardized achievement tests and intelligence tests

The techniques of appraisal are discussed in this chapter, while each of the remaining topics is the subject of following chapters.

Appraisal techniques include the use of nonwritten performance tests, rating sheets, check lists, progress records, anecdotal records, and sociometry.

The Appraisal of Performances and Products

In subjects such as speech, drama, physical education, industrial arts, home economics, music, art, and business education, the development of skills is a major objective. Consequently, in these subjects tests designed to measure a student's ability to perform selected skills in controlled situations are of particular importance. In such tests, factors of correctness and speed of performance, as well as quality of the end product, are usually taken into consideration. Examples of tests of performance in varied subjects might be basketball dribbling and goal shooting, sketching an artistic figure, baking a cake, playing a musical score, or dramatic acting.

PERFORMANCE TESTS In the selection of tasks for performance testing, teachers should consider only those which are realistic and directly related to the most important objectives of the course. Tasks of minor importance, particularly those that are time consuming, should not be included. For example, the teacher of physical education who wished to appraise student ability to control a soccer ball soon found that it was far better to require students to dribble the ball through a 15-yard obstacle course than to have them dribble for the full 100-yard length of the field. Furthermore, problems which test a student's mental alertness or his luck rather than his skill in the subject should be avoided. For instance, the malfunctions to be used in an automobile trouble-shooting test in which time is a major criterion should be selected so that their discovery will be dependent upon efficient use of regular procedures rather than upon haphazard attacks or lucky guesses.

It is generally considered that tasks for which partial scores can be assigned are more appropriate for a performance test than those which can be marked only pass or fail. Observable and significant differences in performance should be revealed in a full distribution of scores, not in just a dichotomous over-all rating. To accomplish this, a teacher can break the task into its necessary steps or elements and assign points or ratings to each part. A further consideration is to keep the score assigned to perfect performance in each part in proper relation to the importance of that part in the whole task. With this type of scoring, the part scores have diagnostic value, and the total score is a valid appraisal of the total performance. For example, a published procedures check list for a woodworking performance test designed to measure ability to square wood stock breaks the task into 35 check points. The final 4 points concerned with working the stock to thickness are shown in Table 15-1.

In the organization of a performance test including several tasks using the same basic tools, instruments, or skills, it is sometimes possible to arrange the tasks in order of increasing difficulty. Much administration time then can be saved by testing students somewhat the way a psychologist uses a scale of intelligence or a physical education teacher conducts the pole vault or high jump at a track meet. In this kind of scaled test, no student takes the entire test. Each one starts at an optional difficulty level and proceeds only as far as his ability will take him. When a test arrangement of this type is possible, it is an extravagant waste of time to use tests which require students to attempt performances below and above their ability. It should be noted that this type of test arrangement has application possibilities in many subjects including mathematics and science as well as music, industrial arts, business, and physical education.

In the administration of performance tests, it is important to: (1) provide opportunity for retrial of simple tasks in which chance success plays a part; (2) provide adequate direction so that the student clearly understands what is expected; (3) where feasible, use squad leaders or other selected students as assistant examiners in order to permit multistation testing in a class period; (4) provide a carefully prepared score card,

Table 15-1. Partial Rating Sheet for a Performance Test

CHECK POINT	PROCEDURE	MAXIMUM CREDIT	EARNED CREDIT
32.	Takes heavy cuts to remove excess stock	2	_____
33.	Reduces cut and planes to center of gauged lines	2	_____
34.	Checks frequently	3	_____
35.	Takes all cuts with the grain	3	_____

SOURCE: Adapted from William J. Micheels and M. Ray Karnes, *Measuring Educational Achievement*. New York: McGraw-Hill Book Company, Inc., 1950, p. 357. Used by permission of McGraw-Hill.

check list, or rating sheet on which to record scores or ratings of the procedure and product of the test activity; and (5) plan learning activities for students not taking the test when only part of the class can be tested at one time.

Occasionally teachers find it convenient and proper to apply performance tests to groups rather than to individuals. In fact, teams in physical education, committees and panels in English and social studies, and play groups in drama are more or less natural units that might be rated on a group basis. A major pitfall in this practice must be carefully avoided, however. Each individual has the right to be rated on his own progress toward the goals of instruction for individuals, even though group ratings are important whenever improvement of group performance is also a goal of instruction. For example, a mediocre individual performance in an otherwise brilliant cast deserves a "D" rating, even though the group effect may be "A" or "B." Likewise, a star performer on a losing team in physical education may deserve an "A" rating even though the team rating is low. It is doubly bad practice in physical education to assign automatically high grades to all members of winning teams and low grades to all members of losing groups. The team grade may misrepresent the achievement of physical education objectives by the individual student and the practice teaches him that winning is more important than how well he played the game.

BETTER USE OF OBSERVATIONAL TECHNIQUES   Observation for the purpose of evaluation can also be valuable in nontesting situations. Teachers for a long time have been judging student achievement to a considerable extent upon the basis of observation of daily work. When used expertly, observational techniques can provide an accurate and continuous record of a student's daily progress. This use of observation has several advantages over performance testing:

1. Regular learning activity can proceed undisturbed.
2. Information gained can be used immediately to guide instruction. In fact, rating and instruction frequently are both carried on in the same class period.
3. Students who tend to become tense in test situations can perform more normally since they frequently are unaware that their performance is being rated.
4. Certain objectives cannot be evaluated in any other way, either by performance or written tests (for example, an intangible such as a student's appreciation of a good book).

However, unless observation is well directed, specific, and recorded, it is of little use. Too many teachers gain only general impressions through observation. To use observation effectively as a basis for instruction and marking, teachers must be certain of what to observe. They must select appropriate sample behavior for observation and must make a careful record of what they see.

Observation should be an integral part of a well-planned evaluation program. It should be planned in relation to the objectives of the course and with full knowledge of the strengths and weaknesses of other means of evaluation. Observation can best be employed to evaluate achievement which eludes evaluation by means of written tests. Devices such as check lists, rating sheets, rating scales, and progress charts serve the double purpose of directing and recording observation. These devices can be constructed rather easily by the classroom teacher.

A rating sheet designed to measure students' status in discussion and listening skills is illustrated. The ratings indicate that Allan Ault is inferior in his contribution to discussion and in his listening attentiveness. Bob Brown is below average in the clarity of his speech, but is an outstanding listener and above average in all other ratings. Sue Smith is average in three ratings and outstanding in two. This kind of sheet is usually arranged to receive the ratings of an entire class. This arrangement facilitates recording and intraclass comparisons, but lacks the flexibility of the individual card system.

Table 15-2. Sample Rating Sheet of Discussion and Listening Skills

STUDENT'S NAME	CONTRIBUTIONS ARE CONCISE AND CONSTRUCTIVE	SPEAKS DISTINCTLY	IS COUR- TEOUS	ASKS PROBING QUESTIONS	LISTENS ATTEN- TIVELY
Allan Ault	1	3	2	2	1
Bob Brown	4	2	4	4	5
Sue Smith	5	3	3	3	5

Ratings: 1 = inferior; 2 = below average; 3 = average; 4 = above average; 5 = outstanding

Rating devices frequently are organized so as to reveal a student's skill on a numerical, descriptive, or graphic scale or any combination of the three. The data for Bob Brown's discussion and listening skills are entered in the illustrative numerical-graphic scale in Table 15-3. This type of rating gives a clear picture of an individual's skills at any given time. Comparisons are facilitated by recording later ratings on the same scale in

Table 15-3. Sample Rating Scale of Discussion and Listening Skills

STUDENT: BOB BROWN.	INFERIOR (1)	BELOW AVERAGE (2)	AVERAGE (3)	ABOVE AVERAGE (4)	OUT- STANDING (5)
Contributions are concise and constructive					
Speaks distinctly					
Is courteous					
Asks probing questions					
Listens attentively					

different colors or codings. It should be noted that ratings need not be restricted to the five division points, but may be placed at any position along the scale to indicate the precise judgment of the rater.

The "Rating of Student-Teaching Performance" is an instrument intended for use in periodic student teacher-supervisor conferences. The rating may be made out by the supervisor, by the student teacher as a guide to self-evaluation, or it may be filled out jointly in conference. The instrument would be called a rating sheet if the appropriate numbers were merely inserted in the blanks preceding each factor. The device would be a true rating scale if the entire scale was repeated after each factor and each rating was marked along a line. The second arrangement would have the advantage of providing a graphic representation.

RATING OF STUDENT-TEACHING PERFORMANCE

FACTOR RATED

_____ Over-all class rapport and control
_____ Effectiveness with individual problems of control
_____ Over-all planning and organization
_____ Daily planning
_____ Long-term planning
_____ Effectiveness with high achievers
_____ Effectiveness with average achievers
_____ Effectiveness with low achievers
_____ Attention to motivation
_____ Use of varied methods and materials
_____ Differentiation for individuals
_____ Evaluation techniques
_____ Attention to management details
_____ Knowledge of subject taught
_____ Skills in writing and speaking (including spelling and grammar)
_____ Personal qualities (including appearance, dependability, and initiative)
_____ Professional attitude
_____ Response to supervision
_____ Over-all performance rating for the period considered
_____ Over-all rating of growth for the period considered

0	2	4	6	8	10	12
Failing	Very weak	Weak	Average	Strong	Very strong	Perfect

N. A. – not attempted
N. O. – not observed

Below is a sample of one element in a graphic descriptive rating scale designed to measure the objective of sportsmanlike behavior.

SAMPLE FROM A GRAPHIC DESCRIPTIVE RATING SCALE IN PHYSICAL EDUCATION

11. Behavior when his team is losing:

Becomes surly and rough	Blames other players and complains about officiating	Eases up or clowns around	Demands to play more than his share	Courteous, fair and active player at all times

Another type of rating device is the progress chart. It provides for the rating of skills which are developed in sequence throughout a unit or course. The sample "Progress Chart in Beginning Swimming" demonstrates an application of this technique. According to the chart, Joan Black has accomplished four steps, Mary Adams has accomplished three steps, and Suzy Cox is trailing with only two steps completed. Ratings or completion dates are frequently entered in the chart in place of the x's used in the illustration. Similar charts may be useful wherever projects or skills are part of the course of instruction.

PROGRESS CHART IN BEGINNING SWIMMING

STUDENT	OPENS EYES UNDER WATER	FRONT FLOATS	FLUTTER KICKS	FRONT GLIDES	GLIDES WITH ARM STROKE
Mary Adams	x	x	x		
Joan Black	x	x	x	x	
Suzy Cox	x	x			

APPRAISAL OF LEARNING EXERCISES, PROJECTS, AND PRODUCTS   Rating devices of all types can be of great value in objectifying the appraisal of learning projects, exercises, and products, just as they are indispensable in the evaluation of skills. However, unless teachers keep the objectives of instruction clearly in mind they may place too great weight on learning exercises and end products alone. In particular, learning exercises are weighted heavily in science, mathematics, and languages. In such areas as art, home economics, and industrial arts, product ratings often form a large part of marks earned.

The validity of these marking practices has been seriously questioned by those who maintain that completed exercises and products reveal in only a limited way the student's achievement of course objectives. The authors of this text agree to a considerable extent with that point of view. In many courses ratings of learning exercises and end products should be given only minor weight in the assignment of final marks.

The key to proper evaluation of projects lies in analysis of the purposes for which projects are carried out. The rating of end products alone is insufficient. A large share of the rating should be devoted to evaluation of students' ability to plan effectively, to employ approved techniques, to work efficiently and independently, and to generalize and apply learning. When projects are evaluated in this manner, their rating might well be a major factor in final marks.

The use of learning exercise (homework) ratings as a major part of marks is of very doubtful value. This is particularly true when there is little evidence that the completed exercises are the independent work of the student. Furthermore, rating of learning exercises, at times, becomes a heavy burden on the teacher. Many devote far too much time to this work. For example, research has indicated that some mathematics teachers average two or more hours per day in scoring and recording learning exercises. At the same time these teachers average less than one hour per day in lesson planning.[7]

It is recommended that whenever objective keys can be prepared, students be permitted to do their own scoring and correcting. Students can also benefit from keeping progress charts. Scoring should seldom be carried on as a group activity during class time. However, class discussions arising from that activity frequently are beneficial. Occasional spot checking of papers by the teacher is advisable. The time saved by following these recommendations can well be devoted to careful analysis of the papers of those who are having difficulty. In general, the evaluation of learning exercises should make a major contribution to lesson planning but only a minor contribution to final marking.

The Appraisal of Attitudes

Check lists, rating sheets, scales, and progress charts are effective aids to the solution of a very difficult problem: the evaluation of attitudes. In addition to the help offered by the tools which have already been discussed, much can be gained from the use of anecdotal records.

ANECDOTAL RECORDS Anecdotal records are objective descriptive accounts of significant student behavior as observed and recorded by the teacher. Their purpose is to provide cumulative evidence basic to more adequate evaluative judgments. Students frequently best reveal their true attitudes and status of social development through their actions; thus, an objective record of actions often yields much more valid evidence than would be obtained by means of recall or by use of written tests, scales, and inventories. To use anecdotal records to the best advantage, teachers should keep in mind that:

1. Anecdotes should be objective. Interpretations and recommendations, if any, should be distinctly separate from the factual account of what took place.

2. Anecdotes should be selective. Limitations of time will force most teachers to record only incidents that they believe to be significant in the development of the individual or in the understanding of that development (more extensive records may be required in special cases).

[7] J. R. Schunert, "The Association of Mathematical Achievement with Certain Factors Resident in the Teacher, in the Teaching, in the Pupil, and in the School," *The Journal of Experimental Education*, vol. 19 (March 1951), p. 236.

3. Anecdotes should be brief. Record the essential facts of the incident and its setting. Extensive discussion, interpretation, and recommendation should be deferred until a summary analysis of many anecdotes is made.

4. Anecdotes should record favorable as well as unfavorable incidents. It is an error to record incidents of one type only.

5. Anecdotes should be recorded on uniform blanks or cards. Filing, analysis, and summarization are facilitated by use of a common format.

SAMPLE ANECDOTE

Name: John Jones   *Date:* October 15, 1963
Incident: John volunteered for the first time today. He told of his recent trip to the desert. Classmates listened attentively.
(John transferred to this school on September 12, 1963)
Interpretation: John is beginning to adjust to his class.
Recommendation: None at present.

Sociometry

Sociometry, the study of social relationships revealed by student choices among their classmates, was originally stimulated by Moreno's writing in 1934.[8] Since that time its use has grown steadily in American schools until today sociometric tests, sociocharts, and sociodiagrams are commonly employed by teachers who wish to obtain objective evidence of the social relationships existing in their classrooms. With these techniques teachers can identify "stars," the students who are most desired as co-workers; "isolates," the students who are not named as desired co-workers; "fringers" or "neglectees," those who have selected no one who reciprocates their desire to work together; and "rejectees," those with whom some individual would particularly dislike to work.

Likewise, teachers can identify sociometric "cliques," groups of individuals who restrict almost all their choices to members of the same group; and "cleavages," the absence of choices between two or more groups. Cleavages are commonly found between boys and girls in the upper elementary grades, between rural and urban students in consolidated high schools, and between members and nonmembers of fraternities and sororities in colleges.

Appropriate use of sociometric data facilitates guidance of the social development of individuals and enables teachers to organize sociometric groups which through working better together increase class attainment of all course objectives, including knowledge and skills as well as attitudes

[8] Jacob L. Moreno, *Who Shall Survive?* Washington, D.C.: Nervous and Mental Disease Publishing Company, 1934.

and appreciations. Also, by repeating sociometric tests at intervals, teachers can trace and evaluate otherwise unmeasurable effects of organization and instruction.

SOCIOMETRIC TESTS   Several principles apply to the selection of a sociometric test question which is to be used as the basis for class analysis.

1. The question should relate to an action that will involve only a whole class.
2. The question should not be biased to favor or disfavor anyone. All students should have an equal opportunity to be selected.
3. The action proposed in the question should be real. It should be in agreement with the interests of the age group concerned and with the goals of instruction.
4. The action proposed should be carried out. Students are more likely to give valid responses when they know that action will follow.

On the basis of the above criteria the following items would be inappropriate for use in sociometric study of a class:

1. "The girls in this class will choose their girls' league representative next week. Whom do you think they should select?" (If any boys are in the class, the first and second principles are violated.)
2. "Name the persons you would like as neighbors in a new seating arrangement." (Unless it is clearly understood that their present neighbors could be selected, the second principle is violated.)
3. "If you were going on a trip to Mars tomorrow, whom would you select as companions?" (This item violates the third and fourth principles.)
4. "Name your five best friends." (This item violates the first, third, and fourth principles.)

Several additional factors must be considered in the construction and administration of sociometric tests. First, research seems to indicate that items requiring five selections yield more useful and reliable data than items which require students to make fewer choices (4:148). Second, the validity of sociometric data is improved when students are assured that their choices will be kept strictly confidential. (Test papers should be folded and turned in directly to the teacher, not passed from student to student. Furthermore, all discussion of choices should be thoroughly prohibited.) Third, tests should not be administered before students have had an opportunity to know every member of the class by name. Bias due to difficulties in spelling of names can be eliminated by listing all names on each test paper so that students need only to check their own names and

mark their choices. Recording of results is also facilitated by this procedure. (See the "committee preferences blank.") Research indicates that
when these principles and considerations are satisfied, student responses
to sociometric tests are informative and reliable (2:1321).

Appropriate items for sociometric use could be similar to the following:

1. "Committees will soon be organized for our next unit of instruction. Name in order of preference five persons with whom you would like
to work. If there should be any persons with whom you prefer not to work,
name them also."

2. "Name the five class members near whom you would most like to
be seated. Present neighbors may be named if you wish."

3. "Name the five class members you would prefer to have as team-
mates in our next physical education activity. Your instructor will balance
the teams in playing ability so select those with whom you would most
like to play." (This item probably still contains bias related to playing
ability. It could be useful in the organization of teams which might play
well together, but it may fail to reveal valid information basic to socio-
analysis.)

A suggested format for a sociometric test is illustrated below. In the
example, John Garr has selected Pete Hanson as his first choice. His
second choice is Jane Nebb; his third is Phil Brown. He also has selected
Jack Johns and Sam Post, but has not indicated any preference between
them. His one rejection is Carl Good. Each student in the class should
fill out a similar form. The data obtained should be put into a sociometric
chart to facilitate interpretation.

COMMITTEE PREFERENCES BLANK (CONFIDENTIAL)

To assist in the formation of committees for our next activity, please do the
following:

1. Place a check (√) in the blank before your name.
2. Place your code letter in the blanks before the five class members with whom
   you would prefer to work.
3. If you have distinct preferences among your choices, also number your
   first choice "1," your second choice "2," and so on.
4. If you would object to being on a committee with anyone, place an X
   through the code letter before his or her name.

CODE		NAME
_____	A.	Mary Adams
3F	B.	Phil Brown
_____	C.	Carol Cook
_____	D.	Della Dugan
_____	E.	Faith Farr
✓	F.	John Garr
_____	~~G~~.	Carl Good
1F	H.	Pete Hanson
F	I.	Jack Johns
_____	J.	Amy Jones
_____	K.	Ole Lyon
_____	L.	Marta Moe
2F	M.	Jane Nebb
_____	N.	Bill Nort
F	O.	Sam Post

Note: When you have finished marking your choices, fold your paper, place it on your desk, and continue with your work. In consideration of the feelings of your classmates, do not discuss your choices with anyone. Your teacher will also keep all choices strictly confidential. Each person will have at least one or two of his choices in the group to which he is assigned.

SOCIOCHARTS   If the format illustrated in the "committee preferences blank" is used, it is a simple matter to transfer the responses to a sociochart. In fact, each column of choices represents a corresponding column

students chosen		choices made by															Totals		
		A	B	C	D	E	F	G	H	I	J	K	L	M	N	O	I	II	III
A	MARY		(1BA)		(DA)							KA		(MA)	NA		5	0	3
B	PHIL	(1AB)					(3FB)		(HB)	IB			LB		NB	(OB)	7	0	4
C	CAROL					EC							(1LC)				2	0	1
D	DELLA	(AD)												(MD)		(OD)	3	0	3
E	FAITH								HE					ME			2	0	0
F	JOHN		(BF)			EF			(HF)		JF					(OF)	5	0	3
G	CARL	AG		CG	DG			X	(HG)	(IG)	(1JG)	(KG)		(1MG)			8	1	5
H	PETE	AH	(BH)	CH	DH		(1FH)	(GH)			JH	KH	LH	(MH)		OH	11	0	4
I	JACK					EI	FI	(GI)				(KI)					4	0	2
J	AMY					EJ		(GJ)		IJ	X		(LJ)		NJ		5	1	2
K	OLE			CK			(GK)		(IK)	JK			LK		NK		6	0	2
L	MARTA			(1CL)		EL					(JL)						3	0	2
M	JANE	(AM)	BM	CM	(DM)		(2FM)	(GM)	(HM)	IM	X	KM			NM	OM	11	1	4
N	BILL									X							0	1	0
O	SAM		(BO)		(DO)		(FO)										3	0	3

Fig. 15-1 Sociometric chart of committee preferences

in the chart (Figure 15-1). The chart can be made by cutting and pasting or by simply lining up each column and transferring its contents to the chart.

When the choices made by each student have been entered in the vertical column headed by his letter code, the total number of choices received by each can be determined by counting the entrees in the horizontal row following his name. This total, known as the student's "group status," should then be entered in column I. Research reveals that little is gained by assigning different weights to choices of different rank; merely counting the number of choices is adequate (4:64). Isolates and stars can be identified on the basis of column I entrees. Examination of Figure 15-1 reveals that Mary Adams has a social status score of 5, average when five selections are made. Pete Hanson and Jane Nebb, each having received eleven choices, are stars; Faith Farr and Bill Nort are neglectees; and in addition, Bill Nort is an isolate.

The number of times a student has been rejected should be recorded in column II. In Figure 15-1 it can be seen that Carl, Amy, Jane, and Bill each have received one rejection.

Mutual choices can most simply be determined by starting in the upper left corner of the chart following down column A and across row A encircling every mutual choice. Then from the diagonal line, repeat the procedure for column B and row B. When all mutual choices have been marked, the total for each row should be recorded in column III. For example, in Figure 15-1 Mary has received three mutual choices, and Phil has received four. The number of mutual choices received by a student gives an indication of the degree to which he is accepted as a working partner by those with whom he would like to associate.

On the basis of sociocharts, a teacher can form better working subgroups within his class and he can identify students who may need guidance in social development. However, the full power of sociometry is not clear until these data are graphically arranged in a sociogram.

SOCIOGRAMS Of the various types of sociograms in common use, the target diagram is perhaps the most popular. It is built by placing symbols representing students on a target of concentric circles so that the distance of each symbol from the center of the target is inversely related to the represented student's sociometric status. Thus stars are placed in the center, and isolates on the periphery. Choice patterns can be revealed by drawing lines between symbols to represent choices given and received. When the number of students in the class exceeds ten or twelve, however, an attempt to represent more than mutual choices usually results in an uninterpretable maze of crossed lines. Therefore, it is common to restrict representations to mutual choices, or to first and second choices at most.

In the target diagram (Figure 15-2) designed for the recording of five-choice data, the innermost circle is reserved for placement of symbols representing individuals who received nine or more choices. The ring next to the innermost circle provides the space in which to record symbols representing students who were selected six to eight times. The next ring, labeled by the number 5, receives symbols representing students selected five times.

A refinement in sociogramming designed to reveal cleavages is brought about by dividing the target into quadrants and placing the symbols representing like classifications in the same quadrant. In the illustrated

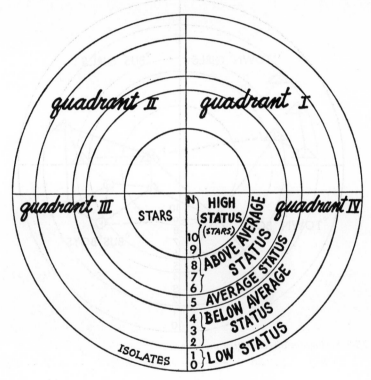

Fig. 15-2 Target on which to plot five-choice sociometric data

sociogram (Figure 15-3), possible cleavages between girls and boys and between students who take buses and students who live in town have been investigated. Figure 15-3 represents the data in Figure 15-1 as follows:

1. From supplementary data in the students' folders it is determined that girls A, D, and M, and boys B. F. H. and O are transported to and from school by bus.

2. Girls A, D, and M, represented by triangles, are placed in quadrant I with M in the center circle, A in ring 5, and D in ring 3 according to the social status of each as recorded in column I of Figure 15-1. (Placement should be sketched lightly in pencil at this stage since minor changes in position are likely to be necessary in step seven.)

3. Circles to represent boys B, F, H, and O are placed in quadrant IV according to the social status total of each.

4. In the same manner town girls and town boys are placed in quadrants II and III respectively.

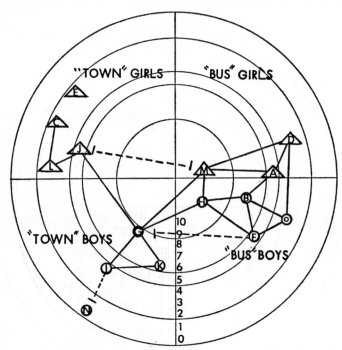

Fig. 15-3 *Sociogram of committee preference*

○ *Boy* △ *Girl* ———— *Mutual choice* - - - - - - - - *Rejection*

5. Lines are drawn lightly between symbols to indicate the mutual choices recorded in column III of Figure 15-1. For example, lines are drawn from A to B, D, and M.

6. Broken lines are drawn to represent the rejections.

7. Symbols are shifted and grouped to reduce the number of crossed lines to a minimum. In this step care must be taken to maintain the correct distance of each symbol from the center of the sociogram. The sociogram is now completed. The problem of interpretation remains.

Examination of the completed sociogram reveals an absence of mutual choices between town girls and students of both sexes who travel by bus. However, restudy of the sociochart (Figure 15-1) shows that seven choices were made between town girls and boys who commute by bus, but verifies almost complete cleavage between the two groups of girls. Furthermore, that cleavage is magnified by the relationship of mutual rejection which has been indicated between the two girls most selected in their respective groups.

On the other hand, cleavages do not exist between students recorded in the other quadrants. In fact, the seven boys and girls who are transported by bus form a fairly close group; and at least one mutual choice and five or six single choices span the possible gaps between the other quadrants.

The sociogram reveals desired association among three of the town boys but isolation and rejection of N, the fourth. It is also clear that town girls, J, L, and C, form a chain but not a closely knit group, while E is a fringer or neglectee. Finally, stars M and H stand out clearly in the center circle, and an additional potential class leader is revealed in G, the only student having mutual choices in all four quadrants. In fact, he could be the key to improved relations among all groups of the class.

USE OF SOCIOMETRIC INFORMATION   Teachers who use sociometric data to guide the formation of groups start by placing a low-status student in each group and then proceed to add one or two persons he has selected. (Top priority should be given to his mutual choice if he shares one, and to his first and second choices if he has ranked his selections.) Additional persons selected by two or more members of the group are then added to bring the group to desired size. Care should be taken to avoid assigning rejectees and their rejectors to the same group. Also, the assignment of two isolates to the same group should be avoided if possible (4:238).

When a teacher decides to reduce or eliminate cleavages and cliques, he may find it helpful to use sociometric grouping which places members of two or more cliques on the same committee. It is considered good practice to keep at least two persons from a clique together since the basic policy is to expand groups rather than to explode them, although the latter technique may be effective in special circumstances (4:239).

Of course, teachers must take all available evidence into consideration whenever they form sociometric groups and not just sociometric data alone. For example, students known to be noisy and disruptive when together would not be assigned to the same group even though they might wish it.

It is also true that teacher action with respect to isolates, neglectees, and rejectees should not be based on sociometry alone. The sociogram serves only to draw the teacher's attention to possible problems which might be investigated more fully through use of observation and case study. Sociometry is useful, but not a panacea. For example, many students of low social status are adequately adjusted and satisfactory in achievement. These individuals can be given minor social assistance by the classroom teacher. However, a few others might be seriously maladjusted and in need of the services of guidance personnel. Obviously, classroom teachers are not expected to handle all cases alone. Their responsibility is to learn to differentiate one type of case from the other and to know when to refer students to specialists.

Finally, teachers should keep in mind that research shows that students identified as stars tend to be elected to leadership roles (4:301). It follows then that teachers would do well to give stars minor leadership training in the classroom. Assignments such as group chairman or class monitor when accompanied by instruction in the responsibilities of those offices have been found to be beneficial.

RELIABILITY AND VALIDITY OF SOCIOMETRY   Two questions that sometimes are asked are: "Isn't sociometry intended for use only in the elementary grades?" and "What faith can one have in sociometric results in the high school?" Research involving use of sociometry in high schools, in the military, in industry, and in hospitals shows that there is a strong tendency for groups to retain quite similar sociometric ratings over a period of several weeks or months. Individual choices may change, but the social status of an individual remains fairly constant unless planned steps are taken to bring about a change. In addition, research at all levels has shown that high-choice individuals are clearly superior to low-choice individuals in personality factors. "Only in rare instances are the low-choice individuals found to be superior to the high ones in any desirable behavior characteristics."[9]

Thus, sociometry can be used with a good deal of confidence. It has proved to be a useful and valuable addition to the evaluation techniques of the modern teacher.

Selected Readings

1. Ahmann, J. Stanley, and Marvin D. Glock, *Evaluating Pupil Growth*. Boston: Allyn and Bacon, Inc., subsidiary of Prentice-Hall, Inc., 1959. Chapters 1, 11, 14.
2. American Educational Research Association, *Encyclopedia of Educational Research*, 3d ed., Chester W. Harris, ed. New York: The Macmillan Company, 1960, pp. 482–485, 1319–1323, 1502–1503.
3. Clark, Leonard H., and Irving S. Starr, *Secondary School Teaching Methods*. New York: The Macmillan Company, 1959. Chapter 10.

[9] Merl E. Bonney, "Sociometric Methods," *Encyclopedia of Educational Research*, 3d ed. New York: The Macmillan Company, 1960, p. 1321. Used by permission of Macmillan.

4. Gronlund, Norman E., *Sociometry in the Classroom.* New York: Harper & Row, Publishers, 1959. Chapters 1–10.
5. Nordberg, H. Orville, James M. Bradfield, and William C. Odell, *Secondary School Teaching.* New York: The Macmillan Company, 1962. Chapter 8.
6. Thomas, R. Murray, *Judging Student Progress,* 2d ed. New York: David McKay Company, Inc., 1960. Chapters 1, 2, 8–11.
7. Thorndike, Robert L., and Elizabeth Hagen, *Measurement and Evaluation in Psychology and Education,* 2d ed. New York: John Wiley & Sons, Inc., 1961. Chapters 1, 2, 13, 14.

CHAPTER 16

Teacher-built tests

Every teacher needs to know how to build effective tests. Estimates based upon research indicate that, on the average, high school classes are tested approximately once each week. The frequency of test usage varies from teacher to teacher and from one subject to another. For example, one study found that in physical education and in fine arts tests were used least frequently, approximately once each month, while at the other ex-treme classes in mathematics and Latin were tested on the average of almost twice each week. Only a small proportion of the tests regularly used in the classroom are purchased. As all but a very few are constructed by the teacher himself, it is apparent that teachers will find it to their ad-vantage to develop skill in test building.

In this chapter the steps in efficient development of tests will be dis-cussed, including: (1) planning tests, (2) building items, (3) organizing tests for use, and (4) improving the items for further use.

PLANNING TESTS

Test construction, like other important elements in the teaching process, requires careful planning. A necessary first step is to get the purpose of the contemplated test clearly in mind.

Clarifying the Purpose

How are the results to be used? Will the test be a diagnostic and instruc-tional device or is it to serve as a basis for determining student marks? In fact, can a test best provide the information desired, or should some other procedure be employed? Clearly identifying the purpose of a proposed test serves to determine the kind of test to be constructed and tends to eliminate tests which lack usefulness.

For example, if a test is to give direction to further instruction, items which reduce chance success to a minimum are to be preferred. It is particularly important in individual diagnosis that items having a high guessing factor be avoided. In diagnostic tests it is better to use completion items than alternate responses, for instance. On the average, half of the students who guess on a true-false item will choose the right answer, making effective diagnosis impossible on the basis of responses to individual items. On the other hand, in tests to be used for marking purposes, the total score is important and chance response to individual items is not critical. Consequently, a greater variety of item types can be used effectively.

In addition to limiting the type of items to be employed, other factors, such as test content and test length, also will vary according to the purpose the instrument is to serve. Thus, definition of purpose sets the stage for the next steps in test planning.

It should be emphasized that no test should be given merely to satisfy an arbitrary time schedule. The beginning teacher who tests her class every Friday fails to comprehend the reasons for testing. Tests are given to serve specific purposes in teaching. To test effectively, teachers need to determine clearly and completely those purposes before test building begins.

Identifying Behaviors to Be Measured

After the purpose has been clarified, the next step is to determine what to include in the test. Assuming that the test is to measure achievement at the conclusion of a unit of instruction, this step is best accomplished by examining the objectives and content of the unit. What learning outcomes are expected at the grade level taught? How are students who have achieved an objective distinguishable from students who have failed to reach the desired goal? Many teachers find that at this stage test construction is facilitated by phrasing course objectives so as to describe exactly what students are expected to be able to do in order to reveal what they have achieved in desired knowledges, skills, and attitudes. Such statements are called behavioral objectives.

To be more explicit, some content topics, such as "understanding democracy," are taught at several grade levels. At each grade the topic is the same, but the behaviors sought are different. To illustrate this point, sample behavioral objectives concerning one element of democratic understandings are listed in Table 16-1 for various grade levels. Study of this table will reveal that the behavior expected in the lower grades is "attentive listening to traditional stories." At the eleventh-grade level students are expected to be able to "identify and interpret the outstanding contributions of an extensive list of American leaders, and to give particular attention to the social, political, military, and economic circumstances from which their contributions arose." Comparable behaviors expected at eighth grade and in college are also included in the table. Suggested evaluation techniques appropriate for each objective are listed in the right-hand column of the table.

Table 16-1. Illustration of Behavioral Objectives
for One Content Topic Taught at Various School Levels

Content: Understanding of Democracy
Specific element: Students will know about the contributions of great Americans.

SCHOOL LEVEL	BEHAVIOR EXPECTED	EVALUATION TECHNIQUE
	Most students will be able to:	
Lower grades	Listen attentively to traditional stories of American heroes	Observation
Eighth grade	Recognize the outstanding contributions of a selected list of American heroes	Objective test
Eleventh grade	Identify and interpret the outstanding contributions of an extensive list of American leaders, and relate their contributions to the social, political, military, and economic development of this nation	Objective and essay tests; ratings of group work and projects
College	Interpret and evaluate the contributions of American leaders while giving attention to the philosophical beliefs of each	Objective and essay tests; term papers
Graduate school	Evaluate the contributions to democracy of specific American leaders, and contrast and compare them with the contributions of important leaders of other ideologies on the world scene	Research papers, essay tests, and objective tests

Objectives to guide testing should be stated so that the described behavior is observable. For example, rather than stating an English class objective as "The students will develop an everlasting appreciation of good literature," it would be better to say "The voluntary reading of each student will increase in volume and quality from month to month during this school year." The first statement describes behavior that is worthy, but not observable. The behavior described in the second statement can be observed, recorded, and evaluated.

Likewise, when objectives have originally been stated to describe the development of an understanding or knowledge, the objective should be restated so as to describe what the student will be able to do when he has developed that understanding or knowledge. For example, the objective "To develop an understanding of the Constitution of the United States" should be restated as: "Students will be able to explain the meaning of the Constitution of the United States in their own words" or "Students will be able to identify which article of the constitution applies to selected circumstances." The first statement does not clarify the level of behavior expected, whereas the second and third statements lead naturally to test items which can measure the behavior described.

Some experienced teachers prefer to base their tests on outlines of subject matter. However, this practice is adequate only when the teacher is thoroughly familiar with the behaviors to be expected at a given grade. Beginning teachers should always use behavioral objectives to guide both instruction and evaluation.

Test Length

A test ordinarily must be built to fit into a given instructional period. Many beginning teachers find it difficult to estimate the amount of time high school students will require to complete a test. Some overestimate the time needed and find that a test planned for thirty minutes is completed in fifteen, leaving an awkward void in the day's lesson. However, the more usual error is that of underestimating the time required. Tests planned for forty minutes or less frequently are still in progress when the bell rings for the next period. The teacher then faces the necessity of collecting the tests before the students are through (a practice that students dislike) or encroaching upon the time allocated to other classes—a practice that arouses the ire of both students and colleagues.

These situations can be avoided by more careful planning. Although the optimum time allocation for any given test can be determined accurately only after the test has been administered, a rough estimate of one minute per item requiring interpretation or application and a half minute per item concerning factual information will be a guideline suitable for many high school classes. Of course, problem items (common in mathematics and science) and essay questions (more frequently used in the social sciences) will require more testing time.

In any event teachers must keep in mind that their students will differ greatly in the speed with which they can successfully complete a test. A test easily finished in fifteen minutes by some students may be a difficult twenty- or twenty-five-minute job for others. Therefore, estimates of testing time requirements should be flexible and take into account the needs of the class. Lesson plans for days on which tests are given should include specific suggestions for profitable use of the entire time by all students.

Those who complete tests early should be advised to proceed on quiet individual projects while the slower students are finishing.

Proportionate Content

After the unit objectives and content have been outlined in some detail, it will become obvious that limitations of time will not permit inclusion of test questions on everything that has been taught. It then becomes necessary to determine what topics should be tested and what proportionate share of the total test should be devoted to each. The more important topics of a unit should receive greater weight in the test than topics of lesser importance. If it is difficult to determine the relative importance of the various topics to be tested, a rough approximation may be achieved

Table 16-2. Plan for a Written Test on Softball

CONTENT	%	NO. OF ITEMS	KNOWLEDGE OF RULES (10%)	KNOWLEDGE OF SKILLS (30%)	APPLICATIONS OF PRINCIPLES (60%)
Fielding	15	6	2	4	
Base running	10	4	1	2	1
Throwing	5	2	–	1	1
Batting	20	8	1	5	2
Offensive strategy	20	8	–	–	8
Defensive strategy	30	12	–	–	12
	100	40	4	12	24

by noting the relative amount of teaching time each received. Then, since assigning different values to various items of a test greatly complicates scoring and since accurate statistical determination of weighting is beyond the skill of most beginning teachers, it is recommended that the number of items covering any given topic be in direct proportion to the relative importance of the topic. For example, four items would be allocated to a topic that is considered twice as important as a topic tested by two items. Admittedly this procedure achieves only a roughly proportionate weighting of the various topics in the test. Nevertheless, the procedure is recommended as most practical for the classroom teacher.

Types of Items to Be Used

The items commonly used in teacher-constructed tests include: (1) alternate response, (2) multiple choice, (3) matching, (4) completion, (5) short answer, (6) essay, and (7) situation.

Each type has its peculiar strengths and weaknesses, which should be taken into consideration in test planning. (Item characteristics are fully discussed in a following section of this chapter.) The first five listed are frequently classified as objective items. However, the scoring of only the first three is fully free from the scorer's personal feelings or prejudices. In truly objective items, each item will have only one correct answer regardless of who does the scoring. Tests made up of the first three types can be scored directly from a key or by a machine. The scoring of completion questions and problems is somewhat less objective in that alternative responses may be acceptable for full or partial credit, while the scoring of essay items is least objective of all. When the planned test is to be scored by someone other than the teacher, fully objective items only should be used.

The selection of item types for a test should be further governed by two factors: the purpose of the test and the conditions under which the test is to be administered. The fact that in diagnostic and instructional tests completion-type items are to be preferred to alternate-response types has been mentioned previously in this chapter. Test administration conditions should be fully considered in test planning. If his classroom is crowded with students or if more than one class section is to be tested, it may be advisable for a teacher to prepare alternate forms of the test. Teachers must be realistic and face the possibility that some students may copy answers when objective tests are used in overcrowded rooms or when information is available from students who have taken the test in an earlier period.

The preparation of alternate forms of objective tests can reduce, if not eliminate, copying. Equivalent forms of matching or multiple-choice items can be constructed easily by merely changing the order of the choices. For example, the following items have different-lettered answers:

FORM I			FORM II		
1. Who discovered the Pacific Ocean?			1. Who discovered the Pacific Ocean?		
A. Magellan	B. Balboa		A. Cortez	B. Columbus	
C. Columbus	D. Cortez		C. Balboa	D. Magellan	

It has been found that essay items also discourage copying on the part of the students. Essay items, however, have the disadvantage of being transferred easily from students in an earlier section to those in a later section.

The selection of items is also affected by the availability of adequate duplication facilities. Wide adoption of the ditto process has made it much easier to prepare objective tests for use in the classroom. The older methods of writing the tests on the chalkboard or of dictating the items to the class are now outmoded. At best these older methods of test presentation were uneconomical. Too much class time was consumed in copying questions from the board or in waiting for the next question to be read aloud by the teacher. When test duplication facilities are not available, teachers are seriously limited in the kinds of tests they can use effectively. Concisely stated problems and essay items are the most efficient to use when it is necessary to dictate a test or to write it on the chalkboard. (Tests are to be presented orally to the class only as a last resort, except in the case of spelling, shorthand, or the foreign languages.)

Opinions differ concerning the advisability of using several types of items in a test or restricting the test to a single type.

Table 16-3. Use and Objectivity of Various Item Types

STUDENT BEHAVIOR TO BE MEASURED	MOST APPROPRIATE ITEM TYPES	OBJECTIVITY OF SCORING
Ability to exercise judgment, recognize relationships, and make associations	1. Alternate response 2. Multiple choice 3. Matching	1–3. Usually most objective
Ability to recall information and solve problems	4. Completion 5. Short answer	4–5. Usually fairly objective
Ability to organize recalled information and express judgments meaningfully	6. Essay	6. Usually least objective
Ability to interpret data, apply learning, think critically, and reason logically	7. Situation	7. Same as basic types (1–6)

Arguments favoring the use of only one type of item in a test point out that a truer score can be obtained by eliminating the confusion sometimes developed by changing the kind of response required. The use of a variety of types with clear directions and sample items for each in a test not only adds interest to the test but makes it possible to use each type to its best advantage. Table 16-3 indicates the recommended use and the relative objectivity of various types of items.

BUILDING TEST ITEMS

The building of good test items is an extremely time-consuming task. Highly trained professional test builders consider it a successful day when they have constructed one, two, or perhaps three unique items which eventually meet the rigorous requirements of a published test.

Teachers cannot devote comparable time to the construction of classroom tests, but they must recognize that tests built in a few hours usually are much in need of improvement. Time, however, is only one element in successful test construction. To build useful test items, a teacher must have knowledge of course objectives and course content, knowledge of item-construction principles, time to practice construction skills, and ideas for item content.

Sources of Ideas for Items

The time to start test construction comes much earlier than most beginning teachers realize. Many of the ideas for test items should evolve in connection with lesson planning. At the time that teachers plan their lessons, the important objectives are clearly in mind. Consequently, at that time ideas for related test questions are much easier to develop than later on when the particulars of any single day's lesson have been forgotten. These ideas should be catalogued, preferably on separate cards, and filed so that they are available when needed. Item ideas in physical education might be statements like the following:

1. Matching item concerning the position of players on a softball diamond in given play situations.
2. True-false item about the infield fly rule.
3. Multiple-choice item concerning choice of plays in a given game situation.

A rich source of ideas for items is the written work of students. Equally important item ideas may be obtained by careful observation of student behavior. Common errors should be recorded for use when item ideas are needed.

Another excellent way to get item ideas is to give a pretest made up of completion items. The erroneous ideas recorded make very useful distracters in later multiple-choice or matching questions.

Some useful ideas for items may be obtained through examination of textbooks, courses of study, and tests in the subject. However, these sources are likely to yield ideas less pertinent to a particular class than the sources discussed above. Under no circumstances should the course textbook be substituted for the test plan. Teachers who use their textbook in lieu of a test plan are very likely to develop inferior tests. If items are based solely on ideas noted while paging through a text, it is almost inevitable that the resulting test will be a mere collection of questions concerning unusual facts which may have little or no relation to the real course objectives.

Item ideas, like fully developed items, should be filed so that they are readily available. Many teachers have solved the problem by recording ideas and items on separate cards and keeping them filed in boxes classified by unit objectives. A record of the effectiveness of each item, determined after its use, can also be kept on the same card.

General Principles of Item Construction

Before starting to build test items, teachers should become thoroughly acquainted with the general principles of item construction listed below.

STATING ITEMS CLEARLY   In order to do this:

1. Use vocabulary suitable to the students' level. Teachers sometimes fail to realize that many high school students are just beginning to develop technical vocabularies. Beginning teachers are particularly susceptible to the error of transferring their collegiate vocabulary almost unchanged to the high school classroom.

2. Avoid the use of figurative, ambiguous, complex, and unnecessarily qualitative expressions. Use specific and direct language in items. Eliminate unnecessary words.

3. Avoid trick questions. Place critical information in the most prominent part of the sentence. When essential information is hidden in minor clauses or complex phrases, the students' mental alertness and reading ability are measured rather than their achievement of the course objectives.

4. Be grammatically correct. Particularly avoid double negatives and inconsistent constructions.

5. Use negative statements sparingly. When they must be used, draw the students' attention to the negative element through use of special direction or underlining. If several such items are to be used, group them together, preferably at the end of the test.

6. Directions for taking the test should be clear, complete, and concise. All directions should be included in the test so that once the test is started interruptions for further directions from the test administrator become unnecessary.

ITEMS CONTAINING CLUES   Items should be stated so that achievement is measured rather than student ability to draw clues from the form or language of the item. Specifically:

1. Avoid using certain words such as "no," "none," and "all" in such manner as to determine specifically the answer desired. (See the discussion of true-false items for examples.)

2. Avoid making the longest answer consistently the best answer. (See the discussion of multiple-choice items for examples.)

ENCOURAGING GOOD STUDY HABITS To accomplish this end:

1. Avoid asking for the mere reproduction or completion of statements taken directly from class discussions or from assigned readings. Such items can be answered on the basis of memorization without any knowledge of meaning. Tests should measure ability to understand, to apply, and to interpret rather than mere ability to memorize by rote.

2. Avoid use of stereotyped phraseology (except in distracters) for the reasons just cited.

STATING ITEMS FOR OBJECTIVE SCORING The final score on a test should depend as little as possible on interpretations peculiar to the scorer.

1. Avoid use of recall and recognition items which unintentionally lead to debatably equivalent answers.

2. Essay questions should be carefully stated and keyed so that scoring can be as objective as possible.

Alternate-Response Items

Alternate-response items are statements or question which require that the student select one of two possible answers. The most common form is true-false, although yes-no, right-wrong, and completion forms are also widely used.

Examples:

T	F	1.	Kennedy was elected president in 1960.
Yes	No	2.	Was Edison the inventor of the telephone?
Right	Wrong	3.	The square root of 64 is 8.
_____		4.	Joan (lent, borrowed) her book to me.

The cluster true-false form is an adaptation of the original true-false type.

Example:

If a painted cube 3 inches on an edge is sawed into 1-inch cubes, then of the 1-inch cubes

T	F	1.	four will be painted on one side.
T	F	2.	six will be painted on two sides.
T	F	3.	eight will be painted on three sides.
T	F	4.	none will be painted on four sides.
T	F	5.	none will be entirely unpainted.

Another modified true-false form requires that the student correct false statements by substituting words or phrases for underlined parts of the original statements. This form has some of the characteristics of completion items. It has been found to have higher reliability than the ordinary true-false form.

Example:

Monday 1. Labor Day comes on a *Sunday*.

<u>True</u> 2. In the United States, national elections are held on a *Tuesday*.

Alternate-response items are comparatively easy to construct and are economical of testing time. A wide sampling of course content is possible in minimum time through use of this type of item. However, these advantages are largely counterbalanced in practice by the accompanying disadvantages of (1) encouragement of memorization of unrelated factual information, (2) negative learning effect of false statements, and (3) low reliability due to the comparatively large possibility of guessing the correct answer. Perhaps the greatest weaknesses of this type of item are its lack of effectiveness in diagnosis and the tendency to overemphasize knowledge of unusual factual content. Nevertheless the alternate-response form remains one of the most frequently used item forms in educational testing. Specific suggestions for its construction follow.

AVOIDING HIDDEN FALSE PHRASES Many readers automatically assume that all qualifying phrases are true.

Poor: 1. California, which in area is the fifth largest state in the United States, has its capital at Sacramento.
                                                                    1. T   F

Improved: 1. California is the fifth largest state in the United States.
                                                                    1. T   F
             2. The capital of California is Sacramento. 2. T   F

STRUCTURING THE SENTENCE In a statement of reason, the false part, if any, should follow the word "because."

Poor: A cubic foot of ice weighs more than a cubic foot of water because water increases in volume when it freezes.

Improved: A cubic foot of ice weighs less than a cubic foot of water because water decreases in volume when it freezes.

AVOIDING USAGE CLUES Avoid consistently using certain words in true statements more frequently than in false statements. It has been found that many teachers inadvertently provide clues to the truth or falsity of items by using such words as "none," "never," "all," "no," and "always" predominantly in false statements just as they use words like "may," "most," "some," "often," and "generally" predominantly in true statements. Before making the final draft of a test, teachers should check to see that these words are used about equally in both true and false items. Research has also shown that in the tests of many teachers, items including specific citations or enumerations as well as items more than twenty words in length are usually true (8:240). These clues, too, can be avoided.

AVOIDING AMBIGUOUS AND QUALITATIVE EXPRESSIONS

Poor:	1.	In 1960 the population of St. Paul was quite large.		
			T	F
Improved:	1.	In 1960 the population of St. Paul exceeded 600,000.		
			T	F
Poor:	2.	Boys usually can run faster than girls.	T	F
Improved:	2.	Ten-year-old boys usually can run faster than girls of the same age.	T	F

AVOIDING STATEMENTS TAKEN DIRECTLY FROM TEXTBOOKS Use of textbook quotes in tests encourages students to squander their study time on educationally sterile rote memorization.

AVOIDING STATEMENTS THAT MAY BE EITHER TRUE OR FALSE True-false statements that are not absolutely true or absolutely false pose an unreasonable problem to the student. He is forced to guess what degree of truth or falsity will be tolerated by the teacher. There is danger that the best students will miss these items merely because they know of unusual exceptions that the scorer has overlooked or considered inconsequential. The same items are answered easily by students with less information.

Poor:	There are 365 days in a year.	T	F
Improved:	An ordinary calendar year contains 365 days.	T	F

The first statement could be scored as true, yet some students would mark it false because they possessed information concerning such exceptions as leap year, solar year, tropical year, lunar year, or astronomical year. (The period of the earth's revolution around the sun is approximately 365 days, 5 hours, 48 minutes, and 46 seconds.)

Multiple-Choice Items

A multiple-choice item is composed of a question or incomplete statement together with at least three possible responses or completions. The student must select the one answer that is correct or best. The part of the item that precedes the responses is called the stem, and the incorrect responses are known as distracters.

Examples:

(Question stem)

_____ 1. From what country was the Alaskan territory purchased?
    A. China
    B. Russia
    C. Japan
    D. England
    E. Canada

(Incomplete-statement stem)

_____ 1. The Alaskan territory was purchased from
    A. China
    B. Russia
    C. Japan
    D. England
    E. Canada

                    A. to
_____ 2. Robert threw the ball B. two fast.
                    C. too

Many experienced constructors of tests rate multiple-choice items superior to all other types. By careful organization of distracters, the builder of this type of item can measure a student's ability to make judgments of predetermined exactness, while at the same time the item is easy to score and comparatively free from the factor of guessing. Some susceptibility to clues and relative difficulty of construction are the chief drawbacks of this item form. Careful attention to the following suggestions should help teachers improve the quality of their multiple-choice items.

USING AN ADEQUATE STEM The stem should include enough to indicate clearly the kind of answer required and also eliminate unnecessary repetition in the responses.

Poor: The mean
    A. is computed by substracting the low score from the high score and dividing by two.
    B. is computed by adding the scores.
    C. is computed by dividing the sum of the scores by the number of scores.
    D. is computed by adding the scores and dividing by two.

Improved: How is the mean computed?
    A. Subtract the low score from the high score and divide by two.
    B. Add the scores.
    C. Divide the sum of the scores by the number of scores.
    D. Add the scores and divide by two.

AVOIDING CLUES Carelessly constructed multiple-choice items frequently include such keys as grammatical inconsistency, lack of homogeneity among the responses, systematic location of the correct answer, and unusual length of the correct response.

Poor: Francis Bacon was an
    A. Dane
    B. Englishman
    C. Frenchman
    D. German
    E. Spaniard

Improved: What was the nationality of Francis Bacon?
    A. Danish
    B. English
    C. French
    D. German
    E. Spanish

Poor: What Spanish explorer looked for the fountain of youth?
    A. Cabot
    B. Ericson
    C. Lafayette
    D. Ponce de León

Improved: What explorer looked for the fountain of youth?
    A. Balboa
    B. De Soto
    C. Coronado
    D. Ponce de León

It has been shown that in some tests the correct answer appears so frequently in the same position (such as the second or fourth choice) that students who discover the clue can improve their score. Another common error is to make the correct answer consistently the longest or most smoothly worded response.

USING ONLY PLAUSIBLE CHOICES To students who lack the achievement being tested, all listed responses should appear to be homogeneous and plausible.

Poor: Who discovered the continent of North America?
      A. Washington
      B. Edison
      C. Cabot
      D. Ford
      E. Lindbergh

Improved: Who discovered the continent of North America?
      A. Columbus
      B. Balboa
      C. Cabot
      D. La Salle
      E. Ponce de León

Poor: The ratio of 8 ounces to a pound is
      A. 16:1
      B. 1:16
      C. 8:16
      D. none of these

Improved: The ratio of 8 ounces to a pound is
      A. 1:2
      B. 2:1
      C. 8:1
      D. 1:8
      E. none of these

Matching Items

A set of matching items is composed of two related groups of materials. The problem is to select for each item in one group the single best associated or matching element in the other group.

These items can be used to advantage in a wide variety of situations. For example, sets could be built using such combinations as a list of men together with a list of their works, a list of terms together with a list of their definitions, a list of play situations together with a list of the rules which apply, a list of events together with a list of their causes or of their effects, a list of problems together with a list of their solutions, or a list of cities together with a chart of their geographical locations.

Matching items have characteristics similar to those of the multiple-choice type. In fact, a matching exercise could be looked upon as a group of multiple-choice stems combined with a single set of possible responses. Matching items are particularly well adapted to measure student ability to recognize relationships and to make associations. However, in the measurement of fine discrimination, understanding, and judgment, this type is inferior to the multiple-choice type. Since a group of matching items is organized into a unit, with one set of responses, the type is economical in its use of test space, and requires less construction time for each item than multiple-choice items of comparable quality. The chief limitation of matching items is the frequency of the presence of clues in exercises constructed by individuals who fail to realize the importance of employing only homogeneous materials and supplying a surplus of choices. The following example is an illustration of these common errors.

Poorly constructed matching exercise:

Directions: Match column I with column II

I	II
1. signal caller	goal line
2. field goal	quarterback
3. illegal use of hands	15-yard penalty
4. number of downs in a series	3 points
5. must be crossed to score a touchdown	4

Any high school student, regardless of the paucity of his knowledge of football, would be able to answer all five items above on the basis of the clues presented. For example, quarterback is the only player listed; therefore it becomes the automatic answer to item 1. In item 3 the word "illegal" is easily associated with the word "penalty" in the list of answers. The word "number" in item 4 limits the possible selections for that item to the only number in column II. Since a "line" is the only feasible choice to be "crossed to score," choice one becomes the automatic answer to item 5. That leaves "3 points" to match effortlessly with "field goal" by the simple process of elimination.

It is obvious that these terms, all relating to the game of football, still lack the degree of homogeneity necessary to make up a usable matching exercise. The items should be revised into separate completion, alternate-response, or multiple-choice questions. They could be made usable in matching forms only by expansion into several separate exercises. These might include (1) players and their functions, (2) scoring plays and their point value, and (3) illegal plays and their penalties. In addition to having relatively heterogeneous content and an undesirable balance between the number of item stems and the number of choices, the sample exercise needs revision in several other respects.

1. No space has been designated for the answers. Blanks should be placed to the left of each numbered item.
2. The terms in column II are not labeled. Upper-case letters (A, B, C, D, and so on) are to be preferred.

3. The directions are inadequate. They might better read, "Match each football term in column I with the best selection from column II. Any lettered choice may be used once, several times, or not at all."

Specific suggestions for the improvement of matching items are discussed below.

LIMITING CONTENT TO HOMOGENEOUS MATERIAL   To the student who lacks the achievement measured, every element among the responses should appear to be a plausible answer to every element in the column of stems. If the material to be tested cannot satisfy this condition, the exercise should be recast into items of a type other than matching.

AVOIDING PROCESS OF ELIMINATION TESTING   Provide more responses than stems in each set, and occasionally use a single response as the match to more than one stem. This will increase the number of distracters and reduce the possibility of answering items by the process of elimination.

LIMITING CONTENT TO MATERIAL THAT SATISFIES THE OVER-ALL PLAN OF THE TEST   Resist the temptation to append additional items to matching exercises merely because they easily fall into the pattern of the matching set. To ignore this restriction is to destroy the validity of the total test. If the content in question would not be important enough to include as separate alternate-response, multiple-choice, or completion items, then it is not of sufficient importance to be tested by matching.

KEEPING MATCHING SETS RELATIVELY SHORT   The maximum number of responses to include in a single exercise should be determined by the reading difficulty and organization of the content. Ordinarily, eight to ten responses is a feasible limit. However, for extremely well-organized and concise responses the limit might be extended to twelve or fifteen without loss of efficiency.

ARRANGING FOR EASY UNDERSTANDING AND SCORING   Each item stem should be numbered, preceded by an answer blank, and placed in a column near the left margin of the page.

Each response should be clearly labeled and placed in a column at the right side of the paper, if possible. Upper-case letters (A, B, C, for example) are to be preferred to numbers or lower-case letters because they are less susceptible to confusing distortions. If the responses are to appear on a chart, diagram, map, or other figure, be sure that the choices are all clearly marked.

The responses should be put in alphabetical, chronological, or other meaningful order if possible.

The responses should be the shorter phrases and the stems the longer ones (with a possible exception of lists of terms and their definitions).

All parts of the exercise, including any necessary charts, diagrams, and figures, should be placed on the same page. It will be necessary to recheck this as the test is being typed for reproduction.

STATING DIRECTIONS CLEARLY   The directions should succinctly explain how the matching is to be done. Particular care should be taken to emphasize whether the responses are to be used only once or more than once.

Sample matching exercise:

Directions for items 1–8: Select the letter which best indicates the location of the following materials in our school library. Any choice may be used once, several times, or not at all.

Library Materials	Choices for Items 1–8
_____ 1. Dictionary	A. bibliography room
_____ 2. Cumulative Book Index	B. curriculum library
_____ 3. School Review	C. office
_____ 4. Encyclopedia	D. periodical desk
_____ 5. Education Index	E. reference desk
_____ 6. School and Society	F. reserve room
_____ 7. Bulletins	G. none of these
_____ 8. NSSE yearbooks	

Completion Items

Completion items are made up of sentences from which key words or phrases have been omitted. The student must think of the appropriate completions and write them in the blanks provided. A completion exercise may involve a single sentence, several sentences, or a paragraph. Each sentence may contain any number of blanks so long as the meaning of the exercise can be distinguished easily by students who possess the achievement being tested.

This kind of item can be used in a wide variety of situations, but is most commonly used to measure recall of factual information. This item type is particularly useful in diagnostic and instructional tests since the factor of guessing is much lower than in items of alternate-response, multiple-choice, and matching types. Good quality completion items are considered relatively easy to construct, but due to the frequent necessity of considering the value of equivalent answers and the problem of reading some handwriting, their scoring is very time consuming.

Sample completion items:

_____ 1. "The Lady of the Lake" was written by (*1*).
_____ 2. In basketball a field goal counts (*2*), and a free throw
_____ 3. counts (*3*).

1–5.   In any right triangle the altitude to the hypotenuse:

_____ 1. is the mean proportional between the (*1*) of

_____ 2. the (*2*),

_____ 3. forms (*3*) with the hypotenuse, and

_____ 4. forms two triangles which are (*4*) to each other

_____ 5. and to (*5*).

_____ 1. The (*1*) of the United States is made up of the House of Representatives and the Senate. Each member of the

_____ 2. House is elected for a term of (*2*) years, whereas mem-

_____ 3. bers of the Senate are elected for terms of (*3*) years.

_____ 4. All states have equal representation in the (*4*) and pro-

_____ 5. portionate representation in the (*5*). The presiding

_____ 6. officer of the Senate is the (*6*).

Specific suggestions for the improvement of completion items are illustrated in the following paragraphs.

OMITTING IMPORTANT WORDS   Avoid asking for details that you would deem unworthy of testing by other means.

Poor: Alexander _____ Bell is _____ for inventing the telephone.

Improved: Alexander Graham Bell is noted for inventing the

_____ .

AVOIDING TOO MANY OMISSIONS   Enough should be left so that the meaning of the item is clear to the student being tested.

Poor: The _____ of a _____ is found by multiplying the _____ by _____ .

Improved: The area of a rectangle is found by multiplying the _____ by the _____ .

AVOIDING AMBIGUOUS STATEMENTS   Phrase statements so that the kind of response desired is clearly indicated. Careful attention to this factor will save much time for the scorer as well as for the examinee.

Poor: Charles Lindbergh made his trans-Atlantic flight in _____ .

Improved: The year in which Charles Lindbergh made his trans-Atlantic flight was _____ .

Improved: The type of airplane in which Charles Lindbergh made his trans-Atlantic flight was _____ .

Improved: The name of the airplane in which Charles Lindbergh made his trans-Atlantic flight was _____ .

AVOIDING UNINTENDED CLUES Do not precede blanks with the articles "a" or "an." Make all blanks the same length. Check all items to see that the omitted words are not automatically associated with any words remaining in the statement.

Poor: A football player is ineligible to receive a forward pass unless he is a back or an _____.

Improved: The only football players eligible to receive forward passes are backs and _____.

Poor: In the circle formula $A = \frac{1}{2}rc$, c and r are symbols for _____ and _____.

Improved: In the circle formula $A = \frac{1}{2}rc$, c and r are symbols for _____ and _____.

Poor: In Alaska the summer days are extremely long just as in the wintertime the _____ are dark and _____.

Improved: Alaskan nights are long in the _____ season of the year.

OMITTING WORDS NEAR THE END OF THE STATEMENT Statements are more difficult to understand when omissions are made at their beginning and clearer when they occur at the end.

Poor: _____ is the longest side of a right triangle.

Improved: The name of the longest side of a right triangle is _____.

AVOIDING STATEMENTS FROM ASSIGNED READING Revise such materials so that mere rote learning will be discouraged. Test application of learning.

Poor: For every action there is an equal and opposite _____.

Improved: Robert can pull 90 pounds and Bill can pull 60 pounds. If they alone are pulling steadily on opposite ends of a rope, the maximum tension in the rope is _____ pounds.

Short-Answer Items

Short-answer items are direct questions or specific directions which require recalled responses. The responses usually are only a few words in length. Since the form is natural, the items are easy for the student to understand and also comparatively easy for the teacher to construct.

This type of item can be used to measure a wide variety of objectives in a manner that reduces to a minimum success on the basis of guessing. However, since the response required is short, there is some tendency to overemphasize the measurement of factual and unorganized learning.

Use of this type is further limited by the fact that scoring frequently is less objective and more time consuming than scoring recognition items.

Sample short-answer items:

_____ 1. In what year did Columbus discover America?
_____ 2. How much annual interest is payable on a 6 percent loan of $10,000?
_____ 3. Compute the cost of burning a 100-watt light for five hours, assuming electricity sells for $.08 a kilowatt hour.
         4–6. Name the capital city of each of the following states.
_____ 4. Oregon
_____ 5. Illinois
_____ 6. Maine
       7–10. List the four largest cities in the United States in the order of their 1960 census population.
_____ 7.
_____ 8.
_____ 9.
_____10.
_____11. Define "adjective."

Construction of short-answer items will be improved by following the suggestions below.

USING SPECIFIC STATEMENTS   Avoid statements that will elicit a wide variety of responses.

Poor:	What do you know about the United Nations?
Improved:	What is the principal purpose of the United Nations?
Poor:	Name the four most beautiful cities in the world.
Improved:	List the four most populous cities in the world.

USING PROBLEM SITUATIONS   Avoid overemphasis on mere recall of factual information. Measure the application of learning.

Poor:	Define kilowatt.
Improved:	How long will a 200-watt lamp burn in consuming one kilowatt of electricity?

AVOIDING ALTERNATE-RESPONSE STATEMENTS   Construct questions so that the guessing factor remains at a minimum.

Poor:	How does the area of Brazil compare with the area of the United States?
Improved:	What South American country, if any, contains an area greater than the United States?

LIMITING ITEMS TO FIVE OR SIX LISTINGS   Do not use items that encourage students to learn long lists of miscellaneous information.

Poor: List the ten largest cities in the world.

Improved: Name the three largest cities of the world in the order of their size.

SPECIFYING ACCURACY IN NUMERICAL RESPONSES

Poor: What is the value of pi?

Improved: What is the value of pi to the nearest one hundredth?

AVOIDING UNNECESSARY COMPLEXITIES   Do not introduce unnecessarily complex computation when knowledge of a principle is the main objective to be measured.

Poor: Find the area of a trapezoid having bases of 4.06 inches and $11\frac{5}{12}$ inches and an altitude of 11.9 centimeters.

Improved: Find the area of a trapezoid having 4-inch and 6-inch bases and an altitude of 8 inches.

Answer: _____ square inches

Essay Items

Essay items are questions or statements which require the student to organize a comparatively long answer in his own words. These items differ from the short-answer type in that they permit the student to express himself freely. His response is not limited to a numerical answer nor to a few words recalled from his learning.

Essay items can be used advantageously to measure ability to organize and express ideas, to discuss issues, to evaluate trends, to interpret meanings, to explain relationships, to criticize constructively, to summarize effectively, to describe application of principles, and the like. This type can be used in all subject matter areas but seems to have greatest applicability in the social studies, in studies of literature, and in some aspects of the sciences. In mathematics, physical education, industrial arts, and in other subjects which emphasize the achievement of specific skills, essay items are somewhat less useful.

A further advantage of considerable importance is the tendency of this type of item to encourage students to study better and to remember their learning longer. When studying for essay items rather than for ordinary recognition or short-answer types, students frequently devote more time to noting relationships and organizing information into larger units.

Essay items are not without their serious limitations, however. Unless they are extremely well constructed and keyed, their scoring is so subjective as to destroy their practical usefulness as diagnostic instruments. Furthermore, they ordinarily take so much time to answer and so much time to score that they seldom can be used efficiently as instructional devices.

One study (11:43–47) is typical of the many which establish an irrefutable fact: essay tests—whether scored by the same teacher, different teachers, or by specially trained experts—yield almost *unbelievably inconsistent* results. This study involved 130 teachers who scored each of five essay papers. A common model response rated at 25 points was provided each teacher. The findings revealed that every paper was given as few as 5 points by at least one teacher and as many as 18 points by other teachers. The minimum range of scores on any paper was nineteen out of twenty-six possible ratings. Furthermore, every paper was ranked poorest among the five by some teachers, and every paper was also ranked best among the five by others. If a percentage scale of 90 percent = A, 80 percent = B, 70 percent = C, 60 percent = D, and less than 60 percent = F had been used, every paper would have received C grades, D grades, and F grades, and three of the five papers would have received all grades A through F. The researchers concluded that their results illustrated ". . . the situation that commonly prevails in evaluating essay responses."[1]

Nevertheless, some respected scholars, expert in fields other than measurement, have become so enamored with the virtues of essay tests that they completely ignore their faults. A few of this group maintain that essay tests should be the only test form used in educational measurement. Such a conclusion is unsupported by scientific evidence. In fact, if a teacher were to adopt such a practice:

1. He would be restricting his measurement procedures to a technique that has changed little in over 100 years of use in American schools.
2. He would be rejecting the scientific developments in objective testing of the last fifty years.
3. He would be ignoring the research facts that reveal the extreme unreliability of essay testing.
4. He would be ignoring the advice of measurement experts that has been accepted by business, industry, government, and the military.
5. He might merely be unwilling to put forth the considerable effort that would be expended in learning how to build and interpret objective tests of high quality.

The proper conclusion is not to abandon the use of all essay testing as some measurement authorities have advocated, but merely to abandon

[1] Robert L. Thorndike and Elizabeth Hagen, *Measurement and Evaluation in Psychology and Education*, 2d ed. New York: John Wiley & Sons, Inc., 1961, p. 47.

the use of the poorly constructed and scored variety. When essay items are well constructed and properly keyed, they can be scored with some objectivity. However, when they are employed in the usual manner, they substitute two guessing factors for the one that is common to recognition types in that students must guess at the meaning of the questions and teachers must guess at their scoring.

Construction of essay items can be improved by following the suggestions below.

USING APPROPRIATE QUESTIONS   Questions beginning with "why," "how," "criticize," "contrast," "evaluate," and similar words, are more appropriate to essay items than those beginning with such terms as "where," "who," "when," "what," "list," and "enumerate" which can be used in other types of testing.

Poor: Discuss basketball with respect to (1) who originated the game, (2) when and where it was originated, (3) what size court and ball are official, (4) the names of the positions, (5) what team won the national AAU championship last year, (6) what defensive style was most popular in that tournament.

Improved: In 100 to 200 words, contrast the zone and man-to-man defenses in basketball. Explain how they differ with respect to (1) basic techniques involved and (2) their appropriate use in typical game situations.

AVOIDING VAGUE GENERAL QUESTIONS   Provide sufficient directions to limit the length and suggest the specific content of the response desired.

Poor: Discuss basketball.
Improved: (See example above.)

ADEQUATE SAMPLING   To evaluate achievement more fully, use several questions requiring answers of approximately 50 to 100 words rather than fewer questions requiring longer responses.

Poor: In 600 to 1000 words trace the westward movement in American history.

Suggested improvement: Six or eight questions, each requiring a 50- to 100-word discussion of a clearly defined aspect of the movement.

OPTIONAL CHOICE OF ITEMS   It is poor practice to ask the student to select his own test by responding to such directions as "answer three of the following four questions" or "answer four of the following seven questions." Test-construction experts agree that permission of optional choices destroys the possibility of making comparative evaluations of student achievement on the basis of the test results. When choice of content is permitted, the students take different tests.

It should be pointed out that it may be advisable for a teacher to ignore this recommendation of the experts if he is teaching in a school in which the provision of optional items is customary. Students almost without exception look upon the optional-choice arrangement as a privilege which safeguards the fairness of the test.

POINT VALUE   Provide specific information concerning the value of each item if different weights are to be assigned to the various items. It appears to be advisable to give the same point value to all essay items unless they vary greatly in length or difficulty. Research is inconclusive but seems to indicate that little or nothing is to be gained by assigning varying weights to items. However, if more than a single weight is used, the weight assigned to each item should be clearly indicated.

TIMING   Include suggestions for the amount of testing time to be given to each item. This practice is particularly helpful to students when time limits for the total test are rigid.

Examples:

1. (5 points—ten minutes) In approximately 50 words compare the
   . . . .
2. (10 points—fifteen minutes) In 100 to 150 words, discuss the
   . . . .

SCORING   Build a complete key to be used in scoring the items. Development of an accurate and usable key will make more efficient scoring of essay items possible. Further suggestions for scoring are discussed later in this chapter.

Situation Items

The items discussed up to this point—alternate response, multiple choice, matching, completion, short answer, and essay—constitute the basic types of test items in common use today. However, innumerable modifications and combinations of these forms are constantly being developed by the builders of educational tests. At least one of these forms, variously referred to as situation, problem solving, and interpretive testing, merits special mention.

In this kind of test, exercise material (in such form as a written description, a chart, a table, or a photograph) is presented, followed by a series of related items in ordinary form. Comprehension and analysis of the presented material, as well as recall of learning, are required to respond successfully to the questions.

This type of item can be used to advantage in the measurement of ability to interpret data, to think critically, to reason logically, and to apply principles to a new situation. Difficulty in finding suitable materials and an increase in the length of time required to take the test are its chief limitations. To construct this type and other modified types, follow the suggestions discussed under the basic item types involved. Two sample situation-type item sets follow.

Sample A: Situation-type item set

Directions for items 31–35: From the table at the right, choose the pupil who *best* answers the following descriptions. Any lettered choice may be used once, several times, or not at all.

Descriptions

_____ 31. Most mature intellectually.

_____ 32. Most mature educationally.

_____ 33. Brightest for his age.

_____ 34. Most *accelerated* educationally, from the standpoint of *chronological* age.

_____ 35. Most *retarded* educationally, from the standpoint of *mental* age.

Choices for items 31 through 35

Pupil	C.A.	M.A.	E.A.
A	12-10	13-8	13-9
B	11-7	13-6	13-0
C	12-11	12-6	13-8
D	12-8	13-10	13-8
E	11-10	12-6	13-7

Sample B: Situation-type item set

Directions: Study the following description of an experiment and then answer the questions as directed below.

The Situation

A teacher of science in the ninth grade of a four-year high school firmly believed that teachers of the lower grades were shamefully mishandling that subject. While at college one summer he determined to prove his point. He collected the following data on his 150 science pupils of the previous year.

1. The number of his pupils who had received previous science instruction, (60). Group A.

2. The number of his pupils who had not received previous science in-struction, (60). Group B.
3. The number of his pupils for whom no data of this kind were available, (30).
4. The final science test scores for all 150 pupils.

His Procedure

With the use of a system of random numbers he assigned 15 of the "no record" pupils to the "previous science" group (A) and the remaining 15 to the other group (B). He computed the average final test scores for each group, the probable error of the difference of these averages, and a set of correlations.

His Findings

1. Group A (with previous science) averaged 77 on the final of 120 points.
2. Group B (no previous science) averaged 80 on the final of 120 points.
3. The probable error of the difference in these averages was one point.
4. The correlation between amount of previous science and science achievement in grade nine was minus .01.

Mark items 1–6 either S, U, or C according to whether the statement is (S) substantiated, (U) unsubstantiated, or (C) contrary, respectively, to the findings of the study.

His Conclusions

_____ 1. Ninth-grade pupils do better in science if they have had no previous science.

_____ 2. Teachers of the lower grades do more harm than good in their attempts to teach science.

_____ 3. The differences noted were significant at the 1 percent level.

_____ 4. Teachers of the lower grades should learn to teach science well or leave it alone.

_____ 5. Instruction in science in the lower grades in his school district reduced the science marks of his average ninth-grade pupils of the last year by 1 percent.

_____ 6. The problem should be given further study.

7. (14 points) Criticize this study from the viewpoint of scientific investigation. Point out specific changes that you would make if you were conducting this study (200–300 words).

ORGANIZING THE TEST

After the items have been constructed, the next step is to organize them into a test that can be administered and scored efficiently. Tests should be attractively and logically arranged. They should be easy to read and easy to score. Too many potentially excellent groups of items have been reduced to mediocrity as a result of haphazard organization. The effectiveness of tests can be enhanced by careful attention to the following principles and suggestions.

Headings

Provide blanks at the top of the first page for the student's name, the class period, the date, and the final score. Also place the test title and the number of each copy at the top of page one.

Example one

Social Studies
Test One, Copy No. 12

Name _____   Date _____
Score _____   Period _____

Answer blanks

Establish definite positions for the answers. Do not scatter these positions about the page. Throughout the test use a column of numbered blanks or symbols on either the left or right margin of the paper. Some teachers prefer the right-hand margin because it is somewhat more convenient for right-handed examinees and test scorers (see example two). However, the answer column placed at the left-hand margin (see example three) is more easily associated with the proper item without extra numbering. In addition, many students, when writing, rest their left hand across the top left-hand portion of the test paper. Thus they effectively, though inadvertently, shield the filled-in answers from students who might be tempted to copy. For tests which exceed one or two pages in length, it may be advisable to prepare separate answer sheets.

Example two

(Use of right-hand margin for various types of answers.)
1. In what year did Columbus discover America?   1. _____
2. Columbus discovered America in 1429.   2.   T   F
3. Columbus discovered America in
   A. 1493
   B. 1494
   C. 1592
   D. 1595
   E. None of these   3. (   )

Example three

(Use of column on left for various types of answers.)

_____ 1. In what year did Columbus discover America?

   T   F   2. Columbus discovered America in 1429.

(   ) 3. Columbus discovered America in

           A. 1493

           B. 1494

           C. 1592

           D. 1595

           E. None of these

Readability

Space items and their parts so as to achieve maximum readability. For example, in matching exercises place the column of item stems on the left side of the paper and the column of choices at the right (see example four, a sample matching exercise).

Example four

Directions for matching items 36–40: Select the day of the week upon which each listed holiday occurs. Place each selected letter in the proper blank at the left. Any lettered choice may be used once, more than once, or not at all. (The first item illustrates correct procedure.)

	Holidays	*Choices for Items 36–40*
____B____	(X) Labor Day	A. Sunday
_____	36. Easter	B. Monday
_____	37. Independence Day	C. Tuesday
_____	38. Thanksgiving	D. Wednesday
_____	39. Christmas	E. Thursday
_____	40. National Election Day	F. Friday
		G. Saturday
		H. Varies from year to year

In multiple-choice items, place the choices in a column beneath the stem. This suggestion may be ignored when the choices are so short that they can all be placed effectively in a single line (see example five, a multiple-choice sample).

Example five

Directions for multiple-choice items 21–35: In the blank at the left of each numbered item write the letter of the answer you have selected for that item.

_____ 21. What color results when equal portions of yellow and blue pigments are mixed?

    A. Black

    B. Green

    C. Purple

    D. Yellow orange

    E. None of these

_____ 22. The sum of 6 plus 3 is

    (A) ½   (B) 2   (C) 3   (D) 9   (E) 18

In completion exercises, the omissions should be numbered in parentheses. Correspondingly numbered blanks for the answers should be placed on the same line in the column at the left (see example six, a sample completion item).

Example six

Directions for completion items 41–46: Each of the numbered spaces in the following paragraph indicates the omission of a word. Complete the meaning of each statement by writing the correct word in the correspondingly numbered blank at the left. The first item is answered as an example.

_____9_____ (X) There are (X) playing positions on a baseball team.

_____ 41. The defensive player positioned about midway between second and third base is the (41). He frequently must

_____ 42. pivot at second base in order to complete (42). If

_____ 43. he is the "clean-up" hitter, he bats in (43) position.

_____ 44. When he hits a home run with the bases full, four (44)

_____ 45. are scored. However, if the (45) calls a third strike

_____ 46. on him, he is (46).

Avoid placing part of the item on one page and the remainder of the item on another. If the bottom of the page is reached with part of an item left over, place the entire item on the next page, or rearrange the items so that they fit the page. An exception must be made for items which are more than a full page in length. For such items place the parts on pages which face each other. Illustrated material should be placed just ahead of the items for which it is intended.

Directions

State directions briefly and clearly. Use vocabulary at the level of the students. Include only information that is essential to their understanding of the general conditions of the test and of how to proceed.

Place general information at the beginning of the test clearly stating the purpose of the test, its time limits, the point value of the items, and whether or not a correction formula is to be used in scoring the test (see example seven).

Example seven

Test information: This is a test which will inform you of how well you are achieving the goals of this unit. The results will *not* be used in marking. Each item will count 1 point. Your score will be found by subtracting one third of the number of your errors from the number of items you answer correctly. Omit those items for which you have little or no knowledge of the answer. *Do not guess wildly.* You will be allowed twenty to thirty minutes to complete the test.

Immediately precede each different group of items with specific direc' tions for that group.

Example eight

(Sample true-false items.)
Directions for true-false items 11–21:
For items that are true, cross out the letter T. For items that are false, cross out the letter F.
(The first two items are marked to illustrate the proper procedure.)

T̸   F   (1) The sum of 2 plus 2 is 4.
T   F̸   (2) The sum of 2 plus 2 is 5.
T   F   11. Thomas Edison invented the sewing machine.
T   F   12. The steamboat was invented by John Claremont.

At the end of the test, place directions for those who finish the test early. These directions should indicate what the student should do after he has completed the test (see example nine).

Example nine

When you have completed this test and have checked your answers, place the test face down on your desk. Do *not* bring it to the teacher's desk. After your test has been picked up, proceed *very quietly* with your assigned studies. Remain in your seat until your teacher has indicated that the testing period is over. Your complete cooperation will be appreciated by everyone.

Use simplified directions when students understand them. After students have become accustomed to a particular testing procedure, directions can be reduced in length and illustrative items eliminated. In particular, teachers who make frequent use of instructional tests find that they can keep their students alert to the requirements of the items employed. It is much better to introduce new item types in practice situations than to take up valuable testing time to give instruction. The following example of simplified directions also indicates appropriate wording when the test is to be scored with a stencil key.

Example ten

General information:

   Purpose: Marking. Approximately 5 percent of semester's mark.

   Scoring: 1 point per item. No correction for guessing.

   Time: Approximately forty to fifty minutes.

Specific directions:

   True-false items 1–30: Cross out T for true, F for false.

   Multiple-choice items 31–65: In the column at the left, cross out the letter representing the best choice.

Ending directions:

   Remember to work quietly on assigned studies after you have completed this test.

Arrangement of Items

Arrange the sequence of items so as to encourage the student and not confuse him. Insofar as possible:

Place items of the same type together in the test. To change frequently from one type of item to another is disconcerting to the student.

Place the easier items at the beginning of the test and the more difficult and time-consuming items near the end.

Items on related objectives or on related content should be kept together in the test.

Elimination of Clues

Avoid patterns of responses which might provide clues to the answers or might easily be transmitted from one class section to another.

   The lettered choices should be used as the correct responses in a random order. Avoid systematic patterns of responses. Students soon become alert to clues of this type.

   No particular choice should be the correct answer noticeably more frequently nor less frequently than any other choice. Keep count of the number of times each selection is used as the answer on the entire test. Revise the items if there is an unreasonable lack of balance in this respect. Many teachers unconsciously favor one letter over others.

Check the entire test to see that clues of all types are eliminated. In particular, make sure that:

Words like "no," "none," "sometimes," and "generally" are used about equally in true and in false items.

The longer choices in multiple choice items are correct responses no more frequently than the shorter choices.

No item contains information that could be used directly to answer a different item.

Duplication of Copies

Tests should be duplicated so that each student has a copy. It is very poor economy to write tests on the board, and even less advisable to read them aloud to the class. Reproduction of the test for class use should be as expert a job as is possible. Only one side of the paper should be used unless it is so heavy that disconcerting shadows do not show through. For clear copies the type must be clean and the duplicating machine operating properly. More than a few tests are reduced in effectiveness through careless attention to details at this stage. If the teacher does this work himself, as is frequently the case, he must be sure to get adequate instructions in the proper use of the machine. If clerks do this work, it should be remembered that they will do a much better job when given adequate time to work carefully.

Proofreading

The master copy should be proofread carefully before it is run off. Any necessary corrections can be made most easily at that time. After the test is duplicated, it is too late to make corrections effectively. Proofreading should be done early. If it is delayed until students are taking the test, it may be found too late that typographical errors have played real tricks with some items.

For example, the following incident actually occurred recently.

A psychology professor, during the administration of a test, became aware of a ripple of ill-concealed amusement among his students. His reaction may well be imagined when he belatedly read his test and discovered that the letter "g" had been dropped from the word "sing" in the following item, with which he had intended to measure knowledge of the effects of heredity upon musical talent:

True-False. "A girl is more likely to be able to sin expertly if her mother is gifted with the same talent."

From that day on, at least one psychology professor has taken special care to proofread his tests.

IMPROVING TEST ITEMS

Clues leading to test items which need improvement can be found by (1) noting items which are difficult for students to understand, (2) examining the responses of students to find choices that have not been selected, and (3) analyzing the difficulty and discrimination of all items.

Observation

While administering a test, teachers can gain many clues to needed improvements by noting the items which are misinterpreted by students. If the questions of students repeatedly concern the same items, those items should be studied for needed revisions. It is good practice to tabulate (on a copy of the test) the number and character of questions which arise during test administration. These notations will be useful when items are revised.

In multiple-choice or matching exercises all choices should appear plausible to at least a few members of the class. If close check of the test reveals that some responses have been selected by no one, those responses should be revised.

Item Analysis

Item analysis is an extremely fruitful technique for test builders to use. More than thirty methods of item analysis have been developed. A method which is effective, yet easy to apply, involves the following steps:

1. Score the tests, then select the highest-scoring quarter and the lowest-scoring quarter of the papers. That is, if 160 students took a test, put the highest-scoring forty papers in one pile and the lowest-scoring forty papers in another.

2. Tabulate the number of errors made on each item by each group. Item 1 may have been missed by eight of the high-scoring students and by thirty of the low scorers.

3. Compute the discrimination index of each item by subtracting the percentage of error of the top group from the percentage of error recorded for the bottom group. For item 1 above, the computation would be: $8 \div 40 = .20$; $30 \div 40 = .75$; $.75-.20 = .55$. The discrimination index of item 1 is .55.

4. Compute the difficulty index of each item by finding the average percentage of error scored by the top and bottom groups. For item 1 above, the computation would be: $(.75 + .20) \div 2 = .475$. The difficulty index of item 1 is .475.

The indices of discrimination and difficulty are important indicators of the quality of items used in tests designed to measure *differences in achievement* among students. (In diagnostic and instructional instruments the indices are of little consequence as measures of item quality.)

For the purpose of measuring differences among students, the theoretically optimum difficulty index is .50. In practice almost the full range of indices from zero to 1.00 is usable, although the greater the deviation from .50, the less effective the item becomes. At the extremes of zero and 1.00 the item adds nothing to the measurement desired. This fact is more easy to understand when it is realized that on a test made up of items each having zero difficulty, every student would have a perfect paper. On the other hand, if a test were composed of items of 1.00 difficulty, all students would miss all the items. In either event, no differences in achievement are measured.

This index of discrimination indicates the degree to which an item is more difficult for the low-scoring group on the whole test than it is for the high-scoring group. If the low group as a whole makes fewer errors on an item than are made by the high group, the index of discrimination is negative. Such items should be revised or replaced before the item is used again. A discrimination index of zero indicates that the item fails to measure differences between the high scorers and the low scorers. These items should also be revised or replaced. The best items have discrimination indices of .60 or higher. In general, a discrimination index of at least .20 is required for effective measurement.

Table 16-4. Analysis of Four Items

ITEM NO.	TABULATION OF ERRORS				ESTIMATED DISCRIMI-NATION A — B	ESTIMATED DIFFI-CULTY (A + B)/2	EVALU-ATION
	40 LOWEST PAPERS (25%)	ERROR (A)	40 HIGHEST PAPERS (25%)	ERROR (B)			
1	卌 卌 卌 卌 卌 卌	.75	卌 ///	.20	.55	.475	Good
2	卌 卌 卌 卌	.50	卌 卌 卌 卌	.50	0	.50	Revise
3	卌 卌	.25	卌 卌 卌	.375	− .125	.31	Replace
4	卌 卌 卌 ///	.45	卌 卌 ////	.35	.10	.40	Revise

Item Judgment Criteria

Although item analysis offers dramatic objective information concerning test items, it cannot, by itself, prove that an item is of high quality. The technique is extremely useful for directing attention to weak items, but should not be taken as the sole criterion of item value. For instance, consider such items as "What is the color of the book assigned yesterday?" and "How many steps are in the stairway leading to the library reading room?" These items might be perfect when judged on the single basis of discrimination and difficulty indices, but completely unacceptable when the criterion of "measurement of valid course objectives" is applied.

Before an item can be accepted for use unconditionally, it must receive affirmative ratings on *all* of the following points:

1. Does the item measure a valid objective of the course?
2. Is the item easy to understand? Is it fair?
3. Is the item's index of discrimination satisfactory (at least .20)?
4. Is the item's index of difficulty satisfactory (between .10 and .90)?
5. Does the item fit the test plan?

ADMINISTERING TESTS

After you have constructed the test items and organized them into a test, you must prepare yourself to administer the test effectively. Test administration is not just sitting at your desk while the students work. In fact a good test administrator is too busy to sit down. The job should not be taken lightly. Unless the test is administered intelligently, all the work of construction will be ineffective. It is up to you to learn to do the job right.

Responsibilities of a Test Administrator

It is the responsibility of the test administrator to do the following:

1. Become thoroughly familiar with the test and its directions. See that the test is ready to be administered.
2. Establish favorable physical and psychological conditions for testing.
3. See that the students have all the necessary materials and understand what to do with them.
4. Maintain proper testing conditions throughout the test period.
5. Collect the test materials and check them for completeness.

Suggestions for Test Administrators

1. Become thoroughly familiar with the test and its directions. See that the test is ready to be administered.

a. Count the tests and number the copies as soon as they have been duplicated. Be sure that you have at least two or three extra copies. One of these extra copies should be used for a key and the others held as reserves to be used if for any reason copies become unusable. Numbering the copies enables you to keep better track of the test and also serves as a code number by which test scores can be reported confidentially.

b. Prepare the key *before* you administer the test. The best way to prepare the key is to take the test yourself. Read each item carefully, then check your key with your answers on the original draft of the test. Correct any discrepancies. In that manner you will become thoroughly familiar with the test and be able to do a better job of administering it.

c. At the time you prepare the key, make written notes of any suggestions or clarifications that should be announced at the time the test is administered. Also make written notes concerning any items which appear potentially difficult for students to understand. With this information you will be better able to answer the most likely questions of students.

d. Put the tests and keys in a safe place, and remember where you put them. Do not leave test materials or keys on your desk, in unlocked drawers or cabinets, or in open shelves about the room. Place them in a securely locked file or storage cabinet. Some teachers prefer to store these materials at home.

2. Establish favorable physical and psychological conditions for testing.

a. Make certain that conditions of light, heat, ventilation, and seating are adequate throughout the entire room. No student should be required to sit at a desk or table which for him is too large or too small. Left-handed students should not be seated at desk-arm chairs designed for right-handed individuals. It is difficult for students to do their best when they are suffering physical discomfort.

b. Determine the best seating arrangement for the test. If the test is to be used for marking purposes, students should be seated far enough apart to provide adequate working space and to discourage copying. Few high school classrooms have enough unoccupied seats to permit an alternate seat arrangement. However, many modern classrooms are furnished with movable desk-arm chairs which easily can be arranged to gain full use of the entire area of the room. It is advisable to have the necessary seating arrangements completed before the arrival of the class which is to be tested.

c. Eliminate distracting noises. For example, window shades that flap persistently in a draft should be adjusted, and desks that creak should be tightened up, oiled, or left vacant. Clanking heating system radiators and noisy ventilator fans are other common distracters which should be reported for repair to the maintenance staff.

d. Discourage visitation in your classroom during testing periods. Testing periods are not suitable for teacher-parent, teacher-teacher, or other conferences. In some instances, it may be necessary to post a sign on the door: "Testing—no visitors, please."

e. Establish testing readiness in your students. Discuss plans for the test with your class a day or two ahead of its scheduled administration. The purposes of the test should be fully explained, the objectives and content to be measured should be outlined, and practice with unfamiliar item types should be provided. This pretest discussion and practice should encourage and direct review on the part of the student, and at the same time reinforce his confidence. Much fear of tests is based on fear of the unknown.

f. Encourage a positive attitude toward tests. A positive attitude can be developed or destroyed in students, depending upon the approach adopted by the teacher. The tone of pretest discussions and practice should not be one of urgency. Neither overlook nor deplore deficiencies. Be businesslike, but pleasant. Tests should be discussed as opportunities to learn more about oneself. Following tests with constructive conferences and using tests principally as diagnostic and instructional devices will go a long way toward establishing a favorable student attitude.

g. Establish control of the class from the beginning of the test period. Do not permit unnecessary communication. Last minute trips to the water fountain or the pencil sharpener should be discouraged. Be pleasant but firm. Insist upon prompt compliance with directions.

3. See that the students receive all of the necessary test materials and know what to do with them.

a. Establish an efficient procedure for distributing test materials. Supplementary materials, such as answer sheets, scratch paper, and pencils, should be passed out before the tests are distributed.

b. Read the directions aloud to the class. Speak clearly and slowly. Be sure that the test purpose, the time limits, and the method of scoring are understood. Be brief; be businesslike but not severe. You should try to reduce tensions in students, not build them up.

c. If any corrections in the test are necessary, announce them before the test is begun. Put the essential corrections on the board so that students can double check their changes.

d. Announce that after the test has begun no one is to speak or to leave his seat without permission. Questions on procedure will be answered at the student's desk. Direct the students to raise their hands quietly when they need assistance.

e. Do not permit students to start the test before you have given the starting order. Unless you insist on compliance with this requirement, you will find that some students will fail to follow directions merely because they were reading test items when they should have been listening to directions or studying them.

f. Permit students to ask questions about the test directions after the oral directions have been completed. Keep any necessary question period to a minimum. Most students will be anxious to start the test.

4. Maintain proper conditions for testing throughout the testing period.

a. Move about the room while the test is under way. Check carefully to see that directions are being followed. A complete circuit of the class should be made for that purpose at the beginning of the test and periodically thereafter. Quietly observe the work of each student, but do not watch any one person so long or intently that he becomes aware of the observation. Under no circumstances should the test administrator remain seated at his desk.

b. While the test is under way, you should answer only the legitimate questions of students who have indicated their need with a raised hand. Do not permit students to direct questions to you from across the room. Nor should students bring questions to you. It is much less distracting to other students if you give assistance only at the desk of the individual who asks for help. Speak very quietly so as not to disturb the rest of the class. Answer questions concerning interpretation of directions or clarification of typographical errors only. If a student understands the directions but still has difficulty in understanding an item on the test, do not define words in the item or give similar helps. Tell the student to work on the other items and return to the most difficult items last. Give no information that indicates the answer to any problem in the test. Furthermore, avoid smiling or frowning in response to answers you read. Some students can derive clues from the facial expressions of the teacher as he observes their work.

c. Be alert to detect any copying which may be taking place. Always be in a position to observe the entire class. In particular, avoid becoming so intent upon helping one student that you ignore the needs or the transgressions of others. If you observe questionable behavior, do not create a disturbance. Most situations can be corrected with a mere glance or by standing near the possible offenders long enough to let them know you are aware of what is being attempted. If your suspicions are confirmed, do not hesitate to act quickly and firmly. Do not seize the test papers and dramatically tear them to bits as one new teacher was observed to do. Merely quietly tell the offender to report after class, at which time the problem should be discussed rationally and without rancor.

Your chief responsibility in moving about the room during the test period is to help answer necessary questions and to help students who are observed to be misinterpreting the test directions. The prevention of cheating is a secondary responsibility of the test administrator. When tests are properly motivated, evaluated, and administered, cheating seldom occurs.

    d. Maintain a quiet working atmosphere throughout the test period. Do not permit students to move about the room while testing is still in progress. Carry several sharpened pencils which can be traded with students who otherwise would wish to use the pencil sharpener.

    e. Urge students to work at their maximum accurate speed. Some students attempt to work too fast while others spend too much time trying to answer every item in sequence. You should become acquainted with students who make these errors and quietly guide them to the most profitable use of their time.

5. Collect the test materials and check them for completeness.

    a. In the case of untimed tests, pick up the completed test and any supplementary test materials as soon as the student indicates that he has finished. If tests are collected by the teacher, much confusion is avoided. Do not permit the students to deliver the tests individually to the teacher's desk.

    b. In case the entire class finishes a test together (frequently so on short-timed tests), the tests and test materials can be returned efficiently through use of student monitors.

    c. Be certain that students who complete the test early immediately begin to work quietly on assignments.

    d. When tests are completed early, it is well for students to check them carefully for unintentionally omitted items.

    e. Count all returned materials and check your records to see that everything is turned in. Arrange the returned tests so that they are ready for scoring.

SCORING TESTS

The question of who should score tests is largely academic. Usually the teacher does the scoring with little or no help from clerks or students. Nevertheless, there is some evidence to indicate that learning could be enhanced by greater use of students in the scoring process. Administrators may eventually provide clerical service for the clerical parts of the job.

Students can be used to advantage in the scoring of instructional tests made up of objectively scored items. Practically all scoring of essay items and most scoring of recall items require subjective judgment which can be supplied by the teacher alone.

It is to be recommended that students score instructional tests employing items of the alternate-response, multiple-choice, and matching types. Students might also score carefully constructed completion and short-answer items. Exchange of papers has been found to increase the accuracy of scoring. Rechecking by the writers of each paper is recommended. Much learning takes place in the process of scoring.

Teachers should score all essay items and all tests to be used for purposes of diagnosis or marking. Well-trained clerks, if available, could adequately score all tests other than those composed of essay items.

Assigning Weights to Items

Strict application of logic would indicate that items be assigned different weights according to their importance or their difficulty. Results of research, however, reveal that little is to be gained by that procedure.[2] Students have been found to retain very nearly the same rank in class regardless of whether unweighted or weighted scores were used. The increase in the difficulty of scoring occasioned by the use of differential weights does not seem to result in a correspondingly more accurate score. Consequently, it is recommended that the same number of points be assigned to each item.

Use of Correction Formulas

Test items of the alternate-response, multiple-choice, and matching types tend to encourage students to guess. Successful guesses increase the number of correctly answered items and, thereby, hide the true achievement of the student. Therefore, many teachers use a correction formula to get an approximation of the score that each student would have earned had he not guessed. In the formula used $S = R - W/(C\text{-}1)$, S is the corrected score, R is the number of items answered correctly, W is the number of errors made, and C is the number of choices provided in each item. The expectation is that, on the average, guesses on alternate-response items will be correct one half of the time, guesses on three-choice items will be correct one third of the time, and so forth. For example, if a student knew the answers to eight items of a 10-point alternate-response test, and

[2] Robert L. Abel and Dora E. Damrin, "Tests and Examinations," *Encyclopedia of Educational Research,* 3d ed. New York: The Macmillan Company, 1960, p. 1512.

guessed at the answers to the other two items, he would get one of them correct. By the formula, he would get a score of 8, the number of answers he actually knew ($8 = 9 - 1/2\text{-}1$). The correction formula is based on the assumption that the laws of chance apply. In practice, this assumption is satisfied part of the time only. For instance, when the student is able to eliminate one or more responses of a multiple-response item, application of the formula will undercorrect. On the other hand, the formula overcorrects when students read the entire item and are drawn by purposely plausible distracters.

The authors of this text do not recommend use of the correction formula to adjust scores of individual students because: (1) The formula is based on a statistical concept, not a purely mathematical one. It can be used correctly to adjust class measures, but for individuals it will overcorrect part of the time and undercorrect at other times. (2) The resulting adjustments in score usually lead to only small changes in the ranking of individuals. These changes are hardly worth the additional scoring effort, particularly when the number of choices in the items is three or more. (3) Pupils disfavor use of the formula. It is difficult for them to understand the loss of points already earned by answering items correctly.

Use of the correction formula has the advantage of discouraging wild guessing on the part of the student. When the formula is used, students tend to give more careful consideration to their responses. Some teachers use the correction formula solely for the purpose of encouraging students to work more carefully.

In case you should want to obtain corrected scores for a test composed of alternate-response items, a recommended procedure is to award 2 points for each correct item, 1 point for each omitted item, and no points for errors. The adjustment accomplished parallels that obtained through use of the formula $S = R - W/(C\text{-}1)$. This adjustment in score is usually considered fairer by all students including those who object to the regular correction formula.

Scoring Keys

The scoring of tests, frequently a tedious task, can be greatly simplified through use of adequate keys. The four types most frequently used to score all items except essay items are the (1) keyed test, (2) strip key, (3) accordion key, and (4) stencil key. The most common form of key is built by writing the answers in the proper blanks on a copy of the test. A strip key is made by cutting the columns of answers from a keyed test or by carefully spacing the answers for each page of items on a separate cardboard strip. An accordion key results when the answer strips are all placed on one sheet of heavy paper which is then folded to the width of a single column of answers in the manner of an accordion. Each of these three types of keys is used in the same manner. The proper column of correct answers is placed alongside the corresponding column of responses, one test page at a time. The stencil type of key is most effective when an answer sheet has been used. A stencil can be made easily by marking the correct answers on an answer sheet and then punching holes in the key corresponding to each correct answer. When the stencil is superimposed on an answer sheet, the correct responses are visible through the punched holes. An entire test can be scored quickly by merely counting the number of marks which show through the holes.

Essay items are much more difficult to score. Keys for essay items should indicate the main points to be discussed in each response. Credit should be allowed for the substitution of equivalent points. If ability to organize and to express ideas is an objective of your course, point credit should be given for organization and expression.

Scoring of essay items has been found to be most efficient when the entire set of test papers is scored on one item before a second item is scored on any paper. In this manner the scorer can become thoroughly familiar with application of the key. Furthermore, this procedure materially reduces the likelihood that the score on one item will affect the objectivity of scoring a following item. Finally, it is recommended that answers be placed on one side of the test paper and the student's name be placed on the reverse side. Objectivity of scoring can be improved by keeping the scorer unaware of the name of the person who wrote the paper being scored.

Selected References

1. Adams, Georgia Sachs, Theodore L. Torgerson, and Ernest R. Wood, *Measurement and Evaluation for the Secondary School Teacher*. New York: Holt, Rinehart and Winston, Inc., 1956. Chapters 11–23.
2. Ahmann, J. Stanley, and Marvin D. Glock, *Evaluating Pupil Growth*. Boston: Allyn and Bacon, Inc., a subsidiary of Prentice-Hall, Inc., 1959. Chapters 7–10.
3. Bean, Kenneth L., *Construction of Educational and Personnel Tests*. New York: McGraw-Hill Book Company, Inc., 1953. Chapters 2–5.
4. Furst, Edward J., *Constructing Evaluation Instruments*. New York: David McKay Company, Inc., 1958. Chapters 7–11.
5. Garrett, Henry E., *Testing for Teachers*. New York: American Book Company, 1959. Chapters 8, 9.
6. Gerberich, J. Raymond, *Specimen Objective Test Items, A Guide to Achievement Test Construction*. New York: David McKay Company, Inc., 1956. Chapters 2–13.
7. Magnuson, Henry W., Melvin W. Gipe, and Thomas A. Shellhammer, *Evaluating Pupil Progress*, 1960 ed. Bulletin of the California State Department of Education, vol. 29, no. 14 (December 1960), chapter 2.

8. Remmers, H. H., N. L. Gage, and J. Francis Rummel, *A Practical Introduction to Measurement and Evaluation.* New York: Harper & Row, Publishers, 1960. Chapters 7, 8.
9. Schwartz, Alfred, and Stuart C. Tiedeman, *Evaluating Student Progress.* New York: David McKay Company, 1957. Chapters 5, 6.
10. Thomas, R. Murray, *Judging Student Progress,* 2d ed. New York: David McKay Company, Inc., 1960. Chapters 1–3.
11. Thorndike, Robert L., and Elizabeth Hagen, *Measurement and Evaluation in Psychology and Education,* 2d ed. New York: John Wiley & Sons, Inc., 1961. Chapters 3, 4.
12. Wood, Dorothy Adkins, *Test Construction: Development and Interpretation of Achievement Tests.* Columbus, Ohio: Charles E. Merrill Books, Inc., 1960, pp. 20–60, 81–125.

CHAPTER 17

Marking and reporting

All teachers face the important problem of how to determine and report marks. In attacking this problem, they must recognize that marking practices to a great extent are defined by the over-all marking policies of each school. The format of the report, the basic standard with which individual student achievement is compared, the achievements marked, and the general distribution of marks are all matters of policy ordinarily determined by the administration of the school. No teacher should attempt to establish his own system nor should he make adaptations without the approval of his principal. Experienced teachers will avoid the error of the beginner who proudly stated that his C grades were as good as any other teacher's B's.

The teacher's first responsibility in marking is to determine and then to follow the policies set by the school. (When revisions in policy are desired by the school and its community, participation on study committees becomes a professional opportunity.) The second responsibility of the teacher is to see that his marks reflect evaluation of student progress toward all important objectives of the course. Too many teachers base their marks exclusively on the most conveniently obtainable evidence. Better marking practices require the teacher to seek and to use a wide variety of evidence concerning the attainment of course objectives.

This chapter contains (1) a discussion of common marking practices, (2) discussion of questions and issues in marking, (3) recommendations on how to combine the achievement data into a single mark, and (4) suggestions for reporting.

Purpose of Marks

Achievement marks serve several purposes: (1) informing parents and the student of educational progress; (2) motivating better study; (3) guiding the selection of course work in both high school and in college; and

(4) providing bases for grouping, promoting, and graduating. In addition, some schools employ marks to determine honors as well as to determine eligibility for participation in extraclass activities. These purposes can be summarized as information, motivation, guidance, and administration.

To accomplish these purposes effectively, a marking system must be easy for students, counselors, and parents to understand. It must be as objective and reliable as possible. It must be economical of time and it must be acceptable to the majority of students, counselors, parents, and teachers in the area where it is employed. No single system now in use fully satisfies all criteria. However, it appears that the most suitable solution would involve both letter marks based on summation of standard scores and descriptive comments to parents based on observation and standardized test interpretation.

MARKING PRACTICES

What marking systems are likely to be encountered in a modern school? Looking to research for an answer, teachers will find that many different systems of marking and reporting achievement are currently used in American schools. Letter symbols, numbers, and descriptive statements, all are used either singly or in combination.[1] It is impractical to study all the variations, but every teacher should be acquainted with the methods from which the variety of systems is derived. With this knowledge he can better adjust to the particular practices of his school and more capably cooperate in their improvement.

The most common system of marking employs five letters: A for excellent, B for above average, C for average, D for below average but passing, and F for failure. This system is used by approximately 75 percent of all schools. A minority of schools denote more fine gradations by addition of letters or by attaching plus or minus signs to the four given passing marks. Other schools use fewer categories, such as H for honors, S for satisfactory, and U for unsatisfactory or S and U alone. The letter systems have the advantage of wide usage, but the disadvantage of grouping a wide range of achievement under a single mark. For example, a grade of C usually is earned by 35 to 50 percent of a class. Thus, many differences in achievement remain unrevealed when only two to five categories of marks are employed.

The numerical systems of marking include (1) percentages, (2) rank orders, (3) percentile ranks, and (4) standard scores. Numerical systems

[1] Ann Z. Smith and John E. Dobbin, "Marks and Marking Systems," *Encyclopedia of Educational Research,* 3d ed. New York: The Macmillan Company, 1960, pp. 783–789.

provide a greatly increased number of marking categories. In this connection it should be recognized that fine discrimination in marking can be both a weakness and a strength. For example, to mark John 75 percent and Mary 76 percent indicates that they differ in achievement, which is quite likely to be true; but these marks also indicate that Mary exceeds John by 1 percent, which may or may not be true, considering the limitations of present evaluation techniques.

Of all numerical systems, percentage marks have been in use the longest and are still the most popular. In this system the standing of each student is computed as a percentage of a theoretically perfect 100 percent performance. An arbitrary passing point is set, usually 60, 70, or 75 percent. Percentage marks differ from other numerical marks in that percentages are based on absolute achievement and not on the attainment of the class. Theoretically, all members of a class could pass or all could fail. However, in practice it is quite possible to manipulate the difficulty of tests so that "appropriate" proportions of students fall into the various categories. At one time, percentage marks were very widely used. However, they have been largely replaced by letter marks.

In the rank order system, the student having the highest achievement is 1, the next highest is ranked 2, and so on. If there were thirty-five students in a class, the lowest in achievement would have a rank of 35. Passing may be set at any point. Ranks are difficult to interpret unless the size of the class is known. A rank of 6 in a class of sixty may represent a quite different level of achievement from that represented by the same rank in a class of only seven or eight students.

Percentile rank marks indicate the percentage of the class exceeded by any given student. That is, a student who achieved better than 75 percent of his class would receive a percentile mark of 75. The basic meaning of this system is fairly easy to understand. However, the system has the disadvantage of being subject to misinterpretation when comparisons are involved. For example, a percentile rank of 40 does not necessarily represent an achievement twice that of a percentile rank of 20. An increase in percentile rank from 10 to 15 exceeds an increase from a rank of 45 to 50 but is frequently interpreted as equivalent by those who do not understand the characteristics of percentiles.

The use of standard scores in marking is a comparatively new technique. In this system the student is marked according to the number of standard deviation units between his position in class achievement and the average achievement of the class. Students at the class average are marked 0. Those below average receive negative marks and those above average get positive marks. The most common adaptation of this system, Z-scores, eliminates algebraic signs and uses 50 as the average score. Marks range from a low of about 20 to a high around 80 with a passing mark most frequently set at about 35. Standard scores overcome several of the defects of other numerical systems. For classes in which achievement is approximately normally distributed, standard scores are quite simple to interpret. Nevertheless, many parents and teachers find it difficult to orient themselves to a system that employs a statistically derived basic unit.

Looking ahead, it appears that standard scores will be used extensively to form basic distributions from which letter marks can be more accurately derived.

In recent years an increasing number of schools have been employing descriptive written reports to parents or teacher-parent conferences as a means of supplementing or replacing traditional reports. Of these practices, the most feasible at the secondary level appears to be the check list of descriptive phrases (see Table 17-10).

QUESTIONS AND ISSUES IN MARKING

In addition to determining school policy concerning the form of marks to be used, teachers must also determine (1) the school policy concerning the bases to be used for marking, and (2) the school-recommended distribution of marks. In other words, teachers must find the answers to questions such as: Should achievement, citizenship, and attendance be marked separately? How can subject matter achievement and citizenship be differentiated? How should citizenship marks be determined? Should marks be adjusted according to student ability? Should marks be based on an absolute scale, a percentage scale, or a relative scale? What proportion of a class should receive each mark? What is the school's policy toward failing marks? Are special notices to parents and conferences with counselors required when failing marks are anticipated? What systems for recording and combining marks are most feasible? The next section of this chapter will be devoted to discussion of these questions.

Marking Achievement and Citizenship Separately

During a marking period teachers are expected to acumulate data concerning the quality of each student's homework, tests, projects, reports, study habits, attention, effort, leadership, cooperation, and the like. There is little wonder that some beginning teachers, amid this maze of information, are overwhelmed with the task of marking and reporting.

While teachers, students, parents, and administrators generally accept that an achievement mark should represent a student's achievement of all objectives of a course, it should be obvious that a single mark cannot portray accurately the standing of a student on so many divergent items. Yet, a few schools attempt to adjust a single mark to assess a student's record in all these factors. Most schools, however, follow the more satisfactory practice of reporting attendance records and citizenship ratings separately from achievement marks.

It is conceded that the attainment of good habits of study, attendance, and citizenship are important school objectives, but to include them in the subject-matter mark reduces the accuracy of the information conveyed by the mark, thereby reducing its effectiveness. Therefore, it is strongly recommended that factors of attendance and citizenship be reported in marks separate from those used for achievement.

Differentiating Subject-Matter Achievement and Citizenship

Some teachers have difficulty differentiating the factors that should be considered in a citizenship mark from those factors which should be part of the mark of subject-matter achievement. Many schools offer specific instruction concerning this point. However, when such information is not provided the following guidelines should prove helpful:

When instruction to bring about a particular behavior is regularly offered as part of a course (or earlier course in a sequence of courses), the behavior is usually a factor to be considered in the achievement mark of the given course.

When, in addition to satisfying the point above, a particular behavior is uniquely sought in a given course, the behavior is always a factor to be considered in the achievement mark for that course.

When the above conditions are not met, the behavior concerned is usually a factor to be considered in the citizenship mark.

The following examples should clarify application of the guidelines:

1. A student is occasionally late in arriving at his class. This behavior belongs in the citizenship category.

2. A student fails to clean up around his desk or bench. This behavior should be reflected in the citizenship mark unless instruction in neatness is regularly and uniquely offered as part of the course.

3. A student uses equipment so as to endanger the safety of his classmates. Assuming that instruction in the safe use of equipment is offered, the behavior should affect the achievement mark. If the student willingly persists in the dangerous behavior after instruction has been offered to him specifically, his citizenship mark should also be affected.

The obvious exceptions to the above guidelines are behaviors in the fundamentals of reading, writing, arithmetic, grammar, spelling, and speech. When behaviors in these fundamentals merit attention in courses not usually offering such instruction, it is likely that neither citizenship marks nor achievement marks in the course will be affected. However, in such circumstances a report under "comments to parents" and a report to the counselor responsible for assignment of students to remedial courses might both be appropriate.

Determining and Using Citizenship Marks

If citizenship marks are to have real significance in secondary schools, teachers must give careful attention to their preparation. The student behaviors to be observed and rated must be clearly identified, the resulting ratings must be carefully recorded and synthesized into final marks, and the final marks themselves must be given meaningful recognition by the school. Examples of the last point are found in schools which provide honor awards or special school privileges for their outstanding citizens. Other schools require students to have average or better citizenship ratings as prerequisites to graduation, or as prerequisites to participation in the cocurricular activities of the school. The supporters of this kind of requirement maintain that the privilege of participation in school activities should be denied to students whose behavior is unsatisfactory.

When they determine citizenship marks, teachers customarily follow either of two procedures. In the first procedure teachers assume all students begin a marking period with a top rating in citizenship. Subsequent misbehaviors during the marking period lower the rating of the transgressors. Thus, students who do not misbehave earn the top mark in citizenship. In the second procedure, teachers assume that all students begin with an average rating in citizenship. During the marking period, the rating is lowered for students who misbehave and raised for students who make positive contributions to the class through acts of leadership or service. Thus, in this system, top citizenship marks are earned only by students who make positive contributions to the class. The students who offer neither trouble nor leadership earn average citizenship marks. Although sound arguments can be developed to support either system, the second system appears to have greater merit.

Some school systems report student citizenship by means of descriptive rating sheets or check lists. Such communications provide parents with much more usable information than is provided by the single-mark report commonly used (see Table 17-10).

Adjusting Marks According to Student Ability

Some educators maintain that each student should be marked according to his ability to achieve. Advocates of this view point out that under other

systems of marking high-ability students can earn top marks while working below their capacity. They also suggest that low-ability students can
earn only low marks even though they work at their utmost capacity. In
other words, advocates of marking according to ability believe that other
systems encourage loafing on the part of high-ability students and frustration leading to ultimate reduction of effort on the part of low-ability
students. Undoubtedly marking according to ability has much to be said
in its favor; however, as a single system of marking it is inadequate. The
resulting marks have no consistent meaning. Such marks can serve only
the motivational purpose of marking. They fail to serve the other common
purposes.

Achievement marks should be kept as independent as possible of factors
other than achievement. As a matter of fact, the motivational purpose of
ability marking can be largely accomplished through use of appropriate
supplementary written and oral comments to students, counselors, and
parents. Such supplementary use of this type of reporting is strongly encouraged.

Basing Marks on Scales

Should marks be based on an absolute scale, a percentage scale, or a
relative scale? Teachers agree that marks should be based on the most
reliable and meaningful scale available. Unfortunately, scales with known
zero points and units of equal size are available in very few subjects.
Typing achievement can be measured in words per minute, and some
performances in physical education can be measured in equally reliable
scales of time and distance. However, for most subjects, the only scales
available are teacher-constructed tests which measure a limited range of
achievement in units of unknown size. Furthermore teacher-built tests
over the same content vary in an uncontrolled manner from test to test
regardless of whether they are built by the same teacher or by different
teachers. In particular, some tests are much more difficult than others
built to measure the same content. As a result, percentage scores for the
same student will vary widely from test to test. Clearly, in most subjects
absolute scales of achievement do not exist, and percentage scales are
highly unreliable. Therefore many teachers follow the practice of professional test builders and base their evaluation of a given test score upon
its position in a distribution of scores for that test. Likewise, they assign
marks according to the position of a student in the distribution of total
scores for his class or grade. This practice is based upon the belief that
in a series of measurements over the same content, a given student is
more likely to maintain his relative position in his class more consistently
than he would maintain a particular percentage score.

In many schools, the practice of assigning marks in approximate agreement with a student's standing in his class or in a group of similar classes has largely replaced marking according to a percentage system. It should be emphasized that this change in procedure has neither increased nor decreased the proportion of high grades earned, since the procedure is only the first step in determining the letter mark earned by a given score. Whether or not the top score has earned a mark of A, B, C, D, or F depends upon several other factors.

In conclusion, since absolute scales in education are seldom available and because percentage scales are highly unreliable, the most meaningful basis for marks is the relative scale: position in a given distribution of scores. Obviously, marks determined in this manner must be interpreted in relation to the group measured. Top positions in a distribution of low-ability students are not given the same marks as comparable positions in a distribution of high-ability students.

It should be noted that classes differ in ability level under several circumstances:

1. The students may be assigned to separate sections according to their intelligence or their proficiency in the subject.

2. The course itself may attract disproportionate enrollment of high-ability students or low-ability students. (Some electives attract students of high ability; other electives, the opposite.)

3. The class may be taught during an instructional period in which an unusual number of classes in the first two categories are also offered. The result may be an unusually high or low grouping.

4. The class may differ from average merely because of chance variation that occurs when no attention is given to grouping.

Marking Standards

What proportion of a class should receive each mark? The proportion of A, B, C, D, and F marks earned by a particular class should depend upon three factors: (1) the marking policy of the school, (2) the ability level of the class, and (3) the achievement level of the class.

A beginning teacher may find that his school has no official marking policy. Actually, in some schools teachers mark completely according to their own standards. In such a situation, the beginner would do well to follow the average practice of teachers having classes like his own. In a great many schools, however, the beginner will find a statement of marking policy in the administration's handbook for teachers. Table 17-1 represents the kind of direction a principal might provide for the teachers

Table 17-1. Suggested Distribution of Marks

MARKS	UNSELECTED STUDENTS	SELECTED STUDENTS			
		LOW	AVERAGE	ADVANCED	HONORS
A	10%	0	0	20%	80%
B	20%	0	20%	60%	20%
C	40%	20%	60%	20%	0
D	25%	60%	20%	0	0
F	5%	20%	0	0	0

in a school having both heterogeneous classes and classes selected according to ability.

The above marking distributions are recommended for consideration of teachers at a particular high school. It is expected that minor deviations from the suggested percentages will be the rule rather than the exception. However, since the honors classes enroll only highly selected students of proven ability, it is expected that no student in those classes will be given a grade lower than B unless he has been issued a deficiency notice and given an opportunity to transfer to a group of lower classification.

In some schools marking policies are worked out in detail by joint committees of teachers and administrators. The following report, "General Philosophy for Determining Scholarship Marks at Y High School," is adapted from the work of such a joint committee. This statement of policy includes the committee's answers to eight frequently asked questions and represents the way administration and faculty can cooperate intelligently to give greater uniformity and meaning to a marking system. It should be recognized that at present marking practices differ so greatly that a similar committee at another school might make quite different recommendations. This variability in opinion makes it all the more imperative that educators work together to bring about more uniform practice.

General Philosophy for Determining Scholarship Marks at "Y" High School[2]

Evaluation is a continuous process for guiding growth in every class. This process is carried on in many ways, such as through written work, group discussions, or individual conferences. The quarter grade is a cumulation of this process.

Periodically the teacher reports student progress to the parents. This procedure becomes increasingly effective when based on a common philosophy which is understood by teachers, students, and parents.

The following statements attempt to establish a uniform policy for grading

[2] Adapted from the report of a joint committee of teachers and administrators at Pacific Beach Junior High School, San Diego, California.

scholarship in this secondary school. Answers are proposed for questions which teachers frequently ask. This report is proposed as a basis for discussion by faculty groups.

A and B grades are recorded when student achievement is definitely above average for the grade level (not necessarily for a particular class). High quality of achievement is the criterion, rather than the quantity of work done or the effort expended. The A and B grades indicate that students receiving such marks could succeed in college or advanced work in the field.

C and D grades are recorded when student achievement is average or below average for the grade level (not necessarily for a particular class). In this category should fall marks (1) for students with superior ability who are doing only average or below average work, (2) for students with average ability who are doing average or below average work, and (3) on a counseling basis for students with inferior ability who would not benefit from repeating the course.

F grades are recorded when student achievement is definitely inferior, and no credit should be granted for the course. If the course is a required one, the student must repeat the course.

Interpretation of Scholastic Grading in Specific Situations

1. Should teachers attempt to follow a grading curve?

    The expression "grading curve" usually refers to a symmetrical curve of distribution in which the percentages of grades, A to F, are 7, 24, 38, 24, 7; 10, 20, 40, 20, 10; 5, 20, 50, 20, 5; or the like. If the philosophy stated above is accepted, then any symmetry which results in the grading pattern is purely coincidental. In actual practice distributions like 12, 25, 38, 20, 5; or 15, 30, 35, 15, 5, are more common. *However, an individual classroom will seldom fit the typical pattern* and departmental distributions will usually vary in predictable ways. Even entire school distributions may be influenced by community factors.

    Students in elective courses, where special aptitude or interest is likely to be evident, will usually earn more high marks than students in required courses. *Students in advanced courses should receive the marks which the same effort and achievement would earn in regular classes; they should not be penalized for being in advanced courses.*

2. How should extra credit assignments be evaluated?

    Extra assignments for able students should represent superior quality and genuine student interest. The completion of average extra credit assignments, however, does not necessarily reflect superior scholarship. For example, twenty assignments representing only average workmanship do not indicate superior student achievement.

3. Should teachers grade by a point system where a certain number of points are given for each completed assignment?

    The point system frequently tends to emphasize quantity rather than quality of work. The student who reads twenty easy books or writes twenty poor compositions is neither a good reader nor a good writer.

4. Should students receive lower grades at the beginning of the year than at the end?

   Students should be graded according to the same general policy throughout the year.

5. How should grades be awarded when the teacher is using ability groups within a class of unselected students?

   The students should be graded in relation to average achievement for the grade level. If students in slower groups consistently make high grades, the work should be made more difficult. In faster groups, the difficulty of the assignment and the quality of achievement should indicate high grades for the student, but students who demonstrate only average achievement should receive average marks. If the work is too difficult for the student, he should be transferred to a group better suited to his ability.

6. How should the teacher grade students in two-track courses, such as advanced and regular mathematics?

   The students should be graded on the same comparative bases as listed above. High marks should indicate work above the average expectancy for the grade. If students in the regular class receive a disproportionate number of high marks, the work should be made more difficult or the students should be transferred to an advanced class.

7. How should students be graded in adjustment and remedial classes?

   These students should be graded on the same basis as regular students. When the student doing remedial work is doing outstanding work in his group, the work should be made more difficult or the student should be transferred to a regular class.

8. How should students in honors courses be graded?

   These students should be graded on the basis of quality the same as students in regular classes. Since these students are selected for their high level of achievement, they would be expected to receive high marks. No student should be penalized in grades for being in an advanced or accelerated class.

After a teacher has determined the marking policy of his school and the ability level of the class to be marked, he must make a decision concerning the quality of achievement attained by his class. If the teacher has adequate evidence to conclude that his class has achieved at a level higher than might be expected for a group of its classification, he should increase the proportion of high grades assigned. On the other hand, when he has evidence that a class is not performing up to expectations for its level, the proportion of low grades should be increased. At no time should the suggested proportions be followed automatically. However, when a teacher finds that his marks regularly deviate in the same direction from the suggested pattern, he should reassess his marking practices.

Whenever an individual teacher's marks are either consistently higher or consistently lower than the pattern established for a given quality of work at a school, then that teacher has failed to act in accord with highest professional standards. Marks that must be interpreted differently for individual teachers are unfair to students, parents, and other teachers. Therefore, it is important that teachers make serious efforts to mark in as similar a manner as possible.

OLDER SYSTEMS OF DETERMINING MARKS

Three methods of recording data and determining marks are in common use: raw scores, percentages, and letter marks. Each will be discussed in the following paragraphs.

Raw Score Marking

Teachers frequently use raw scores as their basic method of recording ratings of student achievement. In this system, students earn points toward marks for items answered correctly on quizzes and examinations, for completeness and accuracy of laboratory exercises and written assignments, and for success on any other factors the teacher wishes to include. The number of points assigned to each type of measurement is an arbitrary decision of the teacher, as is the apparent weighting of each factor to be used in the final distribution of raw scores.

In the use of the raw score system of recording and marking, a teacher might proceed as follows:

Step 1. The teacher decides that he will give 40 percent of the final mark to ratings of learning activities, 40 percent to quizzes, and 20 percent to the final examination. Thus, he intends that the relative weight of scores concerning activities, quizzes, and the final examination will be in the order of 2:2:1.

Step 2. He decides that he will record twenty activity marks and give four quizzes of equal weight during the marking period.

Step 3. Next, he decides to have a total of 100 raw score points on the final examination. Then, to achieve apparent balance, each of the four quizzes will contain a possible total of 50 points, and each of the twenty recorded activity marks will be assigned a possible 10 points.

Table 17-2. Planned Component Weights

	WEIGHTS		TOTAL	POINTS
COMPONENT MEASURED	PERCENT	RATIO	POINTS	EACH
20 assignments, and so on	40	2	200	10
4 quizzes	40	2	200	50
1 final examination	20	1	100	100

Step 4. At the end of the marking period, the teacher merely totals the number of points earned by each student and places the totals in a frequency distribution.

Step 5. He then assigns marks A, B, C, and so on, to various portions of the distribution according to the marking policy of the school. Note: At this point he could follow the "absolute system" and give A's to totals above a set percentage such as 90 percent (450 points), B's to totals between 80 and 90 percent (between 400 and 450 points), and so forth. However, use of this system is justified only when all the component measures are standardized.

LIMITATIONS OF RAW SCORE MARKING   The raw score system explained above appears to work precisely, but careful examination will reveal two debilitating flaws: a student's standing prior to the final computation is difficult to determine, and *the teacher's control of the effective weights of the various components of the final mark is an illusion.*

Not all teachers realize that when final marks are determined according to a student's relative position in a distribution formed by combining scores from separate measures, the effective weights of the different components are directly proportional to the variability (standard deviation) of each component—not proportional to the total score possible on each.

The two examples in Tables 17-3 and 17-4 demonstrate the manner in which the effective weights of components can differ from the weighting planned when a system of raw score marking is used.

Table 17-3. Effective Weights of Component Measures Vary According to Their Respective Standard Deviations (Example One)

COMPONENTS	TOTAL POINTS	STANDARD DEVIATION	PLANNED WEIGHT	EFFECTIVE WEIGHT
Activity ratings	200	9	2	1
Quizzes	200	9	2	1
Final examination	100	9	1	1

Table 17-4. Effective Weights of Component Measures Vary According to Their Respective Standard Deviations (Example Two)

COMPONENTS	TOTAL POINTS	STANDARD DEVIATION	PLANNED WEIGHT	EFFECTIVE WEIGHT
Activity Ratings	200	30	2	6
Quizzes	200	5	2	1
Final examination	100	10	1	2

The preceding illustrations show that teachers who use the raw score system of determining marks have relinquished control of the relative weights of the components of the final mark. To maintain control of the relative weights of all measures used in a total, it is necessary to establish component distributions which have predetermined variability and predetermined means. This is exactly what is accomplished by use of the standard score system which will be discussed later in this chapter.

Percentage Marking

Percentages are commonly used as a basic system of recording data and determining marks. In this system a teacher proceeds as follows:

Step 1. The teacher scores and records each assignment, quiz, exam, laboratory report, as a percentage score. When a paper is judged to be worth 30 of a possible 40 points, a score of 75 is recorded. Likewise, when another paper is judged to be worth 90 points out of a total of 120 points, a score of 75 is recorded. Thus, the number of raw score points on each measure is immaterial.

Step 2. He decides to weight activity ratings, quizzes, and the final examination in the ratio of 3:2:1.

Step 3. At the end of the marking period, the percentage marks in each category are averaged for each student. The teacher then triples the activity average, doubles the quiz average, and adds the two totals to the final examination mark. Thus, the total mark for each student is made up of six parts based on the planned component ratio of 3:2:1.

Step 4. The teacher then forms a distribution of the students' weighted percentage totals and assigns marks of A, B, and C to specified proportions of the distribution according to the policy of the school.

If the teacher in the above illustration had recorded eight activity rankings, five quizzes, and two examinations for each student, the final mark for a student having the scores listed below would be computed in five steps. In the first step of the computation the percentage scores in each category are totaled.

ACTIVITY RATINGS	QUIZZES	EXAMINATIONS
60	70	15
65	80	85
80	96	100
55	74	
85	80	
75	400	
50		
90		
560		

In the second step of the computation, the average for each category is found.

ACTIVITY RATINGS	QUIZZES	EXAMINATIONS
$560 \div 8 = 70$	$400 \div 5 = 80$	$100 \div 2 = 50$

In the third step of the computation, the average score for each category is multiplied by its predetermined weighting factor.

ACTIVITY RATINGS	QUIZZES	EXAMINATIONS
$70 \times 3 = 210$	$80 \times 2 = 160$	$50 \times 1 = 50$

In the fourth step of the computation, the weighted components are totaled.

$$210 + 160 + 50 = 420$$

In the fifth step the student's total of 420 is placed in the class distribution of similar totals and given a letter mark according to the school policy for that particular type of class. (Note: The student's average weighted percentage can be found by dividing his total of 420 by 6. The resulting score of 70 percent sometimes is reported as his mark, or the score is assigned a letter mark according to local practice; that is, if 70 percent is considered barely passing, the student would be given a mark of D. This practice is fairly common, but seldom justified.)

LIMITATIONS OF PERCENTAGE MARKING   Some teachers conclude that use of percentage marks will overcome the flaws existing in the raw score systems of recording and marking. This conclusion is approximately 50 percent correct. It is true that percentage marks on individual measures can be more easily interpreted, but percentages used as components of final letter marks suffer from the same flaw of weighting as that which afflicts the raw score system. The effective weights of the components vary with the standard deviations of the component distributions.

The described procedure of weighting and combining percentages would produce totals having the intended component weights of 3:2:1 only when the components have identical variability. The relationship of three components having different ranges of measurement can be described mathematically by the ratio $a:b:c$. Multiplying a by 3, b by 2, and c by 1, as was done in the foregoing illustration, results in weights of $3a:2b:c$. This relationship is equal to the ratio 3:2:1 only when $a = b = c$.

Perhaps the concept of a test's effective weight will be made more clear by use of a nonmathematical explanation. Suppose that a class studying the skill of dart throwing is to be measured by two tests. Each class member is to throw one dart at each of two targets from a distance of 10 paces. Bull's-eye hits will count 100 points; hits in the first inner ring will count 90 points; hits in the next ring will count 80 points, and so forth.

Each student will be given a letter mark according to his average score on the two tests. Assuming that one target covers a large tablecloth, and the other target is drawn on a small handkerchief, which target will have the greater effect in determining a student's mark? Will their effects be equal?

It should be obvious that even though both targets are scaled from zero to 100, their effective weights in determining marks are not the same. Students will undoubtedly score either 90 or 100 points on the larger target; whereas, on the smaller target their scores may well range all the way from zero to 100. When the two scores for each student are combined and placed in a distribution, the relative positions of students in that distribution will be almost wholly dependent upon the small target scores. Likewise, when the two scores of each student are averaged, the range of averages will be determined almost wholly by the small target scores. Thus, the component which provides the greater range of scores is the component which carries the greater effective weight in determining final marks.

The graphic illustration on page 492 should further clarify the meaning of test weights. Figure 17-1 shows the range of scores on two tests of 100 points each. Scores on the first test ranged from 15 to 95, while on the second test the range was from 65 to 85. By following the appropriate broken line it can be seen that a student who scores at the top of test I and at the bottom of test II would have an average of 80 points $\left(\dfrac{95 + 65}{2} = 80\right)$. However, a student who scores at the bottom of test I and at the top of test II would average only 50 points $\left(\dfrac{15 + 85}{2} = 50\right)$. Thus, test I carries greater effective weight than test II.

Figure 17-1 further reveals that other letter marks assigned on the basis of the average scores would be strongly weighted in favor of test I. A student who scores A on the first test and F on the second test would earn a mark of B on the illustrated combination. On the other hand, the lowest student on test I would fail on the combined average regardless of his success on test II.

It should be clear from the above illustration that teachers who base marks on accumulated raw scores or accumulated percentages bias the results in favor of students who happen to score high on the measures having the greatest spread of scores.

Letter Marking

The most widely used systems of marking base letter marks on class distributions of numerical scores. This type of transfer is seldom automatic since recommendations for the allocation of the various marks usually are

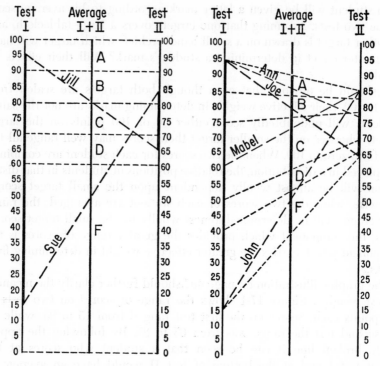

Fig. 17-1   *Graphic representation of the effect of differences in the range of scores upon the average of those scores (A + C frequently does not average B)*

Case 1: Letter marks are given on a percentage basis with F covering the largest range.

Case 2: Letter marks are given on a "curve" basis with C covering the largest range.

	I	II	I + II
Jill	A	D	B
Sue	F	B	F

	I	II	I + II
Ann	A	C	A
Joe	A	F	B
Mabel	C	A	C
John	F	A	F

flexible. The final decisions are left to the judgment of the teacher. In the exercise of their judgment, most teachers find it helpful to arrange numerical scores in a frequency distribution and determine division points between letter marks on the basis of the "breaks" in the distribution. For example, assume that a 120-point test has been given to a class of forty students. Their scores on the test were as follows:

78, 60, 84, 68, 89, 74, 81, 66, 61, 75, 87, 76, 84, 77, 74, 65, 73, 58, 86, 70, 83, 71, 90, 68, 80, 83, 66, 74, 81, 74, 76, 77, 75, 86, 78, 78, 73, 76, 84, 75

Further assume that the class is slightly better than average in a school recommending a policy of A's, 10 percent; B's, 20 percent; C's, 40 percent; D's 20 percent; and F's, 10 percent. A frequency distribution of scores should be made, having the lowest score (58) at the bottom and the highest score (90) at the top (see Table 17-5).

Table 17-5. Determination of Letter Marks
from a Distribution of Numerical Scores

RAW SCORE DISTRIBUTION		LETTER GRADES
90	/	
89	/	
88		
87	/	A
86	//	
85		
84	///	
83	// .	
82		B
81	//	
80	/ .	
79		
78	///	
77	//	
76	///	C
75	///	
74	////	
73	//	
72		
71	/	
70	/	
69		D
68	//	
67		
66	//	
65	/	
64		
63		
62		
61	/	F
60	/	
59		
58	/	

Then, using knowledge of the general quality of the class together with knowledge of the school's marking policy, a teacher will find that convenient breaks in the distribution suggest letter allocation as follows:

five A's (86–90), eight B's (80–84), seventeen C's (73–78), seven D's (65–71), and three F's (58–61).

The slight deviation from the proportions recommended by the school is justified by the character of the distribution and the quality of the class.

Teachers commonly combine letter marks into a single mark in either of two ways: (1) averaging letters by assuming that an A and a C will average B or (2) temporarily assigning numerical equivalents to letter marks and then averaging the numbers before finally changing back to a letter mark.

As an illustration of the first method, marks of C, A, F, B, D would be combined as follows: The A and the F would be changed into two grades of C, the B and the D would also average C. The result would be five C's or an average of C.

MARKS	STEP ONE	STEP TWO	STEP THREE
C	C	C	
A	C	C	
F	C	C	C
B	B	C	
D	D	C	

The same five marks would be combined by the second method (using $A = 4, B = 3, C = 2, D = 1, F = 0$), as follows:

MARKS	STEP ONE	STEP TWO	STEP THREE
C	2		
A	4		
F	0	$10 \div 5 = 2$	$2 = C$
B	3		
D	1		
	$\overline{10}$		

The second method can be further illustrated by a problem frequently encountered at marking time. What mark should be given a student who had earned ten daily marks (A, B, F, C, D, D, C, B, D, A); four quiz marks (C, A, B, C); and a final examination mark of C?

Assumptions:

1. The daily marks are to be weighted equally.
2. The quiz of grade B is to be weighted double that of each of the other quizzes.

3. The final mark is to be made up of daily work 50 percent, quizzes 25 percent, and final examination 25 percent.

The first step toward a solution would be to combine the daily marks.

DAILY MARKS

A	4
B	3
F	0
C	2
D	1
D	1
C	2
B	3
D	1
A	4
	21

$$21 \div 10 = 2.1 = C$$

The second step is to combine the quizzes, giving double weight to the one on which the student earned a mark of B.

QUIZZES

C	2
A	4
B	3 + 3
C	2
	11 + 3 = 14

$$14 \div 5 = 2.8 = B$$

The third step is to combine the averages (giving double weight to the daily marks so as to preserve the recommended 50–25–25 ratio).

Daily marks	2.1
	2.1
Quizzes	2.8
Final exam	2
	9.0

$$9.0 \div 4 = 2.25 = C$$

The earned mark therefore would be C. (If pluses were used, the mark would be C plus.)

LIMITATIONS OF THESE COMPUTATIONS It should be recognized that letter marks also have serious limitations as a basic system of recording and marking. Merely to substitute the letter A for 100 points and B for the score of 90, does not alter the fact that the effective weight of a component in a combination of marks is related to the spread of scores of the component.

Furthermore, neither illustrated method of combining letter marks is defensible unless the underlying assumptions are recognized and judged acceptable. Far too many teachers use marking systems without considering the rational foundations involved. For example, when a teacher combines an A and a C to equate with two grades of B, and when he combines an F and a C to equate with two grades of D, the first underlying assumption involved is that each letter mark represents an equal range of achievement. Also, when the letter marks themselves have been obtained by use of raw score or percentage scales, the tenability of the assumption of equality of resulting letter-mark units depends upon acceptance of assumptions with respect to the uniformity of the basic raw score or percentage units.

That is, when letter marks have been based upon percentage scales using 90 through 100 as A, 80 through 89 as B, 70 through 79 as C, 60 through 69 as D, and 0 through 59 as F, a letter mark of F *cannot* be combined justifiably with a letter mark of A to yield two marks of C *unless* the percentage range of 90 through 100 is accepted as equivalent to the percentage range of 0 through 59. Similar discrepancies exist in letter mark ranges measured in raw score units (see Figure 17-1). Consequently, it is illogical for a teacher to combine A's and F's to obtain C's in either situation.

On the other hand, transfer of letter marks to a numerical scale such as A = 4.0, B = 3.0, reduces the major problem of combining scores but does not eliminate it. Since the component letter distributions are translated to a system having a constant range, the weights of components are brought partially under control. Full control, however, is not achieved until the component distributions have been made identical by conversion to normalized standard scores.

It should also be recognized that transfer of letter grades to the discrete-point scale of A = 4.0, B = 3.0, involves the assumption that differences within the range of a component letter mark are not important, while even smaller differences in range at the division points between letters are critical. Figure 17-2 shows that on a particular test (case 2) all scores from 50 through 74 were transferred to the single point 2.0. No allowance was made for differences as great as 24 points in that part of the scale; whereas, a difference of only 12 points in other parts of the scale (39–51, and 74–86) could raise the letter equivalent from 0.0 to 2.0 or from 2.0 to 4.0. These conditions usually are acceptable only when the frequency of scores in an interval is considered a better marking base than the raw score or percentage units involved.

In spite of its weaknesses, the transfer of letter marks to a scale having constant range is a step in the direction necessary to accomplish scientific control of weighted marks. The logical next step is to transfer the original measures to a controlled scale that represents the original measures with greater fidelity. Without question, standard score scales serve that purpose. It is to be hoped and expected that teachers soon will recognize the inadequacies of older methods and adopt the more accurate method of standard scores.

Fig. 17-2   Transfer of marks and scores to the scale: A = 4, B = 3, C = 2, D = 1, F = 0

Case 1: Marks based on percentages.   *Case 2:* Marks based on a "curve."

Weaknesses

1. Differences of scores within groupings are ignored.
2. The range of scores represented fails to be constant from point to point on the scale. For example, in case 2 the scale score 1.0 represents 10 raw score points (scores between 40 and 50); whereas, the scale score 2.0 represents 25 raw score points (scores between 50 and 75).

NEWER SYSTEMS OF DETERMINING MARKS

Standard scores are of two basic types: linear transformations which establish distributions having the same shape as the original distributions of raw scores or area transformations which change the shape of the original distributions to conform with a normal distribution. The second type, known as normalized standardized scores, is appropriate for use whenever it is logical to assume that valid and reliable measurement in accurate units would result in a normal distribution. That assumption usually is tenable only when the scores of hundreds of students have been placed in a single distribution. When the teacher is concerned with the measurement of only one or two relatively small classes, it is usually more appropriate for him to use standard scores based on a linear transformation. For this reason only standard scores of linear type are discussed here.

Z-Score Marking

The most commonly used standard score of the linear-transformation type is the Z-scale. On a Z-scale, the mean score is 50 and the standard deviation is 10. Thus each unit is equal to one tenth of a standard deviation: a score of 60 is always one standard deviation above average; and a score of 45 is one-half standard deviation below average. Raw scores can be transferred to Z-scores by using the four steps listed below:

Step 1. Put the raw scores into a frequency distribution of unit interval.

Step 2. Determine the mean of the raw scores by adding all the raw scores and dividing the total by the number of scores.

Step 3. Compute or estimate the standard deviation of the raw score distribution. *One* of the following methods should be used.

1. For distributions that are approximately normal and contain no more than fifty individual scores, a rough but useful estimated standard deviation can be found by dividing the range of raw scores by four. Formula: $S = R \div 4$
2. When raw score distributions deviate from the normal at the extremes, a more accurate approximation of the standard deviation is provided by either of the following formulas:
$S = .4\,(C_{90} - C_{10})$; $S = .3$ (*average of the top 10 percent minus the average of the bottom 10 percent*)
3. When a mathematically accurate standard deviation is desired, the following formula should be used:

$$S = \sqrt{\frac{\Sigma(X - \overline{X})^2}{N}}$$

In the above formulas, S represents standard deviation, R stands for range, C indicates centile point, X is any score, $\overline{X}$ is the mean, and N is the number of scores.

Step 4. Determine the Z-score for each raw score by *either* of the following techniques:

1. From Tables 17-6 or 17-7 take the Z-scores in the column headed by the raw score standard deviation and place them alongside the raw score distribution so that 50 is opposite the mean, 60 is opposite the raw score which is one standard deviation above the mean, and so on.
2. Compute each Z-score by substitution in the formula:

$$Z = \frac{10(\textit{raw score} - \textit{raw score mean})}{\textit{standard deviation}} + 50$$

Table 17-6. Z-Scale Equivalents for Raw Scores Having Standard Deviations from 1 to 10.

(Each pattern repeats between Z-scale standard deviation points.)

	RAW SCORE STANDARD DEVIATION									
X−X̄	1	2	3	4	5	6	7	8	9	10
10				75	70	67	64	63	61	60
9			80	73	68	65	63	61	60	59
8			77	70	66	63	61	60	59	58
7			73	68	64	62	60	59	58	57
6		80	70	65	62	60	59	58	57	56
5		75	67	63	60	58	57	56	56	55
4		70	63	60	58	57	56	55	54	54
3	80	65	60	58	56	55	54	54	53	53
2	70	60	57	55	54	53	53	53	52	52
1	60	55	53	53	52	52	51	51	51	51
0	50	50	50	50	50	50	50	50	50	50
−1	40	45	47	48	48	48	49	49	49	49
−2	30	40	43	45	46	47	47	48	48	48
−3	20	35	40	43	44	45	46	46	47	47
−4		30	37	40	42	43	44	45	46	46
−5		25	33	38	40	42	43	44	44	45
−6		20	30	35	38	40	41	43	43	44
−7			27	33	36	38	40	41	42	43
−8			23	30	34	37	39	40	41	42
−9			20	28	32	35	37	39	40	41
−10				25	30	33	36	38	39	40

In Table 17-8, the four steps are applied to the group of forty raw scores used earlier. From this illustration it can be observed that the raw score mean of 76 has an equivalent Z-score of 50, and that every raw score is transferred to the Z-scale in a manner which maintains its relative position in relation to the mean.

When daily work, quizzes, and examinations are recorded in Z-scores, it is a simple matter to control the contribution of each to a combination mark. For example, if daily marks are to count 25 percent, quizzes 50

Table 17-7. Z-Scale Equivalents for Raw Scores
Having Standard Deviations from 11 to 20

(Each pattern repeats between Z-scale standard deviation points.)

	RAW SCORE STANDARD DEVIATION									
X−X̄	11	12	13	14	15	16	17	18	19	20
20										60
19									60	60
18								60	59	59
17							60	59	59	59
16						60	59	59	58	58
15					60	59	59	58	58	58
14				60	59	59	58	58	57	57
13			60	59	59	58	58	57	57	57
12		60	59	59	58	58	57	57	56	56
11	60	59	58	58	57	57	56	56	56	56
10	59	58	58	57	57	56	56	56	55	55
9	58	58	57	56	56	56	55	55	55	55
8	57	57	56	56	55	55	55	54	54	54
7	56	56	55	55	55	54	54	54	54	54
6	55	55	55	54	54	54	54	53	53	53
5	55	54	54	54	53	53	53	53	53	53
4	54	53	53	53	53	53	52	52	52	52
3	53	53	52	52	52	52	52	52	52	52
2	52	52	52	51	51	51	51	51	51	51
1	51	51	51	51	51	51	51	51	51	51
0	50	50	50	50	50	50	50	50	50	50

percent, and examinations 25 percent, marks for a student would be combined as illustrated below:

DAILY WORK	QUIZZES	EXAMINATIONS	WEIGHTED AVERAGE	
61	47	40	Daily work	55
50	61	46	Quizzes	52
55	53	‾86	Quizzes	52
60	45		Exams	43
70	54	$86 \div 2 = 43$		‾202
52	‾260			
45				
48	$260 \div 5 = 52$			
57				
60				
47				
‾605				

$605 \div 11 = 55$

Table 17-8. Transformation of Raw Scores to Z-Scores

SOURCE OF DATA	RESULTANT Z-SCALE	STEP 1: BUILD THE RAW SCORE DISTRIBUTION	STEP 2: COMPUTE THE MEAN	STEP 3: ESTIMATE THE STANDARD DEVIATION
Step 3	70 $+2S$	92	$\overline{X} = \Sigma X \div 40$	$S = R \div 4$
	⎧69	91		
	68	90 /	90	$S = (90 - 58) \div 4$
	66	89 /	89	$S = 32 \div 4$
Step 4	⎨65	88		
	64	87 /	87	$S = 8$
	63	86 //	172	
	⎩61	85		Mark the standard
Step 3	60 $+S$	84 ///	252	deviation points in
	⎧59	83 //	166	the distribution:
	58	82		
	56	81 //	162	$Z_{70} = \overline{X} + 2S =$
Step 4	⎨55	80 /	80	$76 + 16 = 92$
	54	79		$Z_{60} = \overline{X} + S =$
	53	78 ///	234	$76 + 8 = 84$
	⎩51	77 //	154	$Z_{40} = \overline{X} - S =$
Step 2	50 $\overline{X}$	76 ///	228	$76 - 8 = 68$
	⎧49	75 ///	225	$Z_{30} = \overline{X} - 2S =$
	48	74 ////	296	$76 - 16 = 60$
	46	73 //	146	
Step 4	⎨45	72		
	44	71 /	71	
	43	70 /	70	STEP 4:
	⎩41	69		Fill in the remainder
Step 3	40 $-S$	68 //	136	of the Z-scale by use
	⎧39	67		of column "8" in
	38	66 //	132	Table 17-6.
	36	65 /	65	
Step 4	⎨35	64		or
	34	63		
	33	62		Compute each point
	⎩31	61 /	61	by use of the for-
Step 3	30 $-2S$	60 /	60	mula:
	⎧29	59		
	28	58 /	58	
Step 4	⎨26	57		
	⎩25	56	$\overline{3034}$	$Z = \dfrac{10(X - \overline{X})}{S} + 50$
			$3034 \div 40 = 76$	

The student's total of 202 points is then put into a distribution of students' totals from which letter marks are assigned according to the policy of the school.

It should be noted that the precision of the weighting of each component could be slightly increased by building a distribution of average Z-scores for the component and from it determining a new Z-score for each student. It should also be noted that teachers frequently record daily assignment marks in raw scores ranging from 0 to 3 or 4 points. At the end of a marking period, these scores are totaled, placed in a distribution, and transferred to the Z-scale.

Table 17-9 shows that combining two Z-scores gives results different from those obtained by combining the raw scores from the same two tests. In the table, the ratio of the raw score standard deviations of the two tests is 20:5. Test I therefore has four times the weight of test II in a raw score

Table 17-9. Difference between Combined Raw Scores
(Inadvertently Weighted) and Combined Z-Scores (Equally Weighted)

	TEST I $(\overline{X} = 55; S = 20)$			TEST II $(\overline{X} = 75; S = 5)$			COMBINED SCORES	
STUDENT	RAW SCORE	POSI-TION	Z-SCORE	RAW SCORE	POSI-TION	Z-SCORE	RAW SCORE (I:II = 20:5)	Z-SCORE (I:II = 1:1)
Alice	95	+2S	70	85	+2S	70	180	140
Clayton	95	+2S	70	65	−2S	30	160	100
Esther	55	$\overline{X}$	50	75	$\overline{X}$	50	130	100
George	35	−S	40	85	+2S	70	120	110
Manfred	15	−2S	30	85	+2S	70	100	100
Rose	15	−2S	30	65	−2S	30	80	60

combination. This effect can be observed by noting that the two students who scored 95 on test I rank 1 and 2 on the raw score combination. On the other hand, when the tests are weighted equally by use of Z-scores Alice remains in rank 1, but George moves from fourth to second position because his relatively low score on test I no longer is quadrupled in weight.

Advantages and Limitations of Standard Score Marking

Obviously, use of standard scores will not improve the validity of poorly constructed tests, nor will their use guarantee that teachers will assign marks in judicious agreement with school policy. *But use of standard scores will do two things that are not done by older systems of marking.*

1. Standard scores provide measurements that have *consistent meaning* with respect to an individual's standing in a group. That is, a Z-score of

40 always indicates a position 1 standard deviation below the mean of the base group.

2. Standard scores enable a teacher to give whatever weight he wishes to each component of a final mark since each system has a constant mean and a constant standard deviation.

Teachers should recognize that users of Z-scores accept the assumption that marking based upon the relative standing of students in a defined group is more meaningful and reliable than marking based upon students' attainment of arbitrary percentage scores on measures of unknown and variable difficulty. However, class-size groups also can be of "unknown and variable" quality. Consequently, use of standard scores does not obviate the desirability of developing a broad scoring base by occasionally administering tests to all classes in a given subject. When school-wide tests in a subject are not feasible, a teacher should accumulate achievement data from his own classes over several semesters. In that manner he can keep a check on his judgment of the performance level of a particular class.

In conclusion, it again should be emphasized that even the best scoring systems serve only to enable the teacher to combine measurements accurately, and thus to place students accurately in rank order according to the measurements employed. Whether or not the top-ranking students deserve a mark of A, B, or lower is entirely up to the teacher's professional interpretation of the school's marking policy. However, the fairness and accuracy of a teacher's marking will depend upon his ability to build and use valid tests, his ability to collect and record additional evidences of student achievement, his ability to judge the value of student rankings in accordance with school marking policy, *and his ability to use the most accurate scoring system available.*

REPORTING TO PARENTS

Reports to parents concerning the progress of students commonly take three forms: (1) report cards, (2) supplementary reports, and (3) personal conferences. It is unlikely that any one procedure alone will do an adequate job of reporting. Teachers should become proficient in the use of all three.

Report Cards and Supplementary Reports

Report cards in their most common form include a single achievement mark in each subject, citizenship marks, comments to parents, and a record of attendance and tardiness (see Sample Report Card). Such cards are usually sent to the student's home every six to twelve weeks. Most reports require parental signature before they are returned to school. More elaborate reports include ratings on progress toward separate objectives and invite comment and visitation.

In addition to a regular report card, many schools employ supplementary progress reports. These reports are unstructured letters as used

SAMPLE REPORT CARD

Student _____ Jane Doe _____ Grade _11_ Counselor _Jackson_

Report for period ending _____ March 15, 1964 _____ Central High School

PER.	COURSE TITLE	SCHOLAR-SHIP	CITIZEN-SHIP	PERIODS ABSENT	PERIODS TARDY	TEACHER'S SIGNATURE
1	U. S. History	A	S	2	0	J. Jones
2	English	B	E	2	0	S. Smith
3	Homemaking	C	S	2	1	E. Brown
4	Physical Ed.	C	U	5	6	D. White
5	Chemistry	C	S	2	0	A. Evans
6	Algebra	D	E	2	0	F. Olson

Comments to Parents

Per. 1. *Jane is an excellent student of history.*

4. *Jane needs to change her attitude toward Phys. Ed.*

6. *Jane is working hard and showing some improvement.*

Comments from Parents

Parent's signature_____

Parents are cordially invited to comment above or to visit the school to discuss this report. Conferences with teachers, counselors, or administrators may be arranged by telephoning the school: No. 582-3993.

by some schools, but more commonly detailed check lists descriptive of student behavior are employed for this purpose (see Table 17-10).

Supplementary reports are most frequently called for when students are in danger of failing. In fact, many schools require that parents and students be notified of any deficiencies in scholarship or citizenship several weeks before the end of a marking period. (Notification of impending C or D grades should be given to students in advanced classes just as notices of possible failure are given to students in groups of lower classification.)

Table 17-10. Citizenship Report

_____I. RESPONSIBILITY RATING. Behaviors considered:

_____ 1. Comes to class on time
_____ 2. Hands in school work on time
_____ 3. Demonstrates an interest and a will to learn
_____ 4. Brings necessary equipment to class
_____ 5. Prepares and brings to class extra materials
_____ 6. Does not waste school supplies
_____ 7. Takes good care of school building, equipment, and grounds
_____ 8. Works independently
_____ 9. Finds his own material for reports and other activities
_____10. Accepts responsibility for developing projects helpful to the class
_____11. Accepts leadership roles
_____12. Has a positive influence on class morale

_____II. COOPERATION RATING. Behaviors considered:

_____ 1. Listens when someone is talking
_____ 2. Does not talk to other students unnecessarily
_____ 3. Cooperates with class officers and committee chairmen
_____ 4. Respects opinions of others
_____ 5. Controls his voice and actions
_____ 6. Abides by group decisions
_____ 7. Does nothing that would bring criticism on his class or school

_____III. WORK HABITS RATING. Behaviors considered:

_____ 1. Gets to work without urging by the teacher
_____ 2. Does not waste time
_____ 3. Does his work carefully
_____ 4. Prepares written work neatly
_____ 5. Prepares reports in his own words
_____ 6. Is careful to follow directions
_____ 7. Uses intelligently the index, table of contents, and dictionaries
_____ 8. Completes assignments promptly

E = Excellent
U = Unsatisfactory (needs improvement)
no mark = satisfactory

SOURCE: Adapted from a self-rating form used by the Los Angeles City School Districts.

Appropriately used, deficiency notices serve two distinct purposes: they direct the attention of the teacher, student, and parent to the specific needs of a particular student, and they reduce the shock of failure to both student and parent. A basic principle of marking is that unsatisfactory marks should never be a surprise to a student or his parents.

Every teacher should be fully aware of the important public relations aspect of reporting. Little can be gained, except perhaps ill will, by thoroughly negative reports. To tell a mother that her son is a complete rascal and totally ignorant of the purposes of school may be a true representation of at least part of the facts, but as a report it is completely inadequate. Nothing constructive is gained. Parents want facts, but they also have a right to expect competent professional analyses and constructive suggestions which give evidence that the problems are being studied with at least some prospect of successful solution. Too many reports to parents just baldly state that the student is failing. When a parent responds to such a communication, he frequently is angry or annoyed and is psychologically unable to provide the help of which he would be capable under more favorable circumstances. Such situations must be prevented. It is not without design that in many schools all communications to parents must be approved by the principal. Beginning teachers should be prepared to meet such regulations with understanding.

Parent-Teacher Conferences

Under present teaching schedules in secondary schools, it would be practically impossible for teachers to confer with any significant number of parents during regular teaching days even if the parents were able to keep appointments at the school. Consequently, parent-teacher conferences on the secondary level remain the exceptional practice rather than the rule. Nevertheless, it would be advisable for beginning teachers to be ready to participate in parent-teacher conferences concerning student deficiency.

For that type of conference, several guidelines have been developed:

1. Prepare yourself prior to the conference. Review records of the student's ability, background, and performance. Also learn something of the parent if possible. Communication is facilitated when the teacher is aware of the parent's level of familiarity with school purposes and school terminology.

2. Prepare materials to help the parent visualize the student's learning status and progress. Charts and graphs are well understood by some parents, but all will understand a set of well-selected samples of the student's test papers, assignments, and projects. Such concrete materials often tell much more than mere words.

3. Be a good listener. A parent-teacher conference should be a discussion and an interchange of information. It is not intended to be a lecture

on the part of either participant, although there may be times when it would be well for the teacher to permit the parent to present his grievances without interruption.

4. Be constructive. Listening, of course, is not sufficient. The teacher should discuss steps that he expects to take to help the student, and he should also invite the parent to suggest steps that might be taken by the student's home.

5. Keep the conference on a professional level. The discussion should seek remedies, not the assignment of blame. In particular, teachers should avoid evaluation of the contribution other teachers may possibly have made to the development of the student's problem. The matter of scheduling the conference should also be given consideration. Parent conferences with teachers should be by appointment only, scheduled far enough in advance to permit adequate preparation, and held in a school conference room which permits free discussion without overt or accidental eavesdropping. A classroom shared with students, an office shared with colleagues, or a PTA meeting are not adequate places to conduct a professional conference. When parents expect informal discussions in such surroundings, courteously suggest making an appointment. The confidential professional nature of parent-teacher conferences deserves more widespread recognition.

REPORTING STANDARDIZED TEST RESULTS TO PARENTS

Whether or not to report standardized test scores, including IQ's, to parents has long been a perplexing problem for beginning teachers. Research conducted by the American Educational Research Association in 1961 found that roughly 90 percent of the secondary school teachers in a national sample thought that parents, in most cases, should be told the achievement test scores of their children.[3] Slightly more than half of the sample favored giving that information to all parents as standard practice. The research also found that there was almost an even division between secondary school teachers who favored and those who opposed telling parents their child's IQ, although less than 20 percent thought that it should be done as standard practice.

Authorities in the field of educational and psychological testing appear to be in agreement that schools should accept the responsibility of communicating standardized test results to parents as well as to students.[4]

[3] Research Division, National Education Association, *Research Bulletin*, vol. 40, no. 4 (December 1962), p. 122.
[4] Walter N. Durost, "How to Tell Parents about Standardized Test Results," *Test Service Notebook No. 26*. New York: Harcourt, Brace & World, Inc., 1961.

They stress the point, however, that the reporting of scores as single specific numbers does not constitute proper communication. In fact, they insist that unless the meaning of a score is conveyed, no effective communication has taken place. Therefore, it is recommended that teachers recognize the error present in scores, and report achievement test results

Fig. 17-3   Student report of percentile-band results on the Cooperative English Tests

Cooperative English Test Manual for Interpreting Scores, 1960, p. 15. Used with permission of the Educational Testing Service and San Diego State College Photograph Audio-Visual Services.

only in terms of estimated bands like those in Figure 17-3. Grade placement scores have value in discussions among educators, but in communications to parents and students percentile bands are much more
likely to be correctly understood. For example, a high school freshman
might be told: "Jim, your test result in vocabulary is the percentile band
35 through 60. You have scored higher than about 35 percent of high
school freshman and about 40 percent have made scores higher than
yours." Then, if this is one of Jim's weak spots, the discussion might well
be continued to outline steps toward remediation since standardized
achievement test results serve teacher and student best as starting points,
not culminations.

Intelligence test results—if they are to be communicated at all—should
be explained in relation to their expected use. IQ's, in particular, should
be discussed only with the greatest discretion. It is highly unlikely that a
teacher ever should tell a parent, "Your son's IQ is 117," even if that score
is obtained on the best test currently available. As a matter of fact, it
would be better if teachers themselves refrained from thinking of an IQ as
a single number.

When school policy approves communication of intelligence test results,
they should be interpreted as rough estimates of academic potential. If
a parent requests his son's intelligence score for that purpose, he might
be told, "John's estimated academic potential is like that of students who
on the whole make average grades in that course." Or, if selection of a
college is his purpose, the records of the school might permit the teacher
to say, "Forty percent of our graduates having scores like John's have
earned passing grades (or honors, if that is the case) at a certain university." When school records are less adequate, intelligence test results
could well be referred to only in terms of the broad categories: superior,
above average, average, and below average.

In conclusion, it should be emphasized that there is, as yet, no generally
accepted policy with respect to the communication of intelligence test
scores to students and their parents. The trend clearly is toward more free
exchange of this information, but for the time being, the beginning
teacher is well advised to follow very carefully the policy of the school
in which he is employed.

Selected References

1. Adams, Georgia Sachs, Theodore L. Torgerson, and Ernest R. Wood, *Measurement and Evaluation for the Secondary-School Teacher.* New York: Holt, Rinehart and Winston, Inc., 1956. Chapters 25–27.
2. Bradfield, James M., and H. Stewart Moredock, *Measurement and Evaluation in
   Education.* New York: The Macmillan Company, 1957. Chapters 9–13.

3. Carter, William L., Carl W. Hansen, and Margaret G. McKim, *Learning to Teach in the Secondary School.* New York: The Macmillan Company, 1962. Chapter 11.
4. Gorow, Frank F., *Statistical Measures: A Programmed Text.* San Francisco: Chandler Publishing Company, 1962.
5. Grambs, Jean D., William J. Iverson, and Franklin K. Patterson, *Modern Methods in Secondary Education,* revised ed. New York: Holt, Rinehart and Winston, Inc., 1958. Chapter 18.
6. Klausmeier, Herbert J., *Teaching in the Secondary School.* New York: Harper & Row, Publishers, 1958. Chapter 17.
7. Magnuson, Henry W., Melvin W. Gipe, and Thomas A. Shellhammer, *Evaluating Pupil Progress.* Bulletin of the California State Department of Education, Sacramento, vol. 29, no. 14 (December 1960), Chapter 8.
8. Nordberg, H. Orville, James M. Bradfield, and William C. Odell, *Secondary School Teaching.* New York: The Macmillan Company, 1962. Chapter 8.
9. Pounds, Ralph L., and Robert L. Garretson, *Principles of Modern Education.* New York: The Macmillan Company, 1962. Chapter 14.
10. Rothney, John W., *Evaluating and Reporting Pupil Progress.* ("What Research Says to the Teacher," Series No. 7.) Washington, D.C.: National Education Association, 1955.
11. Schwartz, Alfred, and Stuart C. Tiedeman, *Evaluating Student Progress.* New York: David McKay Company, Inc., 1957. Chapter 18.
12. Thorndike, Robert L., and Elizabeth Hagen, *Measurement and Evaluation in Psychology and Education,* 2d ed. New York: John Wiley & Sons, Inc., 1961. Chapter 17.
13. Walker, Helen M., and Joseph Lev, *Elementary Statistical Methods,* revised ed. New York: Holt, Rinehart and Winston, Inc., 1958. Chapters 4–7.

Interpretation and use of standardized tests

The use of a wide variety of standardized measurement instruments has become common practice in American schools.[1] Thousands of standardized tests have been developed to measure a student's general intelligence, specific aptitudes, achievement, and personality characteristics. The results are employed by administrators to appraise the effectiveness of their instructional program, and to enable them to classify students for programming. In addition, school counselors use standardized instruments when they study a student's adjustment status, his educational needs, and his vocational interests. And classroom teachers employ standardized tests:

1. To determine the range of ability and achievement within a class so that appropriate instructional level, goals, pacing, materials, and activities can be selected.

2. To identify individuals who are potentially fast learners and consequently most likely to benefit from special motivation, enrichment work, and acceleration.

3. To identify individuals who are slow learners and laggards in the subject matter of the particular class. For these students the teacher can plan a slower pace of instruction, more concrete illustrations, more frequent drill and review, and—if class size permits—individually adapted remediation.

[1] A standardized instrument is a test or scale for which regularized procedures of administration and scoring have been established and for which scores of norm groups have been determined. In the standardization process, the instrument is administered to norm groups carefully selected to be representative of all those for whom it was designed. The resulting distributions of scores are then used as norms to aid interpretation of scores made in subsequent administrations of the instrument.

4. To identify individuals who are achieving less than might reasonably be expected. These students may benefit from special study by the teacher or counselor.

5. To discover, through item analysis, any broad subject-matter topics which might be given greater instructional emphasis, provided that such emphasis is acceptable within the local course of study.

6. To compare the achievement of a class and its individual members with the national norms for classes and individuals of similar ability. This information can help a teacher evaluate the success of his instruction.

7. To help a student select a program of studies which is compatible with his needs and abilities.

8. To help motivate better teaching and better learning. Knowledge of success, or lack of it, when intelligently interpreted can be a powerful motivator for both teacher and student.

To insure that he gets all the help possible from the standardized testing program of his school, a teacher should study the scores of his classes using analytical lists, charts, graphs, and individual profiles, and then he should supplement that information with careful long-term observation of the students themselves, since tests alone merely give helpful indications, not final answers.

The purpose of this chapter is to acquaint beginning teachers with the general characteristics of the standardized tests and test scores they will be most likely to find in use wherever they teach. Assistance in the reading and interpretation of test scores will be the principal focus of the chapter; however, a necessary first step is an introduction to the nature of educational measurement.

THE NATURE OF SCORES IN EDUCATIONAL MEASUREMENT

A basic problem in the science of education is the development of measurement instruments scaled so as to have a true zero point and units of equal size throughout the range of measurement. Until such instruments are in existence, teachers will be unable to use measures of a student's intelligence, his growth in knowledge of subject matter, or his changes in attitude in the same manner as they use measures of a student's height and weight. That is, when the units involved are not of the same size, measurements made in different parts of a scale cannot be compared accurately. To be more specific, tests of educational achievement yield raw scores that usually indicate the number of items correctly answered. Thus, on any educational scale the basic unit is an individual test item—but such a scale is composed of unequal units unless the items are all of equal difficulty or are individually weighted according to the amount of knowledge measured.

Therefore, gains measured in different parts of many educational scales are not directly comparable. For example, a student who has changed in weight from 120 to 125 pounds has gained exactly as much weight as another student who has changed from a weight of 90 to 95 pounds. A 5-pound change is precisely the same amount in any part of the weight scale. However, when a student's score on an achievement test moves from 120 to 125 points his gain in achievement is not necessarily equal to the gain made by a student whose score changed from 90 to 95 points. The units involved may be of different size. Consequently, educational tests ordinarily do not enable a teacher to make precise comparisons of change.

Furthermore, even when units are equivalent, comparisons involving multiplication or division cannot be made unless zero on the scale represents complete absence of the quality being measured. The problem of developing scales which register zero only when there is complete absence of the quality measured is not peculiar to educational measurement. For example, the same difficulty is encountered in the measurement of temperature. When the familiar Fahrenheit and centigrade scales were developed, the absolute zero point (total absence of heat) was not firmly established. On the centigrade scale the zero point was set at the freezing point of water under certain prescribed conditions, while the zero point on the Fahrenheit scale was set 32 units below the freezing point. The size of a degree on each scale is constant, but differs from one scale to the other. Therefore, it is obvious that a reading of 75 degrees on one scale does not represent the same temperature as a reading of 75 degrees on the other. Also it should be noted that neither scale justifies the statement that a temperature of 80 degrees is twice as warm as a temperature of 40 degrees.

For the same reason, it is incorrect to say that the earth was twice as old in 1000 A.D. as it was in 500 A.D., since the zero point concerning the age of the earth has not been firmly established. In educational measurement it is inaccurate to state that a student having an IQ of 150 is twice as intelligent as a student having an IQ of 75, or that a student who scores 80 points on an arithmetic test has twice the arithmetic skill of a student who scored only 40 points on the test. Zero points in these factors and in many others have not been established.

Because the basic unit of measurement is undefined, a student who scores a certain number of points on a test constructed by one teacher is unlikely to score the same number of points on a test constructed by another teacher to cover the same subject matter. However, if the tests are sound tests of the subject, a student can be expected to hold very nearly the same position among his classmates on each of the two tests. Under these circumstances—and they are the usual circumstances in educational measurement—scores become more stable and informative measurements when they are transformed to numbers which in some manner describe positions in a distribution of scores. For this reason, the building of frequency distributions of raw scores and their transformation to derived scores is common practice in educational measurement. By definition, "a frequency distribution is a tabulation of scores from high to low, or low to high, showing the number of individuals that obtain each score or fall in each score interval."[2]

Points or positions in a frequency distribution are described by use of several variations of two basic procedures:

Procedure one: The position of a particular score in a distribution can be described according to the number or percentage of *individuals* who scored either above or below the given score.

Procedure two: The position of a particular score in a distribution can be described according to its *numerical value* in relation to selected mathematical properties of the distribution.

Scores Based on Counting Individuals

NUMERICAL RANK The simplest of scores derived by counting individuals (frequencies or cases) in the distribution is numerical rank. In this system, every frequency in the distribution is numbered according to its ordered position counted from the top. Whenever the frequency at any score is greater than one, all cases at that score are assigned the average of the numerical positions filled. For example, in Table 18-1, the score of 83 is said to have a numerical rank of 1 since it is the single top score. The two individuals who scored 82 take up positions two and three so each is assigned a rank of 2.5, the average of those positions. In the same way, every case in a distribution can be ranked. Numerical rank, however, is seriously limited in application because identical ranks in groups of different size may have extremely different meanings.

CENTILE POINTS The basis for an improved ranking scale is obtained by designating points in a distribution according to the *percentage* of the frequency falling *below* each point. In Table 18-1 it can be observed that $12/100$ of all frequencies fall below the midpoint of score 58, therefore, 58 can be designated as the twelfth centile point, C_{12}, in the distribution.[3]

---

[2] Roger T. Lennon, "A Glossary of 100 Measurement Terms," *Test Service Notebook*, No. 13. New York: Harcourt, Brace & World, Inc., p. 2.

[3] One half of the frequencies at any score are assumed to fall below the midpoint of that score. In Table 18-1, the two scores of 58 are assumed to spread out evenly between 57.5 and 58.5 so that exactly one frequency falls below 58.0.

Table 18-1. A Sample Distribution of 50 Raw Scores and Their Equivalent Derived Scores

	DERIVED MATHEMATICALLY		DISTRIBUTION OF RAW SCORES			DERIVED BY COUNTING FREQUENCIES				
STANDARD SCORES Z	z	DEVIATION POINTS	X	TABS	f	NUMERICAL RANK	ACCUM. f	CENTILE POINTS	%ILE RANK	T
			84							
71	2.1		83	/	1	1	49.5	C_{99}	99	73
70	2.0	$\bar{X} + 2S$	82	//	2	2.5	48		96	68
69			81							
67			80							
66			79							
64	1.4		78	/	1	4	46.5		93	65
63			77							
61			76	//	2	5.5	45	C_{90}	90	63
60	1.0	$\bar{X} + S$	75	/	1	7	43.5		87	61
59			74	//	2	8.5	42		84	60
57			73	///	3	11	39.5		79	58
56	.6		72	//	2	13.5	37		74	56
54			71	////	4	16.5	34		68	55
53			70	////	4	20.5	30		60	53
51			69	//////	6	25.5	25	median	50	50
50	0.0	mean $(\bar{X})$	68	///	3	30	20.5		41	48
49			67	//	2	32.5	18		36	47
47			66	/	1	34	16.5		33	46
46	−.4		65	//	2	35.5	15		30	45
44			64	///	3	38	12.5	C_{25}	25	43
43			63	//	2	40.5	10		20	42
41			62	/	1	42	8.5		17	41
40	−1.0	$\bar{X} - S$	61	/	1	43	7.5		15	40
39			60							
37			59							
36	−1.4		58	//	2	44.5	6	C_{12}	12	38
34			57							
33			56	/	1	46	4.5		9	37
31			55							
30	−2.0	$\bar{X} - 2S$	54	/	1	47	3.5		7	35
29			53	//	2	48.5	2		4	32
27	−2.3		52	/	1	50	.5	C_1	1	27
			51							
			50							

Annotations along the deviation-points column: "one standard deviation" is marked between each pair of adjacent deviation points. A "Range" bracket spans from C_{25} up.

Procedure

			f	NUMERICAL RANK	ACCUM. f	%ILE RANK	T
$z = \dfrac{X - \bar{X}}{S}$	$S = \sqrt{\dfrac{\Sigma(X - \bar{X})^2}{N}}$		Count tabs	Count f down	Count f up to midpoint of score	$\dfrac{\text{Accum. } f}{N} \times \dfrac{}{100}$	Take from %ile in "normal" table
$Z = 10z + 50$	$\bar{X} = \dfrac{\Sigma X}{N}$						

In this manner, it is possible to designate 100 points of reference in any frequency distribution.

The most commonly used reference point of the centile type, the fiftieth centile point (C_{50}) is also known as the median. In Table 18-1, the median of the distribution of raw scores is 69. Students who score below the median are in the bottom half of the distribution, just as students who score below C_{25} are in the bottom quarter of the distribution.

PERCENTILE RANK   It is important to note that all frequencies at a given centile point are said to have a percentile rank of that particular centile number. That is, all cases at C_{10} have a percentile rank of 10, and all cases at the median have a percentile rank of 50. Likewise, a student who has a percentile rank of 25 exceeds roughly 25 percent of the individuals in the distribution, and roughly 75 percent exceed him.[4] Percentile rank within a school grade is the type of score most commonly used in standardized testing at high school and college levels. Such a score clearly indicates the percentage of the norm group which scored below any given point in the norm group distribution. For example, when 60 percent of high school juniors fall below a score of 37 in the norm group distribution established for a standardized test, a percentile rank of 60 among high school juniors is assigned to anyone scoring 37 on subsequent administrations of the test.

Percentile rank scores are more meaningful than numerical rank scores but are susceptible to unique misinterpretations discussed later in this chapter.

Mathematically Derived Scores

The mathematical properties most used in procedure two are the distribution's arithmetic mean and standard deviation. An arithmetic mean, commonly called average, is the measure of a distribution's central tendency obtained by dividing the sum of all the scores by their total number.[5] In Table 18-1, the sum of the fifty scores is 3400. The arithmetic mean of the scores then, is 68. A standard deviation is a mathematical measure of the variability of scores in a distribution.[6] When the scores are spread

---

[4] The percentile rank of a given score is found by counting half the frequencies at the score and to that number adding all the frequencies below the score. The obtained sum is then divided by the total frequency of the distribution.

[5] The formula for the arithmetic mean $\overline{X} = \dfrac{\Sigma X}{N}$ indicates that the mean ($\overline{X}$) of a set of scores is equal to the sum of (Σ) the scores (X) divided by the number of scores (N).

[6] The formula for the standard deviation $S = \sqrt{\dfrac{\Sigma(X - \overline{X})^2}{N}}$ indicates that the standard deviation of a group of N scores is equal to the square root of the average of their squared differences from the mean.

out widely from the mean, the standard deviation is relatively large, but when the scores cluster closely about the mean, the standard deviation is relatively small. The full range of scores in a distribution practically never is less than twice as large as the standard deviation, nor more than six times as large as that measure. In distributions containing 100 or more scores, the full range is usually from four to six times as large as the standard deviation. In Table 18-1, the range of the fifty scores is 32 points (83.5–51.5), and the standard deviation is 7 points.

In the interpretation of standardized tests, the mean score of a defined age or grade group is commonly used as the basic reference point and their standard deviation is commonly used as the basic unit of measurement.

AGE NORMS   When a test is being designed to measure a characteristic which for a school-age group typically increases with age (such as mental ability or physical development), the test is administered to sample groups of thousands of individuals at each age level for which the test is intended. The arithmetic mean of each age group is then reported as an age norm. Thus, in the standardization of a mental test, it may be found that children 10 years and 4 months old averaged 46 points. Then, any child scoring 46 points on the test would be said to have a mental age of 10 years and 4 months (10-4). Likewise, in the determination of the familiar age norms for height, measurements are made on large groups of persons at each developmental age. The average height of each age group is then tabled so that a child can measure his height, refer to the table, and determine his standing in relation to the average.

Age norms have been developed for educational achievement also. Such norms are called achievement ages, subject ages, educational ages, or age equivalents. Thus, a student whose arithmetic score is average for students 11 years and 6 months old would be said to have an arithmetic age of 11-6. If his score on a battery of achievement tests is average for students 10 years and 9 months old, his educational age is said to be 10-9.

AGE QUOTIENTS   Selected age scores of individuals sometimes are compared by the mathematical process of division so as to yield quotients that help teachers answer three popular questions:

1. How does Johnny's performance on mental ability tests compare with the scores of other children of his chronological age? This question is answered by dividing Johnny's mental age score (MA) by his chronological age (CA) and moving the decimal point two places to the right. The result is Johnny's *intelligence quotient*, the formula for which is

$$IQ = \frac{MA}{CA} \times 100$$

2. How does Johnny's performance on a battery of achievement tests (his educational age) compare with the scores of other children of his chronological age? This question is answered by determining the student's *education quotient* by dividing his educational age (EA) by his chronological age (CA) and multiplying the result by 100:

$$EQ = \frac{EA}{CA} \times 100$$

3. How does Johnny's performance on a battery of achievement tests compare with the scores made by other children of his mental age? To answer this question Johnny's *accomplishment quotient* is obtained by the formula:

$$AQ = \frac{EA}{MA} \times 100 \text{ or } AQ = \frac{EQ}{IQ} \times 100$$

Quotient scores appear to be simple to interpret: scores of 100 indicate performance equal to the group average, scores below 100 indicate lower than average performance, and scores above 100 indicate better than average performance. However, quotient scores are particularly susceptible to errors of interpretation. For example, IQ, by far the most extensively used quotient score, varies so widely in meaning for different age groups, that it is being replaced by the deviation IQ (discussed later in this chapter). Furthermore, the AQ (accomplishment quotient) contains such a strong tendency to overrate the accomplishment of low-ability students and underrate the accomplishment of high-ability students (due to factors associated with the reliability of measurement) that the AQ must be used with extreme caution, if, in fact, it is to be used at all.

GRADE NORMS   In the measurement of educational achievement, scores are commonly reported as averages for given grade levels, called grade norms, grade placements, or grade equivalents. Age norms and grade norms are very similar concepts. Each is an arithmetic mean for a given group. It should be noted that, whereas age norms are based upon a twelve-month year and expressed by two numbers separated by a dash, grade norms are based upon a ten-month school year and expressed as a decimal. An age norm half way between 10 years and no months (10-0) and 11 years and no months (11-0) is 10 years and 6 months (10-6). The grade norm midway between the beginning of the tenth and eleventh grades is 10.5. A grade equivalent of 6.7 would be interpreted to mean that the obtained score was average for a group that had completed half or more of the seventh month of the sixth grade. In actual standardization, however, tests frequently are administered in only one month of each successive grade. The grade equivalent scores of intermediate months are obtained by interpolation. Grade norms are the derived scores most commonly used at elementary school level.

LINEAR DERIVATION OF STANDARD SCORES The position of a score in a distribution also can be described according to its raw score deviation from the mean. Thus, in Table 18-1, a score of 80 could be said to be +12 points (80–68) from the mean, and a score of 64 could be said to be —4 points (64–68) from the mean. Such scores roughly locate positions in reference to the mean, but fail to indicate whether or not a score is near one of the extremes of the distribution. In a distribution having a standard deviation of 36, a score 12 points above the mean is only a third of a standard deviation from the mean—a position relatively close to the center of the distribution. On the other hand, in a distribution having a standard deviation of 4, a score 12 points above the mean is three standard deviations above the mean—a position seldom exceeded by anyone.

To overcome this confusion in meaning, the sigma or z-score system has been evolved. In that system, a score's position is described by a number that indicates its distance from the mean in standard deviation units.[7] A raw score at the mean of a distribution always becomes a z-score of zero, a z-score of —.5 always denotes a position one-half standard deviation below the mean, and so on.

The z-score system is basic to all standard score scales. The Z-scale, for example, is obtained from z-scores by the formula: $Z = 10z + 50$. By use of a mean of 50 and a standard deviation of 10, this scale avoids the negative signs and decimals which complicate the z-scale. Other linear standard scores may be obtained by application of the formula:

new standard score = z(new standard deviation) + new mean

The transformation of a distribution of raw scores to z-scores or Z-scores is known as a linear transformation because the graph of the relationship is a straight line. This fact is pictured in Figure 18-1, a line graph of the relationship between Z-scores and raw scores having a mean of 28 and a standard deviation of 4.

Standard scores of the linear transformation type are extremely useful to teachers when they are determining student marks as explained in Chapter 17. Furthermore, Z-scores derived from distributions of varied shapes maintain precisely consistent mathematical meanings. The mean is always denoted by a Z-score of 50, a Z of 60 is always one standard deviation above the mean, a Z of 40 is always one standard deviation below the mean, and so on. However, Z-scores fail to have consistent percentile rank equivalents unless they are derived from distributions of the same shape.

[7] The z-score of any raw score X can be found by substitution in the formula:
$$z = \frac{X - \bar{X}}{s}.$$

Fig. 18-1 Graphical and computational linear transformation of a sample distribution of twenty-five raw scores ($\overline{X} = 28$, $S = 4$) to their equivalent Z-scores

Sample Computations for Scores in the Above
Distribution in Which $\overline{X} = 28$ and $S = 4$

Computation for a score of 20	Computation for a score of 34
$Z = \dfrac{(\text{raw score} - \text{mean})10}{\text{standard deviation}} + 50$	$Z = \dfrac{(\text{raw score} - \text{mean})10}{\text{standard deviation}} + 50$
$Z = \dfrac{(X - \overline{X})10}{4} + 50$	$Z = \dfrac{(X - \overline{X})10}{4} + 50$
$Z = \dfrac{(20 - 28)10}{4} + 50$	$Z = \dfrac{(34 - 28)10}{4} + 50$
$Z = \dfrac{(-8)10}{4} + 50$	$Z = \dfrac{(6)10}{4} + 50$
$Z = -20 + 50$	$Z = 15 + 50$
$Z = 30$	$Z = 65$

NORMALIZED STANDARD SCORES   Fortunately, when large numbers of students are measured by practically any educational or psychological test, the resulting distribution of scores has a strong tendency to resemble *a normal curve* for which percentile rank scores and standard score equivalents are well known. That is, in a normal distribution a percentile rank of 2 is always two standard deviations below the mean (at $z = -2$), a percentile rank of 16 is always one standard deviation below the mean (at the point z equals -1), a percentile rank of 50 is always at the mean ($z = 0$), and so on. The relationship of percentile rank scores and standard scores when the raw scores are *normally distributed* is shown in Figure 18-2.

Percentile Ranks	.1	2	16	50	84	98	99.9
z-Scores	-3	-2	-1	0	+1	+2	+3
Z-Scores	20	30	40	50	60	70	80
T-Scores	20	30	40	50	60	70	80

Fig. 18-2   Percentile rank scores and equivalent standard scores in a normal distribution

It is sometimes advantageous to transform nonnormal distributions of raw scores to percentile ranks and then assign each percentile rank the standard score it would have in a normal distribution. For example, in Figure 18-3, the frequency of cases (four) below 23.0 is represented by the shaded area. Four cases is 16 percent of the total frequency (twenty-five) in the distribution. Therefore, a raw score of 23 has a percentile rank of 16. From Figure 18-3 or from statistical tables of normal curve data, it is found that the equivalent position (percentile rank equals 16) in a normal distribution is always exactly one standard deviation below the mean, at $z = -1$. The raw score of 23 then is assigned a score which is one standard deviation below the mean on whatever standard score scale is used. Each raw score in the distribution can be transformed to a standard score in the same manner. When standard scores are derived by this transformation technique, they are classified as *normalized standard scores*.

Use of normalized standard scores is appropriate when it is logical to

Fig. 18-3   *Transformation of a sample distribution of twenty-five raw scores* ($\overline{X} = 28$, $S = 4$) *to their equivalent normalized standard scores*

Sample Computation for Scores
in the Above Distribution

	For a Raw Score of	
	23	34
Step 1: Count all frequencies below the score's midpoint.	4	24.5
Step 2: Divide the obtained accumulated frequency by the total frequency in the distribution. (This is the percentile rank of the raw score.)	$\dfrac{4}{25} = .16$	$\dfrac{24.5}{25} = .98$
Step 3: Read the standard score of the obtained percentile rank from a graph or table of a normal distribution.	$z = -1$ $T = 40$	$z = 2$ $T = 70$

assume that a distribution of raw scores deviates from normal because of errors of measurement or when it is necessary to force large sets of data into similar distributions so that various segments of a battery of tests will yield comparable scores. The American Psychological Association, the American Educational Research Association, and the National Council on Measurements Used in Education all recommend that standardized test results be reported as normalized standard scores. This recommendation is followed by a great many publishers of educational and psychological tests. Some of the most common scores of this type are discussed in the following paragraphs and shown in Figure 18-4.

Fig. 18-4 *The relationship of stanines to the normal curve and to a variety of other scores*

T-scores. The most commonly used normalized scale employs 50 as a mean and 10 as a standard deviation. This derived score is called a T-score and should not be confused with the similarly numbered but differently derived Z-score. The T-score was originated as a normalized standard score by McCall, who is said to have named it in honor of the psychologists Terman and Thorndike. Since T-scores are derived from the percentile rank data of normal distributions, a T-score of 50 always indicates the median, a T-score of 40 always indicates a percentile rank of 16, a T-score of 60 always indicates a percentile rank of 84, and so on, as revealed in Figure 18-2. On the other hand, a Z-score will have these percentile rank equivalents only when the original raw score data are normally distributed. However, regardless of the size and shape of a distribution, its Z-scores will have precise meaning in terms of the distribution's mean and standard deviation—an advantage not possessed by the T-score. Consequently, Z-scores, despite restricted interpretation, may be used with distributions of any size and shape, while T-scores ordinarily are appropriate for use only with groups normally distributed.

Deviation IQ. A normalized standard score of special importance is the deviation IQ, a scale which has practically replaced the quotient IQ. This scale has a mean of 100 and a standard deviation of 16 (or 15 as used by some tests) for all chronological ages. Thus, regardless of the age at which a person is tested, if his resulting deviation IQ is 148, his score is three standard deviations above the mean of his age group and his percentile rank is 99.9 in that group. Such was not the case with the outmoded quotient IQ. That long-used intelligence score is plagued by the fact that the IQ's of different age groups frequently have different standard deviations even when measured with the same test. On that scale (quotient IQ) an IQ of 148 for a 16-year-old sometimes represents a percentile ranking inferior to that represented by an IQ of 132 for a person measured at an earlier age. The deviation IQ, like all normalized standard scores, provides consistent interpretation in terms of percentile rank.

Stanines. The stanine (standard nine) scale is a normalized standard scale of bands having a mean of 5 and a standard deviation of 2. The scale divides a normal distribution into nine segments, the middle seven of which are each one-half standard deviation wide. Figure 18-4 shows that the bottom 4 percent of the distribution is in stanine one, the next 7 percent in stanine two, and so forth. Teachers should note the unlimited width of the first and ninth stanines. For example, stanine nine contains IQ's of 129 as well as those of 148 and higher. Thus, the scale is inadequate to identify the top 1 to 2 percent of students who in many schools are classified as gifted and provided special learning opportunities. Nevertheless, the stanine scale has gained wide acceptance in education in the comparatively short time since its origination by psychologists in the U. S. Air Force of World War II.

This section concerning the nature of measurement has sought to develop a general understanding of the scores discussed. The development of computational skill has not been intended. Those beginning teachers who feel the need of computational exercises should consult the readings listed at the end of this chapter or textbooks in elementary statistics. The measurement concepts developed here are basic to the proper use of intelligence tests and standardized achievement tests, the topics which follow.

INTELLIGENCE TESTS AND THE CLASSROOM TEACHER

Some beginning teachers—and more experienced ones, as well—have the erroneous idea that intelligence tests and their resulting scores are intriguing but valueless, having meaning for guidance workers and psychologists only. These teachers do not bother to determine the intelligence ratings of their students and a few profess thereby to be fairer and less biased in their work with students. On the other hand, there are teachers who lean heavily on intelligence testing. These teachers may ignore errors of measurement and expect all students with IQ's measured at a given point to learn less than students with scores a few points higher. They may also ignore other limitations affecting IQ interpretation; for example, they frequently expect all students of low to average IQ to be low to average in all things, with the possible exception of physical stature and strength.

Fortunately, only a small proportion of teachers fall into these two extreme categories. In between these extremes is found the great majority of teachers. They regularly use IQ's in their study of the learning problems of their students, and they expect students of high intelligence to surpass others in academic achievement. However, these teachers realize that IQ differences of 5 or 10 points on a single measurement have little, if any, meaning in relation to the learning potential of individual students. The reasons are simple: single scores frequently are in error by that amount and many variables other than intelligence are involved in learning. In short, the majority of teachers recognize that intelligence tests are useful but not infallible instruments.

Development of Intelligence Tests

Instruments for the measurement of intelligence have an interesting but not mysterious background of development. Prior to the beginning of the twentieth century, men in many countries tried to measure intelligence, but all were unsuccessful. However, during the first decade of this century, two Frenchmen, Binet and Simon, developed an intelligence scale that was an outstanding contribution to the advancement of scientific measurement. Their work is basic to many tests now in world-wide use. In the United States, the Stanford-Binet Intelligence Scale, authored by Terman in 1916 and revised in 1937 and 1960 by Terman and Merrill, has been the adaptation held in highest esteem by psychologists and educators. This test together with two scales developed by Wechsler, the Wechsler Adult Intelligence Scale (WAIS) and the Wechsler Scale for Children (WISC), are used whenever most precise measurement of intelligence is necessary. These tests are particularly important in clinical work and in the measurement of the IQ's of persons having reading difficulties. However, all tests of this type are limited in school application by the fact that they must be administered orally and to only one individual at a time.

The need for a test of intelligence that could be administered to groups was first satisfied by the Army Alpha Test authored in 1917 by Otis and other American psychologists. This test helped solve the World War I classification needs of the United States Army, just as its many successors have been successfully applied to the classification problems of schools, business, and industry.

Several outstanding group tests, including those of Otis, Terman, Cattell, Kuhlmann, and the Thurstones, were developed in the 1920s, 1930s, and 1940s. These tests have been repeatedly published in new editions modified in content, printing style, or scoring procedure. Through this process they have remained in extensive use over a long period of years. They are by no means the only intelligence tests in use, however. According to Buros' *Tests in Print*, there were more than 200 intelligence tests on the world market in 1961.[8] Approximately 150 of these were being published in the United States.

Among the forty or more "individual" tests of intelligence now available are some specially designed to measure the IQ's of children who have defective motor ability, hearing, or vision.[9] Among the group tests are some which claim to be nonverbal (unaffected by individual differences in ability to understand words), culture free or culture fair (unaffected by individual differences in cultural background), or multiracial (unaffected by individual differences in racial origin). In fact, if the need arose—and the test titles could be taken at face value—an intelligence test now could be found to measure almost any type of person at any time from his birth to his dotage!

Obviously, the 200 or more intelligence tests of the 1960s vary greatly

[8] Oscar K. Buros, *Tests in Print*. Highland Park, N. J.: The Gryphon Press, 1961, p. xxvi.
[9] *Ibid.*, pp. 120–127.

in quality and in popularity of use. No teacher could possibly be expected to be informed about all of them. However, every teacher should be able to use and interpret the tests adopted by his school. To help teachers meet this responsibility, six of the most respected and most used group tests of intelligence will be described in the following section.

Six Outstanding Group Tests of Intelligence

The group tests of intelligence discussed below were selected for use in a state-wide testing program by a committee of psychologists and educators who gave major consideration to tests published or revised between 1950 and 1961.[10] It must be acknowledged that many other tests could be judged at least equally meritorious, depending upon the particular biases of the judges and the special testing purposes to be served. Nevertheless, the following tests, listed in the order of their first publication dates, must be accepted as worthy of mention.

KUHLMANN-ANDERSON INTELLIGENCE TESTS This well-established series of tests was first published in 1927. The seventh edition, published in 1960, has separate booklets for each of two levels: grades seven–nine and nine–twelve. In this edition, separate "verbal," "quantitative," and "total" scores are employed. However, the sixth edition, still widely used although published in 1952, yields a single IQ which correlates very highly with the Binet IQ. Furthermore, this IQ is based on the student's median performance on ten subtests. Thus, neither unusually high scores nor unusually low scores on any one segment of the total test have great effect on the resulting IQ—a circumstance assumed to increase test reliability. The sixth edition is organized in nine similarly timed booklets, one for the usual range of student ability found at each grade level: kindergarten, one, two, three, four, five, six, seven–nine, and nine–twelve. This organization permits great flexibility in test administration. Students who are at the extremes of ability in any grade level can be tested with the next higher or lower booklet as needed. Competing tests usually are organized in only three to five levels.

Another strength of the Kuhlmann-Anderson tests is the relatively low level of reading ability required throughout the series. Consequently, scores on these tests, when compared with scores on competing tests, frequently are found to be somewhat less affected by reading-ability differences among the students tested. On the other hand, possible criticisms of this series of tests include:

1. The computation of a median IQ based upon ten separate mental age scores is a more time-consuming procedure than is required by many other tests.

10 State of California Education Code, Chapter 994, Statutes of 1961.

2. The IQ yielded by the sixth edition is the "older" intelligence score which tends to vary in meaning for different age groups.

3. The series is not coordinated with any battery of achievement tests. Consequently, interpretations are more restricted than is the case when an intelligence test and achievement tests are standardized on the same group of students.

HENMON-NELSON TESTS OF MENTAL ABILITY   This series of tests was first published in 1931. The 1961 revision is organized in three levels: grades three–six, six–nine, and nine–twelve. The test at each level is composed of ninety multiple-choice items arranged in order of difficulty. The test manual provides easy conversion of the tests' raw scores to mental ages, percentile ranks within grades, grade equivalent scores, and deviation IQ scores, all based upon an extensive, scientifically selected, and nationwide standardization sample. The major strengths of this series of tests reside in its ease of administration and scoring and in its excellent standardization. At the same time, the tests are somewhat limited in school use by their comparatively high dependence upon reading ability and their lack of common standardization with a battery of achievement tests.

CALIFORNIA TEST OF MENTAL MATURITY (CTMM)   This test series was first published in 1936 and most recently revised in 1958. Its six levels are designed for grades kindergarten–one, one–three, four–eight, seven–nine, nine–thirteen, and ten–sixteen. The complete form requires from ninety minutes to two hours to administer, depending upon the level of test used. The short form of this test requires only about one hour of testing time.

Both forms of the test provide mental age scores and IQ's, as well as grade equivalents, percentile ranks within grade groups, and percentile ranks within grade levels. These derived scores are based on the total test and on its separate language and nonlanguage segments. In addition, the test provides data and a form for a "diagnostic profile" of the various scores on subsections of the test.

The strengths of the CTMM lie in its very adequate standardization, in the relatively high correlation between its total-score IQ and the Binet IQ, in the large number of levels and forms in which the tests are produced, and in its common standardization with the California Achievement Tests.

The major weakness of the CTMM is that it provides too many subscores of questionable reliability. According to the criticism of experts, the subscore errors are so large that its diagnostic profile should be ignored by classroom teachers.[11]

---

[11] Oscar K. Buros, ed., *The Fifth Mental Measurements Yearbook*. Highland Park, N. J.: The Gryphon Press, 1959, pp. 433–439.

LORGE-THORNDIKE INTELLIGENCE TESTS   This test, originally published in 1954, has separate levels for grades kindergarten–one, two–three, four–six, seven–nine, and ten–twelve. The tests for grades four–six, seven–nine, and ten–twelve are available in both verbal and nonverbal forms. The tests provide deviation IQ's, grade percentiles, grade equivalents, and age equivalents. Special features of these tests include: (1) the availability of directions in the Spanish language for the nonverbal forms (except level kindergarten–one) and (2) the provision of separate IQ norms for communities classified according to their average socioeconomic level. In spite of their relatively short background of development, the Lorge-Thorndike Tests are very highly regarded by reviewers.[12] These tests have been commended especially for excellent design and for ease of administration and scoring. On the other hand, the tests lack common standardization with an achievement battery, and they may be somewhat deficient in their ability to measure the very able high school senior.[13]

COOPERATIVE SCHOOL AND COLLEGE ABILITY TESTS (SCAT)   The first level of SCAT was published in 1955, but the entire series including two forms for grades four–six, six–eight, eight–ten, ten–twelve, and twelve–fourteen was not completed until 1957. The tests are rated among the best of all instruments constructed to measure a student's potential for academic achievement.[14] However, SCAT does not yield IQ's. In the place of IQ's, these tests provide verbal, quantitative, and total-score *percentile bands* which clearly portray the measured student's approximate standing in comparison with a national sample of students at his grade level. These tests also yield "converted scores" which facilitate comparison of results obtained from the various levels and forms of the test. Thus, a student's development from grade to grade can be traced and compared with the development of other students. This feature combined with the fact that SCAT is normed jointly with an outstanding achievement battery, the Sequential Tests of Educational Progress, greatly enhances the school use of both sets of tests.

SCIENCE RESEARCH ASSOCIATES TESTS OF EDUCATIONAL ABILITY   This comparatively new series of tests, published in 1957–1958, is designed for three levels: grades four–six, six–nine, and nine–twelve. The tests provide three part scores: language, reasoning, and quantitative, in addition to the total test score. The raw score results are transferred to AQ's (ability quotients) which are standard scores similar to the deviation IQ, except that AQ's are based on grade groups rather than on age groups. Percen-

12 *Ibid.*, pp. 479–484.

13 Anne Anastasi, *Psychological Testing,* 2d ed. New York: The Macmillan Company, 1961, p. 221.

14 Buros, *The Fifth Mental Measurements Yearbook,* pp. 450–457.

tiles in age, percentiles in grade, and estimated IQ's are also provided. A limited program of coordination of norms with the Iowa Tests of Educational Development and the SRA Achievement Series is described in the test manual.

These tests have been commended for their attractive appearance, ease of administration, ease of scoring, and potential ease of interpretation. They have also been severely criticized for lack of multiple forms, for inadequate standardization, and for weaknesses in their procedure of coordination with achievement batteries.[15]

The Interpretation of Intelligence Scores

The preceding discussion revealed that intelligence test results are reported in a variety of scores including: IQ's, mental ages, percentiles, and grade equivalents. The derivation of these scores was discussed earlier, however, a recapitulation may be helpful.

A mental age of 12 indicates that the student has made a test score equivalent to that of the average 12-year-old in the test's standardizing group. Whereas, an IQ of 100 indicates that the student has made a score that is average for his own chronological age. Likewise, a student's percentile rank indicates roughly what percentage of the tested group scored below the student, and his grade equivalent indicates the grade level at which his score would be average. For example, an average 14-year-old would have a mental age of 14, an IQ of 100, a grade equivalent of grade nine, and a percentile rank of fifty in that grade.

Of the common methods of reporting intelligence test results, mental age alone has the advantage of indicating the level of mental ability attained. That is, in any group tested simultaneously, the student who earns the highest mental age score has demonstrated the greatest mental ability. Mental ages, however, have the disadvantage of changing from year to year. Up to the age of about 16, an average student gains one year in mental age for each year gained in chronological age, but a student of an IQ of 75 gains only three fourths of a year each year of his early life. On the other hand, IQ's remain relatively constant from year to year, but fail to denote the relative mental level of members of a group made up of individuals of varying chronological ages. It is only for persons of equal chronological age that IQ's indicate relative mental ability.

In the interpretation of intelligence quotients, teachers should not assume that students of the same IQ necessarily possess the same capacity for learning. In fact, identical IQ ratings are derived from identical intelligence test scores only when the tested students are of identical chronological age. That is, the highest IQ in the class does not necessarily possess

15 *Ibid.*, pp. 510–513.

the greatest problem-solving ability. He merely is best for his age. For example, Tom, 11 years of age, Jim, 12, and Bill, 14, are in the seventh grade. If they made identical scores on an intelligence test, giving each of them a mental age of 12 years, Tom's quotient IQ would be 109, Jim's would be 100, and Bill's would be 86. Yet Tom, Jim, and Bill, as measured by the test, would have the same ability to solve problems involving mental processes.

Teachers should keep alert also to the fact that most commonly used intelligence tests, weighted heavily with verbal factors, are adequate predictors of success in the verbal activities of the school, but do not serve to predict effectively a student's potential in the nonverbal learnings. Furthermore, intelligence tests do not measure native capacity alone. The scores are affected by the kinds and quality of experience available to the student. Students from backgrounds that fail to provide experience considered common to American urban culture are likely to receive lower scores than they would if the tests were more adequate. Students of lower socioeconomic background, those having reading difficulties, and those having adjustment or health problems typically score lower than their potential. Intelligence scores, then, of a particular student are meaningful only when that student is similar to the standardizing group with respect to the nonintellectual factors which might affect test scores. For example, the mental score of a rural youth might not be valid if the standardizing group is predominantly of urban background.

Finally, due to errors of measurement (discussed later in this chapter), any single intelligence score can be interpreted safely only as an indication of the midpoint of a range of scores within which the student's true score can be expected to occur. The range of scores should be at least 10 points wide in the case of total test scores, and at least 15 points wide for all subscores including those termed: "verbal," "nonlanguage," "reasoning," and "quantitative." Thus, even when they are of the same age and background, two students must differ by at least 10 or 15 points in intelligence scores before it is reasonable to assume that one exceeds the other in true intellectual potential. And even then, such a conclusion frequently would be incorrect. Obviously, all teachers must exercise extreme caution when they interpret intelligence measures.

STANDARDIZED ACHIEVEMENT TESTS AND THE CLASSROOM TEACHER

The interpretation of scores from standardized achievement tests also is a regular task of secondary school teachers. To know each student's approximate potential for learning as measured by an intelligence test is of tremendous help in instruction, but this knowledge is only one facet of the teacher's study of the learner. If the teacher is to do the best job of teaching, and if he is to know something of the extent of his teaching success, he must also find answers to questions such as: What is the level of each student's study skills? How well can he read? How does his general educational development compare with that of other students of his ability and grade level? Are each student and the class progressing as well as might be expected? How does their learning compare with local, state, and national norms? Reliable answers to questions like these are not easily determined by observation alone. Fortunately, hundreds of instruments have been produced to help supply the objective evidence needed. The development of these instruments has been the result of efforts which began more than 100 years ago.

The Development of Achievement Testing

The first step toward improved measurement of achievement in American schools was made before the Civil War by Horace Mann who urged that written tests of essay type replace oral examinations, the mode of measurement commonly used at that time. His recommendations were not widely adopted until late in the nineteenth century.

The next addition to testing techniques can be traced back to J. M. Rice, who in the 1890s conducted the first testing survey of educational achievement. His informal study was followed in the early 1900s by the more accurate work of Thorndike, Stone, Ayres, and others who developed tests and scales for use in surveys of achievement in arithmetic, handwriting, and spelling.

The idea of grouping several tests of common school subjects into a single booklet or "battery" evolved about 1920. In the fifteen years immediately following that date, three outstanding and long-lived batteries were published. (The latest revisions of these tests, the Stanford Achievement Test, the Metropolitan Achievement Test, and the California Achievement Test, are among the most popular tests of the 1960s.) In addition to the mentioned batteries, many single-subject tests were published for the first time in the 1920s and 1930s. All of these tests would be classified as inadequately standardized if they were judged according to present-day standards. Nevertheless, in the relatively short period of years between World War I and World War II significant progress in testing techniques was made. It was also in these productive years that two additional kinds of tests came into general use: (1) diagnostic tests which identify a student's specific weaknesses in subjects such as arithmetic and reading and (2) practice tests which provide drill materials accompanied by performance norms.

All of the tests published in this period were characterized by the use of items requiring short and specific answers which could be scored in an objective and impersonal manner. Consequently, the instruments became known as objective-type tests.

The teacher-built tests of the 1920s and 1930s also began to feature objectively scored items. Soon thereafter, true-false, matching, multiple-choice, and completion forms of items practically replaced the use of essay questions in many classrooms. It should be noted that the adoption of objective testing in schools was stimulated by more than mere ease of scoring. The accumulating research evidence of that day indicated that the results of essay testing were highly unreliable. In fact, studies revealed that not only would an essay test frequently be assigned widely different scores by different teachers, but the same teacher often would fail to score a paper the same way on a second reading.[16] Faced with this evidence, classroom teachers as well as local and state officials took action to accelerate the use of objective tests.

Admittedly, objective testing as used by many teachers also had its weakness. It encouraged overemphasis upon the measurement of memorized factual information. Recognition of this fault gave impetus to the "evaluation movement" of the 1940s and 1950s. This movement correctly stressed the necessity of using evidence beyond objective measurement in the assessment of educational achievement. The residual effect upon testing in the 1960s has been that measurement instruments now give greater emphasis to the measurement of understanding, application, interpretation, and problem solving. Regular use of this type of measurement, as part of a broad program of evaluation, is now common in American schools.

Outstanding Standardized Achievement Tests

According to a comprehensive survey completed in 1961, about 1000 achievement tests were then in print and almost that number had ceased publication. The single-subject tests in print include: approximately 200 each in mathematics and English, about 100 each in social studies, science, and foreign languages, about 50 in business education, about 25 each in fine arts and physical education, and lesser numbers in home economics, driver education, and industrial arts. In addition, about 30 achievement batteries were being published for use in elementary and secondary schools.[17]

Outstanding among the tests most commonly used are seven batteries which measure "general educational development." Four of these bat-

---

[16] Robert L. Ebel and Dora E. Damrin, "Tests and Examinations," *Encyclopedia of Educational Research*, 3d ed. New York: The Macmillan Company, 1960, p. 1505.

[17] Buros, *Tests in Print*, p. xxvi.

teries, the Iowa Tests of Basic Skills, the Metropolitan Achievement Tests, the SRA Achievement Series, and the Stanford Achievement Test are designed for both elementary schools and junior high schools. A brief view of each follows.

IOWA TESTS OF BASIC SKILLS

Levels: Grades 3, 4, 5, 6, 7, 8–9 (all levels are in the same reusable booklet)

Administration: Four sessions totaling five hours and twenty-five minutes

Subtests: Vocabulary, reading comprehension, language skills (spelling, capitalization, punctuation, and usage), work-study skills (map reading, reading graphs and tables, knowledge and use of reference materials), arithmetic skills (arithmetic concepts, arithmetic problem solving)

Scores: Percentile ranks and grade equivalents for individuals and for schools are supplied for testing periods at the beginning of the school year, at the middle of the school year, and at the end of the school year.

Comment: This test has received extraordinary praise from measurement experts. Specifically, it has been commended for the technical excellence of the items, the comprehensiveness of the research upon which the test was based, and the high level of its curricular validity.[18] The test has also been praised for accomplishing its purpose, the measurement of basic skills (not information) commonly developed through school curricula. Negative comments have pointed out the lack of items to measure the basic skills of writing, speaking, listening, thinking critically, and using the scientific method.[19] The tests also lack common standardization with an intelligence test.

METROPOLITAN ACHIEVEMENT TESTS

Levels: Grades 1.5, 2, 3–4, 5–6, 7–9

Administration: Five sessions totaling four hours and forty-four minutes for level 7–9

Subtests: Word knowledge, reading, spelling, language (usage, punctuation and capitalization, parts of speech, grammar, kinds of sentences, dictionary skills, sources of information), arithmetic computation, arithmetic problem solving, arithmetic concepts, social studies information (geography, history, civics), social studies study skills (reading maps, and reading tables, charts, and graphs), science

Scores: Percentile ranks, grade equivalents, standard scores, and stanines

[18] Buros, *Mental Measurements Yearbook,* pp. 30–37.
[19] *Ibid.,* p. 31.

Comment: This battery tests knowledge as well as skills. The recognizable relationship of many of its items to the informational content of specific courses will be regarded as a strength by some and as a weakness by others. The wide variety of norms provided are based upon a standardization program which involved 550,000 students. The norms are coordinated with intelligence measurements on the Pintner General Ability Test.

SRA ACHIEVEMENT SERIES

Levels: Grades 1–2, 2–4, 4–6, 6–9
Administration: Three sessions totaling six hours and ten minutes for level 6–9
Subtests: Work-study skills (references, charts), reading (comprehension. vocabulary), language arts (capitalization and punctuation, usage, spelling), arithmetic (reasoning, concepts, computation)
Scores: Percentile ranks and grade equivalents for first semester and for second semester testing.
Comment: This battery has been applauded for its use of imaginative items based on situations of interests to students. It also has been commended for its liberal timing and its suitability for measurement of the above-average student. It has been severely criticized for inadequate measurement of below-average students and the consequent necessity for retesting with lower-level materials.[20] The battery does not provide coordination with an intelligence test.

STANFORD ACHIEVEMENT TEST

Levels: Grades 1.9–3.5, 3–4, 5–6, 7–9
Administration: Six sessions totaling four hours and twenty minutes for level 7–9
Subtests: Paragraph meaning, word meaning, spelling, language, arithmetic reasoning, arithmetic computation, social studies, science, study skills
Scores: Modal-age grade equivalents, total group grade equivalents, percentile ranks within modal-age grades, and standard scores
Comment: This battery has been applauded for use of modal-age norms, for its comprehensive standardization, and for its provision of many forms. On the other hand, the series has been criticized for alleged overemphasis upon miscellaneous and traditional knowledge and lack of emphasis upon problem solving, meanings, and applications.[21] The battery is not standardized in coordination with an intelligence test.

Two of the seven outstanding achievement batteries are designed to

[20] *Ibid.*, pp. 48–55.
[21] *Ibid.*, pp. 76–80.

provide a coordinated program of measurement for the elementary school and for the complete range of grades in secondary schools.

CALIFORNIA ACHIEVEMENT TESTS

Levels: Grades 1–2, 3–4.5, 4–6, 7–9, 9–14

Administration: Three hour sessions each for levels 7–9 and 9–14

Subtests: Reading vocabulary, reading comprehension, mathematics reasoning, mathematics fundamentals, mechanics of English, spelling. Each subtest, with the exception of the spelling test, is composed of either three or four separately scored parts.

Scores: Grade equivalents, percentile ranks, and expected grade placements

Comment: Critics have commended this battery for attractive organization, for extensive standardization, and for provision of separate norms for students at different levels of intelligence as measured by the California Test of Mental Maturity. At the same time, the battery has been criticized on the basis that extension of subtest classifications such as reading, arithmetic, and language skills from elementary grades to senior high school and junior college makes association of scores with actual course content difficult at the higher levels.[22]

SEQUENTIAL TESTS OF EDUCATIONAL PROGRESS (STEP)

Levels: Grades 4–6, 7–9, 10–12, 13–14

Administration: Each subtest, except the thirty-five-minute essay test, may be administered in one ninety-minute session or in two fifty-minute sessions. The total battery requires about ten hours.

Subtests: Reading, writing, social studies, science, mathematics, listening, essay

Scores: Percentile-rank bands and converted scores (norms are provided only for tests administered at the beginning of the school year)

Comment: This battery—more than any competitor—emphasizes the measurement of student ability to apply learned skills to the solution of novel problems. For this emphasis, it has received both praise and reprobation.[23] However, coordination of norms with those of the School and College Ability Test together with the use of percentile-band reporting should appreciably improve the validity of test score interpretation by teachers and parents.

One battery of tests designed for the secondary school only is particularly outstanding.

[22] *Ibid.*, pp. 7–8.
[23] *Ibid.*, pp. 62–75.

THE IOWA TESTS OF EDUCATIONAL DEVELOPMENT

Levels: Grades 9–13
Administration: Nine hours for the regular form, and six hours for the shorter version
Subtests: Understanding of basic social concepts, general background in the natural sciences, correctness and appropriateness of expression, ability to do quantitative thinking, ability to interpret reading materials in the social studies, ability to interpret reading materials in the natural sciences, ability to interpret literary materials, general vocabulary, uses of sources of information
Scores: Percentile ranks and standard scores
Comment: This battery has been praised for its careful standardization, its sound construction, and for the high reliability with which it measures the attainment of important educational objectives sought in common by high schools. The test, however, does not provide separate norms for students at differing levels of intelligence.

Selection of Standardized Tests

A teacher wishing to select a battery subtest, a practice test, a diagnostic test, or a year-end test for use in a particular class can easily determine what tests are published in the subject by using *Tests in Print*.[24] His next step might well be use of the *Mental Measurements Yearbooks* to learn what experts think of each test's weaknesses and strength.[25] He then could order specimen sets of the tests which appear to be most promising. Such materials are frequently available from the publisher at nominal cost. Finally, the teacher could become thoroughly acquainted with the standardized test by actually taking the test, scoring it, and using the test manual to help him interpret the results.

In selecting a test, teachers frequently are aided by department heads or counselors. Teachers, however, shoulder the primary responsibility alone when it comes to interpretation of the results of standardized tests, including the results of test batteries such as those briefly reviewed above.

Graphical Representation of Test Results

The results of testing programs involving use of batteries of standardized tests often are reported to teachers in the form of graphs or profiles that picture a student's standing in each of the tested areas. Consequently, it is highly important that teachers learn to read the various types of profiles with ease.

[24] Buros, *Tests in Print*, pp. 1–238.
[25] Buros, *Mental Measurements Yearbook*, pp. 324–870.

Profiles are two-dimensional graphs constructed so that the scale of scores is along one axis and each test is listed at an assigned position along the other. In the irregular-line type of profile, points representing the student's obtained scores are plotted and connected by straight lines. The lines themselves have no meaning in the graphical sense. They merely serve to guide the reader's eye from one test score to another.

Carol Kramer's profile of percentile scores on the Iowa Test of Educational Development (see Figure 18-5) reveals that she has scored highest in correctness of expression and in the use of sources of information. Her lowest scores are in social studies background and in the reading of literature. This profile places the scale of scores along the vertical axis with lowest scores at the bottom and highest scores at the top.

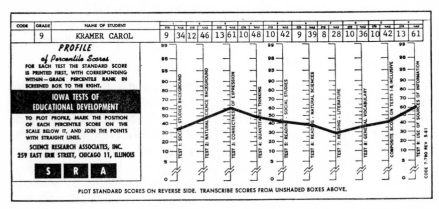

Fig. 18-5 *Profile of percentile scores on the Iowa Tests of Educational Development*
Copyright 1961. Reprinted by permission of Science Research Associates, Inc.

In Figure 18-6, the individual profile chart of Mary Ashland's scores on the Metropolitan Achievement Tests, the scale of scores is on the horizontal axis. Low scores are on the left and higher scores are on the right. It should be noted carefully that the sample interpretation accompanying Mary Ashland's profile correctly gives little or no attention to the minor fluctuations in the line representing the scores. For example, Mary scored below her Pintner intelligence measurement in three tested skills, but in only one case (study skills in social studies) is it presumed that the discrepancy is serious. The use of dashes instead of a solid line to connect scores on the subtests measuring the mechanics of language emphasizes the fact that these scores are less reliable than the total language score.

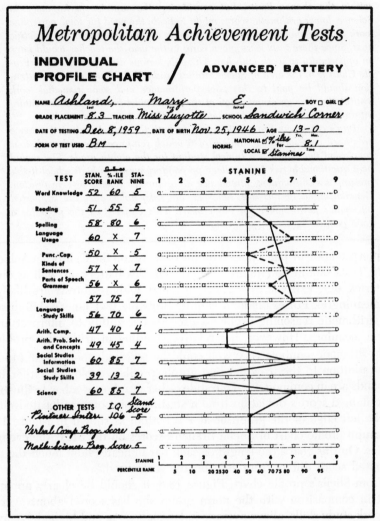

Fig. 18-6 Individual profile chart of stanine scores on the Metropolitan Achievement Tests

Ashland, Mary E. *Mary's age is 13 years and 0 months which makes her about 6 months younger than the median age of children in the early months of the eighth grade. Her Pintner Intermediate IQ is 106 and the mental ability stanine corresponding to the median standard score is 5. Word Knowledge and Reading, the two Metropolitan tests correlating most highly with intelligence, are average. Mary's skills in the mechanics of language seem well developed. The stanines of 4 in the arithmetic area are*

(Continued on page 540)

within the chance limits, but considering the superior performance in Science, lower arithmetic scores might indicate the need for some corrective work if Mary should decide to enter some occupation within the scientific area. Since these tests were given early in the year the teacher would have an opportunity to work with her. The only serious discrepancy on the Profile Chart is in the area of Social Studies Study Skills. Certainly some attention should be paid to this poor performance and some remedial work instituted unless an examination of the test booklet or other supplementary information indicates that for some reason this is not a valid result.

Mary's composite prognostic scores in both the verbal and math-science area have corresponding stanines of 5 which reinforces the rather obvious conclusion that Mary is a typical student for the eighth grade. She would be a questionable risk for a college preparatory course in high school if this presupposes subsequent attendance in a typical liberal arts institution. Generalizations of this sort, however, are risky unless they are supported by similar performance for other years. This emphasizes the need for a good cumulative testing program.

Interpretation of Janet James' profile of scores on the California Achievement Tests should be equally cautious. On this battery, as well as on all batteries, only extreme differences in scores within subtests are likely to be meaningful. For example, it is quite probable that Janet's skill in solving arithmetic reasoning problems exceeds her ability to interpret arithmetic meanings. However, her relative standing in arithmetic problems and arithmetic symbols very well could be reversed upon retest (18–7).

In addition to the irregular-line graph, profiles employing either bars or bands are in common use. One style of bar graph uses a bar to illustrate an obtained score's deviation from a starting point of zero located either at the left edge of the graph or at the bottom as shown in Figure 18-8, the pupil profile chart of Sheila Branch's scores on the SRA Achievement Series. On this chart, the length of each bar indicates how much the represented score differs from zero on the scale used.

From Sheila's profile chart, Figure 18-8, it should be clearly apparent that in comparison with the norm group she has scored about average in work-study skills, above average in language arts, and high above average in arithmetic. Her weak points are in reading comprehension and vocabulary. The teacher probably would be justified in planning special reading experiences for Sheila. However, in the absence of an intelligence measurement which has been standardized on the same norm group, it is impossible to form any sound hypotheses about whether or not Sheila's performance in any of the measured skills represents satisfactory achievement. For example, if Sheila's intelligence happened to be near the 99th percentile in comparison with the norm group used on the SRA Achievement Series, then her performance in at least three of the four skill areas might justify further study by the teacher.

Fig. 18-7 *Diagnostic profile of grade placement scores on the California Achievement Tests*

Copyright 1963. **Used by permission of the California Test Bureau.**

Several weeks ago you took some interesting tests called the SRA Achievement Series. These tests show how well you are doing in school by comparing your scores with those of other boys and girls all over the country.
The types of school work measured by each test are described on the back
of this page. When you look at your score for each test, turn this page over
and read about the test.

Your teacher will help you draw a line showing how you scored on each
of the tests. Look at your line. Is it straight and right next to the center
line? If it is, then you have scored about the same as the average pupil in
your grade in the United States. Most probably, though, it is not straight,
but has some peaks and valleys. The high points show where you are doing
your best work, and the low points show where you are weakest. The
numbers at the side of the chart show how much above or below the
average each score is. For example, if one of your scores is opposite the
number 70, that means that you did better on that test than 70 percent of
the boys and girls who took the tests. In other words, in every group of
100 pupils that took the tests, you scored better than 70 of them. If one of
your scores is 45, then you scored better than 45 of the 100 pupils.

Fig. 18-8   Pupil profile chart of percentile scores on the SRA Achievement Series

How to Use the SRA Achievement Series, 1961, p. 19. Reprinted by permission of Science Research Associates, Inc. and San Diego State College Photograph Audio-Visual Services.

Three additional points should be noted in relation to Sheila's profile:

1. Because percentile ranks do not represent equal raw score units throughout a scale, the numbers along the vertical percentile scales at the left- and right-hand edges of the chart are not equally spaced. They have been adjusted to more nearly represent the position each percentile would have along the base line of a normal distribution of raw scores. When an adjusted scale is not used, teachers must be careful to remember that percentile differences near the middle of the range (near 50) represent much smaller differences in test score than are represented by percentile differences of equal size near either extreme of the scale. In the case of Sheila, the work-study skills scores of the 55th percentile in references and the 45th percentile in charts are correctly separated by less vertical distance than separates her percentile scores of 80 in arithmetic reasoning and 90 in arithmetic concepts. Without adjusted-normal charts these discrepancies in percentile rank scales would be difficult to visualize.

2. Percentile rank scores usually cannot be directly averaged. (When percentile ranks of composite scores are desired, each percentile should be reconverted to its raw score. The raw scores of each individual are then added and the totals are placed in a distribution from which the percentile of each composite raw score can be determined directly.) This principle can be verified in Sheila's case. Her percentile rank on the composite of all scores on the test is correctly reported as 62 even though the arithmetic average of her ten separate percentile scores would be 58.3.

3. Profiles of scores on achievement batteries sometimes are prepared by individual students under the supervision of their teacher. The directions at the bottom of Sheila's profile chart were placed there to help her prepare a broken-line graph which, of course, could be used alone or be superimposed on the bar graph illustrated.

A second style of bar graph is shown in Sherrell Murphy's individual profile of scores on the Metropolitan Achievement Test (Figure 18-9). This graph employs a bar to reveal the extent of an obtained score's deviation from the mean score of the norm group. Each bar starts at the mean and ends at the score represented. Graphs of this type are particularly useful to portray a student's performance in comparison with the average performance of his grade or age.

Likewise, when the picture desirec. is a comparison of a student's performance with his measured potential, each bar is started at the level of the student's intelligence score. Furthermore, when an error allowance of at least one stanine on each side of Sherrell's intelligence stanine of 8 is made, the teacher can analyze Sherrell's profile somewhat as follows:

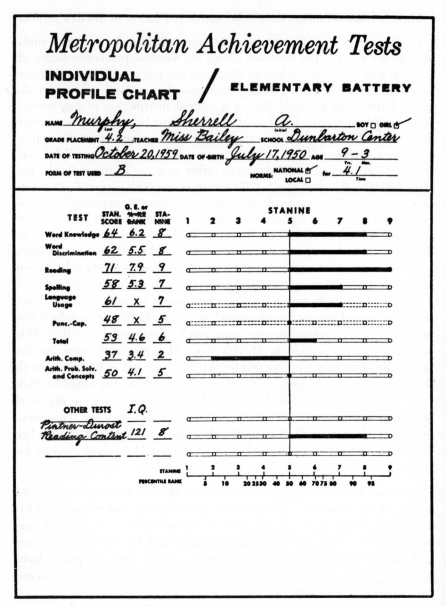

Fig. 18-9   *Individual profile chart of stanine scores on the Metropolitan Achievement Tests*

Except for Punctuation and Capitalization and the two arithmetic tests, deviation from expected performance is well within chance limits, if one assumes that Sherrell's capacity lies somewhere between a 7 and an 8. It would appear to be a good working hypothesis that Sherrell needs to do some additional work in the punctuation and capitalization area. Understanding the pupil's work may be facilitated by carefully examining her paper for clues as to possible reasons for the poor performance.

It would seem to be quite clear that Sherrell is a handicapped child in the area of arithmetic. The very low stanine of 2 in Arithmetic Computation suggests that the difficulty lies in her failure to master fundamentals. Her performance is just average in Arithmetic Problem Solving. Since this test involves more reasoning ability, it is logical for her stanine to be higher here than in Computation. One cannot tell from the profile alone the nature of her difficulty, but an alert teacher would consider this to be a danger signal calling for careful study.[26]

With the help of a profile, a teacher quickly can identify a student's relative strengths and weaknesses. However, the interpretation of profiles is not quite as simple as it first appears to be. Since the graphs are based on tests, each of which involves error, comparisons of the relationship between scores on any two tests must take into consideration both sources of error. For example, is Sheila's (Figure 18-8) percentile rank of 65 in spelling reliably superior to her grammatical-usage score of 55? How frequently do students equal in these abilities make test scores that are ten or more percentile points apart? To answer these important questions, one must have knowledge of the standard errors involved. Usually these figures must be searched for in a test manual or tediously computed. However, the band type of profile shown in Figure 18-10 portrays error information as an integral part of the profile. This practice must be highly recommended.

Band profiles, prepared by the test publisher or by the classroom teacher, re-emphasize the fact that a test score is only an estimate of the range of scores within which the student's true score may be expected to fall. When two bands overlap, it is not possible to say that the tested student is better in one measured subject than in the other.

Technically described, each band is centered at the obtained score and extends one standard error on each side of that point. Consequently, the chances are only about 68 in 100 that the true score lies within the band. Therefore, it should be recognized that there remain about 16 chances in 100 that the band is too low, and 16 chances in 100 that the band is too high, to include the true score. It may be interesting to note that if the

STEP STUDENT PROFILE
SEQUENTIAL TESTS OF EDUCATIONAL PROGRESS

Fig. 18-10 Profile of percentile-band results based on the Sequential Tests of Educational Progress

band were doubled in length, the chances that it would then encompass the true score would be increased to approximately 96 in 100.

From Figure 18-10 it can be concluded with high confidence that in comparison with the norm group the student's ability is considerably above average in listening, science, and mathematics; slightly above average in reading; and average or below in writing. More specifically, the reading percentile band indicates that the chances are about 68 in 100 that the student's true percentile rank in reading lies between 54 and 71. Comparing the various ratings among themselves, a teacher could confidently make conclusions such as: "The student's performances in mathematics and in science exceed his performances in social studies and writing; whereas, his scores in mathematics and science are not significantly different from each other." Clearly, this type of profile offers the teacher a great deal of information.

In addition to their use to portray a student's standing on a single administration of a battery of tests, profiles are also used to picture a student's growth pattern in grade equivalent scores or converted scores as measured by periodic testing. Still another use of profiles involves the graphing of class averages. This procedure enables a teacher to study the relative strengths and weaknesses of different classes and to trace class growth from one testing to another. When this is done, class norms— not norms for individuals—should be used. Furthermore, it is incorrect to use percentile scores as averages or as the basis for growth comparisons. Of course, in these uses and in all uses of profiles, teachers must keep in mind that tests on the same profile must be recorded on the same scale of units, and to be strictly comparable, all tests on the same profile must be standardized on the same norm group.

From the preparation and study of profiles, teachers undoubtedly learn a great deal to help their teaching. However, this task is only part of the job which prepares them to make the best use of standardized measures.

BASIC CONSIDERATIONS IN THE INTERPRETATION OF STANDARDIZED TESTS

Before teachers can adequately interpret the results of standardized tests, they must answer several key questions:

1. With respect to factors which might affect test scores, does the locally tested group differ from the sample group upon which the test was standardized? (Local norms may be necessary.)
2. To what extent does the test usually accomplish the task for which it was intended? Is it valid for your purposes?

3. How accurately does the test measure? What is its reliability and standard error of measurement?

Information pertaining to these questions usually is contained in manuals provided by test publishers.

Adequacy of Norms

In their study of the first question, teachers must realize that standardized tests are intended for use only by individuals and groups similar to those represented in the norm group. For example, achievement test results of a class or school can be expected to differ from national norms when the local group and the norm group differ with respect to such factors as:

1. Intelligence
2. Instructional facilities
3. School curriculum
4. Admission and promotion policies
5. Socioeconomic level and emotional tone of the students' homes
6. Student study habits, student health, and student attitude toward testing and toward school

Neither the adequacy of instruction nor the adequacy of student achievement can be judged fairly unless the norm group and the tested group are known to be similar. Unfortunately, very few test manuals provide sufficient detailed information concerning norm groups. Without such information, interpretation of test results should be limited to description of student status in relation to the norm group; whether or not that status is as high as it should be remains unknown. For example, teachers have little cause for elation when their superior-ability students merely exceed the norms for groups of mixed ability. Likewise, no one should be critical of a teacher merely because his students of inferior ability score below the achievement norm of higher-ability students.

Test Validity

Before they attempt to interpret the scores of a test, teachers should examine evidence concerning the validity of the test. This term has been defined as the measure of the extent to which a test does what it is intended to do. Consequently, tests which have different purposes require different kinds of validating evidence. Such evidence usually is available in test manuals.

To judge the validity of an achievement test, teachers should seek evidence which shows how well the test samples the content of the course to be measured. This type of evidence establishes a test's *content validity.* Evidence which reveals how well the results of a given test agree with other immediate measures of the same thing establishes a test's *concurrent validity*, and evidence which shows how well a test predicts later performance of those tested establishes a test's *predictive validity*.

Content validity is of primary importance for tests used to evaluate achievement and instruction, while concurrent validity and predictive validity are of greatest importance when tests are used for the ordinary administrative and guidance purposes.

Teachers should realize that the single most important characteristic of any test is its validity. Until evidence concerning the validity of a test is established, student scores obtained on the test can have little, if any, meaning.

Standard Error of Measurement

Teachers will fail to interpret tests adequately unless they recognize that a single test score is merely a sample measurement which almost always contains considerable error. Experienced teachers know that when a student is tested more than once with the same test or with equivalent tests, he seldom, if ever, makes the same score twice in succession. Furthermore, it is known that if he were to be retested an unlimited number of times, the resulting scores would form a normal distribution called the sampling distribution of his scores. The mean of a sampling distribution is defined as a *true score*. The standard deviation of the sampling distribution is a measure of the variability of the student's scores and is defined as the *standard error* of his scores. Different individuals are likely to have somewhat different distributions. Obviously, unlimited retesting of individuals is not a feasible procedure, so test publishers substitute appropriate statistical analyses of their standardization data to produce sound estimates of the average standard error involved in measurements made with their tests. This information, termed the standard error of measurement of the test, is made available in test manuals and sometimes is superimposed upon graphical reports of test results. In any event, teachers must be able to associate standard errors of measurement with normal curve data if they are to understand the predictable variability of test scores.

Study of Figure 18-11 will reveal that roughly 68 percent of measures made can be expected to fall within the range of ±1 standard error of the true score, while the remaining 32 percent can be expected to fall above and below that range. Likewise, roughly 96 percent of measures made by a test can be expected to fall within a range of the true score ±2 standard errors, while the remaining 4 percent can be expected to fall outside that range. When applied to the most accurate intelligence tests currently in use (S.E. equals 5 IQ points), these figures reveal that 68 percent of such IQ's are likely to be within ±5 points of the true IQ, while 32 percent will deviate more than 5 points from the true IQ; 96 percent are likely to fall within a range of ±10 points of the true IQ, and roughly 4 percent are likely to be more than 10 points in error. Recognizing these facts, teachers will not be surprised to find that a student's scores fluctuate from one administration of a test to another. Any single obtained score can be accepted only as a fairly rough estimate of the level at which the student may be expected to perform in repeated measurements by the given test.

Knowledge of the standard error of measurement is also essential whenever a teacher wishes to interpret the relationship of scores made on two

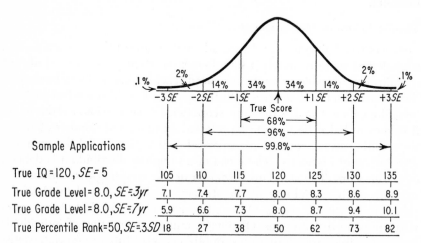

Fig. 18-11 *The standard error of measurement: an estimate of the variability of test scores that would be obtained in repeated measurement of the same individual*

administrations of the same test or of different tests. In practice this problem appears in situations like the following:

Tommy has scored at a grade level of 8.3 on a test of arithmetic and at a grade level of 8.7 on a test of reading. Is his reading skill really better than his skill in arithmetic? What is the likelihood that a difference as large as 0.4 could represent a chance fluctuation of scores due to errors of measurement rather than a difference in true scores in arithmetic and reading?

Assuming that the two tests were standardized on the same sample so that the scaling is consistent, and further assuming that the standard error of the difference in the two test scores is 0.5, then, by applying the standards listed below, the teacher should conclude that the measured difference is too small to be accepted as proof of a difference in true scores.

Tommy's score in reading would have to exceed this score in arithmetic by 2 times 0.5 (a full year), before it would be acceptable to conclude that he is really more skilled in one subject than in the other (and even then, the conclusion would be incorrect about one time in twenty).

The following standards are usually followed when differences in test scores are being interpreted:

1. The difference between two measurements is assumed to be highly reliable when the difference exceeds three times the standard error involved. The chances then are more than 100 to 1 in favor of the existence of a difference in true scores.

2. The difference between two measurements is assumed to be fairly reliable when the difference exceeds twice the standard error involved. The chances then are about 19 to 1 in favor of the existence of a difference in true scores.

3. The difference between two measurements is assumed to be of questionable reliability when it is more than the standard error but less than twice that amount. The chances then are at least 2 to 1 in favor of the existence of a difference in true scores.

4. The difference between two scores is assumed to be unreliable when it is less than the standard error involved. The chances then are less than 2 to 1 in favor of the existence of a difference in true scores.

Test Reliability

The accuracy with which a test measures is also expressed as a reliability coefficient in decimal form ranging from .00 to 1.00. A reliability coefficient of 1.00 indicates perfect consistency in individuals' scores in a test-retest situation. If such a test could be constructed, its standard error of measurement would be zero. A reliability coefficient of zero, on the other hand, indicates a complete lack of consistency in measurement. An individual upon retest might score at any point within the range of scores produced by the test. Such a test would be useless.

In practice, it is generally considered that a test must have a reliability of at least .80 before it can be accepted as a satisfactory measure of individual performance—and higher reliability is much to be desired.

Coefficients of reliability must be employed with a degree of caution, however, as they can be determined by a variety of procedures, each designed to serve a particular purpose and each yielding a slightly different coefficient. The size of reliability coefficients also varies somewhat according to the ability level and variability of the groups upon which they are based. Therefore, classroom teachers should recognize that the relative accuracy of measurement of two tests can be judged accurately on the basis of reliability coefficients only when the coefficients have been computed by application of the same formula to data obtained from measurement of comparable groups. Only then can one be reasonably certain that the test having the higher reliability coefficient will measure with the greater accuracy.

Interpretation of Age and Grade Norms

Age and grade norms are among the easiest norms to understand. The concept involved is simple, but when applied at the secondary school level, age and grade norms have severe limitations.

1. Many student characteristics such as scores on mental tests, computational ability, and physical height show variable and decreasing annual change as students progress through high school. Some characteristics show no measurable increase with age beyond the early teens, and a few reveal a decrease in average test performance. For example, in many schools United States history is offered in the eighth grade and again in the eleventh grade. American history norms, then, would be expected to increase at those grade levels and remain fairly stable or decrease for students not taking the subject.

2. Age and grade norms frequently are inadequate to indicate properly the standing of high- or low-scoring pupils. For instance, tests intended for high school use will be standardized on grades nine through twelve. In an average school, half of the twelfth graders would be expected to score higher than the twelfth-grade norm. If the twelfth-grade norm is 73 points on a particular test, what is the standing of a student who scores 80 points? Test publishers attempt to answer this question, if they answer it at all, by extrapolating their standardization data so as to estimate what groups beyond their sample would score if the assumptions accepted by the publishers were true. Thus, the test publisher might assume that the annual increment beyond grade twelve would be 3.5 points and assign the score of 80 a grade norm of 14, even though no one beyond grade twelve had been tested in the standardization sample. To be specific, the Iowa Tests of Basic Skills, intended for grades three through nine, provide approximate grade equivalent scores for the range 1.0 to 12.5 by extrapolation beyond the measured sample's range of 3.1 to 8.1.

It should be noted that extrapolation upward from one school level to another is particularly subject to misinterpretation. For instance, a student, teacher, or parent might conclude that an eighth-grade student who scored at the eleventh-grade norm in reading on a junior high school test would be able to read eleventh-grade material as well as the average eleventh grader. Such a conclusion would be justified only when the standardization sample included eleventh graders and when the test was composed of content appropriate to that grade level. The eleventh-grade norm on a test designed for the seventh, eighth, and ninth graders usually is an extrapolated score, and at best, it is only the average score of eleventh graders on seventh-, eighth-, and ninth-grade material. An eleventh-grade norm earned on a test intended for junior high schools does not indicate that the junior high school student could perform at average eleventh-grade level on a test designed for use in senior high school. The score merely indicates that the junior high school student has done a particularly good job in the junior high school content covered by the test.

Age norms, in particular, are quite likely to be inaccurate for ages at both extremes of an established range since age norms are frequently determined by administering tests to grade levels and then making separate distributions of scores for each age represented. For example, when a test is standardized on seventh, eighth, and ninth grades, the modal (most common) age at each grade is 12, 13, and 14 respectively. However, some of the most brilliant 14-year-olds will have been accelerated into grades beyond the sample, and the slower 12-year-olds will not yet have reached seventh grade. Thus, the 14-year age norm would be too low and the 12-year age norm would be too high to be truly representative of all students of those ages.

3. Grade norms and age norms are an inadequate basis for comparison of the relative standing of students in schools following admission and promotion policies different from those predominant in the standardization sample. Students who are overage or underage for their grade frequently make average scores different from those made by the age group which is at age for a given grade. In recognition of this problem at least one test publisher reports separate grade norms for students who are at the age most typical for a given grade. These norms are called modal-age grade norms. When modal-age grade norms are not available it is important to know the age composition of the grades in the standardizing sample.

4. Probably the most serious weakness in age and grade norms is their susceptibility to misinterpretation as standards to be achieved by all students of a given age or grade. Half of an average class should be expected to exceed the established norm. Likewise, in an average class, half of the pupils can be expected to score lower than the norm for their age or grade. Ordinarily, age norms and grade norms are midpoints of distributions of typical groups. They can be used as standards only for average students seeking average goals in an average environment.

Interpretation of Percentile Scores

Percentile scores generally are considered to be an improvement over age and grade norms since they are free from errors of extrapolation and are not so likely to be misused as single standards. They provide 100 reference points for an age or grade group rather than a single point. However, percentile scores must also be interpreted with caution because they are subject to the same errors of norm group sampling which affect the validity of age and grade norms and in addition they have certain weaknesses due to the fact that they are directly related to numbers of persons below given points in a distribution and not directly related to raw scores.

1. Percentile scores tend to exaggerate differences in raw scores near the middle of the range and to reduce relative differences of raw scores near the extremes. This aberration is brought about by the fact that on most measures norm groups tend to cluster near the middle of the range of scores and scatter out near the extremes. This fact brings about a serious nonlinear relationship between raw scores and percentile rank equivalents. Consequently, comparisons of the percentile ranks of students are likely to be quite different from comparisons of their equivalent raw scores. For example, a 3-point difference in raw score in the middle of the range on the language segment of the SRA Tests of Educational Ability yields a percentile rank difference of 20 points, while a 3-point difference in raw score near the top of the same scale yields a percentile rank difference of only 3 or 4 points. On practically all tests, individuals who differ as much as 15 or 20 percentile points in the middle range (from about a percentile rank of 35 to a percentile rank of 65) are more alike in raw score than individuals who are only 5 or 10 percentile points apart in either the lower or upper parts of the percentile range.

2. The standard error of percentiles near the middle of the range is much larger than the standard error at the extremes. For example, the manual for the California Achievement Tests gives a standard error of nine months for the eleventh-grade spelling norms. Translated to the percentile scale, this standard error becomes about 15 percentile points for true scores near the 50th percentile, and reduces to a standard error of about 5 percentile points for true scores around the 5th and 95th percentiles. Thus, obtained percentile scores on that test (and on many other tests) will be 15 or more points in error for about one third of the large group of students who in true measurement would score about average for their grade. For the smaller number of students who in true measurement would rate either very low or very high, the California test yields percentile scores in spelling which are 15 or more points in error

only about one or two times in 100. Accordingly, teachers must recognize that on all standardized tests, percentile scores near 50 frequently are in error as much as 10 or 15 points, while errors of that magnitude are much less frequent in high and low percentile scores.

3. Percentiles cannot be averaged directly. A student who has percentile ranks of 60 on half of the tests in a battery and percentile ranks of 80 on each of the remaining tests is not likely to have a percentile rank of 70 on the total battery. When averages or totals of several percentile scores are desired, the percentiles should first be transformed to raw scores or to other scores having an arithmetic base.

4. Percentile scores are meaningless without direct reference to the group upon which they are based. A single raw score total on a test might be described truthfully as the 50th percentile for high school seniors as well as the 90th percentile for students in a lower grade. Consequently, the base group should be named whenever percentile norms are discussed.

THE ETHICS OF STANDARDIZED ACHIEVEMENT TESTING

Many teachers engaged in standardized achievement testing are perplexed by questions of ethics such as: What can a teacher properly do to prepare students for a standardized achievement test? Is it permissible to excuse inferior students from the tests? What legitimate use can be made of test scores and item analyses? Definitive responses to many such questions await the study of authorities. However, valuable, but tentative, answers to some of the important questions have been suggested in a periodical article[27] which is abstracted below.

1. When teachers prepare students for a standardized achievement test:

It is acceptable and proper to explain to students something about the purposes and general form of the test. Such a discussion would not include any references to the specific content of the test. It might properly cover such matters as the various types of objective questions; the fact that some items will be easy and some will be very difficult; the fact that students should not worry if they cannot answer every question; the importance of working rapidly without racing; and the advisability of making intelligent guesses.

It is acceptable and proper to familiarize students with the mechanics of a standardized achievement test through the use of practice

[27] Anton Thompson, "Tentative Guidelines for Proper and Improper Practices with Standardized Achievement Tests," *California Journal of Educational Research*, vol. 9, no. 4 (September 1958), pp. 159–166.

exercises. These exercises should teach students how to mark their answers to the various types of questions but should not offer any clues as to the content of the approaching test.

It is acceptable and proper in giving a machine-scored test to pass around a sample, well-marked answer sheet before the test is begun, and to point out the possibility that the students will lower their test scores if they do not mark their answer sheets in the same way.

It is acceptable and proper to try to bring about optimum motivation of the students for the taking of a standardized test. This means encouraging students to do as well as they can. It does not mean that pupils are to be threatened or made extremely tense and anxious.

It is *not* acceptable and proper for a teacher to coach students on the subject matter of a specific standardized test. Such coaching will invalidate the scores earned by the students. Not only will such scores have no value, they may actually do the student harm if they are recorded and used for guidance or instructional purposes. Testing authorities are in complete agreement that teachers and students should take standardized tests without such preparation.

It is *not* acceptable and proper to use the report of a previous item analysis to prepare other students for that test.

It is *not* acceptable and proper to use a particular standardized test as a model for the construction of an elaborate set of drill exercises that parallel the content and format of that test.

It is *not* acceptable and proper to give one form of a standardized test a few days or weeks before a second form of the test is to be given as a district-wide or school-wide survey.

It is *not* acceptable and proper to make individual students overanxious and tense concerning the outcome of a standardized achievement test, nor to set impossible goals for a class.

It is *not* acceptable and proper to exclude a regular student from taking a district-wide survey on the grounds that his teacher thinks the student is a poor learner or because the student is said to become confused when he takes a test. Presumably the norm group also included some persons who were dull and some who hated to take tests.

It is *not* acceptable and proper to neglect in any way the instruction of any students in order to concentrate more effort on instruction to raise the scores of other students.

2. During the administration of a standardized test:

It is *not* acceptable to alter the directions or time limits. The standard conditions prescribed for the test must be followed exactly.

It is *not* acceptable and proper, after a test is under way, to give students any help beyond that allowed by the test manual. For most tests, this means that the tester cannot help a student who raises his hand to ask the meaning of a particular test question. Although the testers are usually given some leeway in answering questions not dealing with the content of the test, it is a safe rule to err on the side of explaining too little rather than too much.

It is *not* acceptable and proper for the administrator of a standardized test to give special assistance to the poor readers in a class by reading test items aloud. This holds true even though the test is an arithmetic test and a teacher is confident that certain students who could not otherwise do so could correctly solve a test exercise if it were just read aloud to them. If a test was normed without reading items aloud to the students in the standardization sample, then the test must be given the same way if students' scores are to be interpreted through use of the publisher's norms.

3. Shortly after a standardized test has been given:

It is acceptable and proper to make use of the results of an item analysis as a basis for remedial work with the students.

It is acceptable and proper for a teacher to return a student's scored test booklet or answer sheet to the student for use in class discussion or in individual conference. The booklets or answer sheets should not be taken from the classroom, since they may then fall into the hands of others who will be taking the same test. The usual purposes of returning a scored booklet or answer sheet are (1) to inform the students concerning their individual results on the test and (2) to call attention of the class to any group weaknesses in learning revealed by the teacher's study of the frequency of errors on each test item— weaknesses that may suggest a need for subsequent reteaching and relearning.

4. With respect to the long-term effects of a standardized test:

It is *not* acceptable and proper for a teacher to make a collection of various standardized tests for the purpose of using items from them in his own tests.

It is *not* acceptable and proper for a teacher to develop instructional materials which include specific items from a standardized test even though the materials also include other content not taken directly from a test. Once test items have been lifted out of a test and used as instructional material, the value of that test as a standardized measuring instrument has been destroyed.

It is *not* acceptable and proper to use a standardized achievement test as an abbreviated course of study. A standardized test is merely a sampling of many learnings which should be in a complete course of study. It is not intended that the test content influence the teaching emphasis of any teacher. For example, if a course of study in a certain district recommends that one third of an English course be given to the study of American literature, a teacher of the course should not alter his attention to that literature merely because he knows that the standardized test used does not devote one third of its items to the coverage of American literature.

It is acceptable and proper for a teacher whose course of study recommends the development of a given learning to continue to teach the recommended material even though he knows that the standardized test used contains a specific question relating to that particular learning. Knowledge of the general content of an approaching test does not require the teacher to go out of his way to avoid any reference to the learnings in the test. The real criterion of propriety is whether the teacher omits learnings because they are not in a given test, whether he includes materials not in the course of study because they cover items that are in a given test, and also whether he consciously gives undue attention to particular learnings in the course of study because he knows they are in a given test.

Teachers should note that the above suggestions refer to the administration and use of achievement tests only. Tests of intelligence, special aptitude, and personality are administered according to somewhat different sets of regulations. Fortunately, these tests usually are administered under the direct supervision of a psychometrist or counselor. To prepare teachers for that service is not included among the purposes of this textbook.

A brief history of the development of intelligence and achievement tests and an introduction to selected instruments of each type has been sketched in this chapter. The principal concern has been that of preparing beginning teachers to understand the test scores and profiles they will use in the classroom.[28] To that end examples of correct profile interpretation have been included together with discussion of the pitfalls to avoid

[28] Another facet of test score interpretation—communication of scores to parents—is discussed in Chapter 17.

in the interpretation of norms. Also it has been pointed out that among the hundreds of standardized tests published for school use, there are likely to be several specifically designed for the subjects taught by each teacher. To use these instruments intelligently and ethically in the improvement of instruction is both the responsibility and the privilege of the teacher of today.

Selected References

1. Ahmann, J. Stanley, and Marvin D. Glock, *Evaluating Pupil Growth*. Boston: Allyn and Bacon, Inc., a subsidiary of Prentice-Hall, 1959. Chapters 12, 15, 16.
2. American Educational Research Association, *Encyclopedia of Educational Research*, 3d ed., Charles W. Harris, ed. New York: The Macmillan Company, 1960, pp. 807–816, 1510–1514.
3. Anastasi, Anne, *Psychological Testing*, 2d ed. New York: The Macmillan Company, 1961. Chapters 4–6.
4. Buros, Oscar K., ed., *The Fifth Mental Measurements Yearbook*. Highland Park, N. J.: The Gryphon Press, 1959.
5. Cronbach, Lee J., *Essentials of Psychological Testing*, 2d ed. New York: Harper & Row, Publishers, 1960. Chapters 1–6.
6. Garrett, Henry E., *Testing for Teachers*. New York: American Book Company, 1959. Chapters 1, 2, 5.
7. National Council on Measurement Used in Education, *The 15th Yearbook*. Ames, Iowa: National Council on Measurements Used in Education, 1958.
8. Noll, Victor H., *Introduction to Educational Measurement*. Boston: Houghton Mifflin Company, 1957. Chapters 3, 4, 6, 9.
9. Remmers, H. H., N. L. Gage, and J. Francis Rummel, *A Practical Introduction to Measurement and Evaluation*. New York: Harper & Row, Publishers, 1960. Chapters 2–6.
10. Schwartz, Alfred, and Stuart C. Tiedeman, *Evaluating Student Progress*. New York: David McKay Company, Inc., 1957. Chapters 13–16.
11. Thorndike, Robert L., and Elizabeth Hagen, *Measurement and Evaluation in Psychology and Education*, 2d ed. New York: John Wiley & Sons, Inc., 1961. Chapters 6–8, 11.

PART SEVEN

Becoming a
Professional Person

CHAPTER 19

Advancement in the profession

THE TEACHER AS A MEMBER OF THE PROFESSION

This is the true joy in life, the being used for a purpose recognized by yourself as a mighty one. . . . — *George Bernard Shaw*

Teaching is an old and honored profession. Teachers should be proud of their profession, not pompous nor vain, not meek nor spiritless, but individuals with confidence and self-esteem. It was not many years ago that some teachers were reluctant to admit their occupation. Each year sees the teaching profession growing in status, prestige, and recognition.

Anyone who becomes a teacher can be assured of a life's work that will be challenging and rewarding. The noted author James Hilton[1] once wrote that prejudice, greed, and ignorance are eternal. He wrote that if he had a child who wished to enter the teaching profession he would bid him Godspeed. The elimination of ignorance is a kind of vigilant and courageous war and, unlike most wars, some results can be seen in one's lifetime.

Teaching is an appealing but not a glamorous profession. It is an adventure worthy of a lifetime devotion. Teaching is not an easy career; it is more difficult than most; it calls for patience and courage; it offers a challenge to the best mind. But the rewards are satisfying.

Before 1940, school enrollments remained relatively constant; increases were gradual and predictable. Since 1940, enrollments have risen sharply. It is estimated that this condition will continue at least through 1970. The decade of the 1960s will be one of continuing high enrollments in schools. At this time from 1,000,000 to 1,250,000 new pupils start to school each year. From 1950 to 1960 the general population increase was 18.5 percent, whereas the school-age increase was 42.9 percent.[2]

[1] James Hilton, "Who Will Lead?" *This Week Magazine*, copyright 1945 by the United Newspapers Magazine Corporation. This article was reprinted in "I Am a Teacher," Reader's Digest Services, Inc., 1957.

[2] *Rankings of the States, 1962*, Research Report 1962-R1. Washington, D.C.: Research Division, National Education Association (January 1962), p. 7.

More than 150,000 new teachers are needed each year to serve new school enrollments and to replace teachers leaving the profession. Also three other needs for teachers remain unfilled: (1) teachers to relieve overcrowding and to eliminate part-time sessions, (2) teachers to provide services that are not now available, and (3) teachers who are fully certificated to replace partially prepared teachers.

Currently, the teaching profession includes:

1,400,000	teachers in public elementary and secondary schools
220,000	teachers in private elementary and secondary schools
130,000	school administrators, supervisors, consultants, researchers, and other specialists in elementary and secondary schools
350,000	professional personnel in higher educational institutions
25,000	professional staff members in professional organizations, in governmental offices of education, and in private agencies with educational programs
2,125,000	total for the profession

"There are shortages in most high school teaching fields now, and most of these shortages will become greater. In 1960, *there was one additional high-school teacher employed for every two teachers in 1950.* This trend is continuing."[3] A report by the National Education Association states that on the basis of past experience only 83 percent of those qualifying for elementary teaching certificates and 68 percent of those ready for high school certification actually seek teaching positions. The estimated shortage of public school teachers, at least for the years immediately in the future, is between 125,000 and 150,000.[4]

Opportunities in the Profession

Most young people who think of teaching will naturally think of classroom service. The person who has prepared himself for teaching, secondary school teaching in this instance, truly has many types of educational work other than instruction open to him. Of course, about 90 percent of positions are in the classrooms of public and private schools. When a person has completed the basic preparation for the profession, numerous types of service are available. Some of these opportunities require specialized or advanced preparation and nearly all are predicated on successful classroom experience.

[3] *Invitation To Teaching*, revised ed. Washington, D.C.: National Commission on Teacher Education and Professional Standards, National Education Association (May 1961), p. 9.

[4] *Teacher Supply and Demand*, 1962, Research Report 1962-R8. Washington, D.C.: Research Division, National Education Association (April 1962), p. 5.

Some positions entail travel or living in a foreign country. Others are generally available in this country, but are limited to the larger cities where extensive educational programs are supported. Small schools do not have the diversified programs that call for specialized services. Educational opportunities for high school teachers include:

A. Instructional service
   1. Classroom teacher
   2. Critic teacher in a laboratory or experimental school
   3. Departmental head (part-time teaching only)
   4. Athletic coach
B. Administrative service
   1. Principal
   2. Assistant principal
   3. Research director
C. Counseling service
   1. Guidance director
   2. Dean of girls or boys
   3. Vocational counselor or placement officer
   4. Visiting teacher
D. Supervisory service
   1. Departmental head
   2. Subject supervisor
   3. General supervisor
   4. Curriculum consultant
E. Special services
   1. Director of audio-visual materials
   2. Coordinator of language laboratories
   3. TV coordinator
   4. Director of programmed learning materials
   5. Librarian
F. Service outside the United States
   1. Teacher——military bases, embassies, insular territories
   2. Teacher—mission schools
   3. Teacher at corporation installations
G. Miscellaneous
   1. Teacher—Indian schools
   2. Camp director
   3. Director of youth organizations
   4. Teacher—private or church schools

CERTIFICATION Most of the positions above require a certificate or credential. Teaching certificates are granted by the departments of education in the fifty states upon recommendation of colleges and universities where the teachers received their education. The requirements or standards for the certificates are set by the states, but the teacher education departments or schools administer them.

Teaching credentials are granted for periods of time ranging from a few years to life. Conditions for renewal of temporary certificates are also set by the states.

Certificate specialization is unsettled at the moment. In some states subject fields are designated on the certificate and the teacher may teach only these designated subjects. In other states, a broader certification obtains, and a teacher may, for example, teach any subject offered in the junior or senior high school.

SUBJECT COMBINATIONS IN HIGH SCHOOL TEACHING   A matter of concern to high school teachers is that of subject combinations. With broad or even narrow certification regulations, teachers frequently find that they are required to teach in two or more subject fields. This is particularly true in the case of beginning teachers who frequently start in the small school districts. Although teaching combinations tend to be reasonably logical, at times one finds combinations that are utterly devoid of content relationship. The larger high schools tend to place their teachers in one teaching field only.

Most teachers will do a large part of their teaching in their major or minor fields. Combinations of English, speech, and social studies are quite common. The combination of mathematics and science is common. Foreign language teachers may find themselves teaching two different languages, or they may have some teaching in another subject. Teachers of such special subjects as music, art, and home economics are less likely to teach outside their major concentration than are the teachers of the more academic subjects.

In this connection, it should be noted that many college and university schools and departments of education require student teachers to complete a certain amount of their preparation in at least two teaching areas.

LOCAL PROFESSIONAL ORGANIZATION   Professional organizations exist at the local, state, national, and international levels. Most teachers find their greatest interest and involvement in the first three of these levels.

Local professional organizations are so numerous that no attempt has been made to count them. For example, California alone has more than 500 such local groups. They may or may not be affiliated with state or national organizations, but they are important. Usually, any district with twenty-five or more teachers will have one or more local professional organizations. These are the grass-roots groups who speak for teachers in matters of policy formation. Members of these local groups carry their ideas to the state organizations where larger decisions are made. Local organizations hold a great potential for the profession, and all teachers should belong to them and make themselves heard.

It is no exaggeration to say that the increased effectiveness of present-day teachers' organizations is due to the emergence of local professional activity. These groups have been chiefly concerned with teacher welfare, personnel policies, rights, responsibilities, ethics, and public relations.

Local organizations are the training grounds for state and national professional leadership. The democratic concept finds its best expression at this level.

STATE PROFESSIONAL ORGANIZATION   Teachers have professional organizations in each of the fifty states, the District of Columbia, and in Puerto Rico. These organizations enroll a majority of the teachers of the several states and maintain permanent headquarters with full-time staffs.

State organizations are essentially legislative and policy-making bodies. Their functions are carried out through a host of commissions and committees of members (usually nonpaid service). The purpose of the state organizations everywhere is much the same, and the California Teachers Association is typical:

To further the educational interests of the State of California, to give increasing efficiency to its school system, to secure and maintain for the office of teaching its true rank among the professions of the state, to furnish a practicable basis for united action among those devoted to the cause of education in the state.[5]

Legal responsibility for formulating and administering major educational policies for education rests with the state departments of education. These departments are created by constitutional or statutory law, but they work closely with the voluntary self-perpetuating teacher organizations. Legislation concerning teachers originates from many sources, one of the most fertile of which is the professional group. School law, of course, is the prerogative of the legislature.

NATIONAL PROFESSIONAL ORGANIZATION   The National Education Association (NEA) in the United States is an active, aggressive organization of some 800,000 members. All teachers should feel an obligation to join this organization.

Massey and Vineyard summarize the reasons for membership in the NEA as follows:

Some teachers have asked, "What has the NEA done for me?" The answer is easy. Our national professional organization has led the way in placing the importance and needs of the schools before the American people. This powerful

[5] *The Beginning Teachers Guide.* Burlingame, Calif.: Department of Classroom Teachers, California Teachers Association, 1957, p. 9.

public-relations program has had tremendous influence in bringing about greatly increased expenditures for school plants, equipment, materials, and teachers' salaries. The many commissions of the NEA work diligently to improve every aspect of the profession. . . . Its research division conducts studies, gathers data, and furnishes information for a multitude of educational projects. It has an active lobby in Washington, working for legislation favorable to public education and opposing any which would be detrimental. Since every teacher reaps the benefits of NEA activity, it follows that every teacher should support it. Finally, the strength of any profession lies largely in its unity and in the effectiveness of its organization.[6]

A strong national organization, such as the NEA, for example, is needed to coordinate local and state organizations. With coordinated effort, the local, state, and national levels provide a powerful impetus for a maturing, effective profession.

ASSOCIATION OR FEDERATION?   The question of what type of organization shall represent teachers has become a live issue. Essentially, two points of view are represented—unionism and professionalism. To some teachers the two viewpoints are incompatible; other teachers see no over-riding incompatibility.

Over the past decade, the issue of unionism versus professionalism has been brewing. Sporadic teacher strikes over the country seemed to have little or no effect on the issue one way or another. Then, on November 7, 1960, the United Federation of Teachers of New York City called a strike over the issue of collective bargaining and what agency should represent the teachers at the bargaining table. The strike lasted one day, but with no clear settlement of issues.

A second strike (labeled by some as a revolt, not a strike) occurred in New York City on April 11, 1962. It was reported that 20,588 teachers, or 51 percent of the 40,000 in the system stayed away from their class-rooms. Reverberations of this strike were heard throughout the country. On the whole, the professional organizations deplored the strike as illegal, unprofessional, and belittling. There were, however, proponents who claimed that teachers are workers, albeit professional workers, and that their occupational needs and the needs of the society they serve demand forceful action. These individuals feel that youth is being sacrificed if schools are permitted to pay poor salaries, employ poorly trained teachers, and maintain policies inimical to the best interests of society. The New York City strike has been evaluated and re-evaluated, but the basic issue of unionism remains.

[6] Harold W. Massey and Edwin E. Vineyard, *The Profession of Teaching.* New York: The Odyssey Press, Inc., 1961. Used by permission of Odyssey.

Several organizations vie for the right to represent teachers. The National Education Association and its affiliates stand on one side. On the other side are such organizations as the American Federation of Teachers, an affiliate of the AFL-CIO, and the Teachers Union, a once influential organization that has been accused of left-wing domination.

Some educational writers who claim to hold unbiased, objective views on this controversial issue would like to see the organizational house put in order. They plead for a merger of the NEA and the AFT. Desirable as such a positive move is, one must realistically face the obstacles involved. Chief stumbling blocks appear to lie in the fact that NEA has no restrictions on administrator membership, and second, that one organization is at least twelve times larger than the other. Some of the educational writers think that unless a merger is accomplished, in time, a third organization will grow up between the two and replace both.

Whether the strike is a proper weapon for teachers will remain an unanswered question for some years to come. No one at this moment can say what the future holds in this matter of organization. What effect will organization have on such matters as school support, public acceptance, working conditions for teachers, organizational democracy, and even the objectives of education itself?

INTERNATIONAL EDUCATION ORGANIZATIONS   Cultural relations between nations and international groups have been expanding rapidly. Only in recent years have nongovernmental international professional organizations achieved much importance. Today, the World Confederation of Organizations of the Teaching Profession (WCOTP) and the International Association of Universities (IAU) are providing leadership in better understanding among educators around the world. These and other responsible organizations are in a position to do more for international cultural relations than random or self-organized minority groups.

PROFESSIONAL ETHICS   Standards of conduct beyond those governed by law are usually spelled out in a code of ethics. Most professions have such codes. The medical profession, for example, relies on the Hippocratic oath and the Principles of Medical Ethics. The American Bar Association has its Canons of Ethics, and the architects, The Standards of Professional Practice.

A code of ethics is self-imposed and it becomes effective only if the members of the profession abide by it. All the state teachers associations embrace a code of ethics which covers such areas as: (1) teacher-pupil relationships, (2) teacher-parent relationships, (3) teacher-administrator relationships, (4) teacher-board of education relationships, and (5) teacher-professional relationships.

The NEA has subscribed to a Code of Ethics since 1929. The 1952 edition is stated in terms of five principles:[7]

Principle Number One stresses the obligations of teachers to guide learners in the pursuit of knowledge and skills so that they may become "happy, useful, self-supporting citizens."

Principle Number Two states that teachers and parents share the task of "shaping each student's purposes and acts toward socially acceptable ends."

Principle Number Three deals with the teacher's personal conduct both in the classroom and the community.

Principle Number Four defines the ethics of employment and fosters regard for mutual respect and good faith between employer and employee.

Principle Number Five stresses professional relationships among all teachers.

The ethical phases of these five principles are finally broken down into six or more specific obligations.

Professional Growth: In-Service Teacher Education

Many avenues to professional growth are open to teachers. One of the hallmarks of a profession is found in the demand for continuous in-service growth. "The competent teacher is a growing teacher." As a teacher grows, he contributes in increasing degree to his community. This fact is one of the basic reasons why many school boards provide part or all of the costs of in-service education for their teachers. Few professions provide the opportunities for mental and personality growth that teaching does. Both teachers and communities should be aware of the fact that in-service education is to their mutual advantage. To this extent the teacher contributes time, effort, and resources; the school district contributes encouragement and resources.

Opportunities for in-service growth are varied. Those most frequently available to teachers are study programs, group study of school problems, community study or activities, school visitation, travel, workshops, exchange teaching, writing, reading, research, and a miscellany of other activities. These growth opportunities will be described in the paragraphs that follow.

CONTINUED PROFESSIONAL AND CULTURAL DEVELOPMENT   No attempt is made here to separate professional and cultural types of activities. They are treated as two sides of a coin. As a coin is spun the two sides blend; as a teacher grows and matures, culture and professional development blend.

[7] See Appendix.

College and university summer sessions draw their largest enrollments from teachers. At times, school districts provide part or all of the costs of summer study. In some districts salary increments are correlated with advanced college preparation. Some states are mandating additional college study for renewal of certificates, especially for the renewal of substandard certificates. Most American teachers start their teaching careers with the bachelor's degree. No data are available to indicate how many teachers have master's or doctor's degrees. It is safe to say that there is a substantial number of these. It can also be safely assumed that most of these advanced degrees were earned by the teachers after they had begun their careers.

In addition to courses taken for credit, there are noncredit study opportunities offered by colleges and by the school districts themselves. Extension courses are available in practically every community.

Group study of school problems provides another in-service growth opportunity of great value. Such study is usually connected with development of new school programs or projects or the evaluation or redesign of old programs. Other opportunities arise through surveys, census polls, catalogue construction, and through the production of courses of study or curriculums. Often these studies engage sizeable committees who may have the assistance of consultants and valuable resource persons. Projects may involve teachers from a single building or they may bring together teachers from several buildings, or perhaps teachers from different school districts.

Workshops continue to grow in popularity. Teachers join together to study a common problem. They meet after school, during special conferences, on weekends, or during regularly scheduled summer terms. At times the workshop group goes off to an isolated spot at the seashore or in the mountains for relaxed and uninterrupted pursuit of a problem. The workshop, too, may be intergrated with a travel tour at home or abroad. Chandler defines this group study device in this manner:

A workshop is a systematic program of group study which is characterized by a focus on the specific concerns and problems of those involved, as distinguished from formal courses whose content is typically determined by the subject matter organization or by the instructor. Democratic planning under the leadership of a director is an additional characteristic of workshops. Often consultants or specialists in the field of study are obtained to help.[8]

Activities at workshops are as varied as the interests of teachers. They involve previewing films, constructing courses of study, making tests,

[8] B. J. Chandler, *Education and the Teacher.* New York: Dodd, Mead & Company, Inc., 1961, pp. 325–326.

cataloguing lists of resource materials, building crafts, or doing similar useful professional tasks.

Opportunities to work with any of the several aspects of community life are also valuable. Teachers need to know their communities in as much detail as possible: the philanthropic and charitable agencies, cultural resources, economic and vocational aspects, governmental agencies and services, and other ramifications of the community.

School visitation is almost invariably helpful to teachers. This may be home visitation, or equally important, it may be interschool or intraschool visitation. This is an area for teacher growth that has not been fostered by school officials to any considerable extent. Visitation does involve problems such as teachers being away from their classrooms, the payment of substitute teachers, and other administrative details, but the values to teachers remain.

WRITING, READING, RESEARCH, AND TRAVEL   In one sense, reading, writing, studying, and growing in cultural and professional stature are obligations of teachers, but they are also opportunities. Few vocations offer these opportunities, at least to the same extent. Teaching constantly forces its members to clarify their thinking, to re-examine their beliefs because they deal with ideas which are never static. Someone has said that a teacher constantly renews his youth. And, in a very real sense, the teacher is paid for all this.

Teaching is a broad occupation and teachers may range far beyond their specialization in their reading, writing, and the enjoyment of the arts. They may range over every type of composition from biography, fiction, travel, adventure, science, poetry, to journalism. Their interest in music, drama, and the fine arts may be just as catholic. Such interests tend to "elevate and liberate the human spirit."

For the teacher who has the talent and the desire, the opportunities for writing are almost endless. Coupled with writing is research. These activities cannot help but add to the stature of the teacher, and they may be financially profitable. Sir Francis Bacon wrote, "Reading maketh a full man, conference a ready man, and writing an exact man." The applicability of these words for teachers is extremely significant.

Loula Grace Erdman, a teacher in Texas who has found time to write and to teach, wrote in a magazine article a few years ago:

Recently, when I was awarded the *Redbook*-Dodd, Mead prize for a novel I wrote, a newspaper reporter said, "Of course you'll give up teaching now."

Without even stopping to think, I answered, "Of course not."

My answer made the headlines. "She'll stick to teaching!" they cried, as if that, and not the literary award, were the big news.[9]

[9] Loula Grace Erdman, "I'm Going to Stick to Teaching," *Redbook*, 1947, vol. 89, no. 3, p. 51. Reprinted in "I Am a Teacher," Reader's Digest Services, Inc., 1957.

Travel, too, is an enriching experience. Whether limited to one's own country, or whether it extends to foreign lands, it is bound to enhance teaching effectiveness because, if done understandingly, one gets a first-hand knowledge of places, events, peoples, and cultures. Travel is not only fun, it can also "soften prejudices, religious or political, and liberalize a man's mind."[10]

As a group, teachers travel widely, singly or in tour groups. Tour groups are commonplace today, and are sponsored by colleges, universities, state education associations, and the National Education Association. Some school districts recognize travel to the extent of allowing credit toward salary increments.

Many teachers have an opportunity to do an occasional stint of exchange teaching, either in this country or in a foreign country. This is an unusually rewarding experience. Contacts may be made through a state teachers association, the National Education Association, the Office of Cultural Affairs of the State Department, or through any of a large number of private organizations.

The use of teachers as paid consultants is new. Some of them are very knowledgeable specialists whose services are useful to industry, foundations, the military, and to foreign governments.

GROWTH OPPORTUNITIES Most teachers agree wholeheartedly about the advantages their profession offers. These opportunities are wonderful, but are they available to *all* teachers? Undoubtedly, many in-service growth activities are open to all who wish to participate; but other activities are limited and fall to those individuals who have earned a certain amount of recognition. Leadership is a maturing, developing role. It begins in small ways and increases with sincere and systematic effort. Certainly a school system that attempts to promote in-service growth among its teachers will bend every effort to offer opportunities to all teachers. Advanced study, travel, participation in community life, and work with teacher groups and workshops are beneficial and open to all teachers regardless of grade or departmental level. Writing or doing research, for those suited to this type of work, either for pay or for fun, adds another cubit to the stature of the teacher.

There are so many avenues for professional advancement that no one need feel that he is limited or handicapped. Not all teachers may travel, but most will. Not all teachers may attend a workshop, but most will find an activity that makes a fair substiute for it. Such activities are found in committee work, conferences, conventions, or service on survey teams.

People who are active and do things are usually interesting people. They break the bonds of provincialism. The great English scientist.

[10] Charles B. Fairbanks, *The Philosophy of Foreign Travel*, 1853.

Herbert Spencer, once wrote, "That man is best educated who has touched life in most places." And, in a somewhat similar vein, the noted American literary critic, John Mason Brown, has written:

What happiness is, no person can say for another. But no one, I am convinced, can be happy who lives only to himself. The joy of living comes from immersion in something that we know to be bigger, better, more enduring and worthier than we are. People, ideas, causes—these offer the one possible escape not merely from selfishness but from the hungers of solitude and the sorrows of aimlessness. No person is as uninteresting as a person without interests.

The pitiful people are those who in their living elect to be spectators rather than participants; the tragic ones are those sight-seers who turn their backs deliberately on the procession. The only true happiness comes from squandering ourselves for a purpose.[11]

THE TEACHER AND COMMUNITY PARTICIPATION

Every beginning teacher should take a look at his community. This he can do through the pupils in his classes, his colleagues, the parents of the pupils, the organizations and institutions of the community, the occupations and businesses which are the livelihood of the community, and through countless other ways. A community has so many sides that it is impossible to inventory it adequately. Some of its characteristics are tangible; some are not. But all the characteristics and factors that make up a community bear on the citizens who live there. And Haskew and McLendon state and restate, "The total community educates" (3:63–78).

In considering community needs, teachers and administrators may well give thought to such questions as the following: What is meant by "community"? What are the needs of the community? What community needs can be appropriately met by the school? How can the job be done?

When people who live in a particular region or locality have certain laws, customs, and traditions in common, they are said to form a *community*. Boys and girls who enroll in school come from homes and neighborhoods which expect them to observe the laws, traditions, and customs of their particular community. In the process of growing up today, however, youth have to learn more than respect for the laws and mores of a particular community. They need to be able to detect truth from falsehood, to evaluate conflicting points of view, to appreciate their opportunities, and to assume their rightful share of responsibility for community life. All of these needs can be met within the framework of the local community where boys and girls live. Yet this conception of community need

11 William I. Nichols, ed., *Words to Live By*. New York: Simon and Schuster, Inc., 1949, pp. 79–80.

is still too narrow. Living in an unstable society, characterized by a mobile population, youth have no assurance that they will continue to live in one locality. Furthermore, a local, provincial conception of citizenship obligations no longer suffices in a world of expanding human relationships. Both teachers and their students are compelled to gain an understanding of the local, state, national, and world communities. Many will have to learn to make themselves at home in almost any part of the world.

School-Community Relations

For a long time, school administrators have been aware of the need for good school-public relations. For classroom teachers, on the other hand, public relations has been a blind spot. Teachers have tended only to their own business, teaching boys and girls in the classroom, and have given little thought to the attitude of the public toward the school. However, times do change. The role of the classroom teacher in public relations, as well as the concept of public relations itself has been undergoing a transition. It is becoming increasingly evident that the foundations of good school-community relations are laid in the classroom, and that the best messenger of good will is the student who enjoys his schoolwork.

Teacher-Community Relationships

Teachers need to join and to become *active* in parent-teacher groups, churches, civic clubs, youth-service agencies, and the like. In the first place, teachers owe it to themselves, to their own personal development, to work with their peers in community activities. Teachers need to associate with other teachers, but they need also the broadening and stimulating influence provided by association with people from various walks of life. In the past, teachers tended to isolate themselves from the community. Often this social isolation was self-imposed. Nothing is a greater impairment of mental health than this sort of thing.

The teacher often finds his new teaching community different from the one in which he grew up. Such a situation should offer a challenge to any sincere teacher. It is a new and a different world for the teacher from the rural interior to face problems of some urban areas. The adjustment is just as great when the situations are reversed. One community may have problems of undernourished children, another of delinquent children; some may be more privileged, with completely different problems. The true teacher accepts these students and does what he can for their educational development. Of the children of another environment, one teacher said, "I remember only the doors they have opened for me, the prejudices I have shed."

A second reason for teacher participation in community affairs is to vitalize the curriculum. It is stressed elsewhere in this book that some of the most valuable resources in teaching are found *outside* the four walls of the schoolroom. Again it should be pointed out that a school program which fails to take into account other educational forces of the community becomes ineffective and sterile. The ivory tower concept of the school as an institution isolated from the rest of the community is no longer tenable. The teacher who is ignorant of and indifferent to community currents and forces is robbing the taxpayer and shortchanging his students. Other educational agencies, which are competing, conflicting, or cooperating with the school, need to be understood. Teacher participation brings about understanding. Those agencies which work with the school deserve teacher support. Those agencies which misunderstand the purposes and program of the school may be enlightened by an interpreter who is known and respected as an *active* citizen of both the school and the larger community.

The community needs the teacher as much as the teacher needs the community. By exerting the leadership that his profession calls for, the teacher can promote a better social and political climate. He has a heavy responsibility to help make democracy a real, functional way of life. This begins in the classroom, and the teacher whose own life personifies democratic ideals will inevitably affect the outlook of his community. The good will that any teacher develops in a community comes back to the school in better school support and understanding.

Teachers will, of course, want to join organizations in the community. Personal and professional motivations will govern which ones. A PTA membership is probably the foundation of professional associations. Then comes an array of professional affiliations, most of which are discussed elsewhere in this chapter. Church and related organizations are high on the list. Also to be considered are civic and social clubs, recreational agencies, cultural and literary groups, and youth organizations. However, there is the danger of the teacher's spreading his energies and talents too thinly by joining too many organizations. Priorities will have to be considered. Finally, the teacher should realize that he is not expected to build his life entirely around the community. Teachers need to be well-adjusted individuals. They should be a part of the community, but should not be engulfed by it.

THE OUTLOOK IN TEACHING

Factors to Consider

In seeking a first position or in contemplating a change in positions, one should investigate such matters as general philosophy of the school, including the degree of personal freedom allowed teachers both inside and outside the school. It is unwise to accept a position which will in all likelihood be incompatible with one's philosophical and cultural ideas. Other general matters that should be investigated are those pertaining to living conditions, welfare, geography, and one's ultimate professional goal.

The following paragraphs will describe briefly some of the specific factors which should be considered in analyzing the job.

SALARY   The immediate salary offered in any particular teaching position, although of great importance, must be equated with several other factors before a decision is made to accept or reject a position. Is a salary schedule in operation in the school system where employment is desired? If a salary schedule is used, where will the applicant be placed if employed? Are regular increments a part of the schedule? How large are these increments, and what is their number? What is the maximum salary one can obtain, and how many years will it take to reach the maximum? Does the salary schedule reward one for study, for travel, and for other procedures by which professional improvement is made? Is the starting salary large enough to enable a person to live in the community? Will the salary be paid throughout the school year on a yearly basis, or will it be paid only during the months when school is in session? (Many school districts pay salaries throughout the calendar year in an attempt to provide an additional measure of stability for the staff.) Is a single salary schedule, based upon *training* and *experience*, in effect in the school under consideration? (Single salary schedules have no sex differentials with respect to beginning salary, advancement in salary through increments, and maximum salary obtainable.)

The beginning salary, the maximum salary, and the length of service necessary to reach the maximum are important factors in a choice of position. However, they must be weighed against further factors of tenure and retirement benefits before a choice can be made. Finally, what is the attitude of the board of education and the community with respect to teachers' salaries? Has the school a record of consistent attempts to maintain salaries at the highest level possible for the district, or has it been niggardly in respect to salaries?

TENURE   Nearly half of the states in this country have passed legislation, either permissive or mandatory in nature, which protects certificated employees against unjust dismissal by boards of education. Teacher tenure laws provide for a probationary period of service in a school district of from two to three years. If a teacher successfully completes the probationary period and begins to teach the following year, he has reached "permanent" status in the district. Then he may be dismissed only for cause, after a hearing is held to determine the justness of the dismissal. Such tenure laws provide a measure of security for teachers which is unavailable in most other professions. A permanent teacher will be able to plan ahead for the years to come, to finance a home, to make and keep friends in the community, and, as long as he maintains good teaching and moral standards, he will be able to work in his teaching job secure in the knowledge that an unjust dismissal is impossible.

When one chooses a position, the tenure possibilities must be seriously considered. Is tenure available in this particular community by mandatory state legislation? If the district does not qualify under mandatory legislation, has it adopted permissive measures to provide tenure for the teaching staff? If no tenure legislation is available in the state in which a job is sought, the amount of teacher turnover from year to year (in the district in question) is an important factor to be considered. Does a high percentage of the teachers remain in this district year after year or does a major portion move to other districts at the end of each school year? The percentage of teacher turnover each year in a school district is a reflection of the adequacy of salaries, the attitude of the board of education and the administration, the working conditions in each school, and the community conditions under which teachers live and work.

THE COMMUNITY   What can the teacher expect from the community, and what does the community expect from the teacher? Is a teacher able to live a normal life outside of school hours? Is the community large enough to provide the recreational opportunities one desires? Is housing available at a price a teacher can afford to pay? Are teachers accepted by the community and invited to participate in churches, clubs, and other aspects of community life? These are important questions which will determine to a great extent one's happiness outside the classroom.

WORKING CONDITIONS   Labor unions have fought an extended battle for the past century to improve the conditions of safety and health under which their members work. A similar movement has been in existence with much less fanfare in the teaching profession. Boards of education, school administrators, and teachers, along with the help and encouragement of state agencies, have been constantly working to improve school plants, teaching materials, and general working conditions for teachers. The new teacher should consider the following factors which will help make it possible for him to do his best work.

Teaching load. Teaching load is to a certain extent standardized, but the beginning teacher might very well inquire about how many different classes or preparations he will have. Class size is another matter of interest to the beginning teacher; class size affects the load to be carried.

Equipment and facilities. Does the school under consideration possess good equipment and facilities? Information about equipment can be obtained by asking questions of other teachers, or, if feasible, by making a tour of a school building.

Classroom space. Teachers are happier if they have their own class-rooms. Shared classrooms mean shared bulletin boards, storage space, desk. Chalkboards may not be adequate for two teachers; therefore, every-thing must be removed before another teacher comes in.

Teaching assignment. One of the most important things to investigate concerns the teaching assignment. Is the assignment in the area of major or minor preparation? Teaching in peripheral areas in the first year of teaching can be difficult. These assignments always mean more prepara-tion.

Extraclass load. The extraclass load can make the difference between a pleasant assignment and a vexing, time-consuming one. The teacher can expect to participate in extraclass activities, but he must guard against an overload.

The principal. Often, it is possible to find out a few significant things about the principal. The important matters concern philosophy, staff morale, support in crises, status, and similar matters.

No beginning teacher should feel that he must investigate every detail before he accepts a new position, but a few inquiries about basic matters may save misunderstandings and regrets.

LEAVE OF ABSENCE Although nearly half the states and almost every major school system make some mention of leaves of absence for teachers, there is no uniformity. Where leaves are granted without loss of pay, the time may vary from a day or two to a week or two. In some districts un-used sick leave may be cumulated for as much as twenty or twenty-five days. Leaves of absence for sickness, death in the family, and maternity are of major importance. Safeguards in the area of illness, for example, are as important a consideration as retirement, and are a major factor in teacher welfare.

RETIREMENT AND PENSION ALLOWANCES Some kind of retirement laws are in effect in every state. They are being improved all the time. At one time teachers had one of the best retirement outlooks of all professions. Today, the Federal Social Security Act has made liberal retirement allow-ance available to thousands of workers. Several states have integrated their state plans for retirement of teachers with those of the federal system.

Retirement is usually permissible at 60 or 62 years of age; compulsory at 65 or 70. The allowance that goes with retirement is based upon earnings and length of service. Most retirement plans are contributory. The teacher contributes a percentage of his salary, and the state or district contributes a sum based on the salary or the teacher's contribution. This is also the basis of social security.

One of the problems at present is the matter of reciprocity between states. Teachers frequently move to other states. Their retirement ac-counts should go with them.

Effective Applications

Seeking a job should follow accepted procedures for best results. The following paragraphs outline the steps that are likely to produce the most satisfactory results.

THE JOB OUTLOOK   With a long preparation nearly completed, the prospective teacher looks for a job. The labor market goes in cycles. NEA studies show that the market is reasonably good viewed from the standpoint of teacher placement. Supply is likely to be below the demand for some years to come. In 1961, the National Commission on Teacher Education and Professional Standards of the National Education Association made recommendations in connection with identification, admission, and retention of teachers which are the first steps in successful job placement. The commission recommended:

That the selective process at least be based on evaluation of emotional maturity, moral and ethical fitness, health, demonstrated ability to work with children and youth, academic aptitude and intelligence, academic achievement, demonstrated competence in speech and basic skills, and professional interest and motivation (2:203).

With qualifications like these, placement is practically assured. Teachers of this type are readily in demand.

COLLEGE AND UNIVERSITY PLACEMENT SERVICES   More and more employing officials are seeking candidates for their positions rather than waiting for candidates to come to them. It is natural for them to turn first to the college and university placement offices. Practically all colleges have placement offices, and their officers are eager to see their graduates successfully placed.

In 1952, the NEA made a study of placement by asking 1611 school superintendents how they recruited teachers. The methods of recruitment favored at that time are practically the same today. The five most frequently mentioned practices, in order of importance, were:

1. Contacting placement bureaus of colleges and universities, commercial teachers' agencies, state departments of education, state teachers associations, and state employment services.
2. Selecting teachers from applications sent in voluntarily by candidates.
3. Making inquiries at conferences, conventions, and similar gatherings.
4. Making inquiries of other school systems.
5. Advertising and publishing lists of positions vacant.[12]

[12] National Education Association, Research Division, *Teacher Personnel Practices, 1950–51: Appointment and Termination of Service,* Research Bulletin (February 1962), p. 15.

In this connection mention should be made of the fact that there is a growing trend toward direct recruitment by school officials on college campuses. The superintendent, director of personnel, or a similar official visits a number of college campuses each spring expressly seeking the teachers needed by his school district. Such visits may be to colleges and universities in a local area, or the school official may go to other states in his search for teachers.

Placement offices compile recommendations, furnish personal data forms, and obtain transcripts of high school and college courses. Students planning to teach should contact the local placement office long before they reach the completion of their program. Placement opportunities in various subject areas, subject combinations most sought as reflected by the records of the placement office, and other facts will be available to those making inquiry. Placement offices not only assist directly in job placement, but they also act as a certain measure of protection against students making unwise choices.

Prospective teachers should fill out placement office blanks with the utmost care and neatness. These forms will be examined by prospective employers. It is also necessary to file with the application forms photographs made expressly for placement purposes. Good photographs are a solid investment. For the photograph, the person should dress neatly and conservatively. Dark clothing provides contrast and usually photographs best. Good grooming is imperative.

Students completing their education program should file placement papers even though they do not desire immediate placement. Military service, graduate study, marriage, and other conditions may delay placement, but nothing is lost by filing papers.

In connection with filling out application or placement office forms, the prospective teacher should carefully consider the matter of recommendations. The best recommendations can be made by persons who know the candidate's professional ability. Employers give greatest consideration to recommendations written by college supervisors of student teaching, supervising or critic teachers, principals, and other school teachers. Professors of one's major and minor subject areas are also valuable references. At times a character reference is in order. No person's name should ever be used as a reference until permission has been obtained to use the name.

Placement offices assemble all the data about a candidate, including recommendations, and on request send the file to prospective employers. Placement credentials and recommendations are confidential and are not available to the candidate.

STATE TEACHERS ASSOCIATIONS Most state teachers associations maintain a placement service for their members. Membership in the association is required of those who wish the help of the association. The placement bureaus of state teachers associations are highly reputable and perform a valuable service. They are especially valuable for the person seeking employment in a section of the state not reached by the local college placement office.

COMMERCIAL PLACEMENT AGENCIES   Private agencies also assist in the placement of teachers. They are particularly helpful during times of teacher oversupply, and they cover wide geographical areas. Some of them are national in scope. Thus, a prospective teacher can gain contacts well beyond the areas covered by most college and university placement offices. Most commercial agencies are reliable. Their fees range from 5 to 10 percent of the first year's salary, a condition which may place a heavy financial drain on earnings during the first year.

SEEKING A POSITION INDEPENDENTLY   Candidates may wish to canvass the field independently in an attempt to locate a position. This may be likened to a barnstorming adventure, and, although it may be profitable, it can also be frustrating and expensive both in terms of time and money. Barnstorming is like fishing in unknown waters: there are possibilities of a catch, but generally the results are poor.

Teachers should always be on the lookout for positions if they are in the market for a first position, or a change of position. The placement agencies are helpful, but efforts in one's own behalf are in order. Inquiry among friends and acquaintances may furnish clues to openings.

LETTERS OF APPLICATION   Employing officials, consciously or unconsciously, evaluate candidates by their letters of application, and by the manner in which application blanks are filled out. There are three types of letters which may be used in applying for a position: letters of inquiry, letters of application, and follow-up letters.

Although it is not ethical to apply for positions which are not known to exist, it is ethical to write a *letter of inquiry*. There are at least two occasions on which such a letter is in order. First, the candidate may desire to teach in a state or an area of his own state not served by his college placement office. Second, he may have heard rumors of a vacancy in a certain district.

A letter of inquiry should be carefully written and should be predicated upon a sincere desire to learn about a vacancy in a given district. Such letters should be accompanied by a stamped self-addressed envelope, and should be framed in such a way that a reply can be quickly and easily made.

When it is known that a vacancy exists, the candidate should write a *letter of application*. The letter may contain complete information about the candidate, or the information may be set forth in a résumé accompanied by a covering letter. Current practice tends to favor the second type. Letters of application are usually necessary even though the college placement office has forwarded the candidate's credentials. The candidate should state in the first paragraph of his letter how he learned of the vacancy. This should be specific, not, "I have learned of a vacancy in your school." If the candidate has any unusual or special reason for desiring this position, he should state it in as straightforward a manner as possible. He does not beg for the job; he offers his services.

Needless to say, letters of application should be meticulously prepared. Mistakes in grammar, spelling, and composition may cause the letter to be rejected with only passing consideration. Most school officials prefer typed letters, especially for high school positions. Good quality paper, clean typewriter keys, and a fresh typewriter ribbon will help to give a professional look to a letter of application.

Letters of application should supply the usual personal information. Major emphasis should be placed on the educational background in high school and college. The employing official wishes to know about majors and minors, degrees, honors received, teaching credential held, and other educational experience. He is also much interested in any teaching experience the candidate has had. Experience should be considered broadly, and should include paid teaching, student teaching, work experience, and volunteer experience with organizations such as Red Cross and Scouts. Hobbies and extracurricular interests should be included.

The information in the letter of application must be brief and concise, yet the candidate must make a favorable impression if he desires the job. Form letters are usually unsatisfactory and under no circumstances should mimeographed résumés or letters be used. This letter, like the letter of inquiry, requires a self-addressed stamped envelope.

It is customary not to mention salary in these letters. Little is to be gained by a mention of salary since public schedules govern compensation in most school districts.

Whether one should mention church or other affiliations is up to each individual. In most states, employers and placement officials are prevented by law from making inquiry into such affiliations. If the candidate has reason to believe that his affiliations will be received favorably, he is privileged to volunteer the information.

Brief, courteous, *follow-up letters* are in order. They do not reiterate qualifications; they may remind the official of some salient point in the application. The follow-up letter gives the candidate an opportunity to thank the hiring official for his interview. Most of all, the letter serves as a dignified reminder.

THE PERSONAL INTERVIEW   The importance of the first personal contact with a prospective employer cannot be overestimated. First impressions are lasting impressions. The letter of application, the personal data sheet, the photograph, and the letters of recommendation have been carefully examined and analyzed by the prospective employer. The administrator now wishes to talk to the candidate personally. An interview will give him a chance to make up his mind about how well the candidate will fit in with the rest of the faculty. It also gives him an opportunity to appraise such matters as the candidate's interest in teaching, his community interests, and some of his theories concerning the growth and development of boys and girls.

Before the interview, it is well to obtain as much information about the position as possible. If a job is offered and accepted, this community will be home. Caution, however, is in order because undue inquisitiveness and excessive prying are worse than no interest at all. One should use good judgment in seeking information.

Special care should be given to one's personal appearance. Extremes in dress and styles should naturally be avoided; the same is true for cosmetics and jewelry.

During the interview the ability to talk to the school administrator in professional language in a mature manner is of great importance. There will rarely be any questions of competence, unless his qualifications are unsuitable for the position. The administrator will naturally assume that the college has taken care of the matter of subject competence. There will be more questions about classroom control, the likelihood of remaining in teaching as a career, why the individual selected teaching as a vocation, and his general outlook on life. Frequently questions about extracurricular activities and guidance are discussed.

The interview helps the prospective employer to make up his mind about the candidate's general enthusiasm concerning teaching. He senses many things even in a short interview. He observes courtesy, introversion or extroversion, promptness, boastfulness, and general ability to communicate ideas.

Employing officials also learn a great deal from the questions a candidate asks. Were the questions mature and professional? Did they reflect a rich cultural background? Interviews are two-way streets. Both candidate and employer should come away from the interview with some positive opinions.

The candidate should sense the proper ending for the interview. Nothing is gained, often something is lost, by attempting to prolong an interview after it has accomplished its purpose. A question as to when a decision will be reached is perfectly in order. And common courtesy requires the candidate to thank his interviewer for the time he has been given.

The Ethics of Placement

Principle number four of the Code of Ethics of the National Education Association specifically makes recommendations concerning placement and contract. This section of the code resulted from the fact that in the past some of the interpersonal relationships of teachers, job seekers in this instance, have not been entirely satisfactory.

Candidates for teaching positions should not make application for positions that do not exist. Inquiry will determine whether a certain vacancy exists; if it does, an application is in order. In this same connection, it is considered bad taste, if not unethical, to make applications for positions wholesale. When positions are scarce, candidates are likely to feel that many applications should be circulated at one time. School superintendents have let it be known that they have had literally hundreds of applications for a single position. The wasted effort and the disappointments involved in such a situation are unfortunate.

In case a candidate has been offered two or more positions, he must not play one position against the other in the hope of gaining an unusual financial advantage. Harmful effects are almost sure to follow. They may be in the form of ill will either toward the candidate or toward the college from which he is graduating. The fortunate person with two good offers considers them carefully and makes a decision.

One of the most unethical of practices is to underbid another applicant for a position. Abuses of this sort are offset by the fact that most school districts have open salary schedules. This prevents unsavory bargaining.

When a candidate has accepted a position, he should notify all other employing officials who have him under consideration. Also, the college placement officer should be informed of the action. This will enable the placement office to recommend another candidate for the vacancies.

It is unethical to break a contract willfully. In case another position involving an unusual opportunity presents itself, the teacher should present the matter to the employing official and request mutual abrogation of the contract.

Positions involved in a school controversy should be handled with delicacy. It is better to wait until the controversy is cleared before placing an application.

The Characteristics of a Profession

A profession is not easily defined except in a very narrow sense. The concept "teaching profession" is best generalized through its characteristics. It is a way of making a living, yet it is not a business; it has no profit motive. It is, therefore, a form of public service. Individuals who engage in teaching must acquire a large body of general and special knowledge along with specialized professional education. Teachers have been given great freedom to pursue their work with a minimum of outside interference. In the main, those individuals who qualify are accorded prestige and esteem, but they must constantly merit this esteem.

Another characteristic of a profession is *spirit*. It cannot be taught but it crystallizes through professional courses, observation of teachers at work, working with other professionals in workshops and on committees, and through the unpaid services which teachers render their organizations. In the past, too many teachers never seemed to acquire this spirit. Frequently teaching was just a job, but today the situation is different. Greater professional knowledge and maturity, together with a genuine desire to serve, have helped to weld a profession.

Huggett and Stinnett have listed the following eight characteristics which make a true profession (4:57–68). (1) A profession involves intellectual activities, (2) a profession commands a body of specialized knowledge, (3) a profession requires extended professional preparation, (4) a profession demands continuous in-service growth, (5) a profession affords a life career and a permanent membership, (6) a profession sets its own standards, (7) a profession exalts service above personal gain, and (8) a profession has a strong, closely knit professional organization.

Throughout this text strong support has been given to the idea that teaching is a profession, and as such it faces up squarely to the criteria posed above. Terrien made a study in New London, Connecticut, in which he asked teachers the question: "Do you consider high school teaching to be a profession?" Ninety-seven percent answered affirmatively.[13]

THE HALLMARKS OF A PROFESSIONAL PERSON

From the very beginning of his career a teacher should be a "professional teacher." A professional teacher is one who thinks and acts in a professional manner. He possesses and exemplifies the characteristics already described. Although many of these characteristics grow as long as one teaches, the teacher concept is present even in the student teacher.

Centuries ago Sir Francis Bacon wrote a phrase which every professional person should heed: "I hold every man a debtor to his profession." To teachers this phrase is particularly cogent. Teachers belong to a great profession which they have made by their energies and actions, yet the profession is greater than the sum of its parts. Teachers can and should be proud of their profession.

[13] Frederic W. Terrien, "Who Thinks What About Educators," *American Journal of Sociology*, vol. 19 (September 1953), p. 154.

Effective teaching is like the three sides of an equilateral triangle. The sides represent knowledge of teaching techniques and skills, knowledge of subject area, and knowledge of and liking for students. This text has been primarily concerned with the first of these characteristics, but the authors have also repeatedly stressed the importance of the other two. A weakness in one may very well mean an unhappy or an ineffective teacher.

The professional person is one who has concern for his conduct, has regard for his appearance, and has pride in his speech. The professional person is one who seeks to bring dignity and respect to the profession and feels a debt to his profession. The professional person is one who is circumspect about his activities inside and outside the classroom, and is proud to say, "I am a teacher."

Selected References

1. Chandler, B. J., *Education and the Teacher*. New York: Dodd, Mead & Company, Inc., 1961.
2. Educational Policies Commission, *Professional Organizations in American Education*. Washington, D.C.: National Educational Association, 1957.
3. Haskew, Laurence D., and Jonathon C. McLendon, *This Is Teaching*. Chicago: Scott, Foresman and Company, 1962.
4. Huggett, Albert J., and T. M. Stinnett, *Professional Problems of Teachers*. New York: The Macmillan Company, 1956.
5. Lindsey, Margaret, ed., *New Horizons for the Teaching Profession*. Washington, D.C.: National Commission on Teacher Education and Professional Standards, National Education Association, 1961.
6. Massey, Harold W., and Edwin E. Vineyard, *The Profession of Teaching*. New York: The Odyssey Press, Inc., 1961.
7. Risk, Thomas M., *Principles and Practices of Teaching in Secondary Schools*, 3d ed. New York: American Book Company, 1958.
8. Stinnett, T. M., and Laurence D. Haskew, *Teaching in American Schools: A Handbook for the Future Teacher*. New York: Harcourt, Brace & World, Inc., 1962.

Code of Ethics of the National Education Association of the United States[1]

We, the members of the National Education Association of the United States, hold these truths to be self-evident
—that the primary purpose of education in the United States is to develop citizens who will safeguard, strengthen, and improve the democracy obtained through a representative government;
—that the achievement of effective democracy in all aspects of American life and the maintenance of our national ideal depend upon making acceptable educational opportunities available to all;
—that the quality of education reflects the ideals, motives, preparation and conduct of the members of the teaching profession;
—that whoever chooses teaching as a career assumes the obligation to conduct himself in accordance with the ideals of the profession.

As a guide for the teaching profession, the members of the National Education Association have adopted this code of professional ethics. Since all teachers should be members of a united profession, the basic principles herein enumerated apply to all persons engaged in the professional aspects of education—elementary, secondary, and collegiate.

FIRST PRINCIPLE: The primary obligation of the teaching profession is to guide children, youth, and adults in the pursuit of knowledge and skills, to prepare them in the ways of democracy, and to help them to become happy, useful, self-supporting citizens. The ultimate strength of the nation lies in the social responsibility, economic competence, and moral strength of the individual American.

In fulfilling the obligations of this first principle the teacher will—

[1] Used by permission of the National Education Association Committee on Professional Ethics.

1. Deal justly and impartially with students regardless of their physical, mental, emotional, political, economic, social, racial, or religious characteristics.
2. Recognize the differences among students and seek to meet their individual needs.
3. Encourage students to formulate and work for high individual goals in the development of their physical, intellectual, creative, and spiritual endowments.
4. Aid students to develop an understanding and appreciation not only of the opportunities and benefits of American democracy but also of their obligations to it.
5. Respect the right of every student to have confidential information about himself withheld except when its release is to authorized agencies or is required by law.
6. Accept no remuneration for tutoring except in accordance with approved policies of the governing board.

SECOND PRINCIPLE: The members of the teaching profession share with parents the task of shaping each student's purposes and acts toward socially acceptable ends. The effectiveness of many methods of teaching is dependent upon cooperative relationships with the home.

In fulfilling the obligations of this second principle the teacher will—

1. Respect the basic responsibility of parents for their children.
2. Seek to establish friendly and cooperative relationships with the home.
3. Help to increase the student's confidence in his own home and avoid disparaging remarks which might undermine that confidence.
4. Provide parents with information that will serve the best interests of their children, and be discreet with information received from parents.
5. Keep parents informed about the progress of their children as interpreted in terms of the purposes of the school.

THIRD PRINCIPLE: The teaching profession occupies a position of public trust involving not only the individual teacher's personal conduct, but also the interaction of the school and the community. Education is most effective when these many relationships operate in a friendly, cooperative, and constructive manner.

In fulfilling the obligations of this third principle the teacher will—

1. Adhere to any reasonable pattern of behavior accepted by the community for professional persons.
2. Perform the duties of citizenship, and participate in community activities with due consideration for his obligations to his students, his family, and himself.

3. Discuss controversial issues from an objective point of view, thereby keeping his class free from partisan opinions.
4. Recognize that the public schools belong to the people of the community, encourage lay participation in shaping the purposes of the school, and strive to keep the public informed of the educational program which is being provided.
5. Respect the community in which he is employed and be loyal to the school system, community, state, and nation.
6. Work to improve education in the community and to strengthen the community's moral, spiritual, and intellectual life.

FOURTH PRINCIPLE: The members of the teaching profession have inescapable obligations with respect to employment. These obligations are nearly always shared employer-employee responsibilities based upon mutual respect and good faith.

In fulfilling the obligations of this fourth principle the teacher will—

1. Conduct professional business through the proper channels.
2. Refrain from discussing confidential and official information with unauthorized persons.
3. Apply for employment on the basis of competence only, and avoid asking for a specific position known to be filled by another teacher.
4. Seek employment in a professional manner, avoiding such practices as the indiscriminate distribution of applications.
5. Refuse to accept a position when the vacancy has been created through unprofessional activity or pending controversy over professional policy or the application of unjust personnel practices and procedures.
6. Adhere to the conditions of a contract until service thereunder has been performed, the contract has been terminated by mutual consent, or the contract has otherwise been legally terminated.
7. Give and expect due notice before a change of position is to be made.
8. Be fair in all recommendations that are given concerning the work of other teachers.
9. Accept no compensation from producers of instructional supplies when one's recommendations affect the local purchase or use of such teaching aids.
10. Engage in no gainful employment, outside of his contract, where the employment affects adversely his professional status or impairs his standing with students, associates, and the community.
11. Cooperate in the development of school policies and assume his professional obligations thereby incurred.

12. Accept his obligation to the employing board for maintaining a professional level of service.

FIFTH PRINCIPLE: The teaching profession is distinguished from many other occupations by the uniqueness and quality of the professional relationships among all teachers. Community support and respect are influenced by the standards of teachers and their attitudes toward teaching and other teachers.

In fulfilling the obligations of this fifth principle the teacher will—

1. Deal with other members of the profession in the same manner as he himself wishes to be treated.
2. Stand by other teachers who have acted on his behalf and at his request.
3. Speak constructively of other teachers, but report honestly to responsible persons in matters involving the welfare of students, the school system, and the profession.
4. Maintain active membership in professional organizations and, through participation, strive to attain the objectives that justify such organized groups.
5. Seek to make professional growth continuous by such procedures as study, research, travel, conferences, and attendance at professional meetings.
6. Make the teaching profession so attractive in ideals and practices that sincere and able young people will want to enter it.

INDEX